Discovering Computers

Technology in a World of Computers, Mobile Devices, and the Internet

Discovering Computers

Technology in a World of Computers, Mobile Devices, and the Internet

Misty E. Vermaat
Susan L. Sebok
Steven M. Freund

Contributing Authors
Jennifer T. Campbell
Mark Frydenberg, Bentley University

Shelly Cashman Series®
A part of Course Technology, Cengage Learning

CENGAGE
Learning·

Australia • Brazil • Japan • Korea • Mexico • Singapore • Spain • United Kingdom • United States

Discovering Computers: Technology in a World of Computers, Mobile Devices, and the Internet
Misty E. Vermaat
Susan L. Sebok
Steven M. Freund

Vice President, General Manager: Dawn Gerrain

Executive Editor: Kathleen McMahon

Associate Acquisitions Editor: Reed Curry

Senior Product Manager: Emma Newsom

Associate Product Manager: Crystal Parenteau

Editorial Assistant: Sarah M. Ryan

Senior Brand Manager: Elinor Gregory

Market Development Manager: Kristie Clark

Market Development Manager: Gretchen Swann

Marketing Coordinator: Amy McGregor

Print Buyer: Julio Esperas

Senior Content Project Manager: Matthew Hutchinson

Researcher: F. William Vermaat; Jacqueline Vermaat

Development Editor: Lyn Markowicz

Management Services: PreMedialGlobal

Interior Designer: Joel Sadagursky

Art Director: Jackie Bates, GEX

Text Design: Joel Sadagursky

Cover Design: Lisa Kuhn, Curio Press, LLC

Cover Photos: Tom Kates Photography

Illustrator: PreMedialGlobal

Compositor: PreMedialGlobal

Printer: RRD Menasha

For product information and technology assistance, contact us at
Cengage Learning Customer & Sales Support, 1-800-354-9706

For permission to use material from this text or product, submit all requests online at **cengage.com/permissions**
Further permissions questions can be emailed to
permissionrequest@cengage.com

Library of Congress Control Number: 2013908521

ISBN-13: 978-1-285-16176-1

ISBN-10: 1-285-16176-9

Course Technology
20 Channel Center Street
Boston, MA 02210
USA

Cengage Learning is a leading provider of customized learning solutions with office locations around the globe, including Singapore, the United Kingdom, Australia, Mexico, Brazil and Japan. Locate your local office at:
international.cengage.com/region

Cengage Learning products are represented in Canada by Nelson Education, Ltd.

To learn more about Cengage Learning, visit **www.cengage.com**

Purchase any of our products at your local college bookstore or at our preferred online store at **www.cengagebrain.com**

Printed in the United States of America
3 4 5 6 19 18 17 16 15 14

Table of Contents at a Glance

Table of Contents

CHAPTER **3**

Computers and Mobile Devices: Evaluating the Possibilities
103

CHAPTER **4**

Programs and Apps: Using Software at Work, School, and Home
151

CHAPTER **5**

Digital Safety and Security: Identifying Threats, Issues, and Defenses
201

CHAPTER **6**

Inside Computers and Mobile Devices: Exploring the Components
    247

CHAPTER **7**

Input and Output: Examining Popular Devices
    287

CHAPTER 8

Digital Storage: Preserving on Media and in the Cloud — 335

CHAPTER 9

Operating Systems: Managing, Coordinating, and Monitoring Resources — 377

CHAPTER 10

Communications and Networks: Sending and Receiving Digital Content — 415

CHAPTER 11

Information and Data Management: Organizing, Verifying, Maintaining, and Accessing
463

CHAPTER 12

Information Systems and Program Development: Designing and Building Solutions
509

Preface

The Shelly Cashman Series® offers the finest textbooks in computer education. We are proud of the fact that the previous seventeen editions of this textbook have been the most widely used in computer education. With this edition of *Discovering Computers* we have implemented significant improvements based on current computer trends and comments made by instructors and students. *Discovering Computers: Technology in a World of Computers, Mobile Devices, and the Internet* continues with the innovation, quality, and reliability you have come to expect from the Shelly Cashman Series.

In *Discovering Computers: Technology in a World of Computers, Mobile Devices, and the Internet* you will find an educationally sound, highly visual, interactive, and easy-to-follow pedagogy that, with the help of animated figures, relevant video, and interactive activities in the e-book, presents an in-depth treatment of introductory computer subjects. Students will finish the course with a solid understanding of computers, how to use computers, and how to access information on the Web.

Objectives of this Text, e-Book, and CourseMate Web Site

Discovering Computers: Technology in a World of Computers, Mobile Devices, and the Internet is intended for use

as a stand-alone solution or in combination with an applications, Internet, or programming textbook in a full-semester introductory computer course. No experience with computers is assumed. The objectives of this offering are to:

- Present the most-up-to-date technology in an ever-changing discipline
- Give students an in-depth understanding of why computers are essential in business and society
- Teach the fundamentals of and terms associated with computers and mobile devices, the Internet, programs and apps, and digital safety and security
- Present the material in a visually appealing, interactive, and exciting manner that motivates students to learn
- Provide exercises, lab assignments, and interactive learning activities that allow students to learn by actually using the computer, mobile devices and the Internet
- Present strategies for purchasing desktop computers, mobile computers, and mobile devices
- Provide alternative learning techniques and reinforcement via the Web
- Offer distance-education providers a textbook with a meaningful and exercise-rich digital learning experience

Hallmarks of Discovering Computers

To date, more than six million students have learned about computers using *Discovering Computers*. With the Web integration and interactivity, streaming up-to-date audio and video, extraordinary step-by-step visual drawings and photographs, unparalleled currency, and the Shelly and Cashman touch, this book will make your computer concepts course exciting and dynamic. Hallmarks of Shelly Cashman Series *Discovering Computers* include:

A Proven Pedagogy

Careful explanations of complex concepts, educationally-sound elements, and reinforcement highlight this proven method of presentation.

A Visually Appealing Book that Maintains Student Interest

The latest technology, pictures, drawings, and text are combined artfully to produce a visually appealing and

easy-to-understand book. Many of the figures include a step-by-step presentation, which simplifies the more complex computer concepts. Pictures and drawings reflect the latest trends in computer technology. This combination of pictures, step-by-step drawings, and easy-to-read text layout sets the standard for computer textbook design.

Latest Technologies and Terms

The technologies and terms your students see in *Discovering Computers* are those they will encounter when they start using computers. Only the latest application software is shown throughout the book.

Web Integrated

This book uses the Web as a major learning tool. The purpose of integrating the Web into the book is to (1) offer students additional information and currency

Distinguishing Features

Discovering Computers: Technology in a World of Computers, Mobile Devices, and the Internet includes a variety of compelling features, certain to engage and challenge students, making learning with *Discovering Computers* an enriched experience. These compelling features include:

- **Strong Content.** Based on market research and in-depth assessment of organization and each chapter's content, Discovering Computers has been restructured and reorganized to improve retention of material and promote transference of knowledge. The text's visually engaging presentation showcases current technology as well as course fundamentals in order to reinforce classroom and real world applications.
- **Balanced Presentation.** The print book provides students only with what they really need to know to be successful digital citizens in the classroom and beyond. The media-rich ebook addresses timely content, such as statistics, trends, prices, models, and expands on the print, with content appropriate for Computing majors. Students and instructors can choose to utilize this digital-only content, empowering each to fit the content to their specific needs and goals for the course.

- **Thematic Approach.** Chapter boxes, marginal elements, and accompanying digital-only content are linked by common themes to facilitate class discussions and help students make connections. These connections shed light on the integral role technology plays in business and society.
- **Media Engagement.** Enrichment content is available only in the e-book to enhance student knowledge and understanding through links to content and interactive media embedded at locations most appropriate for learning. Developed by the authors, activities providing deeper understanding and encourage learning by doing as well as offer practical skill development.
- **Reinforcement and Support.** End-of-chapter student assignments, along with the accompanying CourseMate web site, offer students an exceptional learning solution in addition to significant practice opportunities in the form of study guide materials, flash cards, practice tests and critical thinking opportunities.

on important topics; (2) use its interactive capabilities to offer creative reinforcement and online quizzes; (3) make available alternative learning techniques with Web-based learning games, practice tests, and interactive labs; (4) underscore the relevance of the Web as a basic information tool that can be used in all facets of society; (5) introduce students to doing research on the Web; and (6) offer instructors the opportunity to organize and administer their traditional campus-based or distance-education-based courses on the Web using various learning management systems.

Extensive End-of-Chapter Student Assignments

A notable strength of *Discovering Computers* is the extensive student assignments and activities at the end of each chapter. Well-structured student assignments can make the difference between students merely participating in a class and students

retaining the information they learn. End-of-chapter student assignments include the following:

- Study Guide exercises reinforce material for the exams
- Key Terms pages review chapter terms
- Checkpoint exercises test knowledge of chapter concepts
- How To — Your Turn exercises require that students learn new practical skills
- Problem Solving exercises require that students seek solutions to practical technology problems
- Internet Research exercises require that students search for information on the web
- Critical Thinking exercises challenge student assessment and decision-making skills
- Beyond the Book exercises expand understanding of chapter animations, boxes, figures, mini features, social media posts, and third-party links and videos through thought-provoking questions

Instructor Resources

The Instructor Resources include both teaching and testing aids.

Instructor's Manual   Includes lecture notes summarizing the chapter sections, figures and boxed elements found in every chapter, teacher tips, classroom activities, lab activities, and quick quizzes in Microsoft Word files.

Syllabus   Easily customizable sample syllabi that cover policies, assignments, exams, and other course information.

Figure Files   Illustrations for every figure in the textbook in electronic form. Figures are provided both with and without callouts.

Solutions to Exercises   Includes solutions for all end-of-chapter student assignments.

PowerPoint Presentations — Course Presenter   A one-click-per-slide presentation system that provides PowerPoint slides for every subject in each chapter. Course Presenter provides consistent coverage for multiple lecturers.

Test Bank & Test Engine   Test banks include 220 questions for every chapter, featuring objective-based and critical thinking question types, and including page number references and figure references, when appropriate. Also included is the test engine, ExamView, the ultimate tool for your objective-based testing needs.

Printed Test Bank   A Rich Text Format (.rtf) version of the test bank that you can print.

Test Out/Final Exam   Objective-based exam that can be used to test students out of your course, or as a final examination.

Pretest/Posttest   Carefully prepared tests that can be used at the beginning and the end of the semester to measure student progress.

Computer Concepts CourseMate

The Computer Concepts CourseMate for *Discovering Computers* is the most expansive digital site for any computer concepts text in the market today! The content in the CourseMate solution is integrated into each page of the text, giving students easy access to current information on important topics, reinforcements activities, and alternative learning techniques. Integrating the Computer Concepts CourseMate into the classroom keeps today's students engaged and involved in the learning experience.

The Computer Concepts CourseMate includes an integrated, multi-media rich and interactive digital book, powered by MindTap, and a variety of interactive quizzes and learning games, exercises, videos, and other features that specifically reinforce and build on the concepts presented in the chapter. These interactive activities are captured within the CourseMate EngagementTracker, making it easy to assess students' retention of concepts. This digital solution encourages students to take learning into their own hands and explore related content on their own to learn even more about subjects in which they are especially interested.

All of these resources on the Computer Concepts CourseMate for *Discovering Computers* enable students to get more comfortable using technology and help prepare students to use the Internet as a tool to enrich their lives.

Contact Us

Colleges, Universities, Continuing Education Departments, Post-Secondary Vocational Schools, Career Colleges, Business, Industry, Government, Trade, Retailer, Wholesaler, Library, and Resellers
Call Cengage Learning at 800-354-9706

K-12 Schools, Secondary Vocational Schools, Adult Education, and School Districts
Call Cengage Learning at 800-354-9706

In Canada
Call Nelson Cengage Learning at 800-268-2222

Anywhere
www.cengage.com/coursetechnology

Visual Walkthrough of the Book

Current. Relevant. Innovative.
Teaching the Significance of Today's Digital World.

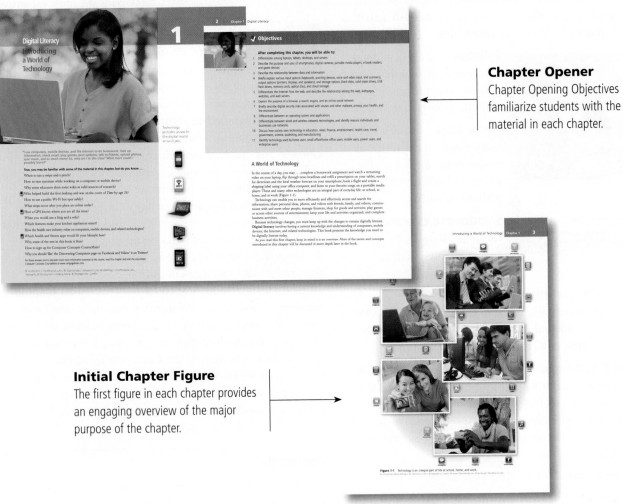

Chapter Opener
Chapter Opening Objectives familiarize students with the material in each chapter.

Initial Chapter Figure
The first figure in each chapter provides an engaging overview of the major purpose of the chapter.

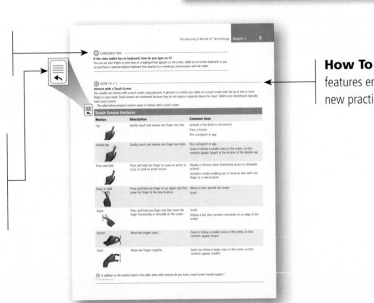

Consider This
features provide readers with critical thinking opportunities.

How To
features enable readers to learn new practical skills

Interactive e-Book Activity Icon
Several elements in each chapter are interactive learning activities in the e-book and are identified by this icon or by blue text.

Mini Feature

throughout the text explore various real world topics to deepen concept understanding.

Secure IT

features allow students to broaden their knowledge with details regarding security issues they will face.

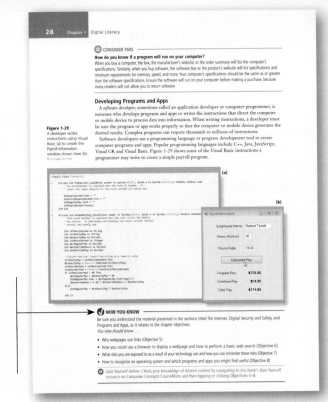

Now You Know

feature provides assessment opportunity and integrates directly to chapter learning objectives to assess learning outcomes.

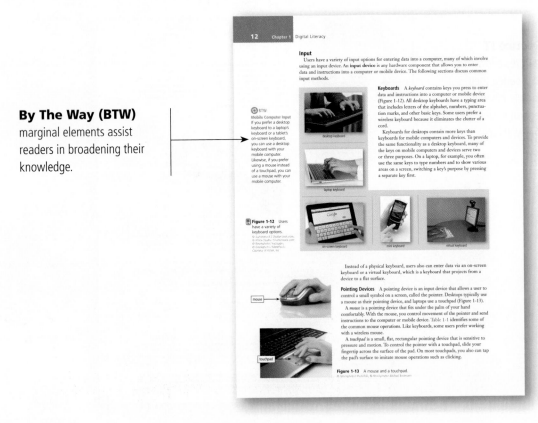

By The Way (BTW)

marginal elements assist readers in broadening their knowledge.

Ethics and Issues

boxes raise controversial, computer-related topics, challenging readers to carefully consider general concerns of computers in society.

Chapter Summary

allows another review of materials presented in the chapter to reinforce learning and provide additional self assessment opportunities.

Technology @ Work

features put chapter information to practical use and provide context within students' lives

STUDENT ASSIGNMENTS

End-of-Chapter Student Assignments

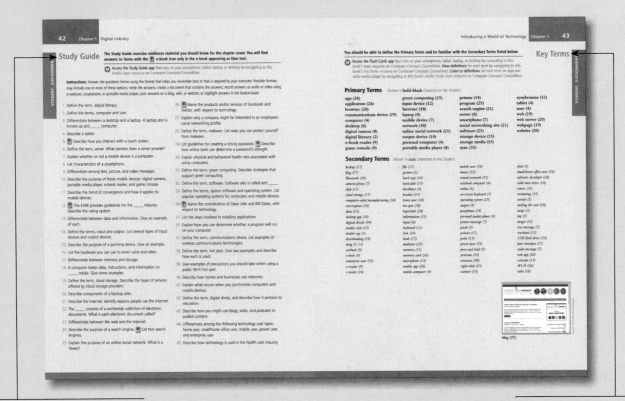

Study Guide
materials reinforce chapter content while **Study Guide mobile app** provides practice opportunities on the go.

Key Terms
Before taking a test, use the Key Terms page as a checklist of terms to know.

Checkpoint
Use these pages of multiple-choice, true/false, matching, and short answer exercises to reinforce understanding of the topics presented in the chapter.

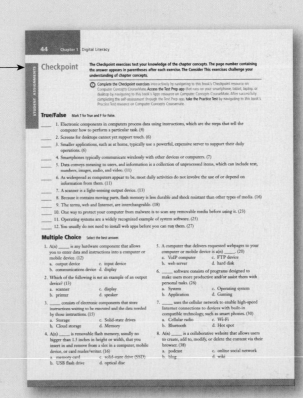

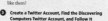

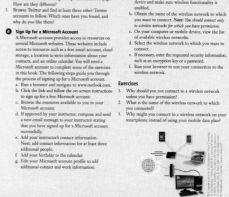

STUDENT ASSIGNMENTS

How To: Your Turn

activities enable readers to learn
and to reinforce new practical
skills with personally meaningful
and applicable exercies.

Problem Solving
Personal activities call on students to relate concepts to their own lives.

---

50 Chapter 1 Digital Literacy

⊘ Problem Solving

The Problem Solving exercises extend your knowledge of chapter concepts by seeking solutions to practical problems with technology that you may encounter at home, school, or work. The Collaboration exercise should be completed with a team.

Challenge yourself with additional Problem Solving exercises by navigating to this book's Problem Solving resource on Computer Concepts CourseMate.

Instructions: You often can solve problems with technology in multiple ways. Determine a solution to the problems in these exercises by using one or more resources available to you (such as a computer or mobile device, articles on the web or in print, blogs, podcasts, videos, television, user guides, other individuals, electronics or computer stores, etc.). Describe your solution, along with the resource(s) used, in the format requested by your instructor (brief report, presentation, discussion, blog post, video, or other means).

Personal

1. **Shopping for Software** You are shopping for software that will assist you with your home's interior design. The package for the program you would like to purchase states that it was designed for the most recent version of Windows, but an older version is installed on your computer. How can you determine whether the program will run on your computer?

2. **Bad Directions** You are driving to your friend's house and are using your smartphone for directions. While approaching your destination, you realize that your smartphone app instructed you to turn the wrong way on your friend's street. How could this have happened?

3. **Bank Account Postings** While reviewing your checking account balance online, you notice that debit card purchases have not posted to your account for the past several days. Because you use online banking to balance your account, you become concerned about your unknown account balance. What steps will you take to correct this situation?

4. **Inaccessible Media** You insert a memory card with digital photos from your most recent family vacation and discover that your computer will not read the memory card. What might be wrong?

5. **Problematic Camera** After charging your digital camera battery overnight, you insert the battery and turn on the camera only to find that it is reporting a low battery. Seconds later, the camera shuts off automatically. What might be wrong?

Professional

6. **Discarding Old Computer Equipment** Your company has given you a new laptop to replace your current, outdated desktop. Because of the negative environmental impact of discarding the old computer in the trash, your supervisor asked you to suggest options for its disposal. How will you respond?

7. **Dead Battery** While traveling for business, you realize that you forgot to bring the battery charger for your laptop. Knowing that you need to use the laptop to give a presentation tomorrow, what steps will you take tonight to make sure you have enough battery power?

8. **Software Installation** You are attempting to install a program on your office computer. After inserting the installation disc and specifying that you would like to begin the installation, your computer appears to begin installing the program. Halfway through the installation process, an error message appears stating that you must have administrative privileges to perform the installation. Why were you not informed immediately upon beginning the installation? What are your next steps?

9. **Incorrect Sign-In Credentials** Upon returning to the office from a well-deserved two-week vacation, you turn on your computer. When you enter your user name and password, an error message appears stating that your password is incorrect. What are your next steps?

10. **Synchronization Error** You added appointments to the calendar on your computer, but these appointments are not synchronizing with your smartphone. Your calendar has synchronized with your smartphone in the past, but it has stopped working without explanation. What are your next steps?

Collaboration

11. **Technology in Health Care** Your dentist is moving from a shared office so that he can open his own practice. He mentioned that he would like to use technology in his office that not only will improve the patient experience, but also make his job easier. Form a team of three people to determine the types of technology your dentist can use in his new office. One team member should research ways that technology can help improve patient check-in and billing. Another team member should research the types of technology your dentist can use while he is working with patients, and the third team member should research any additional technology that can be used in the office to improve the patient experience. Compile your findings in a report and submit it to your instructor.

Internet Research
Internet Research exercises require follow-up research on the Web and suggest writing a short article or presenting the findings of the research to the class.

---

48 Chapter 1 Digital Literacy

⊘ Internet Research

The Internet Research exercises broaden your understanding of chapter concepts by requiring that you search for information on the web.

Instructions: Use a search engine or another search tool to locate the information requested or answers to questions presented in the exercises. Describe your findings, along with the search term(s) you used and your web source(s), in the format requested by your instructor (brief report, presentation, discussion, blog post, video, or other means).

① Making Use of the Web
Search Engines and Research
Sixty percent of all American adults use a search engine every day, according to Pew Internet, and they generally are pleased with the outcome of their research experience. In How To 1-2 and 1-3 on pages 20 and 21 in this chapter, you learned to use a browser to display a webpage and to perform a basic web search.

Using these skills, find the answers to the following questions. (1) Visit the Pew Internet website and locate the latest Search Engine Use report. What are three of the users' positive search experiences? Which search engine is the most popular among the people surveyed? When was the survey conducted, and how many adults were surveyed? (2) Visit the CNET website and read at least three reviews of products. Create a table listing the product name, price, editors' and users' ratings, and "bottom line" summary. (3) Use a search engine or research website to locate articles about banning mobile devices in schools. What policies have schools created in lieu of a total ban on this technology? How have schools integrated mobile devices in the classroom as a vehicle to enhance learning?

many of the same basic principles by allowing members to communicate common interests, play games, and share photos, videos, and music. Some of these social networking sites are for personal use, while others are for entrepreneurs, business owners, and professionals to share job-related topics.

Compare the features of the top personal social networks, and create a table listing the number of active members in the United States and worldwide, the number of years the sites have existed, the more popular features, and the amount of content, such as photos, news stories, and links, that is shared each month. What types of advertisements are featured in each of these sites? Which sites are marketed toward younger and older users? Then, research the social networks used for business. How does their content differ from that found on the personal social networks? How many companies use these sites as a recruiting tool? How many native languages are supported? How are professionals using these websites to find potential clients and business partners?

② Social Media
Historians place the birth of online social networking with the BBS (Bulletin Board System), where users communicated with a central computer and sent messages to other BBS members and also downloaded files and games. The next phase of social networking evolved when CompuServe, AOL (America Online), and Prodigy were among the services linking people with similar interests. Today's social networks share

③ Search Sleuth
(1) Which magazine introduced the first microcomputer kit for the MITS Altair in its January 1975 issue? (2) Which company sold the TRS-80, one of the more popular personal computers introduced in 1977? (3) What material did Douglas Engelbart use to create the first mouse? (4) What is the code name for the 12 engineers who developed the IBM PC? (5) Who received the first text message in 1992? What was the content of this message? (6) Which company developed the first digital camera? How many pounds did this camera weigh? (7) What is the title of Stephen King's e-book that was released in 2000? (8) In which year did Amazon.com report that for the first time sales of e-books exceeded the sales of hardcover books? (9) What is the name of the keyboard developed in the 1930s with a layout designed to maximize efficiency and reduce hand stress? (10) When did the first USB flash drive appear on the retail market? Which company developed this storage medium?

STUDENT ASSIGNMENTS

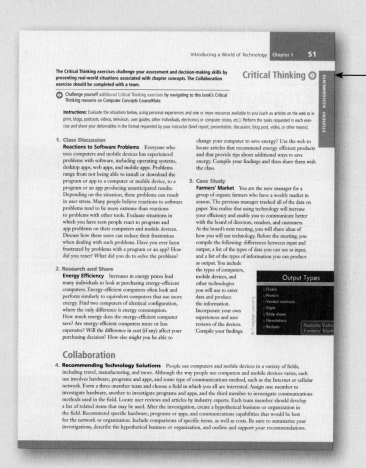

Critical Thinking

activities provide opportunities for creative solutions to these thought-provoking activities presented in each chapter. The Critical Thinking exercises are constructed for class discussion, presentation, and independent research. The Collaboration exercise is designed for a team environment.

Beyond the Book

exercises expand student understanding by allowing research and supported learning opportunities.

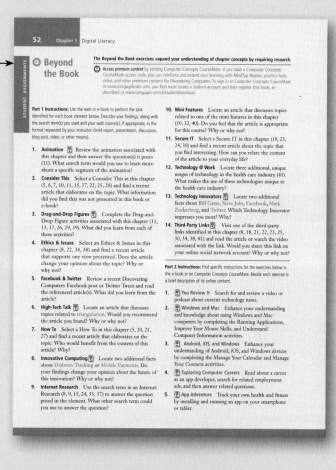

*Visual Walkthrough of the Computer Concepts
CourseMate for Discovering Computers*

Interactive. Current. Engaging.
Your Interactive Guide to the Digital World!

Introduce the most current technology into the classroom with the Computer Concepts CourseMate for Discovering Computers. An integrated e-book and a wide range of online learning games, quizzes, practice tests, and Web links expand on the topics covered in the text with hands-on reinforcement.

Who Wants to Be a Computer Genius?

The Who Wants to Be a Computer Genius? learning game allows students to quiz themselves on chapter content within a dynamic and entertaining game scenario. Question results are provided instantly so that students quickly see which concepts they understand and which concepts they need to study. Page remediation is included with question results so students know exactly where in the text to find the information they need.

EngagementTracker

EngagementTracker makes assessing students easy by tracking student progress on the interactive activities. Clear and visual reports illustrate the class progress as a whole.

Wheel of Terms

Wheel of Terms is an interactive study tool for learning the Key Terms in each chapter. This learning game presents students with a short definition of one of the chapter's Key Terms and prompts them to type the correct term as the answer.

Online Content

SAM: Skills Assessment Manager

Get your students workplace-ready with SAM, the market-leading proficiency-based assessment and training solution for Microsoft Office! SAM's active, hands-on environment helps students master Microsoft Office skills and computer concepts that are essential to academic and career success, delivering the most comprehensive online learning solution for your course!

Through skill-based assessments, interactive trainings, business-centric projects, and comprehensive remediation, SAM engages students in mastering the latest Microsoft Office programs on their own, giving instructors more time to focus on teaching. Computer concepts labs supplement instruction of important technology-related topics and issues through engaging simulations and interactive, auto-graded assessments. With enhancements including streamlined course setup, more robust grading and reporting features, and the integration of fully interactive MindTap Readers containing Cengage Learning's premier textbook content, SAM provides the best teaching and learning solution for your course.

Learn Online

CengageBrain.com is the premier destination for purchasing or renting Cengage Learning textbooks, eBooks, eChapters, and study tools at a significant discount (eBooks up to 50% off Print). In addition, CengageBrain.com provides direct access to all digital products including eBooks, eChapters and digital solutions (i.e., CourseMate and SAM) regardless of where purchased.

MindLinks

MindLinks is a new Cengage Learning Service designed to provide the best possible user experience and facilitate the highest levels of learning retention and outcomes, enabled through a deep integration of Cengage Learning's digital suite into an instructor's Learning Management System (LMS). MindLinks works on any LMS that supports the IMS Basic LTI open standard. Advanced features, including gradebook exchange, are the result of active, enhanced LTI collaborations with industry-leading LMS partners to drive the evolving technology standards forward.

CourseCasts Learning on the Go

Always available. . . always relevant.

Our fast-paced world is driven by technology. You know because you are an active participant — always on the go, always keeping up with technological trends, and always learning new ways to embrace technology to power your life. Let CourseCasts, hosted by Ken Baldauf of Florida State University, be your guide to weekly updates in this ever-changing space. These timely, relevant podcasts are produced weekly and are available for download at http://coursecasts.course.com or directly from iTunes (search by CourseCasts). CourseCasts are a perfect solution to getting students (and even instructors) to learn on the go!

CourseNotes — Technology in a Flash!

Course Technology's CourseNotes are six-panel quick reference cards that reinforce the most important and widely used features of a software application in a visual and user-friendly format. CourseNotes serve as a great reference tool during and after the student completes the course. CourseNotes are available for software applications, such as Microsoft Office 2013, Word 2013, PowerPoint 2013, Excel 2013, Access 2013, and Windows 8. Topic-based CourseNotes are available for Best Practices in Social Networking, Hot Topics in Technology, and Web 2.0. Visit www.cengage.com to learn more!

About Our Covers

The Shelly Cashman Series is continually updating our approach and content to reflect the way today's students learn and experience new technology. This focus on student success is reflected on our covers, which feature real students from the University of Rhode Island using the Shelly Cashman Series in their courses, and reflect the varied ages and backgrounds of the students learning with our books. When you use the Shelly Cashman Series, you can be assured that you are learning computer skills using the most effective courseware available.

Digital Literacy
Introducing a World of Technology

Technology provides access to the digital world around you.

"I use computers, mobile devices, and the Internet to do homework, look up information, check email, play games, post updates, talk to friends, upload photos, sync music, and so much more! So, why am I in this class? What more could I possibly learn?"

True, you may be familiar with some of the material in this chapter, but do you know . . .

When to use a swipe and a pinch?

How to ease eyestrain while working on a computer or mobile device?

Why some educators shun some wikis as valid sources of research?

Who helped build the first desktop and was on the cover of *Time* by age 26?

How to use a public Wi-Fi hot spot safely?

What steps occur after you place an online order?

How a GPS knows where you are all the time?

When you would use a blog and a wiki?

Which features make your kitchen appliances smart?

How the health care industry relies on computers, mobile devices, and related technologies?

Which health and fitness apps would fit your lifestyle best?

Why some of the text in this book is blue?

How to sign up for Computer Concepts CourseMate?

Why you should 'like' the Discovering Computers page on Facebook and 'follow' it on Twitter?

For these answers and to discover much more information essential to this course, read this chapter and visit the associated Computer Concepts CourseMate at www.cengagebrain.com.

© Andre Blais / Shutterstock.com

✓ Objectives

After completing this chapter, you will be able to:

1 Differentiate among laptops, tablets, desktops, and servers

2 Describe the purpose and uses of smartphones, digital cameras, portable media players, e-book readers, and game devices

3 Describe the relationship between data and information

4 Briefly explain various input options (keyboards, pointing devices, voice and video input, and scanners), output options (printers, displays, and speakers), and storage options (hard disks, solid-state drives, USB flash drives, memory cards, optical discs, and cloud storage)

5 Differentiate the Internet from the web, and describe the relationship among the web, webpages, websites, and web servers

6 Explain the purpose of a browser, a search engine, and an online social network

7 Briefly describe digital security risks associated with viruses and other malware, privacy, your health, and the environment

8 Differentiate between an operating system and applications

9 Differentiate between wired and wireless network technologies, and identify reasons individuals and businesses use networks

10 Discuss how society uses technology in education, retail, finance, entertainment, health care, travel, government, science, publishing, and manufacturing

11 Identify technology used by home users, small office/home office users, mobile users, power users, and enterprise users

A World of Technology

In the course of a day, you may . . . complete a homework assignment and watch a streaming video on your laptop, flip through news headlines and refill a prescription on your tablet, search for directions and the local weather forecast on your smartphone, book a flight and create a shipping label using your office computer, and listen to your favorite songs on a portable media player. These and many other technologies are an integral part of everyday life: at school, at home, and at work (Figure 1-1).

Technology can enable you to more efficiently and effectively access and search for information; share personal ideas, photos, and videos with friends, family, and others; communicate with and meet other people; manage finances; shop for goods and services; play games or access other sources of entertainment; keep your life and activities organized; and complete business activities.

Because technology changes, you must keep up with the changes to remain digitally literate. **Digital literacy** involves having a current knowledge and understanding of computers, mobile devices, the Internet, and related technologies. This book presents the knowledge you need to be digitally literate today.

As you read this first chapter, keep in mind it is an overview. Most of the terms and concepts introduced in this chapter will be discussed in more depth later in the book.

Figure 1-1   Technology is an integral part of life at school, home, and work.

Computers

A **computer** is an electronic device, operating under the control of instructions stored in its own memory, that can accept data (*input*), process the data according to specified rules, produce information (*output*), and store the information for future use. Computers contain many electric, electronic, and mechanical components known as *hardware*.

Electronic components in computers process data using instructions, which are the steps that tell the computer how to perform a particular task. A collection of related instructions organized for a common purpose is referred to as software or a program. Using software, you can complete a variety of activities, such as search for information, type a paper, balance a budget, create a presentation, or play a game.

One popular category of computer is the personal computer. A **personal computer** (PC) is a computer that can perform all of its input, processing, output, and storage activities by itself and is intended to be used by one person at a time. Most personal computers today also can communicate with other computers and devices.

Types of personal computers include laptops, tablets, and desktops, with the first two sometimes called mobile computers. A *mobile computer* is a portable personal computer, designed so that a user can carry it from place to place. A **user** is anyone who interacts with a computer or mobile device, or utilizes the information it generates.

Laptops

A **laptop**, also called a *notebook computer*, is a thin, lightweight mobile computer with a screen in its lid and a keyboard in its base (Figure 1-2). Designed to fit on your lap and for easy transport, laptops weigh up to 10 pounds (varying by manufacturer and specifications). A laptop that is less than one inch thick and weighs about 3 pounds or less sometimes is referred to as an ultrathin laptop. Most laptops can operate on batteries or a power supply or both.

Tablets

Usually smaller than a laptop but larger than a phone, a **tablet** is a thin, lighter-weight mobile computer that has a touch screen (read How To 1-1 for ways to interact with a touch screen). A popular style of tablet is the slate, which does not contain a physical keyboard (Figure 1-3). Like laptops, tablets run on batteries or a power supply or both; however, batteries in a tablet typically last longer than those in laptops.

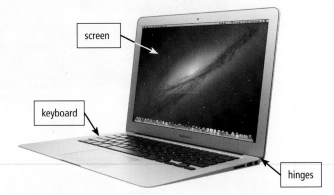

Figure 1-2 A typical laptop has a keyboard in the base and a screen in the lid, with the lid attaching to the base with hinges.
© iStockphoto / Stephen Krow

Figure 1-3 A slate tablet.
© iStockphoto / franckreporter

CONSIDER THIS

If the slate tablet has no keyboard, how do you type on it?
You can use your fingers to press keys on a keyboard that appears on the screen, called an *on-screen keyboard,* or you can purchase a separate physical keyboard that attaches to or wirelessly communicates with the tablet.

 HOW TO 1-1

Interact with a Touch Screen
You usually can interact with a touch screen using gestures. A *gesture* is a motion you make on a touch screen with the tip of one or more fingers or your hand. Touch screens are convenient because they do not require a separate device for input. Tablets and smartphones typically have touch screens.

The table below presents common ways to interact with a touch screen.

Touch Screen Gestures

Motion	Description	Common Uses
Tap	Quickly touch and release one finger one time.	Activate a link (built-in connection) Press a button Run a program or app
Double-tap	Quickly touch and release one finger two times.	Run a program or app Zoom in (show a smaller area on the screen, so that contents appear larger) at the location of the double-tap
Press and hold	Press and hold one finger to cause an action to occur, or until an action occurs.	Display a shortcut menu (immediate access to allowable actions) Activate a mode enabling you to move an item with one finger to a new location
Drag, or *slide*	Press and hold one finger on an object and then move the finger to the new location.	Move an item around the screen Scroll
Swipe	Press and hold one finger and then move the finger horizontally or vertically on the screen.	Scroll Display a bar that contains commands on an edge of the screen
Stretch	Move two fingers apart.	Zoom in (show a smaller area on the screen, so that contents appear larger)
Pinch	Move two fingers together.	Zoom out (show a larger area on the screen, so that contents appear smaller)

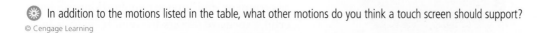 In addition to the motions listed in the table, what other motions do you think a touch screen should support?

Desktops

A **desktop**, or desktop computer, is a personal computer designed to be in a stationary location, where all of its components fit on or under a desk or table. On many desktops, the screen is housed in a device that is separate from a tower, which is a case that contains the processing circuitry (Figure 1-4a). Other desktops, sometimes called all-in-one desktops, do not contain a tower and instead use the same case to house the screen and the processing circuitry (Figure 1-4b). Some screens for desktops support touch.

Figure 1-4   Some desktops have a separate tower; others do not.
© iStockphoto / Oleksiy Mark; Source: Microsoft; © iStockphoto / hocus-focus; Apple, Inc.

CONSIDER THIS

Which type of computer — laptop, tablet, or desktop — is best?
It depends on your needs. Because laptops can be as powerful as the average desktop, more people today choose laptops over desktops so that they have the added benefit of portability. Tablets are ideal for those not needing the power of a laptop or for searching for information, communicating with others, and taking notes in lectures, at meetings, conferences, and other forums where a laptop is not practical.

Figure 1-5   A server provides services to other computers or devices on a network.
© iStockphoto / alxpin

Servers

A **server** is a computer dedicated to providing one or more services to other computers or devices on a network. A network is a collection of computers and devices connected together, often wirelessly. Services provided by servers include storing content and controlling access to hardware, software, and other resources on a network.

A server can support from two to several thousand connected computers and devices at the same time. Servers are available in a variety of sizes and types for both small and large business applications (Figure 1-5). Smaller applications, such as at home, sometimes use a high-end desktop as a server. Larger corporate, government, and Internet applications use powerful, expensive servers to support their daily operations.

Mobile and Game Devices

A **mobile device** is a computing device small enough to hold in your hand. Because of their reduced size, the screens on mobile devices are small — often between 3 and 5 inches.

Some mobile devices are Internet capable, meaning that they can connect to the Internet wirelessly. You often can exchange information between the Internet and a mobile device or between a computer or network and a mobile device. Popular types of mobile devices are smartphones, digital cameras, portable media players, and e-book readers.

 CONSIDER THIS

Are mobile devices computers?
The mobile devices discussed in this section can be categorized as computers because they operate under the control of instructions stored in their own memory, can accept data, process the data according to specified rules, produce or display information, and store the information for future use.

Smartphones

A **smartphone** is an Internet-capable phone that usually also includes a calendar, an appointment book, an address book, a calculator, a notepad, games, and several other apps (which are programs on a smartphone). Smartphones typically communicate wirelessly with other devices or computers. With several smartphone models, you also can listen to music and take photos.

Many smartphones have touch screens. Instead of or in addition to a touch screen, some smartphones have a built-in mini keyboard on the front of the phone or a keyboard that slides in and out from behind the phone (Figure 1-6). Others have keypads that contain both numbers and letters.

mini keyboard

touch screen

slide out keyboard

Figure 1-6 Smartphones may have a touch screen and/or a mini keyboard or slide out keyboard.
© iStockphoto / Cagri Özgür; © iStockphoto / serts; © iStockphoto / Oleksiy Mark

Instead of calling someone's phone to talk, you can send messages to others by pressing images on an on-screen keyboard, keys on the mini keyboard, or buttons on the phone's keypad. Three popular types of messages that you can send with smartphones include text messages, picture messages, and video messages.
- A *text message* is a short note, typically fewer than 300 characters, sent to or from a smartphone or other mobile device.
- A *picture message* is a photo or other image, sometimes along with sound and text, sent to or from a smartphone or other mobile device. A phone that can send picture messages sometimes is called a *camera phone*.
- A *video message* is a short video clip, usually about 30 seconds, sent to or from a smartphone or other mobile device.

Read Ethics & Issues 1-1 on the next page to consider whether sending text messages affects writing skills.

 BTW
Messaging Services
Providers of wireless communications services may charge additional fees for sending text, picture, or video messages, depending on the service plan.

❋ ETHICS & ISSUES 1-1

📖 Do Text Messages Affect Writing Skills?

When you send text messages, the goal is to communicate the most amount of information using the fewest words and characters. This type of rapid-fire communications places a higher priority on brevity and speed than spelling, capitalization, and punctuation. Educators wonder about the effect that text messages might have on the writing habits and grammar skills of today's students. Their use of text acronyms such as LOL (laugh out loud) and text abbreviations that include numbers, such as gr8 (for great) or 2 (for to, too, or two), is working its way into their formal writing. While adults also use text acronyms and abbreviations, the concern is

that teens and young adults use them so often before developing formal writing skills. The result could be students who are less able to use formal language when needed.

Research indicates that the more text messages students send, the more likely it is that they may have difficulty with formal writing. On the positive side, by reducing a message to as few words as possible, students learn to present the most important content first, without rambling or exaggeration. The downside is this can lead to short, choppy sentences that do not connect with each other and a lack of supporting details, which are essential in formal writing. Other positives are that students are writing more than ever, and that this

type of writing can be considered a form of journaling, or recording of thoughts, activities, and opinions. Some educators argue that rather than worrying about the writing style that students use in their text messages, they should focus on helping students distinguish between formal and informal communications, and what is appropriate in each.

Does the use of text messages make students less likely to perform well in formal writing assignments? Why or why not? Should teachers allow students to use text acronyms and abbreviations in formal writing? Why or why not? Do text messages have any positive impact on communications skills? Why or why not?

Digital Cameras

A **digital camera** is a device that allows you to take photos and store the photographed images digitally (Figure 1-7). While many digital cameras look like a traditional camera, some are built into smartphones and other mobile devices.

🔄 **Internet Research**

What is a digital SLR camera?

Search for: digital slr camera introduction

Digital cameras typically allow you to review, and sometimes modify, images while they are in the camera. You also can transfer images from a digital camera to a computer, so that you can review, modify, share, organize, or print the images. Digital cameras often can connect to or communicate wirelessly with a computer, a printer, or the Internet, enabling you to access the photos on the camera without using a cable. Some also can record videos. Many digital devices, such as smartphones and tablets, include an integrated digital camera.

Figure 1-7 With a digital camera, you can view photographed images immediately through a small screen on the camera to see if the photo is worth keeping.
© iStockphoto / Oktay Ortakcioglu; © iStockphoto / Oktay Ortakcioglu; © Louis Bourgeois / Shutterstock.com

Portable Media Players

🔄 **Internet Research**

What are popular portable media players?

Search for: portable media players

A **portable media player**, sometimes called a *personal media player*, is a mobile device on which you can store, organize, and play or view digital media (Figure 1-8). Digital media includes music, photos, and videos. Portable media players enable you to listen to music, view photos, and watch videos, movies, and television shows. With most, you transfer the digital media from a computer (or the Internet, if the device is Internet capable) to the portable media player.

earbuds

Figure 1-8 Portable media players, such as the iPod shown here, typically include a set of earbuds.
© iStockphoto / Sebastien Cote

Portable media players usually include a set of *earbuds*, which are small speakers that rest inside each ear canal. Some portable media player models have a touch screen, while others have a pad that you operate with a thumb or finger, so that you can navigate through digital media, adjust volume, and customize settings. Some portable media players also offer a calendar, address book, games, and other apps (discussed later in this chapter).

🔍 Internet Research

What are the features of the top e-book readers?

Search for: e-book reader comparison

E-Book Readers

An **e-book reader** (short for electronic book reader), or *e-reader*, is a mobile device that is used primarily for reading e-books (Figure 1-9). An *e-book*, or digital book, is an electronic version of a printed book, readable on computers and other digital devices. In addition to books, you typically can purchase and read other forms of digital media such as newspapers and magazines.

Most e-book reader models have a touch screen, and some are Internet capable. These devices usually are smaller than tablets but larger than smartphones.

Figure 1-9   An e-book reader.
© iStockphoto / Michael Bodmann

Game Devices

A **game console** is a mobile computing device designed for single-player or multiplayer video games. Gamers often connect the game console to a television so that they can view their gameplay on the television's screen (Figure 1-10). Many game console models are Internet capable and also allow you to listen to music and watch movies or view photos. Typically weighing between three and eleven pounds, the compact size of game consoles makes them easy to use at home, in the car, in a hotel, or any location that has an electrical outlet and a television screen.

A handheld game device is small enough to fit in one hand, making it more portable than the game console. Because of their reduced size, the screens are small — similar in size to some smartphone screens. Some handheld game device models are Internet capable and also can communicate wirelessly with other similar devices for multiplayer gaming.

game console

handheld game device

Figure 1-10   Game consoles often connect to a television; handheld game devices contain a built-in screen.
© iStockphoto / Gene Chutka; © Barone Firenze / Shutterstock.com

CONSIDER THIS

Are digital cameras, portable media players, e-book readers, and handheld game devices becoming obsolete because more and more smartphones and tablets include their functionality?

True, many smartphones and tablets enable you to take and store photos; store, organize, and play or view your digital media; read e-books; and play games. This trend of computers and devices with technologies that overlap, called *convergence,* means that consumers may need fewer devices for the functionality that they require.

Still, consumers often purchase separate stand-alone devices (i.e., a separate digital camera, portable media player, etc.) for a variety of reasons. The stand-alone device (i.e., a digital camera) may have more features and functionality than the combined device offers (i.e., a smartphone). You might want to be able to use both devices at the same time, for example, send text messages on the phone while reading a book on an e-book reader. Or, you might want protection if your combined device (i.e., smartphone) breaks. For example, you still can listen to music on a portable media player if your smartphone becomes nonfunctional.

 MINI FEATURE 1-1

Living Digitally – Gaming

Video gamers spend billions of dollars each year making the most of their downtime with game consoles and devices. With outstanding 3-D graphics and challenging gameplay, nearly three-fourths of U.S. households own game hardware and software/apps. The popularity is due, in large part, to the social aspect of gathering families and friends to play together as a group or online with each other and those around the world.

Game Accessories and Input Techniques

The more popular game consoles work with a wide variety of accessories and input techniques for directing movements and actions of on-screen players and objects, some of which are described below and shown in the images to the left:

- **Gamepads:** Holding the gamepad with both hands, press buttons with your thumbs or move sticks in various directions to trigger events.
- **Air gestures:** Moving your body or a handheld device in predetermined directions through the air, you may need at least six feet of open space to accommodate your motions.
- **Voice commands:** Speaking instructions toward the game console, ensure no background noise is in the room, or use a headset.
- **Fitness accessories:** Working with fitness accessories, such as balance boards and resistance bands, you can make fitness fun and functional.

Games

Gamers have several options available for purchasing games for game consoles. They can (1) purchase or rent discs or other media that contain games; (2) download games, or transfer them from online stores, to a game console; or (3) sign up for cloud gaming services that stream games, or transfer games on demand.

For tablets and smartphones, you can download games from an app store to your mobile computer or device. Games are the most popular downloaded app category. Two of the major factors for this attractiveness are price, for many of the games can be downloaded at no or little cost, and impressive, fast graphics that draw users into the action.

The wide variety of categories offers a gaming experience for practically everyone. Numerous games are available in each genre (some of these games are shown on the next page).

- **Action and adventure:** Characters move through their world by running, jumping, and climbing in an attempt to reach the next level of play and eventually defeat a villain or rescue a prisoner.
- **Education:** Engaging and entertaining puzzles and problems present practical instruction and possible assessment to teach skills and concepts that are applicable in real-world circumstances.
- **Music and fitness:** Individuals and groups improve their physical and mental fitness while engaging in athletic competitions, aerobics, dance, and yoga.
- **Puzzle and strategy:** Players use their skills and intelligence to solve problems, generally with the goal of moving objects to create a pattern.
- **Racing and sports:** Athletes and drivers strive to complete a course or to cross a finish line in record time.
- **Role-playing:** Gamers assume the role of a character and experience adventures while on a major quest.
- **Simulation:** Players control an activity in a simulated situation, such as piloting an airplane or playing an instrument in a rock band.

The Entertainment Software Rating Board (ESRB) assigns ratings to provide guidance of a game's age-appropriateness and content.

✳ The number of hours spent playing games has increased steadily each year, and the tablet and smartphone industry is partly responsible for this rise in popularity. Is game playing advantageous to society? What are the advantages of playing games, and do they outweigh the disadvantages?

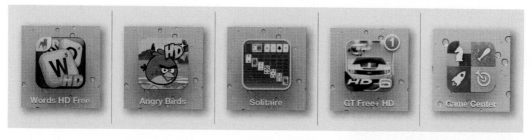

© iStockphoto / Ivan Vasilev

Data and Information

Computers process data (input) into information (output) and often store the data and resulting information for future use. *Data* is a collection of unprocessed items, which can include text, numbers, images, audio, and video. *Information* conveys meaning to users. Both business and home users can make well-informed decisions because they have instant access to information from anywhere in the world.

Many daily activities either involve the use of or depend on information from a computer. For example, as shown in Figure 1-11, computers process several data items to print information in the form of a cash register receipt.

✳ **CONSIDER THIS**

Can you give another example of data and its corresponding information?
Your name, address, term, course names, course sections, course grades, and course credits all represent data that is processed to generate your semester grade report. Other information on the grade report includes results of calculations such as total semester hours, grade point average, and total credits.

✳ **BTW**
Links to Media
When you see the ▤ e-book icon in this book, it means you can tap or click corresponding material in the Discovering Computers e-book for related interactive content, such as viewing an animation, interacting with a figure, visiting a website, or watching a video.

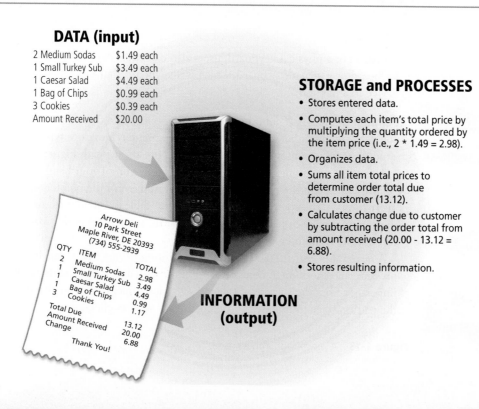

DATA (input)

2 Medium Sodas	$1.49 each
1 Small Turkey Sub	$3.49 each
1 Caesar Salad	$4.49 each
1 Bag of Chips	$0.99 each
3 Cookies	$0.39 each
Amount Received	$20.00

STORAGE and PROCESSES

• Stores entered data.

• Computes each item's total price by multiplying the quantity ordered by the item price (i.e., 2 * 1.49 = 2.98).

• Organizes data.

• Sums all item total prices to determine order total due from customer (13.12).

• Calculates change due to customer by subtracting the order total from amount received (20.00 - 13.12 = 6.88).

• Stores resulting information.

INFORMATION (output)

Arrow Deli
10 Park Street
Maple River, DE 20393
(734) 555-2939

QTY	ITEM	TOTAL
2	Medium Sodas	2.98
1	Small Turkey Sub	3.49
1	Caesar Salad	4.49
1	Bag of Chips	0.99
3	Cookies	1.17
	Total Due	13.12
	Amount Received	20.00
	Change	6.88

Thank You!

▤ **Figure 1-11**
A computer processes data into information. In this simplified example, the item ordered, item price, quantity ordered, and amount received all represent data (input). The computer processes the data to produce the cash register receipt (information, or output).
© Cengage Learning;
© iStockphoto / Norman Chan

Input

Users have a variety of input options for entering data into a computer, many of which involve using an input device. An **input device** is any hardware component that allows you to enter data and instructions into a computer or mobile device. The following sections discuss common input methods.

BTW

Mobile Computer Input
If you prefer a desktop keyboard to a laptop's keyboard or a tablet's on-screen keyboard, you can use a desktop keyboard with your mobile computer. Likewise, if you prefer using a mouse instead of a touchpad, you can use a mouse with your mobile computer.

desktop keyboard

laptop keyboard

Keyboards   A *keyboard* contains keys you press to enter data and instructions into a computer or mobile device (Figure 1-12). All desktop keyboards have a typing area that includes letters of the alphabet, numbers, punctuation marks, and other basic keys. Some users prefer a wireless keyboard because it eliminates the clutter of a cord.

Keyboards for desktops contain more keys than keyboards for mobile computers and devices. To provide the same functionality as a desktop keyboard, many of the keys on mobile computers and devices serve two or three purposes. On a laptop, for example, you often use the same keys to type numbers and to show various areas on a screen, switching a key's purpose by pressing a separate key first.

on-screen keyboard

mini keyboard

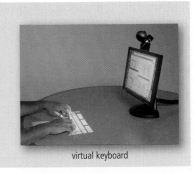

virtual keyboard

Figure 1-12 Users have a variety of keyboard options.
© skyfotostock / Shutterstock.com;
© Africa Studio / Shutterstock.com;
© iStockphoto / kycstudio;
© iStockphoto / MorePixels;
Courtesy of Virtek, Inc.

Instead of a physical keyboard, users also can enter data via an on-screen keyboard or a virtual keyboard, which is a keyboard that projects from a device to a flat surface.

Pointing Devices   A pointing device is an input device that allows a user to control a small symbol on a screen, called the pointer. Desktops typically use a mouse as their pointing device, and laptops use a touchpad (Figure 1-13).

A *mouse* is a pointing device that fits under the palm of your hand comfortably. With the mouse, you control movement of the pointer and send instructions to the computer or mobile device. Table 1-1 identifies some of the common mouse operations. Like keyboards, some users prefer working with a wireless mouse.

A *touchpad* is a small, flat, rectangular pointing device that is sensitive to pressure and motion. To control the pointer with a touchpad, slide your fingertip across the surface of the pad. On most touchpads, you also can tap the pad's surface to imitate mouse operations such as clicking.

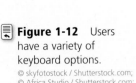

mouse

touchpad

Figure 1-13 A mouse and a touchpad.
© iStockphoto / PhotoTalk; © iStockphoto / Michael Bodmann

Table 1-1   Mouse Operations

Operation	Description	Common Uses
Point	Move the mouse until the pointer is positioned on the item of choice.	Position the pointer on the screen.
Click	Press and release the primary mouse button, which usually is the left mouse button.	Select or deselect items on the screen or start a program or feature.
Right-click	Press and release the secondary mouse button, which usually is the right mouse button.	Display a shortcut menu.
Double-click	Quickly press and release the primary mouse button twice without moving the mouse.	Start a program or program feature.
Drag	Point to an item, hold down the primary mouse button, move the item to the desired location on the screen, and then release the mouse button.	Move an object from one location to another or draw pictures.

Voice and Video Input   Some mobile devices and computers enable you to speak data instructions using voice input and to capture live full-motion images using video input. With your smartphone, for example, you may be able to use your voice to send a text message, schedule an appointment, and dial a phone number. Or, you may opt for video calling instead of a traditional phone call, so that you and the person you called can see each other as you chat on a computer or mobile device. As in this example, video input usually works in conjunction with voice input. For voice input, you use a microphone, and for video input you use a webcam (Figure 1-14).

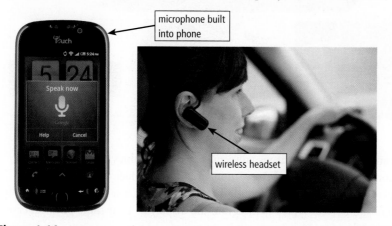

microphone built into phone

wireless headset

webcam

Figure 1-14   You can speak instructions into a microphone or wireless headset and capture live video on a webcam for a video call.
© iStockphoto / Stephen Krow; © iStockphoto / pierrephoto; © iStockphoto / Suprijono Suharjoto

A *microphone* is an input device that enables you to speak into a computer or mobile device. Many computers and most mobile devices contain built-in microphones. You also can talk into a *headset*, which contains both a microphone and a speaker. Many headsets can communicate wirelessly with the computer or mobile device. A *webcam* is a digital video camera that allows you to capture video and usually audio input for your computer or mobile device.

Scanners   A *scanner* is a light-sensing input device that converts printed text and images into a form the computer can process (Figure 1-15). A popular type of scanner works in a manner similar to a copy machine, except that instead of creating a paper copy of the document or photo, it stores the scanned document or photo electronically.

Figure 1-15   A scanner.
© iStockphoto / Edgaras Marozas

Output

Users have a variety of output options to convey text, graphics, audio, and video — many of which involve using an output device. An **output device** is any hardware component that conveys information from a computer or mobile device to one or more people. The following sections discuss common output methods.

Printers A **printer** is an output device that produces text and graphics on a physical medium such as paper. Printed content sometimes is referred to as a *hard copy* or *printout*. Most printers today print text and graphics in both black-and-white and color on a variety of paper types (Figure 1-16). Some printer models also can print lab-quality photos. A variety of printers support wireless printing, where a computer or other device communicates wirelessly with the printer.

Figure 1-16 A printer can produce a variety of printed output.

Courtesy of Epson America, Inc.; © designsstock / Shutterstock.com; © iStockphoto / Henrik Jonsson; © maigi / Shutterstock.com

Displays A display is an output device that visually conveys text, graphics, and video information. Displays consist of a screen and the components that produce the information on the screen. The display for a desktop typically is a monitor, which is a separate, physical device. Mobile computers and devices typically integrate the display in their same physical case (Figure 1-17). Some displays have touch screens.

smartphone display

digital camera display

tablet display

laptop display

monitor display

Figure 1-17 Displays vary depending on the computer or mobile device.

© iStockphoto / Sebastien Cote; © David Lentz / Photos.com; © Dmitry Rukhlenko / Photos.com; © Mrallen / Dreamstime.com; © Pakhnyushcha / Shutterstock.com

What can you do to ease eyestrain while using a computer or mobile device?
Position the display about 20 degrees below eye level. Clean the screen regularly. Blink your eyes every five seconds. Adjust the room lighting. Face into an open space beyond the screen. Use larger fonts or zoom the display. Take an eye break every 30 minutes. If you wear glasses, ask your doctor about computer glasses.

Speakers   Speakers allow you to hear audio, that is, music, voice, and other sounds. Most personal computers and mobile devices have a small internal speaker. Many users attach higher-quality speakers to their computers and mobile devices, including game consoles.

So that only you can hear sound, you can listen through earbuds (shown in Figure 1-8 on page 8) or headphones, which cover or are placed outside of the ear (Figure 1-18). Both earbuds and head-phones usually include noise-cancelling tech-nology to reduce the interference of sounds from the surround-ing environment. To eliminate the clutter of cords, users can opt for wireless speakers or wireless headphones.

🔵 **Internet Research**
What types of earbuds are available?
Search for: earbud reviews

Figure 1-18   In a crowded environment where speakers are not practical, users can wear headphones to hear music, voice, and other sounds.
© iStockphoto / Photo_Alto

Memory and Storage

Memory consists of electronic components that store instructions waiting to be executed and the data needed by those instructions. Although some forms of memory are permanent, most memory keeps data and instructions temporarily, which means its contents are erased when the computer is shut off.

Storage, by contrast, holds data, instructions, and information for future use. For example, computers can store hundreds or millions of student names and addresses permanently. A computer keeps data, instructions, and information on **storage media**. Examples of storage media are hard disks, solid-state drives, USB flash drives, memory cards, and optical discs. The amount of storage for each type of storage media varies, but hard disks, solid-state drives, and optical discs usually hold more than USB flash drives and memory cards. Some storage media are portable, meaning you can remove the medium from one computer and carry it to another computer.

A **storage device** records (writes) and/or retrieves (reads) items to and from storage media. Storage devices often also function as a source of input and output because they transfer items from storage to memory and vice versa. Drives and readers/writers, which are types of storage devices, accept a specific kind of storage media. For example, a DVD drive (storage device) accepts a DVD (storage media).

Hard Disks   A *hard disk* is a storage device that contains one or more inflexible, circular platters that use magnetic particles to store data, instructions, and information. The entire device is enclosed in an airtight, sealed case to protect it from contamination. Desktops and laptops often contain at least one hard disk that is mounted inside the computer's case, called a fixed disk because this hard disk is not portable (Figure 1-19a on the next page).

✺ **BTW**
Disk vs. Disc
The spelling, disk, is used for hard disks and other magnetic media, and disc is used for CDs, DVDs, and other optical media.

Figure 1-19 A fixed disk is mounted inside a laptop's case; an external hard disk is a separate, freestanding device.
© iStockphoto / Brian Balster; © iStockphoto / murat sarica

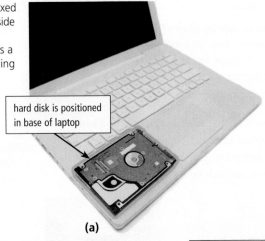

hard disk is positioned in base of laptop

(a)

External hard disks are separate, portable, freestanding hard disks that usually connect to the computer with a cable (Figure 1-19b).

external hard disk connected to laptop

(b)

hard disk contains moving parts

SSD contains no moving parts

Figure 1-20 A solid-state drive (SSD) is about the same size as a laptop hard disk.
© iStockphoto / Ludovit Repko

Solid-State Drives A *solid-state drive* (SSD) is a storage device that typically uses flash memory to store data, instructions, and information. Flash memory contains no moving parts, making it more durable and shock resistant than other types of media. For this reason, some manufacturers are using SSDs instead of hard disks in their desktops, laptops, and tablets (Figure 1-20).

USB Flash Drives A *USB flash drive* is a portable flash memory storage device that you plug in a USB port, which is a special, easily accessible opening on a computer or mobile device (Figure 1-21). USB flash drives are convenient for mobile users because they are small and lightweight enough to be transported on a keychain or in a pocket.

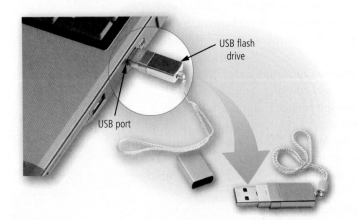

USB flash drive

USB port

Figure 1-21 You insert a USB flash drive in a USB port on a computer.
© Pakhnyushcha / Shutterstock.com

Memory Cards A *memory card* is removable flash memory, usually no bigger than 1.5 inches in height or width, that you insert in and remove from a slot in a computer, mobile device, or card reader/writer (Figure 1-22). With a card reader/writer, you can transfer the stored items, such as digital photos, from a memory card to a computer or printer that does not have a built-in card slot.

Figure 1-22
Computers and mobile devices use a variety of styles of memory cards to store documents, photos, and other items.
© Verisakeet / Fotolia;
© Sonar / Fotolia;
© Xuejun li / Fotolia;
© uwimages / Fotolia

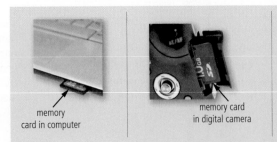

memory card in computer

memory card in digital camera

memory card in phone

memory card in card reader/writer, which is attached to computer

Optical Discs   An optical disc is a type of storage media that consists of a flat, round, portable metal disc made of metal, plastic, and lacquer that is written and read by a laser. CDs (compact discs) and DVDs (digital versatile discs) are two types of optical discs (Figure 1-23).

DVD

DVD drive

Figure 1-23   You can insert a DVD in a DVD drive on a computer.
© iStockphoto / Hanquan Chen

 CONSIDER THIS

What is the general use for each type of storage media?
Hard disks and SSDs store software and all types of user files. A *file* is a named collection of stored data, instructions, or information and can contain text, images, audio, and video. Memory cards and USB flash drives store files you intend to transport from one location to another, such as a homework assignment or photos. Optical discs generally store software, photos, movies, and music.

Cloud Storage   Instead of storing data, instructions, and information locally on a hard disk or other media, you can opt for cloud storage. *Cloud storage* is an Internet service that provides storage to computer users (Figure 1-24).

Types of services offered by cloud storage providers vary. Some provide storage for specific types of media, such as photos, whereas others store any content and provide backup services. A *backup* is a duplicate of content on a storage medium that you can use in case the original is lost, damaged, or destroyed. Read Secure IT 1-1 on the next page for suggestions for backing up your computers and mobile devices.

Figure 1-24   JustCloud is an example of a website that provides cloud storage solutions to home and business users.
Source: JustCloud.com

✳ SECURE IT 1-1

Backing Up Computers and Mobile Devices

Many factors, including power outages and hardware failure, can cause loss of data, instructions, or information on a computer or mobile device. To protect against loss, you should back up the contents of storage media regularly. Backing up can provide peace of mind and save hours of work attempting to recover important material in the event of loss.

A backup plan for computers could include the following:

- Use a backup program, either included with your computer's operating system or one that you purchased separately, to copy the contents of your entire hard disk to a separate device.

- Regularly copy music, photos, videos, documents, and other important items to a USB flash drive, external hard disk, or DVD.

- Subscribe to a cloud storage provider.

- Schedule your files to be backed up regularly.

Backup plans for mobile devices are less specific. Apps for backing up your smartphone or tablet's content are available. You also can back up a mobile device to your computer's hard disk using synchronization software that runs on your computer (synchronization software is discussed later in this chapter). Some mobile device manufacturers, such as Apple, provide cloud storage solutions to owners of their devices. Other services allow subscribers to use a friend's computer as a backup storage location.

Overall, the best advice is to back up often using a variety of methods.

✳ Do you back up files regularly? If not, why not? What would you do if you had no backup and then discovered that your computer or mobile device had failed?

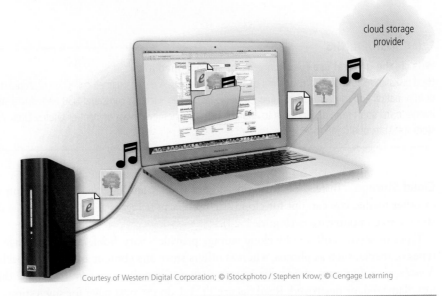

cloud storage provider

Courtesy of Western Digital Corporation; © iStockphoto / Stephen Krow; © Cengage Learning

---

✔ NOW YOU KNOW

Be sure you understand the material presented in the sections titled Computers, Mobile and Game Devices, and Data and Information, as it relates to the chapter objectives.

You now should know . . .

- Which type of computer might be suited to your needs (Objective 1)

- Why you would use a smartphone, digital camera, portable media player, and an e-book reader, and which game software/apps you find interesting (Objective 2)

- How to recognize the difference between data and information (Objective 3)

- When you might use the various methods of input, output, and storage (Objective 4)

⊡ Quiz Yourself Online: Check your knowledge of related content by navigating to this book's Quiz Yourself resource on Computer Concepts CourseMate and then tapping or clicking Objectives 1–4.

The Internet

The **Internet** is a worldwide collection of computer networks that connects millions of businesses, government agencies, educational institutions, and individuals (Figure 1-25). The Internet provides society with access to global information and instant communications.

Businesses, called Internet service providers (ISPs), offer users and organizations access to the Internet free or for a fee. By subscribing to an ISP, you can connect to the Internet through your computers and mobile devices.

Today, more than two billion home and business users around the world access a variety of services on the Internet. The World Wide Web is one of the more widely used Internet services. Other popular services include email, instant messaging, VoIP, and FTP (all discussed later in this chapter).

 BTW

Web vs. Internet
The terms, web and Internet, should not be used interchangeably. The web is a service of the Internet.

Figure 1-25 The Internet is the largest computer network, connecting millions of computers and devices around the world.

© Cengage Learning; © Mmaxer / Shutterstock.com; © Alfonso de Tomas /Shutterstock.com; © SSSCCC / Shutterstock.com; © iStockphoto / Petar Chernaev; © amfoto / Shutterstock.com; © iStockphoto / Oleksiy Mark; © iStockphoto / Oleksiy Mark; © iStockphoto / sweetym; Source: Microsoft; © Oleksiy Mark / Shutterstock.com; Source: Cengage Learning; © iStockphoto / Stephen Krow; © Cengage Learning; © iStockphoto / Skip O'Donnell;Source: Apple Inc; © iStockphoto / Skip O'Donnell; Source: Nutrition Blog Network; © iStockphoto / Ayaaz Rattansi; Source: Microsoft; © Oleksiy Mark / Shutterstock.com; Source: Microsoft; © Cengage Learning;

The World Wide Web

The World Wide Web (or web, for short) is a global library of information available to anyone connected to the Internet. People around the world access the web to accomplish a variety of online tasks, including:

- Search for information
- Conduct research
- Communicate with and meet other people
- Share information, photos, and videos with others
- Access news, weather, and sports

- Participate in online training
- Shop for goods and services
- Play games with others
- Download or listen to music
- Watch videos
- Download or read books

The **web** consists of a worldwide collection of electronic documents. Each electronic document on the web is called a **webpage**, which can contain text, graphics, audio, and video (Figure 1-26).

🌐 **BTW**
Downloading
Downloading is the process of transferring content from a server on the Internet to a computer or mobile device.

Figure 1-26 Webpages, such as the one shown here, can display text, graphics, audio, and video on a computer or mobile device. Pointing to a link on the screen typically changes the shape of the pointer to a small hand with a pointing index finger.
Source: WTMJ

Webpages often contain links. A *link*, short for *hyperlink*, is a built-in connection to other documents, graphics, audio files, videos, webpages, or websites. To activate an item associated with a link, you tap or click the link. In Figure 1-26 on the previous page, for example, tapping or clicking the audio link connects to a live radio show so that you can hear the broadcast. A text link often changes color after you tap or click it to remind you visually that you previously have visited the webpage or downloaded the content associated with the link.

Links allow you to obtain information in a nonlinear way. That is, instead of accessing topics in a specified order, you move directly to a topic of interest. Some people use the phrase *surfing the web* to refer to the activity of using links to explore the web.

A **website** is a collection of related webpages, which are stored on a web server. A **web server** is a computer that delivers requested webpages to your computer or mobile device.

Web Browsing

A **browser** is software that enables users with an Internet connection to access and view webpages on a computer or mobile device. Some widely used browsers include Internet Explorer, Firefox, Safari, and Google Chrome. Read How To 1-2 for instructions about using a browser to display a webpage on a computer or mobile device.

✸ HOW TO 1-2

Use a Browser to Display a Webpage
The following steps describe how to use a browser to display a webpage on a computer or mobile device:

1. Run the browser. (For instructions on running programs and apps, see How To 1-4 and How To 1-5 on page 27.)

2. If necessary, tap or click the address bar to select it and any previously displayed web address it may contain. (A web address is a unique address that identifies a webpage.)

3. In the address bar, type the web address of the webpage you want to visit and then press the ENTER key or tap or click the Go (or similar) button to display the webpage. For example, www.cengagebrain.com is a valid web address, which displays the CengageBrain webpage shown in the figure below. (Chapter 2 discusses the components of a web address in more detail.)

4. If necessary, scroll to view the entire webpage. You can scroll either by sliding your finger across a touch screen or by using a pointing device, such as a mouse, to drag the scroll bar.

5. Tap or click links on the webpage to navigate to the link's destination.

✸ What should you do if the web address you enter does not display a webpage or you receive an error message?

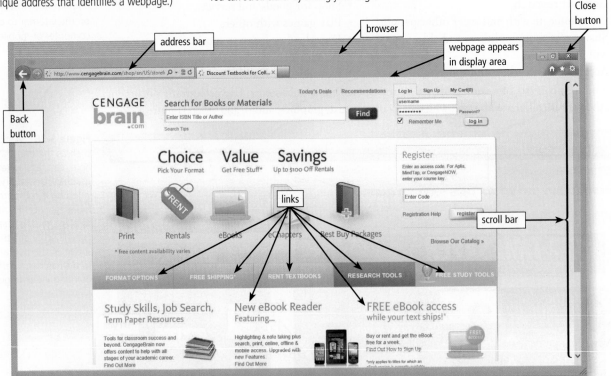

Web Searching

A primary reason that people use the web is to search for specific information, including text, photos, music, and videos. The first step in successful searching is to identify the main idea or concept in the topic about which you are seeking information. Determine any synonyms, alternate spellings, or variant word forms for the topic. Then, use a search engine, such as Google, to help you locate the information. A **search engine** is software that finds websites, webpages, images, videos, news, maps, and other information related to a specific topic. Read How To 1-3 for instructions about how to perform a basic web search using a search engine on a computer or mobile device.

 HOW TO 1-3

Perform a Basic Web Search

The following steps describe how to use a search engine on a computer or mobile device to perform a basic web search:

1. Run a browser. (For instructions on running programs and apps, see How To 1-4 and How To 1-5 on page 27.)

2. If the browser does not contain a separate Search box near the address bar, display the search engine's webpage on the screen by entering its web address in the address bar. For example, you could type `google.com` to display the Google search engine, `bing.com` to display the Bing search engine, or `yahoo.com` to display the Yahoo! search engine.

3. Tap or click the Search box and then type the desired search text in the Search box. The more descriptive the search text, the easier it will be to locate the desired search results. As the figure shows, the search engine may provide search text suggestions as you type search text in the Search box.

4. To display search results based on your typed search text, press the ENTER key or tap or click the Search button. To display search

results based on one of the suggestions provided by the search engine, tap or click the desired search text suggestion.

5. Scroll through the search results and then tap or click a search result to display the corresponding webpage.

6. To return to the search results, tap or click the Back button in your browser, which typically looks like a left-pointing arrow.

 What search text would you enter to locate the admission criteria for your school?

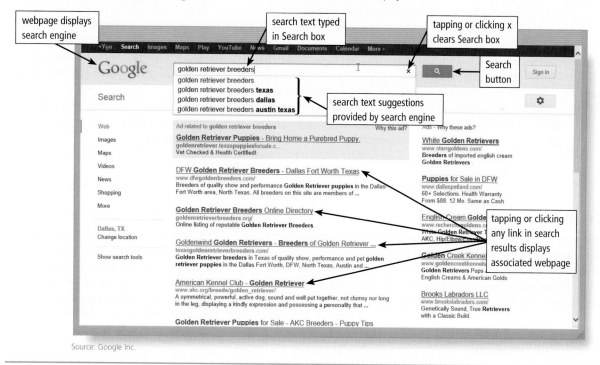

Source: Google Inc.

Online Social Networks

An **online social network**, also called a **social networking site**, is a website that encourages members in its online community to share their interests, ideas, stories, photos, music, and videos with other registered users (Figure 1-27 on the next page). Popular social networking sites include Facebook, Twitter, and LinkedIn.

Some social networking sites have no specialized audience; others are more focused. A photo sharing site, for example, is a specific type of social networking site that allows users to create an online photo album and store and share their digital photos. Similarly, a video sharing site is a type of social networking site that enables users to store and share their personal videos.

 BTW

Facebook and Twitter

Technology Innovators: You should be familiar with Facebook, Mark Zuckerberg, and Twitter.

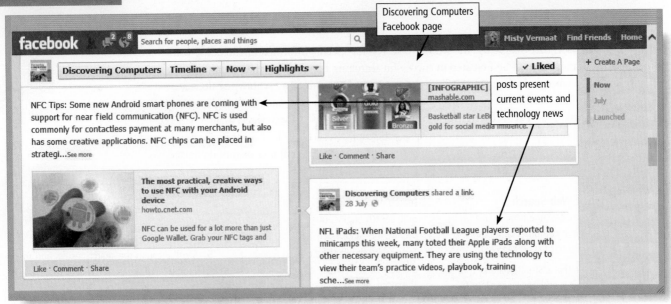

Figure 1-27 When Facebook users 'like' this Discovering Computers Facebook page, the posts shown here appear on their own personal pages. As a student in this class, you should 'like' the Discovering Computers page so that you easily can keep up to date with relevant technology changes and events in the computing industry. If you do not have a Facebook account, use a search engine to search for the text, discovering computers facebook, to display the page in a browser.
Source: Facebook

 CONSIDER THIS

 BTW

Blogs
Posts on Twitter also form a blog, because of its journal format with the most recent entry at the top.

How do Facebook, Twitter, and LinkedIn differ?

With Facebook, you share messages, interests, activities, events, photos, and other personal information — called posts — with family and friends. You also can 'like' pages of celebrities, companies, products, etc., so that posts on these pages appear on your Facebook page. With Twitter, you 'follow' people, companies, and organizations in which you have an interest. Twitter enables you to stay current with the daily activities of those you are following via their Tweets, which are short posts (messages) that Tweeters broadcast for all their followers.

On LinkedIn, you share professional interests, education, and employment history, and add colleagues or coworkers to your list of contacts. You can include recommendations from people who know you professionally. Many employers post jobs using LinkedIn and consider information in your profile as your online resume.

Read Ethics & Issues 1-2 to consider whether employees should be held accountable for their social networking posts.

 ETHICS & ISSUES 1-2

Should Employees Be Held Accountable for Their Social Networking Posts?

Companies no longer solely rely on a resume and interview to consider you as a potential employee. At a minimum, the hiring manager may search the web to find out any information readily available about you. This includes your use of social networking or blogging sites, such as Facebook or Twitter. Once employed, your manager still may track and review your online presence. You might believe your posts and photos should be your own business. Some companies, however, feel that what you say and do online, as well as what others say about you, could reflect poorly on them and, thus, should affect your employment. These companies are worried not only about their reputations but also

potential red flags. For example, companies may be on the lookout for employees who discuss company sales activity on their blogs, gripe about their managers on Twitter, or have Facebook photos that show them taking part in unethical, illegal, or unsavory activities.

Social network-related firings have made headlines. Two examples include a CFO (chief financial officer) fired for blogging details about his publicly traded company and a teacher fired for making disparaging remarks on her Facebook page about students and their parents. Accessing an employee's or a potential employee's social networking profile also could have consequences for the company. For example, if a company realizes that a person is a member of a minority group or has a disability, the company could face

discrimination charges if it does not hire or later fires the employee. Debate regarding what falls under free speech is ongoing. Remember that what you post online is not deleted easily. Whether or not you currently are searching for a job, online posts you make now can damage your future employment opportunities.

What are the results when you search for yourself online? What steps can you take to clean up and protect your online reputation? Would you share social networking accounts or passwords with an employer or potential employer? Why or why not? Should companies be allowed to view and monitor employees' accounts? Why or why not?

Internet Communications

The web is only one of the services on the Internet. Some of the other services on the Internet facilitate communications among users:

- Email allows you to send messages to and receive messages and files from other users via a computer network.
- With instant messaging (IM), you can have a real-time typed conversation with another connected user (real-time means that both of you are online at the same time).
- VoIP enables users to speak to other users over the Internet.
- With FTP, users can transfer items to and from other computers on the Internet.

Digital Security and Safety

People rely on computers to create, store, and manage their information. To safeguard this information, it is important that users protect their computers and mobile devices. Users also should be aware of health risks and environmental issues associated with using computers and mobile devices.

Viruses and Other Malware

Malware, short for malicious software, is software that acts without a user's knowledge and deliberately alters the computer's and mobile device's operations. Examples of malware include viruses, worms, trojan horses, rootkits, spyware, adware, and zombies. Each of these types of malware attacks your computer or mobile device differently. Some are harmless pranks that temporarily freeze, play sounds, or display messages on your computer or mobile device. Others destroy or corrupt data, instructions, and information stored on the infected computer or mobile device. If you notice any unusual changes in the performance of your computer or mobile device, it may be infected with malware. Read Secure IT 1-2 for ways to protect computers from viruses and other malware.

BTW

Malware
A leading maker of security software claims its software blocked more than five billion malware attacks in a single year.

 SECURE IT 1-2

Protection from Viruses and Other Malware

Although it is impossible to ensure a virus or malware never will attack a computer, you can take steps to protect your computer by following these practices:

- **Use virus protection software.** Install a reputable antivirus program and then scan the entire computer to be certain it is free of viruses and other malware. Update the antivirus program and the virus signatures (known specific patterns of viruses) regularly.

- **Use a firewall.** Set up a hardware firewall or install a software firewall that protects your network's resources from outside intrusions.

- **Be suspicious of all unsolicited email attachments.** Never open an email attachment unless you are expecting it *and* it is from a trusted source. When

in doubt, ask the sender to confirm the attachment is legitimate before you open it. Delete or quarantine flagged attachments immediately.

- **Disconnect your computer from the Internet.** If you do not need Internet access, disconnect the computer from the Internet. Some security experts recommend disconnecting from the computer network before opening email attachments.

- **Download software with caution.** Download programs or apps only from websites you trust, especially those with music and movie sharing software.

- **Close spyware windows.** If you suspect a pop-up window (rectangular area that suddenly appears on your screen) may be spyware, close the window. Never click an Agree or OK button in a suspicious window.

- **Before using any removable media, scan it for malware.** Follow this procedure even for shrink-wrapped software from major developers. Some commercial software has been infected and distributed to unsuspecting users. Never start a computer with removable media inserted in the computer unless you are certain the media are uninfected.

- **Keep current.** Install the latest updates for your computer software. Stay informed about new virus alerts and virus hoaxes.

- **Back up regularly.** In the event your computer becomes unusable due to a virus attack or other malware, you will be able to restore operations if you have a clean (uninfected) backup.

What precautions do you take to prevent viruses and other malware from infecting your computer? What new steps will you take to attempt to protect your computer?

Privacy

Nearly every life event is stored in a computer somewhere . . . in medical records, credit reports, tax records, etc. In many instances, where personal and confidential records were not protected properly, individuals have found their privacy violated and identities stolen. Some techniques you can use to protect yourself from identity theft include shredding financial documents before discarding them, never tapping or clicking links in unsolicited email messages, and enrolling in a credit monitoring service.

Adults, teens, and children around the world are using online social networks to share their photos, videos, journals, music, and other personal information publicly. Some of these unsuspecting, innocent computer users have fallen victim to crimes committed by dangerous strangers. Protect yourself and your dependents from these criminals by being cautious in email messages and on websites. For example, do not share information that would allow others to identify or locate you and do not disclose identification numbers, user names, passwords, or other personal security details. A user name is a unique combination of characters, such as letters of the alphabet or numbers, that identifies one specific user. A password is a private combination of characters associated with a user name. Read Secure IT 1-3 for tips on creating strong passwords.

Internet Research

What are other techniques that deter identity theft?

Search for: prevent identity theft

SECURE IT 1-3

Creating Strong Passwords

A good password is easy for you to remember but difficult for criminals and password-breaking software to guess. Use these guidelines to create effective, strong passwords:

- **Personal information:** Avoid using any part of your first or last name, your family members' names, phone number, street address, license plate number, Social Security number, or birth date.

- **Length:** Use at least eight characters.

- **Difficulty:** Use a variety of uppercase and lowercase letters, numbers, punctuation, and symbols. Select characters located on different parts of the keyboard, not the ones you commonly use or that are

adjacent to each other. Criminals use software that converts common words to symbols, so changing the word, two, to the numeral, 2, or the word, and, to the ampersand symbol, &, is not likely to foil a thief.

- **Modify:** Change the password frequently, at least every three months.

- **Variation:** Do not use the same password for all accounts. Once criminals have stolen a password, they attempt to use that password for other accounts they find on your computer or mobile device, especially banking websites.

- **Passphrase:** A *passphrase*, which is similar to a password, consists of several words separated by spaces. Security experts

recommend misspelling a few of the words and adding several numerals. For example, the phrase, "Create a strong password," could become the passphrase, "Creaet a strang pasword42."

- **Common sequences:** Avoid numbers or letters in easily recognized patterns, such as "asdfjkl;," "12345678," "09870987," or "abcdefg." Also, do not spell words backwards or use common abbreviations.

- **Test:** Use online tools to evaluate password strength.

How strong are your passwords? How will you modify your passwords using some of these guidelines?

Health Concerns

Prolonged or improper computer use can lead to injuries or disorders of the hands, wrists, elbows, eyes, neck, and back. Computer users can protect themselves from these health risks through proper workplace design, good posture while at the computer, and appropriately spaced work breaks.

Two behavioral health risks are technology addiction and technology overload. Technology addiction occurs when someone becomes obsessed with using technology. Individuals suffering from technology overload feel distressed when deprived of computers and mobile devices. Once recognized, both technology addiction and technology overload are treatable disorders.

Environmental Issues

Manufacturing processes for computers and mobile devices along with *e-waste*, or discarded computers and mobile devices, are depleting natural resources and polluting the environment. When computers and mobile devices are stored in basements or other locations, disposed in landfills, or burned in incinerators, they can release toxic materials and potentially dangerous levels of lead, mercury, and flame retardants.

Green computing involves reducing the electricity consumed and environmental waste generated when using a computer. Strategies that support green computing include recycling, using energy efficient hardware and energy saving features, regulating manufacturing processes, extending the life of computers, and immediately donating or properly disposing of replaced computers. When you purchase a new computer, some retailers offer to dispose of your old computer properly. To learn more about green computing, complete the Green Computing exercise in the Internet Research section of the student assignments in each chapter of this book.

 CONSIDER THIS —————————————————————————————

How can you contribute to green computing?

Some habits you can alter that will help reduce the environmental impact of computing include the following:

1. Do not leave a computer or device running overnight.
2. Turn off your monitor, printer, and other devices when you are not using them.
3. Use energy efficient hardware.
4. Use paperless methods to communicate.
5. Recycle paper and buy recycled paper.
6. Recycle toner, computers, mobile devices, printers, and other devices.
7. Telecommute.
8. Use videoconferencing and VoIP for meetings.

Programs and Apps

Software, also called a **program**, consists of a series of related instructions, organized for a common purpose, that tells the computer what tasks to perform and how to perform them.

Two categories of software are system software and application software. System software consists of the programs that control or maintain the operations of the computer and its devices. Operating systems are a widely recognized example of system software. Other types of system software, sometimes called tools, enable you to perform maintenance-type tasks usually related to managing devices, media, and programs used by computers and mobile devices. The next sections discuss operating systems and application software.

Operating Systems

An *operating system* is a set of programs that coordinates all the activities among computer or mobile device hardware. It provides a means for users to communicate with the computer or mobile device and other software. Many of today's computers and mobile devices use a version of Microsoft's Windows, Apple's Mac OS, Apple's iOS, or Google's Android (Figure 1-28).

To use application software, your computer or mobile device must be running an operating system.

Figure 1-28   Shown here are the Mac OS and Windows operating systems for personal computers and the Android and iOS operating systems for smartphones. You interact with these operating system interfaces by tapping or clicking their icons or tiles.

Source: Apple Inc.; Apple Inc.; Google Inc.; Microsoft.

Applications

Application software, usually simply called an **application** (or **app** for short), consists of programs designed to make users more productive and/or assist them with personal tasks. Browsers, discussed in an earlier section, are an example of an application that enables users with an Internet connection to access and view webpages. Table 1-2 identifies the categories of applications with samples of ones commonly used in each category.

Applications include programs stored on a computer, as well as those on a mobile device or delivered to your device over the Internet. The term, *desktop app*, often is used to describe applications stored on a computer. The term, *web app* is an application stored on a web server that you access through a browser. A *mobile app* is an application you download from a mobile device's application store or other location on the Internet to a smartphone or other mobile device. Some applications are available as both a web app and a mobile app. For practice working with web apps and mobile apps, see the exercises called App Adventure on the Beyond the Book student assignment page in each chapter of this book.

Table 1-2 Categories of Applications

Category	Sample Applications	Sample Uses
Productivity 	Word Processing	Create letters, reports, and other documents.
	Presentation	Create visual aids for presentations.
	Schedule and Contact Management	Organize appointments and contact lists.
	Personal Finance	Balance checkbook, pay bills, and track income and expenses.
Graphics and Media	Photo Editing	Modify digital photos, i.e., crop, remove red-eye, etc.
	Video and Audio Editing	Modify recorded movie clips, add music, etc.
	Media Player	View images, listen to audio/music, watch videos.
Personal Interest	Travel, Mapping, and Navigation	View maps, obtain route directions, locate points of interest.
	Reference	Look up material in dictionaries, encyclopedias, etc.
	Educational	Learn through tutors and prepare for tests.
	Entertainment	Receive entertainment news alerts, check movie times and reviews, play games.
Communications	Browser	Access and view webpages.
	Email	Send and receive messages.
	VoIP	Speak to other users over the Internet.
	FTP	Transfer items to and from other computers on the Internet.
Security 	Antivirus	Protect a computer against viruses.
	Personal Firewall	Detect and protect against unauthorized intrusions.
	Spyware, Adware, and other Malware Removers	Detect and delete spyware, adware, and other malware.

Installing and Running Applications

Installing software is the process of setting up software to work with a computer, printer, and other hardware. When you buy a computer, it usually has some software such as an operating system preinstalled on its hard disk so that you can use the computer the first time you turn it on. Installed operating systems often include other programs such as a browser, media player, and calculator. To use additional desktop apps on a computer, you usually need to install the software. Mobile apps typically install automatically after you transfer the app's files to your device from its website. You usually do not need to install web apps before you can run them.

Once installed, you can run an application so that you can interact with it. When you instruct a computer or mobile device to run an application, the computer or mobile device *loads* its software, which means the application is copied from storage to memory. Once in memory, the computer or mobile device can carry out, or execute, the instructions in the application so that you can use it.

You interact with a program or application through its user interface. The *user interface* controls how you enter data and instructions and how information is displayed on the screen. Often, you work with icons or tiles (shown in Figure 1-28 on page 25), which are miniature images that link to programs, media, documents, or other objects. Read How To 1-4 for instructions about installing, running, and exiting applications; and read How To 1-5 for instructions about locating, installing, and running mobile apps.

 HOW TO 1-4

Install, Run, and Exit an Application

The following steps describe how to install, run, and exit an application on a computer.

Locate the Application
- Locate the application to install. Applications are available from retail stores, websites, and from other services such as Apple's App Store or Google Play.

Download and/or Install the Application
- If you are installing an application from physical media such as a CD or DVD, insert the media in your computer. If the installation does not start automatically, locate the installation program on the media and then double-tap or double-click the installation program.

- If the application is available from a website or online store, download the application to your computer. Once the download is complete, if the installation does not start automatically, locate and then double-tap or double-click the downloaded file to begin the installation.

Run the Application
- You have various options for running an application:
  ○ Tap or click the application's tile or double-tap or double-click the application's icon in the desktop.
  ○ Display a list of all applications on your computer and then tap or click the icon representing the application to run (some computers may require

you to double-tap or double-click the icon).
  ○ Use the search feature in the operating system to locate the newly installed application and then tap or click the search result to run the application.

Exit the Application
- Locate and tap or click an Exit or Close button or an Exit or Close command, which often can be found on an application's File menu.
- Locate and tap or click the Close button on the application's title bar (horizontal space at top of window).

✹ If you run a second application without first exiting the one you are using, how can you return to the first application?

 HOW TO 1-5

Locate, Install, and Run a Mobile App

The following steps describe how to locate, install, and run an app on a mobile device:

1. Navigate to the online store for your device. Common stores used to obtain apps include Apple's App Store and Google Play.
2. Use the search feature to browse for the type of app you would like to download

and install. If the app is not free, follow the payment instructions.

3. Tap or click the appropriate button to download the desired app. Depending on your device, you may need to enter additional information, such as a password, to download the app. Once the app downloads, it should install automatically.

4. Locate the app's icon on your device and then tap or click the icon to run the app. Depending on the app, you may have to create a profile, which contains personal data about a user, or enter your email address.

✹ After installing an app on your device, what are some locations you might look to find the new app's icon or tile?

✳ **CONSIDER THIS**

How do you know if a program will run on your computer?
When you buy a computer, the box, the manufacturer's website, or the order summary will list the computer's specifications. Similarly, when you buy software, the software box or the product's website will list specifications and minimum requirements for memory, speed, and more. Your computer's specifications should be the same as or greater than the software specifications. Ensure the software will run on your computer before making a purchase, because many retailers will not allow you to return software.

Developing Programs and Apps

A *software developer*, sometimes called an application developer or computer programmer, is someone who develops programs and apps or writes the instructions that direct the computer or mobile device to process data into information. When writing instructions, a developer must be sure the program or app works properly so that the computer or mobile device generates the desired results. Complex programs can require thousands to millions of instructions.

Software developers use a programming language or program development tool to create computer programs and apps. Popular programming languages include C++, Java, JavaScript, Visual C#, and Visual Basic. Figure 1-29 shows some of the Visual Basic instructions a programmer may write to create a simple payroll program.

Figure 1-29
A developer writes instructions using Visual Basic (a) to create the Payroll Information window shown here (b).
© Cengage Learning

(a)

```
Public Class frmPayroll

    Private Sub frmPayroll_Load(ByVal sender As System.Object, ByVal e As System.EventArgs) Handles MyBase.Load
        ' The eventhandler is executed when the form is loaded.  It
        ' clears the Label objects for the hours worked and weekly pay.

        lblHoursWorked.Text = ""
        lblExtraMinutesWorked.Text = ""
        lblRegularPay.Text = ""
        txthoursWorked.Focus()
    End Sub

    Private Sub btnWeeklyPay_Click(ByVal sender As System.Object, ByVal e As System.EventArgs) Handles btnWeekl
        ' This event handler is executed when the user clicks the Weekly
        ' Pay button.  It calculates and displays the hours worked, minutes
        ' worked, and weekly pay.

        Dim strHoursWorked As String
        Dim strHourlyPay As String
        Dim decHourlyPay As Decimal
        Dim intHoursWorked As Integer
        Dim decRegularPay As Decimal
        Dim decOverTimeHours As Decimal
        Dim decOvertimePay As Decimal

        ' Convert the user input from string to a numeric value
        strHourlyPay = txtHourlyPayRate.Text
        decHourlyPay = Convert.ToDecimal(strHourlyPay)
        strHoursWorked = txtHoursWorked.Text
        intHoursWorked = Convert.ToInt32(strHoursWorked)
        If intHoursWorked > 40 Then
            decRegularPay = decHourlyPay * 40
            lblRegularPay.Text = decRegularPay.ToString("C")
            decOvertimePay = 1.5D * decOverTimeHours + decHourlyPay
        Else
            decRegularPay = decHourlyPay * decHourlyPay

        End If
```

(b)

🖳 Payroll Information		
Employee Name	Robert Terrell	
Hours Worked	42	
Hourly Rate	18.00	
Calculate Pay		
Regular Pay	**$720.00**	
Overtime Pay	**$54.00**	
Total Pay	**$774.00**	

✅ **NOW YOU KNOW**

Be sure you understand the material presented in the sections titled The Internet, Digital Security and Safety, and Programs and Apps, as it relates to the chapter objectives.
You now should know . . .

- Why webpages use links (Objective 5)
- How you could use a browser to display a webpage and how to perform a basic web search (Objective 6)
- What risks you are exposed to as a result of your technology use and how you can minimize those risks (Objective 7)
- How to recognize an operating system and which programs and apps you might find useful (Objective 8)

 Quiz Yourself Online: Check your knowledge of related content by navigating to this book's Quiz Yourself resource on Computer Concepts CourseMate and then tapping or clicking Objectives 5–8.

Communications and Networks

Communications technologies are everywhere. Many require that you subscribe to an Internet service provider. With others, an organization such as a business or school provides communications services to employees, students, or customers.

In the course of a day, it is likely you use, or use information generated by, one or more of the communications technologies in Table 1-3.

Table 1-3   Uses of Communications Technologies

Type	Brief Description
Chat rooms	Real-time typed conversation among two or more people on a computers or mobile devices connected to a network
Email	Transmission of messages and files via a computer network
Fax	Transmission and receipt of documents over telephone lines
FTP	Permits users to transfer files to and from servers on the Internet
GPS	Navigation system that assists users with determining their location, ascertaining directions, and more
Instant messaging	Real-time typed conversation with another connected user where you also can exchange photos, videos, and other content
Internet	Worldwide collection of networks that links millions of businesses, government agencies, educational institutions, and individuals
Newsgroups	Online areas in which users have written discussions about a particular subject
RSS	Specification that enables web content to be distributed to subscribers
Videoconference	Real-time meeting between two or more geographically separated people who use a network to transmit audio and video
Voice mail	Allows users to leave a voice message for one or more people
VoIP	Conversation that takes place over the Internet using a telephone connected to a computer, mobile device, or other device
Wireless Internet access points	Enables users with computers and mobile devices to connect to the Internet wirelessly
Wireless messaging services	Send and receive wireless messages to and from smartphones, mobile phones, handheld game devices, and other mobile devices using text messaging and picture/video messaging

© Cengage Learning

Wired and Wireless Communications

Computer communications describes a process in which two or more computers or devices transfer (send and receive) data, instructions, and information over transmission media via a communications device(s). A **communications device** is hardware capable of transferring items from computers and devices to transmission media and vice versa. Examples of communications devices are modems, wireless access points, and routers. As shown in Figure 1-30, some communications involve cables and wires; others are sent wirelessly through the air.

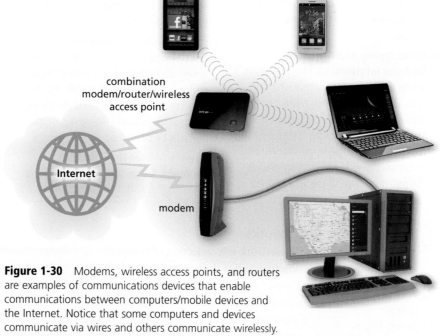

combination modem/router/wireless access point

Internet

modem

Figure 1-30   Modems, wireless access points, and routers are examples of communications devices that enable communications between computers/mobile devices and the Internet. Notice that some computers and devices communicate via wires and others communicate wirelessly.

© Cengage Learning; © iStockphoto / Petar Chernaev; © iStockphoto / Oleksiy Mark; Courtesy of Verizon Wireless; © Patryk Kosmider / Shutterstock.com.; © Pablo Eder / Shutterstock.com; © iStockphoto / 123render.; Source: Microsoft

Wired communications often use some form of telephone wiring, coaxial cable, or fiber-optic cables to send communications signals. The wiring or cables typically are used within buildings or underground between buildings.

Because it is more convenient than installing wires and cables, many users opt for wireless communications, which sends signals through the air or space. Examples of wireless communications technologies include Wi-Fi, Bluetooth, and cellular radio:

BTW
Wireless Communications
Innovative Computing:
You should be familiar with innovative uses of technology related to wireless communications.

- *Wi-Fi* uses radio signals to provide high-speed Internet and network connections to computers and devices capable of communicating via Wi-Fi. Most computers and many mobile devices, such as smartphones and portable media players, can connect to a Wi-Fi network.
- *Bluetooth* uses short-range radio signals to enable Bluetooth-enabled computers and devices to communicate with each other. For example, Bluetooth headsets allow you to connect a Bluetooth-enabled phone to a headset wirelessly.
- Cellular radio uses the cellular network to enable high-speed Internet connections to devices with built-in compatible technology, such as smartphones. Cellular network providers use the categories 3G, 4G, and 5G to denote cellular transmission speeds, with 5G being the fastest.

Wi-Fi and Bluetooth are both hot spot technologies. A *hot spot* is a wireless network that provides Internet connections to mobile computers and devices. Wi-Fi hot spots provide wireless network connections to users in public locations such as airports and airplanes, train stations, hotels, convention centers, schools, campgrounds, marinas, shopping malls, bookstores, libraries, restaurants, coffee shops, and more. Bluetooth hot spots provide location-based services, such as sending coupons or menus, to users whose Bluetooth-enabled devices enter the coverage range. Read Secure IT 1-4 for tips on protecting your personal data while using a public hot spot.

✳ SECURE IT 1-4 ──────────────────────────────

📖 Using Public Wi-Fi Hot Spots Safely

Connecting wirelessly to a public hot spot at your local coffee shop or at the airport can be convenient and practical. Using this free service can be risky, however, because cybercriminals lurk in these areas hoping to gain access to confidential information on your computer or mobile device. Follow these guidelines for a safer browsing experience:

- **Avoid typing passwords and financial information.** Identity thieves are on the lookout for people who sign in to accounts, enter their credit card account numbers in shopping websites, or conduct online banking transactions. If you must type this personal information, be certain the web address begins with "https," not "http." If the web address

changes to "http," sign out of (end your Internet session) immediately.

- **Sign out of websites.** When finished using an account, sign out of it and close the window.
- **Disable your wireless connection.** If you have finished working online but still need to use the computer, disconnect from the wireless connection.
- **Do not leave the computer unattended.** It may seem obvious, but always stay with your computer or mobile device. Turning your back to talk with a friend or to refill your coffee gives thieves a few seconds to steal sensitive information that may be displayed on the screen.
- **Beware of over-the-shoulder snoopers.** The person sitting behind you

may be watching or using a camera phone to record your keystrokes, read your email messages and social networking posts, and view your photos and videos.

✳ How will you apply these precautions the next time you use a public Wi-Fi hot spot? Should businesses post signs alerting customers about Wi-Fi security issues?

© DeiMosz / Shutterstock.com

Networks

A **network** is a collection of computers and devices connected together, often wirelessly, via communications devices and transmission media. Networks allow computers to share *resources*, such as hardware, software, data, and information. Sharing resources saves time and money. In many networks, one or more computers act as a server. The server controls access to the resources on a network. The other computers on the network, each called a client, request resources from the server (Figure 1-31). The major differences between the server and client computers are that the server typically has more power, more storage space, and expanded communications capabilities.

BTW
The Internet
The world's largest computer network is the Internet.

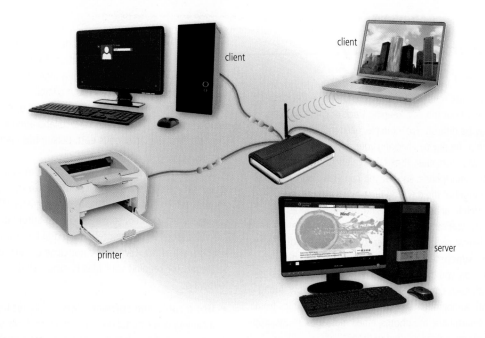

Figure 1-31 A server manages the resources on a network, and clients access the resources on the server. This network enables three separate computers to share the same printer, one wirelessly.

© iStockphoto / sweetym; Source: Microsoft; © iStockphoto / Skip Odonnell; © Jennifer Nickert / Shutterstock.com; © Serg64 / Shutterstock.com; © Oleksiy Mark / Shutterstock.com; Source: Cengage Learning; © Cengage Learning

Many homes and most businesses and schools network their computers and devices. Most allow users to connect their computers wirelessly to the network. Users often are required to sign in to, or log on, a network, which means they enter a user name and password (or other credentials) to access the network and its resources.

Home Networks   Home networks save the home user money and provide many conveniences. Each networked computer or mobile device on a home network has the following capabilities:

- Connect to the Internet at the same time
- Share a single high-speed Internet connection
- Access photos, music, videos, and other content on computers and devices throughout the house
- Share devices such as a printer, scanner, or external hard disk
- Play multiplayer games with players on other computers and mobile devices in the house
- Connect game consoles to the Internet
- Subscribe to and use VoIP

Home networks usually are small, existing within a single structure, and use wireless technologies such as those shown in Figure 1-30 on page 29. You do not need extensive knowledge of networks to set up a home network. You will need a communications device, such as a router, which usually includes setup instructions. Most operating systems also provide tools enabling you easily to connect all the computers and devices in your house.

Business Networks   Business and school networks can be small, such as in a room or building, or widespread, connecting computers and devices across a city, country, or the globe. Some reasons that businesses network their computers and devices together include the following:

- **Facilitate communications.** Using a network, employees and customers communicate efficiently and easily via email, instant messaging, blogs, online social networks, video calls, online meetings, video conferencing, VoIP, wireless messaging services, and more.
- **Share hardware.** In a networked environment, each computer on the network can access the hardware on the network, instead of providing each user with the same piece of hardware. For example, computer and mobile device users can access the laser printer on the network, as they need it.
- **Share data, information, and software.** In a networked environment, any authorized computer user can access data, information, and software stored on other computers on the network. A large company, for example, might have a database of customer information that any authorized user can access.

MINI FEATURE 1-2

Living Digitally: Staying in Sync

If you use multiple computers and mobile devices throughout the day, keeping track of common files may be difficult. For example, each morning, you may begin the day by checking your appointment calendar on your computer. That same calendar appears on your smartphone, so that you can view your schedule throughout the day. You may, however, add, change, or delete appointments using the smartphone, so when you return home you will need to update the calendar on your computer to reflect these edits. When you **synchronize**, or **sync**, computers and mobile devices, you match the files in two or more locations with each other, as shown in the figure below. Along with appointments, other commonly synced files from a smartphone are photos, email messages, music, apps, contacts, calendars, and ringtones.

Syncing can be a one-way or a two-way process. With a one-way sync, also called mirroring, you add, change, or delete files in a destination location, called the *target*, without altering the same files in the original location, called the *source*. For example, you may have a large collection of music stored on your computer at home (the source), and you often copy some of these songs to your mobile device (the target). If you add or delete songs from your computer, you also will want to add or change these songs on your mobile device. If, however, you add or change the songs on your mobile device, you would not want to make these changes on your computer.

In two-way sync, any change made in one location also is made in any other sync location. For example, you and your friends may be working together to create one document reflecting your combined ideas. This document could be stored on a network or on cloud storage on the Internet. Your collaboration efforts should reflect the latest edits each person has made to the file.

You can use wired or wireless methods to sync. In a wired setup, cables connect one device to another, which allows for reliable data transfer. While wireless syncing offers convenience and automation, possible issues include battery drain and low signal strength when the devices are not close to each other. Strategies for keeping your files in sync include the following:

- **Use a cable and software.** Syncing photos from a camera or a smartphone to a computer frees up memory on the mobile device and creates a backup of these files. You easily can transfer photos using a data sync cable and synchronization software. Be certain not to disconnect the mobile device from the computer until the sync is complete. You also can copy your photos and documents from the computer to a smartphone, an external hard disk, a USB flash drive, or some other portable storage device.

- **Use cloud storage.** Cloud storage can provide a convenient method of syncing files stored on multiple computers and accessing them from most devices with Internet access. Several cloud storage providers offer a small amount of storage space at no cost and additional storage for a nominal fee per month or per year. Each provider has specific features, but most allow users to share files with other users, preview file contents, set passwords, and control who has permission to edit the files.

- **Use web apps.** By using web apps for email, contacts, and calendars, your information is stored online, so that it is accessible anywhere you have an Internet connection, and can sync with multiple devices.

✳ Synchronization is an effective method of organizing and sharing common files. What files have you synced, such as photos, music, and email? Which sync method did you use?

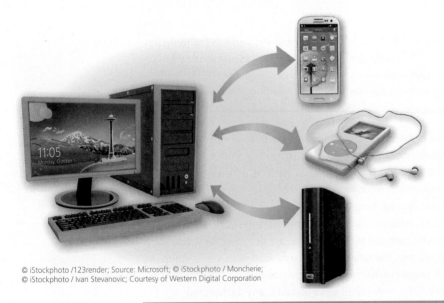

© iStockphoto /123render; Source: Microsoft; © iStockphoto / Moncherie;
© iStockphoto / Ivan Stevanovic; Courtesy of Western Digital Corporation

Uses of Technology in Society

 BTW
Technology @ Work
For more information about how technology is used in a variety of fields, read the Technology @ Work feature at the end of each chapter in this book.

Technology has changed society today as much as the industrial revolution changed society in the eighteenth and nineteenth centuries. People interact directly with technology in fields such as education, government, finance, retail, entertainment, health care, travel, science, publishing, and manufacturing.

Education

Educators and teaching institutions use technology to assist with education. Most equip labs and classrooms with computers. Some even provide computers to students. Many require students to have a mobile computer or mobile device to access the school's network or Internet wirelessly, or to access digital-only content provided by a textbook publisher. To promote education by computer, vendors often offer substantial student discounts on hardware and software.

Educators may use an interactive whiteboard, which is a touch-sensitive device resembling a dry-erase board, that displays images on a connected computer screen (Figure 1-32). They also may use a course management system, sometimes called a learning management system, which is software that contains tools for class preparation, distribution, and management. For example, through the course management system, students access course materials, grades, assessments, and a variety of collaboration tools. Read Ethics & Issues 1-3 on the next page to consider issues related to schools integrating technology into the classroom.

Many schools offer distance learning classes, where the delivery of education occurs at one place while the learning occurs at other locations. Distance learning courses provide time, distance, and place advantages for students who live far from a campus or work full time. A few schools offer entire degrees online. National and international companies offer distance learning training because it eliminates the costs of airfare, hotels, and meals for centralized training sessions.

 Internet Research
How do educators use iTunes U?
Search for: itunes u

Figure 1-32 Teachers and students can write directly on an interactive whiteboard.

ETHICS & ISSUES 1-3

Does Technology Create a Divide between the More and Less Fortunate?

A teacher assigns a research paper that requires students to read several articles on the web. A school requires that all students type papers on a computer and submit the papers using email. While these may be valid ways to integrate technology in a curriculum or to help instructors manage their classroom, they assume all students have ample access to technology outside of school. School districts that assume all students have computers at home place less fortunate students at a further disadvantage. These students may have to stay after school to use a computer or study at the local library to access the Internet. Students at school districts in disadvantaged areas may fall further behind if the school is unable to provide access to the technology taken for granted at other schools, including interactive whiteboards and dedicated technology specialists. These discrepancies are known collectively as the *digital divide*, a term used to illustrate the gap between those with and without access to technology.

With the recent widespread growth of mobile device users, some aspects of the digital divide are closing. Students can email and do research on Internet-capable mobile devices, as well as access education-related apps. Mobile device capabilities, however, are limited. You cannot use a mobile device to write a research paper, prepare a resume, or submit a college application. Some companies and organizations are trying to provide better access. One cable company provides low-cost Internet access to families who receive free or reduced school lunches. Schools can apply for technology grants to purchase classroom computers. These grants may be able to provide access to students, but if no one can teach the students or their teachers how to use the technology, it may not solve the problem.

Is it the school's responsibility to provide an even playing field regarding technology access? Why or why not? Should schools be allowed to require students to use technology? Why or why not? What steps can society take to narrow the digital divide?

Government

Most government offices have websites to provide citizens with up-to-date information. People in the United States access government websites to view census data, file taxes, apply for permits and licenses, pay parking tickets, buy stamps, report crimes, apply for financial aid, and renew vehicle registrations and driver's licenses.

Employees of government agencies use computers as part of their daily routine. North American 911 call centers use computers to dispatch calls for fire, police, and medical assistance. Military and other agency officials use the U.S. Department of Homeland Security's network of information about domestic security threats to help protect against terrorist attacks. Law enforcement officers have online access to the FBI's National Crime Information Center (NCIC) through in-vehicle laptops, fingerprint readers, and mobile devices (Figure 1-33). The NCIC contains more than 15 million missing persons and criminal records, including names, fingerprints, parole/probation records, mug shots, and other information.

Figure 1-33 Law enforcement officials have in-vehicle computers and mobile devices to access emergency, missing person, and criminal records in computer networks in local, state, and federal agencies.
© David R. Frazier Photolibrary, Inc. / Alamy

Finance

Many people and companies use online banking or finance software to pay bills, track personal income and expenses, manage investments, and evaluate financial plans. The difference between using a financial institutions' website versus finance software on your computer is that all your account information is stored on the bank's computer instead of your computer. The advantage is you can access your financial records from anywhere in the world.

Investors often use online investing to buy and sell stocks and bonds — without using a broker. With online investing, the transaction fee for each trade usually is much less than when trading through a broker.

Retail

You can purchase just about any product or service on the web, including groceries, flowers, books, computers and mobile devices, music, movies, airline tickets, and concert tickets. To purchase from an online retailer, a customer visits the business's storefront, which contains product descriptions, images, and a shopping cart. The shopping cart allows the customer to collect purchases. When ready to complete the sale, the customer enters personal data and the method of payment, which should be through a secure Internet connection. Figure 1-34 illustrates the steps involved when a customer purchases from an online retailer.

Many mobile apps make your shopping experience more convenient. Some enable you to manage rewards, use coupons, locate stores, or pay for goods and services directly from your phone or other mobile device. Other mobile apps will check a product's price and availability at stores in your local area or online.

 BTW
Mobile Payments
Innovative Computing: You should be familiar with innovative uses of technology related to mobile payments.

Purchasing from an Online Retailer

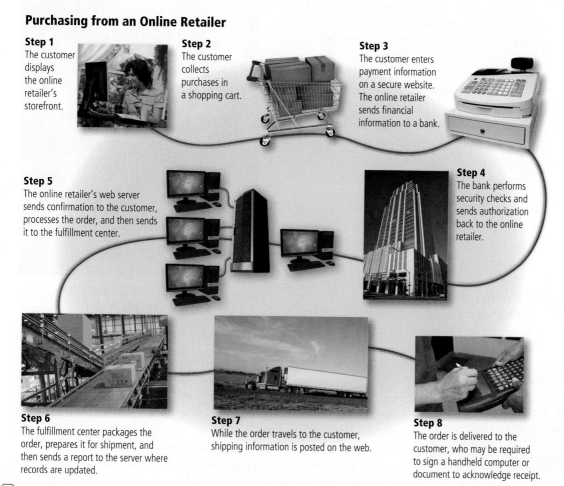

Step 1 The customer displays the online retailer's storefront.

Step 2 The customer collects purchases in a shopping cart.

Step 3 The customer enters payment information on a secure website. The online retailer sends financial information to a bank.

Step 4 The bank performs security checks and sends authorization back to the online retailer.

Step 5 The online retailer's web server sends confirmation to the customer, processes the order, and then sends it to the fulfillment center.

Step 6 The fulfillment center packages the order, prepares it for shipment, and then sends a report to the server where records are updated.

Step 7 While the order travels to the customer, shipping information is posted on the web.

Step 8 The order is delivered to the customer, who may be required to sign a handheld computer or document to acknowledge receipt.

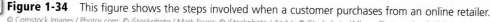

Figure 1-34 This figure shows the steps involved when a customer purchases from an online retailer.
© Comstock Images / Photos.com; © iStockphoto / Mark Evans; © iStockphoto / AndyL; © iStockphoto / Mlenny Photography; © Oleksiy Mark / Photos.com; © Oleksiy Mark / Shutterstock.com.; © iStockphoto / Ed Hidden; © iStockphoto / Oksana Perkins; © Bill Aron / PhotoEdit; © Cengage Learning

Entertainment

You can use computers and mobile devices to listen to audio clips or live audio; watch video clips, television shows, or live performances and events; read a book, magazine, or newspaper; and play a myriad of games individually or with others. In some cases, you download the media from the web to a computer or mobile device so that you can watch, listen to, view, or play later. Some websites support *streaming*, where you access the media content while it downloads. For example, radio and television broadcasts often use streaming media to broadcast music, interviews, talk shows, sporting events, news, and other segments so that you can listen to the audio or view the video as it downloads to your computer. You also can create videos, take photos, or record audio and upload (transfer) your media content to the web to share with others, such as on an online social network.

Health Care

Nearly every area of health care today uses computers. Whether you are visiting a family doctor for a regular checkup, having lab work or an outpatient test, filling a prescription, or being rushed in for emergency surgery, the medical staff around you will be using computers for various purposes:

- Hospitals and doctors use computers and mobile devices to maintain and access patient records.
- Computers and mobile devices monitor patients' vital signs in hospital rooms and at home; patients use computers to manage health conditions, such as diabetes.
- Robots deliver medication to nurses' stations in hospitals.
- Computers and computerized devices assist doctors, nurses, and technicians with medical tests (Figure 1-35).
- Doctors use the web and medical software to assist with researching and diagnosing health conditions.
- Doctors use email, text messaging, and other communications services to correspond with patients.

 BTW

Managing Health Conditions
Innovative Computing: You should be familiar with innovative uses of technology related to managing health conditions.

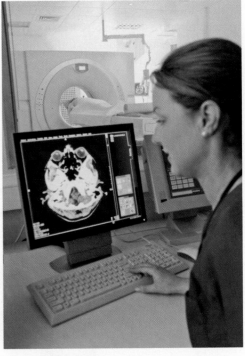

Figure 1-35 Doctors, nurses, technicians, and other medical staff use computers and computerized devices to assist with medical tests.
© Jupiterimages / Photos.com

- Patients use computers and mobile devices to refill prescriptions, and pharmacists use computers to file insurance claims and provide customers with vital information about their medications.
- Surgeons implant computerized devices, such as pacemakers, that allow patients to live longer.
- Surgeons use computer-controlled devices to provide them with greater precision during operations, such as for laser eye surgery and robot-assisted heart surgery.

Travel

Whether traveling by car or plane, your goal is to arrive safely at your destination. As you make the journey, you may interact with a navigation system or GPS, which uses satellite signals to determine a geographic location. GPS technology also assists people with creating maps, determining the best route between two points, locating a lost person or stolen object, monitoring a person's or object's movement, determining altitude, calculating speed, and finding points of interest. Vehicles manufactured today typically include some type of onboard navigation system (Figure 1-36). Many mobile devices such as smartphones also have built-in navigation systems.

Figure 1-36 Many vehicles include an onboard navigation system.
© kaczor58 / Shutterstock.com

In preparing for a trip, you may need to reserve a car, hotel, or flight. Many websites offer these services to the public where you can search for and compare flights and prices, order airline tickets, or reserve a rental car. You also can print driving directions and maps from the web.

BTW
Determining a Location
High-Tech Talk: Navigation systems, mobile phone trackers, and game consoles use the concept of triangulation to determine the location of an object such as a phone or person.

Science

All branches of science, from biology to astronomy to meteorology, use computers to assist them with collecting, analyzing, and modeling data. Scientists also use the Internet to communicate with colleagues around the world. Breakthroughs in surgery, medicine, and treatments often result from scientists' use of computers. Tiny computers now imitate functions of the central nervous system, retina of the eye, and cochlea of the ear. A cochlear implant allows a deaf person to listen. Electrodes implanted in the brain stop tremors associated with Parkinson's disease.

A *neural network* is a system that attempts to imitate the behavior of the human brain. Scientists create neural networks by connecting thousands of processors together much like the neurons in the brain are connected. The capability of a personal computer to recognize spoken words is a direct result of scientific experimentation with neural networks.

Publishing

Many publishers of books, magazines, newspapers, music, film, and video make their works available online. Organizations and individuals publish their thoughts and ideas using a blog, podcast, or wiki.

- A *blog* is an informal website consisting of time-stamped articles (posts) in a diary or journal format, usually listed in reverse chronological order (Figure 1-37). Posts can contain text, photos, links, and more. As others read articles in your blog, you can enable them to reply with their own thoughts. A blog that contains video is called a video blog.
- Podcasts are a popular way to distribute audio or video on the web. A *podcast* is recorded media that users can download or stream to a computer or portable media player. Examples of podcasts include lectures, political messages, radio shows, and commentaries. Podcasters register their podcasts so that subscribers can select content to automatically download when they are connected.

Internet Research
How can you create a blog?
Search for: create a blog

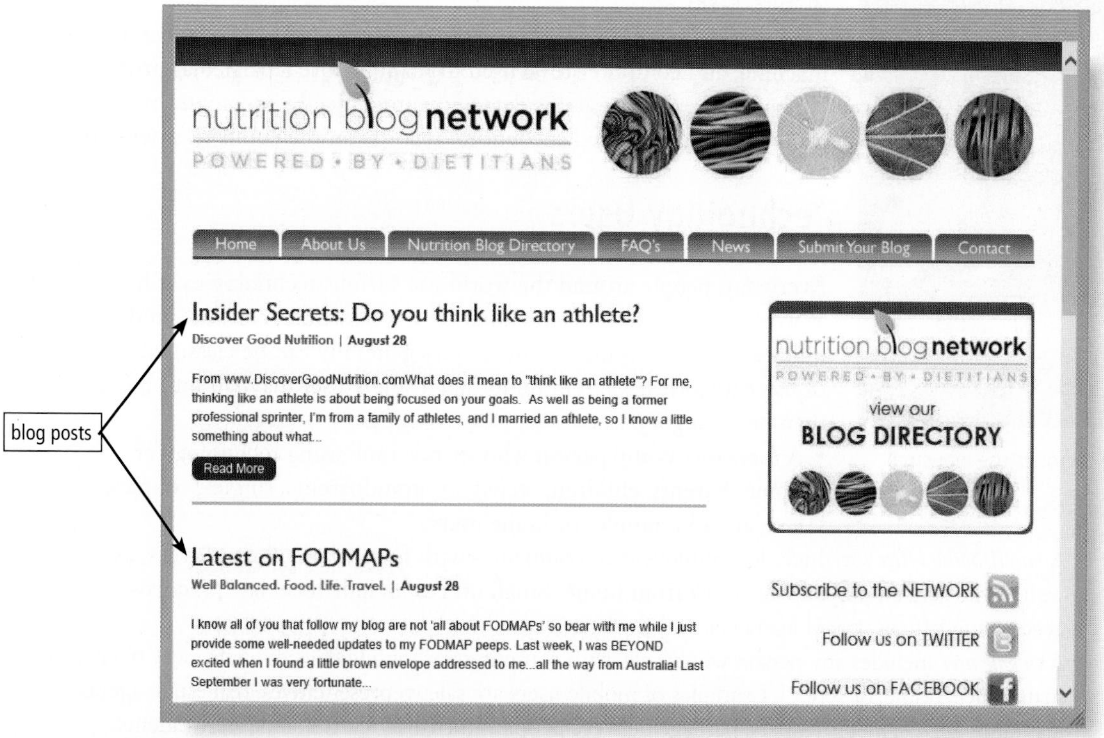

Figure 1-37 Any group or individual can create a blog, so that they can share thoughts and ideas.
Source: Nutrition Blog Network

- A *wiki* is a collaborative website that allows users to create, add to, modify, or delete the content via their browser. Many wikis are open to modification by the general public. The difference between a wiki and a blog is that users cannot modify original posts made by a blogger. Read Ethics & Issues 1-4 for an issue related to using wikis as a source for research.

❋ ETHICS & ISSUES 1-4

Should Wikis Be Allowed as Valid Sources for Academic Research?

As wikis have grown in number, size, and popularity, many educators and librarians have shunned the sites as valid sources of research. While some wikis are tightly controlled with a limited number of contributors and expert editors, these usually focus on narrowly defined, specialized topics. Most large online wikis, such as Wikipedia, often involve thousands of editors, many of whom remain anonymous.

Critics of wikis cite the lack of certified academic credentials by the editors, as well as political or gender bias by contributors. Wikis also are subject to vandalism. Vandals'

motives vary; some enter false information to discredit the wiki, and others for humorous results. On occasion, rival political factions have falsified or embellished wiki entries in an attempt to give their candidate an advantage. Some wiki supporters argue that most wikis provide adequate controls to correct false or misleading content quickly and to punish those who submit it. One popular wiki now requires an experienced editor to verify changes made to certain types of articles. Other wiki protection methods include locking articles from editing, creating a list of recently edited articles, enabling readers to report vandalism, and allowing people to be notified about changes to a wiki

page that they have edited or that is about them. Some proponents propose that people should use wikis as a starting point for researching a fact, but that they should verify the fact using traditional sources.

Should instructors allow wikis as valid sources for academic research? Why or why not? Would you submit a paper to your instructor that cites a wiki as a source? Why or why not? What policies might wikis enforce that could garner more confidence from the public? If a wiki provided verification of the credentials of the author, would you trust the wiki more? Why or why not?

Figure 1-38 Automotive factories use industrial robots to weld car bodies.
© Small Town Studio / Shutterstock.com

Manufacturing

Computer-aided manufacturing (CAM) refers to the use of computers to assist with manufacturing processes such as fabrication and assembly. Industries use CAM to reduce product development costs, shorten a product's time to market, and stay ahead of the competition. Often, robots carry out processes in a CAM environment. CAM is used by a variety of industries, including oil drilling, power generation, food production, and automobile manufacturing. Automobile plants, for example, have an entire line of industrial robots that assemble a car (Figure 1-38).

Special computers on the shop floor record actual labor, material, machine, and computer time used to manufacture a particular product. The computers process this data and automatically update inventory, production, payroll, and accounting records on the company's network.

Technology Users

Every day, people around the world use various technologies at home, at work, and at school. Depending on the hardware, software, and communications requirements, these users generally can be classified in one of five categories. Keep in mind that a single user may fall into more than one category.

- A *home user* is any person who spends time using technology at home. Parents, children, teenagers, grandparents, singles, couples, etc., are all examples of home users.
- A *small/home office user* includes employees of companies with fewer than 50 employees, as well as the self-employed who work from home. Small offices include local law practices, accounting offices, travel agencies, and florists.
- A *mobile user* includes any person who works with computers or mobile devices while away from a main office, home, or school. Examples of mobile users are sales representatives, real estate agents, insurance agents, meter readers, package delivery people, journalists, consultants, and students.

- A *power user* is a user who requires the capabilities of a powerful computer. Examples of power users include engineers, scientists, architects, desktop publishers, and graphic artists.
- An enterprise has hundreds or thousands of employees or customers who work in or do business with offices across a region, the country, or the world. Each employee or customer who uses computers, mobile devices, and other technology in the enterprise is an *enterprise user*.

Table 1-4 illustrates the range of hardware, programs/apps, and communications forms used in each of these categories.

Table 1-4 Categories of Users

User	Sample Hardware	Sample Desktop Apps	Sample Mobile or Web Apps	Forms of Communications
All Users	– Smartphone – Digital camera – Printer	– Word processing – Schedule and contact management – Browser – Security	– Alarm clock – Calculator – News, weather, sports – Reference – Finance	– Email – Online social networks – Blogs
Home User	– Desktop or laptop – Portable media player and earbuds – Game console – E-book reader – Webcam – Headset	– Personal finance – Photo and video editing – Media player – Educational – Entertainment	– Banking – Travel – Mapping – Navigation – Health and fitness – Retail – Media sharing – Educational	– Instant messaging – VoIP
Small/Home Office User	– Desktop(s) or laptop(s) – Server – Webcam – Scanner	– Spreadsheet – Database – Accounting	– Travel – Mapping	– Instant messaging – VoIP – FTP
Mobile User	– Laptop or tablet – Video projector – Wireless headset	– Note taking – Presentation – Educational – Entertainment	– Travel – Mapping – Navigation – Retail – Educational	
Power User	– Desktop – Scanner	– Desktop publishing – Multimedia authoring – Computer-aided design – Photo, audio, video editing		– FTP – Videoconferencing
Enterprise User	– Server – Desktop(s) or laptop(s) – Industry-specific handheld computer – Webcam – Scanner	– Spreadsheet – Database – Accounting	– Travel – Mapping – Navigation	– Instant messaging – VoIP – FTP – Videoconferencing

MINI FEATURE 1-3

Living Digitally: Digital Home

Technology has made homes efficient, safe, and entertaining. Although computers are found throughout today's home, the concept of home automation can be traced back to 1898 when Nikola Tesla invented the first remote control.

Home Automation

New home builders and existing homeowners are integrating features that automate a wide variety of tasks, save time and money, and enhance the overall at-home environment.

- **Lighting:** Controlling lighting is one of the more common uses of technology in the home. Remotes turn light fixtures on and off, motion sensors turn on lights when a car or a visitor approaches the driveway or walkway, and light sensors brighten or dim lighting based on outdoor conditions.

- **Thermostats:** Programmable thermostats adjust to seasonal needs and can be set to control temperatures in individual rooms. Homeowners can use their smartphones to monitor heating and cooling systems, adjust temperatures, and manage energy consumption.

- **Appliances:** Smart appliances, such as dishwashers, can be programmed to run at nonpeak electrical times. Coffeemakers can turn on at set times and shut off if an overheating coffeepot has been left on accidentally. Refrigerators can track expiration dates and create shopping lists.

- **Security:** Alarm system networks monitor many areas of the home. They can detect break-ins at doors, glass breakage, and heat from fires. Surveillance cameras keep a watchful eye on the outside premises and on interior rooms; homeowners can view the images on televisions and computers within the house or on a webpage when they are away from home, as shown in the figure to the left. The security systems can send text and email messages to alert a homeowner when someone has entered or left the home.

- **Vacuums:** Vacuum systems can clean rugs and floors automatically. Sensors prevent the cleaning unit from falling down stairs or bumping into walls. When the cleaning process is complete, the unit returns to the charging station.

Home Entertainment

Televisions have become devices that allow you to do much more than watch a movie or weekly program. By connecting televisions to the Internet and subscribing to online services, users can encounter a wide variety of entertaining options.

- **Gaming:** Although many games are played using a controller, several systems operate by allowing the player to be the controller. Arcade, strategy, and adventure games can be played individually, with a group, or with online friends. Fitness fans can experience a full body workout with yoga sessions, fitness bands, and weights, and new songs, workouts, and difficulty levels.

- **Streaming and sharing content:** Users instantly can watch streaming HD (high-definition) movies, television programs, and sports. They also can connect their tablets and smartphones to share content, including photos and music, chat face-to-face, and update their social networking status.

- **Remotes:** Choosing, configuring, and using remote controls for a home entertainment system can require some time and patience. Although universal remotes are popular choices, many people are turning to using their smartphones and tablets to control all the devices in the room. As shown in the figure below, users enjoy the convenience of customizing apps to operate their television, DVD player, and speakers and to perform other functions anywhere in the home.

✹ How has your life become more efficient, safe, and enjoyable by using home automation and entertainment features?

NOW YOU KNOW

Be sure you understand the material presented in the sections titled Communications and Networks, Uses of Technology in Society, and Technology Users, as it relates to the chapter objectives.
You now should know...

- When you might use wired and wireless communications, and why you would use a network (Objective 9)

- How you would use technology in education, government, finance, retail, entertainment, health care, travel, science, publishing, and manufacturing (Objective 10)

- What types of hardware, software, and communications you could use at home, school, and work (Objective 11)

Quiz Yourself Online: Check your knowledge of related content by navigating to this book's Quiz Yourself resource on Computer Concepts CourseMate and then tapping or clicking Objectives 9–11.

Chapter Summary

Chapter 1 introduced you to basic computer concepts. You learned about laptops, tablets, desktops, servers, smartphones, digital cameras, portable media players, e-book readers, and game devices. The chapter introduced various methods for input, output, memory, and storage. It discussed the Internet, browsing and searching the web, and online social networks. Next, the chapter introduced digital security and safety risks and precautions, along with various types of programs, applications, communications, and networks. The many different uses of technology applications in society also were presented, along with types of users.

This chapter is an overview. Many of the terms and concepts introduced will be discussed further in later chapters.

Test your knowledge of chapter material by accessing the Study Guide, Flash Cards, and Practice Test apps that run on your smartphone, tablet, laptop, or desktop.

TECHNOLOGY @ WORK

Health Care

During an intramural volleyball game, you suffer an injury that requires a trip to an emergency room, which is extremely crowded. Upon check-in, the employee at the front desk uses a computer to record your personal data and symptoms. She also uses the computer to verify that your insurance coverage is current and informs you of your co-payment amount. After waiting several minutes, a triage nurse takes your temperature and blood pressure and then asks a series of questions about your symptoms. The nurse also records this data in a tablet and asks you to remain in the waiting room until someone from the radiology department is available to perform a CT scan. The radiology department is located in a different area of the hospital, so the technicians watch a computer screen that displays a list of patients who currently are waiting for their services.

About 30 minutes later, a technician calls your name and escorts you to the radiology department for your CT scan. As she is performing the scan, a computer records the images that later will be reviewed by a physician. When the CT scan is complete, you return to the waiting room until a physician reviews the results. Once he receives the results and reviews them, a hospital employee takes you to a consultation room.

The physician informs you that other than a few bumps and bruises, he believes that you have sustained no permanent damage and prescribes medication to help ease the pain. He then returns to a computer at the nurses' station and adds his diagnosis to the database that stores your medical records. He also sends your prescription electronically to the hospital's pharmacy. Once discharged, you visit the cashier to pay the bill. You then use a tablet to sign an electronic version of your discharge paperwork so that the hospital can store it electronically. The hospital bills your insurance company electronically. If you owe a balance after the insurance company pays its portion, a computer at the

hospital will generate a bill that will be mailed to you. After purchasing your medication and leaving the hospital, you realize that despite the hospital being busy, computers decreased the time of your visit by automating processes that otherwise would have been performed manually and reduced possible errors by storing all of your personal information centrally.

How else might computers and technology be used in the health care industry?

STUDENT ASSIGNMENTS

Study Guide

The Study Guide exercise reinforces material you should know for the chapter exam. You will find answers to items with the 📄 e-book icon only in the e-book appearing as blue text.

Access the **Study Guide app** that runs on your smartphone, tablet, laptop, or desktop by navigating to this book's Apps resource on Computer Concepts CourseMate.

Instructions: Answer the questions below using the format that helps you remember best or that is required by your instructor. Possible formats may include one or more of these options: write the answers; create a document that contains the answers; record answers as audio or video using a webcam, smartphone, or portable media player; post answers on a blog, wiki, or website; or highlight answers in the book/e-book.

1. Define the term, digital literacy.

2. Define the terms, computer and user.

3. Differentiate between a desktop and a laptop. A laptop also is known as a(n) _____ computer.

4. Describe a tablet.

5. 📄 Describe how you interact with a touch screen.

6. Define the term, server. What services does a server provide?

7. Explain whether or not a mobile device is a computer.

8. List characteristics of a smartphone.

9. Differentiate among text, picture, and video messages.

10. Describe the purpose of these mobile devices: digital camera, portable media player, e-book reader, and game console.

11 Describe the trend of convergence and how it applies to mobile devices.

12. 📄 The ESRB provides guidelines for the _____ industry. Describe the rating system.

13. Differentiate between data and information. Give an example of each.

14. Define the terms, input and output. List several types of input devices and output devices.

15. Describe the purpose of a pointing device. Give an example.

16. List the hardware you can use to enter voice and video.

17. Differentiate between memory and storage.

18. A computer keeps data, instructions, and information on _____ media. Give some examples.

19. Define the term, cloud storage. Describe the types of services offered by cloud storage providers.

20. Describe components of a backup plan.

21. Describe the Internet. Identify reasons people use the Internet.

22. The _____ consists of a worldwide collection of electronic documents. What is each electronic document called?

23. Differentiate between the web and the Internet.

24. Describe the purpose of a search engine. 📄 List two search engines.

25. Explain the purpose of an online social network. What is a Tweet?

26. 📄 Name the products and/or services of Facebook and Twitter, with respect to technology.

27. Explain why a company might be interested in an employee's social networking profile.

28. Define the term, malware. List ways you can protect yourself from malware.

29. List guidelines for creating a strong password. 📄 Describe how online tools can determine a password's strength.

30. Explain physical and behavioral health risks associated with using computers.

31. Define the term, green computing. Describe strategies that support green computing.

32. Define the term, software. Software also is called a(n) _____.

33. Define the terms, system software and operating system. List popular operating systems for computers and mobile devices.

34. 📄 Name the contributions of Steve Jobs and Bill Gates, with respect to technology.

35. List the steps involved in installing applications.

36. Explain how you can determine whether a program will run on your computer.

37. Define the term, communications device. List examples of wireless communications technologies.

38. Define the term, hot spot. Give two examples and describe how each is used.

39. Give examples of precautions you should take when using a public Wi-Fi hot spot.

40. Describe how homes and businesses use networks.

41. Explain what occurs when you synchronize computers and mobile devices.

42. Define the term, digital divide, and describe how it pertains to education.

43. Describe how you might use blogs, wikis, and podcasts to publish content.

44. Differentiate among the following technology user types: home user, small/home office user, mobile user, power user, and enterprise user.

45. Describe how technology is used in the health care industry.

You should be able to define the Primary Terms and be familiar with the Secondary Terms listed below.

Key Terms

Access the Flash Cards app that runs on your smartphone, tablet, laptop, or desktop by navigating to this book's Apps resource on Computer Concepts CourseMate. **View definitions** for each term by navigating to this book's Key Terms resource on Computer Concepts CourseMate. **Listen to definitions** for each term on your portable media player by navigating to this book's Audio Study Tools resource on Computer Concepts CourseMate.

Primary Terms (shown in **bold-black** characters in the chapter)

app (26)	green computing (25)	printer (14)	synchronize (32)
application (26)	input device (12)	program (25)	tablet (4)
browser (20)	Internet (18)	search engine (21)	user (4)
communications device (29)	laptop (4)	server (6)	web (19)
computer (4)	mobile device (7)	smartphone (7)	web server (20)
desktop (6)	network (30)	social networking site (21)	webpage (19)
digital camera (8)	online social network (21)	software (25)	website (20)
digital literacy (2)	output device (14)	storage device (15)	
e-book reader (9)	personal computer (4)	storage media (15)	
game console (9)	portable media player (8)	sync (32)	

Secondary Terms (shown in *italic* characters in the chapter)

backup (17)	*file (17)*	*mobile user (38)*	*slide (5)*
blog (37)	*gesture (5)*	*mouse (12)*	*small/home office user (38)*
Bluetooth (30)	*hard copy (14)*	*neural network (37)*	*software developer (28)*
camera phone (7)	*hard disk (15)*	*notebook computer (4)*	*solid-state drive (16)*
click (13)	*hardware (4)*	*online (6)*	*source (32)*
cloud storage (17)	*headset (13)*	*on-screen keyboard (5)*	*streaming (35)*
computer-aided manufacturing (38)	*home user (38)*	*operating system (25)*	*stretch (5)*
convergence (10)	*hot spot (30)*	*output (4)*	*surfing the web (20)*
data (11)	*hyperlink (20)*	*passphrase (24)*	*swipe (5)*
desktop app (26)	*information (11)*	*personal media player (8)*	*tap (5)*
digital divide (34)	*input (4)*	*picture message (7)*	*target (32)*
double-click (13)	*keyboard (12)*	*pinch (5)*	*text message (7)*
double-tap (5)	*link (20)*	*podcast (37)*	*touchpad (12)*
downloading (19)	*loads (27)*	*point (13)*	*USB flash drive (16)*
drag (5, 13)	*malware (23)*	*power user (39)*	*user interface (27)*
earbuds (9)	*memory (15)*	*press and hold (5)*	*video message (7)*
e-book (9)	*memory card (16)*	*printout (14)*	*web app (26)*
enterprise user (39)	*microphone (13)*	*resources (30)*	*webcam (13)*
e-reader (9)	*mobile app (26)*	*right-click (13)*	*Wi-Fi (30)*
e-waste (24)	*mobile computer (4)*	*scanner (13)*	*wiki (38)*

blog (37)

Checkpoint

The Checkpoint exercises test your knowledge of the chapter concepts. The page number containing the answer appears in parentheses after each exercise. The Consider This exercises challenge your understanding of chapter concepts.

Complete the Checkpoint exercises interactively by navigating to this book's Checkpoint resource on Computer Concepts CourseMate. **Access the Test Prep app** that runs on your smartphone, tablet, laptop, or desktop by navigating to this book's Apps resource on Computer Concepts CourseMate. After successfully completing the self-assessment through the Test Prep app, **take the Practice Test** by navigating to this book's Practice Test resource on Computer Concepts Coursemate.

True/False   Mark T for True and F for False.

_____ 1. Electronic components in computers process data using instructions, which are the steps that tell the computer how to perform a particular task. (4)

_____ 2. Screens for desktops cannot yet support touch. (6)

_____ 3. Smaller applications, such as at home, typically use a powerful, expensive server to support their daily operations. (6)

_____ 4. Smartphones typically communicate wirelessly with other devices or computers. (7)

_____ 5. Data conveys meaning to users, and information is a collection of unprocessed items, which can include text, numbers, images, audio, and video. (11)

_____ 6. As widespread as computers appear to be, most daily activities do not involve the use of or depend on information from them. (11)

_____ 7. A scanner is a light-sensing output device. (13)

_____ 8. Because it contains moving parts, flash memory is less durable and shock resistant than other types of media. (16)

_____ 9. The terms, web and Internet, are interchangeable. (18)

_____ 10. One way to protect your computer from malware is to scan any removable media before using it. (23)

_____ 11. Operating systems are a widely recognized example of system software. (25)

_____ 12. You usually do not need to install web apps before you can run them. (27)

Multiple Choice   Select the best answer.

1. A(n) _____ is any hardware component that allows you to enter data and instructions into a computer or mobile device. (12)
   a. output device
   b. communications device
   c. input device
   d. display

2. Which of the following is *not* an example of an output device? (13)
   a. scanner
   b. printer
   c. display
   d. speaker

3. _____ consists of electronic components that store instructions waiting to be executed and the data needed by those instructions. (15)
   a. Storage
   b. Cloud storage
   c. Solid-state drives
   d. Memory

4. A(n) _____ is removable flash memory, usually no bigger than 1.5 inches in height or width, that you insert in and remove from a slot in a computer, mobile device, or card reader/writer. (16)
   a. memory card
   b. USB flash drive
   c. solid-state drive (SSD)
   d. optical disc

5. A computer that delivers requested webpages to your computer or mobile device is a(n) _____. (20)
   a. VoIP computer
   b. web server
   c. FTP device
   d. hard disk

6. _____ software consists of programs designed to make users more productive and/or assist them with personal tasks. (26)
   a. System
   b. Application
   c. Operating system
   d. Gaming

7. _____ uses the cellular network to enable high-speed Internet connections to devices with built-in compatible technology, such as smart phones. (30)
   a. Cellular radio
   b. Bluetooth
   c. Wi-Fi
   d. Hot spot

8. A(n) _____ is a collaborative website that allows users to create, add to, modify, or delete the content via their browser. (38)
   a. podcast
   b. blog
   c. online social network
   d. wiki

Checkpoint

Matching   Match the terms with their definitions.

_____ 1. laptop (4)

_____ 2. server (6)

_____ 3. picture message (7)

_____ 4. convergence (10)

_____ 5. touchpad (12)

_____ 6. storage device (15)

_____ 7. hard disk (15)

_____ 8. file (17)

_____ 9. software (25)

_____ 10. operating system (25)

a. term that describes the trend of computers and devices with technologies that overlap

b. storage device that contains one or more inflexible, circular platters that use magnetic particles to store data, instructions, and information

c. thin, lightweight mobile computer with a screen in its lid and a keyboard in its base

d. small, flat, rectangular pointing device that is sensitive to pressure and motion

e. set of programs that coordinates all the activities among computer or mobile device hardware

f. named collection of stored data, instructions, or information

g. a photo or other image, sometimes along with sound and text, sent to or from a smartphone or mobile device

h. series of related instructions, organized for a common purpose, that tells the computer what tasks to perform and how to perform them

i. computer that is dedicated to providing one or more services to other computers or devices on a network

j. component that records and/or retrieves items to and from storage media

Short Answer   Write a brief answer to each of the following questions.

1. Define an online social network. (21) Differentiate among Facebook, Twitter, and LinkedIn. (22)

2. Name several different types of malware. (23) List steps you can take to protect your computer from malware and viruses. (23)

3. What is a passphrase? (24) List the guidelines you should use when creating strong passwords. (24)

4. Define green computing. (25) List steps you can take to contribute to green computing. (25)

5. Define application software. (26) Differentiate among desktop apps, web apps, and mobile apps. (26)

✳ Consider This   Answer the following questions in the format specified by your instructor.

1. Answer the critical thinking questions posed at the end of these elements in this chapter: Ethics & Issues (8, 22, 34, 38), How To (5, 20, 21, 27, 27), Mini Features (10, 32, 40), Secure IT (18, 23, 24, 30), and Technology @ Work (41).

2. What does it mean to be digitally literate, and why is it important? (2)

3. 🗒 What are the different touch screen gestures and the actions they may cause to occur? (5)

4. Can a smartphone replace the need for a desktop or laptop? Why or why not? What tasks would be more difficult to accomplish on a smartphone? (7)

5. What types of keyboards are available for smartphones and tablets? (5, 7)

6. In what circumstances is it appropriate or inappropriate to use text acronyms and abbreviations? (8)

7. Do video calls and web conferencing replace the need for face-to-face meetings? Why or why not? (13)

8. Are USB flash drives an appropriate method of backing up data and files? Why or why not? (16)

9. When is it better to use email instead of IM? (23)

10. How do you know if you are addicted to computers or suffer from technology overload? (24)

11. Why is green computing important? (25)

12. What is the difference between system and application software? (25)

13. 🗒 How does the cellular transmission speed change from 3G, 4G, and 5G? (30)

14. When should you use a one-way sync or a two-way sync? (32)

15. What types of websites are legitimate sources of streaming video? (35)

✳ How To: Your Turn

The How To: Your Turn exercises present general guidelines for fundamental skills when using a computer or mobile device and then require that you determine how to apply these general guidelines to a specific program or situation.

Instructions: You often can complete tasks using technology in multiple ways. Figure out how to perform the tasks described in these exercises by using one or more resources available to you (such as a computer or mobile device, articles on the web or in print, online or program help, user guides, blogs, podcasts, videos, other individuals, trial and error, etc.). Summarize your 'how to' steps, along with the resource(s) used, in the format requested by your instructor (brief report, presentation, discussion, blog post, video, or other means).

① Use Computer Concepts CourseMate

Computer Concepts CourseMate provides access to multiple resources to supplement the concepts and skills you are learning in this text. The following steps guide you through the process of signing in to Computer Concepts CourseMate, navigating the website, and accessing various resources.

a. Run your browser and then navigate to www.cengagebrain.com.
b. Sign in with your CourseMate user name and password. If you do not have a user name, tap or click the link to sign up and then follow the instructions to obtain an account.
c. If necessary, add this textbook to your CourseMate account.
d. Tap or click the link to access Computer Concepts CourseMate.
e. Select the desired chapter.
f. Tap or click the resource you want to use.
g. When you are finished viewing the first resource, tap or click the next resource you want to use.
h. Sign out of your CourseMate account when you are finished viewing available resources.

Exercises

1. Summarize the process you use to sign in to your Computer Concepts CourseMate account.
2. Describe each Computer Concepts CourseMate resource available for this book and for each chapter.
3. Which resources on Computer Concepts CourseMate do you feel will best help you reinforce the chapter content? Why?

② Create a Facebook Account, Find the Discovering Computers Facebook Page, and Like It

The Discovering Computers Facebook page contains links to current events and other technology news, as well as relating the link to content in this book. The following steps guide you through the process of signing up for a Facebook account, navigating to the Discovering Computers Facebook page, and liking the page.

a. Run your browser and then navigate to www.facebook.com.
b. Follow the steps on the Facebook webpage to sign up for a new account. If you already have an account, enter your login information and log into your Facebook account.
c. Search for the Discovering Computers Facebook page using the search text, Discovering Computers.
d. Select the Discovering Computers Product/ Service in the search results.
e. Click the Like button to like the page.
f. If your screen displays a Subscribe button, click it to see information from the Discovering Computers Facebook page in your news feed.
g. View the posts and click links on the page that are of interest to you.
h. When you are finished, sign out of Facebook.

Exercises

1. Summarize the process you use to sign up for or sign in to your Facebook account.
2. Which links on the Discovering Computers Facebook page are of interest to you? Why?
3. Browse Facebook and find at least three other Facebook pages that are of interest to you. Which pages have you found, and why do you like them?

Source: Facebook

③ Create a Twitter Account, Find the Discovering Computers Twitter Account, and Follow It

The Discovering Computers Twitter account contains links to current events and other technology news, as well as how it relates to the content in this textbook. The following steps guide you through the process of signing up for a Twitter account, navigating to the Discovering Computers Twitter account, and following it.

a. Run your browser and then navigate to www.twitter.com.

How To: Your Turn ✸

b. Follow the steps on the Twitter webpage to sign up for a new account. If you already have an account, enter your sign-in information and sign in to your Twitter account.

c. Search for the Discovering Computers Twitter account using the search text, DiscoveringComp.

d. Select the Shelly Cashman @DiscoveringComp in the search results.

e. Click the Follow button to follow the account.

f. View the posts and click links on the page that are of interest to you.

g. When you are finished, sign out of Twitter.

Exercises

1. Summarize the process you use to sign up for or sign in to your Twitter account.

2. How is the Discovering Computers Twitter account similar to the Discovering Computers Facebook page? How are they different?

3. Browse Twitter and find at least three other Twitter accounts to follow. Which ones have you found, and why do you like them?

④ Sign Up for a Microsoft Account

A Microsoft account provides access to resources on several Microsoft websites. These websites include access to resources such as a free email account, cloud storage, a location to store information about your contacts, and an online calendar. You will need a Microsoft account to complete some of the exercises in this book. The following steps guide you through the process of signing up for a Microsoft account.

a. Run a browser and navigate to www.outlook.com.

b. Click the link and follow the on-screen instructions to sign up for a free Microsoft account.

c. Browse the resources available to you in your Microsoft account.

d. If approved by your instructor, compose and send a new email message to your instructor stating that you have signed up for a Microsoft account successfully.

e. Add your instructor's contact information. Next, add contact information for at least three additional people.

f. Add your birthday to the calendar.

g. Edit your Microsoft account profile to add additional contact and work information.

Exercises

1. If necessary, navigate to and view your new outlook.com email account. What are some ways to prevent junk email using the mail settings? What is junk email?

2. What is SkyDrive? How much space do you have available on SkyDrive to post files?

3. How can you see yourself using the various features in your newly created Microsoft account?

⑤ Connect to a Wireless Network

Wireless networks are available in many homes and businesses. Connecting to a wireless network can provide you with high-speed access to the Internet and other network resources. The following steps guide you through the process of connecting to a wireless network from a computer or mobile device.

a. If necessary, turn on your computer or mobile device and make sure wireless functionality is enabled.

b. Obtain the name of the wireless network to which you want to connect. **Note:** *You should connect only to wireless networks for which you have permission.*

c. On your computer or mobile device, view the list of available wireless networks.

d. Select the wireless network to which you want to connect.

e. If necessary, enter the requested security information, such as an encryption key or a password.

f. Run your browser to test your connection to the wireless network.

Exercises

1. Why should you not connect to a wireless network unless you have permission?

2. What is the name of the wireless network to which you connected?

3. Why might you connect to a wireless network on your smartphone instead of using your mobile data plan?

© Cengage Learning; © iStockphoto / Petar Chernaev; © iStockphoto / Oleksiy Mark; © Courtesy of Verizon Wireless; © topseller / Shutterstock.com; © alexmisu / Shutterstock.com; © Pablo Eder / Shutterstock.com; © iStockphoto / 123render; Source: Microsoft

✳ Internet Research

The Internet Research exercises broaden your understanding of chapter concepts by requiring that you search for information on the web.

Instructions: Use a search engine or another search tool to locate the information requested or answers to questions presented in the exercises. Describe your findings, along with the search term(s) you used and your web source(s), in the format requested by your instructor (brief report, presentation, discussion, blog post, video, or other means).

❶ Making Use of the Web
Search Engines and Research

Sixty percent of all American adults use a search engine every day, according to Pew Internet, and they generally are pleased with the outcome of their research experience. In How To 1-2 and 1-3 on pages 20 and 21 in this chapter, you learned to use a browser to display a webpage and to perform a basic web search.

Using these skills, find the answers to the following questions. (1) Visit the Pew Internet website and locate the latest Search Engine Use report. What are three of the users' positive search experiences? Which search engine is the most popular among the people surveyed? When was the survey conducted, and how many adults were surveyed? (2) Visit the CNET website and read at least three reviews of products. Create a table listing the product name, price, editors' and users' ratings, and "bottom line" summary. (3) Use a search engine or research website to locate articles about banning mobile devices in schools. What policies have schools created in lieu of a total ban on this technology? How have schools integrated mobile devices in the classroom as a vehicle to enhance learning?

many of the same basic principles by allowing members to communicate common interests, play games, and share photos, videos, and music. Some of these social networking sites are for personal use, while others are for entrepreneurs, business owners, and professionals to share job-related topics.

Compare the features of the top personal social networks, and create a table listing the number of active members in the United States and worldwide, the number of years the sites have existed, the more popular features, and the amount of content, such as photos, news stories, and links, that is shared each month. What types of advertisements are featured in each of these sites? Which sites are marketed toward younger and older users? Then, research the social networks used for business. How does their content differ from that found on the personal social networks? How many companies use these sites as a recruiting tool? How many native languages are supported? How are professionals using these websites to find potential clients and business partners?

❸ Search Sleuth

(1) Which magazine introduced the first microcomputer kit for the MITS Altair in its January 1975 issue? (2) Which company sold the TRS-80, one of the more popular personal computers introduced in 1977? (3) What material did Douglas Engelbart use to create the first mouse? (4) What is the code name for the 12 engineers who developed the IBM PC? (5) Who received the first text message in 1992? What was the content of this message? (6) Which company developed the first digital camera? How many pounds did this camera weigh? (7) What is the title of Stephen King's e-book that was released in 2000? (8) In which year did Amazon.com report that for the first time sales of e-books exceeded the sales of hardcover books? (9) What is the name of the keyboard developed in the 1930s with a layout designed to maximize efficiency and reduce hand stress? (10) When did the first USB flash drive appear on the retail market? Which company developed this storage medium?

Source: Microsoft

❷ Social Media

Historians place the birth of online social networking with the BBS (Bulletin Board System), where users communicated with a central computer and sent messages to other BBS members and also downloaded files and games. The next phase of social networking evolved when CompuServe, AOL (America Online), and Prodigy were among the services linking people with similar interests. Today's social networks share

Internet Research ✳

4 Green Computing

The average American household has 24 electronic products, according to the Consumer Electronics Association. When these devices, such as televisions, computers, and mobile devices become outdated or inoperable, the owner is left with the challenge of disposing or donating them. Many options exist to prevent these electronics from being discarded in landfills and, in turn, producing toxic waste. The United States Environmental Protection Agency (EPA) lists many eCycling resources on its website, including information about locations to donate or recycle electronics, answers to common questions about electronic waste, and regional and state eCycling programs. Visit the EPA site and read about recycling electronics. What toxic substances are found in computer components? Most major computer manufacturers provide recycling services. Identify which companies provide this service and how donations are made. For example, do users mail their electronics, drop them off at a store, or arrange for pickup?

The Electronics TakeBack Coalition encourages consumer electronics manufacturers to take responsibility for the entire life cycle of their products, from manufacture to disposal. Visit the Electronics TakeBack website and read what actions consumers can take to buy and dispose of their products responsibly and to urge companies to practice safe and environmentally friendly policies. Find a computer or phone recycling center in your area and then use an online mapping app (such as Google or Bing Maps) to find directions to these locations. In addition, many nonprofit organizations accept donations of electronic equipment, including computers. Locate several of these organizations and determine which devices they accept as donations. Some electronics retailers will accept used equipment and also sponsor recycling events. Which of these stores are near your residence? What products will they accept?

5 Security

Secure IT 1-1 on page 18 discusses the benefits of creating a backup plan for computers and mobile devices. One backup method is subscribing to a cloud storage provider. Consumer subscriptions to cloud storage services are experiencing double-digit growth each year, with an estimated 1.3 billion users predicted by 2017. Amazon, Google, Microsoft, and Apple are among the many companies offering cloud storage services.

Locate information about two of these services and review the features. Then, locate at least two independent cloud service providers, such as JustCloud, and read about accounts. How much free storage is available? What is the charge for additional storage? Are both limited and unlimited storage plans available? What is the maximum individual file size allowed? What methods do these companies take to secure the files? For example, how do they check the authenticity of the person signing in to the account? How do they monitor suspicious activity? Do they allow users to review all the sign-ins within a set period of time? Do they require account holders to modify their passwords occasionally? Is live customer support available 24 hours each day at no charge? In which country is the company and server located?

Source: JustCloud, Inc.

6 Ethics in Action

The Internet has increased the ease with which students can plagiarize material for research paper assignments. In an attempt to detect plagiarized material, teachers and students are using online services to check for original writing and offer feedback on methods of rewriting and citing sources correctly. For example, Turnitin and WriteCheck both use the same database of millions of student papers and billions of websites to compare phrases. Many other plagiarism checking services exist, and their cost, features, and reliability vary widely.

Visit the Turnitin and WriteCheck sites and then summarize of how these services are used. Compare these services with at least one other service. What are the fees to use these websites? How accurate are the results? How large are the databases of online and offline publications and papers? What features, such as allowing multiple resubmissions and grammar checking, do they offer? What types of reports are generated that give feedback and show plagiarized sources? What help and support are available? In general, how prevalent is plagiarism on your campus? What is your schools' official policy on disciplining students who submit plagiarized papers? Does your school have an honor code?

✳ Problem Solving

The Problem Solving exercises extend your knowledge of chapter concepts by seeking solutions to practical problems with technology that you may encounter at home, school, or work. The Collaboration exercise should be completed with a team.

💻 Challenge yourself with additional Problem Solving exercises by navigating to this book's Problem Solving resource on Computer Concepts CourseMate.

Instructions: You often can solve problems with technology in multiple ways. Determine a solution to the problems in these exercises by using one or more resources available to you (such as a computer or mobile device, articles on the web or in print, blogs, podcasts, videos, television, user guides, other individuals, electronics or computer stores, etc.). Describe your solution, along with the resource(s) used, in the format requested by your instructor (brief report, presentation, discussion, blog post, video, or other means).

Personal

1. **Shopping for Software** You are shopping for software that will assist you with your home's interior design. The package for the program you would like to purchase states that it was designed for the most recent version of Windows, but an older version is installed on your computer. How can you determine whether the program will run on your computer?

2. **Bad Directions** You are driving to your friend's house and are using your smartphone for directions. While approaching your destination, you realize that your smartphone app instructed you to turn the wrong way on your friend's street. How could this have happened?

3. **Bank Account Postings** While reviewing your checking account balance online, you notice that debit card purchases have not posted to your account for the past several days. Because you use online banking to balance your account, you become concerned about your unknown account balance. What steps will you take to correct this situation?

4. **Inaccessible Media** You insert a memory card with digital photos from your most recent family vacation and discover that your computer will not read the memory card. What might be wrong?

5. **Problematic Camera** After charging your digital camera battery overnight, you insert the battery and turn on the camera only to find that it is reporting a low battery. Seconds later, the camera shuts off automatically. What might be wrong?

Professional

6. **Discarding Old Computer Equipment** Your company has given you a new laptop to replace your current, outdated desktop. Because of the negative environmental impact of discarding the old computer in the trash, your supervisor asked you to suggest options for its disposal. How will you respond?

7. **Dead Battery** While traveling for business, you realize that you forgot to bring the battery charger for your laptop. Knowing that you need to use the laptop to give a presentation tomorrow, what steps will you take tonight to make sure you have enough battery power?

8. **Software Installation** You are attempting to install a program on your office computer. After inserting the installation disc and specifying that you would like to begin the installation, your computer appears to begin installing the program. Halfway through the installation process, an error message appears stating that you must have administrative privileges to perform the installation. Why were you not informed immediately upon beginning the installation? What are your next steps?

9. **Incorrect Sign-In Credentials** Upon returning to the office from a well-deserved two-week vacation, you turn on your computer. When you enter your user name and password, an error message appears stating that your password is incorrect. What are your next steps?

10. **Synchronization Error** You added appointments to the calendar on your computer, but these appointments are not synchronizing with your smartphone. Your calendar has synchronized with your smartphone in the past, but it has stopped working without explanation. What are your next steps?

Collaboration

11. **Technology in Health Care** Your dentist is moving from a shared office so that he can open his own practice. He mentioned that he would like to use technology in his office that not will only improve the patient experience, but also make his job easier. Form a team of three people to determine the types of technology your dentist can use in his new office. One team member should research ways that technology can help improve patient check-in and billing. Another team member should research the types of technology your dentist can use while he is working with patients, and the third team member should research any additional technology that can be used in the office to improve the patient experience. Compile your findings in a report and submit it to your instructor.

The Critical Thinking exercises challenge your assessment and decision-making skills by presenting real-world situations associated with chapter concepts. The Collaboration exercise should be completed with a team.

Critical Thinking ✸

 Challenge yourself additional Critical Thinking exercises by navigating to this book's Critical Thinking resource on Computer Concepts CourseMate.

Instructions: Evaluate the situations below, using personal experiences and one or more resources available to you (such as articles on the web or in print, blogs, podcasts, videos, television, user guides, other individuals, electronics or computer stores, etc.). Perform the tasks requested in each exercise and share your deliverables in the format requested by your instructor (brief report, presentation, discussion, blog post, video, or other means).

1. Class Discussion

Reactions to Software Problems Everyone who uses computers and mobile devices has experienced problems with software, including operating systems, desktop apps, web apps, and mobile apps. Problems range from not being able to install or download the program or app to a computer or mobile device, to a program or an app producing unanticipated results. Depending on the situation, these problems can result in user stress. Many people believe reactions to software problems tend to be more extreme than reactions to problems with other tools. Evaluate situations in which you have seen people react to program and app problems on their computers and mobile devices. Discuss how these users can reduce their frustration when dealing with such problems. Have you ever been frustrated by problems with a program or an app? How did you react? What did you do to solve the problem?

2. Research and Share

Energy Efficiency Increases in energy prices lead many individuals to look at purchasing energy-efficient computers. Energy-efficient computers often look and perform similarly to equivalent computers that use more energy. Find two computers of identical configuration, where the only difference is energy consumption. How much energy does the energy-efficient computer save? Are energy-efficient computers more or less expensive? Will the difference in cost (if any) affect your purchasing decision? How else might you be able to

change your computer to save energy? Use the web to locate articles that recommend energy efficient products and that provide tips about additional ways to save energy. Compile your findings and then share them with the class.

3. Case Study

Farmers' Market You are the new manager for a group of organic farmers who have a weekly market in season. The previous manager tracked all of the data on paper. You realize that using technology will increase your efficiency and enable you to communicate better with the board of directors, vendors, and customers. At the board's next meeting, you will share ideas of how you will use technology. Before the meeting, you compile the following: differences between input and output, a list of the types of data you can use as input, and a list of the types of information you can produce as output. You include the types of computers, mobile devices, and other technologies you will use to enter data and produce the information. Incorporate your own experiences and user reviews of the devices. Compile your findings.

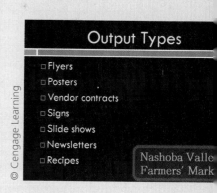

Collaboration

4. **Recommending Technology Solutions** People use computers and mobile devices in a variety of fields, including travel, manufacturing, and more. Although the way people use computers and mobile devices varies, each use involves hardware, programs and apps, and some type of communications method, such as the Internet or cellular network. Form a three-member team and choose a field in which you all are interested. Assign one member to investigate hardware, another to investigate programs and apps, and the third member to investigate communications methods used in the field. Locate user reviews and articles by industry experts. Each team member should develop a list of related items that may be used. After the investigation, create a hypothetical business or organization in the field. Recommend specific hardware, programs or apps, and communications capabilities that would be best for the network or organization. Include comparisons of specific items, as well as costs. Be sure to summarize your investigations, describe the hypothetical business or organization, and outline and support your recommendations.

✺ Beyond the Book

The Beyond the Book exercises expand your understanding of chapter concepts by requiring research.

Access premium content by visiting Computer Concepts CourseMate. If you have a Computer Concepts CourseMate access code, you can reinforce and extend your learning with MindTap Reader, practice tests, video, and other premium content for Discovering Computers. To sign in to Computer Concepts CourseMate at www.cengagebrain.com, you first must create a student account and then register this book, as described at www.cengage.com/ct/studentdownload.

Part 1 Instructions: Use the web or e-book to perform the task identified for each book element below. Describe your findings, along with the search term(s) you used and your web source(s), if appropriate, in the format requested by your instructor (brief report, presentation, discussion, blog post, video, or other means).

1. **Animation** 📱 Review the animation associated with this chapter and then answer the question(s) it poses (11). What search term would you use to learn more about a specific segment of the animation?

2. **Consider This** Select a Consider This in this chapter (5, 6, 7, 10, 11, 15, 17, 22, 25, 28) and find a recent article that elaborates on the topic. What information did you find that was not presented in this book or e-book?

3. **Drag-and-Drop Figures** 📱 Complete the Drag-and-Drop Figure activities associated with this chapter (11, 13, 17, 26, 29, 39). What did you learn from each of these activities?

4. **Ethics & Issues** Select an Ethics & Issues in this chapter (8, 22, 34, 38) and find a recent article that supports one view presented. Does the article change your opinion about the topic? Why or why not?

5. **Facebook & Twitter** Review a recent Discovering Computers Facebook post or Twitter Tweet and read the referenced article(s). What did you learn from the article?

6. **High-Tech Talk** 📱 Locate an article that discusses topics related to triangulation. Would you recommend the article you found? Why or why not?

7. **How To** Select a How To in this chapter (5, 20, 21, 27) and find a recent article that elaborates on the topic. Who would benefit from the content of this article? Why?

8. **Innovative Computing** 📱 Locate two additional facts about Diabetes Tracking or Mobile Payments. Do your findings change your opinion about the future of this innovation? Why or why not?

9. **Internet Research** Use the search term in an Internet Research (8, 9, 15, 24, 33, 37) to answer the question posed in the element. What other search term could you use to answer the question?

10. **Mini Features** Locate an article that discusses topics related to one of the mini features in this chapter (10, 32, 40). Do you feel that the article is appropriate for this course? Why or why not?

11. **Secure IT** Select a Secure IT in this chapter (18, 23, 24, 30) and find a recent article about the topic that you find interesting. How can you relate the content of the article to your everyday life?

12. **Technology @ Work** Locate three additional, unique usages of technology in the health care industry (41). What makes the use of these technologies unique to the health care industry?

13. **Technology Innovators** 📱 Locate two additional facts about Bill Gates, Steve Jobs, Facebook, Mark Zuckerberg, and Twitter. Which Technology Innovator impresses you most? Why?

14. **Third-Party Links** 📱 Visit one of the third-party links identified in this chapter (8, 18, 21, 22, 23, 25, 30, 34, 38, 41) and read the article or watch the video associated with the link. Would you share this link on your online social network account? Why or why not?

Part 2 Instructions: Find specific instructions for the exercises below in the e-book or on Computer Concepts CourseMate. Beside each exercise is a brief description of its online content.

1. 📱 **You Review It** Search for and review a video or podcast about current technology news.

2. 📱 **Windows and Mac** Enhance your understanding and knowledge about using Windows and Mac computers by completing the Running Applications, Improve Your Mouse Skills, and Understand Computer Information activities.

3. 📱 **Android, iOS, and Windows** Enhance your understanding of Android, iOS, and Windows devices by completing the Manage Your Calendar and Manage Your Contacts activities.

4. 📱 **Exploring Computer Careers** Read about a career as an app developer, search for related employment ads, and then answer related questions.

5. 📱 **App Adventure** Track your own health and fitness by installing and running an app on your smartphone or tablet.

The Internet

Accessing, Searching, Sharing, and Communicating

2

You can access the Internet using a variety of computers and devices.

"I use the Internet and web to shop for bargains, browse Google for all sorts of information, manage my fantasy sports teams, download music, check email on my phone, and so much more! What more could I gain from using the Internet?"

True, you may be familiar with some of the material in this chapter, but do you know …

How to protect yourself from identity theft?

How you can write search text to improve results of web searches?

Why some smartphones include GPS receivers?

How to check the speed of your Internet connection?

When you would use a hashtag?

How to search for a job online?

Who created the web and why?

How to create a blog?

How devices on the Internet locate each other?

Why you would want accounts on multiple social networking sites?

What you can do to combat cyberbullying?

Which email app is best suited to your needs?

How the transportation industry relies on computers, mobile devices, and related technologies?

What wording you should avoid in online communications?

How you can publish a webpage?

For these answers and to discover much more information essential to this course, read this chapter and visit the associated Computer Concepts CourseMate at www.cengagebrain.com.

© iStockphoto / kupicoo

✔ Objectives

After completing this chapter, you will be able to:

1 Discuss the evolution of the Internet

2 Briefly describe various broadband Internet connections

3 Describe the purpose of an IP address and its relationship to a domain name

4 Describe features of browsers and identify the components of a web address

5 Describe ways to enter effective search text

6 Explain benefits and risks of using social networking sites

7 Describe uses of various types of websites: search engines; online social networks; informational; media sharing and bookmarking; news, weather, sports, and other mass media; educational; business, governmental, and organizational; blogs; wikis; health and science; entertainment; financial; travel and mapping; shopping and auctions; careers and employment; e-commerce; and portals

8 Identify and briefly describe the steps required for web publishing

9 Explain how the web uses graphics, animation, audio, video, and virtual reality

10 Explain how email, email lists, instant messaging, chat rooms, discussion forums, VoIP, and FTP work

11 Identify the rules of netiquette

The Internet

One of the major reasons business, home, and other users purchase computers and mobile devices is for Internet access. The **Internet** is a worldwide collection of networks that connects millions of businesses, government agencies, educational institutions, and individuals. Each of the networks on the Internet provides resources that add to the abundance of goods, services, and information accessible via the Internet.

Today, billions of home and business users around the world access a variety of services on the Internet using computers and mobile devices. The web, email, and VoIP are three of the more widely used Internet services (Figure 2-1). Other Internet services include instant messaging, chat rooms, discussion forums, and FTP. To enhance your understanding of Internet services, the chapter begins by discussing the history of the Internet and how the Internet works and then explains each of these services.

Evolution of the Internet

The Internet has its roots in a networking project started by the Pentagon's Advanced Research Projects Agency (ARPA), an agency of the U.S. Department of Defense. ARPA's goal was to build a network that (1) allowed scientists at different physical locations to share information and work together on military and scientific projects and (2) could function even if part of the network were disabled or destroyed by a disaster such as a nuclear attack. That network, called *ARPANET*, became functional in September 1969, linking scientific and academic researchers across the United States.

The original ARPANET consisted of four main computers, one each located at the University of California at Los Angeles, the University of California at Santa Barbara, the Stanford Research Institute, and the University of Utah. Each of these computers served as a host on the network. A *host*, more commonly known today as a server, is any computer that provides services and connections to other computers on a network. Hosts often use high-speed communications to transfer data and messages over a network. By 1984, ARPANET had more than 1,000 individual computers linked as hosts. Today, millions of hosts connect to this network, which now is known as the Internet.

BTW

Internet2
Innovative Computing:
You should be familiar
with innovations of
Internet2, whose goal
is to develop and test
advanced technologies
that will benefit Internet
users in the future.

access information

send email

converse with others

Figure 2-1 People around the world use the Internet in daily activities, such as accessing information, sending email messages, and conversing with others from their computers and mobile devices.

The Internet consists of many local, regional, national, and international networks. Both public and private organizations own networks on the Internet. These networks, along with phone companies, cable and satellite companies, and the government, all contribute toward the internal structure of the Internet.

 CONSIDER THIS

Who owns the Internet?

No single person, company, institution, or government agency owns the Internet. Each organization on the Internet is responsible only for maintaining its own network.

The World Wide Web Consortium (*W3C*), however, oversees research and sets standards and guidelines for many areas of the Internet. The mission of the W3C is to ensure the continued growth of the web. Nearly 400 organizations from around the world are members of the W3C, advising, defining standards, and addressing other issues.

Internet Research

How can you learn more about the World Wide Web Consortium?

Search for: w3c

Connecting to the Internet

Users can connect their computers and mobile devices to the Internet through wired or wireless technology and then access its services free or for a fee. With wired connections, a computer or device physically attaches via a cable or wire to a communications device, such as a modem, that transmits data and other items over transmission media to the Internet. For wireless connections, many mobile computers and devices include the necessary built-in technology so that they can transmit data and other items wirelessly. Computers without this capability can use a wireless modem or other communications device that enables wireless connectivity. A *wireless modem*, for example, uses the cellular radio network to provide Internet connections. Figure 2-2 shows examples of modems. The wireless modem shown in the figure is known as a *dongle*, which is a small device that connects to a computer.

Today, users often connect to the Internet via *broadband* Internet service because of its fast data transfer speeds and its always-on connection. Through broadband Internet service, users can download webpages quickly, play online games, communicate in real time with others, and more. Table 2-1 shows examples of popular wired and wireless broadband Internet service technologies for home and small business users.

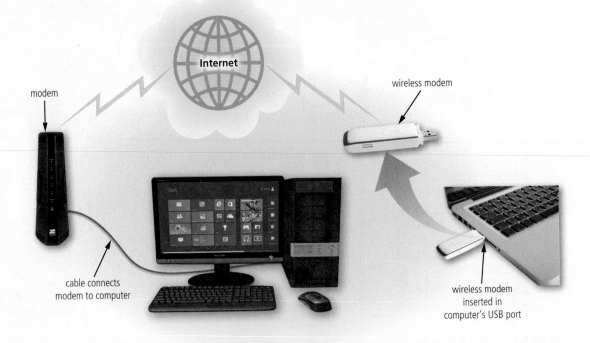

Figure 2-2 Using a modem is one way to connect computers and mobile devices to the Internet.

Courtesy of Zoom Telephonics Inc; © Oleksiy Mark / Shutterstock.com; Source: Microsoft; © Kristina Postnikova / Shutterstock.com; Kristina Postnikova / Shutterstock.com; © Cengage Learning

Table 2-1 Popular Broadband Internet Service Technologies

	Technology	Description
Wired	Cable Internet service	Provides high-speed Internet access through the cable television network via a cable modem
	DSL (digital subscriber line)	Provides high-speed Internet connections through the telephone network via a DSL modem
	Fiber to the Premises (FTTP)	Uses fiber-optic cable to provide high-speed Internet access via a modem
Wireless	Wi-Fi (wireless fidelity)	Uses radio signals to provide high-speed Internet connections to computers and devices with built-in Wi-Fi capability or a communications device that enables Wi-Fi connectivity
	Mobile broadband	Offers high-speed Internet connections over the cellular radio network to computers and devices with built-in compatible technology (such as 3G, 4G, or 5G) or a wireless modem or other communications device
	Fixed wireless	Provides high-speed Internet connections using a dish-shaped antenna on a building, such as a house or business, to communicate with a tower location via radio signals
	Satellite Internet service	Provides high-speed Internet connections via satellite to a satellite dish that communicates with a satellite modem

© Cengage Learning

Employees and students typically connect their computers and mobile devices to the Internet wirelessly through a business or school network, which, in turn, usually connects to a very high-speed Internet service. When away from the office, home, or school, mobile users access the Internet using a variety of Internet services. Some use a **cybercafé**, or Internet café, which is a location that provides computers with Internet access, usually for a fee. Cybercafés exist in cities around the world. Hotels and airports often provide wired or wireless Internet connections as a free service to travelers.

Many public locations, such as airports, hotels, schools, shopping malls, coffee shops, and city parks are Wi-Fi hot spots. Recall that a *hot spot* is a wireless network that provides Internet connections to mobile computers and devices. Although most hot spots enable unrestricted or open access, some require that users agree to terms of service, obtain a password (for example, from the hotel's front desk), or perform some other action in order to connect to the Internet.

Home and small business users can share and provide wireless Internet connections by creating their own Wi-Fi hot spot through a communications device in the home or business that is connected to broadband Internet service. Instead of a stationary Wi-Fi hot spot, some users opt to create mobile hot spots through mobile broadband Internet service via a separate communications device or a tethered Internet-capable device (Figure 2-3). *Tethering* transforms

Internet Research

What is a MiFi device?

Search for: what is mifi

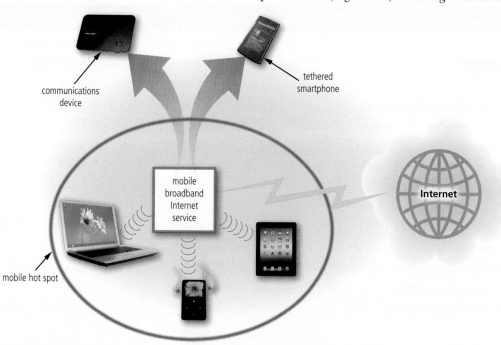

communications device

tethered smartphone

mobile broadband Internet service

Internet

mobile hot spot

Figure 2-3 You can create a mobile hot spot using a communications device or by tethering a smartphone.

Courtesy of Verizon Wireless © figarro / Can Stock Photo; © iStockphoto / Dane Wirtzfeld; © amfoto / Shutterstock.com; © Alex Staroseltsev / Shutterstock.com; Source: Microsoft; © Cengage Learning a smartphone or Internet-capable tablet into a portable communications device that shares its Internet access with other computers and devices wirelessly. Users typically pay additional fees for mobile hot spot and tethering services.

 CONSIDER THIS

Does everyone use broadband Internet?
No. Some home users connect computers to the Internet via slower-speed dial-up access because of its lower cost or because broadband access is not available where they live. *Dial-up access* takes place when a modem in a computer connects to the Internet via a standard telephone line that transmits data and information using an analog (continuous wave pattern) signal.

Internet Service Providers

An **Internet service provider** (**ISP**), sometimes called an Internet access provider, is a business that provides individuals and organizations access to the Internet free or for a fee. ISPs often charge a fixed amount for an Internet connection, offering customers a variety of plans based on desired speeds, bandwidth, and services. In addition to Internet access, ISPs typically include services such as news, weather, financial data, games, travel guides, email, instant messaging, photo communities, and online storage.

Bandwidth represents the amount of data that travels over a network. A higher bandwidth means more data transmits. Data sizes typically are stated in terms of megabytes and gigabytes. A *megabyte* (*MB*) is equal to approximately one million characters, and a *gigabyte* (*GB*) is equal to approximately one billion characters. Table 2-2 shows approximate data usage for various Internet activities.

Wi-Fi networks often provide free Internet access, while some charge a daily or per use fee. Instead of locating a hot spot, some users prefer to subscribe to a mobile service provider, such as Verizon Wireless, so that they can access the Internet wherever they have mobile phone access. A *mobile service provider*, sometimes called a wireless data provider, is an ISP that offers wireless Internet access to computers and mobile devices with the necessary built-in wireless capability (such as Wi-Fi), wireless modems, or other communications devices that enable wireless connectivity. An antenna on or built into the computer or device, wireless modem, or communications device typically sends signals through the airwaves to communicate with a mobile service provider.

Table 2-2   Data Usage Examples

Activity	Quantity	Approximate Data Usage
Send and receive email messages (with no attachments)	100 messages	3–6 MB
Post on social networking sites	100 posts	0.75–1 GB
Send and receive email messages (with attachments)	100 messages	0.75–1 GB
Visit webpages	200 visits	1 GB
Talk with others using VoIP (without video)	1 hour	1.25 GB
Upload or download photos	10 photos	1.5 GB
Listen to streaming music	1 hour	1–2 GB
Play online games	1 hour	1.75 GB
Watch smaller, standard-quality streaming video	1 hour	2–5 GB
Download apps, games, music, e-books	25 downloads	3 GB
Talk with others using VoIP (with video)	1 hour	5–7.5 GB
Watch HD streaming video	1 hour	5–20 GB

© Cengage Learning

How Data and Information Travel the Internet

Computers connected to the Internet work together to transfer data and information around the world using servers and clients and various wired and wireless transmission media. On the Internet, your computer is a client that can access data, information, and services on a variety of servers. Wired transmission media used includes phone line, coaxial cable, and fiber-optic cable. Wireless transmission media includes radio waves and satellite signals.

The inner structure of the Internet works much like a transportation system. Just as interstate highways connect major cities and carry the bulk of the automotive traffic across the country, several main transmission media carry the heaviest amount of *traffic*, or communications activity, on the Internet. These major carriers of network traffic are known collectively as the *Internet backbone*.

In the United States, the transmission media that make up the Internet backbone exchange data and information at several different major cities across the country. That is, they transfer data and information from one network to another until reaching the final destination (Figure 2-4).

BTW

DNS Servers and IPv6
High-Tech Talk: DNS servers work with the IPv4 and IPv6 addressing schemes to locate computers and devices on the Internet.

How a Home User's Request for a Webpage Might Travel the Internet Using Cable Internet Service

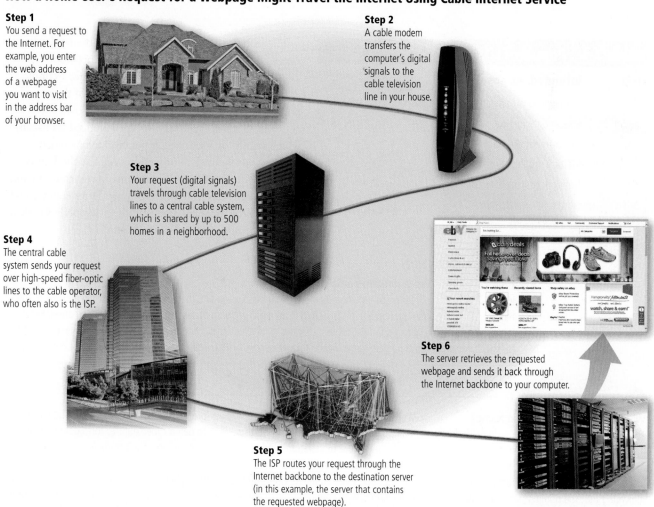

Step 1
You send a request to the Internet. For example, you enter the web address of a webpage you want to visit in the address bar of your browser.

Step 2
A cable modem transfers the computer's digital signals to the cable television line in your house.

Step 3
Your request (digital signals) travels through cable television lines to a central cable system, which is shared by up to 500 homes in a neighborhood.

Step 4
The central cable system sends your request over high-speed fiber-optic lines to the cable operator, who often also is the ISP.

Step 6
The server retrieves the requested webpage and sends it back through the Internet backbone to your computer.

Step 5
The ISP routes your request through the Internet backbone to the destination server (in this example, the server that contains the requested webpage).

Figure 2-4 This figure shows how a home user's request for eBay's webpage might travel the Internet using cable Internet service.
© romakoma / Shutterstock.com; © Pablo Eder / Shutterstock.com; © dotshock / Shutterstock.com; © TonyV3112 / Shutterstock.com; Donna Cox and Robert Patterson, courtesy of the National Center for Supercomputing Applications (NCSA) and the Board of Trustees of the University of Illinois; © iStockphoto / luismmolina; Source: eBay

Domain Names and IP Addresses

The Internet relies on an addressing system much like the postal service to send data and information to a computer or device at a specific destination. An **IP address**, short for Internet Protocol address, is a sequence of numbers that uniquely identifies the location of each computer or device connected to the Internet.

The Internet uses two IP addressing schemes: IPv4 and IPv6. Due to the growth of the Internet, the original scheme, IPv4, began dwindling in availability. To rectify the problem, the IPv6 scheme lengthened the addresses, which increased the available number of IP addresses exponentially. Because all-numeric IP addresses are difficult to remember and use, the Internet supports domain names. A **domain name** is a text-based name that corresponds to the IP address of a server that hosts a website (Figure 2-5). A domain name is part of the web address that you type in a browser's address bar to access a website.

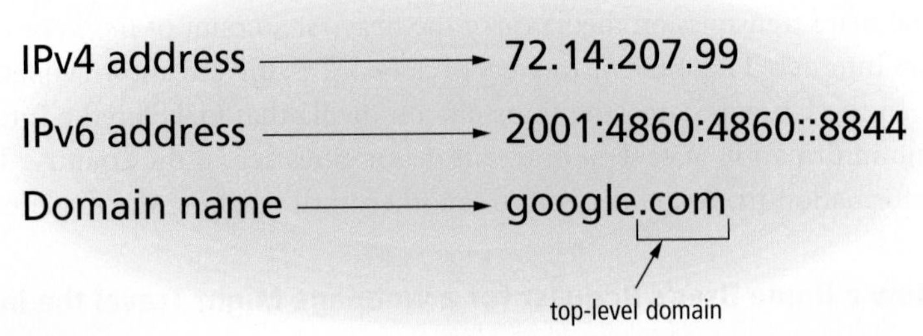

IPv4 address ──────→ 72.14.207.99

IPv6 address ──────→ 2001:4860:4860::8844

Domain name ──────→ google.com
                              └─┬─┘
                         top-level domain

Figure 2-5 The IPv4 and IPv6 addresses, along with the domain name for Google's website.
© Cengage Learning

Table 2-3	Popular TLDs
TLD	**Intended Purpose**
.com	Commercial organizations, businesses, and companies
.edu	Educational institutions
.gov	Government agencies
.mil	Military organizations
.net	Network providers or commercial companies
.org	Nonprofit organizations

© Cengage Learning

The suffix of the domain name, called the *top-level domain* (*TLD*), identifies the type of organization associated with the domain. In Figure 2-5, for example, the .com is the TLD. Table 2-3 lists some of the more popular TLDs. The organization that approves and controls TLDs is called *ICANN* (pronounced EYE-can), which stands for Internet Corporation for Assigned Names and Numbers. For websites outside the United States, the suffix of the domain name may include a country code TLD (*ccTLD*), which is a two-letter country code, such as au for Australia. For example, www.philips.com.au is the domain name for Philips Australia.

✳ **CONSIDER THIS**

How can you secure a domain name?
Individuals and companies register domain names so that people can find their websites easily using a browser. You register a domain name through a registrar, which is an organization that sells and manages domain names. Before purchasing a domain name, you must confirm that it is available, select your desired TLD, and specify the length of time for which you want to reserve the name. Read Ethics & Issues 2-1 to consider issues related to rights of domain names.

✳ **ETHICS & ISSUES 2-1**

Who Has Rights to a Domain Name?
You learn from a registrar that a domain name containing your company name is not available. When you enter the web address in a browser, however, a webpage appears indicating that the domain name is available for purchase, likely by a cybersquatter. Cybersquatters buy and register unused or lapsed domain names so that they can profit from selling them. Cybersquatters sometimes will sell you the domain name, but some take advantage of people trying to reach a more popular website and redirect to a website for their own business.

Website owners periodically must renew domain name registrations. Cybersquatters look for out-of-date registrations and buy them so that the original website owner must buy them back. Cybersquatters may purchase domain names with common words, alternate spellings of trademarked terms, or celebrity names. For example, Google won a case that awarded them the rights to more than 750 domain names that included the word, google.

More than 10 years ago, lawmakers enacted the *Anticybersquatting Consumer Protection Act* (ACPA). The ACPA's goal is to protect trademark owners from being forced to pay a cybersquatter for a domain name that includes their trademark. To win a case against a cybersquatter, you must prove that the cybersquatter acted in bad faith, meaning they tried knowingly to profit from purchasing a domain name with a trademarked term.

Should cybersquatters be prosecuted? Why or why not? Does a large company have the right to sue a smaller company in order to purchase their domain? How should companies protect their brands when registering for domain names?

The *domain name system* (*DNS*) is the method that the Internet uses to store domain names and their corresponding IP addresses. When you enter a domain name (i.e., google.com) in a browser, a DNS server translates the domain name to its associated IP address so that the request can be routed to the correct computer (Figure 2-6). A *DNS server* is a server on the Internet that usually is associated with an ISP.

How a Browser Displays a Requested Webpage

Step 1
Run the browser and enter the web address in the browser's address bar.

web address contains domain name

Step 2
The browser communicates with a DNS server maintained by your ISP or another provider. The DNS server looks up the domain name portion of the web address, finds its associated IP address, and then sends the IP address to your computer or mobile device.

Step 3
The browser uses the IP address to contact the web server at the specified IP address to request the content of the desired webpage. The web server fulfills the user's request by sending the desired content to the user's browser, which formats the page for display on the screen.

72.14.207.99
2001:4860:4860::8844

Figure 2-6   This figure shows how a user's entered domain name (google.com) uses a DNS server to display a webpage (Google, in this case).
Source: Apple Inc.; © Cengage Learning; © Cengage Learning; © Sashkin / Shutterstock.com; Source: Google Inc.

The World Wide Web

While the Internet was developed in the late 1960s, the World Wide Web emerged in the early 1990s. Since then, it has grown phenomenally to become one of the more widely used services on the Internet.

Recall that the **World Wide Web** (**WWW**), or **web**, consists of a worldwide collection of electronic documents. Each electronic document on the web is called a **webpage**, which can contain text, graphics, animation, audio, and video. Some webpages are static (fixed); others are dynamic (changing). Visitors to a *static webpage* all see the same content. With a *dynamic webpage*, by contrast, visitors can customize some or all of the viewed content, such as desired stock quotes, weather for a region, or ticket availability for flights. The time required to download a webpage varies depending on the speed of your Internet connection and the amount of graphics and other media involved.

A **website** is a collection of related webpages and associated items, such as documents and pictures, stored on a web server. A **web server** is a computer that delivers requested webpages to your computer or mobile device. The same web server can store multiple websites.

BTW

Tim-Berners Lee
Technology Innovator:
You should be familiar with Tim Berners-Lee (creator of the World Wide Web).

As web technologies matured in the mid-2000s, industry experts introduced the term *Web 2.0* to refer to websites that provide a means for users to share personal information (such as online social networks), allow users to modify website content (such as wikis), and provide applications through a browser (such as web apps).

Browsing and Navigating the Web

Recall from Chapter 1 that a **browser** is an application that enables users with an Internet connection to access and view webpages on a computer or mobile device. Internet-capable mobile devices such as smartphones use a special type of browser, called a *mobile browser*, which is designed for their smaller screens and limited computing power. Many websites can detect if you are accessing their content on a mobile device (Figure 2-7).

When you run a browser, it may retrieve and display a starting webpage, sometimes called a home page. The initial home page that is displayed is specified in the browser. You can change your browser's home page at any time through its settings, options, or similar commands.

Another use of the term, **home page**, refers to the first page that is displayed on a website. Similar to a book cover or a table of contents, a website's home page provides information about its purpose and content. Many websites allow you to personalize the home page so that it contains areas of interest to you.

Desktop browsers typically support **tabbed browsing**, where the top of the browser shows a tab (similar to a file folder tab) for each webpage you display (shown in Figure 2-7). To move from one displayed webpage to another, you tap or click the tab in the browser. Tabbed browsing allows users to have multiple home pages that automatically are displayed when the browser runs. You also can organize tabs in a group, called a tab group, and save the group as a favorite, so that at any time you can display all tabs at once.

Because some websites attempt to track your browsing habits or gather personal information, current browsers usually include a feature that allows you to disable and/or more tightly control the dissemination of your browsing habits and personal information. Read Secure IT 2-1 for safe browsing tips.

Internet Research

How do I change my browser's home page?

Search for: change browser home page

⊛ SECURE IT 2-1

📰 Safe Browsing Techniques

Browsing the web resembles crossing a busy street: you need to exercise caution and look carefully for unexpected traffic. Cybercriminals are on the lookout to prey upon unsuspecting users, so you should follow these guidelines when browsing:

- **Verify the website is safe.** Type the website address of your email, banking, social networking, and other personal accounts directly in a browser; never visit these websites merely by tapping or clicking links found in email messages. Before you sign in, double-check the web address to verify it is correct. Most browsers change the color of the address bar to verify the website is legitimate. Also, check that the web address begins with https instead of the less secure http, and look for a closed padlock symbol beside it.

- **Clear your browsing history.** A copy of every website you visit is stored in the browser's *cache* (pronounced cash) folder. If you perform online banking or view your credit card transactions, the cache could contain personal information such as passwords and account numbers. You can specify to clear cache automatically each time you close a browser.

- **Use a phishing filter.** *Phishing* is a scam in which a perpetrator attempts to obtain your personal and/or financial information. Many browsers include a *phishing filter*, which is a program that warns or blocks you from potentially fraudulent or suspicious websites.

- **Enable a pop-up blocker.** Malicious software creators can develop a *pop-up ad*, which is an Internet advertisement that suddenly appears in a new window on top of a webpage displayed in a browser. A **pop-up blocker** is a filtering program that stops pop-up ads from displaying on webpages. Many browsers include a pop-up blocker. You also can download pop-up blockers from the web at no cost.

- **Browse anonymously.** To protect your online identity, use a *proxy server*, which is another computer that screens all your incoming and outgoing messages. The proxy server will prevent your browsing history, passwords, user names, and other personal information from being revealed.

⊛ What pop-ups have you encountered while browsing? What new techniques will you use to browse the web safely?

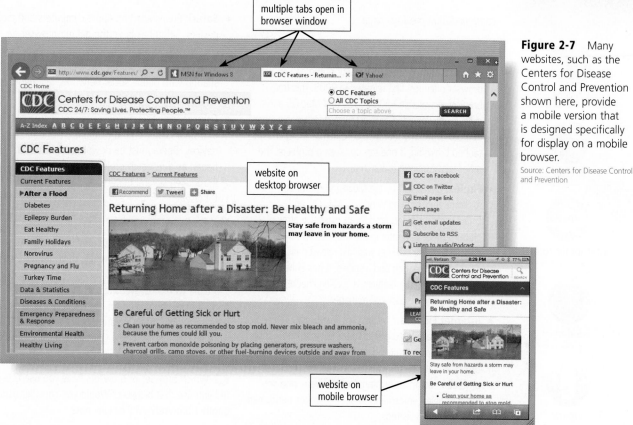

Figure 2-7 Many websites, such as the Centers for Disease Control and Prevention shown here, provide a mobile version that is designed specifically for display on a mobile browser.

Source: Centers for Disease Control and Prevention

 **MINI FEATURE 2-1**

Browsers

The decision of which browser to use is a topic of discussion among computer experts and novices alike. All browsers can retrieve and display webpages, but their features and ease of use vary.

Configuring Options

Users can customize some settings to improve their browsing experience, such as those listed below.

- **Favorites**, also called *bookmarks*, are links to preferred websites. When you add a website to the list of favorites, you can visit that website simply by tapping or clicking its name in a list instead of typing its web address. Favorites can be organized into folders, alphabetized, and sorted by date or how frequently you view the websites.

- Security features, such as filters and secure connections, help protect you from fraudulent and malicious websites that might attempt to steal your identity and personal information. These features also can block websites you do not want to display and can instruct the browser to save passwords.

- Privacy features help prevent thieves from accessing information about your browsing history, such as websites you have visited, data about your browsing session, and content you have seen on specific webpages.

Obtaining Browsers

A browser often is included in the operating system of a computer or mobile device. For example, many computer manufacturers include Internet Explorer when they install Windows and include Safari when they install Mac OS. To locate a particular browser, you can visit the software developer's website and download the program at no cost. Several browsers also are available at shareware websites. Keep your browser up to date to prevent security holes. You can set your browser to perform updates automatically.

Making a Decision

Selecting the best browser for your needs involves some careful thought. You may decide to install several and then use each one for specific needs. Perform some research to compare browsers and then consider the following factors:

- How old is your computer or mobile device? A newer browser may not work properly on older hardware.

- How much memory is in your computer or mobile device? Some browsers work best with a lot of memory.

- Which platform are you using? Some browsers are available for specific operating systems.

- What do you want the browser to do? Some browsers are best suited for performing simple searches while others excel when running media-laden websites.

continued on next page

Chrome

Firefox

Internet Explorer

Safari

Opera

Source: Google Inc; Mozilla
Foundation; Microsoft; Apple Inc;
Opera Software

continued from previous page

Specific Browsers

- **Chrome:** Google's Chrome is one of the newer browser offerings, first released in 2008. This free browser is available for Windows and Mac OS and must be downloaded and installed. It includes a large number of security features. Chrome has independent tabbed browsing; if one tab develops a problem, the other tabs continue to function.

- **Firefox:** Developed by the Mozilla Corporation for computers running Windows, Mac OS, and Linux, Firefox is recognized for its extensive array of plug-ins (discussed later in the chapter). This free general-purpose browser was first released in 2004 and must be downloaded and installed. It has enhanced privacy and security features, a spelling checker, tabbed browsing, and a password manager.

- **Internet Explorer:** Microsoft's free browser, Internet Explorer, is available primarily for Microsoft Windows and comes preinstalled. First released in 1995, the browser features the capability to rearrange tabs, protection against phishing and malware, and settings to delete information about searches performed and webpages visited.

- **Safari:** Preinstalled on Apple computers and mobile devices, Safari has been the default browser for Mac OS since 2003 and is relatively new to Windows. The browser is recognized for its sleek design, built-in sharing with online social networks, fast performance, parental controls, and ease of use.

- **Opera:** This second-oldest browser is free, fast, and small. Used on both computers and mobile devices, Opera must be downloaded and installed. It began as a research project in Norway in 1994 and introduced several features found on most of today's browsers.

Mobile Browsers

Many browsers are included by default with some mobile devices and smartphones. Their features vary greatly. Some allow users to zoom and use keyboard shortcuts with most websites, while others display only websites optimized for mobile devices. The more popular mobile browsers are Opera Mini, Safari, Google Android's browser, Google Chrome, Firefox Mobile, and Internet Explorer Mobile.

 Which browser or browsers have you used? Why did you use that browser? Would you consider using another browser? Why or why not?

Web Addresses

A webpage has a unique address, called a **web address** or *URL* (Uniform Resource Locator). For example, the web address of http://www.nps.gov identifies the U.S. Department of the Interior National Park Service home page. A browser retrieves a webpage using its web address.

If you know the address of a webpage, you can type it in the address bar in of the browser. For example, if you type the address http://www.nps.gov/history/places.htm in the address bar and then press the ENTER key or tap or click the Search, Go, or similar button, the browser downloads and displays the webpage shown in Figure 2-8. The path, history/places.htm, in this web address identifies a webpage that is specified in a file named places.htm, which is located in a folder named history on the server that hosts the nps.gov website. When you enter this web address, after obtaining the IP address for the nps.gov domain name, the browser sends a request to the web server to retrieve the webpage named places.htm, and delivers it to your browser to be displayed.

A web address consists of a protocol, domain name, and sometimes the host name, path to a specific webpage, or file name of the webpage. The *http*, which stands for Hypertext Transfer Protocol, is a set of rules that defines how webpages transfer on the Internet. Many web addresses begin with http:// as the protocol. The text between the protocol and the domain name, called the host name, identifies the type of Internet server. The www, for example, indicates a web server.

✳ CONSIDER THIS

Do you need to type the protocol and host name in a web address?

Many browsers and websites do not require that you enter the http:// or the host name (www) in the web address. For example, you could enter nps.gov instead of http://www.nps.gov. As you begin typing a web address or if you enter an incorrect web address, browsers often display a list of similar addresses or related websites from which you can select.

Figure 2-8   After entering http://www.nps.gov/history/places.htm in the address bar and then pressing the ENTER key or tapping or clicking the Search, Go, or similar button in a browser, the U.S. Department of the Interior National Park Service home page shown here is displayed.

Source: National Park Service U.S. Department of the Interior

Web Feeds   When you enter a web address in a browser, you request, or *pull*, information from a web server. Another way users can pull content is by subscribing to a *web feed*, which contains content that has changed on a website. Mass media, blogs, and online social networks often provide web feeds, saving users the time spent checking the websites for updated content. Websites that use web feeds usually display a feed icon (Figure 2-9). Most browsers contain the capability to read web feeds. *RSS*, which stands for Really Simple Syndication, and *Atom* are popular specifications used to distribute content, such as web feeds, to subscribers. A feed reader, sometimes called an aggregator, is a type of software for computers and mobile devices that reads a user's specified web feeds and collects their most recent content.

Figure 2-9   Websites commonly use this symbol to indicate you can subscribe to their web feed.

Source: Mozilla Foundation

Web Apps and Mobile Apps

Recall from Chapter 1 that a *web app* is an application stored on a web server that you access through a browser. Users typically interact with web apps directly at a website, sometimes referred to as the host. Web app hosts usually provide storage for users' data and information on their servers, known as *cloud storage*.

Many web app hosts provide free access to their software, such as the Word Web App shown in Figure 2-10 on the next page. Others offer part of their web app free and charge for access to a more comprehensive program. Many include advertisements in the free version and charge for an advertisement-free version. Some allow you to use the web app free and pay a fee when a certain action occurs. For example, you can prepare your tax return free, but if you elect to print it or file it electronically, you pay a minimal fee.

A *mobile app* is an application you download from a mobile device's app store or other location on the Internet to a smartphone or other mobile device. Mobile apps often take advantage of features of the device, such as touch screens, digital cameras, microphones, and embedded GPS receivers, to enable you to enter and capture data.

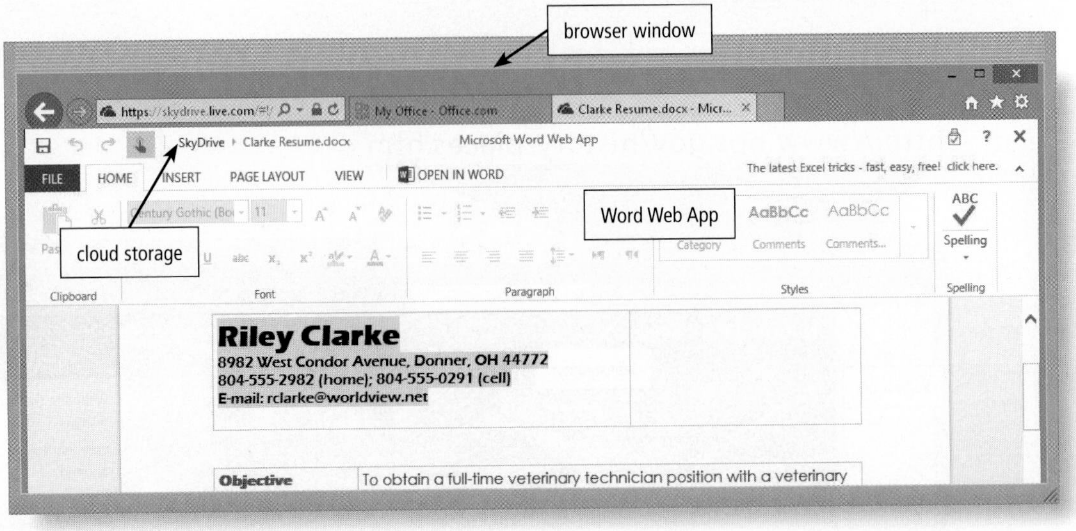

browser window

cloud storage

Word Web App

Riley Clarke
8982 West Condor Avenue, Donner, OH 44772
804-555-2982 (home); 804-555-0291 (cell)
E-mail: rclarke@worldview.net

Objective   To obtain a full-time veterinary technician position with a veterinary

Figure 2-10 Through a browser, you can create documents using the Word Web App and save them on cloud storage, which in this case is Microsoft's SkyDrive.
Source: Microsoft Corporation

Web apps and mobile apps often work together. You might have an account on a website, such as a banking app, that you access from a desktop or laptop. The website may provide a mobile app that you install on a smartphone so that you can access the same information from a mobile device. Because the data and information for each app is stored on cloud storage, all data is synchronized and accessible from anywhere you have an Internet connection, regardless of the computer or device used. The functionality of the app across computers and devices generally is the same, although the mobile app sometimes has fewer features. Some tasks may be easier to accomplish on one device or the other. For example, if a lot of typing is required, you may opt to use the web app on a laptop so that you can use a standard keyboard.

Internet Research
What are popular mobile apps?
Search for: top mobile apps

CONSIDER THIS

What are GPS receivers?
GPS (global positioning system) is a navigation system that consists of one or more earth-based receivers that accept and analyze signals sent by satellites in order to determine the receiver's geographic location. A *GPS receiver* is a handheld, mountable, or embedded device that contains an antenna, a radio receiver, and a processor. Most smartphones include embedded GPS receivers so that users can determine their location, obtain directions, and locate points of interest. Read Ethics & Issues 2-2 to consider issues related to apps that track your location.

ETHICS & ISSUES 2-2

Should Apps Be Allowed to Track Your Location?
When you download an app to your smartphone, you unintentionally may be allowing the app to send personal data. Apps can transmit your location, as well as the time you spend using the app. Apps also can collect personal information, including gender and birth year, if you access the app through an online social network profile. Although apps often present an option to review their security policies, some track user data without permission. Further, the

U.S. Circuit Court of Appeals ruled that police can track GPS signals without a warrant or probable cause, meaning that the government can track activities without permission or knowledge.

If you search for driving directions, coupons, or restaurant tips based on your current location or past activities, you might be using apps that openly use this type of tracking. For example, a check in app posts your location to online social networks, and another app enables you to locate friends by tracking their Bluetooth signals. Even when

you opt to share data, use of these types of apps is not without risk. When people use location-tracking apps, for instance, they run the risk of someone stalking or robbing them.

Do you have an expectation of privacy when you download an app? Should the police be allowed to track GPS data without warrants? Why or why not? Would you use apps that post your location to your online social network profile or otherwise alert others of your whereabouts? Why or why not?

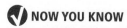 **NOW YOU KNOW**

Be sure you understand the material presented in the sections titled The Internet, Connecting to the Internet, and The World Wide Web, as it relates to the chapter objectives.
You now should know...

- Why you interact with hosts and networks on the Internet (Objective 1)
- Which broadband Internet service and ISP is best suited to your needs (Objective 2)
- How your browser works with domain names and IP addresses when you enter a web address (Objectives 3 and 4)
- Which browser(s) you would use and why (Objective 4)

 Quiz Yourself Online: Check your knowledge of related content by navigating to this book's Quiz Yourself resource on Computer Concepts CourseMate and then tapping or clicking Objectives 1–4.

Types of Websites

The web contains several types of websites: search engines; online social networks; informational; media sharing and bookmarking; news, weather, sports, and other mass media; educational; business, governmental, and organizational; blogs; wikis; health and science; entertainment; financial; travel and mapping; shopping and auctions; careers and employment; e-commerce; and portals. Many websites fall into more than one of these types. All of these websites can be accessed from computers or mobile devices but often are formatted differently and may have fewer features on mobile devices.

Search Engines

A web **search engine** is software that finds websites, webpages, images, videos, news, maps, and other information related to a specific topic. Thousands of search engines are available. Some search engines, such as Bing, Google, and Yahoo!, are helpful in locating information on the web for which you do not know an exact web address or are not seeking a specific website. Those that work with GPS devices or services are location based, meaning they display results related to the device's current geographical position. For example, your smartphone may be able to display all gas stations within a certain distance of your current location. Some search engines restrict searches to a specific type of information, such as jobs or recipes.

Search engines typically allow you to search for one or more of the following items:

- Images: photos, diagrams, and drawings
- Videos: home videos, music videos, television programs, and movie clips
- Maps: maps of a business or address, or driving directions to a destination
- Audio: music, songs, recordings, and sounds
- Publications: news articles, journals, and books
- People or Businesses: addresses and telephone numbers
- Blogs: specific opinions and ideas of others

Search engines require that you enter a word or phrase, called *search text*, to describe the item you want to find. Search text can be broad, such as spring break destinations, or more specific, such as Walt Disney World. If you misspell search text, search engines may correct the misspelling or identify alternative search text. Some also provide suggested search text, links, and/or images as you type your search text.

Depending on your search text, search engines may respond with thousands to billions of search results, sometimes called *hits*. The content of the search results varies depending on the type of information you are seeking and your search text. Some search results contain links to webpages or articles; others are media, such as images or videos. Most search engines sequence the search results based on how close the words in the search text are to one another in the titles and descriptions of the results. Thus, the first few links probably contain more relevant information.

 BTW

Yahoo! and Google

Technology Innovators: You should be familiar with Yahoo! and Google.

 Internet Research

What is a natural language search engine?

Search for: natural language search

 Internet Research

What is a search engine spider?

Search for: search engine spider

If you enter a phrase with spaces between the words in search text, most search engines display results that include all of the keywords. Because keywords describe content, search results exclude articles, conjunctions, and other similar words (e.g., to, the, and). Table 2-4 lists some operators you can use in search text to refine searches. Instead of working with operators to refine search text, many search engines provide an advanced search feature or search tools that assist with limiting search results based on items such as date, TLD, language, etc.

Table 2-4 Search Engine Operators

Operator	Description	Examples	Explanation
Space or +	Display search results that include specific words.	art + music art music	Results have both words, art and music, in any order.
OR	Display search results that include only one word from a list.	dog OR puppy	Results have either the word, dog, or the word, puppy.
		dog OR puppy OR canine	Results have the word, dog, or the word, puppy, or the word, canine.
( )	Combine search results that include specific words with those that include only one word from a list.	Kalamazoo Michigan (pizza OR subs)	Results include both words, Kalamazoo Michigan, and either the word, pizza, or the word, subs.
–	Exclude a word from search results.	automobile –convertible	Results include the word, automobile, but do not include the word, convertible.
" "	Search for an exact phrase in a certain order.	"19th century literature"	Results include the exact phrase, 19th century literature.
*	Substitute characters in place of the asterisk.	writer*	Results include any word that begins with the text, writer (e.g., writer, writers, writer's)

© Cengage Learning

✺ CONSIDER THIS

How can you improve search results?
You may find that many items listed in the search results have little or no bearing on the item you are seeking. You can eliminate superfluous items in search results by carefully crafting search text and use search operators to limit search results. Other techniques you can use to improve your searches include the following:

- Use specific nouns.
- Put the most important terms first in the search text.
- List all possible spellings, for example, email, e-mail.
- Before using a search engine, read its Help information.
- If the search is unsuccessful with one search engine, try another.

Subject Directories A *subject directory* classifies webpages in an organized set of categories, such as sports or shopping, and related subcategories. A subject directory provides categorized lists of links arranged by subject. Using a subject directory, you locate a particular topic by tapping or clicking links through different levels, moving from the general to the specific. A disadvantage with a subject directory is that users sometimes have difficulty deciding which categories to choose as they work through the menus of links presented.

Online Social Networks

Recall from Chapter 1 that an **online social network**, or **social networking site**, is a website that encourages members in its online community to share their interests, ideas, stories, photos, music, and videos with other registered users. Some social networking sites also enable users to communicate through text, voice, and video chat, and play games together online. You interact with a social networking site through a browser or mobile app on your computer or mobile device.

 **MINI FEATURE 2-2**

Social Networking Sites

People you know through personal and professional circles form your social networks. You share common interests, work or spend leisure time together, and know many of one another's friends. Social networking sites allow you to manage your social networks online.

Your account on a social networking site includes profile information, such as your name, location, photos, and personal and professional interests. You might create accounts on a variety of social networking sites to better separate your personal and professional activities. Social networking sites allow you to view the profiles of other users and designate them as your *friends* or contacts. Some social networking sites, such as Facebook and LinkedIn, require friends to confirm a

friendship, while others, such as Twitter and Google+ allow users to follow one another without confirmation.

You can expand your own online social network by viewing your friends' friends and then, in turn, designating some of them as your friends. Friends of your friends and their friends form your *extended contacts*.

- Extended contacts on a personal social networking site such as Facebook can introduce you to others at your college or from your hometown, connect you with long-distance friends or relatives, or enable you to stay in touch with those who have interests similar to yours.

- Extended contacts on a professional social networking site such as LinkedIn can introduce you to people who work at companies where you

might be seeking employment. You can share employment history and skills in your profile, enabling

potential employers who look at your profile to learn about your specific skills.

Read Secure IT 2-2 on the next page for tips about securing your privacy when using social networking sites.

Personal Uses

Many people use social networking sites to share photos and videos, personal greetings, or status updates. A *status update* informs friends about what you are doing. Watching television becomes a social activity as broadcasts encourage viewers to share comments on Twitter or Facebook.

You can *like*, or recommend, online content as a way to share interests with your friends. Your activity updates appear on a designated activity stream, often called a *timeline* or *wall*, which is associated with your account. Activity updates from your friends often appear on a separate page associated with your account, often called a *news feed*.

Many mobile devices have GPS capabilities. Accessing a social networking site with a GPS-enabled device allows you to *check in* at a location, which reveals your location as part of a status update. Mobile social networking apps can share your location with friends, find others nearby, and alert you to promotional deals from local businesses.

Check In button

Business Uses

Businesses use social networking sites to connect with their customers, provide promotional offers, and offer targeted advertising. For example, users who recommend online content about travel services may see travel-related advertising on their social networking site's webpage.

Businesses also use data from social networking sites to better connect with and understand customers. They can review comments from customers about their experiences using companies' products or services. Monitoring these feeds continuously gives companies immediate feedback from customers.

Nonprofit organizations use social networking sites to promote activities and causes, accept donations, and allow volunteers to contact one another online.

❋ Do the benefits of using social networking sites outweigh the risks? Why or why not? Does your answer differ based on whether it is personal or business use?

Source: © iStockphoto / SchulteProductions; © iStockphoto / Slobodan Vasic; © iStockphoto / Gonzalo Andres Aragon Orejuela

Privacy and Security Risks with Online Social Networks

Social networking sites can be excellent places to share messages, photos, and videos. They can, however, be risky places to divulge personal information. Follow these tips to help protect against thieves who are following the traffic and attempting to invade private facets of your life.

- **Choose friends carefully.** You may receive a friend request that appears to be from someone you know. In reality, this message may originate from an identity thief who created a fake profile in an attempt to obtain your personal information. Confirm with the sender that the request is legitimate.

- **Limit friends.** While many online social networks encourage the practice, do not try to gather too many friends in your social network. Some experts believe that a functional online social network should not exceed 150 people. Occasionally review what your friends are posting about you.

- **Prohibit email address book scans.** Online social networks occasionally ask users to enter their email address and password to determine if their friends also are members of the network. In turn, the network obtains access to contacts in your address book and can send spam (unsolicited email messages) to your friends.

- **Divulge only relevant information.** Write details about yourself that are relevant to the reasons you are participating in an online social network. When posting information, be aware that the message may be accessible publicly and associated with your identity permanently. Do not post anything you would not want to be made public.

- **Be leery of urgent requests for help.** Avoid responding to emergency pleas for financial assistance from alleged family members. In addition, do not reply to messages concerning lotteries you did not enter and fabulous deals that sound too good to be true.

- **Read the privacy policy.** Evaluate the website's privacy policy, which describes how it uses your personal information. For example, if you watch a video while signed in to your account, an external website or app may have access to this information and post this activity as an entry in both your activity stream and your friends' news feeds.

- **Manage your profile.** Check for privacy settings, usually found on the Settings or Options tabs, to set permissions so that you can control who can review your profile and photos, determine how people can search for you and make comments, and if desired, block certain people from viewing your page.

⊛ Should social networking sites do a better job of telling their users what information is safe or unsafe to share? What role should parents play in overseeing their child's involvement in social networking sites?

Informational

An informational website contains factual information. Examples include libraries, encyclopedias, dictionaries, directories, guides (Figure 2-11), and other types of reference. You can find guides on numerous topics such as health and medicine, research paper documentation styles, and grammar rules. Many of the other types of websites identified in this section also are used to look up information.

Media Sharing and Bookmarking Sites

A *media sharing site* is a website that enables members to manage and share media such as photos, videos, and music. These websites are sometimes called photo sharing sites, video sharing sites (Figure 2-12), and music sharing sites, respectively. Media sharing sites, which

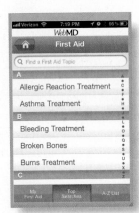

Figure 2-11 You can look up first aid treatments on a medical website, such as WebMD, shown here formatted for display on a mobile device.
Source: WebMD, LLC

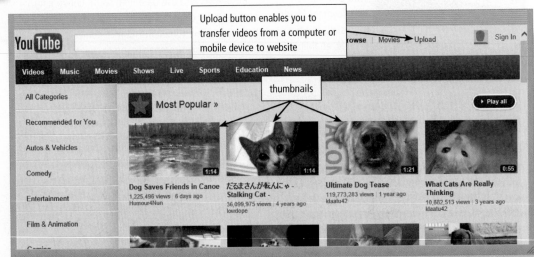

Figure 2-12 YouTube is an example of a video sharing site. You tap or click the thumbnail to view the video.
Source: YouTube, Inc.

may be free or charge a fee, provide a quick and efficient way to upload, organize, store, share, and download media.

 CONSIDER THIS ———————————————————————————————

Why would you use a media sharing site instead of a social networking site?
If you simply want to post photos, videos, or music to share with others and do not require the full functionality of an online social network, consider using a media sharing site. Before you allow someone to take your photo or record video of you, however, remember that the photo or video may end up on a media sharing site. These photos or videos may be accessible publicly and associated with your identity for a long time. Also, once posted, you may be giving up certain rights to the media. Further, do not post photos or videos that are protected by copyright.

⚙ **BTW**
Pinterest and Delicious
Innovative Computing:
You should be familiar
with the bookmarking
sites, Pinterest and
Delicious.

A *bookmarking site* is a website that enables members to organize, tag, and share links to media and other online content. A *tag* is a short descriptive label that you assign to webpages, photos, videos, blog posts, email messages, and other digital content so that it is easier locate at a later time. Many websites and web apps support tagging, which enables users to organize their online content.

News, Weather, Sports, and Other Mass Media

News, weather, sports, and other mass media websites contain newsworthy material, including stories and articles relating to current events, life, money, politics, weather (Figure 2-13), and sports. You often can customize these websites so that you can receive local news or news about specific topics. Some provide a means to send you alerts, such as weather updates or sporting event scores, via text or email messages.

Newsprint on the web is not replacing the newspaper but enhancing it and reaching different populations. Although some exist solely online, many magazines and newspapers sponsor websites that provide summaries of printed articles, as well as articles not included in the printed versions. Newspapers, magazines, and television and radio stations often have corresponding news, weather, or sports websites and mobile apps.

Figure 2-13 Forecasts, radar, and other weather conditions are available on the WEATHER webpage on USA TODAY's website.
Source: Gannett

Educational

An educational website offers exciting, challenging avenues for formal and informal teaching and learning. The web contains thousands of tutorials from learning how to fly airplanes to learning how to cook a meal. For a more structured learning experience, companies provide online training to employees, and colleges offer online classes and degrees. Instructors often use the web to enhance classroom teaching by publishing course materials, grades, and other pertinent class information.

Business, Governmental, and Organizational

A business website contains content that increases brand awareness, provides company background or other information, and/or promotes or sells products or services. Nearly every enterprise has a business website. Examples include Allstate Insurance Company, Dell Inc., General Motors Corporation, Kraft Foods Inc., and Walt Disney Company.

Most United States government agencies have websites providing citizens with information, such as census data, or assistance, such as filing taxes (Figure 2-14). Many other types of organizations use the web for a variety of reasons. For example, nonprofit organizations raise funds for a cause and advocacy groups present their views or opinions.

Figure 2-14
Government agencies, such as the IRS webpage shown here, have websites providing assistance and information to citizens.
Source: IRS

Discovering Computers Twitter feed

Tweets present current events and technology news

search for related posts by entering a hashtag

Figure 2-15 When Twitter users 'follow' this Discovering Computers feed, Tweets such as those shown here appear on their own personal accounts. As a student in this class, you should 'follow' @DiscoveringComp so that you easily can keep current with relevant technology changes and events in the computing industry.
Source: Twitter

Blogs

As described in Chapter 1, a **blog** (short for weblog) is an informal website consisting of time-stamped articles, or posts, in a diary or journal format, usually listed in reverse chronological order. The term *blogosphere* refers to the worldwide collection of blogs. A blog that contains video sometimes is called a video blog, or *vlog*. A *microblog* allows users to publish short messages usually between 100 and 200 characters, for others to read. The collection of a user's Tweets, or posts on Twitter, for example, forms a microblog (Figure 2-15).

✳ **CONSIDER THIS**

How can you locate Tweets about certain topics?

When searching Twitter, you can use hashtags to find related posts. A *hashtag*, which consists of a number sign (#) followed by a keyword, describes and categorizes a Tweet. Similarly, you can tag any word(s) in your Tweets by typing it as a hashtag, such as #election.

Similar to an editorial section in a newspaper, blogs reflect the interests, opinions, and personalities of the author, called the **blogger**, and sometimes website visitors. Blogs have become an important means of worldwide communications. Businesses create blogs to communicate with employees, customers, and vendors. They may post announcements of new information on a corporate blog. Teachers create blogs to collaborate with other teachers and students. Home users create blogs to share aspects of their personal lives with family, friends, and others.

Wikis

Whereas blogs are a tool for publishing and sharing messages, wikis enable users to organize, edit, and share information. A **wiki** is a collaborative website that allows users to create, add, modify, or delete the website content via a browser. Wikis can include articles, documents, photos, or videos. Some wikis are public, accessible to everyone (Figure 2-16). Others are private so that content is accessible only to certain individuals or groups. Many companies, for example, set up wikis for employees to collaborate on projects or access information, procedures, and documents.

Contributors to a wiki typically register before they can edit content or add comments. Wikis usually collect edits on a webpage so that someone can review them for accuracy. Unregistered users typically can review the content but cannot edit it or add comments.

Internet Research

Have errors been found in Wikipedia?

Search for: wikipedia factual errors

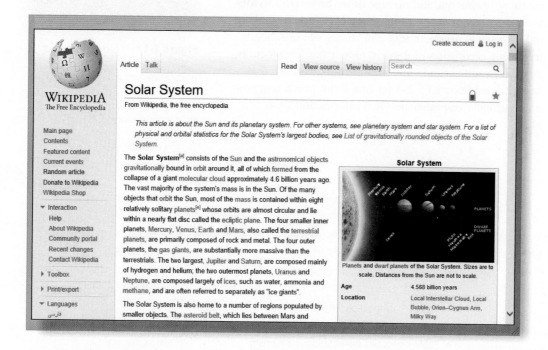

Figure 2-16 Wikipedia is a popular public wiki.
Source: Wikimedia Foundation

Health and Science

Many websites provide up-to-date medical, fitness, nutrition, or exercise information for public access. Some offer the capability of listening to health-related seminars and discussions. Consumers, however, should verify the online information they read with a personal physician. Health service organizations store your personal health history, including prescriptions, lab test results, doctor visits, allergies, and immunizations. Doctors use the web to assist with researching and diagnosing health conditions.

Several websites contain information about space exploration, astronomy, physics, earth sciences, microgravity, robotics, and other branches of science. Scientists use online social networks to collaborate on the web. Nonprofit science organizations use the web to seek public donations to support research.

Entertainment

Entertainment is a growing part of the web's future. An entertainment website offers music, videos, shows, performances, events, sports, games, and more in an interactive and engaging environment. Many entertainment websites support streaming media. **Streaming** is the process of transferring data in a continuous and even flow, which allows users to access and use a file while it is transmitting. You can listen to streaming audio or watch streaming video, such as a live performance or broadcast, as it downloads to your computer, mobile device, or an Internet-connected television.

Sophisticated entertainment websites often partner with other technologies. For example, you can cast your vote about a topic on a television show via your phone or online social network account.

Financial

Online banking and online trading enable users to access their financial records from anywhere in the world, as long as they have an Internet connection. Using online banking, users can access accounts, pay bills, transfer funds, calculate mortgage payments, and manage other financial activities from their computer or mobile device (Figure 2-17). With online trading, users can invest in stocks, options, bonds, treasuries, certificates of deposit, money market accounts, annuities, mutual funds, and so on, without using a broker. Read Secure IT 2-3 for tips about protecting your bank accounts and other personal information from identity theft.

Figure 2-17 Many banks, such as Busey shown here, provide mobile versions of their online banking website so that users can manage financial accounts from their smartphones.
Source: First Busey Corporation

✹ SECURE IT 2-3

📄 Protecting Yourself from Identity Theft

More than eight million U.S. households are victims of identity theft each year, with the unauthorized use of an existing credit card accounting for much of the growing problem. The National Crime Victimization Survey reports that household identity theft losses amount to more than $13 billion each year, and that figure does not account for the aggravation and time required to repair the accounts. Practice these techniques to thwart attempts to steal your personal data:

- Do not tap or click links in or reply to spam for any reason.
- Install a personal firewall (software that protects network resources from outside intrusions).
- Clear or disable web cookies (small text files that web servers store on a computer) in your browser. This action might prevent some cookie-based websites from functioning, but you will be able to decide which cookies to accept or reject.
- Turn off file and printer sharing on your Internet connection.

- Set up a free email account. Use this email address for merchant forms.
- Sign up for email filtering through your ISP or use an anti-spam program.
- Shred financial documents before you discard them.
- Provide only the required information on website forms.
- Public computers are notorious for running *keyloggers*, which record keystrokes in a hidden file, and other tracking software. Avoid checking your email or performing banking activities at these computers. If you must use a public computer for critical activities, be certain to sign out of any password-protected website and to clear the browser's cache.
- Request a free copy of your medical records each year from the Medical Information Bureau.
- Obtain your credit report once a year from each of the three major credit reporting agencies and correct any errors. Enroll in a credit monitoring service.
- Request, in writing, to be removed from mailing lists.

- Place your phone number on the National Do Not Call Registry.
- Avoid shopping club and buyer cards.
- Do not write your phone number on charge or credit receipts. Ask merchants not to write this number or any other personal information, especially your Social Security Number and driver's license number, on the back of your personal checks.
- Do not preprint your phone number or Social Security Number on personal checks.
- Fill in only the required information on rebate, warranty, and registration forms.
- Learn how to block your phone number from displaying on the receiver's system.

If your identity has been stolen, immediately change any passwords that may have been compromised. If you have disclosed your debit or credit card numbers, contact your financial institutions. You also should visit the Federal Trade Commission website or call the FTC help line.

✹ Do you know anyone who has been a victim of identity theft? What steps will you take to protect your identity using some of these guidelines?

Travel and Mapping

Travel websites, sometimes called online travel agencies, enable users to reserve a flight, hotel, or vehicle. On these websites, you can read travel reviews, search for and compare flights and prices, order airline tickets, book a room, or reserve a rental car.

Several mapping web apps, sometimes called web maps, exist that enable you to display up-to-date maps by searching for an address, postal code, telephone number, or point of interest (such as an airport, lodging, or historical site). The maps can be displayed in a variety of views, including terrain, aerial, maps, streets, buildings, traffic, and weather. These websites also provide directions when a user enters a starting and destination point (Figure 2-18). Many work with GPS to determine where a user is located, eliminating the need for a user to enter the starting point and enabling the website to recommend nearby points of interest.

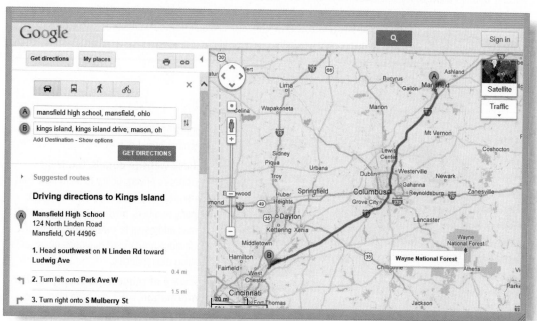

Figure 2-18 Using mapping web apps, such as Google Maps shown here, you can obtain driving directions from one destination to another.
Source: Google Inc.

Shopping and Auctions

You can purchase just about any product or service on the web, a process that sometimes is called *e-retail* (short for electronic retail). To purchase online, the customer visits the business's *electronic storefront*, which contains product descriptions, images, and a shopping cart (Figure 2-19).

Figure 2-19 Shown here is Amazon's storefront for Professional and Technical Books.
Source: Amazon.com, Inc.

The *shopping cart* allows the customer to collect purchases. When ready to complete the sale, the customer enters personal data and the method of payment, which should be through a secure Internet connection.

With an **online auction**, users bid on an item being sold by someone else. The highest bidder at the end of the bidding period purchases the item. eBay is one of the more popular online auction websites.

 CONSIDER THIS

Is it safe to enter financial information online?

As an alternative to entering credit card, bank account, or other financial information online, some shopping and auction websites allow consumers to use an online payment service such as PayPal. To use an online payment service, you create an account that is linked to your credit card or funds at a financial institution. When you make a purchase, you use your online payment service account, which transfers money for you without revealing your financial information. Read Secure IT 2-4 for additional tips to help you shop safely online.

 SECURE IT 2-4

📑 **Shopping Safely Online**

Browsing electronic storefronts and making online purchases can be convenient and economical, but the experience can be a disaster if you encounter unscrupulous vendors. These tips can help you enjoy a safe and productive online shopping trip.

- **Read customer reviews.** Shoppers frequently post comments about merchandise quality, pricing, and shipping. Their evaluations may help you decide whether a company is legitimate. Be aware, however, that the Federal Trade Commission has sued companies for posting false positive reviews and that some companies remove negative comments. Make it a habit to rate merchants as often as possible so that others can learn from your experiences.

- **Look for seals of approval.** Online businesses can display seals if they have met rigorous standards. Some unscrupulous

Source: TRUSTe

Source: Better Business Bureau

merchants, however, will place the seals on their websites even if they have not been approved. To check a seal's legitimacy, click the logo and be certain you are directed to the issuing agency's website.

- **Create a strong password and password questions.** If the merchant requires you to create a user name and password, be certain to develop a long, complex password with at least eight characters that include letters, numbers, and special characters. The website also may ask for answers to security questions; if so, do not supply information that hackers could locate easily, such as your

high school, place of birth, or family member or pet names.

- **Check website details.** Locate the business's privacy policy to learn how your information will be stored. Also, look for phone numbers, physical addresses, and email addresses to contact the vendor if questions arise about damaged goods or billing discrepancies.

- **Beware of requests to supply further information.** After you have placed an order, you may receive an email message asking you to confirm the transaction or to supply additional account information. A reputable business will not solicit these requests, so do not reply to the message.

✹ Have you made online purchases? If so, have you followed the precautions listed here? How will you change your activities the next time you shop online?

Careers and Employment

You can search the web for career information and job openings. Job search websites list thousands of openings in hundreds of fields, companies, and locations. This information may include required training and education, salary data, working conditions, job descriptions, and more. In addition, many organizations advertise careers on their websites. Read How To 2-1 for instructions about how to use a job search website.

When a company contacts you for an interview, learn as much about the company and the industry as possible before the interview. Many have websites with detailed company profiles.

HOW TO 2-1

Search for a Job Online

If you know the company for which you would like to work, you may be able to visit that company's website and search for a webpage with current job postings. If you would like to search for openings in multiple companies, consider using a job search website. The following steps describe how to search for a job online using a job search website.

1. Run a browser.

2. Use a search engine to locate a job search website and then navigate to the website.

3. Many job search websites allow you to search for jobs by criteria, such as keyword, category, or location. If you are searching for a job in a specific field, enter relevant keyword(s) (i.e., loan officer) or select an appropriate category (i.e., finance). To limit your search results to a specific geographical area, specify a location (i.e., Seattle).

4. Some websites allow you to search for jobs based on additional criteria, such as company, salary, job type, education, and experience. To specify these additional criteria, tap or click a link to perform an advanced search.

5. After entering the job search criteria, start the search by tapping or clicking a Search button (or similar feature on the website).

6. When the search results appear, scroll through the results. To find out more about a particular job, you may be able to tap or click the job listing.

7. If desired, follow the instructions in the job listing to apply for the job.

⊛ Which keywords would you use on a job search website to search for a job in your desired field?

Source: Monster

E-Commerce

E-commerce, short for electronic commerce, is a business transaction that occurs over an electronic network such as the Internet. Anyone with access to a computer or mobile device, an Internet connection, and a means to pay for purchased goods or services can participate in e-commerce. Some people use the term *m-commerce* (mobile commerce) to identify e-commerce that takes place using mobile devices. Popular uses of e-commerce by consumers include shopping and auctions, finance, travel, entertainment, and health.

Three types of e-commerce are business-to-consumer, consumer-to-consumer, and business-to-business.

- *Business-to-consumer (B2C) e-commerce* consists of the sale of goods and services to the general public, such as at a shopping website.

- *Consumer-to-consumer (C2C) e-commerce* occurs when one consumer sells directly to another, such as in an online auction.

- *Business-to-business (B2B) e-commerce* occurs when businesses provide goods and services to other businesses, such as online advertising, recruiting, credit, sales, market research, technical support, and training.

Portals

A **portal** is a website that offers a variety of Internet services from a single, convenient location (Figure 2-20). A wireless portal is a portal designed for Internet-capable mobile devices. Most portals offer these free services: search engine; news, sports, and weather; web publishing; reference tools such as yellow pages, stock quotes, and maps; shopping; and email and other communications services.

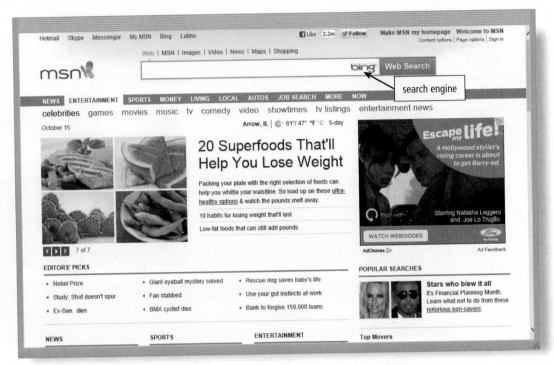

Figure 2-20 Portals, such as MSN, offer a variety of Internet services from a single location.
Source: Microsoft

✻ CONSIDER THIS

Can you assume that content on a website is correct and accurate?
No. Any person, company, or organization can publish a webpage on the Internet. No one oversees the content of these webpages.
   Use the criteria below to evaluate a website or webpage before relying on its content.
- Affiliation: A reputable institution should support the website without bias in the information.
- Audience: The website should be written at an appropriate level.
- Authority: The website should list the author and the appropriate credentials.
- Content: The website should be well organized and the links should work.
- Currency: The information on the webpage should be current.
- Design: The pages at the website should download quickly, be visually pleasing, and easy to navigate.
- Objectivity: The website should contain little advertising and be free of preconceptions.

Web Publishing

By creating their own websites, businesses and individuals can convey information to billions of people. The content of the webpages ranges from news stories to product information to blogs. **Web publishing** is the development and maintenance of websites. To develop a website, you do not have to be a computer programmer. For the small business or home user, web publishing is fairly easy as long as you have the proper tools.

The five major steps in web publishing are as follows:

1. **Plan the website.** Identify the purpose of the website and the characteristics of the people you want to visit the website. Determine ways to differentiate your website from other similar ones. Decide how visitors will navigate the website.

2. **Design the website.** Design the appearance and layout of elements on the website. Decide colors and formats. Determine content for links, text, graphics, animation, audio, video, virtual reality, and blogs. To complete this step, you may need specific hardware such as a digital camera, webcam, video camera, scanner, and/or audio recorder. You also may need software that enables you to create images or edit photos, audio, and video.

3. **Create the website.** To create a website, you have several options:
   a. Use the features of a word processing program that enable you to create basic webpages from documents containing text and graphics.
   b. Use a *content management system*, which is a program that assists you with creating, editing, and hosting content on a website.
   c. Use website authoring software to create more sophisticated websites that include text, graphics, animation, audio, video, special effects, and links.
   d. More advanced users create sophisticated websites by using a special type of software, called a text editor, to enter codes that instruct the browser how to display the text, images, and links on a webpage.
   e. For advanced features such as managing users, passwords, chat rooms, and email, you may need to purchase specialized website management software.

4. **Host the website.** Options for transferring the webpages from your computer to a web server include the following:
   a. Many ISPs offer their customers storage space on a web server.
   b. Content management systems usually include hosting services for free or a fee.
   c. A *web hosting service* provides storage space on a web server for a reasonable monthly fee. To help others locate your webpage, register your web address with various search engines to ensure your website appears in the search results.

5. **Maintain the website.** Visit the website regularly to ensure its contents are current and all links work properly.

ⓥ NOW YOU KNOW

Be sure you understand the material presented in the section titled Types of Websites as it relates to the chapter objectives.
You now should know…

- How to enter search text and improve your search results (Objective 5)
- How you can benefit from social networking sites (Objective 6)
- When you would use specific types of websites (Objective 7)
- How you can publish your own website (Objective 8)

Quiz Yourself Online: Check your knowledge of related content by navigating to this book's Quiz Yourself resource on Computer Concepts CourseMate and then tapping or clicking Objectives 5–8.

Media on the Web

Most webpages include more than just formatted text and links. The more exciting webpages use *multimedia*, which refers to any application that combines text with media. Media includes graphics, animation, audio, video, and/or virtual reality. The sections that follow discuss how the web uses these types of media. Read Ethics & Issues 2-3 on the next page to consider issues related to website accessibility for everyone.

✳ **ETHICS & ISSUES 2-3**

Should Websites Be Required to Meet Accessibility Guidelines?

The W3C (World Wide Web Consortium) publishes accessibility guidelines for websites. The W3C first published the guidelines in 1999 and updates them periodically. Website designers use the guidelines to increase access for all users, including those with poor eyesight or color blindness; tremors and loss of muscle control; hearing loss; seizure disorders, which may be affected by flashing effects; and other disabilities, including dyslexia. The W3C urges website designers to provide alternate text for audio or visual content, include features that allow objects to be activated and understood using a variety of input and output devices, and make the user interface easy to navigate using screen readers or other adaptive technologies.

Several web design programs include built-in tools that web designers use to find potential issues. Companies also employ user testing, or they hire experts to review and test a website for potential issues. Many websites, including several for disability organizations, fail to comply with the standards. Users who cannot access a website's features can bring a lawsuit against the website owners. Many organizations lack the funding necessary to review, test, and rework their website to meet the accessibility standards.

Should the government require that all websites meet the W3C accessibility guidelines? Why or why not? Do websites hosted by disability organizations have a moral obligation to meet the guidelines? Why? What can be done to encourage people and organizations to make their websites more accessible?

Graphics

A **graphic** is a visual representation of nontext information, such as a drawing, chart, or photo. Many webpages use colorful graphics to convey messages (Figure 2-21). Some websites use thumbnails on their pages because graphics can be time-consuming to display. A *thumbnail* is a small version of a larger object that you usually can tap or click to display a larger image or object.

The web often uses infographics to present concepts, products, and news. An *infographic* (short for information graphic) is a visual representation of data or information, designed to

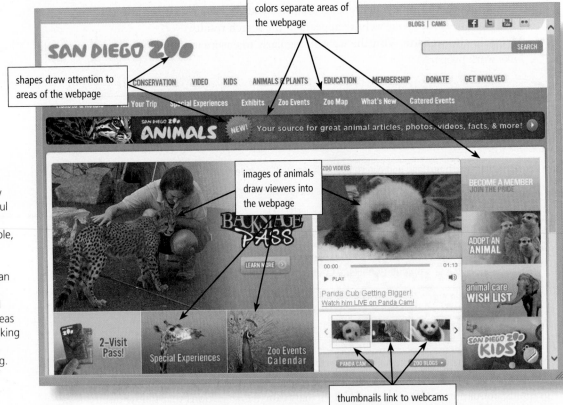

Figure 2-21 Many webpages use colorful graphics to convey messages. For example, the variety of colors, images, shapes, and thumbnails on the San Diego Zoo webpage visually separate and draw attention to areas of the webpage, making the webpage more dynamic and enticing.
Source: Zoological Society of San Diego

communicate quickly, simplify complex concepts, or present patterns or trends (Figure 2-22). Many forms of infographics exist: maps, signs, charts, and diagrams.

Of the graphics formats for displaying images on the web (Table 2-5), the JPEG and PNG formats are more common. *JPEG* (pronounced JAY-peg) is a compressed graphics format that attempts to reach a balance between image quality and file size. With JPG files, the more compressed the file, the smaller the image and the lower the quality. *PNG* (pronounced ping) is a patent-free compressed graphics format that restores all image details when the file is viewed. That is, the PNG format does not lose image quality during compression.

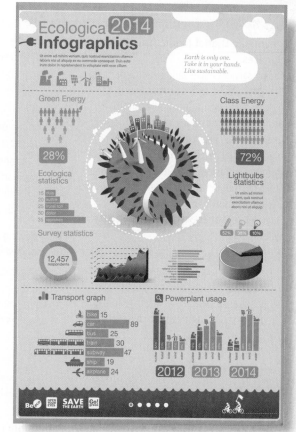

Figure 2-22   An infographic presents complex concepts at a glance.
© radoma / Shutterstock.com

Table 2-5 Graphics Formats Used on the Web

Abbreviation	Name	Uses
BMP	Bitmap	Desktop backgrounds Scanned images
GIF	Graphics Interchange Format	Images with few colors Simple diagrams Shapes
JPEG	Joint Photographic Experts Group	Digital camera photos Game screenshots Movie still shots
PNG	Portable Network Graphics	Comic-style drawings Line art Web graphics
TIFF	Tagged Image File Format	Photos used in printing industry

© Cengage Learning

✳ **CONSIDER THIS**

What is a PDF file?

PDF, which stands for Portable Document Format, is an electronic image format by Adobe Systems that mirrors the appearance of an original document. Users can view a PDF without needing the software that originally created the document.

Animation   Many webpages use *animation*, which is the appearance of motion created by displaying a series of still images in sequence. For example, text that animates by scrolling across the screen can serve as a ticker to display stock updates, news, sports scores, weather, or other information. Web-based games often use animation.

Audio

On the web, you can listen to audio clips and live audio. *Audio* includes music, speech, or any other sound. Simple applications consist of individual audio files available for download to a computer or device. Once downloaded, you can play (listen to) the content of these files. Read How To 2-2 on the next page for instructions about downloading digital media from online services. Other applications use streaming audio so that you can listen to the audio while it downloads.

HOW TO 2-2

Download Digital Media from Online Services

Online services make various forms of digital media available, such as books, music, movies, and apps. You typically can use a program, such as iTunes, or an app, such as the Google Play Store, to access digital media. Digital media also may be available from these services' websites. The following steps describe how to download digital media from online services when you know the name or keyword(s) for the digital media you want to find.

1. On your computer or mobile device, run the program or app from which the digital media is available. If a program or app is not accessible easily, navigate to the online service using your browser.

2. Enter the name or keyword(s) in the Search box.

3. Tap or click the Search button to perform the search.

4. Navigate through the search results and then tap or click the search result for the item you want to download.

5. Locate and then tap or click the Download button or link to download the digital media to your computer or mobile device.

The following steps describe how to browse for and download digital media.

1. On your computer or mobile device, run the program or app from which the digital media is available. If a program or app is not accessible easily, navigate

to the online service using your browser.

2. Tap or click the category corresponding to the type of digital media you want to browse. Common categories include music, movies, books, and apps.

3. Browse the items in the category.

4. When you find an item you want to download, tap or click the item to display additional information.

5. Look for and then tap or click the Download button or link to download the digital media to your computer or mobile device.

 In addition to the online services listed in this box, what are three additional resources from which you can download digital media?

Audio files are compressed to reduce their file sizes. For example, the *MP3* format reduces an audio file to about one-tenth its original size, while preserving much of the original quality of the sound.

To listen to an audio file on your computer, you need special software called a *media player*. Most current operating systems contain a media player; for example, the Windows operating system includes Windows Media Player. Some audio files, however, might require you to download a media player. Media players available for download include iTunes (Figure 2-23) and RealPlayer. You can download media players free from the web.

 **Internet Research**

How do you subscribe to an iTunes podcast?

Search for: subscribe itunes podcast

Figure 2-23 iTunes is a popular media player, through which you can access the iTunes Store to purchase and/or download music, movies, television shows, apps, books, and podcasts.
Source: Apple Inc.

Video

On the web, you can view video clips or watch live video. *Video* consists of images displayed in motion. Most video also has accompanying audio. You also can upload, share, or view video clips at a video sharing site. Educators, politicians, and businesses use video blogs and video podcasts to engage students, voters, and consumers.

Simple video applications on the web consist of individual video files, such as movie or television clips, that you must download completely before you can play them on a computer or mobile device. Video files often are compressed because they are quite large in size. Videos posted to the web often are short in length, usually less than 10 minutes, because they can take a long time to download. As with streaming audio files, streaming video files allows you to view longer or live videos by playing them as they download to your computer.

Internet Research

What is a Smart TV?

Search for: smart tv

Virtual Reality   **Virtual reality (VR)** is the use of computers to simulate a real or imagined environment that appears as a three-dimensional (3-D) space. VR involves the display of 3-D images that users explore and manipulate interactively. Using special VR software, a developer creates an entire 3-D environment that contains infinite space and depth, called a *VR world* (Figure 2-24). A VR world on the web, for example, might show a house for sale where potential buyers walk through rooms in the VR house by sliding their finger on a touch screen or moving an input device forward, backward, or to the side.

In addition to games and simulations, many practical applications of VR also exist. Science educators create VR models of molecules, organisms, and other structures for students to examine. Companies use VR to showcase products or create advertisements. Architects create VR models of buildings and rooms so that clients can see how a completed construction project will look before it is built.

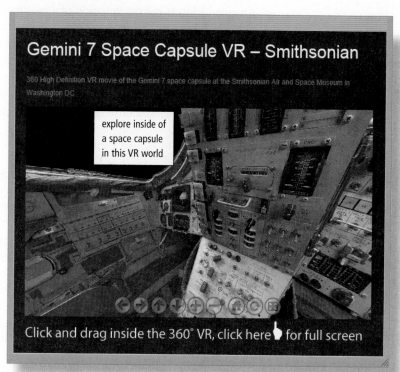

Figure 2-24   Users can explore a VR world using a touch screen or their input device. For example, users can explore the inside of the Gemini 7 space capsule, located at the Smithsonian Air and Space Museum in Washington, D.C., from their computer or mobile device.
Source: World VR

Plug-Ins

Most browsers have the capability of displaying basic multimedia elements on a webpage. Sometimes, however, a browser requires an additional program, called a plug-in, to display multimedia. A *plug-in*, or add-on, is a program that extends the capability of a browser. For example, your browser may require Adobe Reader to view and print PDF files, or Flash Player to view certain graphics or animations. You typically can download plug-ins at no cost from various websites. Some plug-ins run on all sizes of computers and mobile devices; others have special versions for mobile devices. Some mobile browsers do not support the use of plug-ins.

Other Internet Services

As previously mentioned, the web is only one of the many services on the Internet. Other Internet services include the following: email, email lists, instant messaging, chat rooms, discussion forums, VoIP (Voice over IP), and FTP (File Transfer Protocol).

Email

Email (short for electronic mail) is the transmission of messages and files via a computer network. Email was one of the original services on the Internet, enabling scientists and researchers working on government-sponsored projects to communicate with colleagues at other locations. Today, email is one of the primary communications methods for personal and business use.

You use an **email program** to create, send, receive, forward, store, print, and delete email messages. Email programs are available as desktop apps, web apps, and mobile apps. An email message can be simple text or can include an attachment such as a document, a graphic, an audio clip, or a video clip.

Just as you address a letter when using the postal system, you address an email message with the email address of your intended recipient. Likewise, when someone sends you a message, he or she must have your email address. Read How To 2-3 for the steps you can follow to send an email message.

An email address is a combination of a user name and a domain name that identifies a user so that he or she can receive Internet email. A **user name** is a unique combination of characters, such as letters of the alphabet and/or numbers, that identifies a specific user. Your user name must be different from the other user names in the same domain. For example, a user named Rick Claremont whose server has a domain name of esite.com might want to select rclaremont as his user name. If esite.com already has an rclaremont (for Rita Claremont) user name, then Rick will have to select a different user name, such as rick.claremont or r_claremont.

⚙ HOW TO 2-3

Send Email Messages Using Various Email Programs and Web Apps

The process required to send an email message using a computer or mobile device from various email programs and web apps is very similar. The following steps describe how to send an email message using an email program or web app.

1. Run the email program or navigate to the email web app on your computer or mobile device.

2. Look for, and then tap or click the button to compose a new email message.

3. Type the recipient's email address in the To text box. If you are sending the email message to multiple recipients, separate each email address with a semicolon (;).

4. If you would like to send a copy of the email message to one or more people, type their email address(es) in the Cc text box (which stands for carbon copy).

5. To send a copy of the email message to someone while hiding their email address from the other recipients, enter his or her email address in the Bcc text box (which stands for blind carbon copy). The email recipients listed in the To or Cc text boxes will not be able to see the recipients you specified in the Bcc text box.

6. Enter a descriptive subject in the Subject text box. It is not good practice to leave the subject blank when you send email

messages because the recipient's email server may place messages without a subject in a spam or junk mail folder.

7. Type the body of the email message in the appropriate area.

8. If your email program supports it, check the spelling of your email message and correct any errors found.

9. Click the Send button, which sends the email message to everyone listed in the To, Cc, and Bcc text boxes.

❋ Under what circumstances might you want to send a blind carbon copy of an email message to one or more people?

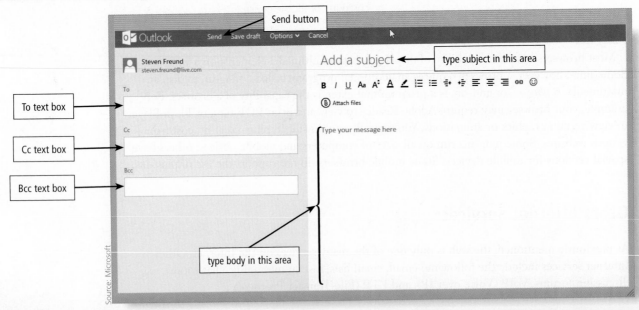

Send button

To text box

Cc text box

Bcc text box

type subject in this area

type body in this area

Source: Microsoft

Sometimes, organizations decide the format of user names for new users so that the user names are consistent across the company. In many cases, however, users select their own user names, often selecting a nickname or any other combination of characters for their user name. Many users select a combination of their first and last names so that others can remember it easily.

In an Internet email address, an @ (pronounced at) symbol separates the user name from the domain name. Your service provider supplies the domain name. A possible email address for Rick Claremont would be rclaremont@esite.com, which would be read as follows: R Claremont at e site dot com. Most email programs allow you to create a *contacts folder*, which contains a list of names, addresses, phone numbers, email addresses, and other details about people with whom you communicate.

Figure 2-25 illustrates how an email message may travel from a sender to a receiver. When you send an email message, an outgoing mail server determines how to route the message through the Internet and then sends the message. As you receive email messages, an incoming mail server holds the messages in your mailbox until you use your email program to retrieve them. Most email programs have a mail notification alert that informs you via a message and/or sound when you receive new mail.

 CONSIDER THIS

What are good practices to follow when using email?

1. Keep messages brief.
2. Respond to messages promptly.
3. Use proper grammar, spelling, and punctuation.
4. Never respond to unsolicited messages.
5. Use meaningful subject lines.
6. Read the message before you send it.
7. Use email when you want a permanent record of a communication.

How an Email Message May Travel from a Sender to a Receiver

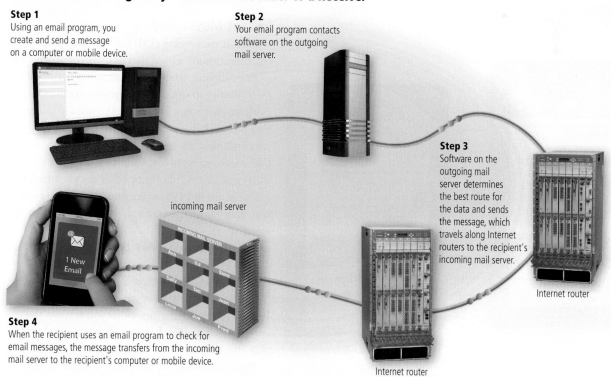

Step 1
Using an email program, you create and send a message on a computer or mobile device.

Step 2
Your email program contacts software on the outgoing mail server.

Step 3
Software on the outgoing mail server determines the best route for the data and sends the message, which travels along Internet routers to the recipient's incoming mail server.

Internet router

incoming mail server

1 New Email

Step 4
When the recipient uses an email program to check for email messages, the message transfers from the incoming mail server to the recipient's computer or mobile device.

Internet router

 Figure 2-25   This figure shows how an email message may travel from a sender to a receiver.

Email Lists

An **email list**, or electronic mailing list, is a group of email addresses used for mass distribution of a message. When a message is sent to an email list, each person on the list receives a copy of the message in his or her mailbox. You *subscribe* to an email list by adding your email address to the mailing list, which is stored on a list server. To remove your name, you *unsubscribe* from the mailing list.

The original use of email lists, such as LISTSERV, allowed any subscriber to send a message, which created a discussion-type forum among all subscribers via email. Many mailing lists today, such as in Figure 2-26, however, are one-way communications and do not allow subscribers to send messages.

Figure 2-26 When you subscribe to a mailing list, you and all others in the list receive messages from the website. Shown here is a user who receives newsletters and alerts from FoxNews.com.
Source: FOX News Network, LLC

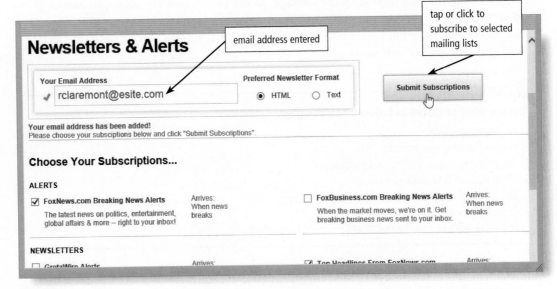

Instant Messaging

Instant messaging (IM) is a real-time Internet communications service that notifies you when one or more of your established contacts are online and then allows you to exchange messages or files or join a private chat room with them (Figure 2-27). *Real time* means that you and the people with whom you are conversing are online at the same time. Some IM services support voice and video conversations, allow you to send photos or other documents to a recipient, listen to streaming music, and play games with another online contact. Many can alert you to information such as calendar appointments, stock quotes, weather, or sports scores.

For IM to work, both parties must be online at the same time. Also, the receiver of a message must be willing to accept messages. To use IM, you may have to install instant messenger software on the computer or mobile device, such as a smartphone, you plan to use.

Many online social networks include an IM feature. To ensure successful communications, all individuals on the friend list need to use the same or a compatible instant messenger.

Figure 2-27 With IM, you and the person(s) with whom you are conversing are online at the same time. The conversation appears on all parties' screens at the same time.
© iStockphoto / Petar Chernaev; © Cengage Learning; © iStockphoto / Oleksiy Mark; © Cengage Learning

Chat Rooms

A **chat** is a real-time typed conversation that takes place on a computer or mobile device with many other online users. A **chat room** is a website or application that permits users to chat with others who are online at the same time. A server echoes the user's message to everyone in the chat room. Anyone in the chat room can participate in the conversation, which usually is specific to a particular topic. Businesses sometimes use chat rooms to communicate with customers.

As you type on your keyboard, others connected to the same chat room server also see what you have typed (Figure 2-28). Some chat rooms support voice chats and video chats, in which people hear or see each other as they chat. Most browsers today include the capability to connect to a chat server.

Figure 2-28 As you type, others in the same chat room see what you have typed.

© ARENA Creative / Shutterstock.com; © Cengage Learning; © topseller / Shutterstock.com; © Alex Staroseltsev / Shutterstock.com; © Oleksiy Mark / Shutterstock.com; © Oleksiy Mark / Shutterstock.com; © Tom Wang / Shutterstock.com; © vlad_star / Shutterstock.com; © artjazz / Shutterstock.com

Discussion Forums

A **discussion forum**, or *message board*, is an online area in which users have written discussions about a particular subject (Figure 2-29). To participate in a discussion, a user posts a message, called an article, to the newsgroup, and other users in the newsgroup read and reply to the message. A *thread*, or threaded discussion, consists of the original article and all subsequent related replies.

Some discussion forums require that you enter a user name and password to participate in the discussion. For example, a discussion forum for students taking a college course may require a user name and password to access the forum. This ensures that only students in the course participate in the discussion. Posts in a discussion forum usually are stored for a certain amount of time, such as a semester, in this example.

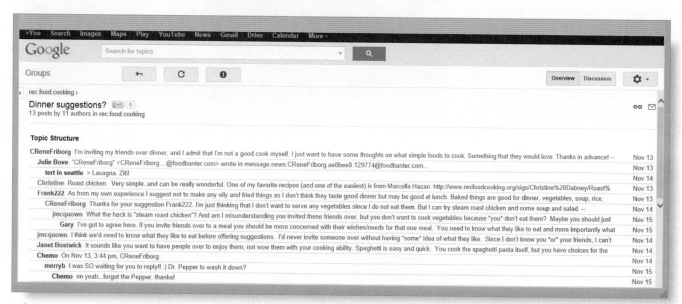

Figure 2-29 Users in a discussion forum read and reply to other users' messages.

© Google Inc.

VoIP

VoIP, short for Voice over IP (Internet Protocol), enables users to speak to other users via their Internet connection. That is, VoIP uses the Internet (instead of the public switched telephone network) to connect a calling party to one or more local or long-distance called parties.

To place an Internet telephone call, you need a broadband Internet connection, a microphone and speaker, both of which are included with a standard computer or mobile device, and VoIP software, such as Skype. Some VoIP services require that you purchase a separate telephone and VoIP router, and subscribe to their service. Others offer certain services free and require a subscription for additional services. Read How To 2-4 for instructions about how to set up a personal VoIP service and make a call.

HOW TO 2-4

Set Up a Personal VoIP Service and Make a Call

VoIP services enable you to make free video or voice calls to others around the world. In many cases, the person you are calling also must use the same VoIP service. The following steps describe how to set up a VoIP service and make a call.

1. If you do not know the VoIP service you want to use, search for a program or app that enables you to place and receive VoIP calls.

2. If necessary, download the program or app for the VoIP service you will use.

3. Most VoIP services require you to have an account with their service before you can place or receive a call. When you start the VoIP program or app, search for the button or link to create a new account. Follow the steps in the program or app to finish creating the account.

4. Once the account has been created, if necessary, sign in to the VoIP service with your user name and password.

5. Make sure the person you are calling also has an account with the same VoIP service. You should know at least one person using this service to successfully

place a call. VoIP services typically allow you to locate and call someone by entering their user name or adding them to your list of contacts. If necessary, add the person you want to call to your list of contacts.

6. On the list of contacts, select the person you want to call and then tap or click the appropriate button to place the call.

7. When the other person answers, you can start your voice or video call.

8. When you are ready to end the call, tap or click the button to end the call.

9. When you are finished using the VoIP service, you should sign out of and exit the VoIP program or app.

Survey your friends and family to see if they use a VoIP service. If so, which service is the most popular among them?

Source: Microsoft

FTP

FTP (File Transfer Protocol) is an Internet standard that permits file uploading and downloading to and from other computers on the Internet. *Uploading* is the process of transferring files from your computer or mobile device to a server on the Internet. Recall that downloading is the process of transferring files from a server on the Internet to your computer or mobile device. Webpage developers, for example, often use FTP to upload their webpages to a web server.

Many operating systems include FTP capabilities. If yours does not, you can download FTP programs from the web, usually for a small fee.

An *FTP server* is a computer that allows users to upload and/or download files using FTP. An FTP site is a collection of files that reside on an FTP server. Many FTP sites have *anonymous FTP*, whereby anyone can transfer some, if not all, available files. Some FTP sites restrict file transfers to those who have authorized accounts (user names and passwords) on the FTP server.

✳ **MINI FEATURE 2-3**

Digital Communications

People, including home users, small/home office users, mobile users, power users, and enterprise users, use technology for many reasons, including communications, productivity, and information. This scenario, which assumes you are a student who balances school with a new internship, presents situations and questions regarding technology use during a single day.

7:30 a.m. Using your smartphone, you update your social networking status to say that today you start an internship. Within minutes, you receive many comments wishing you luck. Before leaving, you send a quick text message to your friends confirming they still want to meet for lunch today and then check the weather app on your smartphone. The local forecast calls for rain, so you take an umbrella.

✳ Should you include the company name for which you are interning in a social networking status? How might an app provider use your location information in ways you have not authorized?

© Cheng Xin / Getty Images

8:15 a.m. At the subway station, you use your smartphone to pay the subway fare. On the subway, you receive a call from your new boss and debate whether you should answer it.

✳ How safe are mobile payment apps? Are you obligated to answer work calls on personal time? What courtesies should you extend to those around you while on a call in a public place?

8:45 a.m. In class, you use a tablet to take notes on the instructor's lecture. As she talks, you remember reading an article about the topic. You use the tablet to search for the article and share what you have learned. The sound is turned off, but you see notifications on your tablet about messages of congratulations based on your social networking post, as well as incoming email messages regarding a group presentation.

✳ Should your school or instructor be able to restrict Internet access during class? Is it acceptable to answer or look at email messages, text messages, or online social network posts when in class?

11:00 a.m. Before meeting friends for lunch, you use an app that uses search criteria, GPS, and user reviews to locate a Mexican restaurant between campus and your job. Once you find a restaurant that you like, you send the location to your friends via text message and then check in to the restaurant via a status update through your online social network.

✳ How can you evaluate user reviews on websites for bias or accuracy? What should you consider when using apps or websites that enable you to check in to locations?

1:00 p.m. Taking a deep breath, you enter the advertising agency and introduce yourself to the receptionist. Your boss brings a laptop to the cubicle where you will be working. He shows you how to check company email and hands you a memo with the company's acceptable use policies.

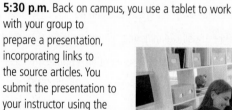
© iStockphoto / somethingway

✳ Can you use company resources, such as your email address, for personal use? Should you use your smartphone to send text messages or check your personal email during company time?

5:30 p.m. Back on campus, you use a tablet to work with your group to prepare a presentation, incorporating links to the source articles. You submit the presentation to your instructor using the school's educational portal.

✳ How important is it to credit sources when researching information on the web? When is it acceptable not to credit sources?

© iStockphoto / svetikd

8:30 p.m. At home, you read assignments for tomorrow's classes using the e-book app on your tablet. You access the e-book's online content and take a quiz. You use the tablet to update your blog with a post about your first day, including a photo of your cubicle taken with your smartphone.

✳ How can technology be used to enhance education? What steps should you take to ensure your privacy on a blog?

11:30 p.m. You exchange several text messages with your brother to share information about your day, plug your phone and tablet into chargers, set the alarm on your smartphone, and then head to bed.

✳ How does technology enhance your daily life?

Netiquette

Netiquette, which is short for Internet etiquette, is the code of acceptable behaviors users should follow while on the Internet; that is, it is the conduct expected of individuals while online. Netiquette includes rules for all aspects of the Internet, including the web, social media, instant messaging, chat rooms, discussion forums, and FTP. Figure 2-30 outlines some of the rules of netiquette, with respect to online communications. Read Ethics & Issues 2-4 to consider issues related to an extreme misuse of online communications — online bullying.

 CONSIDER THIS

What are the various kinds of social media?

Social media consists of content that users create and share online, such as photos, videos, music, links, blog posts, Tweets, wiki entries, podcasts, and status updates. Social media websites facilitate the creation or publishing of social media online and include media sharing sites (for photo, video, and audio files), bookmarking sites, blogs and microblogs, wikis, podcasts, online social networks, and online gaming sites.

Netiquette Guidelines for Online Communications
Golden Rule: Treat others as you would like them to treat you.

Be polite. Avoid offensive language.

Avoid sending or posting *flames*, which are abusive or insulting messages. Do not participate in *flame wars*, which are exchanges of flames.

Be careful when using sarcasm and humor, as it might be misinterpreted.

Do not use all capital letters, which is the equivalent of SHOUTING!

Use **emoticons** to express emotion. Popular emoticons include:

:) Smile	:| Indifference	:o Surprised	:(Frown	:\ Undecided	;) Wink

Use abbreviations and acronyms for phrases:

BTW	by the way	IMHO	in my humble opinion	FWIW	for what it's worth
FYI	for your information	TTFN	ta ta for now	TYVM	thank you very much

Clearly identify a spoiler, which is a message that reveals an outcome to a game or ending to a movie or program.

Be forgiving of other's mistakes.

Read the *FAQ* (frequently asked questions), if one exists.

Figure 2-30 Some of the rules of netiquette, with respect to online communications.
© Cengage Learning

NOW YOU KNOW

Be sure you understand the material presented in the sections titled Media on the Web and Other Internet Services as it relates to the chapter objectives.
You now should know . . .

- Why you use media on the web (Objective 9)

- How you can benefit from using email, email lists, instant messaging, chat rooms, discussion forums, VoIP, and FTP (Objective 10)

- What rules you should follow in online communications (Objective 11)

Quiz Yourself Online: Check your knowledge of related content by navigating to this book's Quiz Yourself resource on Computer Concepts CourseMate and then tapping or clicking Objectives 9–11.

Chapter Summary

This chapter presented the evolution of the Internet, along with various ways to connect to the Internet, how data travels the Internet, and how the Internet works with domain names and IP addresses. It discussed the web at length, including topics such as browsing, navigating, web addresses, web apps and mobile apps, searching, and online social networks. It presented various types of websites, web publishing, and media on the web. It also introduced other services available on the Internet, such as email, email lists, instant messaging, chat rooms, discussion forums, VoIP, and FTP. Finally, the chapter listed rules of netiquette.

Test your knowledge of chapter material by accessing the Study Guide, Flash Cards, and Practice Test apps that run on your smartphone, tablet, laptop, or desktop.

TECHNOLOGY @ WORK

Transportation

What is transportation like without computers and mobile devices? Delivery drivers use clipboards to hold their records. Human navigators use paper maps to track routes for pilots. Ship captains rely solely on experience to navigate through shallow waters. Today, the transportation industry relies heavily on computer and mobile device usage.

Many vehicles include onboard navigation systems to help you navigate from one location to another. These systems usually provide other services such as dispatching roadside assistance, unlocking the driver's side door if you lock the keys in your vehicle, and tracking the vehicle if it is stolen.

The shipping and travel industries identify items during transport using bar codes, which are identification codes that consist of lines and spaces of different lengths. When you ship a package, the shipping company, such as UPS or FedEx, places a bar code on the package to indicate its destination to a computer. Because a package might travel to its destination by way of several trucks, trains, and airplanes,

computers automatically route the package as efficiently as possible. You are able to visit a website to track a package's progress during shipment.

When you travel by airplane, baggage handling systems ensure that your luggage reaches its destination on time. When you check in your baggage at the airport, a bar code identifies the airplane on which the bags should be placed. If you change planes, automated baggage handling systems route your bags to connecting flights with very little, if any, human intervention. When the bags reach their destination, they are routed automatically to the baggage carousel in the airport's terminal building.

Pilots of high-technology commercial, military, and space aircraft today work in a glass cockpit, which features computerized instrumentation, navigation, communication, weather reports, and an autopilot. The electronic flight information shown on high-resolution displays is designed to reduce pilot workload, decrease fatigue, and enable pilots to concentrate on flying safely.

Boats and ships also are equipped with computers that include detailed electronic maps, which help the captain navigate, as well as calculate the water depth and provide a layout of the underwater surface so that the captain can avoid obstructions.

As you travel the roadways, airways, and waterways, bear in mind that computers often are responsible for helping you to reach your destination as quickly and safely as possible.

In what other ways do computers and technology play a role in the transportation industry?

© Digital Vision / Getty Images

Study Guide

The Study Guide exercise reinforces material you should know for the chapter exam. You will find answers to items with the 📄 icon only in the e-book.

🖥 **Access the Study Guide app** that runs on your smartphone, tablet, laptop, or desktop by navigating to this book's Apps resource on Computer Concepts CourseMate.

Instructions: Answer the questions below using the format that helps you remember best or that is required by your instructor. Possible formats may include one or more of these options: write the answers; create a document that contains the answers; record answers as audio or video using a webcam, smartphone, or portable media player; post answers on a blog, wiki, or website; or highlight answers in the book/e-book.

1. Explain how ARPANET contributed to the growth of the Internet.

2. Describe the role of a host on a network.

3. Identify the role of the W3C.

4. Define the term, broadband. List popular wired and wireless broadband Internet services.

5. State the purpose of a hot spot and where you might find one.

6. ISP stands for _____.

7. Briefly describe how data and information travel the Internet.

8. Describe the purpose and composition of an IP address. 📄 What are IPv4 and IPv6?

9. Define the term, domain name.

10. Identify the purpose of several generic TLDs. Identify ICANN's role with TLDs.

11. Describe how and why cybersquatters register domain names.

12. State the purpose of a DNS server.

13. Differentiate between static and dynamic webpages.

14. Distinguish among the web, a webpage, a website, and a web server.

15. Explain the purpose of a browser. List ways you can browse safely.

16. Name examples of popular browsers for personal computers and mobile devices.

17. Describe the function of tabbed browsing.

18. 📄 Explain how a phishing filter can protect you.

19. Define the term, web address. Name a synonym.

20. Name and give examples of the components of a web address.

21. Describe the purpose of a web feed and the role of a feed reader.

22. Explain the relationship between web and mobile apps.

23. Describe the purpose of GPS receivers, and why they are embedded in smartphones.

24. Besides webpages, identify other items a search engine can find.

25. 📄 Name the products or services of Yahoo! and Google, with respect to browsing.

26. Describe how to use a search engine. What are some ways you can refine a search?

27. Differentiate between a search engine and a subject directory.

28. Explain how to use a social networking site for personal or business use.

29. List ways to use social networking sites securely.

30. Describe the purpose of these types of websites: informational; media sharing and bookmarking; news, weather, and sports; educational; business, governmental, and organizational; blogs; wikis; health and science; entertainment; financial; travel and mapping; shopping and auctions; career and employment; and portals.

31. List techniques to protect yourself from identity theft.

32. Describe ways you can shop online safely.

33. List some criteria you can use to narrow your search for a job online.

34. Define the term, e-commerce. Differentiate among B2C, C2C, and B2B e-commerce.

35. List the seven criteria for evaluating a website's content.

36. Identify and briefly describe the steps in web publishing.

37. _____ refers to any application that combines text with media.

38. Describe website accessibility guidelines.

39. Explain how webpages use graphics, animation, audio, video, virtual reality, and plug-ins.

40. Define the terms, thumbnail and infographic.

41. Name the types of graphics formats used on the web and how they use compression.

42. Describe the purpose of these Internet services and explain how each works: email, email lists, instant messaging, chat rooms, discussion forums, VoIP, and FTP.

43. Describe the components of an email address.

44. _____ refers to Internet communications in which both parties communicate at the same time.

45. 📄 Describe how the following use digital communications: home users, small/home office users, mobile users, power users, and enterprise users.

46. Define the term, netiquette.

47. Define the term, social media. List forms of social media.

48. Describe cyberbullying, and explain why it is difficult to catch the perpetrators.

You should be able to define the Primary Terms and be familiar with the Secondary Terms listed below.

Key Terms

Access the Flash Cards app that runs on your smartphone, tablet, laptop, or desktop by navigating to this book's Apps resource on Computer Concepts CourseMate. **View definitions** for each term by navigating to this book's Key Terms resource on Computer Concepts CourseMate. **Listen to definitions** for each term on your portable media player by navigating to this book's Audio Study Tools resource on Computer Concepts CourseMate.

Primary Terms (shown in **bold-black** characters in the chapter)

blog (72)
blogger (72)
browser (62)
chat (87)
chat room (87)
Chrome (64)
cybercafé (57)
discussion forum (87)
domain name (60)
e-commerce (77)
email (84)
email list (86)
email program (84)

emoticons (90)
favorites (63)
Firefox (64)
FTP (88)
graphic (80)
home page (62)
instant messaging
   (IM) (86)
Internet (54)
Internet Explorer (64)
Internet service provider
   (ISP) (58)
IP address (59)

netiquette (90)
online auction (76)
online social
   network (68)
Opera (64)
pop-up blocker (62)
portal (78)
Safari (64)
search engine (67)
social media (90)
social networking
   site (68)
streaming (73)

tabbed browsing (62)
user name (84)
virtual reality (VR) (83)
VoIP (88)
web (61)
web address (64)
web publishing (78)
web server (61)
webpage (61)
website (61)
wiki (73)
World Wide Web
   (WWW) (61)

Secondary Terms (shown in *italic* characters in the chapter)

animation (81)
anonymous FTP (88)
Anticybersquatting Consumer
   Protection Act (60)
ARPANET (54)
Atom (65)
audio (81)
bandwidth (58)
blogosphere (72)
bookmarks (63)
bookmarking site (71)
broadband (56)
business-to-business (B2B)
   e-commerce (77)
business-to-consumer (B2C)
   e-commerce (77)
cable Internet service (57)
cache (62)
ccTLD (60)
check in (69)
cloud storage (65)
consumer-to-consumer (C2C)
   e-commerce (77)
contacts folder (85)
content management system (79)
cyberbullying (90)
dial-up access (58)
DNS server (61)
domain name system (DNS) (61)
dongle (56)

DSL (57)
dynamic webpage (61)
electronic storefront (75)
e-retail (75)
extended contacts (69)
FAQ (90)
Fiber to the Premises (FTTP) (57)
fixed wireless (57)
flames (90)
flame wars (90)
friends (69)
FTP server (88)
gigabyte (GB) (58)
GPS (66)
GPS receiver (66)
hashtag (72)
hits (67)
host (54)
hot spot (57)
http (64)
ICANN (60)
infographic (80)
Internet backbone (59)
JPEG (81)
keyloggers (74)
like (69)
m-commerce (77)
media player (82)
media sharing site (70)
megabyte (MB) (58)

message board (87)
microblog (72)
mobile app (65)
mobile broadband (57)
mobile browser (62)
mobile service provider (58)
MP3 (82)
multimedia (79)
news feed (69)
PDF (81)
phishing (62)
phishing filter (62)
plug-in (83)
PNG (81)
pop-up ad (62)
proxy server (62)
pull (65)
real time (86)
RSS (65)
satellite Internet service (57)
search text (67)
shopping cart (76)
static webpage (61)
status update (69)
subject directory (68)
subscribe (86)
tag (71)
tethering (57)
thread (87)
thumbnail (80)

timeline (69)
top-level domain (TLD) (60)
traffic (59)
unsubscribe (86)
uploading (88)
URL (64)
video (83)
VR world (83)
W3C (56)
wall (69)
Web 2.0 (62)
web app (65)
web feed (65)
web hosting service (79)
Wi-Fi (57)
wireless modem (56)

infographic (80)

Checkpoint

The Checkpoint exercises test your knowledge of the chapter concepts. The page number containing the answer appears in parentheses after each exercise. The Consider This exercises challenge your understanding of chapter concepts.

Complete the Checkpoint exercises interactively by navigating to this book's Checkpoint resource on Computer Concepts CourseMate. **Access the Test Prep app** that runs on your smartphone, tablet, laptop, or desktop by navigating to this book's Apps resource on Computer Concepts CourseMate. After successfully completing the self-assessment through the Test Prep app, **take the Practice Test** by navigating to this book's Practice Test resource on Computer Concepts Coursemate.

True/False   Mark T for True and F for False.

_____ 1. No single person or government agency controls or owns the Internet. (56)

_____ 2. The W3C is responsible for maintaining all networks and content on the Internet. (56)

_____ 3. Users typically pay additional fees for mobile hot spot and tethering services. (58)

_____ 4. A gigabyte (GB) is the basic storage unit on a computer or mobile device and represents a single character. (58)

_____ 5. Visitors to a dynamic webpage can customize some or all of the viewed content, such as desired stock quotes, weather, or ticket availability for flights. (61)

_____ 6. Browsers usually are not included by default with mobile devices and smartphones. (63)

_____ 7. Mobile apps sometimes have fewer features than a web app. (66)

_____ 8. A subject directory is software that finds websites, webpages, images, videos, news, maps, and other information related to a specific topic. (67)

_____ 9. One technique you can use to improve search results is to use specific nouns. (68)

_____ 10. The term, blogosphere, refers to the worldwide collection of blogs. (72)

_____ 11. Unregistered wiki users can review the content, as well as edit it and add comments. (73)

_____ 12. Tethering is the process of transferring data in a continuous and even flow, which allows users to access and use a file while it is transmitting. (73)

Multiple Choice   Select the best answer.

1. A(n) _____ is any computer that provides services and connections to other computers on a network. (54)
   a. host
   b. client
   c. FTP site
   d. subject directory

2. _____ access takes place when a modem in a computer connects to the Internet via a standard telephone line that transmits data and information using an analog signal. (58)
   a. Wireless
   b. Broadband
   c. Dial-up
   d. Mobile

3. A(n) _____ is a sequence of numbers that uniquely identifies the location of each computer or device connected to the Internet. (59)
   a. Internet backbone
   b. domain name
   c. IP address
   d. ccTLD

4. You register a domain name through _____, which is an organization that sells and manages domain names. (60)
   a. a cybersquatter
   b. a registrar
   c. ICANN
   d. an ISP

5. One way to protect your identity while browsing is to use a(n) _____, which is another computer that screens all your incoming and outgoing messages. (62)
   a. password
   b. anonymous FTP
   c. phishing filter
   d. proxy server

6. _____ is a set of rules that defines how webpages transfer on the Internet. (64)
   a. Top-level domain
   b. Hypertext Transfer Protocol
   c. IPv4
   d. Web 2.0

7. A(n) _____ website contains factual information, such as libraries, encyclopedias, dictionaries, directories, guides, and other types of reference. (70)
   a. online social network
   b. media sharing
   c. business
   d. informational

8. A(n) _____, which consists of a number sign (#) followed by a keyword, describes and categorizes a Tweet. (72)
   a. hashtag
   b. microblog
   c. blog
   d. hit

Checkpoint

Matching   Match the terms with their definitions.

_____ 1. tethering (57)

_____ 2. Internet backbone (59)

_____ 3. domain name (60)

_____ 4. web server (61)

_____ 5. URL (64)

_____ 6. web feed (65)

_____ 7. plug-in (83)

_____ 8. chat (87)

_____ 9. cyberbullying (90)

_____ 10. social media (90)

a. text-based name that corresponds to the IP address of a server that hosts a website

b. program that extends the capability of a browser

c. harassment, often involving teens and preteens, using technology

d. websites and tools that foster communications and/or interactions among users, including online social networks, media sharing sites, blogs and microblogs, wikis, podcasts, and online gaming

e. technique that transforms a smartphone or Internet-capable tablet into a portable communications device that shares its Internet access with other computers and devices wirelessly

f. real-time typed conversation that takes place on a computer or mobile device with many other online users

g. computer that delivers requested webpages to your computer or mobile device

h. method of pulling content that has changed on a website

i. term used to refer to the major carriers of network traffic

j. a webpage's unique address

Short Answer   Write a brief answer to each of the following questions.

1. What is a cybersquatter? (60) What is the goal of the Anticybersquatting Consumer Protection Act (ACPA)? (60)

2. Define phishing. (62) What are some safe browsing techniques? (62)

3. Describe the different types of websites. (67) List some tips you can follow to protect yourself from privacy and security risks when using online social networks. (70)

4. List some tips to shop safely online. (76) Differentiate between e-commerce and m-commerce. (77–78)

5. What are some criteria you can use to evaluate a website or webpage before relying on its content? (78) List the steps in web publishing. (79)

✳ Consider This   Answer the following questions in the format specified by your instructor.

1. Answer the critical thinking questions posed at the end of these elements in this chapter: Ethics & Issues (60, 66, 80, 90), How To (77, 82, 84, 88), Mini Features (63, 69, 89), Secure IT (62, 70, 74, 76), and Technology @ Work (91).

2. What are the advantages of using a broadband Internet service? (56)

3. What is the relationship between domain names and IP addresses? (59)

4. Is cybersquatting ethical? Why or why not? (60)

5. How does Web 2.0 technology affect the way you interact with the Internet? (62)

6. What type of information is protected when you browse the web anonymously? (62)

7. What are the advantages and risks associated with allowing an app to track your location? (66)

8. Would you use a wiki as a resource when writing a research paper? Why or why not? (73)

9. Would you use a public computer to check email or do online banking? Why or why not? What are the risks? (74)

10. What information should you avoid using when answering a security question on a website? Why? (76)

11. 📖 Why is it important to have a LinkedIn account? (76)

12. What should you determine during the planning stage of a website? (79)

13. What is the purpose of website accessibility guidelines? (80)

14. What should you keep in mind when using email? (85)

15. 📖 How does a home user's use of digital communications differ from that of a power user? (89)

✳ How To: Your Turn

The How To: Your Turn exercises present general guidelines for fundamental skills when using a computer or mobile device and then require that you determine how to apply these general guidelines to a specific program or situation.

Instructions: You often can complete tasks using technology in multiple ways. Figure out how to perform the tasks described in these exercises by using one or more resources available to you (such as a computer or mobile device, articles on the web or in print, online or program help, user guides, blogs, podcasts, videos, other individuals, trial and error, etc.). Summarize your 'how to' steps, along with the resource(s) used, in the format requested by your instructor (brief report, presentation, discussion, blog post, video, or other means).

1 Perform an Advanced Search

Performing an advanced search will help you locate desired search results more easily by filtering irrelevant content. The following steps guide you through the process of performing an advanced search using your browser.

a. Run your browser and then navigate to a search engine of your choice, such as google.com, bing.com, or yahoo.com.

b. Locate and then tap or click the link or button to perform an advanced search. You may have to perform a basic search before the link for an advanced search appears.

c. Enter as much information as possible on the advanced search form. Entering more information helps the search engine return more relevant results.

d. Tap or click the search (or similar) button to display the search results.

Source: Google Inc.

Exercises

1. Perform a basic search for a topic of your choice. Then, perform an advanced search for the same topic, but enter additional criteria on the advanced search form. How many results did the basic search return? How many results did the advanced search return? Are the advanced search results more relevant? Why or why not?

2. Which search engine did you use to perform your advanced search? Perform the same advanced search using a different search engine. After reviewing the search results, which search engine do you prefer? Why?

3. Will you use the advanced search feature more often? Why or why not?

2 Create a Blog

Several websites are available that can assist you with setting up a blog for free or for a fee. The following steps guide you through the process of creating a blog.

a. Run your browser and then navigate to a search engine of your choice.

b. Perform a search for websites that allow you to create a free blog.

c. Review the search results and visit at least two websites that allow you to create a free blog.

d. After reviewing these websites, navigate to the website you want to use to create the blog.

e. Tap or click the button or link to sign up for a new account.

f. Follow the steps to sign up for a new account.

g. Once you have finished creating your account, configure the desired settings for your blog.

h. Tap or click the button or link to create a new post.

i. Specify a title for your post and then compose the post.

j. When you have finished creating your post, tap or click the button or link to save and publish the post.

k. Sign out of the blog website.

Source: Blog.com

Exercises

1. Summarize the process you used to sign up for an account on the blog website.

2. What topics will your blog discuss? What topics, if any, might not be appropriate for blogs?

3. Do you read other blogs on a regular basis? If so, which ones? If not, search the Internet for blogs that might interest you. Which ones did you find?

How To: Your Turn ☀

③ Determine Your IP (Internet Protocol) Address

Knowing a computer or mobile device's IP address can help you identify it on a network and can help you troubleshoot any problems you may experience connecting to the Internet or other computers and devices on your network. The following steps guide you through the process of determining your IP address.

a. Run your browser and then navigate to a search engine of your choice.

b. Search for a website that can determine your IP address and then navigate to one of these websites.

c. Your IP address should be displayed upon navigating to the website. If it does not, return to the search results and navigate to a different site.

or

a. Run your browser and then navigate to a search engine of your choice.

b. Search for a website that explains how to determine the IP address for your specific operating system and version (such as Windows 8, Mac OS X, iOS, or Android).

c. View the search results and then navigate to the website that provides you with the best guidance.

d. Follow the instructions on your computer or mobile device to determine the IP address.

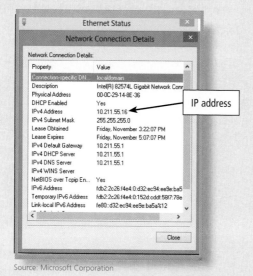

Source: Microsoft Corporation

Exercises

1. Summarize the process you used to determine your IP address.

2. What is your IP address?

3. Is it possible for a computer to have more than one IP address at the same time? Why or why not?

④ Use an Online Auction

Online auctions allow consumers to bid on products that other people are selling. If you are the highest bidder at the end of the bidding period, you often can arrange payment through the online auction. The following steps guide you through the process of using an online auction.

WARNING: Do not purchase or bid on an item if you do not intend to purchase it. If you win the auction, you legally may be obligated to provide payment for the item.

a. Run your browser and then navigate to www.ebay.com.

b. Tap or click the link to register for a new account.

c. Enter the requested information to create the account.

d. Search for an item on which you would like to bid. If you want to browse items in a specific category instead, tap or click the link to browse for items by category.

e. When the search results appear, tap or click an item that interests you to see more details about the item.

f. Review the item details to determine whether you would like to bid on this item. If the item does not interest you, return to the search results and select another item.

g. The seller may have a "Buy It Now" option that allows you to purchase the item immediately at a predetermined price. Alternatively, you can bid on the item by making an offer. The highest bidder at the end of the auction will win the item. **Remember: if you bid on and win an item, you are obligated to provide payment.**

h. You will be notified if you are the winning bidder when the auction closes. At that time, follow the instructions to arrange to pay the seller.

i. When you are finished, sign out of eBay.

Exercises

1. What item(s) did you view? If the buyer had the "Buy It Now" option available, do you think the asking price was fair?

2. Would you purchase an item from an online auction? Why or why not?

3. What items might you post for sale on an online auction?

STUDENT ASSIGNMENTS

✸ Internet Research

The Internet Research exercises broaden your understanding of chapter concepts by requiring that you search for information on the web.

Instructions: Use a search engine or another search tool to locate the information requested or answers to questions presented in the exercises. Describe your findings, along with the search term(s) you used and your web source(s), in the format requested by your instructor (brief report, presentation, discussion, blog post, video, or other means).

❶ Making Use of the Web
Social Networks and Media Sharing

When Facebook recorded its one billionth user, the world took notice of this social networking site's milestone. Indeed, this service has experienced monumental growth since its inception in 2004. Other social networking sites, especially those featured in Mini Feature 2-2 on page 69, are some of the more popular among users of all ages. Likewise, media sharing sites, such as YouTube, which is shown in Figure 2-12 on page 70, are popular means of managing and sharing photos, videos, and music.

Visit two of the websites discussed in Mini Feature 2-2 or other social networking sites and create a profile if you do not currently have one. What personal information is required to join? Does either website ask for personal information that you are uncomfortable sharing? How does the content of these two websites differ? Which features are beneficial for casual users, and which are targeted toward business or professional users? Then, visit two social media sites. What personal information is required to join? Are these websites supported by advertisements? Locate the instructions for posting media. Are these instructions straightforward? Do these websites impose a limit on the number and/or size of media files a user can post?

Source: Facebook

❷ Social Media

Most social media sites permit subscribers to create accounts and profiles at no cost. The companies have invested millions of dollars to develop and maintain the services. Unlike other commercial media, such as television, radio, and newspapers, advertisements generally are not used to fund the majority of operating costs, nor are users required to pay monthly or annual fees for basic services. One method that social media sites use to generate start-up and ongoing subsidies is through venture capitalists' funding. These investors scrutinize business plans and market trends in an effort to locate Internet start-up companies with the potential to generate substantial returns. Once the businesses are running, additional monies are needed to maintain and improve the websites. At this point, some websites display advertisements. The charge for companies to place an advertisement generally increases as the number of subscribers grows. Another method of generating income is to charge users for accessing premium content. Online dating services use this tactic successfully, for they allow people to browse online profiles free of charge but require them to pay to contact a potential dating match.

Locate venture capitalists who are seeking Internet start-up companies. Which criteria do they use to make investment decisions? Who are the successful venture capitalists, and which companies have they funded? Which types of ads are displayed on specific social media and social networking sites? How does the content of these ads pertain to the demographics and interests of users?

❸ Search Sleuth

(1) Who were the original developers of Skype, and how did they determine the name of their company? (2) Which partial word was the first message transmitted on ARPANET? (3) What is the cost of membership for a country to join the World Wide Consortium (W3C)? (4) In which city was the first public, commercial Internet café opened in the United States? In which year did this café open? What was the name of this cybercafé? (5) What was the first registered domain name? Which company registered this name? When was it registered? (6) What was the content of Twitter founder Jack Dorsey's first tweet? (7) Which browser first used the current web feed icon shown in Figure 2-9 on page 65 in this chapter?

Internet Research ☀

(8) Which U.S. president issued the first directive making GPS technology freely available for civilian use? Which branch of the U.S. military operates the GPS satellites orbiting the Earth? (9) Who is responsible for translating Twitter text into more than 20 languages so that it is available throughout the world? Which photo was retweeted the most in the history of Twitter? (10) What was eBay's original name, and what was the first item offered for auction?

4 Green Computing 📖

Employees' interest in working from home, or telecommuting, has steadily risen as apps, hardware, and increased broadband availability and speed have created more opportunities to take advantage of this perk. In one study, 83 percent of respondents claim to have worked at home, and 66 percent project their office will become completely virtual. They credit work-at-home tools such as Skype and other VoIP and collaboration software for helping them enjoy the benefits of telecommuting. They also would trade free meals, employer-paid mobile phone plans, paid vacation days, and a salary reduction in return for the benefit of working at home.

The environment also benefits in many ways when employers permit telecommuting. One major advantage is a reduction in the carbon footprint, or greenhouse gas emissions. Many websites offer tools to calculate individuals' carbon footprints, and a variety of apps measure CO_2 emissions and provide details about how to reduce this footprint.

Locate studies discussing employers' and employees' opinions of telecommuting. What are the advantages and challenges of working from home? Which companies are proponents of telecommuting? Which benefits would you relinquish in return for not commuting to the office at least part of a day? Visit some of the webpages or download at least two apps that allow you to calculate your ecological footprint. Which factors are used to determine your carbon footprint? What measures can you take to reduce greenhouse gas emissions?

5 Security

Secure IT 2-4 on page 76, which offers advice for shopping securely online, recommends creating a strong password and password questions. Despite suggestions and constant reminders from security experts to develop and then periodically change passwords, users continue to create weak passwords. These common passwords are broken easily and, therefore, never should be used. For many years, the most common password has been the word, password.

Locate at least two different company's lists of the 10 or 20 more common passwords in the past two years. Which passwords appear on both lists? Why do consumers continue to use these passwords despite repeated warnings to avoid them? Do you have accounts using one or more of these passwords? What advice is given for developing strong passwords, such as using the lyrics to the first line of a favorite song? How do the companies gather data to determine common passwords?

6 Ethics in Action

The conflict of Internet surveillance versus individuals' privacy rights has been raging for years. Major Internet and technology companies, including Microsoft, Google, eBay, Intel, and AT&T, are seeking to update the Electronic Communications Privacy Act (ECPA). The ECPA prohibits Internet service providers (ISPs) from releasing personal information, including names, addresses, phone numbers, and credit card account numbers, about their subscribers without a court order and protects the contents of files stored on individuals' personal computers.

With the advent of cloud storage and ubiquitous mobile phone usage since the ECPA was passed in 1986, prosecutors and the general public are at odds about whether police should be required to obtain a search warrant to retrieve an individual's email communications or to identify the location of a smartphone or mobile device. Some ISPs have monitored their users' bandwidth to monitor trafficking of copyrighted material. Some, however, have gone a step further by monitoring their users' website surfing activities without giving notice of this eavesdropping practice. Privacy experts claim these ISPs' practices violate the ECPA.

Should Congress enact laws requiring ISPs to formally track their customers' activities in an attempt to aid police investigating crimes, attorneys litigating divorce and insurance fraud cases, and the entertainment industry in locating illegally downloaded files? Should software companies such as Google, Yahoo!, and Facebook develop means for government surveillance of users? Do individuals have a privacy interest in their smartphones' locations? Should police be required to obtain a search warrant to read users' email?

✳ Problem Solving

The Problem Solving exercises extend your knowledge of chapter concepts by seeking solutions to practical problems with technology that you may encounter at home, school, work, or with nonprofit organizations. The Collaboration exercise should be completed with a team.

💻 **Challenge yourself** with additional Problem Solving exercises by navigating to this book's Problem Solving resource on Computer Concepts CourseMate.

Instructions: You often can solve problems with technology in multiple ways. Determine a solution to the problems in these exercises by using one or more resources available to you (such as a computer or mobile device, articles on the web or in print, blogs, podcasts, videos, television, user guides, other individuals, electronics or computer stores, etc.). Describe your solution, along with the resource(s) used, in the format requested by your instructor (brief report, presentation, discussion, blog post, video, or other means).

Personal

1. New Browser Windows While browsing the web, each time you tap or click a link, the link's destination opens in a new browser window. You prefer to have each link open in a new tab so that your taskbar does not become cluttered. How will you resolve this?

Source: Amazon.com, Inc.

2. Unsolicited Friend Requests You recently signed up for an account on the Facebook social networking site. When you log in periodically, you find that people you do not know are requesting to be your friend. How should you respond?

3. Unexpected Search Engine A class project requires that you conduct research on the web. After typing the web address for Google's home page and pressing the ENTER key, your browser redirects you to a different search engine. What could be wrong?

4. Images Do Not Appear When you navigate to a webpage, you notice that no images are appearing. You successfully have viewed webpages with images in the past and are not sure why images suddenly are not appearing. What steps will you take to show the images?

5. Incorrect Home Page After running your browser, you notice that your home page has changed. You change your home page back to its previous setting, exit the browser, and then run the browser again. Surprisingly, your browser still navigates to a website other than the one you chose. What is your next step?

Professional

6. Suspicious Website Visits The director of your company's information technology department sent you an email message stating that you have been spending an excessive amount of time viewing websites not related to your job. You periodically visit websites not related to work, but only on breaks, which the company allows. How does he know your web browsing habits? How will you respond to this claim?

7. Automatic Response When you return from vacation, a colleague informs you that when she sent email messages to your email address, she would not always receive your automatic response stating that you were out of the office. Why might your email program not respond automatically to every email message received?

8. Email Message Formatting A friend sent an email message containing a photo to your email account at work. Upon receiving the email message, the photo does not appear. You also notice that email messages never show any formatting, such as different fonts, font sizes, and font colors. What might be causing this?

9. Sporadic Email Message Delivery The email program on your computer has been delivering new messages only every hour, on the hour. Historically, new email messages would arrive and be displayed immediately upon being sent by the sender. Furthermore, your coworkers claim that they sometimes do not receive your email messages until hours after they are sent. What might be the problem?

Collaboration

10. Technology in Transportation Your project team has been accepted to present a business proposal to a group of potential investors. Because the presentation will take place in Kansas City, Missouri, you will need to transport people and ship some materials to that location. Form a team of three people and determine how to use technology to ship materials and how to make travel arrangements. One team member should research the steps required to use a website to make flight reservations, one team member should determine the steps necessary to print a package shipping label from his or her computer and track the package while it is en route, and another team member should find directions from Kansas City International Airport to a nearby hotel.

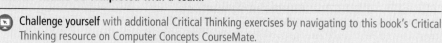
The Critical Thinking exercises challenge your assessment and decision-making skills by presenting real-world situations associated with chapter concepts. The Collaboration exercise should be completed with a team.

Critical Thinking ✳

Challenge yourself with additional Critical Thinking exercises by navigating to this book's Critical Thinking resource on Computer Concepts CourseMate.

Instructions: Evaluate the situations below, using personal experiences and one or more resources available to you (such as articles on the web or in print, blogs, podcasts, videos, television, user guides, other individuals, electronics or computer stores, etc.). Perform the tasks requested in each exercise and share your deliverables in the format requested by your instructor (brief report, presentation, discussion, blog post, video, or other means).

1. Class Discussion

Mobile Browser Comparison   Although most mobile devices include a mobile browser, users have

the option of downloading and installing other browsers. Evaluate and compare reviews of at least four mobile browsers, such as Opera, Android, Firefox, or Safari. Discuss the major differences among the browsers you researched, including number and types of features, for which devices they are available, how they display webpages, security

Source: Google Inc.

features, and the speed at which they perform. Discuss any experiences you or your classmates have had with various browsers. Include in your discussion which mobile browser you would recommend and why.

2. Research and Share

Acceptable Use Policy   Most businesses provide Wi-Fi and Internet access to employees while they are at work. While the intention is for the Internet to be used for work-related purposes, employees often find it easy to become distracted with other activities on the Internet, such as social media, checking personal email, or visiting websites for entertainment. These activities can degrade Internet access for others or lead to poor performance, as well as expose the company to malware or other risks. Many businesses create an Acceptable Use Policy (AUP) that outlines how employees should use the Internet. It also may outline consequences for unauthorized Internet use. Locate two AUPs that are

published online. Compare the two policies and then create a policy you believe would be fair to employees of a small business. Include guidelines for Internet use during breaks, use of smartphones, and restrictions for using social media. Compile your findings and then share them with the class.

3. Case Study

Farmers' Market   You are the new manager for a group of organic farmers who have a weekly market in season. The farmers' market needs a website. You prepare information about the website to present to the board of directors. First, you plan the website by determining its purpose and audience. Use a search engine to locate two farmers' market websites, and print their home pages. Identify what you like and do not like about each. Think about the design of the website for the farmers' market, and select the colors you would recommend. Describe the types of multimedia you would include on the webpage and give specific examples, such as a logo, photos or a slide show, or links to videos. Make a sketch of the home page layout, including navigation, multimedia, and text. Research content management systems. Evaluate whether you could use a preformatted template to meet your needs, and find what types of customization options are available. Determine whether you need a separate ISP for hosting the website, and calculate the costs. List ways you will maintain and update the site content. Compile your findings.

Collaboration

4. Website Evaluation   You and three teammates want to open a new chain of fast food sandwich shops. You envision a website that includes a menu, nutritional options, and allergy information, and that has regular promotions and special offers. With your teammates, evaluate existing fast food and sandwich websites by comparing the advantages and disadvantages of each. Assign each member the task of evaluating one chain. Team members should print the home page of the website to which they are assigned and evaluate their respective restaurants' websites, paying particular attention to the following areas: (1) design, (2) ease of use, (3) menu, (4) nutritional information, (5) allergy information, (6) special offers, (7) location information and directions, and (8) hours and contact information. Summarize your evaluations and rank the websites in terms of their effectiveness. Be sure to include brief explanations supporting your rankings.

⊛ Beyond the Book

The Beyond the Book exercises expand your understanding of chapter concepts by requiring research.

🔘 **Access premium content** by visiting Computer Concepts CourseMate. If you have a Computer Concepts CourseMate access code, you can reinforce and extend your learning with MindTap Reader, practice tests, video, and other premium content for Discovering Computers. To sign in to Computer Concepts CourseMate at www.cengagebrain.com, you first must create a student account and then register this book, as described at www.cengage.com/ct/studentdownload.

Part 1 Instructions: Use the web or e-book to perform the task identified for each book element below. Describe your findings, along with the search term(s) you used and your web source(s), if appropriate, in the format requested by your instructor (brief report, presentation, discussion, blog post, video, or other means).

1. **Animations** 📃 Review the animations associated with this chapter and then answer the questions they pose (77, 85). What search term would you use to learn more about a specific segment of each animation?

2. **Consider This** Select a Consider This in this chapter (56, 58, 60, 64, 66, 68, 71, 72, 76, 78, 81, 85, 90) and find a recent article that elaborates on the topic. What information did you find that was not presented in this book or e-book?

3. **Drag-and-Drop Figures** 📃 Complete the Drag-and-Drop Figure activities associated with this chapter (57, 59, 61, 65, 68, 81). What did you learn from each of these activities?

4. **Ethics & Issues** Select an Ethics & Issues in this chapter (60, 66, 80, 90) and find a recent article that supports one view presented. Does the article change your opinion about the topic? Why or why not?

5. **Facebook & Twitter** Review a recent Discovering Computers Facebook post or Twitter Tweet and read the referenced article(s). What did you learn from the article?

6. **High-Tech Talk** 📃 Locate an article that discusses topics related to the IPv6 addressing scheme. Would you recommend the article you found? Why or why not?

7. **How To** Select a How To in this chapter (77, 82, 84, 88) and find a recent article that elaborates on the topic. Who would benefit from the content of this article? Why?

8. **Innovative Computing** 📃 Locate two additional facts about Internet2 or Pinterest and Delicious. Do your findings change your opinion about the future of this innovation? Why or why not?

9. **Internet Research** Use the search term in an Internet Research (56, 57, 58, 62, 66, 67, 73, 82, 83) to answer the question posed in the element. What other search term could you use to answer the question?

10. **Mini Features** Locate an article that discusses topics related to one of the mini features in this chapter (63, 69, 89). Do you feel that the article is appropriate for this course? Why or why not?

11. **Secure IT** Select a Secure IT in this chapter (62, 70, 74, 76) and find a recent article about the topic that you find interesting. How can you relate the content of the article to your everyday life?

12. **Technology @ Work** Locate three additional, unique usages of technology in the transportation industry (91). What makes the use of these technologies unique to the transportation industry?

13. **Technology Innovators** 📃 Locate two additional facts about Tim Berners-Lee, Google, Yahoo!, and LinkedIn. Which Technology Innovator impresses you most? Why?

14. **Third-Party Links** 📃 Visit one of the third-party links identified in this chapter (60, 61, 62, 66, 67, 70, 74, 76, 77, 91) and read the article or watch the video associated with the link. Would you share this link on your online social network account? Why or why not?

Part 2 Instructions: Find specific instructions for the exercises below in the e-book or on Computer Concepts CourseMate. Beside each exercise is a brief description of its online content.

1. 📃 **You Review It** Search for and review a video, podcast, or blog post about popular social media sites.

2. 📃 **Windows and Mac** Enhance your understanding and knowledge about using Windows and Mac computers by completing the Configure Your Browser and Find Your IP Address activities.

3. 📃 **Android, iOS, and Windows Mobile** Enhance your understanding of mobile devices by completing the Manage Airplane Mode, Configure Your Mobile Browser, and View Data Usage activities.

4. 📃 **Exploring Computer Careers** Read about a career as a web designer, search for related employment ads, and then answer related questions.

5. 📃 **App Adventure** Configure, read, send, and manage email using an app on your smartphone or tablet.

Computers and Mobile Devices
Evaluating the Possibilities

3

People use or interact with a variety of computers and mobile devices every day.

"I use desktops at work and my laptop at home and school. I send messages and access the Internet on my smartphone, take photos with my digital camera, and read books on my e-book reader. What more do I need to know about computers and mobile devices?"

True, you may be familiar with some of the material in this chapter, but do you know . . .

Whether you can be photographed in public without your knowledge?

How to protect devices from malware infections?

How a digital camera converts a photographed image to a digital signal?

How to connect your phone to a Wi-Fi network to save data charges?

How to identify a DVI or an HDMI port?

Which news, sports, and weather apps are best suited to your needs?

What to consider when purchasing a desktop, mobile computer, or mobile device?

How a touch screen recognizes taps and other gestures?

How you can minimize your risk of technology-related tendonitis or carpal tunnel syndrome?

How the meteorology field uses computers, mobile devices, and related technologies?

What NFC is, and when you might use it?

Which company's digital camera face recognition technology originally was developed for its toy robots?

How you can contribute to scientific research using your home or office computer?

What measures you can take to keep your computers and mobile devices from overheating?

For these answers and to discover much more information essential to this course, read this chapter and visit the associated Computer Concepts CourseMate at www.cengagebrain.com.

© Dragon Images / Shutterstock.com

✔ Objectives

After completing this chapter, you will be able to:

1 Describe the characteristics and uses of desktops, laptops, tablets, and handheld computers

2 Describe the characteristics and types of servers

3 Differentiate among POS terminals, ATMs, and self-service kiosks

4 Describe cloud computing and identify its uses

5 Describe the characteristics and uses of smartphones, digital cameras, portable media players, and e-book readers

6 Describe the characteristics of and ways to interact with game devices, including gamepads, joysticks and wheels, dance pads, and motion-sensing controllers

7 Identify uses of embedded computers

8 Differentiate a port from a connector, identify various ports and connectors, and differentiate among Bluetooth, Wi-Fi, and NFC wireless device connections

9 Identify safeguards against hardware theft and vandalism and hardware failure

10 Discuss ways to prevent health-related injuries and disorders caused from technology use, and describe ways to design a workplace ergonomically

Computers and Mobile Devices

 BTW

Peripheral Devices
A *peripheral device* is a device you connect to a computer or mobile device to expand its capabilities. Examples include a keyboard, mouse, microphone, monitor, printer, scanner, webcam, and speakers.

As Chapter 1 discussed, a **computer** is an electronic device, operating under the control of instructions stored in its own memory, that can accept data (input), process the data according to specified rules, produce information (output), and store the information for future use. A **mobile device** is a computing device small enough to hold in your hand. Types of computers and mobiles devices include desktop and mobile computers; servers and terminals; smartphones, digital cameras, e-book readers, and portable media players; game devices; and embedded computers. Figure 3-1 shows a variety of people using computers and mobile devices.

In addition to discussing features, functions, and purchasing guidelines of computers and mobile devices, this chapter also presents ways to connect peripheral devices, protect computers and mobile devices from theft and failure, and minimize your health risks while using computers and mobile devices.

Desktops and Mobile Computers

A **personal computer** (PC) is a computer that can perform all of its input, processing, output, and storage activities by itself and is intended to be used by one person at a time. Personal computers often are differentiated by the type of operating system they use, with Windows and Mac personal computers leading the market share. Companies such as Dell, Lenovo, and HP (Hewlett-Packard) sell personal computers that use the Windows operating system, and Apple sells personal computers that use the Mac operating system.

Types of personal computers include desktops, laptops, and tablets, and the latter two also are considered mobile computers. A *mobile computer* is a portable personal computer, designed so that a user easily can carry it from place to place.

Read Secure IT 3-1 on page 106 for suggestions about how to avoid malware infections on your computers and mobile devices.

laptop

desktop with monitor

portable media player

game console

camera on a smartphone

tablet

Figure 3-1 People use a variety of computers and mobile devices at home, at work, and at school.

SECURE IT 3-1

Avoid Malware Infections

Some websites contain tempting offers to download free games and music, enter contests, and receive coupons on your computers or mobile devices. Danger, however, may lurk in those files, for they secretly could install malware with effects ranging from a mild annoyance to a severe problem such as identity theft. Recall that malware is malicious software that acts without your knowledge and deliberately alters operations of your computer or mobile device. As a general rule, do not install or download unfamiliar software. Follow these guidelines to minimize the chance of your computer or mobile device becoming infected with malware:

- **Websites:** Websites you visit or pop-up windows may present instructions to download new software or update current programs installed on a computer or mobile device. If you are uncertain of their legitimacy, exit and research the software by reading reviews online before you decide to install it.

- **Social media:** Malware authors often focus on social media, with the goal of stealing personal information, such as passwords, profiles, contact lists, and credit card account details. Their websites urge unsuspecting users to take surveys, click links to obtain free merchandise and games, and download antivirus programs. Ignore these deceitful tactics.

- **Email:** Spam (unsolicited email messages) can be loaded with malware, but even email messages from friends can be a culprit. If the message does not contain a subject line or contains links or an attachment, exercise caution. One option is to save the attachment to your computer so that antivirus software can scan the file for possible malware before you open it. Your best practice is to avoid opening suspicious messages at all costs.

- **Flash memory storage:** Colleagues and friends may hand you a USB flash drive or memory card with software, photos, and other files. Scan these media with security software before opening any files.

- **Pop-up windows:** At times, a window may open suddenly (called a pop-up window), with a warning that your computer is infected with a virus or that a security breach has occurred, and then make an urgent request to download free software to scan your computer and correct the alleged problem. Beware. Many of these offers actually are rogue security software that will infect a computer.

- **Software:** Occasionally, some seemingly safe software attempts to install malware. Read the dialog boxes that are displayed on your screen before tapping or clicking the OK or Agree buttons. If you are uncertain, cancel the installation. If possible, update software directly from manufacturers' websites.

※ What online activities might cause malware to be installed on your computer? What new techniques will you use to avoid malware?

※ **CONSIDER THIS**

What is inside a personal computer?

The electronic components and circuitry of a personal computer usually are part of or are connected to a motherboard (Figure 3-2). A *motherboard*, sometimes called a system board, is the main circuit board of the personal computer. Many electronic components attach to the motherboard; others are built into it. Two main components on the motherboard are the processor and memory. Many motherboards also integrate sound, video, and networking capabilities.

A *processor*, also called a *CPU* (central processing unit), is the electronic component that interprets and carries out the basic instructions that operate a computer. *Memory* consists of electronic components that store instructions waiting to be executed and data needed by those instructions.

 Internet Research

What is a computer chip?
Search for: computer chip

motherboard

Figure 3-2 Shown here is the motherboard in a laptop.
© Raw Group / Shutterstock.com

Desktops

A **desktop**, or desktop computer, is a personal computer designed to be in a stationary location, where all of its components fit on or under a desk or table (Figure 3-3). Components include input devices such as a keyboard, mouse, and webcam; output devices such as a monitor, speakers, and printer; storage devices such as a hard disk drive and optical disc drive; system unit; and possibly a communications device(s) such as a modem, network card, or router.

Some people use the term, *system unit*, to refer to the case that contains and protects the motherboard, hard disk drive, memory, and other electronic components of the computer from damage. Many desktops have a system unit tower that is a separate device from a monitor. A *tower*, which is made of metal or plastic, is a frame that houses the system unit on a desktop.

  BTW

Dell
Technology Innovator:
You should be familiar with Dell and its founder, Michael Dell.

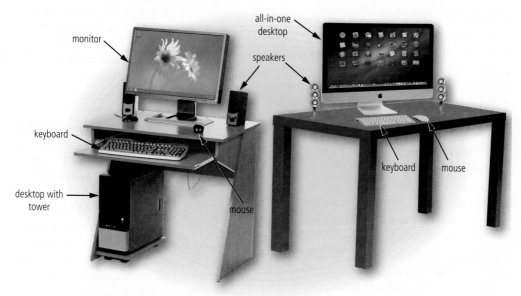

Figure 3-3   The desktop with a tower shown in this figure is a Windows computer, and the all-in-one desktop is a Mac computer.
© George Dolgikh / Shutterstock.com;
© iStockphoto / Skip Odonnell;
© iStockphoto / Evgeny Kuklev;
© Cengage Learning

Towers are available in a variety of form factors, or shapes and sizes. Although they can range in height from 12 inches to 30 inches or more, the trend is toward smaller desktop tower form factors. Some desktops, called an *all-in-one desktop*, do not have a tower and instead house the screen and system unit in the same case. Many peripheral devices, such as keyboard, mouse, printer, speakers, and external hard disk, often occupy space outside a system unit.

 CONSIDER THIS

Who uses desktops?
Home and business users who do not require the portability of a mobile computer may work with desktops for their everyday computing needs. Gaming enthusiasts often choose a *gaming desktop*, which offers high-quality audio, video, and graphics with optimal performance for sophisticated single-user and networked or Internet multiplayer games. Power users may work with a high-end desktop, sometimes called a *workstation*, that is designed to handle intense calculations and sophisticated graphics. For example, architects use powerful desktops to design buildings and homes, and graphic artists use them to create computer-animated special effects for full-length motion pictures and video games. Some users configure a desktop to function as a server on a network (servers are discussed later in this chapter).

 BTW
Monitor Speakers
Many monitors have integrated speakers.

 Internet Research
Which movies use computer animation?
Search for: movies using computer animation

 MINI FEATURE 3-1

Desktop Computer Buyer's Guide

Desktops are a suitable option if you work mostly in one place and have plenty of space in a work area. Today, desktop manufacturers emphasize desktop style by offering bright colors, trendy displays, and theme-based towers so that the computer looks attractive if it is in an area of high visibility. If you have decided that a desktop is most suited to your technology needs, the next step is to determine specific software, hardware, peripheral devices, and services to purchase, as well as where to buy the computer. The following considerations will help you determine the appropriate desktop to purchase.

1. Determine the specific software to use on the desktop. Decide which software contains the features necessary for the tasks you want to perform. Your hardware requirements depend on the minimum requirements of the software you plan to use on the desktop.

2. Know the system requirements of the operating system. Determine the operating system you want to use because this also dictates hardware requirements. If, however, you purchase a new desktop, chances are it will have the latest version of your preferred operating system (Windows, Mac OS, or Linux).

3. Look for bundled software. Purchasing software at the same time you purchase a desktop may be less expensive than purchasing the software

continued on next page

continued from previous page

at a later date. At the very least, you probably will want word processing software and an antivirus program.

4. Avoid purchasing the least powerful desktop available. Computer technology changes rapidly, which means a desktop that seems powerful enough today may not serve your computing needs in the future. Purchasing a desktop with the most memory, largest hard disk, and fastest processor you can afford will help delay obsolescence.

5. Consider upgrades to the keyboard, mouse, monitor, printer, microphone, and speakers. You use these peripheral devices to interact with the desktop, so make sure they meet your standards.

6. Consider a touch screen monitor. A touch screen monitor will enable you to interact with the latest operating systems and apps using touch input.

© Alexey Salo / Photos.com

7. Evaluate all-in-one desktops. All-in-one desktops may be less expensive than purchasing a system unit and monitor separately. In addition, all-in-one desktops take up less space and often look more attractive than desktops with separate towers.

8. If you are buying a new desktop, you have several purchasing options: buy directly from a school bookstore, a local computer dealer, or a large retail store, or order from a vendor by mail, phone, or the web. Each purchasing option has its advantages. Explore each option to find the best combination of price and service.

9. Be aware of hidden costs. Along with the desktop itself, you also may need to make additional purchases. For example, you might purchase computer furniture, an uninterruptable power supply (UPS) or surge protector (discussed later in the chapter), an external hard disk, a printer, a router, a USB flash drive, or computer training classes.

10. Consider purchasing an extended warranty or service plan. If you use your computer for business or require fast resolution to major computer problems, consider purchasing an extended warranty or a service plan through a local dealer or third-party company. Most extended warranties cover the repair and replacement of computer components beyond the standard warranty.

✳ Shop around for a desktop that meets your current needs. Which desktop would you purchase? Why?

Laptops and Tablets

A **laptop**, also called a *notebook computer*, is a thin, lightweight mobile computer with a screen in its lid and a keyboard in its base (Figure 3-4). Designed to fit on your lap and for easy transport, laptops weigh up to 10 pounds (varying by manufacturer and specifications) and can be as powerful as the average desktop. Like desktops, laptops have input devices such as a keyboard, touchpad, and webcam; output devices such as a screen and speakers; a storage device(s) such as a hard disk and maybe an optical disc drive; and usually built-in wireless communications capability. Some laptops have touch screens. Most can operate on batteries or a power supply or both. Read Ethics & Issues 3-1 to consider issues related to laptops and other devices with cameras.

Figure 3-4 Traditional laptops weigh more than ultrathin laptops.
© Sergey Peterman / Shutterstock.com; © iStockphoto / Skip Odonnell

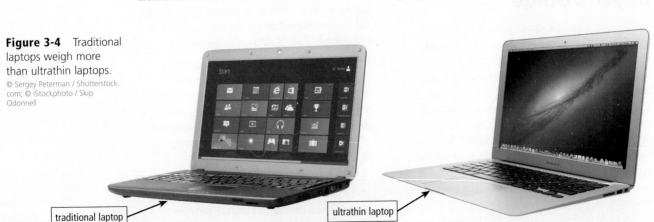

traditional laptop

ultrathin laptop

Netbooks and ultrathin laptops weigh less than traditional laptops, usually have a longer battery life, and do not include an optical disc drive. The difference is that a netbook focuses on affordability, while an ultrathin laptop focuses on power, speed, and durability. While netbooks are adequate for everyday computing tasks, you would want to use an ultrathin laptop to complete processor-intensive tasks, such as editing videos, working with complex software, or playing games.

Usually smaller than a laptop but larger than a smartphone, a **tablet** is a thin, lightweight mobile computer that has a touch screen. Two popular form factors of the tablet, or Tablet PC, are the slate and convertible (Figure 3-5). Resembling a letter-sized pad, a *slate tablet* is a type of tablet that does not contain a physical keyboard. A *convertible tablet* is a tablet that has a screen it its lid and a keyboard in its base, with the lid and base connected by a swivel-type hinge. You can use a convertible tablet like a traditional laptop, or you can rotate the display and fold it down over the keyboard so that it looks like a slate tablet. As with laptops, tablets run on batteries or a power supply or both; however, batteries in a tablet typically last longer than those in laptops.

Some tablets include a *stylus*, which looks like a small ink pen, that you can use instead of a fingertip to enter data, make selections, or draw on a touch screen. A stylus may include buttons you can press to simulate clicking a mouse. As an alternative to interacting with the touch screen, some users prefer to purchase a separate physical keyboard that attaches to or wirelessly communicates with the tablet.

Tablets are useful especially for taking notes in lectures, at meetings, at conferences, and in other forums where the standard laptop is not practical. Because slate tablets can have a more durable construction, they often are used in the medical field and other areas where exposure to heat, humidity, and dust is greater.

 BTW
Ultrabooks
An ultrathin laptop that uses the Windows operating system often is called an *ultrabook*.

 BTW
Pens
Some tablet manufacturers refer to a stylus as a pen.

slate tablet in stand

convertible tablet

Figure 3-5 Examples of slate and convertible tablets.
© iStockphoto / Pedro Castellano; Courtesy of Lenovo

✹ **ETHICS & ISSUES 3-1**

What Punishment for Webcam Spying Is Appropriate?

While webcams and other cameras have many practical and harmless uses, they can also be used for spying. For example, a school district used software, which was supposed to track the school-distributed laptops in case of theft, to take 66,000 photos and screen captures of students. Wiretapping laws in general do not cover these types of acts. New Jersey was one of the first states to rule that secretly recording and broadcasting people without their

permission is a crime. Previously, people could bring civil charges against the person who recorded them, but could not press criminal charges. Lawmakers continue to debate and expand current laws, as well as pass new ones.

While you assume that your at-home activities will remain private, this technology also allows people to take photos or videos in a public setting and broadcast them without your knowledge. A director at the American Civil Liberties Union stated that when you are in a public place, people have the right

to photograph you. Privacy advocates criticize the Google Street View feature, however, which takes images captured using moving vehicles equipped with GPS and cameras, and then creates a panoramic view of an area, including people entering and exiting buildings or relaxing on a beach.

Should webcam spying be comparable to other types of spying? Why or why not? What kind of privacy should you expect when you are in a public place?

CONSIDER THIS

What is a phablet?

Some people use the term, *phablet*, to refer to a device that combines features of a smartphone with a tablet (Figure 3-6). These devices are larger than smartphones but smaller than full-sized tablets. The screen on a phablet usually measures five to seven inches diagonally. Some include a stylus.

Figure 3-6 A phablet combines features of a smartphone and a tablet.
© Iain Masterton / Alamy

 MINI FEATURE 3-2

Mobile Computer Buyer's Guide

If you need computing capability while traveling and during lectures or meetings, you may find a laptop or tablet to be an appropriate choice. With the abundance of mobile computer manufacturers, research each before making a purchase. The following are purchasing considerations unique to mobile computers.

1. Determine which mobile computer form factor fits your needs. Consider a tablet or netbook if you primarily will use the device to access the Internet and email. If you will use the computer to create and edit documents, work on spreadsheets, play graphic intensive games, or use other software that requires greater processing power, consider purchasing a traditional or ultrathin laptop.

2. Consider a mobile computer with a sufficiently large screen. Laptops and tablets are available with various screen sizes. For example, most traditional and ultrathin laptop screens range in size from 11 to 18 inches, while most tablet and netbook screens range in size from 7 to 10 inches.

3. Experiment with different keyboards and pointing devices. Mobile computers often vary in size, and for that reason have different keyboard layouts. Familiarize yourself with the keyboard layout of the computer you want to purchase, and make sure it is right for you. If you have large fingers, for example, you should not purchase a computer with a small, condensed keyboard. Laptops typically include a touchpad to control the pointer. Tablets have a touch screen and an on-screen keyboard.

4. Consider processor, memory, and storage upgrades at the time of purchase. As with a desktop, upgrading a mobile computer's memory and disk storage may be less expensive at the time of initial purchase.

Some disk storage is custom designed for mobile computer manufacturers, meaning an upgrade might not be available in the future.

5. The availability of built-in ports and slots is important. Determine which ports and slots (discussed later in this chapter) you require on the mobile computer. If you plan to transfer photos from a digital camera using a memory card, consider a mobile computer with a built-in card slot compatible with your digital camera's memory card. If you plan to connect devices such as a printer or USB flash drive to your mobile computer, consider purchasing one with one or more USB ports. In addition, evaluate mobile computers with ports enabling you to connect an external monitor.

© iStockphoto / Rüstem GÜRLER

ports and slots

6. If you plan to use your mobile computer for a long time without access to an electrical outlet, or if the battery life for the mobile computer you want to purchase is not sufficient, consider purchasing a second battery. Some mobile computers, such as most tablets, have built-in batteries that can be replaced only by a qualified technician. In that case, you might look into options for external battery packs or power sources.

7. Purchase a well-padded and well-designed carrying case. An amply padded carrying case will protect your mobile computer from the bumps it will receive while traveling. A well-designed carrying case will have room for accessories such as USB flash drives, pens, and paperwork. Although a mobile computer may be small enough to fit in a handbag, make sure that the bag has sufficient padding to protect the computer.

8. If you plan to connect your mobile computer to a video projector, make sure the mobile computer is compatible with the video projector. You should check, for example, to be sure that your mobile computer will allow you to display an image on the screen and projection device at the same time. Also, ensure that the mobile computer has the ports required or that you have the necessary dongle and cables to connect to the video projector.

✳ Based on your current computing needs, should you purchase a traditional laptop, ultrathin laptop, netbook, or tablet? What are the specifications of the mobile computer you would purchase?

Handheld Computers

A **handheld computer** is a computer small enough to fit in one hand. Many handheld computers communicate wirelessly with other devices or computers. Some handheld computers have miniature or specialized keyboards. Others have a touch screen and also include a stylus for input.

Many handheld computers are industry-specific and serve the needs of mobile employees, such as parcel delivery people or warehouse employees (Figure 3-7), whose jobs require them to move from place to place. Handheld computers often send data wirelessly to central office computers.

Figure 3-7 This handheld computer is a lightweight computer that enables warehouse employees to take inventory and check supplies.
© iStockphoto / Ermin Gutenberger

Servers

A **server** is a computer dedicated to providing one or more services to other computers or devices on a network. Services provided by servers include storing content and controlling access to hardware, software, and other resources on a network. In many cases, a server accesses data, information, and programs on another server. In other cases, personal computers, devices, or terminals (discussed later in this chapter) access data, information, and programs on a server. Servers can support from two to several thousand connected computers or devices at the same time.

Some servers, called dedicated servers, perform a specific service and can be placed with other dedicated servers to perform multiple services (Table 3-1). Each type of dedicated server uses

Table 3-1   Dedicated Servers

Type	Main Service Provided
Application server	Stores and runs apps
Backup server	Backs up and restores files, folders, and media
Database server	Stores and provides access to a database
Domain name server	Stores domain names and their corresponding IP addresses
File server (or *storage server*)	Stores and manages files
FTP server	Stores files for user upload or download via FTP
Game server	Provides a central location for online game play
Home server	Provides storage, Internet connections, or other services to computers and devices in a household
List server	Stores and manages email lists
Mail server	Stores and delivers email messages
Network server	Manages network traffic
Print server	Manages printers and documents being printed
Web server	Stores and delivers requested webpages to a computer via a browser

rack server

blade server

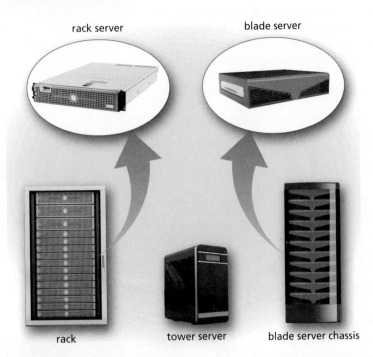

rack

tower server

blade server chassis

Figure 3-8 Shown here are a rack server, blade server, and tower server.
© iStockphoto / Godfried Edelman; © iStockphoto / luismmolina; © iStockphoto / evirgen; © iStockphoto / Alexander Shirokov; © iStockphoto / luismmolina

software designed specifically to manage its service. Dedicated servers typically require a faster processor, more memory, and additional storage.

Servers include a processor, memory, storage, and network connections. Depending on its function, a server may not require a monitor or input device. Some are controlled remotely. Form factors for servers include rack server, blade server, and tower server (Figure 3-8):

- A *rack server*, sometimes called a rack-mounted server, is a server that is housed in a slot (bay) on a metal frame (rack). A rack can contain multiple servers, each in a different bay. The rack is fastened in place to a flat surface.
- A *blade server* is a server in the form of a single circuit board, or blade. The individual blades insert in a blade server chassis that can hold many blades. Like a rack server, the chassis is fastened in place to a flat surface.
- A *tower server* is a server built into an upright cabinet (tower) that stands alone. The tower can be similar in size and shape to a desktop tower or larger.

 CONSIDER THIS

Which server should you use?
Home or small business users and organizations with ample floor space often choose tower servers. (Some home users even use a desktop tower or powerful laptop to act as a home server.) Data centers and other organizations looking to conserve floor space often choose rack servers or blade servers. Organizations that require a large quantity of servers usually opt for blade servers.

Figure 3-9 Server farms and mainframes can handle thousands of connected computers and process millions of instructions per second.
© Sashkin / Shutterstock.com

Some organizations use virtualization to improve utilization of technology. *Virtualization* is the practice of sharing or pooling computing resources, such as servers and storage devices. *Server virtualization* uses software to divide a physical server logically into many virtual servers. That is, virtual servers use software to configure and emulate physical servers. From the end user's point of view, a virtual server behaves just like a physical server. The advantages are that a virtual server can be created and configured quickly, does not require a new physical server, and is easier to manage. Cloud computing, discussed later in this chapter, uses server virtualization.

Major corporations use server farms, mainframes, or other types of servers for business activities to process everyday transactions (Figure 3-9). A *server farm* is a network of several servers together in a single location. Server farms make it possible to combine the power of multiple servers. A *mainframe* is a large, expensive, powerful server that can handle hundreds or thousands of connected users simultaneously. Enterprises use server farms, mainframes, or other large servers to bill millions of customers, prepare payroll for thousands of employees, and manage millions of items in inventory.

⚙ BTW

Watson
Innovative Computing: You should be familiar with innovations of IBM's Watson, such as how it helps transform health care.

Supercomputers

A *supercomputer* is the fastest, most powerful computer — and the most expensive (Figure 3-10). Supercomputers are capable of processing many trillions of instructions in a single second. With weights that exceed 100 tons, these computers can store more than 20,000 times the data and information of an average desktop.

Applications requiring complex, sophisticated mathematical calculations use supercomputers. For example, large-scale simulations and applications in medicine, aerospace, automotive design, online banking, weather forecasting, nuclear energy research, and petroleum exploration use a supercomputer.

Figure 3-10 Supercomputers can process more than one quadrillion instructions in a single second.
Los Alamos National Laboratory

Terminals

A *terminal* is a computer, usually with limited processing power, that enables users to send data to and/or receive information from a server, or host computer. The host computer processes the data and then, if necessary, sends information (output) back to the terminal. Terminals may include a monitor and/or touch screen, keyboard, and memory.

A *thin client* is a terminal that looks like a desktop but has limited capabilities and components. Because thin clients typically do not contain a hard disk, they run programs and access data on a network or the Internet. Public locations, such as libraries and schools, and enterprises sometimes use thin clients because they cost less, are easier to maintain, last longer, use less power, and are less susceptible to malware attacks than desktops.

Special-purpose terminals perform specific tasks and contain features uniquely designed for use in a particular industry. Three widely used special-purpose terminals are point-of-sale terminals, ATMs, and self-service kiosks.

🧭 Internet Research

How is the fastest supercomputer used?
Search for: fastest supercomputer

Point-of-Sale Terminals

The location in a retail or grocery store where a consumer pays for goods or services is the point of sale (POS). Most retail stores use a *POS terminal* to record purchases, process credit or debit cards, and update inventory.

In a grocery store, the POS terminal is a combination of an electronic cash register, bar code reader, and printer (Figure 3-11). A *bar code reader* is an input device that uses laser beams to read bar codes on products. When the checkout clerk or customer scans the bar code on the grocery item, the computer uses the manufacturer name and item numbers to look up the price of the item and the complete product name. Then, the price of the item shows on the display device, the name of the item and its price print on a receipt, and the item being sold is recorded so that the inventory can be updated. Thus, the output from a POS terminal serves as input to other computers to maintain sales records, update inventory, verify credit, and perform other activities associated with the sales transactions that are critical to running the business. Some POS terminals are Internet capable, which allows updates to inventory at geographically separate locations.

touch screen

bar code reader scans bar code on item being purchased

Figure 3-11 Many grocery stores offer self-service checkouts, where consumers use POS terminals to scan purchases, scan their store or saver card and coupons, and then pay for the goods.
© Dennis Macdonald / Getty Images

card reader

Figure 3-12 An ATM is a self-service banking terminal that allows customers to access their bank accounts.
© AlikeYou / Shutterstock.com

Many POS terminals handle credit card or debit card payments. After swiping your card through the reader, the POS terminal connects to a system that authenticates the purchase. Once the transaction is approved, the terminal prints a receipt for the customer.

ATMs

An *ATM* (automated teller machine) is a self-service banking terminal that connects to a host computer through a network (Figure 3-12). Banks place ATMs in public locations, including grocery stores, convenience stores, retail outlets, shopping malls, sports and concert venues, and gas stations, so that customers can access their bank accounts conveniently.

Using an ATM, people withdraw cash, deposit money, transfer funds, or inquire about an account balance. Some ATMs have a touch screen; others have special buttons or keypads for entering data. To access a bank account, you insert a plastic bank card in the ATM's card reader. The ATM asks you to enter a numeric password, called a *PIN* (personal identification number), which verifies that you are the holder of the bank card. When your transaction is complete, the ATM prints a receipt for your records. Read Secure IT 3-2 for ATM safety tips.

 SECURE IT 3-2

ATM Safety

Visiting an ATM to withdraw or deposit money is convenient, but it also is riddled with potential for criminal activity. Avoid being a victim by exercising common sense and following these guidelines.

- **Location:** Choose an ATM in a well-lit public area away from bushes and dividers and near the center of a building. If using a drive-up ATM, keep the engine running and doors locked, roll windows up while waiting for the ATM to process your request, and leave adequate room to maneuver between your vehicle and the one in the lane in front of you. Observe your surroundings and be suspicious of people sitting in vehicles or loitering nearby.

- **ATM card and PIN:** Handle the ATM card like cash by keeping it in a safe location and storing it in a protective sleeve. Do not write the PIN on the back of the card; instead, memorize the numbers. Report a lost or stolen card immediately.

- **Transaction:** Minimize time by having the ATM card ready as you approach the machine. Do not allow people to watch your activity. Cover the keypad or screen with one hand as you enter the PIN, and use your body to block as much of the area as possible. If the ATM screen appears different, behaves unusually, or offers options with which you are unfamiliar or uncomfortable, cancel the transaction and leave the area.

- **Be suspicious of skimmers:** Thieves can capture a credit card number and PIN by placing a *skimmer* on an ATM (shown in the figure to the right). A sophisticated skimmer is an entire panel placed directly on top of the ATM face and virtually is undetectable, but less-technical devices are false card readers secured to the card slot with double-sided tape and a hidden camera or an overlay on the keypad.

- **Valuables:** Expensive clothes and jewelry can be incentives to potential assailants. Dress modestly and leave jewels at home.

- **Exiting:** Do not count cash in public; immediately put it in your pocket or fold it in your hand. If you receive a receipt, take it with you and do not discard it in a trash can near the area. As you leave, be certain you are not being followed. If you suspect

skimmer

© Jochen Tack / Alamy

someone is tracking you, immediately walk to a crowded location or business, or drive to a police or fire station.

- **Statements:** Review your balances and bank statements frequently. Be certain all deposits and withdrawals are listed, and look for unusual or unfamiliar activity.

Which of these tips do you follow, and how will you change your behavior the next time you visit an ATM? Which ATMs in your neighborhood appear to be in safe locations?

Self-Service Kiosks

A self-service *kiosk* is a freestanding terminal that usually has a touch screen for user interaction. Table 3-2 identifies several widely used self-service kiosks. Because users interact with self-service kiosks independently, without a salesperson nearby, it is important the kiosk is simple and easy to use.

Table 3-2 Self-Service Kiosks

Type	Typical Services Provided
Financial kiosk	Pay bills, add minutes to phone plans, add money to prepaid cards, and perform other financial activities.
Photo kiosk	Print photos from digital images. Some allow editing of digital photos. Users may print directly at the kiosk or may send an order to a photo lab to be printed.
Ticket kiosk	Print tickets. Located in airports, amusement parks, movie theaters, rental companies, and train stations.
Vending kiosk	Dispense item after payment is received. Examples include DVD rentals and license plate renewals.
Visitor kiosk	Manage and track visitors upon check-in. Located in businesses, schools, hospitals, and other areas where access is controlled or registration is required.

© Cengage Learning

A *DVD kiosk*, for example, is a self-service DVD rental machine that connects to a host computer through a network (Figure 3-13). DVD kiosks are associated with a particular vendor. To rent a movie online, for example, a customer establishes an account or connects to an existing account on the vendor's website, selects the desired movie, and then chooses a nearby DVD kiosk where the movie will be picked up. Customers also usually can select movies directly at the DVD kiosk via a touch screen or some other input device on the kiosk. After presenting identifying information and swiping a credit card through the reader, the DVD kiosk dispenses the rented movie to the customer. The customer returns it to any of the vendor's nationwide DVD kiosks, at which time the customer's account is charged a fee based on the time elapsed.

touch screen

insert returned DVDs in this slot

Figure 3-13 A DVD kiosk is a self-service DVD rental terminal.
© Getty Images

✔ NOW YOU KNOW

Be sure you understand the material presented in the sections titled Computers and Mobile Devices, Desktops and Mobile Computers, Servers, Supercomputers, and Terminals, as it relates to the chapter objectives.
You now should know . . .

- What you should consider when purchasing a desktop or mobile computer (Objective 1)
- When you would use specific types of servers (Objective 2)
- How you use a POS terminal, ATM, and self-service kiosk (Objective 3)

Quiz Yourself Online: Check your knowledge of related content by navigating to this book's Quiz Yourself resource on Computer Concepts CourseMate and then tapping or clicking Objectives 1–3.

Cloud Computing

Cloud computing refers to an environment of servers that house and provide access to resources users access through the Internet (Figure 3-14). Resources include email messages, schedules, music, photos, videos, games, websites, programs, web apps, servers, storage, and more. That is, instead of accessing these resources locally, you access them on the cloud. For example, you use cloud computing capabilities when you store or access documents, photos, videos, and other media online; use programs and apps online (i.e., email, productivity, games, etc.); and share ideas, opinions, and content with others online (i.e., social networking sites).

Businesses use cloud computing to more efficiently use resources, such as servers and programs, by shifting usage and consumption of these resources from a local environment to the Internet. For example, an employee working during the day in California could use computing resources located in an office in Paris that is closed for the evening. When the company uses the computing resources, it pays a fee that is based on the amount of computing time and other resources it consumes, much in the way that consumers pay utility companies for the amount of electricity used.

Cloud computing allows a company to diversify its network and server infrastructure. Some cloud computing services automatically add more network and server capacity to a company's website as demand for services of the website increases. The network and server capacity may be duplicated around the world so that, for example, an outage of a single server does not affect the company's operations.

 CONSIDER THIS

Are all cloud services available to everyone?
Some cloud services are public and others are private. A public cloud is made available free or for a fee to the general public or a large group, usually by a cloud service provider. A private cloud is dedicated to a single organization. Some cloud services are hybrid, combining two or more cloud types.

 **Internet Research**

How secure is the cloud?
Search for: cloud privacy issues

 BTW

The Cloud
The cloud-shaped symbol, which today universally represents cloud computing, stems from early diagrams that visually portrayed the Internet as a cloud, intangible and widespread.

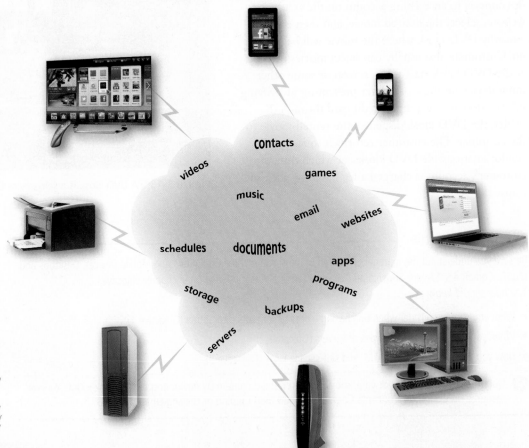

Figure 3-14 Users access resources on the cloud through their Internet connections.

© iStockphoto / Petar Chernaev; © iStockphoto / cotesebastien; © Cengage Learning; © iStockphoto / Jill Fromer; © Cengage Learning; © iStockphoto / 123 render; © Cengage Learning; © Pablo Eder / Shutterstock.com; © Peter Gudella / Shutterstock.com; © Mr.Reborn55 / Shutterstock.com; Courtesy of LG Electronics USA Inc.; © Cengage Learning

Mobile Devices

A mobile device is a computing device small enough to hold in your hand. Because of their reduced size, the screens on mobile devices are small — often between 3 and 5 inches. Popular types of mobile devices are smartphones, digital cameras, portable media players, and e-book readers. Read Ethics & Issues 3-2 to consider issues related to recycling computers and mobile devices.

 ETHICS & ISSUES 3-2

Should Recycling of Electronics Be Made Easier?

As technology advances and prices fall, many people think of computers and mobile devices as disposable. Americans discard millions of electronic items annually, resulting in tons of e-waste. E-waste releases lead, mercury, barium, and other elements into soil and water. A large amount of e-waste ends up polluting developing countries, who accept the materials for profit.

Only about 20 percent of e-waste is recycled. Electronics recycling can take several forms: reusing parts from computers, mobile

devices, and other electronics; creating new products from old products; or melting down or reducing parts to basic elements or materials. In the past, recycling programs that focused on outdated electronic equipment have not been as accessible as recycling programs for paper, glass, and plastic. Today, however, electronic recycling programs have become successful business ventures, with many companies focusing exclusively on e-waste recycling.

Lawmakers at the federal and state levels are working to address e-waste problems. A proposed bill makes it illegal for companies

to export e-waste to developing countries. Currently, several states have laws that mandate e-waste recycling.

How can companies make it easier to recycle electronics? Should the government, manufacturers, or users be responsible for recycling of obsolete equipment? Why? What impact does exporting toxic waste have on developing nations? Should the state or federal government mandate a recycling program for electronics? Why or why not?

Smartphones

A **smartphone** is an Internet-capable phone that usually also includes a calendar, an appointment book, an address book, a calculator, a notepad, games, browser, and numerous other apps. In addition to basic phone capabilities, many smartphones include these features:

- Send and receive email messages and access the web — via Wi-Fi or a mobile data plan
- Communicate wirelessly with other devices or computers
- Function as a portable media player
- Include a built-in digital camera
- Talk directly into the smartphone's microphone or into a Bluetooth headset that wirelessly communicates with the phone
- Conduct live video calls, where the parties can see each other as they speak
- Receive GPS signals to provide users with maps and directions from their current location
- Synchronize data and information with a computer or another mobile device
- Support voice control so that you can speak instructions to the phone and it speaks responses back to you
- Serve as a wireless access point

Many smartphones have touch screens. Instead of or in addition to a touch screen, some have a built-in mini keyboard on the front of the phone or a keyboard that slides in and out from behind the phone. Others have keypads that contain both numbers and letters. Some also include a stylus.

 BTW
Samsung
Technology Innovator: You should be familiar with Samsung.

 CONSIDER THIS

How do you type text messages on a phone that has only a numeric keypad and no touch screen?
Each key on the keypad represents multiple characters, which are identified on the key. For example, the 2 key on the phone's keypad displays the letters a, b, and c on the key's face. On many phones, you cycle through the number, letters, and other symbols associated with a particular key by pressing a key on the keypad multiple times. To type the word, hi, for instance, you would press the 4 key (labeled with the letters g, h, and i) twice to display the letter h, pause momentarily to advance the cursor, and then press the 4 key three times to display the letter i.

A variety of options are available for typing on a smartphone (Figure 3-15). Many can display an *on-screen keyboard*, where you press keys on the screen using your fingertip or a stylus. Some phones support a swipe keyboard app, on which users enter words by tracing a path on an on-screen keyboard with their fingertip or stylus from one letter to the next in a continuous motion. With other phones, you press letters on the phone's keyboard or keypad. Some phones use *predictive text input*, where you press one key on the keyboard or keypad for each letter in a word, and software on the phone predicts the word you want. Swipe keyboard apps and predictive text input save users time when entering text on the phone.

Instead of typing on a phone's keyboard or keypad, users can enter text via a *portable keyboard*, which is a full-sized keyboard that communicates with a smartphone via a dock, cables, or wirelessly. Some portable keyboards physically attach to and remove from the device; others are wireless. Another option is a *virtual keyboard* that projects an image of a keyboard on a flat surface.

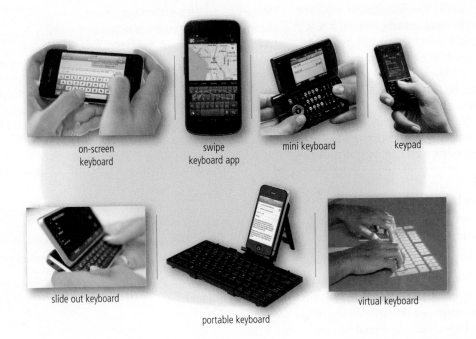

on-screen keyboard

swipe keyboard app

mini keyboard

keypad

slide out keyboard

portable keyboard

virtual keyboard

Figure 3-15 A variety of options for typing on a smartphone.
© iStockphoto / TommL; Courtesy of Nuance; © FreezeFrameStudio / Photos.com; © iStockphoto / webphotographeer; Bloomberg via Getty Images; Courtesy of Jorno; © Italianestro / dreamstime.com

Wireless messaging services enable users to send and receive text messages and picture/video messages to and from smartphones, mobile phones, handheld game devices, and other mobile devices and computers. The type of messages you send depends primarily on the services offered by the mobile service provider that works with the phone or other mobile device you select. Many users have unlimited wireless messaging plans, while others pay a fee per message sent or received.

Text Message Services With text message service, or *SMS* (*short message service*), users can send and receive short text messages, typically fewer than 300 characters, on a phone or other mobile device or computer. Text message services typically provide users with several options for sending and receiving messages:

- Mobile to Mobile: Send a message from your mobile device to another mobile device.
- Mobile to Email: Send a message from your mobile device to an email address anywhere in the world.
- Web to Mobile: Send a message from a text messaging website to a mobile device, or request that a website alert a mobile device with messages of breaking news and other updates, such as sports scores, stock prices, and weather forecasts.
- Mobile to Provider: Send a message by entering a *common short code* (*CSC*), which is a four- or five-digit number assigned to a specific content or mobile service provider, sometimes followed by the message, for example, to a vote for a television program contestant or donate to a charity.

Picture/Video Message Services   With picture message services, users can send photos and audio files, as well as short text messages, to a phone or other mobile device or computer. With video messages services, users can send short video clips, usually about 30 seconds in length, in addition to all picture message services. Smartphones and other mobile devices with picture/video message services, also called *MMS (multimedia message service)*, typically have a digital camera built into the device. Users who expect to receive numerous picture/video messages should verify the phone has sufficient memory.

Picture/video message services typically provide users these options for sending and receiving messages:

- Mobile to Mobile: Send the picture/video from your mobile device to another mobile device.
- Mobile to Email: Send the picture/video from your mobile device to any email address.

If you send a picture message to a phone that does not have picture/video message capability, the phone usually displays a text message directing the user to a webpage that contains the picture/video message. Some online social networks allow you to send a picture/video message directly to your online profile.

Voice mail, which functions much like an answering machine, allows someone to leave a voice message for one or more people. Unlike answering machines, however, a computer in the voice mail system converts an analog voice message into digital form. Once digitized, the message is stored in a voice mailbox. A voice mailbox is a storage location on a hard disk in the voice mail system. To help users manage voice mail messages, some systems offer visual voice mail. With *visual voice mail*, users can view message details such as the length of calls and, in some cases, read message contents instead of listening to them. Some voice mail systems can convert a voice mail message to a text message for display on a computer or mobile device such as a smartphone, which you then can manage like any other text message.

Wireless messaging services and voice mail systems also may be able to send messages to groups of phone numbers or email addresses. Read Secure IT 3-3 for tips about safely using smartphones and other mobile devices in public.

 BTW

Analog vs. Digital
Human speech is analog because it uses continuous (wave form) signals that vary in strength and quality. Most computers and electronic devices are digital, which use only two discrete states: on and off.

SECURE IT 3-3

Safe Mobile Device Use in Public Areas

Sending a text message, updating a Facebook status, posting a Tweet, selecting a new play-list, and checking email messages are tasks you may perform using a mobile device many times each day. They all require some concentration as you focus on the device, usually while looking downward, and they distract you from events occurring around you. Using technology responsibly and safely can prevent theft and injuries.

One common method of thwarting a smartphone thief is to not use the phone to check the time. Potential thieves randomly ask people for the correct time. If a person stops and takes a phone out of a pocket or purse, the thief glances at the make and model and decides if it is worth snatching.

Bus stops and train stations are common places for mobile device theft. People in these locations tend to use their smartphones to check schedules, send text messages, and make phone calls. Headphones and earbuds are giveaways that you are using a mobile device and may not be focused on your surroundings. Apple's white earbuds or EarPods are a clear indication that the person is using an Apple product; one out of every seven crimes in New York City is an Apple theft. Thieves are likely to snatch the devices while the doors are closing just before the train or bus departs from a station so that the victim is unable to pursue the thief. To decrease the chance of theft or pickpocketing, keep your mobile device(s) in a front pocket or in a zippered backpack. Keep your head up and look around at the surroundings. If possible, when in public, avoid using accessories that indicate the type of device to which they are connected.

Cognitive psychologists have studied the effects of *inattentional blindness*, which occurs when a person's attention is diverted while performing a natural activity, such as walking. The researchers have determined that diverted attention is particularly pronounced when people are talking on a mobile phone and, to a lesser extent, using a portable media player. Emergency room reports indicate that distracted walking accidents are on the rise, especially when people trip over cracks in sidewalks or run into fixed objects, such as parked cars and telephone poles.

 Do you know anyone who has had a mobile device stolen? If so, how did the theft occur? Have you ever experienced inattentional blindness or distracted walking?

Digital Cameras

A **digital camera** is a mobile device that allows users to take photos and store the photographed images digitally. While many digital cameras look like a traditional camera, mobile devices such as smartphones and portable media players often have a built-in digital camera.

In addition to cameras built into phones and other devices, types of digital cameras include point-and-shoot cameras and SLR cameras (Figure 3-16). A *point-and-shoot camera* is an affordable and lightweight digital camera with lenses built into it and a screen that displays an approximation of the image to be photographed. Point-and-shoot cameras, which range in size and features, provide acceptable quality photographic images for the home or small business user. An *SLR camera* (single-lens reflex camera), by contrast, is a high-end digital camera that has interchangeable lenses and uses a mirror to display on its screen an exact replica of the image to be photographed. SLR cameras are much heavier and larger than point-and-shoot cameras. They also can be quite expensive, with a variety of available lens sizes and other attachments.

Most point-and-shoot cameras include zoom and autofocus capability, use a built-in flash, store images on memory cards, and enable you to view and sometimes edit images directly on the camera. Many can take video in addition to still photos. Some have a GPS; others are waterproof. Figure 3-17 illustrates how a point-and-shoot digital camera might work.

Digital cameras store captured images on storage in the camera or on some type of memory card. Although many cameras enable you to edit, print, and share photos directly from the camera, some users prefer to download photos from a digital camera or the memory card to a computer's hard disk to perform these tasks. Read How To 3-1 for instructions about how to transfer photos to a computer.

 **BTW**

Sony
Technology Innovator: You should be familiar with Sony.

Internet Research

What is an SD card?
Search for: sd card information

Figure 3-16 SLR digital cameras have lenses and other attachments, whereas the lenses on point-and-shoot cameras are built into the device. Many smartphones also have built-in digital cameras.
© iStockphoto / andrew-thief; © Pawel Gaul / Photos.com; © iStockphoto / Stephen Krow

How a Digital Camera Might Work

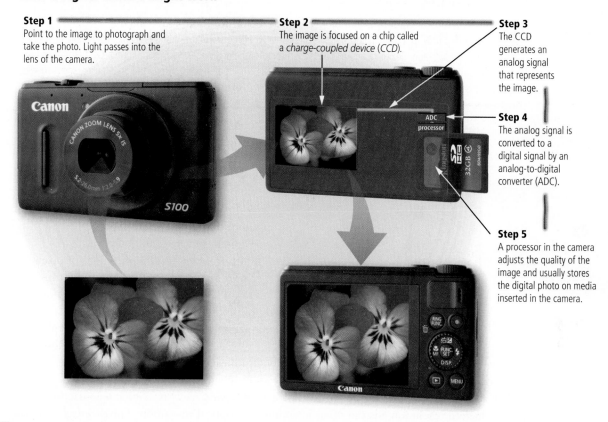

Step 1
Point to the image to photograph and take the photo. Light passes into the lens of the camera.

Step 2
The image is focused on a chip called a *charge-coupled device* (CCD).

Step 3
The CCD generates an analog signal that represents the image.

Step 4
The analog signal is converted to a digital signal by an analog-to-digital converter (ADC).

Step 5
A processor in the camera adjusts the quality of the image and usually stores the digital photo on media inserted in the camera.

Figure 3-17 This figure shows how a point-and-shoot digital camera might work.
© iStockphoto / David Birkbeck; © iStockphoto / David Birkbeck; © Johan Larson / Shutterstock.com; Courtesy of Kingston Technology Company, Inc

---

✸ HOW TO 3-1

Transfer Photos from a Mobile Device to a Computer

Many individuals take hundreds of photos each year using mobile devices such as digital cameras, smartphones, and tablets. After taking the photos, transferring them to a computer allows you easily to create backup copies, edit the photos using photo editing software, and create digital photo albums. The following steps describe multiple ways to transfer photos from a mobile device to a computer.

To transfer photos from a mobile device to a computer using a memory card:

1. Safely remove the memory card from the mobile device.
2. Properly insert the memory card into the appropriate memory card slot on the computer.

3. When the computer detects the memory card, navigate to the location of the photos to transfer.
4. Select the files to transfer and then drag them to the destination folder on the computer.
5. Safely remove the memory card from the computer and insert it back in the mobile device.

To transfer photos from a mobile device to a computer using a USB cable:

1. Connect the cable to the mobile device and to the computer.
2. When the computer detects the mobile device, navigate to the location on the mobile device containing the photos to transfer.
3. Select the files to transfer and then drag them to the destination folder on the computer.

4. Disconnect the USB cable from the computer and from the mobile device.

Some mobile devices also allow you to transfer photos using wireless technologies such as Bluetooth and Wi-Fi. The steps required to transfer photos wirelessly vary greatly for each device. Thus, read your mobile device's documentation to see if and how you can transfer photos to your computer wirelessly. Be aware that transferring photos wirelessly could increase your data charges.

✸ Of the above techniques, which way do you find is easiest to transfer files from your mobile device to a computer? Why? What other techniques might you use to accomplish this task?

Do you need a digital camera if you have a camera built into your mobile phone?
If you use a camera only for posts on social media sites, then your mobile phone's built-in camera probably is adequate. If you want more flexibility and options when photographing images, you should purchase a digital camera. Features typically not found in cameras built into mobile phones include optical zoom, additional lenses, scene modes, autofocus, image stabilization, and burst mode (capturing a series of images in rapid succession).

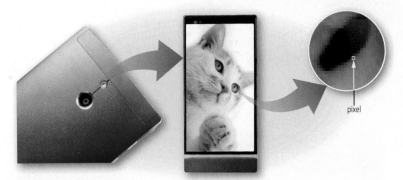

pixel

Figure 3-18 A pixel is a single point in an electronic image.
© Lingong / Dreamstime.com

Photo Quality Resolution affects the quality of digital camera photos. **Resolution** is the number of horizontal and vertical pixels in a display device. A *pixel* (short for picture element) is the smallest element in an electronic image (Figure 3-18). Digital camera resolution typically is stated in megapixels, or millions of pixels. For example, a 16 MP resolution means 16 million pixels. The greater the number of pixels the camera uses to capture a picture, the better the quality of the picture but the larger the file size and the more expensive the camera. Most digital cameras provide a means to adjust the resolution. At a lower resolution, you can capture and store more images in the camera.

The actual photographed resolution is known as the *optical resolution*. Some manufacturers state enhanced resolution, instead of, or in addition to, optical resolution. The *enhanced resolution* usually is higher because it uses a special formula to add pixels between those generated by the optical resolution. Be aware that some manufacturers compute a digital camera's megapixels from the enhanced resolution, instead of optical resolution.

Portable Media Players

A **portable media player**, sometimes called a *personal media player*, is a mobile device on which you can store, organize, and play or view digital media (Figure 3-19). Smartphones and other mobile devices often can function as a portable media player. Portable media players enable you to listen to music; view photos; watch videos, movies, and television shows; and even record audio and video. Some include a digital camera and also offer a calendar, address book, games, and other apps. Others communicate wirelessly with other devices or computers and enable you to synchronize your digital media with a computer, another mobile device, or cloud storage.

Figure 3-19 Some portable media players have touch screens; others have touch-sensitive pads or buttons that enable you to access your media library.
© iStockphoto / Stephen Krow;
© iStockphoto / rzelich;
© iStockphoto / AleksVF

earbuds

portable media player with button controls

portable media player with touch screen

portable media player with touch-sensitive pad

Portable media players usually include a set of *earbuds*, which are small speakers that rest inside each ear canal. Available in a variety of sizes and colors, some portable media player models have a touch screen. Others have a *touch-sensitive pad*, which is an input device that contains buttons and/or wheels you operate with a thumb or finger. Using the touch-sensitive pad, you can scroll through and play music; view pictures; watch videos or movies; navigate through song, picture, or movie lists; display a menu; adjust volume; customize settings; and perform other actions. Some portable media players have only button controls.

Your collection of stored digital media is called a *media library*. Portable media players house your media library on a storage device in the player and/or on some type of memory card. With most, you transfer the digital media from a computer or the Internet, if the device is Internet capable, to the portable media player's media library. Read How To 2-2 on page 82 for instructions about how to transfer digital media from online services to a mobile device, such as a portable media player.

 BTW

EarPods

Apple uses the term, *EarPods*, to refer to earbuds they designed to match the shape of the human ear.

 MINI FEATURE 3-3

Mobile Device Buyer's Guide

Mobile devices such as smartphones, digital cameras, and portable medial players are quite popular among people who are frequently on the go. Research the manufacturers and then consider the following guidelines before purchasing a mobile device.

Smartphone Purchase Guidelines

1. Choose a wireless carrier and plan that satisfies your needs and budget.
2. Decide on the size, style, and weight of the smartphone that will work best for you.
3. Determine whether you prefer an on-screen keyboard, keypad, or mini keyboard.
4. Select a smartphone that is compatible with the program you want to use for synchronizing your email messages, contacts, calendar, and other data.
5. Choose a smartphone with sufficient battery life that meets your lifestyle.
6. Make sure your smartphone has enough memory and storage for contacts, email messages, photos, videos, and apps.
7. Consider purchasing accessories such as extra batteries, earbuds, screen protectors, and carrying cases.

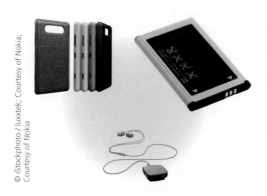

Digital Camera Purchase Guidelines

1. Determine the type of digital camera that meets your needs, such as a point-and-shoot camera or SLR camera.
2. Choose a camera with an appropriate resolution.
3. Evaluate memory cards because different cameras require different memory cards.

4. Consider a camera with built-in photo editing features.
5. Make sure that you can see the screen easily.
6. If the photos you plan to take will require you to zoom, choose a camera with an appropriate optical zoom.
7. Purchase accessories such as extra batteries and battery chargers, extra memory cards, lenses, and carrying cases.

Portable Media Player Purchase Guidelines

1. Choose a portable media player with sufficient storage capacity for your media library.
2. Consider a portable media player that can play video.

continued on next page

continued from previous page

3. Read reviews about sound quality. Consider higher-quality earbuds, headphones, or external speakers.

4. Select an appropriate size and style.

5. Consider additional memory cards to increase the storage capacity of your portable media player.

6. Consider rechargeable batteries instead of disposable batteries.

☀ Although most smartphones also can function as portable media players and digital cameras, would you have a separate portable media player and digital camera? Why?

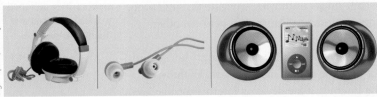

E-Book Readers

An **e-book reader** (short for electronic book reader), or *e-reader*, is a mobile device that is used primarily for reading e-books and other digital publications (Figure 3-20). An *e-book*, or digital book, is an electronic version of a printed book, readable on computers and other mobile devices. Digital publications include books, newspapers, and magazines. Mobile computers and devices that display text also can function as e-book readers.

E-book readers usually are smaller than tablets but larger than smartphones. Most e-book reader models can store thousands of books, have a touch screen, and are Internet capable with built-in wireless technology. You use an on-screen keyboard to navigate, search, make selections, take notes, and highlight. Some have a text-to-speech feature, where the device speaks the contents of the printed page. E-book readers are available with an electronic paper black-and-white screen or with a color screen. Most have settings to adjust text size and for various lighting conditions, such as bright sunlight or dim lighting. Batteries usually have a long life, providing more than 75 hours of use before needing to be recharged.

Similar to how a portable media player stores digital media, e-book readers store digital publications in a library on a storage device in the e-book reader and/or on memory cards. You typically transfer the digital publication from a computer or the Internet, if the device is Internet capable, to the e-book reader. Read How To 2-2 on page 82 for instructions about how to transfer digital media from online services to a mobile device such as an e-book reader. Read Ethics & Issues 3-3 to consider library circulation of e-books.

BTW

Electronic Paper Screen
Some users of e-books prefer the electronic paper black-and-white screen over the models with color screens because the electronic paper resembles a paper page from a book.

Figure 3-20
E-book readers enable you to read e-books and other digital publications such as newspapers and magazines.
© iStockphoto / pressureUA

☀ **ETHICS & ISSUES 3-3**

Should Limits Be Placed on Libraries' Lending of E-Books?
Each time you check out a printed book from the library, the mere act of thumbing through the pages as you read causes subtle damage to the book. E-books have no wear and tear, which means that libraries can circulate them an unlimited number of times. Libraries add e-books to their circulation by partnering with companies that offer an inventory system and enable libraries and library networks to license content from publishers.

These companies allow the publishers to set certain limits, such as number of consecutive checkouts, length of checkout, and so forth.

One publisher states that, on average, libraries replace a print book after 26 checkouts. That publisher used the statistic to set its policy so that libraries have to repurchase e-book content after 26 checkouts. The publisher cited loss of revenue and author royalties if libraries do not repurchase e-books as they do print books. Some publishers do not offer e-books to

libraries at all because of the same concern. Criticism from some librarians is that when a print book is purchased, the library can circulate it as many times as it wants, or until the book falls apart; therefore, no limits should be placed on e-books.

Should publishers be able to put a limit on how many times a library can circulate an e-book? Why or why not? How do the limits affect library patrons, libraries, authors, and publishers?

Do you need a separate e-book reader if you have a tablet or other device that can function as an e-book reader?

If you want the flexibility of reading on one device while using a tablet or other device for separate tasks, you will want to purchase a separate e-book reader. Also, e-book readers have a design suited for optimal readability of on-screen text and a longer battery life.

Game Devices

A **game console** is a mobile computing device designed for single-player or multiplayer video games. Gamers often connect the game console to a television or a monitor so that they can view gameplay on the screen. Some models also allow you to listen to music and watch movies or view photos. Typically weighing between 3 and 11 pounds, many game console models include internal disk drives or memory to store games and other media. Optical disc drives in the game consoles provide access to games and movies on optical disc. Some use memory cards and accept USB flash drives. Game consoles that are Internet capable enable gamers to download games, stream games or movies, and play with others online. Some gamers connect keyboards or webcams so that they more easily can send text messages or conduct video chats with other gamers.

A **handheld game device** is a small mobile device that contains a screen, speakers, controls, and game console all in one unit. Some include a stylus. Some handheld game device models have touch screens and built-in digital cameras. Some are Internet capable for downloading games and apps. Most handheld game devices can communicate wirelessly with other similar devices for multiplayer gaming.

With a game console or computer video game, players direct movements and actions of on-screen objects via a controller, voice, or air gestures. Game controllers include gamepads, joysticks and wheels, dance pads, and a variety of motion-sensing controllers (Figure 3-21). The list on the next page describes each of these types of game controllers. Most communicate via wired or wireless technology.

🔅 BTW

📄 Nintendo
Technology Innovator: You should be familiar with Nintendo.

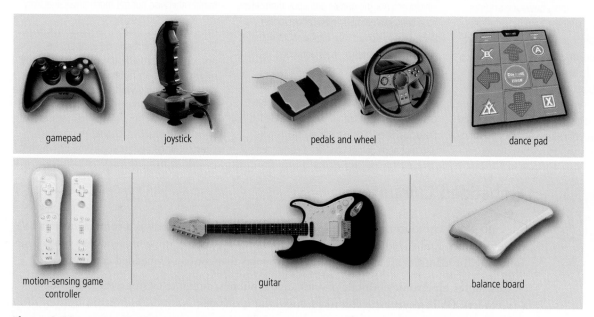

gamepad   joystick   pedals and wheel   dance pad

motion-sensing game controller   guitar   balance board

Figure 3-21   Game players have a variety of ways to direct movements and actions of on-screen objects.

Internet Research

Which video games are the most widely used?

Search for: popular video games

- A *gamepad*, which is held with both hands, controls the movement and actions of players or objects in video games or computer games. On the gamepad, users press buttons with their thumbs or move sticks in various directions to trigger events. Several gamepads can communicate with the game console simultaneously for multiplayer gaming.

- Users running flight and driving simulation software often use a joystick or wheel. A *joystick* is a handheld vertical lever, mounted on a base, that you move in different directions to control the actions of the simulated vehicle or player. The lever usually includes buttons, called triggers, that you press to initiate certain events. A *wheel* is a steering-wheel-type input device that users turn to simulate driving a car, truck, or other vehicle. Most wheels also include foot pedals for acceleration and braking actions.

- A *dance pad* is a flat, electronic device divided into panels that users press with their feet in response to instructions from a music video game. These games test the user's ability to step on the correct panel at the correct time, following a pattern that is synchronized with the rhythm or beat of a song.

- *Motion-sensing game controllers* allow the user to guide on-screen elements with air gestures, that is, by moving their body or a handheld input device through the air. Some motion-sensing game controllers are sold with a particular type of game; others are general purpose. Sports games, for example, use motion-sensing game controllers, such as baseball bats and golf clubs. With general-purpose motion-sensing game controllers, you simulate batting, golfing, and other actions with a universal handheld device or no device at all.

- Controllers that resemble musical instruments, such as guitars, drums, keyboards, and microphones work with music video games that enable game players to create sounds and music by playing the instrument.

- Fitness games often communicate with a *balance board*, which is shaped like a weight scale and contains sensors that measure a game player's balance and weight. Read Ethics & Issues 3-4 to consider whether games and apps are qualified to provide medical advice.

 ETHICS & ISSUES 3-4

Are Fitness Video Games and Apps Qualified to Provide Medical Advice?

Most video games and smartphone apps provide a workout only for your fingers. A host of games and apps, however, attempt to track calories, suggest workout routines, and more. Because you can take your smartphone anywhere, one advantage is that apps can provide tips for eating healthfully at a restaurant, act as a pedometer to track your steps, and send reminders to exercise. Another advantage is you can receive instant feedback and support from fitness apps and games that allow you to post workouts,

calorie counts, and even weight loss to social media sites.

Some critics find fault with these systems, claiming that neither the game or app developers, nor the games and apps themselves, have been evaluated by medical personnel. Because they do not take into account the amount of lean muscle mass and body fat, health and weight loss goals can be miscalculated. Experts say that games that simulate sports, such as tennis, burn half the calories you would burn if you participated in the actual sport. Some medical experts note also that apps do not consider a participant's

medical history when recommending activities. Proponents of fitness-related games and apps say that the games encourage people to be more active, especially the elderly and children who might otherwise not get much physical activity.

Should game and app developers be permitted to provide medical advice? Why or why not? Can fitness-related games provide a quality workout? Can an app give accurate calorie recommendations? Why or why not? As long as the games make people more active, should the games' shortcomings be ignored? Why or why not?

Embedded Computers

An **embedded computer** is a special-purpose computer that functions as a component in a larger product. Embedded computers are everywhere — at home, in your car, and at work. The following list identifies a variety of everyday products that contain embedded computers.

- **Consumer electronics:** Mobile phones, digital phones, digital televisions, cameras, video recorders, DVD players and recorders, answering machines
- **Home automation devices:** Thermostats, sprinkling systems, security systems, vacuum systems, appliances, lights
- **Automobiles:** Antilock brakes, engine control modules, electronic stability control, airbag controller, cruise control, navigation systems and GPS receivers

- **Process controllers and robotics:** Remote monitoring systems, power monitors, machine controllers, medical devices
- **Computer devices and office machines:** Keyboards, printers, fax and copy machines

Because embedded computers are components in larger products, they usually are small and have limited hardware. These computers perform various functions, depending on the requirements of the product in which they reside. Embedded computers in printers, for example, monitor the amount of paper in the tray, check the ink or toner level, signal if a paper jam has occurred, and so on. Figure 3-22 shows some of the many embedded computers in vehicles. Read Ethics & Issues 3-5 to consider whether in-vehicle technology fosters a false sense of security.

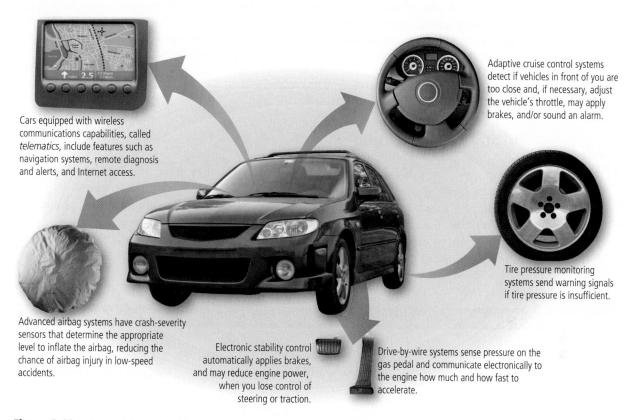

Cars equipped with wireless communications capabilities, called *telematics*, include features such as navigation systems, remote diagnosis and alerts, and Internet access.

Adaptive cruise control systems detect if vehicles in front of you are too close and, if necessary, adjust the vehicle's throttle, may apply brakes, and/or sound an alarm.

Tire pressure monitoring systems send warning signals if tire pressure is insufficient.

Advanced airbag systems have crash-severity sensors that determine the appropriate level to inflate the airbag, reducing the chance of airbag injury in low-speed accidents.

Electronic stability control automatically applies brakes, and may reduce engine power, when you lose control of steering or traction.

Drive-by-wire systems sense pressure on the gas pedal and communicate electronically to the engine how much and how fast to accelerate.

Figure 3-22 Some of the embedded computers designed to improve your safety, security, and performance in today's vehicles.
© Nir Levy / Shutterstock.com; © Santiago Cornejo / Shutterstock.com; © Patti McConville / Getty Images; © iStockphoto / narvikk; © iStockphoto / kenneth-cheung; © iStockphoto / Marcin Laska

---

❄ **ETHICS & ISSUES 3-5** ─────────────────────────────────

Does In-Vehicle Technology Foster a False Sense of Security?

Embedded computers in vehicles can guide you when backing out of a driveway or alert you to unsafe road conditions. You can use GPS technology to help reach a destination. Hands-free and voice-activated technology allows you to use a phone and play music or send text messages while driving. Apps can track gas mileage or tell you when an oil change is due. Recently, all new cars were required to include electronic stability control, which can assist with steering the car in case of skidding. All of this technology is supposed to make driving safer.

Critics of in-vehicle technology claim that it can provide drivers with a false sense of security. If you rely on a sensor for assistance while backing up, for example, you may fail to look for obstructions behind the vehicle. Using GPS and hands-free technology to find a location or talk on the phone ultimately can be distracting. The electronic stability control may cause you to drive faster than conditions allow.

Teen drivers statistically are more susceptible to being distracted while driving. If they learn to drive using vehicles equipped with features such as video rearview mirrors, they may be unable to drive older, less-equipped vehicles

safely. Without GPS step-by-step guidance, teen drivers may have difficulty navigating using a paper map. Many apps and devices help parents protect their teens while driving. Mobile devices can be programmed to block incoming calls or text messages while the vehicle is moving. GPS can be used to track a vehicle's location and speed, as well as seatbelt usage and number of passengers in the vehicle.

Does in-vehicle technology make driving safer? Why or why not? What basic skills should all drivers have, regardless of their vehicle's technology?

CONSIDER THIS ———————————————————————————

Can embedded computers use the Internet to communicate with other computers and devices?

Many already do, on a small scale. For example, a *Smart TV* enables you to browse the web, stream video from online media services, listen to Internet radio, communicate with others on social media sites, play online games, and more — all while watching a television show.

A trend, called the *Internet of Things,* describes an environment where processors are embedded in every product imaginable (things), and those 'things' communicate with each other via the Internet (i.e., alarm clocks, coffeemakers, apps, vehicles, refrigerators, phones, washing machines, doorbells, streetlights, thermostats, navigation systems, etc.). For example, when your refrigerator detects the milk is low, it sends your phone a text message that you need milk and adds a 'buy milk' task to your scheduling app. On the drive home, your phone determines the closest grocery store that has the lowest milk price and sends the address of that grocery store to your vehicle's navigation system, which in turn gives you directions to the store. In the store, your phone directs you to the dairy aisle, where it receives an electronic coupon from the store for the milk. Because this type of environment provides an efficient means to track or monitor status, inventory, behavior, and more — without human intervention — it sometimes is referred to as machine-to-machine (M2M) communications.

Putting It All Together

Industry experts typically classify computers and mobile devices in six categories: personal computers (desktop), mobile computers and mobile devices, game consoles, servers, supercomputers, and embedded computers. A computer's size, speed, processing power, and price determine the category it best fits. Due to rapidly changing technology, however, the distinction among categories is not always clear-cut. Table 3-3 summarizes the categories of computers discussed on the previous pages.

Table 3-3   Categories of Computers and Mobile Devices

Category	Physical Size	Number of Simultaneously Connected Users	General Price Range
Personal computers (desktop)	Fits on a desk	Usually one (can be more if networked)	Several hundred to several thousand dollars
Mobile computers and mobile devices	Fits on your lap or in your hand	Usually one	Less than a hundred dollars to several thousand dollars
Game consoles	Small box or handheld device	One to several	Several hundred dollars or less
Servers	Small cabinet to room full of equipment	Two to thousands	Several hundred to several million dollars
Supercomputers	Full room of equipment	Hundreds to thousands	Half a million to several billion dollars
Embedded computers	Miniature	Usually one	Embedded in the price of the product

Be sure you understand the material presented in the sections titled Cloud Computing, Mobile Devices, Game Devices, Embedded Computers, and Putting It All Together as it relates to the chapter objectives.
You now should know…

- When you are using cloud computing (Objective 4)
- What you should consider when purchasing a mobile device (Objective 5)
- What types of controllers you might use with game consoles (Objective 6)
- When you are using an embedded computer (Objective 7)

💻 Quiz Yourself Online: Check your knowledge of related content by navigating to this book's Quiz Yourself resource on Computer Concepts CourseMate and then tapping or clicking Objectives 4–7.

Ports and Connections

Computers and mobile devices connect to peripheral devices through ports or by using wireless technologies. A **port** is the point at which a peripheral device (i.e., keyboard, printer, monitor, etc.) attaches to or communicates with a computer or mobile device so that the peripheral device can send data to or receive information from the computer or mobile device. Most computers and mobile devices have ports (Figure 3-23). Some ports have a micro or mini version for mobile devices because of the smaller sizes of these devices.

 BTW

Jacks
Instead of the term, port, the term, *jack*, sometimes is used to identify audio and video ports (i.e., audio jack or video jack).

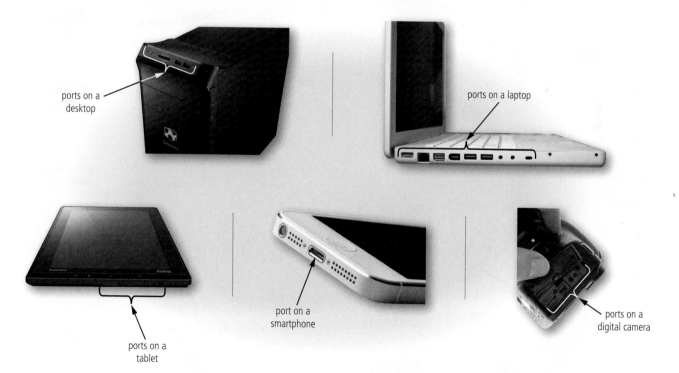

ports on a desktop

ports on a laptop

ports on a tablet

port on a smartphone

ports on a digital camera

Figure 3-23 Most computers and mobile devices have ports so that you can connect the computer or device to peripherals.
Courtesy of Gateway; © Ultraone / Dreamstime.com; Courtesy of Lenovo; © iStockphoto / Nikada; © David Kilpatrick / Alamy

A **connector** joins a cable to a port. A connector at one end of a cable attaches to a port on the computer or mobile device, and a connector at the other end of the cable attaches to a port on the peripheral device. Table 3-4 shows a variety of ports you may find on a computer or mobile device. Notice that many are color-coded to help you match the connector to the correct port. USB and Thunderbolt are more general-purpose ports that allow connections to a wide variety of devices; other ports are more specific and connect a single type of device. Read How To 3-2 on page 131 for instructions about how to connect peripheral devices and accessories to a computer or mobile device.

Table 3-4 Popular Ports and Connectors

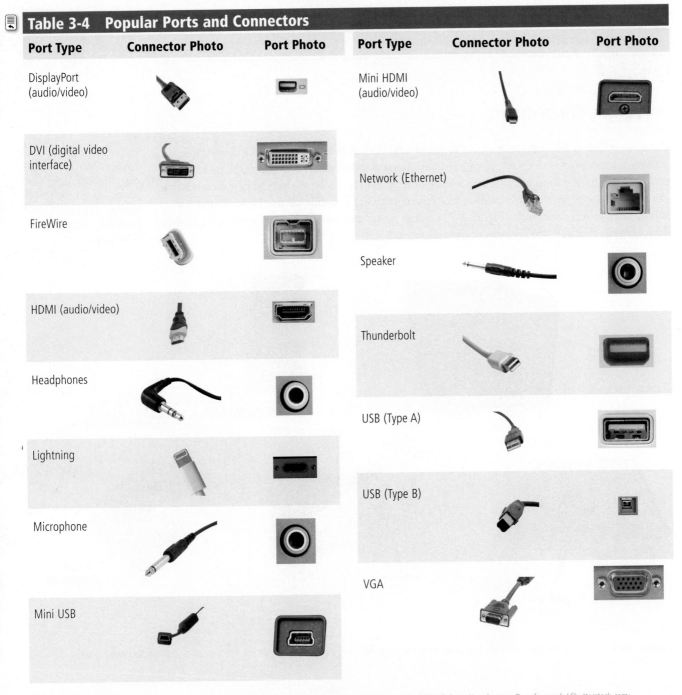

Port Type	Connector Photo	Port Photo	Port Type	Connector Photo	Port Photo
DisplayPort (audio/video)			Mini HDMI (audio/video)		
DVI (digital video interface)					
FireWire			Network (Ethernet)		
			Speaker		
HDMI (audio/video)			Thunderbolt		
Headphones					
			USB (Type A)		
Lightning			USB (Type B)		
Microphone					
			VGA		
Mini USB					

© Cengage Learning; © Steveheap / Dreamstime.com; © iStockphoto / Hans Martens; © iStockphoto / Ksenia Krylova; © iStockphoto / Lusoimages; © ronfromyork / Shutterstock.com; © Jorge Salcedo / Shutterstock.com; © Aarrows / Dreamstime.com; © iStockphoto / Lusoimages; © Pcheruvi / Dreamstime.com; © iStockphoto / Potapova Valeriya; © iStockphoto / Jivko Kazakov; © iStockphoto / TimArbaev; © iStockphoto / Ashok Rodrigues; © iStockphoto / Jon Larson; © Aarrows / Dreamstime.com; © iStockphoto / Li Ding; © iStockphoto / TimArbaev; © iStockphoto / Matthew Brown; © Jorge Salcedo / Shutterstock.com; © David Kilpatrick / Alamy; © Aarrows / Dreamstime.com; © David Kilpatrick / Alamy; © iStockphoto / Li Ding; © iStockphoto / TimArbaev; © iStockphoto / Matthew Brown; © Jorge Salcedo / Shutterstock.com; © Pcheruvi / Dreamstime.com; © Anton Malcev / Photos.com; © iStockphoto / alexander kirch; © iStockphoto / Nick Smith; © iStockphoto / Mohamed Badawi; © Jorge Salcedo / Shutterstock © iStockphoto / Brandon Laufenberg; © getIT / Shutterstock.com; © stavklem / Shutterstock.com; © iStockphoto / Lusoimages

🌐 HOW TO 3-2

Connect Peripheral Devices and Accessories to a Computer or Mobile Device

You connect peripheral devices and accessories to computers or mobile devices either to enhance the capabilities of the computer or mobile device or to transfer data or information from a peripheral device or an accessory to a computer or mobile device. The following steps describe how to connect peripheral devices and accessories to a computer or mobile device.

1. If the peripheral device or accessory packaging included an installation disc, insert the disc in the computer. Install any necessary software and drivers required for the computer to recognize the device or accessory.

2. Connect the peripheral device or accessory to the computer or mobile device using the cable that came with the device or accessory. If a cable was not included or you are unable to locate the cable, you may be able to purchase one either from the device's or accessory's manufacturer or from a company that sells various cables. Cables also are available with multiple connectors that fit many common devices.

3. If the computer recognizes the device or accessory, you should be able to begin using it.

4. If the computer does not recognize the device or accessory, refer to its documentation to determine whether any additional steps are required to use the device or accessory.

🌼 Why is it sometimes necessary to install a program on a computer before the computer is able to recognize the device or accessory you are connecting?

© Dmitry DG / Fotolia

USB Ports

A **USB port**, short for universal serial bus port, can connect up to 127 different peripheral devices together with a single connector. Devices that connect to a USB port include the following: card reader, digital camera, external hard disk, game console, joystick, modem, mouse, optical disc drive, portable media player, printer, scanner, smartphone, speakers, USB flash drive, and webcam. In addition to computers and mobile devices, you find USB ports in vehicles, airplane seats, and other public locations.

Several USB versions have been released, with newer versions (i.e., USB 3.0) transferring data and information faster than earlier ones (i.e., USB 2.0). Newer versions are *backward compatible*, which means they support older USB devices as well as newer ones. Keep in mind, though, that older USB devices do not run any faster in a newer USB port. In addition to transferring data, cables plugged into USB ports also may be able to transfer power to recharge many smartphones and tablets. Newer versions of USB can charge connected mobile devices even when the computer is not in use.

To attach multiple peripheral devices using a single USB port, you can use a USB hub. A *USB hub* is a device that plugs in a USB port on the computer or mobile device and contains multiple USB ports, into which you plug cables from USB devices. Some USB hubs are wireless. That is, a receiver plugs into a USB port on the computer and the USB hub communicates wirelessly with the receiver.

Port Replicators and Docking Stations

Instead of connecting peripheral devices directly to ports on a mobile computer, some mobile users prefer the flexibility of port replicators and docking stations. A *port replicator* is an external device that provides connections to peripheral devices through ports built into the device. The mobile user accesses peripheral devices by connecting the port replicator to a USB port or a special port on the mobile computer. Port replicators sometimes disable ports on the mobile computer to prevent conflicts among the devices on the computer and port replicator.

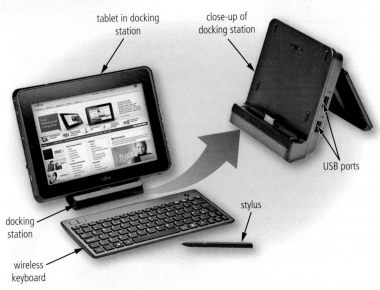

tablet in docking station

close-up of docking station

USB ports

docking station

wireless keyboard

stylus

Figure 3-24 Docking stations often are used with tablets and other mobile computers, providing connections to peripheral devices.
Courtesy of Fujitsu Technology Solutions; © Cengage Learning

A docking station is similar to a port replicator, but it has more functionality. A *docking station*, which is an external device that attaches to a mobile computer or device, contains a power connection and provides connections to peripheral devices (Figure 3-24). Docking stations also may include slots for memory cards, optical disc drives, and other devices. With the mobile computer or device in the docking station, users can work with a full-sized keyboard, a mouse, and other desktop peripheral devices from their traditional laptop, ultrathin laptop, or tablet.

Wireless Device Connections

Instead of connecting computers and mobile devices to peripheral devices with a cable, some peripheral devices use wireless communications technologies, such as Bluetooth, Wi-Fi, and NFC.

Bluetooth Bluetooth technology uses short-range radio signals to transmit data between two Bluetooth-enabled computers or devices. In addition to computers, mobile devices and many peripheral devices, such as a mouse, keyboard, printer, or headset, and many vehicles and consumer electronics are Bluetooth enabled. Bluetooth devices have to be within about 33 feet of each other, but the range can be extended with additional equipment. If you have a computer that is not Bluetooth enabled, you can purchase a *Bluetooth wireless port adapter* that will convert an existing USB port into a Bluetooth port. Read How To 3-3 for instructions about setting up two Bluetooth devices to communicate with each other.

✹ HOW TO 3-3

Pair Bluetooth Devices
Before two Bluetooth devices will communicate with each other, they might need to be paired. **Pairing** is the process of initiating contact between two Bluetooth devices and allowing them to communicate with each other. It is important to have the documentation for the Bluetooth devices you are pairing readily available. The following steps will help you pair two Bluetooth devices.

1. Make sure the devices you intend to pair are charged completely or plugged into an external power source.

2. Turn on the devices to pair, ensuring they are within your immediate reach.

3. If necessary, enable Bluetooth on the devices you are pairing.

4. Place one device in *discoverable mode*, which means it is waiting for another Bluetooth device to locate its signal. If you

are connecting a smartphone to a Bluetooth headset, for example, the smartphone would need to be in discoverable mode.

5. Refer to the other device's documentation and follow the necessary steps to locate the discoverable device from the other device you are pairing.

6. After no more than about 30 seconds, the devices should initiate communications.

7. You may be required to enter a passkey (similar to a PIN) on one device for the other device with which you are pairing. For example, if you are pairing a smartphone with a Bluetooth headset, you may be required to enter the Bluetooth headset's passkey on the smartphone. In this case, you would refer to the Bluetooth headset's documentation to obtain the passkey. Common passkeys are 0000 and 1234.

8. After entering the correct passkey, the two devices should be paired successfully.

✹ Why is a passkey required when pairing two Bluetooth devices? Do you need to pair Bluetooth devices before each use?

© iStockphoto / Moncherie; © Norman Chan / Shutterstock.com

Wi-Fi Short for wireless fidelity, **Wi-Fi** uses radio signals that conform to 802.11 standards, which were developed by the Institute of Electrical and Electronics Engineers (IEEE). Computers and devices that have the appropriate Wi-Fi capability can communicate via radio waves with other Wi-Fi computers or devices. Most mobile computers and devices are Wi-Fi enabled, along with routers and other communications devices. For successful Wi-Fi communications in open or outdoor areas free from interference, the Wi-Fi computers or devices should be within 300 feet of each other. In closed areas, the wireless range is about 100 feet. To obtain communications at the maximum distances, you may need to install extra hardware. Read How To 3-4 for instructions about connecting a phone to a Wi-Fi network.

✴ HOW TO 3-4

Connect Your Phone to a Wi-Fi Network to Save Data Charges

Many of today's data plans limit the amount of data you can transfer each month on your mobile service provider's network. Connecting a smartphone to a Wi-Fi network enables you to transfer data without using your phone's data plan and risking costly overages. The following steps describe how to connect your phone to a Wi-Fi network.

1. Make sure you are in a location where a Wi-Fi network is available. Obtain any necessary information you need to connect to the Wi-Fi network.
2. Navigate to the settings on your phone.
3. Locate and enable Wi-Fi in your phone's settings.
4. When your phone displays a list of available wireless networks, choose the network to which you want to connect.

5. If necessary, enter any additional information, such as a password, required to connect to the network.
6. Your phone should indicate when it successfully is connected to the network.
7. When you are finished using the Wi-Fi connection or are not within range of the Wi-Fi network, disable Wi-Fi on your phone to help conserve battery life.

✴ If you have a data plan allowing unlimited data and you are within range of a Wi-Fi network, is it better to use your mobile service provider's network or the Wi-Fi network? Why?

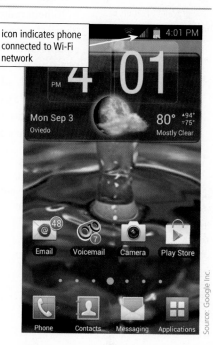

icon indicates phone connected to Wi-Fi network

Source: Google Inc.

NFC **NFC** (*near field communications*) uses close-range radio signals to transmit data between two NFC-enabled devices. Examples of NFC-enabled devices include smartphones, digital cameras, computers, televisions, and terminals. Other objects, such as credit cards and tickets, also use NFC technology. For successful communications, the devices either touch or are within an inch or two of each other.

✴ CONSIDER THIS

What are some uses of NFC devices?

- Pay for goods and services (i.e., smartphone to terminal)
- Share contacts, photos, and other files (i.e., smartphone to smartphone or digital camera to television)
- Download apps (i.e., computer to smartphone)
- Gain access or admittance (i.e., smartphone to terminal)

Protecting Hardware

Users rely on computers and mobile devices to create, store, and manage important information. Thus, you should take measures to protect computers and devices from theft, vandalism, and failure.

Hardware Theft and Vandalism

Companies, schools, and other organizations that house many computers are at risk of hardware theft and vandalism, especially those with smaller computers that easily can fit in a backpack or briefcase. Mobile users are susceptible to hardware theft because the size and weight of their computers and devices make them easy to steal. Thieves may target laptops of company executives so that they can use the stolen computer to access confidential company information illegally.

To help reduce the chances of theft, companies and schools use a variety of security measures. Physical access controls, such as locked doors and windows, usually are adequate to protect the equipment. Many businesses, schools, and some homeowners install alarm systems for additional security. School computer labs and other facilities with a large number of semifrequent users often attach additional physical security devices such as cables that lock the equipment to a desk (Figure 3-25), cabinet, or floor. Mobile users sometimes lock their mobile computers temporarily to a stationary object, for example, a table in a hotel room. Small locking devices also exist that require a key to access a hard disk or optical disc drive.

Figure 3-25 Using cables to lock computers can help prevent theft of equipment.
Courtesy of Kensington

Figure 3-26 Some mobile computers include fingerprint readers, which can be used to verify a user's identity.
© Jochen Tack / Alamy

Some users install a security or device-tracking app on their mobile computers and devices. Some security apps shut down the computer and sound an alarm if the computer moves beyond a specified distance. Others can be configured to photograph the thieves when they use the computer. Device-tracking apps use GPS, Wi-Fi, IP addresses, and other means to determine the location of a lost or stolen computer or device.

Users can configure computers and mobile devices to require identification before allowing access. For example, you can require entry of a user name and password to use the computer or device. Some computers have built-in or attached fingerprint readers (Figure 3-26), which can be used to verify a user's identity before allowing access. A *fingerprint reader* captures curves and indentations of a fingerprint. This type of security does not prevent theft, but it renders the computer or device useless if it is stolen.

Hardware Failure

Hardware can fail for a variety of reasons: aging hardware; random events such as electrical power problems; and even errors in programs or apps. Not only could hardware failure require you to replace or repair a computer or mobile device, but it also can cause loss of software, data, and information.

One of the more common causes of system failure is an electrical power variation, which can cause loss of data and loss of equipment. If computers and mobile devices are connected to a network, a single power disturbance can damage multiple devices at once. Electrical disturbances that can cause damage include undervoltages and overvoltages.

- An **undervoltage** occurs when the electrical supply or voltage drops, often defined as more than five percent, below the normal volts. A *brownout* is a prolonged (more than a minute) undervoltage. A *blackout* is a complete power failure. Undervoltages can cause data loss but generally do not cause equipment damage.

- An **overvoltage**, or **power surge**, occurs when the incoming electrical supply or voltage increases, often defined as more than five percent, above the normal volts. A momentary overvoltage, called a *spike*, occurs when the increase in power lasts for less than one millisecond (thousandth of a second). Uncontrollable disturbances such as lightning bolts can cause spikes. Overvoltages can cause immediate and permanent damage to hardware.

To protect against electrical power variations, use a surge protector. A **surge protector**, also called a *surge suppressor*, uses electrical components to provide a stable current flow and minimize the chances of an overvoltage reaching the computer and other electronic equipment (Figure 3-27). Sometimes resembling a power strip, the computer and other devices plug in the surge protector, which plugs in the power source.

Figure 3-27   Circuits inside a surge protector safeguard against electrical power variations.
Courtesy of Tripp Lite

The surge protector absorbs small overvoltages — generally without damage to the computer and equipment. To protect the computer and other equipment from large overvoltages, such as those caused by a lightning strike, some surge protectors stop working completely when an overvoltage reaches a certain level. Surge protectors also usually protect the computer from undervoltages. No surge protectors are 100 percent effective. Large power surges can bypass the protector. Repeated small overvoltages can weaken a surge protector permanently. Some experts recommend replacing a surge protector every two to three years.

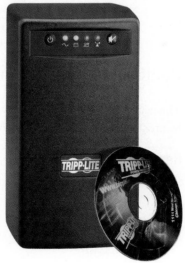

For additional electrical protection, some users connect an uninterruptible power supply to the computer. An **uninterruptible power supply** (**UPS**) is a device that contains surge protection circuits and one or more batteries that can provide power during a temporary or permanent loss of power (Figure 3-28). A UPS connects your computer and a power source. Read Secure IT 3-4 on the next page for purchasing suggestions regarding surge protectors and UPSs.

Figure 3-28   If power fails, a UPS uses batteries to provide electricity for a limited amount of time.
Courtesy of Tripp Lite

 CONSIDER THIS

What other measures can organizations implement if their computers must remain operational at all times?

Some companies use duplicate components or duplicate computers to protect against hardware failure. A *fault-tolerant computer* has duplicate components so that it can continue to operate when one of its main components fail. Airline reservation systems, communications networks, ATMs, and other systems that must be operational at all times use duplicate components, duplicate computers, or fault-tolerant computers.

SECURE IT 3-4

Avoid System Failure with Surge Protectors and UPSs

Electrical power surges are a part of everyday life, and they are especially prevalent during thunderstorms and peak energy consumption periods. These unavoidable occurrences can damage or ruin sensitive electronic equipment. The processor in a computer is particularly sensitive to the current fluctuations. Two devices can help protect electronic components: a surge protector and an uninterruptible power supply (UPS).

Purchase the best surge protector you can afford. Typically, the amount of protection offered by a surge protector is proportional to its cost. That is, the more expensive the surge protector, the more protection it offers. At a minimum, it should cost more than $15 and meet or exceed these specifications:

- Sufficient outlets to accommodate each device needing protection
- Individual on/off switch for each device
- Built-in fuse
- UL 1449 rating (ensures quality control and testing)

- Joule rating of at least 600 (a Joule is the unit of energy the device can absorb before it can be damaged; the higher the Joule rating, the better the protection)
- Indicator light (shows it is functioning properly)
- Warranty for damages to any connected equipment (best units offer replacement guarantee)
- Low clamping voltage (the level when electricity is diverted)
- High energy-absorption rating (allows electricity to flow before failing)
- Low response time (time between the spike and the protector's response), preferably less than ten nanoseconds (billionths of a second)
- Protection for a modem, communications lines, and cables, if your computer connects to a network or the Internet

If the home has many audio and video technologies in different rooms, a whole-house surge protector may be convenient and cost effective. Another advantage is that it might prevent a house fire caused when faulty wiring overheats and then ignites. A whole-house surge protector, which costs at least $300, connects to the electric meter or to the breaker box. This device should be installed by a licensed electrician.

If your electric service fails frequently, a UPS may offer peace of mind. Two types of UPS devices are standby and online. A *standby UPS*, sometimes called an *offline UPS*, switches to battery power when a problem occurs in the power line. The amount of time a standby UPS allows a user to continue working depends on the electrical requirements of the computer and the size of the batteries in the UPS. A UPS for a home user should provide enough time to save current work and shut down the computer properly. An *online UPS* always runs off the battery, which provides continuous protection. An online UPS is much more expensive than a standby UPS.

✳ How do you protect your computer and other electrical devices from power surges? Would a UPS be a good investment given the reliability of your electric service?

Health Concerns of Using Technology

The widespread use of technology has led to some important user health concerns. You should be proactive and minimize your chance of risk.

Repetitive Strain Injuries

A *repetitive strain injury* (*RSI*) is an injury or disorder of the muscles, nerves, tendons, ligaments, and joints. Technology-related RSIs include tendonitis and carpal tunnel syndrome.

- Tendonitis is inflammation of a tendon due to repeated motion or stress on that tendon.
- Carpal tunnel syndrome (CTS) is inflammation of the nerve that connects the forearm to the palm of the wrist.

Repeated or forceful bending of the wrist can cause tendonitis or CTS of the wrist. Symptoms of tendonitis of the wrist include extreme pain that extends from the forearm to the hand, along with tingling in the fingers. Symptoms of CTS include burning pain when the nerve is compressed, along with numbness and tingling in the thumb and first two fingers.

Long-term computer work can lead to tendonitis or CTS. Factors that cause these disorders include prolonged typing, prolonged mouse usage, or continual shifting between the mouse and the keyboard. If untreated, these disorders can lead to permanent physical damage.

✳ **CONSIDER THIS** ────────────────────────────────

What can you do to prevent technology-related tendonitis or CTS?
Follow these precautions:

- Take frequent breaks to exercise your hands and arms (Figure 3-29).
- Do not rest your wrists on the edge of a desk. Instead, place a wrist rest between the keyboard and the edge of your desk.
- Place the mouse at least six inches from the edge of the desk. In this position, your wrist is flat on the desk.
- Minimize the number of times you switch between the mouse and the keyboard.
- Keep your forearms and wrists level so that your wrists do not bend.
- Avoid using the heel of your hand as a pivot point while typing or using the mouse.
- Keep your shoulders, arms, hands, and wrists relaxed while you work.
- Maintain good posture.
- Stop working if you experience pain or fatigue.

Hand Exercises

- Spread fingers apart for several seconds while keeping wrists straight.
- Gently push back fingers and then thumb.
- Dangle arms loosely at sides and then shake arms and hands.

Figure 3-29 To reduce the chance of developing tendonitis or carpal tunnel syndrome, take frequent breaks during computer sessions to exercise your hands and arms.
© iStockphoto / Denis Kartavenko; © Oleksiy Mark / Shutterstock.com; © Cengage Learning

Other Physical Risks

Computer vision syndrome (*CVS*) is a technology-related health condition that affects eyesight. You may have CVS if you have sore, tired, burning, itching, or dry eyes; blurred or double vision; distance blurred vision after prolonged staring at a display device; headache or sore neck; difficulty shifting focus between a display device and documents; difficulty focusing on the screen image; color fringes or after-images when you look away from the display device; and increased sensitivity to light. Eyestrain associated with CVS is not thought to have serious or long-term consequences. Figure 3-30 outlines some techniques you can follow to ease eyestrain.

People who spend their workday using the computer sometimes complain of lower back pain, muscle fatigue, and emotional fatigue. Lower back pain sometimes is caused from poor posture. Always sit properly in the chair while you work. To alleviate back pain, muscle fatigue, and emotional fatigue, take a 15- to 30-minute break every 2 hours — stand up, walk around, stretch, and relax.

Techniques to Ease Eyestrain

- Every 10 to 15 minutes, take an eye break.
  - Look into the distance and focus on an object for 20 to 30 seconds.
  - Roll your eyes in a complete circle.
  - Close your eyes and rest them for at least one minute.
- Blink your eyes every five seconds.
- Place your display device about an arm's length away from your eyes with the top of the screen at or below eye level.
- Use large fonts.
- If you wear glasses, ask your doctor about computer glasses.
- Adjust the lighting.

Figure 3-30 Following these tips may help reduce eyestrain while using technology.
© grublee / Shutterstock.com

Internet Research

What is a treadmill desk?

Search for: treadmill desk

Another way to help prevent these injuries is to be sure your workplace is designed ergonomically. **Ergonomics** is an applied science devoted to incorporating comfort, efficiency, and safety into the design of items in the workplace. Ergonomic studies have shown that using the correct type and configuration of chair, keyboard, display device, and work surface helps users work comfortably and efficiently and helps protect their health (Figure 3-31). You can hire an ergonomic consultant to evaluate your workplace and recommend changes.

viewing angle: 20° to center of screen **viewing distance:** 18 to 28 inches

arms: elbows at about 90° and arms and hands approximately parallel to flooor

keyboard height: 23 to 28 inches depending on height of user

adjustable height chair with 4 or 5 legs for stability

feet flat on floor

Figure 3-31 A well designed work area should be flexible to allow adjustments to the height and build of different individuals. Good lighting and air quality also are important considerations.
© C Squared Studios / Getty Images

Behavioral Health Risks

Some technology users become obsessed with computers, mobile devices, and the Internet. **Technology addiction** occurs when the technology consumes someone's entire social life. Technology addiction is a growing health problem but can be treated through therapy and support groups.

People suffering from *technology overload* feel distressed when deprived of technology, even for a short length of time, or feel overwhelmed with the amount of technology they are required to manage. To cope with the feelings of distraction and to control the impact that technology can have on work and relationships, set aside technology-free time.

 CONSIDER THIS

How can you tell if you are addicted to technology?
Symptoms of a user with technology addiction include the following:

- Craves computer time
- Overjoyed when using a computer or mobile device
- Unable to stop using technology
- Irritable when not using technology
- Neglects family and friends
- Problems at work or school

NOW YOU KNOW

Be sure you understand the material presented in the sections titled Ports and Connections, Protecting Hardware, and Health Concerns of Using Technology as it relates to the chapter objectives.
You now should know…

- How you can connect a peripheral device to a computer or mobile device (Objective 8)

- How you can protect your hardware from theft, vandalism, and failure (Objective 9)

- How you can minimize your risk of health-related injuries and disorders that can result from using technology (Objective 10)

> Quiz Yourself Online: Check your knowledge of related content by navigating to this book's Quiz Yourself resource on Computer Concepts CourseMate and then tapping or clicking Objectives 8–10.

Chapter Summary

This chapter presented characteristics of and purchasing guidelines for desktops, laptops, tablets, smartphones, digital cameras, and portable media players. It also discussed handheld computers, servers, supercomputers, point-of-sale terminals, ATMs, self-service kiosks, e-book readers, game devices, embedded computers, and cloud computing. It presented a variety of ports and connections, ways to protect hardware, and health concerns of using technology use along with preventive measures.

Test your knowledge of chapter material by accessing the Study Guide, Flash Cards, and Practice Test apps that run on your smartphone, tablet, laptop, or desktop.

TECHNOLOGY @ WORK

Meteorology

With the television tuned to the local weather station, you anxiously are awaiting to see the projected path of a hurricane in the tropics. Having experienced hurricanes in the past, you rely heavily on the accuracy of weather forecasts so that you can prepare adequately if a storm travels through the area. Computers allow meteorologists to better estimate the severity and path of storms, enabling people to make potentially life-saving preparations.

The National Hurricane Center uses powerful computers to generate multiple computer models to determine a storm's path. These models consider factors such as the storm's current strength, the effects of nearby weather systems, the storm's central pressure, and whether the storm may travel over land. These models also may consider previous storms that traveled a similar path. While these models are not 100 percent accurate, they do ensure that everyone who may be affected by the storm has enough time to prepare.

Violent, rotating thunderstorms potentially can spawn tornadoes, which

sometimes cause catastrophic damage. For this reason, it is important for everyone to watch or listen closely to the weather during the storm. Meteorologists can monitor weather systems on multiple radars and send additional severe weather warnings automatically to weather radios and apps. Computer technology enables these messages to be broadcast automatically to weather radios and apps only in areas that may be affected.

In addition to computers helping us stay safe during severe storms, they also assist with day-to-day weather forecasting. Several years ago, meteorologists could predict the weather for only a few days into the future. Beyond that point, the forecast was very uncertain. Meteorologists presently are able to predict the weather, including temperature and chance of precipitation, one week or more into the future with much greater accuracy because computers create models using historical weather data and behavior to predict the future path of various weather systems.

News and weather stations have weather apps and also post their weather forecasts

National Oceanographic and Atmospheric Administration

online. In fact, several websites have interactive radars that allow visitors to zoom in and view how weather is affecting their immediate neighborhood.

The meteorology field has made significant advancements because of computer technologies. Weather forecasts are more accurate, which not only helps us prepare on land, but also helps to protect those traveling by air or by sea.

✺ In what other ways do computers and technology play a role in the meteorology field?

Study Guide

The Study Guide exercise reinforces material you should know for the chapter exam. You will find answers to items with the 📄 icon only in the e-book.

🔘 **Access the Study Guide app** that runs on your smartphone, tablet, laptop, or desktop by navigating to this book's Apps resource on Computer Concepts CourseMate.

Instructions: Answer the questions below using the format that helps you remember best or that is required by your instructor. Possible formats may include one or more of these options: write the answers; create a document that contains the answers; record answers as audio or video using a webcam, smartphone, or portable media player; post answers on a blog, wiki, or website; or highlight answers in the book/e-book.

1. List types of computers and mobile devices.

2. Explain how to avoid malware infections.

3. Describe how personal computers often are differentiated.

4. 📄 Name the contributions of Dell and Michael Dell, with respect to personal computers and peripherals.

5. Define the term, motherboard.

6. Describe the roles of the processor and memory.

7. Identify types of desktop users and explain how each user's computer needs may differ.

8. List considerations when purchasing a desktop. A(n) _____ desktop may be less expensive and take up less space.

9. Differentiate among traditional and ultrathin laptops, netbooks, tablets, phablets, and handheld computers.

10. To interact with a tablet, you may use a touch screen or a(n) _____.

11. List considerations when purchasing a mobile computer. Explain the importance of built-in ports and slots.

12. Describe the purpose and functions of a server. Differentiate among rack, blade, and tower servers.

13. Define virtualization as it relates to servers. Define the terms, server farm and mainframe.

14. A(n) _____ is used to solve complex, sophisticated mathematical calculations such as petroleum exploration.

15. Define the terms, terminal and thin client. List the advantages of a thin client.

16. Identify situations where POS terminals, ATMs, and self-service kiosks might be used. List ATM safety guidelines.

17. List cloud computing resources. Describe how businesses use cloud computing to manage resources.

18. List types of mobile devices. Describe features of a smartphone.

19. Explain the issues surrounding the recycling of e-waste.

20. Differentiate among types of smartphone keyboards.

21. 📄 Name the products and/or services of Samsung, with respect to technology.

22. List options provided by text and picture/video message services.

23. _____ occurs when a person's attention is diverted, such as by talking on a mobile phone.

24. Describe the types of digital cameras, how they store captured images, and how to transfer photos to a computer.

25. Explain how resolution affects digital picture quality.

26. Identify the features of a portable media player.

27. 📄 List considerations when purchasing mobile devices. List accessory options for various device types.

28. List features of e-book readers. Explain the issues surrounding library circulation of e-books.

29. Identify types of game controllers.

30. Explain whether fitness video games are an effective form of exercise.

31. List products that contain embedded computers. List the disadvantages of in-vehicle technology.

32. 📄 With _____ computing, you can donate your computer's resources for scientific research.

33. Explain how a computer uses ports and connectors.

34. List devices that connect to a USB port. Explain the role of a USB hub.

35. Define the term, backward compatible.

36. Distinguish between a port replicator and a docking station.

37. Describe the following technologies: Bluetooth, Wi-Fi, and NFC.

38. _____ is the process of initiating contact between two Bluetooth devices.

39. List steps to connect your phone to a Wi-Fi network.

40. List methods for securing against hardware theft and vandalism.

41. Define the terms, undervoltage and overvoltage, and explain how each can damage a computer or data.

42. Describe the purposes of surge protectors and UPS devices. Explain the purpose a fault-tolerant computer.

43. Identify causes and types of repetitive strain injuries.

44. List symptoms of CVS.

45. Describe the role of ergonomics in a workplace.

46. List symptoms of technology addiction. Define the term, technology overload.

You should be able to define the Primary Terms and be familiar with the Secondary Terms listed below.

Key Terms

Access the Flash Cards app that runs on your smartphone, tablet, laptop, or desktop by navigating to this book's Apps resource on Computer Concepts CourseMate. View definitions for each term by navigating to this book's Key Terms resource on Computer Concepts CourseMate. Listen to definitions for each term on your portable media player by navigating to this book's Audio Study Tools resource on Computer Concepts CourseMate.

Primary Terms   (shown in **bold-black** characters in the chapter)

Bluetooth (132)
cloud computing (116)
computer (104)
computer vision
   syndrome (137)
connector (129)
desktop (106)
digital camera (120)
e-book reader (124)

embedded computer (126)
ergonomics (138)
game console (125)
handheld computer (111)
handheld game device (125)
laptop (108)
mobile device (104)
NFC (133)
overvoltage (135)

pairing (132)
personal computer (104)
port (129)
portable media player (122)
power surge (135)
resolution (122)
server (111)
smartphone (117)
surge protector (135)

tablet (109)
technology addiction (138)
undervoltage (135)
uninterruptible power
   supply (UPS) (135)
USB port (131)
Wi-Fi (133)

Secondary Terms   (shown in *italic* characters in the chapter)

all-in-one desktop (107)
application server (111)
ATM (114)
backup server (111)
backward compatible (131)
balance board (126)
bar code reader (113)
blackout (135)
blade server (112)
Bluetooth wireless port adapter
   (132)
brownout (135)
charge-coupled device (CCD) (121)
common short code (CSC) (118)
convertible tablet (109)
CPU (106)
CVS (137)
dance pad (126)
database server (111)
discoverable mode (132)
docking station (132)
domain name server (111)
DVD kiosk (115)
earbuds (123)
EarPods (123)
e-book (124)

enhanced resolution (122)
e-reader (124)
fault-tolerant computer (135)
file server (111)
fingerprint reader (134)
FTP server (111)
game server (111)
gamepad (126)
gaming desktop (107)
home server (111)
inattentional blindness (119)
Internet of Things (128)
jack (129)
joystick (126)
kiosk (115)
list server (111)
mail server (111)
mainframe (112)
media library (123)
memory (106)
MMS (multimedia message service)
   (119)
mobile computer (104)
motherboard (106)
motion-sensing game controller (126)
near field communications (133)

network server (111)
notebook computer (108)
offline UPS (136)
online UPS (136)
on-screen keyboard (117)
optical resolution (122)
peripheral device (104)
personal media player (122)
phablet (110)
PIN (114)
pixel (122)
point-and-shoot camera (120)
port replicator (131)
portable keyboard (118)
POS terminal (113)
predictive text input (117)
print server (111)
processor (106)
rack server (112)
repetitive strain injury (RSI)
   (136)
server farm (112)
server virtualization (112)
skimmer (114)
slate tablet (109)
SLR camera (120)

Smart TV (128)
SMS (short message service)
   (118)
spike (135)
standby UPS (136)
storage server (111)
stylus (109)
supercomputer (113)
surge suppressor (135)
system unit (106)
technology overload (138)
telematics (127)
terminal (113)
thin client (113)
touch-sensitive pad (123)
tower (106)
tower server (112)
ultrabook (109)
USB hub (131)
virtual keyboard (118)
virtualization (112)
visual voice mail (119)
voice mail (119)
web server (111)
wheel (126)
workstation (107)

slate tablet (109)

Checkpoint

The Checkpoint exercises test your knowledge of the chapter concepts. The page number containing the answer appears in parentheses after each exercise. The Consider This exercises challenge your understanding of chapter concepts.

Complete the Checkpoint exercises interactively by navigating to this book's Checkpoint resource on Computer Concepts CourseMate. **Access the Test Prep app** that runs on your smartphone, tablet, laptop, or desktop by navigating to this book's Apps resource on Computer Concepts CourseMate. After successfully completing the self-assessment through the Test Prep app, **take the Practice Test** by navigating to this book's Practice Test resource on Computer Concepts Coursemate.

True/False   Mark T for True and F for False.

_____ 1. Malware authors focus on social media, with the goal of stealing personal information. (106)

_____ 2. Although they can save space, all-in-one desktops usually are more expensive than a system unit and monitor purchased separately. (108)

_____ 3. Most traditional and ultrathin laptop and ultrabook screens range in size from 7 to 10 inches, and most tablet and netbook screens range in size from 11 to 18 inches. (110)

_____ 4. Dedicated servers typically require a faster processor, more memory, and additional storage. (112)

_____ 5. Most computers and electronic devices are analog, which use only two discrete states: on and off. (119)

_____ 6. Some mobile devices allow you to transfer photos using wireless technologies such as Bluetooth and Wi-Fi. (121)

_____ 7. Most smartphones also can function as portable media players and digital cameras. (122)

_____ 8. Because embedded computers are components in larger products, they usually are small and have limited hardware. (127)

_____ 9. Instead of the term, port, the term, connector, sometimes is used to identify audio and video ports. (129)

_____ 10. Newer versions of USB are backward compatible, which means they support only new USB devices, not older ones. (131)

_____ 11. Because the processor in a computer is particularly sensitive to current fluctuations, you always should use a surge protector. (136)

_____ 12. An offline UPS always runs off the battery. (136)

Multiple Choice   Select the best answer.

1. Examples of a(n) _____ device include keyboard, mouse, microphone, monitor, printer, USB flash drive, scanner, webcam, and speakers. (104)
   a. output
   b. input
   c. mobile
   d. peripheral

2. Some people use the term _____ to refer to the case that contains and protects the motherboard, hard disk drive, memory, and other electronic components of the computer from damage. (106)
   a. system unit
   b. phablet
   c. thin client
   d. USB hub

3. Some desktops, called a(n) _____, do not have a tower and instead house the screen and system unit in the same case. (107)
   a. peripheral unit
   b. system unit
   c. all-in-one desktop
   d. gaming computer

4. Power users may work with a high-end desktop, sometimes called a(n) _____, that is designed to handle intense calculations and powerful graphics. (107)
   a. laptop
   b. gaming desktop
   c. server farm
   d. workstation

5. Services provided by _____ include storing content and controlling access to hardware, software, and other resources on a network. (111)
   a. jacks
   b. servers
   c. fault-tolerant computers
   d. mainframes

6. A dedicated server that backs up and restores files, folders, and media is referred to as a(n) _____. (111)
   a. web server
   b. file server
   c. storage server
   d. backup server

7. A four- or five-digit number assigned to a specific content or mobile service provider is referred to as a(n) _____. (118)
   a. CSC
   b. MMS
   c. SMS
   d. SLR

8. A(n) _____ can connect up to 127 different peripheral devices together with a single connector. (131)
   a. SLR device
   b. USB port
   c. port replicator
   d. docking station

Checkpoint

Matching   Match the terms with their definitions.

_____ 1. peripheral device (104)

_____ 2. motherboard (106)

_____ 3. CPU (106)

_____ 4. tower (106)

_____ 5. phablet (110)

_____ 6. virtualization (112)

_____ 7. thin client (113)

_____ 8. resolution (122)

_____ 9. pairing (132)

_____ 10. standby UPS (136)

a. term used to refer to a device that combines the features of a smartphone with a tablet

b. power supply that switches to battery power when a problem occurs in the power line

c. metal or plastic frame that houses the system unit on a desktop

d. component you connect to a computer or mobile device to expand its capabilities

e. terminal that looks like a desktop but has limited capabilities and components

f. the practice of sharing or pooling computing resources, such as servers and storage devices

g. electronic component that interprets and carries out the basic instructions that operate a computer

h. the number of horizontal and vertical pixels in a display device

i. process of initiating contact between two Bluetooth devices and allowing them to communicate with each other

j. the main circuit board of a personal computer

Short Answer   Write a brief answer to each of the following questions.

1. Describe the different types of desktops. (107) What should you consider when purchasing a desktop? (107–108)

2. How do netbooks and ultrathin laptops differ from traditional laptops? (109) What privacy issues have arisen with webcams in mobile devices? (109)

3. Describe the different types of tablets. (109) What is a stylus? (109)

4. List the three form factors for servers. (112) What are the advantages of virtual servers? (112)

5. What typing options are available on smartphones? (117–118) Differentiate between predictive text input and a swipe keyboard app. (117)

✳ Consider This   Answer the following questions in the format specified by your instructor.

1. Answer the critical thinking questions posed at the end of these elements in this chapter: Ethics & Issues (109, 117, 124, 126, 127), How To (121, 131, 132, 133), Mini Features (107, 110, 123), Secure IT (106, 114, 119, 136), and Technology @ Work (139).

2. How do malware authors use social media to spread infection? (106)

3. What are the two main components of the motherboard? What is in the system unit? (106)

4. What are the features of a gaming desktop? What is a workstation? (107)

5. How do netbooks and ultrathin laptops differ? When might you use each? (109)

6. What additional requirements are associated with a dedicated server? (111)

7. How does a POS terminal serve as input? Why would a grocery store use a POS terminal? (113)

8. What information might you receive from a web to mobile text message? For what purpose is a common short code (CSC) used? (118)

9. What is the difference between enhanced and optical resolution? (122)

10. 📱 When purchasing a smartphone, what should you consider when choosing a wireless plan? (123)

11. What is the purpose of a docking station? (132)

12. Why might you want to connect your phone to a Wi-Fi network? (133)

13. How can you configure your computer or mobile device to help track it in case of theft? (134)

14. How does a surge protector work? What is the purpose of an uninterruptible power supply? (135)

15. How can you prevent technology-related tendonitis and CTS? (136)

❋ How To: Your Turn

The How To: Your Turn exercises present general guidelines for fundamental skills when using a computer or mobile device and then require that you determine how to apply these general guidelines to a specific program or situation.

Instructions: You often can complete tasks using technology in multiple ways. Figure out how to perform the tasks described in these exercises by using one or more resources available to you (such as a computer or mobile device, articles on the web or in print, online or program help, user guides, blogs, podcasts, videos, other individuals, trial and error, etc.). Summarize your 'how to' steps, along with the resource(s) used, in the format requested by your instructor (brief report, presentation, discussion, blog post, video, or other means).

❶ Synchronize a Device

Synchronizing a mobile device with the cloud or a computer provides a backup location for your data should your device fail, or become lost or stolen. While companies such as Google and Apple typically will allow you to download your purchased apps again free of charge, you also should synchronize your data so that it is available in the event a problem with your device arises. The following steps guide you through the process of synchronizing a device.

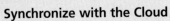

© Iain Masterton / Alamy

Synchronize with the Cloud

a. Search for an app compatible with your device that allows you to synchronize the data on your device with the cloud. Some device manufacturers, such as Apple, provide a service to synchronize your device with the cloud.
b. If necessary, download and install the app.
c. The first time you run the app, you may need to enter some personal information so that you are able to sign in and access your data in the future.
d. Configure the app to synchronize at your desired interval. If you are synchronizing a smartphone, keep in mind that synchronizing with the cloud will require a data plan. Be sure your data plan supports the amount of data that will be synchronized.
e. Once you have configured the synchronization settings successfully, select the option to manually synchronize your device at this time.

Synchronize with a Computer

a. Install and run the app designed to synchronize your device with your computer. For instance, iTunes is used to synchronize Apple devices with a computer.
b. Connect the device to the computer using the synchronization cable provided.
c. When the synchronization is complete, a message will inform you that it is safe to disconnect the device. Do not disconnect the device before the synchronization is complete, as that may damage the data on the device.

Retrieve Synchronized Data

If you lose your device or the data on your device, you can retrieve the data previously synchronized. To retrieve data synchronized previously, follow the instructions in the program or app used to synchronize your data.

Exercises

1. What type of device are you attempting to synchronize? What programs and apps are available to synchronize your device with the cloud? What programs and apps are available to synchronize your device with a computer?
2. Which program or app did you use to synchronize your device? Why did you choose that program or app instead of the others?
3. How long did it take to synchronize your device? What data on your device did the program or app synchronize?

❷ Evaluate Earbuds and Headphones

Earbuds and headphones are used to listen to music and other audio files on computers and mobile devices. Selecting the proper product not only depends on the style you prefer, but also the type of audio you will be playing. Prices for earbuds and headphones can range from only a few dollars to several hundred dollars, so it is important to know what you are purchasing. The following guidelines describe what to look for when evaluating earbuds and headphones.

- Determine which style you prefer. Earbuds rest inside your ear, while headphones rest over your ear. Experiment with both types and determine which is more comfortable for you.
- Determine the quality you desire. If you listen to music casually and typically do not notice variations in sound quality, a higher-end product might not be necessary. Alternatively, if sound quality is important, you may consider a more expensive set. Note that a higher price does not always indicate better quality; read online product reviews for information about the sound quality of various products.

How To: Your Turn

- Decide whether you would like a noise cancelling feature. Noise cancelling headphones help block external noise while you are listening to the audio on your device. Noise cancelling headphones sometimes require batteries, and you are able to turn the noise cancelling feature on and off. If you will be listening to audio in locations where you also need to hear what is going on around you, consider purchasing a product without this feature.

Exercises

1. Do you prefer earbuds or headphones? Why?
2. Is sound quality important to you? Why or why not?
3. Based on your preferences and needs, which type of product (earbuds or headphones) is best for you? Locate a product online that meets your specifications. What brand is it? How much does it cost? Where is this product available?

❸ Ergonomically Arrange Your Computer Work Area

Maintaining an ergonomic work area will help keep you comfortable while working with your computer. In addition to providing comfort, an ergonomic work area also will help minimize health risks associated with using a computer frequently. The following guidelines will help you set up an ergonomic work area:

- Set up a work area of at least two feet by four feet.
- The viewing angle between your eyes and the center of the screen should be 20 degrees, and your eyes should be 18 to 28 inches away from the screen.
- Your elbows should be at about 90 degrees and your arms and hands should be approximately parallel to the floor.
- The height of the keyboard from the floor should be 23 to 28 inches, depending on the height of the user.
- Use a chair with four or five legs that allows you to adjust the height.
- Your feet should rest flat on the floor.

Exercises

1. Evaluate your current work area. Is it ergonomic? Why or why not?
2. What types of health risks might a nonergonomic work area pose?
3. What are some additional guidelines you can follow to help minimize health risks while using your computer?

❹ Find, Download, and Read an E-Book on an E-Book Reader

Most e-book readers enable you to find and download new e-books without having to connect to a computer first. To search for and download an e-book, you need to establish an Internet connection through either Wi-Fi or a mobile data plan. The following steps guide you through the process of finding, downloading, and reading an e-book on an e-book reader.

a. Turn on your e-book reader and establish an Internet connection.
b. Navigate to the store on your e-book reader where you can search for and download e-books.
c. Locate the option to search available e-books and then enter the desired search text. You usually can search by the book's title, author, or genre.
d. Perform the search and then browse the search results for the book you want to download and install.
e. Select the option to download the book. Please note that many books cost money to download. If your payment information was entered previously, you may be charged for downloading this e-book. If you do not want to be charged, locate and download an e-book that is free.
f. When the download is complete, return to your list of installed e-books.
g. Select the e-book you have just downloaded to read the e-book.

Exercises

1. What type of e-book reader do you have? Are you happy with the selection of e-books on your e-book reader?
2. In addition to e-book readers, what other types of devices allow you to read e-books?
3. Do e-books cost more or less than traditional print books? What are the advantages and disadvantages of using e-books?

✳ Internet Research

The Internet Research exercises broaden your understanding of chapter concepts by requiring that you search for information on the web.

Instructions: Use a search engine or another search tool to locate the information requested or answers to questions presented in the exercises. Describe your findings, along with the search term(s) you used and your web source(s), in the format requested by your instructor (brief report, presentation, discussion, blog post, video, or other means).

❶ Making Use of the Web
Shopping and Auctions

E-retailers are changing the ways consumers shop for goods. One market research firm reports that nearly three-fourths of shoppers complete one-half of all their transactions online. As shoppers grow increasingly loyal to e-commerce, shopping sites have become more sophisticated, and brick-and-mortar stores have adapted to the online presence. Nearly 50 percent of smartphone and mobile device owners use apps to compare prices and purchase items every month.

Online auctions offer another convenient method of shopping for and selling practically anything imaginable. Most auction sites organize products in categories and provide photos and descriptions. eBay is one of thousands of Internet auction websites and is the world's largest personal online trading community. In addition, craigslist is a free online equivalent of classified advertisements.

(a) Visit two shopping websites and search for the latest iPhone or Android phone. Which features do these websites offer compared with the same offerings in brick-and-mortar stores? What are the advantages and disadvantages of shopping online? What policies do these websites offer for returning items? Which items have you purchased online?

(b) Visit an auction website and search for two objects pertaining to your hometown or a favorite vacation destination. For example, if you are from Boston, search for a Red Sox or Bruins jersey. Describe these two items. How many people have bid on these items? Who are the sellers? What are the opening and current bids?

❷ Social Media

Businesses are discovering that using social media is an efficient and effective method of building brand loyalty and promoting the exchange of ideas. According to a recent study, 80 percent of American Internet users visit social networking sites and blogs, and 60 percent discover particular brands and companies by reading material posted on these websites when conducting research using a variety of online sources. The informal communication between consumers and company representatives can help maintain credibility and promote trust. Twitter, Facebook, and other social media often are used to befriend customers, give a positive feeling about services and goods, engage readers, and market new ideas. Subscribers share their opinions, thoughts, and experiences, either positive or negative, through product and service reviews.

Visit at least three Twitter, Facebook, or other social media sites and review the content. How many Twitter followers or Facebook 'likes' does the website have? Which posts are engaging and promote positive attitudes about the companies and the products or services offered? How many user-generated reviews and product ratings are shown? How do the websites encourage sharing opinions? In which ways do the companies respond to and interact with customers? If negative posts are written, does the company respond professionally and positively?

❸ Search Sleuth
(1) What are four 10-letter words composed of letters on a keyboard's top row? (2) Which company is

Source: ebay

Internet Research ✳

credited with developing the first phablet? (3) Who wrote the official five-note Intel signature jingle? How many weeks did he need to write this jingle? (4) What trait do Belle, Deep Blue, Hydra, Gravity Pipe, MDGRAPE-3, and Deep Crack share? (5) For which purpose was the Barcode Battler developed? (6) In which shopping center was the first ATM installed in the United States? When was it installed? (7) Which company has self-service kiosks located in the Empire State Building in New York City and the Willis Tower in Chicago? (8) What is the name of the predictive text input method that Martin King and Cliff Kushler developed? (9) JPL's Frederic C. Billingsley used the word, pixel, to describe which images in 1965? (10) Who created the first video game joystick in 1967?

❹ Green Computing

When your computer is turned on, many of the components generate heat. The processor and video card become so hot that, in theory, they could be used as a hot plate to cook food. If heat builds up inside the case, the components could become seriously damaged.

Most computers have a cooling system that consists of an intake fan on the front and sometimes the sides of the case and an exhaust fan on the back inside the power supply. These two fans work together to move cool air over the components and force hot air out the opposite side.

It is important to keep the computer as cool as possible, and the most effective method of meeting this requirement is to not restrict the airflow. Remove all obstructions on all sides of the case, especially the rear. Most likely the fans will become caked with dust and pet hair, so occasionally unplug the computer, open the case, and blow canned air over the fins. Place a cooling mat with an integrated fan under a laptop to keep temperatures in the normal range. If you are interested in checking the computer's internal heat, install temperature monitoring software.

Locate the intake and exhaust fans in your computer. How much space is allocated on all sides of the computer so that these fans can work efficiently? Can you remove any obstructions or position the case in a location that increases the airflow? Visit some websites that advertise cooling mats and temperature monitoring software. What are their costs, and which features do they have?

❺ Security

Surge protectors and uninterruptible power supplies offer electrical protection, and Secure IT 3-4 on page 136 gives suggestions about features to consider when purchasing these devices. Visit an electronics store or view websites with a variety of surge protectors from several manufacturers. Read the packaging to determine many of the specifications listed in Secure IT 3-4. Compare at least three surge protectors by creating a table using these headings: manufacturer, model, price, Joule rating, warranty, clamping voltage, energy-absorption rating, response time, and other features. Which surge protector do you recommend?

❻ Ethics in Action

Instant background checks on United States citizens are available through several websites. Computers search several decades of public record databases with billions of records containing warrants, state and local arrests, convictions, felonies, probation violations, revoked licenses, driving infractions, average income, bankruptcies, marriage and divorce history, reverse phone and email lookups, estimated income, property sales transactions, births, deaths, and census figures.

The companies that provide this information in an uncensored format offer a variety of methods of looking into an individual's criminal history. For example, some websites offer a free trial or have a free directory that allows a preliminary search for a person's name. If the name is found, then a full criminal background check can be ordered.

Do you believe people who run a background check are using the report only for personal reasons, or is the information being used to make employment or leasing decisions? When might a background check be useful, in addition to the desire to locate lost family members and friends or to verify that a babysitter does not have a criminal history? Would you consider running a background check on yourself? Visit at least two background check sites. What is the cost to run a search? Which databases are used? Do the websites offer an opportunity to individuals to remove information, or opt out, from the page?

✸ Problem Solving

The Problem Solving exercises extend your knowledge of chapter concepts by seeking solutions to practical problems with technology that you may encounter at home, school, work, or with nonprofit organizations. The Collaboration exercise should be completed with a team.

🔲 **Challenge yourself** with additional Problem Solving exercises by navigating to this book's Problem Solving resource on Computer Concepts CourseMate.

Instructions: You often can solve problems with technology in multiple ways. Determine a solution to the problems in these exercises by using one or more resources available to you (such as a computer or mobile device, articles on the web or in print, blogs, podcasts, videos, television, user guides, other individuals, electronics or computer stores, etc.). Describe your solution, along with the resource(s) used, in the format requested by your instructor (brief report, presentation, discussion, blog post, video, or other means).

Personal

1. **Slow Computer Performance**   Your computer is running exceptionally slow. Not only does it take the operating system a long time to start, but programs also are not performing as well as they used to perform. How might you resolve this?

2. **Faulty ATM**   When using an ATM to deposit a check, the ATM incorrectly reads the amount of the check and credits your account the incorrect amount. What can you do to resolve this?

3. **Insufficient Memory**   When trying to download a photo to your smartphone, an error message is displayed stating that no more storage space is available. What types of items might you remove from your phone to obtain additional storage space?

4. **Touch Input Does Not Work**   While working with your tablet, it suddenly stops responding to your touch gestures. What might be wrong, and how can you try to fix this problem?

5. **Potential Virus Infection**   While using your laptop, a message is displayed stating that your computer is infected with a virus and you should click a link to download a program designed to remove the virus. How will you respond?

Professional

6. **New Computer**   Your boss has given you the authority to purchase a new computer, but you are unsure of which one to buy. Each computer you review has a different type of processor, and you are having difficulty determining which one will suit your needs. How will you obtain this information?

7. **Server Not Connecting**   While traveling on a business trip, your phone suddenly stops synchronizing your email messages, calendar information, and contacts. Upon further investigation you notice an error message stating that your phone is unable to connect to the server. What are your next steps?

8. **Mobile Device Synchronization**   When you plug your smartphone into your computer to synchronize the data, the computer does not recognize that the smartphone is connected. What might be the problem?

9. **Cloud Service Provider**   Your company uses a cloud service provider to back up the data on each employee's computer. Your computer recently crashed, and you need to obtain the backup data to restore to your computer; however, you are unable to connect to the cloud service provider's website. What are your next steps?

10. **Connecting to a Projector**   Your boss asked you to give a presentation to your company's board of directors. When you enter the boardroom and attempt to connect your laptop to the projector, you realize that the cable to connect your laptop to the projector does not fit in any of the ports on your laptop. What are your next steps?

Collaboration

11. **Technology in Meteorology**   Your environmental sciences instructor is teaching a lesson about how technology has advanced the meteorology field. Form a team of three people to prepare a brief report about how technology and meteorology are connected. One team member should research how meteorologists predicted weather patterns before computer use became mainstream. Another team member should create a timeline illustrating when and how technology was introduced to the meteorology field, and the third team member should research the technology required for a typical news station to forecast and present the weather.

The Critical Thinking exercises challenge your assessment and decision-making skills by presenting real-world situations associated with chapter concepts. The Collaboration exercise should be completed with a team.

Critical Thinking ✳

 Challenge yourself with additional Critical Thinking exercises by navigating to this book's Critical Thinking resource on Computer Concepts CourseMate.

Instructions: Evaluate the situations below, using personal experiences and one or more resources available to you (such as articles on the web or in print, blogs, podcasts, videos, television, user guides, other individuals, electronics or computer stores, etc.). Perform the tasks requested in each exercise and share your deliverables in the format requested by your instructor (brief report, presentation, discussion, blog post, video, or other means).

1. Class Discussion

Technology Purchases You are the director of information technology at a company that specializes in designing and selling customizable sportswear for local high school and college sports teams. Most of the computer equipment is out of date and must be replaced. You need to evaluate the technology requirements of individual employees so that you can order replacements. Determine the type of computer or mobile device that might be most appropriate for the following employees: a graphic designer who exclusively works in the office, a cashier who is responsible for assisting customers with purchases, and a sales representative who travels to various locations and needs wireless communications capabilities. Consider the varying requirements of each, including mobility, security, and processing capabilities. Discuss various options that might work for each user, and considerations when purchasing each type of device.

2. Research and Share

Game Devices You manage a youth recreation center and have been given a grant to purchase a game console and accessories, along with fitness games, for use at the center. Use the web to research three popular recent game consoles. Choose five characteristics to compare the game consoles, such as Internet capabilities, multiplayer game support, storage capacity, television connection, and game controllers. Research fitness games for each console and what accessories are needed to run the games. Determine the goals of each game, such as skill-building, weight loss, or entertainment. Read user reviews of each game as well as professional reviews by gaming industry experts. If possible, survey your friends and classmates to learn about their experiences with each game, such as heart rate while playing the games, any fitness goals reached, and their enjoyment of the game. Compile your findings and then share with the class.

3. Case Study

Farmers' Market You are the new manager for a group of organic farmers who have a weekly market in season. The farmers' market would like to purchase a digital camera to upload pictures of its vendors and events to its Facebook page and its website. You prepare information about digital camera options to present to the board of directors. First, you research the cost and quality differences between point-and-shoot cameras and SLR cameras. Use the web to find a recent model of both camera types and compare the reviews, as well as the costs, for each. Make a list of additional features, such as video capabilities, editing capabilities, lens, megapixels, GPS, flash, and zoom. Determine how each camera stores the images, the amount of storage available, and how to transfer images to a computer. Explore whether software is included with the camera that can be used to edit, store, or organize the images after they are transferred to a computer. Compare your findings with the camera capabilities of a recent model smartphone. Determine what type of camera would be best for the market's needs and the capabilities that are most important. Compile your findings.

© Skylines / Shutterstock.com

Collaboration

4. **Technology in the Military** Technology is an integral part of military operations. Many military research projects use simulators that resemble civilian computer games. Your company has been contacted by the Department of Defense for a research project. Form a four-member team, and then form two two-member groups. Assign each group one of the following topics to research: (1) How have mobile computers and cloud computing affected issues of national security? (2) How can the utilization of microchips worn by soldiers, or wearable computers, be integrated into civilian use? Meet with your team and discuss your findings. Compile and organize your findings to include both topics and share with your class. Include any advantages or disadvantages, as well as any legal ramifications that may arise.

Beyond the Book

The Beyond the Book exercises expand your understanding of chapter concepts by requiring research.

Access premium content by visiting Computer Concepts CourseMate. If you have a Computer Concepts CourseMate access code, you can reinforce and extend your learning with MindTap Reader, practice tests, video, and other premium content for Discovering Computers. To sign in to Computer Concepts CourseMate at www.cengagebrain.com, you first must create a student account and then register this book, as described at www.cengage.com/ct/studentdownload.

Part 1 Instructions: Use the web or e-book to perform the task identified for each book element below. Describe your findings, along with the search term(s) you used and your web source(s), if appropriate, in the format requested by your instructor (brief report, presentation, discussion, blog post, video, or other means).

1. **Animation** 🖥 Review the animation associated with this chapter and then answer the question(s) it poses (121). What search term would you use to learn more about a specific segment of the animation?

2. **Consider This** Select a Consider This in this chapter (106, 107, 110, 112, 116, 118, 122, 125, 128, 133, 135, 137, 138) and find a recent article that elaborates on the topic. What information did you find that was not presented in this book or e-book?

3 **Drag-and-Drop Figures** 🖥 Complete the Drag-and-Drop Figure activities associated with this chapter (111, 112, 115, 118, 120, 121, 128, 140). What did you learn from each of these activities?

4. **Ethics & Issues** Select an Ethics & Issues in this chapter (109, 117, 124, 126, 127) and find a recent article that supports one view presented. Does the article change your opinion about the topic? Why or why not?

5. **Facebook & Twitter** Review a recent Discovering Computers Facebook post or Twitter Tweet and read the referenced article(s). What did you learn from the article?

6. **High-Tech Talk** 🖥 Locate an article that discusses topics related to touch screens. Would you recommend the article you found? Why or why not?

7. **How To** Select a How To in this chapter (121, 131, 132, 133) and find a recent article that elaborates on the topic. Who would benefit from the content of this article? Why?

8. **Innovative Computing** 🖥 Locate two additional facts about IBM's Watson or volunteer computing. Do your findings change your opinion about the future of this innovation? Why or why not?

9. **Internet Research** Use the search term in an Internet Research (106, 107, 113, 116, 120, 125, 134, 138) to answer the question posed in the element. What other search term could you use to answer the question?

10. **Mini Features** Locate an article that discusses topics related to one of the mini features in this chapter (107, 110, 123). Do you feel that the article is appropriate for this course? Why or why not?

11. **Secure IT** Select a Secure IT in this chapter (106, 114, 119, 136) and find a recent article about the topic that you find interesting. How can you relate the content of the article to your everyday life?

12. **Technology @ Work** Locate three additional, unique usages of technology in the meteorology industry (139). What makes the use of these technologies unique to the meteorology industry?

13. **Technology Innovators** 🖥 Locate two additional facts about Dell and Michael Dell, Samsung, Sony, and Nintendo. Which Technology Innovator impresses you most? Why?

14. **Third-Party Links** 🖥 Visit one of the third-party links identified in this chapter (104, 106, 107, 109, 110, 114, 117, 119, 120, 121, 123, 124, 125, 126, 133, 136, 139) and read the article or watch the video associated with the link. Would you share this link on your online social network account? Why or why not?

Part 2 Instructions: Find specific instructions for the exercises below in the e-book or on Computer Concepts CourseMate. Beside each exercise is a brief description of its online content.

1. 🖥 **You Review It** Search for and review a video, podcast, or blog post about current models and features of desktops, traditional laptops, or ultrathin laptops.

2. 🖥 **Windows and Mac** Enhance your understanding and knowledge about using Windows and Mac computers by completing the Power Management and Using Removable Flash Memory activities.

3. 🖥 **Android, iOS, and Windows Mobile** Enhance your understanding of mobile devices by completing the Power Management and Transfer Photos from a Digital Camera or Mobile Device to a Computer activities.

4. 🖥 **Exploring Computer Careers** Read about a career as a help desk specialist, search for related employment ads, and then answer related questions.

5. 🖥 **App Adventure** Check the news, sports, and weather using apps on your smartphone or tablet.

Programs and Apps

Using Software at Work, School, and Home

4

People use a variety of programs and apps on their computers and mobile devices.

"I use my computer and mobile devices to complete homework assignments, pay bills, edit digital photos, post social media updates, and play games. I also use an antivirus program. What other programs and apps could I need?"

True, you may be familiar with some of the material in this chapter, but do you know . . .

How to recognize a virus hoax?

If you should copy information from the web into a research paper?

Whether health and fitness apps can help you reach your goals?

How to back up your computer?

Why you should use a personal firewall?

Who uses iTunes U?

How to avoid risks when using payment apps?

Why you would use a QR code?

How antivirus programs detect viruses?

How the entertainment industry uses programs and apps?

Which office web and mobile apps are best suited to your needs?

Which software company is named after a creek?

How to recognize a phishing message?

How to defragment a hard disk?

For these answers and to discover much more information essential to this course, read this chapter and visit the associated Computer Concepts CourseMate at www.cengagebrain.com.

✔ Objectives

After completing this chapter, you will be able to:

1 Identify the general categories of programs and apps

2 Describe how an operating system interacts with applications and hardware

3 Differentiate among the ways you can acquire programs and apps: retail, custom, web app, mobile app, open source, shareware, freeware, and public-domain

4 Identify the key features of productivity applications: word processing, presentation, spreadsheet, database, note taking, calendar and contact management, project management, accounting, personal finance, legal, tax preparation, document management, support services, and enterprise computing

5 Identify the key features of graphics and media applications: computer-aided design, desktop publishing, paint/image editing, photo editing and photo management, clip art/image gallery, video and audio editing, multimedia and website authoring, media player, and disc burning

6 Identify the uses of personal interest applications: lifestyle, medical, entertainment, convenience, and education

7 Identify the purpose of software used in communications

8 Identify the key features of security tools: personal firewall, antivirus programs, malware removers, and Internet filters

9 Identify the key features of file and disk management tools: file manager, search, image viewer, uninstaller, disk cleanup, disk defragmenter, screen saver, file compression, PC maintenance, and backup and restore

Programs and Apps

Using programs and apps, you can accomplish a variety of tasks on computers and mobile devices. Recall from Chapter 1 that a **program**, or **software**, consists of a series of related instructions, organized for a common purpose, that tells the computer what tasks to perform and how to perform them. An **application**, or **app**, sometimes called *application software*, consists of programs designed to make users more productive and/or assist them with personal tasks.

An *operating system* is a set of programs that coordinates all the activities among computer or mobile device hardware. Other programs, often called *tools* or *utilities*, enable you to perform maintenance-type tasks usually related to managing devices, media, and programs used by computers and mobile devices. The operating system and other tools are collectively known as *system software* because they consist of the programs that control or maintain the operations of the computer and its devices.

With programs and apps, you can create letters, memos, reports, and other documents; develop presentations; prepare and file taxes; draw and alter images; record and enhance audio and video clips; obtain directions or maps; play games individually or with others; compose email messages and instant messages; protect your computers and mobile devices from malware; organize media; locate files; and much more. Table 4-1 categorizes popular categories of programs and apps by their general use.

Table 4-1   Programs and Apps by Category

Category	Types of Programs and Apps	
Productivity (Business and Personal)	• Word Processing • Presentation • Spreadsheet • Database • Note Taking • Calendar and Contact Management • Project Management	• Accounting • Personal Finance • Legal • Tax Preparation • Document Management • Support Services • Enterprise Computing
Graphics and Media	• Computer-Aided Design (CAD) • Desktop Publishing • Paint/Image Editing • Photo Editing and Photo Management • Clip Art/Image Gallery	• Video and Audio Editing • Multimedia and Website Authoring • Media Player • Disc Burning
Personal Interest	• Lifestyle • Medical • Entertainment • Convenience • Education	
Communications	• Blogging • Browser • Chat Room • Discussion Forum • Email • FTP	• Instant Messaging • VoIP • Videoconference • Web Feeds • Wireless Messaging
Security	• Personal Firewall • Antivirus • Malware Removers • Internet Filters	
File and Disk Management	• File Manager • Search • Image Viewer • Uninstaller • Disk Cleanup	• Disk Defragmenter • Screen Saver • File Compression • PC Maintenance • Backup and Restore

CONSIDER THIS

Are the categories of programs and apps shown in Table 4-1 mutually exclusive?

Programs and apps listed in one category may be used in other categories. For example, photo editing applications, which appear in the graphics and media category, often also are used for business or personal productivity. Additionally, the programs and apps in the last three categories (communications, security, and file and disk management) often are used in conjunction with or to support programs and apps in the first three categories (productivity, graphics and media, and personal interest). For example, users may use file transfer software (FTP) to publish webpages created with website authoring programs.

 **Internet Research**

Which mobile operating system is the most widely used?

Search for: mobile operating system market share

The Role of the Operating System

The operating system serves as the interface between the user, the applications, and the computer or mobile device's hardware (Figure 4-1). To use applications, such as a browser or email program on a personal computer, your computer must be running an operating system. Similarly, a mobile device must be running an operating system to run a mobile app, such as a navigation or payment app. Desktop operating systems include Mac OS, Windows, and Linux. Mobile operating systems include Android, iOS, and Windows Phone.

Each time you start a computer or mobile device, the operating system is loaded (copied) from the computer's hard disk or mobile device's storage media into memory. Once the operating system is loaded, it coordinates all the activities of the computer or mobile device.

An Example of How an Operating System Interacts with a User, an Application, and Hardware

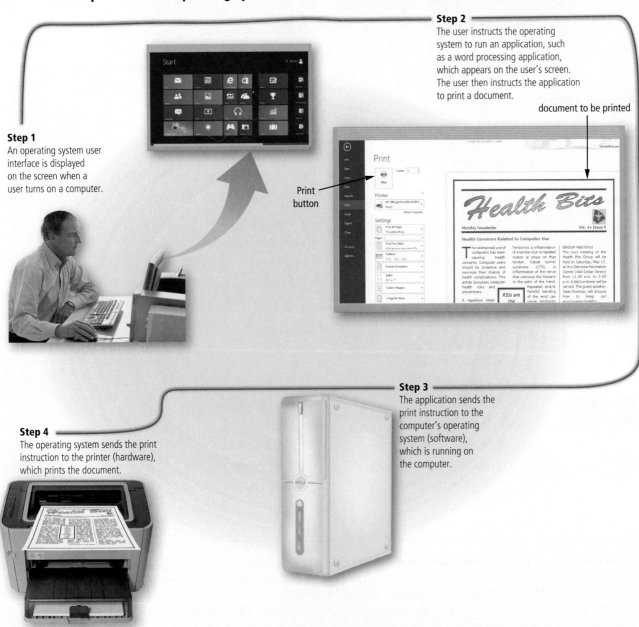

Step 1
An operating system user interface is displayed on the screen when a user turns on a computer.

Step 2
The user instructs the operating system to run an application, such as a word processing application, which appears on the user's screen. The user then instructs the application to print a document.

document to be printed

Print button

Step 3
The application sends the print instruction to the computer's operating system (software), which is running on the computer.

Step 4
The operating system sends the print instruction to the printer (hardware), which prints the document.

Figure 4-1   This figure shows how the operating system is the interface between the user, the application, and the hardware.

This includes running applications and transferring data among input and output devices and memory. While the computer or mobile device is running, the operating system remains in memory.

Software Availability

Software is available in a variety of forms: retail, custom, web app, mobile app, mobile web app, open source, shareware, freeware, and public domain.

- *Retail software* is mass-produced, copyrighted software that meets the needs of a wide variety of users, not just a single user or company. Some retail software, such as an operating system, typically is preinstalled on new computers. You also can purchase retail software from local stores and on the web. With online purchases, you may be able to download purchased programs immediately instead of waiting for the software to arrive by mail. Some retail programs have a *trial version*, which is an application you can use at no charge for a limited time, to see if it meets your needs. Some trial versions have limited functionality.

- *Custom software* performs functions specific to a business or industry. Sometimes a company cannot locate retail software that meets its unique requirements. In this case, the company may use software developers to create tailor-made custom software. Custom software usually costs more than retail software.

- A *web app* is an application stored on a web server that you access through a browser. Users typically interact with web apps directly at a website. Many websites provide free access to their apps. Some charge a one-time fee, while others charge recurring monthly or annual subscription fees. You may be able to use part of a web app free and pay for access to a more comprehensive program or pay a fee when a certain action occurs.

- A *mobile app* is an application you download from a mobile device's app store, sometimes called a marketplace, or other location on the Internet to a smartphone or other mobile device. Some mobile apps are preinstalled on a new mobile computer or device. Many mobile apps are free; others have a minimal cost — often less than a few dollars.

- A *mobile web app* is a web app that is optimized for display in a browser on a mobile device. Many app developers opt for web delivery because they do not have to create a different version for each mobile device's app store. Many web apps use a responsive design, which means the app displays properly on any computer or device.

- *Open source software* is software provided for use, modification, and redistribution. This software has no restrictions from the copyright holder regarding modification of the software's internal instructions and its redistribution. Open source software usually can be downloaded from a web server on the Internet, often at no cost. Promoters of open source software state two main advantages: users who modify the software share their improvements with others, and customers can personalize the software to meet their needs.

- *Shareware* is copyrighted software that is distributed at no cost for a trial period. To use a shareware program beyond that period, you send payment to the software developer. Some developers trust users to send payment if software use extends beyond the stated trial period. Others render the software useless if no payment is received after the trial period expires. In some cases, a scaled-down version of the software is distributed free, and payment entitles the user to the fully functional product.

- *Freeware* is copyrighted software provided at no cost by an individual or a company that retains all rights to the software. Thus, software developers typically cannot incorporate freeware in applications they intend to sell. The word, free, in freeware indicates the software has no charge.

- *Public-domain software* has been donated for public use and has no copyright restrictions. Anyone can copy or distribute public-domain software to others at no cost.

BTW

Copyright
A copyright gives authors, artists, and other creators of original work exclusive rights to duplicate, publish, and sell their materials.

Thousands of shareware, freeware, and public-domain programs are available on the Internet for users to download. Examples include communications, graphics, and game programs. Read Secure IT 4-1 for tips about safely downloading shareware, freeware, or public-domain software.

Recall from Chapter 1 that you typically need to install desktop apps on a computer. Installing is the process of setting up the software to work with a computer, printer, and other hardware. Mobile apps typically install automatically after you download the app from the device's app store. You usually do not need to install web apps before you can use them.

During installation of software or before the first use, a program or app may ask you to register and/or activate the software. *Software registration* typically is optional and usually involves submitting your name and other personal information to the software manufacturer or developer. Registering the software often entitles you to product support. *Product activation* is a technique that some software manufacturers use to ensure that you do not install the software on more computers than legally licensed. Usually, the software can be run a preset number of times, has limited functionality, or does not function until you activate it via the Internet or by phone. Thus, activation is a required process for programs that request it. Some software allows multiple activations; for example, you can install it and run it on a desktop and a laptop. Registering and/or activating software also usually entitles you to free program updates for a specified time period, such as a year.

Many desktop and mobile apps use an *automatic update* feature, where the updates can be configured to download and install automatically. With web apps, by contrast, you always access the latest version of the software.

 CONSIDER THIS

What is a license agreement?

A *license agreement* is the right to use a program or app. The license agreement provides specific conditions for use of the software, which a user typically must accept before using the software (Figure 4-2). Unless otherwise specified by a license agreement, you do not have the right to copy, loan, borrow, rent, or in any way distribute programs or apps. Doing so is a violation of copyright law; it also is a federal crime.

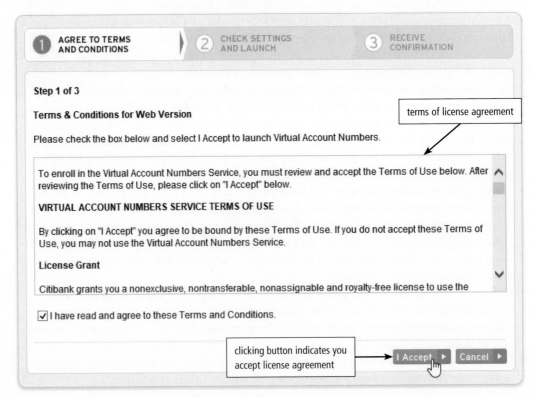

Figure 4-2 A user must accept the terms in a license agreement before using the software.
Source: Citigroup Inc

SECURE IT 4-1

Safe Downloading Websites

The temptation to download shareware, freeware, and public-domain software is high, especially when the cost of such useful or fun programs is free or extremely reasonable. Danger lurks, however, when websites tempt potential customers with catchy offers promising to speed up the computer or to acquire the latest versions of games and music. Many of these websites are filled with virus-infected software just waiting to be installed on an unsuspecting user's computer or mobile device.

Before downloading any software, consider these factors when locating and evaluating shareware, freeware, or public-domain websites:

- Search for popular shareware, freeware, and public-domain download websites.

The software generally is organized into evaluation categories, such as outstanding and recommended, or grouped into purpose, such as tools and gaming.

- Look for websites with programs for your particular type of computer or mobile device. Some websites exclusively offer Windows- or Apple-based products.

- Determine whether the latest versions of shareware, freeware, or public-domain software are available. Many developers update their programs frequently in an effort to thwart viruses and include new features. The newest versions, therefore, often are safer and easier to use than previous versions.

- Find websites with search engines to help you locate a variety of programs in a specific category. For example, if you need

antivirus software, you can search to find which shareware, freeware, and public-domain software is available.

- Seek websites with ratings for and reviews of products. Often, comments from users provide guidance in selecting the most desirable software for your needs.

If you follow these tips, you may find shareware, freeware, and public-domain software to be one of the best software bargains in the marketplace.

Have you ever used or downloaded programs or apps from a shareware, freeware, or public-domain software website? If so, what software did you acquire? If not, would you consider locating shareware, freeware, or public-domain software for your particular needs? Why or why not?

Productivity Applications

Productivity applications can assist you in becoming more effective and efficient while performing daily activities at work, school, and home. Productivity applications include word processing, presentation, spreadsheet, database, note taking, calendar and contact management, project management, accounting, personal finance, legal, tax preparation, document management, support services, and enterprise computing.

A variety of manufacturers offer productivity apps in each of these areas, ranging from desktop to mobile to web apps. Many have a desktop version and a corresponding mobile version adapted for smaller screen sizes and/or touch screens.

  BTW

Apple and Microsoft

Technology Innovators: You should be familiar with Microsoft and Apple.

Project Development

With productivity applications, users often create, edit, format, save, and distribute projects. Projects include documents, presentations, calendars, and more. During the process of developing a project, you likely will switch back and forth among these activities.

1. When you *create* a project, you enter text or numbers, insert images, and perform other tasks using a variety of input methods, such as a keyboard, a mouse, touch, or voice.
2. To *edit* a project means to make changes to its existing content. Common editing tasks include inserting, deleting, cutting, copying, and pasting.
   a. Inserting involves adding text, images, or other content.
   b. Deleting means that you are removing text, images, or other content.
   c. Cutting is the process of removing content and storing it in a temporary storage location, called a *clipboard*.
   d. Copying is the process of placing content on a clipboard, with the content remaining in the document. Read Ethics & Issues 4-1 on the next page for a discussion about unethical copying.
   e. Pasting is the process of transferring content from a clipboard to a specific location in a project.
3. When users *format* a project, they change its appearance. Formatting is important because the overall look of a document significantly can affect its capability to communicate

BTW

Points
The text you are reading in this book is about 10 points, which makes each character about 10/72, or approximately one-sixth, of an inch in height.

clearly. Examples of formatting tasks are changing the font, font size, and font style (Figure 4-3).

a. A *font* is a name assigned to a specific design of characters. Cambria and Calibri are examples of fonts.

b. *Font size* indicates the size of the characters in a particular font. Font size is gauged by a measurement system called points. A single point is about 1/72 of an inch in height.

c. A *font style* adds emphasis to a font. Bold, italic, underline, and color are examples of font styles.

4. During the process of creating, editing, and formatting a project, the computer or mobile device holds it in memory. To keep the project for future use requires that you save it. When you *save* a document, the computer transfers the project from memory to a local storage medium, such as a USB flash drive or hard disk, or cloud storage. Once saved, a project is stored permanently as a file.

5. You can distribute a project as a hard copy or electronically. A *hard copy* is information that exists on a physical medium, such as paper. To generate a hard copy, you *print* a project. Sending electronic files via email or posting them for others to view, on websites for example, saves paper and printer supplies. Many users opt for electronic distribution because it contributes to green computing.

 CONSIDER THIS

How often should you save a project?
Saving at regular intervals, such as every 5 or 10 minutes, ensures that the majority of your work will not be lost in the event of a power loss or system failure. Many programs have an AutoSave feature that automatically saves open projects at specified time intervals, such as every 10 minutes. Some web apps save your work instantly as you type.

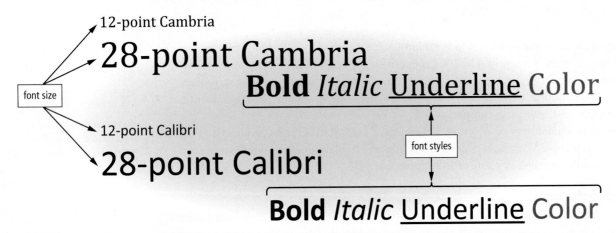

Figure 4-3 The Cambria and Calibri fonts are shown in two font sizes and a variety of font styles.
© Cengage Learning

 ETHICS & ISSUES 4-1

How Should Schools Deal with Internet Plagiarism?
If you ask a student whether plagiarism and cheating are ethical, would you be surprised to receive a response other than a resounding "No"? According to a survey, 55 percent of college presidents believe that plagiarism has increased during the last 10 years. Further, 89 percent of college presidents blame the Internet and computers for the increase. The Internet offers many ways to cheat purposefully, including websites that allow you to purchase or download a research paper. What students may not realize is

that copying information without properly citing it also is plagiarism.

Students who intentionally plagiarize blame peer pressure and competition as some reasons to cheat. Teachers have several tools to catch plagiarists, including a variety of Internet-based services that compare suspect papers to those found on the Internet and produce a report highlighting text that may have been copied. Some instructors, however, are reluctant to confront students with the evidence of plagiarism.

Some educators argue that the best way to prevent cheating is to educate students. First, teach them values and discuss the

consequences of cheating. Next, teach students how to cite sources properly and summarize information in their own words. Armed with this information, the student fully knows right from wrong and hopefully will make the responsible decision not to cheat.

How should educators deal with plagiarism? How should schools educate students about using the Internet for research? Should schools use a paper-comparison service in an attempt to stop cheating? Why or why not? Would you notify an instructor if you knew a classmate had plagiarized material for a research paper? Why or why not?

Word Processing

Word processing software, sometimes called a word processor, is an application that allows users to create and manipulate documents containing mostly text and sometimes graphics (Figure 4-4). Millions of people use word processing software on their computers and mobile devices every day to develop documents such as letters, memos, reports, mailing labels, newsletters, and webpages.

A major advantage of using word processing software is that it enables users to change their written words easily. Word processing software also has many features to make documents look professional and visually appealing. For example, you can change the shape, size, and color of characters; apply special effects, such as three-dimensional shadows; use built-in styles to format documents; and organize text in newspaper-style columns.

Most word processing software allows users to incorporate graphics, such as digital photos and clip art, in documents. **Clip art** is a collection of drawings, photos, and other images. In Figure 4-4, a user inserted an graphic of a tractor in the document. With word processing software, you easily can modify the appearance of an image after inserting it in the document.

You can use word processing software to define the size of the paper on which to print and to specify the margins. A feature, called wordwrap, allows users to type words in a paragraph continually without pressing the ENTER key at the end of each line. As you type more lines of text than can be displayed on the screen, the top portion of the document moves upward, or scrolls, off the screen.

Word processing software typically includes a spelling checker, which reviews the spelling of individual words, sections of a document, or the entire document.

⚡ Internet Research

What are the guidelines for writing business letters?

Search for: business letter writing

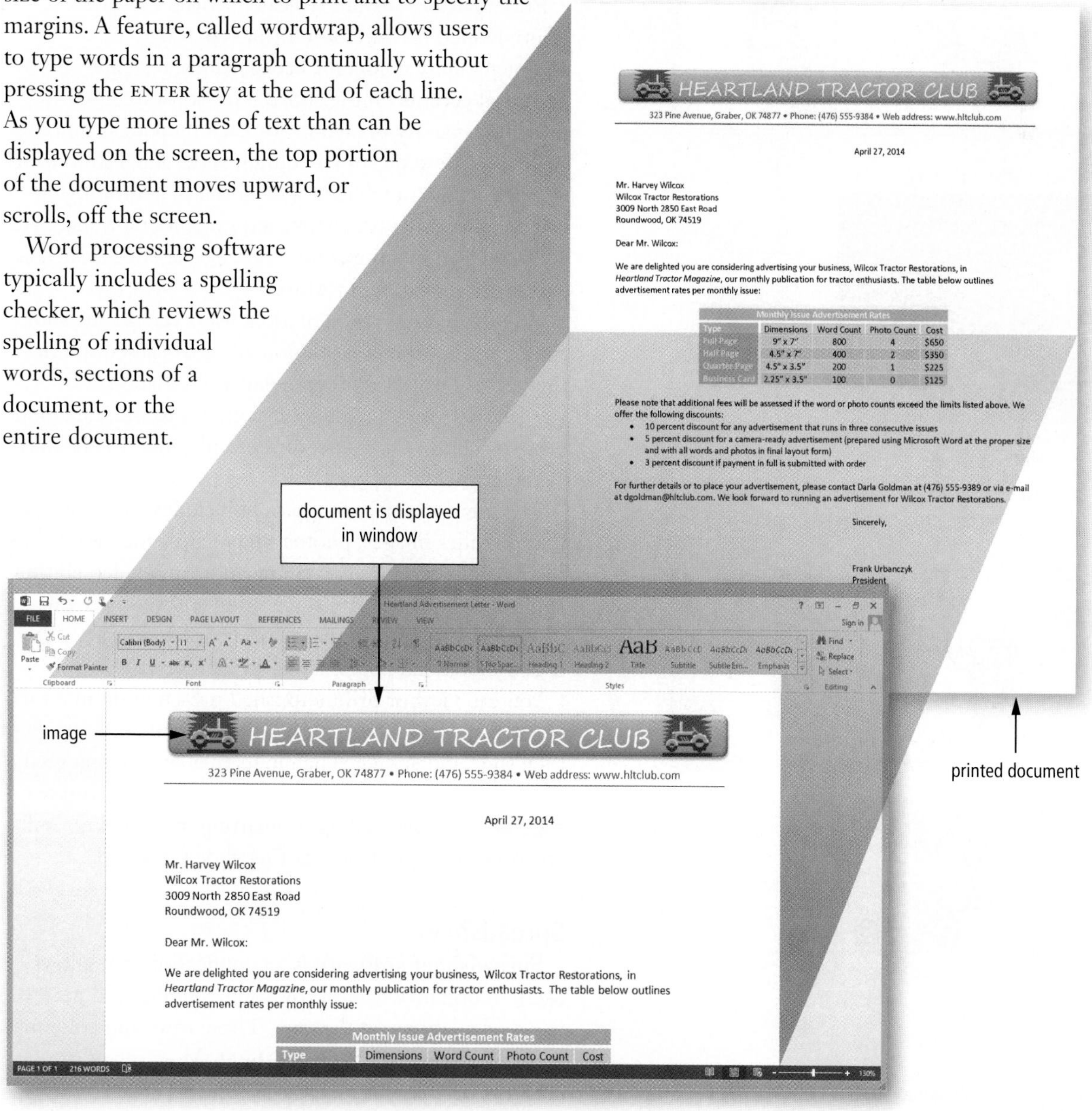

Figure 4-4 Word processing software enables users to create professional and visually appealing documents.
Source: Microsoft; © Cengage Learning

Figure 4-5 This presentation created with presentation software consists of five slides.

The spelling checker compares the words in the document with an electronic dictionary that is part of the word processing software. Some word processing programs also check for contextual spelling errors, such as a misuse of homophones (words pronounced the same but have different spellings or meanings, such as one and won).

Presentation

Presentation software is an application that allows users to create visual aids for presentations to communicate ideas, messages, and other information to a group. The presentations can be viewed as slides, sometimes called a *slide show*, that are displayed on a large monitor or on a projection screen from a computer or mobile device (Figure 4-5).

Presentation software typically provides a variety of predefined presentation formats that define complementary colors for backgrounds, text, and graphical accents on the slides. This software also provides a variety of layouts for each individual slide such as a title slide, a two-column slide, and a slide with clip art, a chart, a table, or a diagram. In addition, you can enhance any text, charts, and graphics on a slide with 3-D effects, animation, and other special effects, such as shading, shadows, and textures.

When building a presentation, users can set the slide timing so that the presentation automatically displays the next slide after a preset delay. Presentation software allows you to apply special effects to the transition between slides. One slide, for example, might fade away as the next slide appears.

Presentation software typically includes a clip gallery that provides images, photos, video clips, and audio clips to enhance presentations. Some audio and video editing applications work with presentation software, providing users with an easy means to record and insert video, music, and audio commentary in a presentation.

You can view or print a finished presentation in a variety of formats, including a hard copy outline of text from each slide and audience handouts that show completed slides. Presentation software also incorporates features such as checking spelling, formatting, researching, and creating webpages from existing slide shows.

Spreadsheet

Spreadsheet software is an application that allows users to organize data in rows and columns and perform calculations on the data. These rows and columns collectively are called a **worksheet**. Most spreadsheet software has basic features to help users create, edit, and format worksheets. A spreadsheet file is similar to a spiral notebook that can contain thousands of related individual worksheets. Data is organized vertically in columns and horizontally in rows on each worksheet (Figure 4-6).

Each worksheet usually can have thousands of columns and rows. One or more letters identify each column, and a number identifies each row. Only a small fraction of these columns and rows are visible on the screen at one time. Scrolling through the worksheet displays different parts of it on the screen.

A cell is the intersection of a column and row. The spreadsheet software identifies cells by the column and row in which they are located. For example, the intersection of column B and row 4 is referred to as cell B4. As shown in Figure 4-6, cell B4 contains the number, $1,000.29, which represents the wages for January.

Many of the worksheet cells shown in Figure 4-6 contain a number, called a value, that can be used in a calculation. Other cells, however, contain formulas that generate values. A formula performs calculations on the data in the worksheet and displays the resulting value in a cell, usually the cell containing the formula. When creating a worksheet, you can enter your own formulas. In Figure 4-6, for example, cell B17 could contain the formula =B9+B10+B11+B12+ B13+B14+B15+B16, which would add (sum) the contents of cells B9, B10, B11, B12, B13, B14, B15, and B16. That is, this formula calculates the total expenses for January.

A *function* is a predefined formula that performs common calculations such as adding the values in a group of cells or generating a value such as the time or date. For example, the function =SUM(B9:B16) instructs the spreadsheet application to add all of the numbers in the range of cells B9 through B16. Spreadsheet applications contain many built-in functions.

One of the more powerful features of spreadsheet software is its capability of recalculating the rest of the worksheet when data in a worksheet changes. Spreadsheet software's capability of recalculating data also makes it a valuable budgeting, forecasting, and decision-making tool. Another standard feature of spreadsheet software is charting, which depicts the data in graphical form, such as bar charts or pie charts. A visual representation of data through charts often makes it easier for users to see at a glance the relationship among the numbers.

BTW

Dan Bricklin

Technology Innovator: You should be familiar with Dan Bricklin (cocreator of the first spreadsheet program).

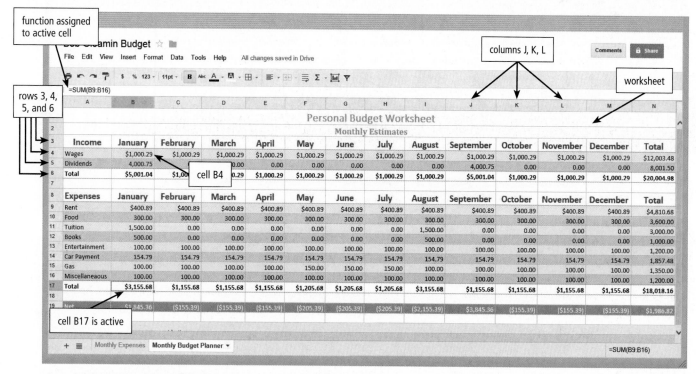

Figure 4-6   With spreadsheet software, you create worksheets that contain data arranged in rows and columns, and you can perform calculations on the data in the worksheets.
Source: Google Inc.

Database

A **database** is a collection of data organized in a manner that allows access, retrieval, and use of that data. In a manual database, you might record data on paper and store it in a filing cabinet. With a computerized database, such as the one shown in Figure 4-7, the computer stores the data in an electronic format on a local storage medium, such as a hard disk or optical disc, or on cloud storage.

Database software is an application that allows users to create, access, and manage a database. Using database software, you can add, change, and delete data in a database; sort and retrieve data from the database; and create forms and reports using the data in the database.

With most personal computer database programs, a database consists of a collection of tables, organized in rows and columns. Each row, called a record, contains data about a given item in the database, which is often a person, product, object, or event. Each column, called a field, contains a specific category of data within a record. The Publisher database shown in Figure 4-7 consists of two tables: a Customer table and a Book Rep table. The Customer table contains 15 records (rows), each storing data about one customer. The customer data is grouped into 10 fields (columns): CU # (customer number), Customer Name, Street, City, State, Postal Code, Amount Paid, Current Due, Returns, and BR # (book rep number). The Current Due field, for instance, contains the amount of money the customer owes the publisher. The Customer and Book Rep tables relate to one another through a common field, BR # (book rep number).

Users run queries to retrieve data. A query is a request for specific data from the database. For example, a query might request a list of customers whose balance is greater than $20,000. After obtaining the results of a query, database applications can present them on the screen, send them to the printer, or save them in a file.

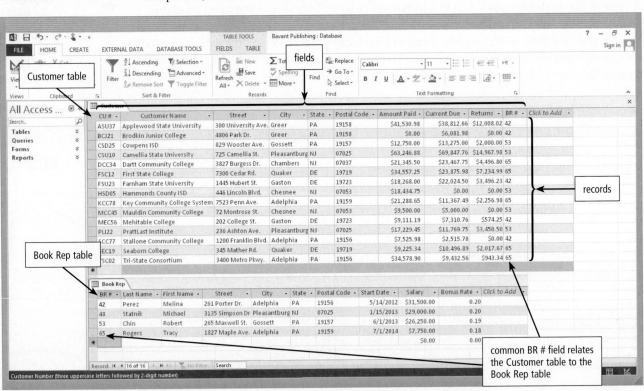

Figure 4-7 This database contains two tables: one for customers and one for book reps. The Customer table has 15 records and 10 fields; the Book Rep table has 4 records and 10 fields.
Source: Microsoft

Note Taking

Note taking software is an application that enables users to enter typed text, handwritten comments, drawings, sketches, photos, and links anywhere on a page and then save the page as part of a notebook (Figure 4-8). Users also can include audio recordings as part of their notes. Many note taking applications also include a calendar feature.

Users find note taking software convenient during meetings, class lectures and conferences, and in libraries and other settings that previously required a pencil and tablet of paper for recording thoughts and discussions.

Calendar and Contact Management

Calendar and contact management software is an application that helps you organize your calendar, keep track of contacts, and share this information with other devices or users (Figure 4-9). This software provides a way for individuals and workgroups to organize,

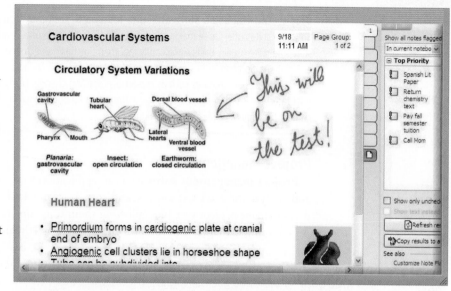

Figure 4-8 With note taking software, mobile users can handwrite notes, draw sketches, insert photos and links, and type text.
Source: Microsoft

find, view, and share appointment and contact information easily. Although sometimes available separately, calendar and contact management software typically exists as a unit in a single program. Many email applications include calendar and contact management features.

Calendar and contact management applications enable you to synchronize information. This means that all of your computers and mobile devices, along with your organization's server or cloud storage, have the latest version of any updated information.

Figure 4-9 Users can share schedules with other computers, mobile devices, and users via calendar and contact management applications.
Source: Google Inc.

Software Suite

A **software suite** is a collection of individual applications available together as a unit. Productivity software suites typically include, at a minimum, word processing, presentation, spreadsheet, and email applications.

Why would you use a software suite instead of a stand-alone application?

Software suites offer three major advantages: lower cost, ease of use, and integration. When you purchase a software suite, the suite usually costs significantly less than purchasing each application individually, or as stand-alone applications. Software suites provide ease of use because the applications in the suite normally use a consistent interface and share features such as clip art and spelling checker. Lastly, applications in a software suite often are integrated, which makes it easy to share information among them. For example, your email program can access your contact list to find recipients' email addresses.

Project Management

Project management software is an application that allows a user to plan, schedule, track, and analyze the events, resources, and costs of a project. Project management software helps users manage project variables, allowing them to complete a project on time and within budget. A marketing manager, for example, might use project management software to schedule the processes required in an advertising campaign (Figure 4-10).

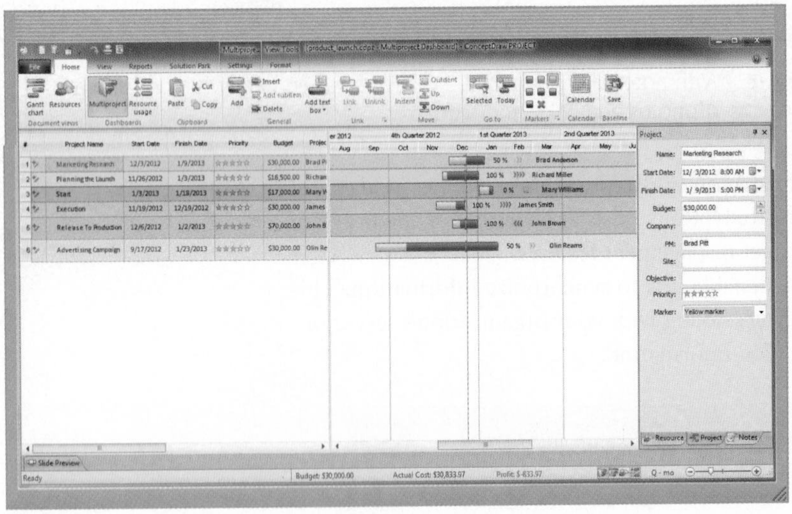

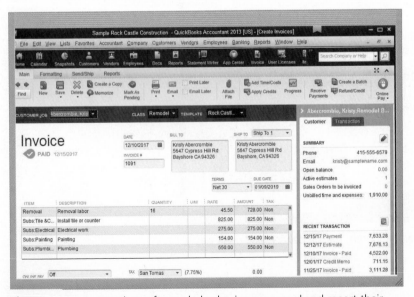

Figure 4-10 With project management software, you can plan and schedule a project.
Courtesy of CS Odessa

Figure 4-11 Accounting software helps businesses record and report their financial transactions.
Courtesy of Intuit

Accounting

Accounting software is an application that helps businesses of all sizes record and report their financial transactions. With accounting software, business users perform accounting activities related to the general ledger, accounts receivable, accounts payable, purchasing, invoicing (Figure 4-11), and payroll functions. Accounting software also enables business users to write and print checks, track checking account activity, and update and reconcile balances on demand.

Most accounting software supports online credit checks, bill payment, direct deposit, and payroll services. Some offer more complex features, such as job costing and estimating, time tracking, multiple company reporting, foreign currency reporting, and forecasting the amount of raw materials needed for products. The cost of accounting software for small businesses ranges from less than one hundred to several thousand dollars. Accounting software for large businesses can cost several hundred thousand dollars.

Personal Finance

Personal finance software is a simplified accounting application that helps home users and small/home office users balance their checkbooks, pay bills, track personal income and expenses, verify account balances, transfer funds, track investments, and evaluate financial plans (Figure 4-12). Personal finance software helps determine where, and for what purpose, you are spending money so that you can manage your finances.

Most personal finance software includes financial planning features, such as analyzing home and personal loans, preparing income taxes, and managing retirement savings. Other features include managing home inventory and setting up budgets. Most of these applications also offer a variety of online services, such as online banking and online investing. Read Secure IT 4-2 for safety tips when using personal finance apps on your smartphone or other mobile device.

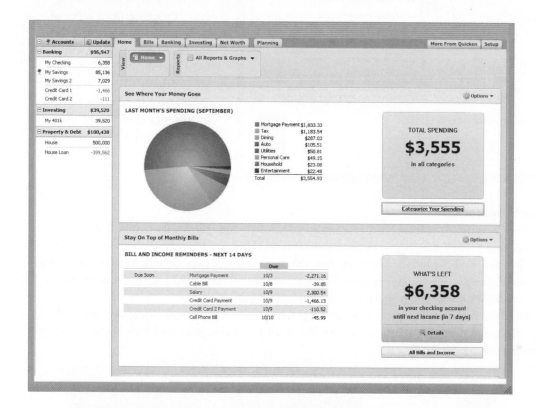

Figure 4-12 Personal finance software assists home users with tracking personal accounts.
Courtesy of Intuit

 SECURE IT 4-2

Using Personal Finance Apps Safely

Using personal finance apps on a smartphone to pay bills, deposit checks, verify payments, and transfer funds is convenient and easy. It also is a magnet for cybercriminals to snatch personal information and money from unsuspecting users. In recent years, Google and other companies with app marketplaces have removed more than 50 finance apps filled with malicious instructions to invade users' smartphones and gain access to information stored on their devices. By using caution and common sense, however, you can take steps to safeguard your funds and your identity by following these practices:

• **Evaluate the apps.** Fraudulent apps may resemble legitimate apps from financial institutions. They often, however, are riddled with misspellings and awkward

sentences. In addition, legitimate companies rarely promote downloading an app from a pop-up advertisement. If you desire an app from a bank or other financial institution, visit that company's website for instructions about downloading and installing its authentic apps.

• **Use strong passwords to access the apps.** Many of the more secure personal finance apps have dual passwords that involve typing a string of characters and also validating a picture.

• **Guard your smartphone.** One security firm estimates that the collective value of smartphones lost each year exceeds $30 billion. With that figure in mind, store as little personal information as possible on your phone so that if the mobile device is lost, the chances of losing your identity

and having your accounts compromised is lessened. Be certain to password protect your mobile device. Also install software to locate your lost or stolen device and to wipe (erase) its content remotely.

• **Verify the transactions.** Always verify your transactions by scrutinizing monthly statements. In addition, periodically check balances and alert your financial institution if any activity seems abnormal.

☀ Have you used finance apps? If so, which ones? When making transactions, do you follow some of the tips described above? If not, would you consider downloading an app to complete some common banking transactions? Why or why not?

Legal

Legal software is an application that assists in the preparation of legal documents and provides legal information to individuals, families, and small businesses (Figure 4-13). Legal software provides standard contracts and documents associated with buying, selling, and renting property; estate planning; marriage and divorce; and preparing a will or living trust. By answering a series of questions or completing a form, the legal software tailors the legal document to specific needs. Read Ethics & Issues 4-2 on the facing page to consider whether an attorney should review documents created with legal software.

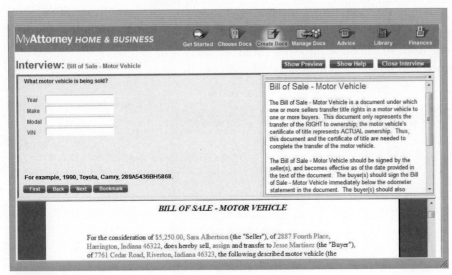

Figure 4-13 Legal software assists individuals, families, and small businesses in the preparation of legal documents.
Source: Avanquest Software

Tax Preparation

Tax preparation software is an application that can guide individuals, families, or small businesses through the process of filing federal taxes (Figure 4-14). These programs forecast tax liability and offer money-saving tax tips, designed to lower your tax bill. After you answer a series of questions and complete basic forms, the software creates and analyzes your tax forms to search for missed potential errors and deduction opportunities.

Once the forms are complete, you can print any necessary paperwork; then, they are ready for filing. Some tax preparation programs also allow you to file your tax forms electronically, a process called *e-filing*.

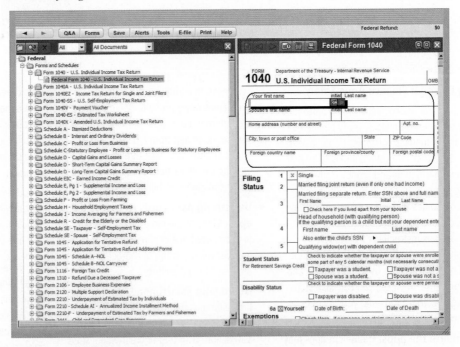

Figure 4-14 Tax preparation software guides individuals, families, or small businesses through the process of filing federal taxes.
Source: 2nd Story Software

🌐 BTW

📄 Adobe

Technology Innovator: You should be familiar with Adobe Systems.

Document Management

Document management software is an application that provides a means for sharing, distributing, and searching through documents by converting them into a format that can be viewed by any user. The converted document, which mirrors the original document's

 **ETHICS & ISSUES 4-2**

Should an Attorney Review Documents Created with Legal Software?
Hiring an attorney to create a will or prepare a contract can cost you thousands of dollars. Legal software or website services, on the other hand, typically cost less than $100 and sometimes are free. While it is tempting to opt for the route that will save money, you should evaluate the program to make sure it is up to date, addresses the latest laws and provisions that are specific to your state, and includes a legal dictionary. If you use a program that is out of date or creates an incomplete or invalid legal document, the cost for an attorney to correct the

document could exceed the amount you originally spent on the program.

In nearly all states in the U.S., it is legal to create your own will. Each state, however, has complex laws that govern the types of information a will should contain, how any taxes associated with the estate are paid, and more. Legal software, therefore, should account for all laws, allow you to create and change your will easily, and cost less than using an attorney. Regardless of whether you use an attorney or legal software, in most states a will must be printed, signed, witnessed, and notarized in order to be valid.

Attorneys caution against using legal software unless you intend to have an attorney review the document. Not only can they validate the accuracy of the document, attorneys claim they can provide for gaps in the software, such as successors to businesses, complexities that arise from second marriages, and provisions for children with special needs.

Would you use legal software to create a will or contract? Why or why not? Do you think it is wise to prepare a will using legal software? Why or why not? How do mistakes made as a result of using legal software differ from mistakes that result from human error?

---

appearance, can be viewed and printed without the software that created the original document. Some document management software allows users to edit content and add comments to the converted document (Figure 4-15).

Many businesses use document management software to share and distribute company brochures, literature, and other documents electronically. Home users distribute flyers, announcements, and graphics electronically. A popular electronic image file format that document management software uses to save converted documents is **PDF** (Portable Document Format), developed by Adobe Systems. To view and print a PDF file, you need Acrobat Reader software, which can be downloaded free from Adobe's website.

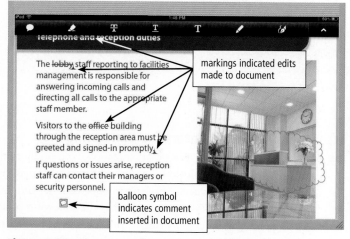

Figure 4-15 Users can edit content and add comments to a converted document.
Source: Adobe Systems Incorporated

 **CONSIDER THIS**

Can you create a PDF file only in document management applications?
No. Many productivity applications, such as word processing and spreadsheet programs, provide a method of saving a project as a PDF. This enables other users to view your document without requiring the application that created the project.

Internet Research
Are there alternatives to Adobe Reader?
Search for: adobe reader alternatives

Support Services

A variety of desktop, mobile, and web apps provide a service intended to make business or personal tasks easier to accomplish. Some applications focus on a single service, while others provide several services in a single application. Examples include reference, travel, and retail applications.

- Reference applications: Look up definitions, synonyms, addresses, directions, and more; or translate text from one language to another.
- Travel applications: Compare rates and prices of flights, hotels, and rental cars; order airline tickets; print boarding passes; make hotel or vehicle reservations; check traffic conditions; or send a package.
- Retail applications: Check product availability, compare prices locally or online, locate stores, pay for purchases (read Secure IT 4-3 on the next page for safety tips when using payment apps), manage rewards, use coupons, or track a shipment.

SECURE IT 4-3

Avoiding Risks Using Payment Apps

Paying for coffee at Starbucks or purchasing clothing at Macy's has become streamlined with the advent of mobile payment apps. More than 12 percent of smartphone users have paid for items at the cash register using an app, such as Google Wallet, on their phone instead of using cash or credit cards; this number is expected to increase as more merchants accept this form of payment and the apps become more secure. The users enjoy the convenience of maintaining control when they scan the phone at the checkout counter instead of handing a credit card to a clerk. This security factor becomes even more pronounced at restaurants, where unscrupulous employees take credit cards away from the table and then have full access to the personal information the cards contain.

Mobile payment providers state that using their apps is more secure than using plastic credit cards. The apps use a payment system on phones with a GPS system, which allows the provider to verify that the sales transition is legitimate. A smartphone user never enters an account number at the cash register because all the financial information is stored on the mobile payment system. If, however, an unauthorized charge is made, the Electronic Fund Transfer Act protects users as long as the claim is made promptly, generally within two days.

If you use your smartphone to make purchases, follow this advice from the security experts:

- Use a password on your phone.
- Select a payment app that requires you to enter a password to start the transaction.
- Choose a payment app that issues a receipt so that you can verify every purchase.
- Be vigilant about checking mobile transactions against monthly statements from the credit card company.

Should additional merchants allow payments using mobile apps? Should merchants be required to pay when customers use payment apps (like they do when customers use credit cards)? Why or why not? Where would you like to pay for transactions using your smartphone?

Source: Google Inc.

Enterprise Computing

A large organization, commonly referred to as an enterprise, requires special computing solutions because of its size and geographic distribution. A typical enterprise consists of a wide variety of departments, centers, and divisions — collectively known as functional units. Nearly every enterprise has the following functional units: human resources, accounting and finance, engineering or product development, manufacturing, marketing, sales, distribution, customer service, and information technology.

Software used in functional units is not mutually exclusive; however, each functional unit in an enterprise uses specific software, as outlined below.

- Human resources software manages employee information such as pay rate, benefits, personal information, performance evaluations, training, and vacation time.
- Accounting software manages everyday transactions, such as sales and payments to suppliers. Finance software helps managers budget, forecast, and analyze.
- Engineering or product development software allows engineers to develop plans for new products and test their product designs.
- Manufacturing software assists in the assembly process, as well as in scheduling and managing the inventory of parts and products.
- Marketing software allows marketing personnel to create marketing campaigns, target demographics, and track their effectiveness.
- Sales software enables the salesforce to manage contacts, schedule meetings, log customer interactions, manage product information, and take customer orders.
- Distribution software analyzes and tracks inventory and manages product shipping status.
- Customer service software manages the day-to-day interactions with customers, such as phone calls, email messages, web interactions, and instant messaging sessions.
- Information technology staff use a variety of programs and apps to maintain and secure the hardware and software in an enterprise.

⭐ **MINI FEATURE 4-1**

Web and Mobile Apps for Personal and Business Productivity

Whether you are checking appointments, sending or reading email messages, scanning business cards or bar codes, banking or looking up information online, making a purchase, arranging travel, or checking in with friends on social networking sites, web and mobile apps can assist your personal and business productivity.

Office Productivity

Maintaining an appointment calendar, accessing and editing documents, and checking email messages are common tasks of office productivity web and mobile apps. Calendar apps keep track of your appointments and synchronize information entered on a mobile device with your online or desktop calendar software. Email mobile apps assist you by displaying names from your phone's contact list that match a recipient's name as you enter it. Advanced features often found in office productivity web apps, such as sending email messages with attachments and formatting documents with fonts and colors, usually are omitted from their mobile counterparts to simplify the interaction.

Scanning

QR code readers, bar code scanners, and business card scanning apps all require use of the camera on a mobile device to scan a code or card. A *QR code* (quick response code) is a square-shaped coded graphic that corresponds to a web address or other information. A *QR code reader* app scans the QR code, as shown on the phone in the figure, and then displays the corresponding webpage in a browser. A bar code scanner reads the code and then looks up the product's ratings and reviews online. A business card scanner takes a photo of a business card and deciphers the name, address, and other information on the card to add it immediately to your device's contacts list.

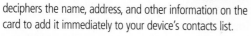
© iStockphoto / franckreporter

Financial

You can access bank accounts or investments using a financial app. Financial mobile apps help you track expenses as you spend money and notify you when a bill is due. To help secure information, financial mobile apps can disable access if your device is stolen or lost. Some banking mobile apps allow you to take a photo of a check with the device's camera and upload it to a server to process the deposit.

Reference

Dictionaries, encyclopedias, books, and directories are available online as reference apps. Many have associated mobile apps that format information for or take advantage of features on mobile devices. For example, rather than typing a search term in a dictionary web app to look up its definition, the corresponding mobile app also might offer voice input. On the mobile version of an encyclopedia app, you might shake the device to display random topics or redisplay the app's home screen. Some reference mobile apps also can download information directly to your phone for offline access.

Retail

Online marketplaces and payment services support buying and selling items and transferring funds from one party to another. Marketplace apps enable customers to read about products, enter or examine product reviews, and make purchases. A retail store mobile app might use a device's GPS to determine sellers or special deals closest to the customer's location. You also might use a device's camera to scan a product's bar code and then place the item in a shopping cart. Payment services allow customers to send money or pay for items using mobile devices.

Travel

Researching or purchasing flights, hotels, rental cars, or travel services is a common online task for personal and business travelers. Travel apps allow you to display and filter the results. Many allow you to share travel plans with others in your online social networks or display your itinerary and destination information on a map.

Source: KAYAK.com

Social Networking

Many users connect with their family, friends, and coworkers on social networking sites using mobile apps. Social networking web apps integrate instant messaging, video chat, and other interactive communications. Social networking mobile web apps use GPS technology to locate others nearby and generally do not have the real-time audio and video capabilities as their web-based counterparts.

☀ Compare the web and mobile versions of the same app for personal and business productivity. What features are common to both? Are there any features in the mobile version that are not found in the web version? Are there any features in the web version that are not found in the mobile version? Why do you think the developers made these decisions? What features would you like to see that are missing from either version of the app?

Graphics and Media Applications

 BTW

3-D Graphics
High-Tech Talk: Game developers spend many hours creating 3-D graphics, which appear to have height, width, and depth, giving realistic qualities to objects.

In addition to productivity applications, many people work with software designed specifically for their field of work. Power users such as engineers, architects, desktop publishers, and graphic artists often use sophisticated software that allows them to work with graphics and media. Many of these applications incorporate user-friendly interfaces or scaled-down versions, making it possible for the home and small business users also to create documents using these types of programs.

Graphics and media applications include computer-aided design, desktop publishing, paint/image editing, photo editing and photo management, clip art/image gallery, video and audio editing, multimedia and website authoring, media players, and disc burning.

Figure 4-16　Architects use CAD software to design building structures.
© Cyberstock / Alamy

Computer-Aided Design

Computer-aided design (CAD) software is a type of application that assists professionals and designers in creating engineering, architectural, and scientific designs and models. For example, engineers create design plans for vehicles and security systems. Architects design building structures and floor plans (Figure 4-16). Scientists design drawings of molecular structures.

Three-dimensional CAD programs allow designers to rotate designs of 3-D objects to view them from any angle. Some CAD software even can generate material lists for building designs.

Home and small business users work with less sophisticated design and modeling software. These applications usually contain thousands of predrawn plans that users can customize to meet their needs. For example, *home design/landscaping software* is an application that assists users with the design, remodeling, or improvement of a home, deck, or landscape.

 BTW

Online Photo Storage
Many online photo storage services enable you to create scrapbooks — selecting photos, adding captions, selecting backgrounds, and more.

Desktop Publishing

Desktop publishing software (DTP software) is an application that enables designers to create sophisticated publications that contain text, graphics, and many colors. Professional DTP software is ideal for the production of high-quality color documents such as textbooks, corporate newsletters, marketing literature, product catalogs, and annual reports. Designers and graphic artists can print finished publications on a color printer, take them to a professional printer, or post them on the web in a format that can be viewed by those without DTP software.

Home and small business users create newsletters, brochures, flyers, advertisements, postcards, greeting cards, letterhead, business cards, banners, calendars, logos, and webpages using personal DTP software (Figure 4-17). Although many word processing programs include DTP features, home and small business users often prefer to create DTP documents using DTP software because of its enhanced features. These programs typically guide you through the development of a project by asking a series of questions. Then, you can print a finished publication on a color printer or post it on the web.

Many personal DTP programs also include paint/image editing software and photo editing and photo management software (discussed next), enabling users to embellish their publications with images.

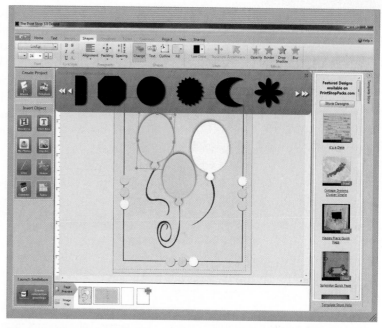

Figure 4-17 With personal DTP software, home users can create greeting cards.
Courtesy of Broderbund / Encore Software

Paint/Image Editing

Graphic artists, multimedia professionals, technical illustrators, and desktop publishers use paint software and image editing software to create and modify graphics such as those used in DTP documents and webpages. **Paint software**, also called *illustration software*, is an application that allows users to draw pictures, shapes, and other graphics with various on-screen tools such as a pen, brush, eyedropper, and paint bucket. **Image editing software** is an application that provides the capabilities of paint software and also includes the capability to enhance and modify existing photos and images. Modifications can include adjusting or enhancing image colors, adding special effects such as shadows and glows, creating animations, and image stitching (combining multiple images into a larger image).

Paint/image editing software for the home or small business user provides an easy-to-use interface; includes various simplified tools that allow you to draw pictures, shapes, and other images (Figure 4-18); and provides the capability of modifying existing graphics and photos. These products also include many templates to assist you in adding images to documents such as greeting cards, banners, calendars, signs, labels, business cards, and letterhead.

 BTW
Built-In Image Editing
Word processing, presentation, and other productivity applications usually include basic image editing capabilities.

Photo Editing and Photo Management

Photo editing software is a type of image editing software that allows users to edit and customize digital photos. With photo editing software, users can retouch photos, crop images, remove red-eye, erase blemishes, restore aged photos, add special effects, enhance image quality, change image shapes, color-correct images, straighten images, remove or rearrange

Figure 4-18 Home users can purchase affordable paint/image editing programs that enable them to draw images.
DrawPlus X5 © Serif (Europe) Ltd, | www.serif.com

objects in a photo, and more (Figure 4–19). Many applications also provide a means for creating digital photo albums.

When you purchase a digital camera, it usually includes photo editing software. Some digital cameras even have basic photo editing software built in so that you can edit the image directly on the camera. Read How To 4-1 for instructions about editing photos.

Figure 4-19 With photo editing software, users can edit digital photos, such as by adjusting the appearance of images as shown here.

PhotoPlus X6 © Serif (Europe) Ltd | www.serif.com

HOW TO 4-1

Edit Photos

When you take a photo using a digital camera or smartphone, you sometimes may want to edit the photo to remove unwanted areas, correct imperfections, or change its file size. Many apps allow you to edit photos easily. Several are easy to use and do not require advanced photo editing experience. Before editing a photo, you first should make a backup of the original photo. The table below describes common ways to edit photos using a photo editing app.

After you have edited a photo to your satisfaction, you may want to share the photo with others. Many mobile devices such as smartphones and tablets, as well as most photo editing apps, have built-in options that allow you to share photos. To share a photo on a mobile device or from within a photo editing app, follow these steps:
1. Open the photo to share.
2. Select the sharing option in the photo editing app or on the mobile device.

3. Choose the method by which to share the photo. Common ways to share photos include sending the photo as an email attachment, posting the photo to a social media site, and sending the photo as a picture message to another mobile device.

Examine your digital camera or other mobile device with a camera feature. Which of the photo editing features discussed here does it have? Did you notice any photo editing features in addition to those listed here?

ACTION	PURPOSE	STEPS
Crop	Removes unwanted areas of a photo	1. Select cropping tool. 2. Adjust photo border to define area(s) of the photo to keep and discard.
Remove red-eye	Removes the appearance of red eyes caused by the camera flash	1. Select red-eye removal tool. 2. Tap or click areas of the photo with the red-eye effect or drag a border around the affected areas.
Resize	Changes the physical dimensions of the photo	1. Select resizing tool. 2. Drag sizing handles to increase or decrease the photo's dimensions or type the desired height and width in the appropriate text boxes.
Compress	Decreases the photo's file size	1. Select option to compress photo. 2. Choose desired level of compression.
Adjust sharpness	Increases or decreases crispness of objects in the photo	1. Select option to adjust sharpness. 2. Drag sharpness slider to desired value or type the desired sharpness level into appropriate text box.
Adjust brightness	Adjusts lightness or darkness in the photo	1. Select option to adjust brightness. 2. Drag brightness slider to desired value or type the desired brightness level into appropriate text box.
Adjust contrast	Adjusts the difference in appearance between light and dark areas of the photo	1. Select option to adjust contrast. 2. Drag contrast slider to desired value or type the desired contrast level into appropriate text box.

With **photo management software**, you can view, organize, sort, catalog, print, and share digital photos. Some photo editing software includes photo management functionality. Read Ethics & Issues 4-3 to consider issues related to altering digital photos.

 ETHICS & ISSUES 4-3

Is It Ethical to Alter Digital Photos?
Many commercial artists, photojournalists, and creators of cartoons, book covers, and billboards use photo editing software to alter photos. Artists can use graphic software to alter digital photos by changing colors, resizing, adding or removing objects, and more.

In several high-profile cases, major news sources published intentionally altered photos. The alterations were more than just touching up a blemish. Instead, they were attempts to alter the facts, such as the instance where an unknown person combined separate photos of an anti-war activist and

a presidential candidate so that it looked like the candidate was protesting. Also making news are celebrity or model photos that artists retouch to change their physical appearance. Real estate agents on occasion have altered photos of homes for online listings or print brochures.

The National Press Photographers Association expresses reservations about digital altering and subscribes to the following belief: "As [photo]journalists we believe the guiding principle of our profession is accuracy; therefore, we believe it is wrong to alter the content of a photo in any way

... that deceives the public." Yet, some insist that the extent to which a photo "deceives the public" is in the eye of the beholder.

Is it ethical to alter digital photos? Why or why not? Does the answer depend on the reason for the alteration, the extent of the alteration, or some other factor? If some alteration is accepted, can photographic integrity still be guaranteed? Why or why not? Should magazines stop altering pictures of people to change their appearance? Why or why not?

Clip Art/Image Gallery

Applications often include a **clip art/image gallery**, which is a collection of clip art and photos. Some applications contain links to additional clips available on the web or are available as web apps. You also can purchase clip art/image gallery software that contains thousands of images (Figure 4-20).

In addition to clip art, many clip art/image galleries provide fonts, animations, sounds, video clips, and audio clips. You can use the images, fonts, and other items from the clip art/image gallery in all types of projects, including documents, brochures, worksheets, and slide shows.

Video and Audio Editing

Video editing software is an application that allows professionals to modify a segment of a video, called a clip. For example, users can reduce the length of a video clip, reorder a series of clips, or add special effects such as words that move across the screen. Video editing software typically includes audio editing capabilities. **Audio editing software** is an application that enables users to modify audio clips, produce studio-quality soundtracks, and add audio to video clips (Figure 4-21). Most television shows and movies are created or enhanced using video and audio editing software.

Figure 4-20 Clip art/image gallery software contains thousands of images.
Courtesy of IMSI / Design, LLC

 **BTW**

Instagram
Innovative Computing: You should be familiar with the photo sharing app, Instagram.

Figure 4-21 With audio editing software, users modify audio clips.
Source: Adobe Systems Incorporated

Many home users work with easy-to-use video and audio editing software, which is much simpler to use than its professional counterpart, for small-scale movie making projects. With these programs, home users can edit home movies, add music or other sounds to the video, and share their movies on the web. Some operating systems include video editing and audio editing applications.

Multimedia and Website Authoring

Multimedia authoring software allows users to combine text, graphics, audio, video, and animation in an interactive application (Figure 4-22). With this software, users control the placement of text and images and the duration of sounds, video, and animation. Once created, multimedia presentations often take the form of interactive computer-based presentations or web-based presentations designed to facilitate learning, demonstrate product functionality, and elicit direct-user participation. Training centers, educational institutions, and online magazine publishers use multimedia authoring software to develop interactive applications. These applications may be distributed on an optical disc, over a local area network, or via the Internet as web apps.

Website authoring software helps users of all skill levels create webpages that include graphics, video, audio, animation, and special effects with interactive content. In addition, many website authoring programs allow users to organize, manage, and maintain websites. Website authoring software often has capabilities of multimedia authoring software.

Productivity apps, such as word processing and spreadsheets, often include the capability of saving projects as webpages. This allows home and small business users to create basic webpages using an application they already own. For more sophisticated websites, however, users work with website authoring software.

 CONSIDER THIS

What is computer-based or web-based training?
Computer-based training (CBT) is a type of education in which students learn by using and completing exercises with instructional software. *Web-based training* (WBT) is a type of CBT that uses Internet technology to deliver the training. CBT and WBT typically consist of self-directed, self-paced instruction about a topic so that the user becomes actively involved in the learning process instead of being a passive recipient of information. Beginning athletes use CBT programs to learn the intricacies of participating in a sport. The military and airlines use CBT simulations to train pilots to fly in various conditions and environments. WBT is popular in business, industry, and schools for teaching new skills or enhancing existing skills of employees, teachers, and students.

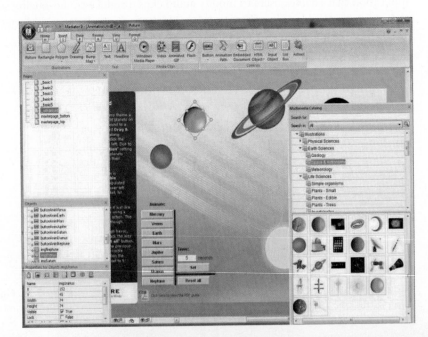

Figure 4-22
Multimedia authoring software allows you to create dynamic presentations that include text, graphics, audio, video, and animation.
Courtesy of Matchware Inc.

Media Player

A **media player** is a program that allows you to view images and animations, listen to audio, and watch video files on your computer or mobile device (Figure 4-23). Media players also may enable you to organize media files by genre, artist, or other category; create playlists; convert files to different formats; connect to and purchase media from an online media store or marketplace; tune into radio stations; download podcasts; burn audio CDs; and transfer media to portable media players. Read Ethics & Issues 4-4 to consider whether media downloads should be taxed.

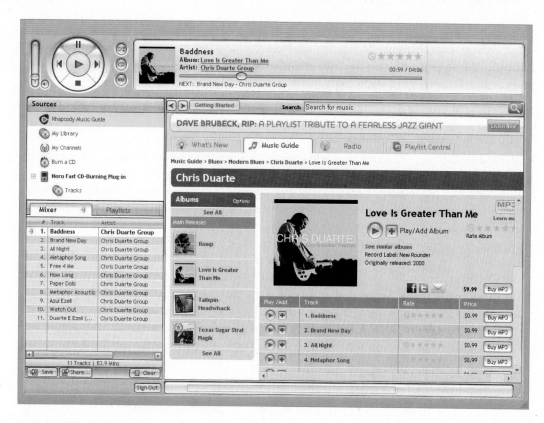

Figure 4-23
A media player.
Source: Rhapsody

☀ ETHICS & ISSUES 4-4

Should the Government Tax Media Downloads?

When you walk into a store and purchase a DVD of your favorite movie, chances are you also pay a state and/or local sales tax. If you purchase and download or stream the same movie online digitally, however, you are less likely to pay a sales tax. Some government taxing bodies seek to change that discrepancy. The main reason for the pressure to tax is lost revenue. State and local governments lose sales tax revenue when consumers purchase and legally download digital content instead of purchasing taxable, physical media. Another reason for pressure to tax stems

from the media industry looking to recoup lost sales due to illegally downloaded digital content. Some state laws attempt to distinguish between tangible goods (that include packaging and/or printed documentation) and intangible goods (that have no physical components to them), such as streaming video. Other laws express that if you can sense the goods (i.e., you can view or hear them), they are taxable.

Critics of the taxes claim that government should not tax the greenest form of media purchases. When you download and stream digital media, you eliminate packaging, optical discs, and use of delivery vehicles.

Critics also argue that governments single out media content due to pressure from the media industry. For example, some governments tax the purchase of newspapers, magazines, and books, but often the same content is sold online and is not taxed.

Should the government tax media downloads, such as music, video, e-books, newspaper articles, and magazine articles? Why or why not? Should digital content delivery be considered a service rather than a good by taxing bodies? Why?

Disc Burning

Disc burning software writes text, graphics, audio, and video files on a recordable or rewritable disc. This software enables home users easily to back up contents of their hard disk on an optical disc (CD/DVD) and make duplicates of uncopyrighted music or movies. Disc burning software usually also includes photo editing, audio editing, and video editing capabilities. When you buy a recordable or rewritable disc, it typically includes disc burning software.

Personal Interest Applications

Countless desktop, mobile, and web apps are designed specifically for lifestyle, medical, entertainment, convenience, or education activities. Most of the programs in this category are relatively inexpensive; many are free. Some applications focus on a single service, while others provide several services in a single application.

- Lifestyle applications: Access the latest news or sports scores, check the weather forecast, compose music, research genealogy, find recipes, or locate nearby restaurants, gas stations, or points of interest.
- Medical applications: Research symptoms, establish a fitness or health program, track exercise activity, refill prescriptions, count calories, or monitor sleep patterns.
- Entertainment applications: Listen to music or the radio, view photos, watch videos or shows, read a book or other publication, organize and track fantasy sports teams, and play games individually or with others.
- Convenience applications: Obtain driving directions or your current location, remotely start your vehicle or unlock/lock the doors, set an alarm or timer, check the time, calculate a tip, or use a flashlight.
- Education applications: Access how-to guides, learn or fine-tune a particular skill, follow a tutorial, run a simulation, assist children with reading and other elementary skills, or support academics (read How To 4-2 for instructions about using help with programs and apps).

 **Internet Research**
What is geocaching?
Search for: geocaching basics

 BTW
iTunes U
Innovative Computing: You should be familiar with the education app, iTunes U.

 HOW TO 4-2

Obtain Help about Programs and Apps
Multiple ways are provided to obtain help while using the programs and apps on a computer or mobile device. The program or app developer usually includes a Help feature in the program and/or online. In addition, third parties often post resources online that can provide further assistance. The following sections describe the various ways to obtain help about a program or app.

Help System
You typically can access help in a program or app using one of the following methods:
- Tap or click the Help or Information icon in the program or app. The appearance of Help or Information icons may vary, but they typically are identified by a question mark or the letter 'i' formatted in italic.

- Navigate the program or app's menu to locate the Help command.
- If you are using a program or app on a Windows desktop or laptop, press the F1 key on the keyboard to display Help content.

Online Help
Online help usually is available from the program or app developer. The following steps describe how to obtain online help.
1. Navigate to the program or app developer's website.
2. Search for, and then tap or click a Help or Support link.
3. Select the program or app for which you wish to obtain help to display the help information.

Searching for Help
In addition to obtaining help from within a program or app or on the developer's website, you also can search the web for help as described in the following steps.

1. Navigate to a search engine such as google.com or yahoo.com.
2. Type the program or app name, as well as the type of help for which you are searching, as the search text, and then press the ENTER key or tap or click the search button.
3. Scroll the search results and then tap or click the search result to display more information. Be aware that not all help originates from reputable or accurate sources.

 Under what circumstances would you use each of these methods to obtain help with a program or app you are using? Justify your answer.

 **MINI FEATURE 4-2**

Web and Mobile Apps for Graphics, Media, and Personal Interests

Whether sharing, viewing, and purchasing media, such as photos; streaming audio and video; or playing games by yourself or with others, countless web and mobile apps are available to meet your needs. You also can use web and mobile apps to look up news, sports, and weather; obtain maps and directions; help you reach your health and fitness goals; and assist you with academic objectives.

Media Sharing

With media sharing mobile apps, you use the digital camera on your mobile device to take quality photos and/or videos and then instantly can share the photos or videos on social media sites. Using the corresponding media sharing web app, you can categorize, tag, organize, and rank the media posted by you, your friends, and your contacts.

Streaming Audio and Video

Podcasts, video blogs, clips or episodes from a television show, or even an entire movie are available through a variety of streaming media web and mobile apps, often with a membership or monthly fee. Streaming media enables you to view and listen to content without downloading it to your computer or device, saving valuable disc or media storage space.

Game

Game web and mobile apps often offer a social component, enabling you to chat within the game environment, find friends who play the same game apps, and post your scores on social media. Word, puzzle, and board games are just some examples of apps you can play by yourself or with friends or others using the same apps.

Source: Zynga, Inc.

News, Sports, and Weather

Many apps provide access to the latest news, stories, current events, sports scores, sporting events, and weather forecasts. Some of these mobile apps use GPS technology to provide current or customized information based on the location of your mobile device. You also can configure these apps to send text messages and other types of alerts when certain events occur, such as when a football team scores a touchdown or when severe weather is near.

Mapping

Using GPS technology in your mobile device, you can use mapping mobile apps to obtain directions, maps, and recommendations for restaurants or other points of interest based on your current location. Some mapping apps even help you to locate friends based on their GPS signals (if they enable you to do so). Others allow you to share your current location on social media using a check-in feature. Web apps help you decide on a route, print directions or a map, and even find amenities along your route, such as public rest stops or restaurants.

Health and Fitness

Losing weight, training for a race, or following a low-calorie diet are some uses of health and fitness apps. Using a mobile device as a pedometer or GPS receiver can help you count your steps or create a map of a route you run and then update your profile with the data it tracked. You can use corresponding web apps to chart and analyze your progress, schedule your next workout, or determine the next steps to reach your goals. These apps also can help plan your meals and track the nutritional value of food you consume.

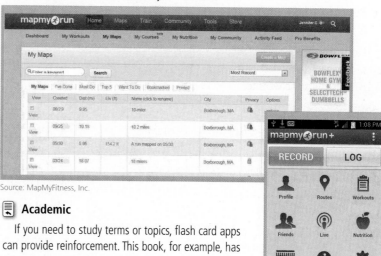

Source: MapMyFitness, Inc.

📖 Academic

If you need to study terms or topics, flash card apps can provide reinforcement. This book, for example, has an accompanying Flash Cards app designed to improve your retention of chapter key terms. Schools often subscribe to educational web apps that provide students with games, quizzes, and lessons about course topics. Using these apps, teachers can keep track of students' progress and pinpoint where they may need extra help. You even can access complete college or high school courses and take advantage of free or fee-based digital content provided by publishers and teachers.

✳ Which web and mobile apps have you used for media sharing; streaming audio and video; gaming; news, sports, and weather; mapping; health and fitness; and education? Will you try others after reading this mini feature? Why or why not?

Communications Applications

One of the main reasons people use computers is to communicate and share information with others. Earlier chapters presented a variety of communications applications, which are summarized in Table 4-2.

Table 4-2   Communications Applications

Blogging
- Time-stamped articles, or posts, in diary or journal format, usually listed in reverse chronological order
- Blogger (author) needs *blog software*, or blogware, to create/maintain blog
  - Some websites do not require installation of blog software

Browsing
- Allows users to access and view webpages on the Internet
- Requires browser
  - Integrated in some operating systems
  - Available for download on the web, usually for free

Chat Room
- Real-time, online typed conversation with many users
- Requires chat client software
  - Integrated in some operating systems and browsers
  - Available for download on the web, usually for free
  - Included with some paid ISPs
  - Built into some websites

Discussion Forum
- Online areas where users have written discussions
- May require a reader program
  - Integrated in some operating systems, email programs, and browsers

Email
- Messages and files sent via a network such as the Internet
- Requires an email program
  - Integrated in many software suites and operating systems
  - Available free at portals on the web
  - Included with a paid ISP
  - Can be purchased separately

FTP
- Method of uploading and downloading files with other computers on the Internet
- May require an FTP program
  - Integrated in some operating systems
  - Available for download on the web, usually for a small fee

Instant Messaging
- Real-time exchange of messages, files, audio, and/or video with another online user
- Requires instant messenger software
  - Integrated in some operating systems
  - Available for download on the web, usually for free
  - Included with some paid ISPs

Videoconference
- Meeting between geographically separated people who use a network to transmit video/audio
- Requires videoconferencing software, a microphone, a speaker, and a webcam

VoIP
- Allows users to speak to other users via an Internet connection
- Requires a microphone, a speaker, a high-speed Internet connection, and VoIP software
  - Some subscription services also require a separate phone and VoIP router
  - With a webcam, some services also support video chat or videoconferences

Web Feeds
- Keeps track of changes made to websites by checking feeds
- Requires a feed reader
  - Integrated in some email programs and browsers
  - Available for download on the web, usually for free

Wireless Messaging
- Short text, picture, or video messages sent and received, mainly on mobile devices
- May require messaging plan from mobile service provider
- Requires messaging software
  - Integrated in most mobile devices
  - Available for download on the web, usually for free

NOW YOU KNOW

Be sure you understand the material presented in the sections titled Graphics and Media Applications, Personal Interest Applications, and Communications Applications, as it relates to the chapter objectives.
You now should know . . .

- When you might use a graphics or media application (Objective 5)
- Which personal interest applications you would find useful (Objective 6)
- When you are interacting with communications applications (Objective 7)

 Quiz Yourself Online: Check your knowledge of related content by navigating to this book's Quiz Yourself resource on Computer Concepts CourseMate and then tapping or clicking Objectives 5–7.

Security Tools

To protect your computers and mobile devices, you can use one or more security tools. Security tools include personal firewalls, antivirus programs, malware removers, and Internet filters. Although some of these tools are included with the operating system, you also can purchase stand-alone programs that offer improvements or added functionality.

Personal Firewall

A **personal firewall** is a security tool that detects and protects a personal computer and its data from unauthorized intrusions (Figure 4-24). Personal firewalls constantly monitor all transmissions to and from a computer and may inform a user of attempted intrusions. When connected to the Internet, your computer is vulnerable to attacks from nefarious individuals who try to access a computer or network illegally. These attacks may destroy your data, steal information, damage your computer, or carry out some other malicious action.

⊛ **BTW**
Security Suites
A *security suite* is a collection of individual security tools available together as a unit. These programs often are called Internet security programs.

⊛ **BTW**
Hacker
The term, *hacker,* refers to someone who accesses a computer or network illegally.

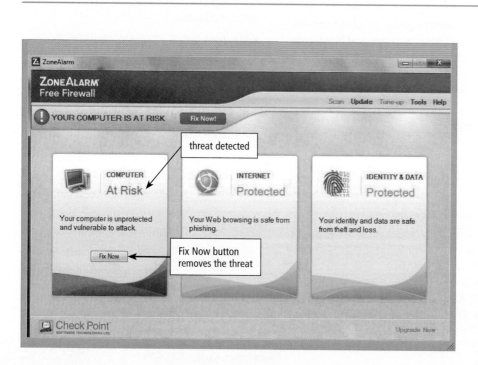

Figure 4-24
This personal firewall detected a threat to the computer and provided a means to remove the threat.
Courtesy of Checkpoint Software Technologies Ltd.

MINI FEATURE 4-3

Viruses and Malware

A computer **virus** is a potentially damaging computer program that affects, or infects, a computer negatively by altering the way the computer works without the user's knowledge or permission. Once the virus is in a computer, it can spread throughout and may damage your files and operating system.

Computer viruses do not generate by chance. The programmer of a virus, known as a virus author, intentionally writes a virus program. Writing a virus program usually requires significant programming skills. The virus author ensures the virus can replicate itself, conceal itself, monitor for certain events, and then deliver its *payload* — the destructive event or prank the virus was created to deliver. Viruses can infect all types of computers and mobile devices, including smartphones and tablets. Despite the many variations of viruses, most have two phases involved in their execution: infection and delivery.

To start the infection phase, the virus must be activated. Today, the most common way viruses spread is by users running infected programs or apps. During the infection phase, viruses typically perform one or more of the following actions:

1. First, a virus replicates by attaching itself to program files. A macro virus hides in a macro, which is a standard feature of many productivity applications such as word processing and spreadsheet apps. A boot sector virus targets the computer's start-up files. A file virus attaches itself to program files. The next time an infected program or app is run, the virus executes and infects the computer.

2. Viruses also conceal themselves to avoid detection. A stealth virus disguises itself by hiding in fake code sections, which it inserts within working code in a file. A polymorphic virus actually changes its code as it infects computers.

3. Finally, viruses watch for a certain condition or event and activate when that condition or event occurs. The event might be starting the computer or reaching a date on the system clock. A logic bomb activates when it detects a specific condition (say, a name deleted from the employee list). A time bomb

is a logic bomb that activates on a particular date or time. If the triggering condition does not exist, the virus simply replicates.

During the delivery phase, the virus unleashes its payload, which might be a harmless prank that displays a meaningless message — or it might be destructive, corrupting or deleting data and files. The most dangerous viruses do not have an obvious payload; instead they quietly modify files. One way antivirus software detects computer viruses is by monitoring files for unknown changes.

In addition to viruses, other malware includes worms, trojan horse programs, and rootkits.

- A *worm* resides in active memory and replicates itself over a network to infect computers and devices, using up the system resources and possibly shutting down the system.

- A *trojan horse* is a destructive program disguised as a real program, such as a screen saver. When a user runs a seemingly innocent program, a trojan horse hiding inside can capture information, such as user names and passwords, from your computer or enable someone remotely to control your computer. Unlike viruses, trojan horses do not replicate themselves.

- A *rootkit* is a program that easily can hide and allow someone to take full control of your computer from a remote location, often for nefarious purposes. For example, a rootkit can hide in a folder on your computer, and the folder will appear empty. This is because the rootkit has instructed your computer not to display the contents of the folder. Rootkits can be very dangerous and often require special software to detect and remove.

Studies show that an unprotected computer can be infected by malware within minutes after being connected to the Internet. Due to the increasing threat of viruses attacking your computer, it is more important than ever to protect your computer from viruses and other malware. Secure IT 1-2 on page 23 in Chapter 1 lists steps you can follow to protect your computer from a virus infection.

 If your computer or mobile device becomes infected with a virus or malware, where can you obtain information about removing the virus or malware?

Signs of Virus Infection

- An unusual message or image is displayed on the computer screen.
- An unusual sound or music plays randomly.
- The available memory is less than what should be available.
- A program or file suddenly is missing.
- An unknown program or file mysteriously appears.
- The size of a file changes without explanation.
- A file becomes corrupted.
- A program or file does not work properly.
- System properties change.
- The computer operates much slower than usual.

Antivirus Programs

To protect a computer from virus attacks, users should install an antivirus program and keep it updated by purchasing revisions or upgrades to the software. An **antivirus program** protects a computer against viruses by identifying and removing any computer viruses found in memory, on storage media, or on incoming files (Figure 4-25). Antivirus programs scan for programs that attempt to modify a computer's start-up files, the operating system, and other programs that normally are read from but not modified. In addition, many antivirus programs automatically scan files downloaded from the web, email attachments, opened files, and all types of removable media inserted in the computer or mobile device.

If an antivirus program identifies an infected file, it attempts to remove the malware. If the antivirus program cannot remove the infection, it often quarantines the infected file. A *quarantine* is a separate area of a hard disk that holds the infected file until the infection can be removed. This step ensures other files will not become infected. Quarantined files remain on your computer or mobile device until you delete them or restore them.

Most antivirus programs also include protection against other malware such as worms, trojan horses, and spyware. When you purchase a new computer, it may include a trial version of antivirus software. Many email servers also have antivirus programs installed to check incoming and outgoing email messages for viruses and other malware. Read Secure IT 4-4 for tips about recognizing virus hoaxes.

Figure 4-25 An antivirus program scans memory, media, and incoming email messages and attachments for viruses and attempts to remove any viruses it finds.
Source: AVG Technologies

 SECURE IT 4-4

Recognizing Virus Hoaxes

Many years ago, people mailed chain letters to friends and relatives promising riches, good health, and other unverifiable claims. Today's equivalent of the chain letter is a computer hoax, which spreads across the Internet in record time and often is the source of urban legends. The hoaxes take several forms and often disappear for months or years at a time, only to resurface some time later.

Most alarming to some users are the computer virus hoaxes, which warn that the computer is infected and needs immediate attention. Occasionally, the claims state the problem is so severe that the computer will explode or that the entire hard disk will be erased in a matter of seconds. The warning cites prominent companies, such as Microsoft and McAfee. These messages claim to offer a solution to the problem, generally requesting a fee for a program to download. Snopes.com compiles these hoaxes and describes their sources and histories.

In reality, these fake messages are generated by unscrupulous scammers preying upon gullible people who panic and follow the directions in the message. These users divulge credit card information and then often download files riddled with viruses.

If you receive one of these virus hoaxes, never respond to the message. Instead, delete it. Most importantly, never forward it to an unsuspecting friend or coworker. If you receive the virus hoax from someone you know, send him or her a separate email message with information about the hoax.

Have you ever received a virus hoax? If so, what action did you take?

CONSIDER THIS

How do antivirus programs detect viruses?

Many antivirus programs identify viruses by looking for virus signatures. A *virus signature*, also called a virus definition, is a known specific pattern of virus code. Computer users should update their antivirus program's signature files regularly. This extremely important activity allows the antivirus program to protect against viruses written since the antivirus program was released and/or its last update. Most antivirus programs contain an automatic update feature that regularly prompts users to download the updated virus signatures, usually at least once a week. The vendor usually provides this service to registered users at no cost for a specified time.

Spyware, Adware, and Other Malware Removers

Spyware is a program placed on a computer or mobile device without the user's knowledge that secretly collects information about the user and then communicates the information it collects to some outside source while the user is online. Some vendors or employers use spyware to collect information about program usage or employees. Internet advertising firms often collect information about users' web browsing habits. Spyware can enter your computer when you install a new program, through a graphic on a webpage or in an email message, or through malware.

Adware is a program that displays an online advertisement in a banner or pop-up window on webpages, email messages, or other Internet services. Sometimes, Internet advertising firms hide spyware in adware.

A **spyware remover** is a program that detects and deletes spyware and similar programs. An **adware remover** is a program that detects and deletes adware. Malware removers detect and delete spyware, adware, and other malware. Read Secure IT 4-5 for measures you can take to protect your mobile device from malware.

 CONSIDER THIS

Are cookies spyware?

A *cookie* is a small text file that a web server stores on your computer. Cookie files typically contain data about you, such as your user name, viewing preferences, or shopping cart contents. Cookies are not considered spyware because website programmers do not attempt to conceal the cookies.

 SECURE IT 4-5

Malware Risks to Mobile Devices

Hackers aggressively are taking advantage of the surge in mobile device purchases and are spreading malware to unsuspecting users. Threats to Android devices are growing in record numbers due to the rising popularity of tablets and smartphones and the variety of marketplace sources for downloading apps. The Federal Bureau of Investigation issues consumer alerts warning users of the serious risks for theft of personal and sensitive information. Often the malware steals phone numbers; it also can allow hackers to control the mobile device from remote locations. Once the hacker takes over the device, all the information on it is available, including

passwords and account numbers. One of the fastest growing threats within mobile apps is *toll fraud malware*, which is a malicious mobile app that uses a variety of fraudulent schemes to charge unsuspecting users for premium messaging services.

Smartphone users can take several precautions to guard against malware threats. They include:

- Read reviews of apps and the company that creates them before downloading the apps to your mobile device.
- Use mobile malware and antivirus protection.
- Turn off location-based apps that track your movements.

- Do not connect to unknown wireless networks.
- Keep the operating system up to date.
- Enable the screen lock feature, and use a strong password to unlock the device.
- Reset the mobile device before selling or trading it in.
- Practice the same safe computing measures you take on your home computer.

Which of these guidelines do you follow now when using your mobile device? How will you modify your usage after reading these tips?

Internet Filters

Filters are programs that remove or block certain items from being displayed. Four widely used Internet filters are anti-spam programs, web filters, phishing filters, and pop-up blockers.

Anti-Spam Programs   **Spam** is an unsolicited email message or posting sent to many recipients or forums at once. Spam is considered Internet junk mail. The content of spam ranges from selling a product or service, to promoting a business opportunity, to advertising offensive material. Spam also may contain links or attachments that contain malware.

An **anti-spam program** is a filtering program that attempts to remove spam before it reaches your Inbox or forum. If your email program does not filter spam, many anti-spam programs are available at no cost on the web. ISPs often filter spam as a service for their subscribers.

Web Filters   **Web filtering software** is a program that restricts access to certain material on the web. Some restrict access to specific websites; others filter websites that use certain words or phrases. Many businesses use web filtering software to limit employee's web access. Some schools, libraries, and parents use this software to restrict access to websites that are not educational.

Internet Research
What are current phishing scams?
Search for: recent phishing scams

Phishing Filters   **Phishing** is a scam in which a perpetrator sends an official looking email message that attempts to obtain your personal and/or financial information (Figure 4-26). Some phishing messages ask you to reply with your information; others direct you to a phony website or a pop-up window that looks like a legitimate website, which then collects your information.

A **phishing filter** is a program that warns or blocks you from potentially fraudulent or suspicious websites. Some browsers include phishing filters.

Pop-Up Blockers   A *pop-up ad* is an Internet advertisement that suddenly appears in a new window on top of a webpage. A **pop-up blocker** is a filtering program that stops pop-up ads from displaying on webpages. Many browsers include a pop-up blocker. You also can download pop-up blockers from the web at no cost.

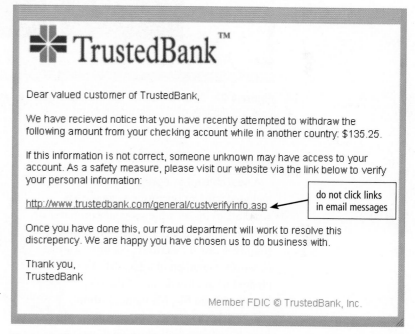

Figure 4-26   An example of a phishing email message.
Source: Andrew Levine

File and Disk Management Tools

To perform maintenance-type tasks related to managing a computer, its devices, or its programs, you can use one or more file and disk management tools. Functions provided by these tools include the following: managing files, searching, viewing images, uninstalling software, cleaning up disks, defragmenting disks, setting up screen savers, compressing files, maintaining a personal computer, and backing up files and disks. Although some of these tools are included with the operating system, you also can purchase stand-alone programs that offer improvements or added functionality.

File Manager

A **file manager** is a tool that performs functions related to file management. Some of the file management functions that a file manager performs are displaying a list of files on a storage medium (Figure 4-27); organizing files in folders; and copying, renaming, deleting, moving, and sorting files. A **folder** is a specific named location on a storage medium that contains related documents. Operating systems typically include a file manager.

Figure 4-27 With a file manager, you can view files containing documents, photos, and music. In this case, thumbnails of photos are displayed.
Source: Microsoft

Search

A **search tool** is a program, usually included with an operating system, that attempts to locate a file on your computer or mobile device based on criteria you specify (Figure 4-28). The criteria could be a word or words contained in a file, date the file was created or modified, size of the file, location of the file, file name, author/ artist, and other similar properties. Search tools can look through documents, photos, music, and other files on your computer or mobile device and/or on the Internet, combining search results in a single location.

Search tools typically use an index to assist with locating files quickly. An *index* stores a variety of information about a file, including its name, date created, date modified, author name, and so on. When you enter search criteria, instead of looking through every file and folder on the storage medium, the search tool looks through the index first to find a match. Each entry in the index contains a link to the actual file on the storage media for easy retrieval.

Figure 4-28 This search displays all files on the mobile device that match the search critieria, Map. Notice the search results show map apps, email with a map, and a calendar event.
Source: Apple Inc

Image Viewer

An **image viewer** is a tool that allows users to display, copy, and print the contents of a graphics file, such as a photo (Figure 4-29). With an image viewer, users can see images without having to open them in a paint or image editing program. Many image viewers include some photo editing capabilities. Most operating systems include an image viewer.

Uninstaller

An **uninstaller** is a tool that removes a program, as well as any associated entries in the system files. When you install a program, the operating system records the information it uses to run the software in the system files. The uninstaller deletes files and folders from the hard disk, as well as removes program entries from the system files. Read How To 4-3 for instructions about uninstalling programs and apps from your computers and mobile devices.

Figure 4-29　An image viewer allows users to see the contents of a photo file.
Source: Microsoft

 CONSIDER THIS

Can you use a file manager to delete a program?
If an uninstaller exists and you remove software from a computer by deleting the files and folders associated with the program without running the uninstaller, the system file entries might not be updated. This may cause the operating system to display error messages when you start the computer.

 HOW TO 4-3

Uninstall a Program or Remove an App

You may choose to uninstall a program or remove an app from your computer or mobile device for a variety of reasons. For example, you may uninstall a program if you need more space on your hard disk, or if you no longer have a use for that program. Uninstalling unwanted programs and apps will keep your hard disk free from clutter and maximize your computer or mobile device's performance. The following steps describe how to uninstall a program or remove an app.

Windows
1. Open the Control Panel.
2. Tap or click the option to uninstall a program.

3. Tap or click to select the program to uninstall.
4. Tap or click the Uninstall button and then follow the prompts on the screen.

Mac
1. Open the Finder.
2. Tap or click Applications in the left pane.
3. Scroll to display the app you wish to uninstall.
4. Drag the app's icon to the Trash.

iPhone, iPad, or iPod Touch
1. Press and hold the icon for the app you wish to delete until the app icons begin to animate.

2. Tap the X on the icon for the app you wish to delete to remove the app from your device.

Android
1. Display the Settings menu.
2. Tap Applications.
3. Tap the application to uninstall.
4. Tap the Uninstall button.
5. Tap the OK button.

✹ In addition to the reasons stated here, what other reasons might you choose to uninstall an app from your computer or mobile device?

Disk Cleanup

A **disk cleanup** tool searches for and removes unnecessary files (Figure 4-30). Unnecessary files may include downloaded program files, temporary Internet files, deleted files, and unused program files. Operating systems usually include a disk cleanup tool.

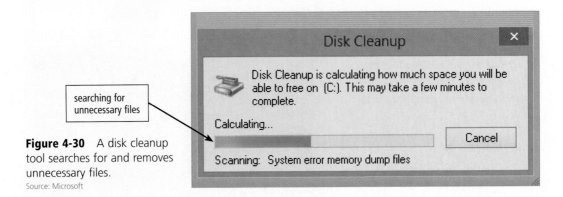

searching for unnecessary files

Figure 4-30 A disk cleanup tool searches for and removes unnecessary files.
Source: Microsoft

Disk Defragmenter

A **disk defragmenter** is a tool that reorganizes the files and unused space on a computer's hard disk so that the operating system accesses data more quickly and programs run faster. When an operating system stores data on a disk, it places the data in the first available sector (a storage location on a disk in the shape of an arc). The operating system attempts to place data in sectors that are contiguous (next to each other), but this is not always possible. When the contents of a file are scattered across two or more noncontiguous sectors, the file is fragmented.

Fragmentation slows down file access and thus the performance of the entire computer. **Defragmenting** the disk, or reorganizing it so that the files are stored in contiguous sectors, solves this problem (Figure 4-31). Operating systems usually include a disk defragmenter. Read How To 4-4 for instructions about defragmenting a hard disk.

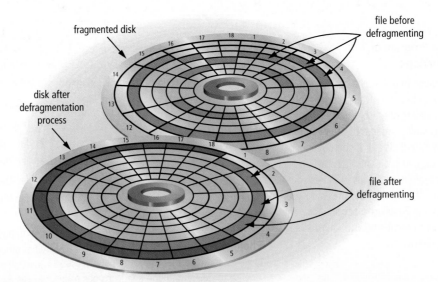

Figure 4-31 A fragmented disk has many files stored in noncontiguous sectors. Defragmenting reorganizes the files so that they are located in contiguous sectors, which speeds access time.
© Cengage Learning

HOW TO 4-4

Defragment a Hard Disk

Defragmenting a hard disk can improve your computer's performance by storing all related files for a particular program together. This can reduce the amount of time it takes the hard disk to locate and access the files necessary for programs to run. Windows has a built-in tool to defragment a computer's hard disk. If you are using a Mac, you should obtain a program to defragment your hard disk. The following steps describe how to defragment a hard disk using the Windows 8 operating system.

1. Tap or click the Desktop tile to run the Desktop app.
2. Swipe from the right or point to the upper-right corner of the screen to display the Charms bar.
3. Tap or click the Settings charm.
4. Tap or click the Control Panel link on the Settings menu to display the Control Panel.
5. Tap or click the 'System and Security' link.
6. If necessary, scroll to display the 'Defragment and optimize your drives' link.

7. Tap or click the 'Defragment and optimize your drives' link.
8. Tap or click the hard disk you wish to defragment.
9. Tap or click the Optimize button to begin defragmenting the selected hard disk. This process may take from several minutes to more than one hour.

❋ What other tools can help optimize the performance of your computer?

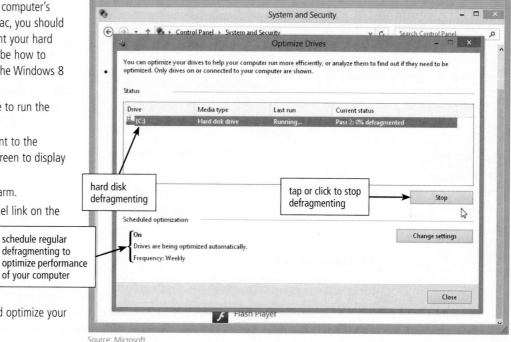

Source: Microsoft

Screen Saver

A **screen saver** is a tool that causes a display device's screen to show a moving image or blank screen if no keyboard or mouse activity occurs for a specified time. When you press a key on the keyboard or move the mouse, the screen saver disappears and the screen returns to the previous state.

❋ **CONSIDER THIS**

What is the purpose of a screen saver?

Screen savers originally were developed to prevent a problem called ghosting, in which images could be etched permanently on a monitor's screen. Although ghosting is not as severe of a problem with today's displays, manufacturers continue to recommend that users install screen savers for this reason. Screen savers also are popular for security, business, and entertainment purposes. To secure a computer, users configure their screen saver to require a password to deactivate.

File Compression

A **file compression tool** shrinks the size of a file(s). A compressed file takes up less storage space than the original file. Compressing files frees up room on the storage media. You may need to compress a file so that it will fit on a smaller storage medium, such as a USB flash drive. Attaching a compressed file to an email message, for example, reduces the time needed for file transmission. Uploading and downloading compressed files to and from the Internet reduces the file transmission time.

 **Internet Research**

How are files compressed?

Search for: how file compression works

Compressed files sometimes are called **zipped files**. When you receive or download a compressed file, you must uncompress it. To **uncompress** (or unzip or expand) a file, you restore it to its original form. Some operating systems include file compression and uncompression capabilities. Read How To 4-5 for instructions about using file compression tools.

HOW TO 4-5

Compress and Uncompress Files and Folders

While the operating system may be able to compress some files by 50 percent or more, other files' sizes may not decrease significantly when they are compressed. Compressed files typically are stored by default in a file with a .zip file extension. The following steps describe how to compress a file or folder and then uncompress (expand or extract) the compressed file.

1. Press and hold or right-click the file(s) or folders you wish to compress to display a shortcut menu.

2. Tap or click the option to compress the file(s) or folder(s). (You may need to select a Send to or other command to display the compression options.)

3. If necessary, type the desired file name for the compressed file.

Uncompressing (or expanding) compressed files or folders returns them to their original form. The following steps uncompress a compressed file.

1. Double-tap or double-click the compressed file.

2. If necessary, tap or click the option to uncompress (expand or extract) the file.

or

1. Press and hold or right-click the compressed file to display a shortcut menu.

2. Tap or click the option to uncompress (expand or extract) the file.

In addition to the operating system's built-in functionality to compress files and folders, what other programs and apps exist that can compress files and folders?

PC Maintenance

A **PC maintenance tool** is a program that identifies and fixes operating system problems, detects and repairs disk problems, and includes the capability of improving a computer's performance. Additionally, some personal computer maintenance utilities continuously monitor a computer while you use it to identify and repair problems before they occur.

Backup and Restore

A **backup tool** allows users to copy, or back up, selected files or the contents of an entire storage medium to another storage location, such as another hard disk, optical disc, USB flash drive, or cloud storage (Figure 4-32). During the backup process, the backup tool monitors progress and alerts you if it needs additional media, such as another disc. Many backup programs compress files during the backup process. By compressing the files, the backup program requires less storage space for the backup files than for the original files.

Because they are compressed, you usually cannot use backup files in their backed up form. In the event you need to use a backup file, a **restore tool** reverses the process and returns backed up files to their original form. Backup tools work with a restore tool. You should back up files and disks regularly in the event your originals are lost, damaged, or destroyed.

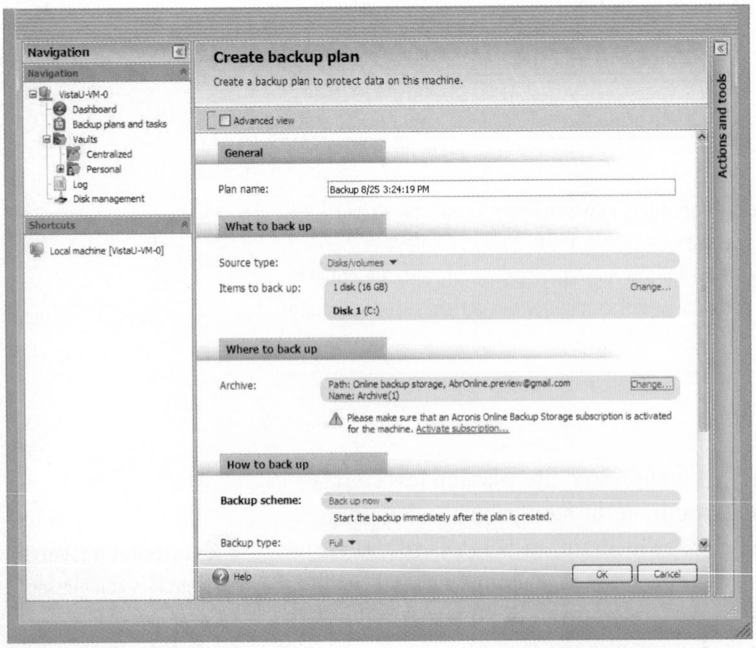

Figure 4-32 A backup tool allows users to copy files, folders, or the entire contents from one storage medium to another location.
Source: Acronis

✔ NOW YOU KNOW

Be sure you understand the material presented in the sections titled Security Tools and File and Disk Management Tools as it relates to the chapter objectives.
You now should know . . .

- Why you should use personal firewalls, antivirus programs, malware removers, and Internet filters (Objective 8)
- Which file and disk management tools you would find useful (Objective 9)

🖵 Quiz Yourself Online: Check your knowledge of related content by navigating to this book's Quiz Yourself resource on Computer Concepts CourseMate and then tapping or clicking Objectives 8–9.

✔ Chapter Summary

This chapter presented a variety of programs and apps available for computers and mobile devices. You learned about the role of the operating system and the various ways software is distributed. The chapter presented the features of a variety of productivity applications, graphics and media applications, and personal interest applications. It reviewed several communications applications and then presented features of a variety of security tools and file and disk management tools.

📑 Test your knowledge of chapter material by accessing the Study Guide, Flash Cards, and Practice Test apps that run on your smartphone, tablet, laptop, or desktop.

⚡ TECHNOLOGY @ WORK

📑 Entertainment

Do you wonder how music on the radio sounds so perfectly in tune, how animated motion pictures are created, or how one controls lighting during a concert? Not only does the entertainment industry rely on computers to advertise and sell their services, computers also assist in other aspects, including audio and video composition, lighting control, computerized animation, and computer gaming.

Entertainment websites provide music and movies you can purchase and download to your computer or mobile device; live news broadcasts, performances, and sporting events; games you can play with other online users; and much more.

As early as 1951, computers were used to record and play music. Today, computers play a much larger role in the music industry. For example, if you are listening to a song on the radio and notice that not one note is out of tune, it is possible that a program or app was used to change individual notes without altering the rest of the song.

Many years ago, creating cartoons or animated motion pictures was an extremely time-consuming task because artists were responsible for sketching thousands of drawings by hand. Currently, artists use computers to create these drawings in a fraction of the time, which significantly reduces the time and cost of development.

Computers also are used in the game industry. While some game developers create games from scratch, others might use game engines that simplify the development process. For example, LucasArts created the GrimE game engine, which is designed to create adventure games.

During a concert, lighting technicians use computer programs to control lights by turning them off and on, changing their color, or changing their placement at specified intervals. In fact, once a performance begins, the technicians often merely are standing by, monitoring the computer as it performs most of the work. A significant amount of time and effort, however, is required to program the computer to execute its required tasks during a live show.

The next time you listen to a song, watch a movie, play a game, or attend a concert, think about the role computers play in contributing to your entertainment.

✳ How else might computers and technology be used in the entertainment industry?

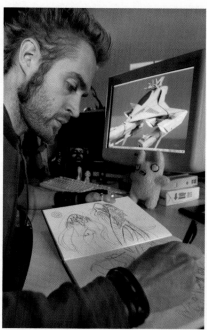

© Horizons WWP / Alamy

Study Guide

The Study Guide exercise reinforces material you should know for the chapter exam. You will find answers to items with the icon only in the e-book.

Access the Study Guide app that runs on your smartphone, tablet, laptop, or desktop by navigating to this book's Apps resource on Computer Concepts CourseMate.

Instructions: Answer the questions below using the format that helps you remember best or that is required by your instructor. Possible formats may include one or more of these options: write the answers; create a document that contains the answers; record answers as audio or video using a webcam, smartphone, or portable media player; post answers on a blog, wiki, or website; or highlight answers in the book/e-book.

1. List categories of programs and apps.

2. Define the terms: operating system, tools, and system software.

3. List examples of desktop and mobile operating systems.

4. Describe how an operating system interacts with the computer.

5. _____ software is tailor-made for a specific business or industry.

6. Differentiate among web apps, mobile apps, and mobile web apps.

7. List any restrictions for open source, shareware, freeware, and public-domain software.

8. Describe steps to register and activate software.

9. Explain the purpose of a license agreement.

10. List types of productivity applications.

11. Name the contributions of Microsoft and Apple, with respect to productivity applications.

12. Describe the activities that occur during project development.

13. Differentiate among font, font size, and font style.

14. Explain how the Internet has expanded plagiarism.

15. Identify functions of the following software: word processing, presentation, spreadsheet, database, note taking, calendar and contact management, project management, accounting, personal finance, legal, tax preparation, and document management.

16. List advantages of using a software suite.

17. Define the following terms: worksheet and function.

18. Name the contributions of Dan Bricklin, with respect to spreadsheet programs, and of Adobe Systems, with respect to document management software.

19. Name the products and/or services of Evernote.

20. List safety considerations when using personal finance apps.

21. Describe issues that might arise when using legal software.

22. Describe the functions of reference, travel, and retail applications.

23. Identify risks when using payment apps.

24. Name the types of software used by various functional units in an enterprise.

25. Identify functions of the following apps: office productivity, scanning, financial, reference, retail, travel, and social networking.

26. Identify functions of the following software: computer-aided design, desktop publishing, paint/image editing, photo editing and photo management, clip art/image gallery, video and audio editing, multimedia and website authoring, media player, and disc burning.

27. List ways to edit digital photos.

28. Identify issues surrounding altered digital photos.

29. Name the products and/or services of Instagram, with respect to photo sharing.

30. Define the terms, CBT and WBT.

31. List types of personal interest applications.

32. Describe ways to obtain help about a program or app.

33. Identify functions of the following apps: media sharing; streaming audio and video; game; news, sports, and weather; mapping; health and fitness; and academic.

34. Name the products and/or services of iTunes U.

35. Identify types of communications applications.

36. A(n) _____ includes time-stamped articles in a journal format.

37. Identify functions of the following tools: personal firewalls, antivirus programs, malware removers, and Internet filters.

38. Describe ways a virus infects programs or apps.

39. List types of malware. Identify signs of a virus infection.

40. Explain the risks of and how to avoid computer virus hoaxes.

41. Identify ways to avoid malware when using a mobile device.

42. Identify functions of the following tools: file manager, search, image viewer, uninstaller, disk cleanup, disk defragmenter, screen saver, file compression, PC maintenance, and backup and restore.

43. Define the terms, folder and index.

44. List steps to uninstall a program or remove an app.

45. Describe the disk defragmentation process.

46. Compressed files are sometimes called _____ files. List steps to uncompress a file.

47. List storage media for backups.

48. Describe uses of technology in the entertainment industry.

You should be able to define the Primary Terms and be familiar with the Secondary Terms listed below.

Key Terms

Access the **Flash Cards** app that runs on your smartphone, tablet, laptop, or desktop by navigating to this book's Apps resource on Computer Concepts CourseMate. **View definitions** for each term by navigating to this book's Key Terms resource on Computer Concepts CourseMate. **Listen to definitions** for each term on your portable media player by navigating to this book's Audio Study Tools resource on Computer Concepts CourseMate.

Primary Terms (shown in **bold-black** characters in the chapter)

accounting software (164)
adware remover (182)
anti-spam program (183)
antivirus program (181)
app (152)
application (152)
audio editing software (173)
backup tool (188)
calendar and contact management software (163)
clip art (159)
clip art/image gallery (173)
computer-aided design (170)
database (162)
database software (162)
defragmenting (186)

desktop publishing software (170)
disc burning software (176)
disk cleanup (186)
disk defragmenter (186)
document management software (166)
file compression tool (187)
file manager (183)
folder (184)
image editing software (171)
image viewer (185)
legal software (166)
media player (175)
multimedia authoring software (174)
note taking software (162)
paint software (171)

PC maintenance tool (188)
PDF (167)
personal finance software (164)
personal firewall (179)
phishing (183)
phishing filter (183)
photo editing software (171)
photo management software (173)
pop-up blocker (183)
presentation software (160)
program (152)
project management software (164)
restore tool (188)
screen saver (187)
search tool (184)

software (152)
software suite (163)
spam (183)
spreadsheet software (160)
spyware remover (182)
tax preparation software (166)
uncompress (188)
uninstaller (185)
video editing software (173)
virus (180)
web filtering software (183)
website authoring software (174)
word processing software (159)
worksheet (160)
zipped files (188)

Secondary Terms (shown in *italic* characters in the chapter)

adware (182)
application software (152)
automatic update (156)
blog software (178)
brightness (172)
clipboard (157)
compress (172)
computer-based training (CBT) (174)
contrast (172)
cookie (182)
create (157)
crop (172)
custom software (155)
edit (157)
font (158)

font size (158)
font style (158)
format (157)
freeware (155)
function (161)
hacker (179)
hard copy (158)
home design/landscaping software (170)
illustration software (171)
index (184)
license agreement (156)
mobile app (155)
mobile web app (155)
open source software (155)
operating system (152)

payload (180)
pop-up ad (183)
print (158)
product activation (156)
productivity applications (157)
public-domain software (155)
QR code (169)
QR code reader (169)
quarantine (181)
red-eye (172)
resize (172)
retail software (155)
rootkit (180)
save (158)
security suite (179)
shareware (155)

sharpness (172)
slide show (160)
software registration (156)
spyware (182)
system software (152)
toll fraud malware (182)
tools (152)
trial version (155)
trojan horse (180)
utilities (152)
virus signature (182)
web app (155)
web-based training (WBT) (174)
worm (180)

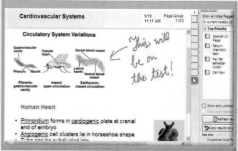

note taking software (162)
Source: Microsoft

Checkpoint

The Checkpoint exercises test your knowledge of the chapter concepts. The page number containing the answer appears in parentheses after each exercise. The Consider This exercises challenge your understanding of chapter concepts.

Complete the Checkpoint exercises interactively by navigating to this book's Checkpoint resource on Computer Concepts CourseMate. **Access the Test Prep app** that runs on your smartphone, tablet, laptop, or desktop by navigating to this book's Apps resource on Computer Concepts CourseMate. After successfully completing the self-assessment through the Test Prep app, **take the Practice Test** by navigating to this book's Practice Test resource on Computer Concepts Coursemate.

True/False   Mark T for True and F for False.

_____ 1. Application software serves as the interface between the user, the apps, and the computer's or mobile device's hardware. (154)

_____ 2. Each time you start a computer or mobile device, the system software is loaded from storage into memory. (154)

_____ 3. Open source software is mass-produced, copyrighted software that meets the needs of a wide variety of users. (155)

_____ 4. When downloading shareware, freeware, or public-domain software, it is good practice to seek websites with ratings for and reviews of products. (157)

_____ 5. While a computer or mobile device is running, the operating system remains in memory. (155)

_____ 6. With database software, users run functions to retrieve data. (162)

_____ 7. Software suites offer three major advantages: lower cost, ease of use, and integration. (164)

_____ 8. A PDF file can be viewed and printed without the software that created the original document. (167)

_____ 9. The military and airlines might use CBT simulations to train pilots to fly in various conditions and environments. (174)

_____ 10. An antivirus program automatically deletes quarantined files. (181)

_____ 11. One of the fastest growing threats in mobile apps is toll fraud malware. (182)

_____ 12. Cookies typically are considered a type of spyware. (182)

Multiple Choice   Select the best answer.

1. Programs called _____ enable you to perform maintenance-type tasks usually related to managing devices, media, and programs used by computers and mobile devices. (152)
   a. productivity tools
   b. tools or utilities
   c. operating systems
   d. multimedia software

2. _____ software performs functions specific to a business or industry. (155)
   a. Retail   c. Shareware
   b. Open source   d. Custom

3. A(n) _____ is the right to use a program or app. (156)
   a. license agreement   c. software registration
   b. product activation d. automatic update

4. _____ software is an application that allows users to organize data in rows and columns and perform calculations on the data. (160)
   a. Spreadsheet   c. Presentation
   b. Database   d. Document management

5. _____ is a type of application that assists professionals and designers in creating engineering, architectural, and scientific designs and models. (170)
   a. Enterprise software
   b. CAD software
   c. Public-domain software
   d. A software suite

6. The term _____ refers to decreasing a photo's file size. (172)
   a. crop   c. compress
   b. resize   d. shrink

7. A _____ is a destructive program disguised as a real program. (180)
   a. worm   c. pop-up ad
   b. trojan horse   d. rootkit

8. A(n) _____ is a known, specific pattern of virus code. (182)
   a. index
   b. quarantine
   c. cookie
   d. virus signature

Checkpoint

Matching   Match the terms with their definitions.

_____ 1. tools (152)

_____ 2. open source software (155)

_____ 3. shareware (155)

_____ 4. QR code (169)

_____ 5. payload (180)

_____ 6. rootkit (180)

_____ 7. worm (180)

_____ 8. quarantine (181)

_____ 9. phishing (183)

_____ 10. defragmenting (186)

a. destructive event or prank a virus was created to deliver

b. copyrighted software that is distributed at no cost for a trial period

c. malware that resides in active memory and replicates itself over a network to infect computers and devices, using up the system resources and possibly shutting down the system

d. program that enables you to perform maintenance-type tasks usually related to managing devices, media, and programs used by computers and mobile devices

e. software provided for use, modification, and redistribution that has no restrictions from the copyright holder regarding modification of the software

f. process of reorganizing a hard disk's files so that the files are stored in contiguous sectors

g. malware that can hide and allow someone to take full control of a computer from a remote location

h. scam in which a perpetrator sends an official looking email message that attempts to obtain personal and/or financial information

i. square-shaped coded graphic that corresponds to a web address or other information

j. separate area of a hard disk that holds an infected file until the infection can be removed

Short Answer   Write a brief answer to each of the following questions.

1. What is the difference between software registration and product activation? (156) What activities does a license agreement restrict? (156)

2. What is the clipboard? (157) List some uses of the clipboard. (157)

3. List some security tools you can use to protect your computers and mobile devices. (179) What is a personal firewall? (179)

4. Differentiate among a virus, worm, trojan horse, and rootkit. (180) In reference to malware, what is a quarantine? (181)

5. List the different types of file and disk management tools. (183) What functions do they provide? (183)

✳ Consider This   Answer the following questions in the format specified by your instructor.

1. Answer the critical thinking questions posed at the end of these elements in this chapter: Ethics & Issues (158, 166, 173, 175), How To (172, 176, 185, 187, 188), Mini Features (169, 177, 180), Secure IT (156, 165, 168, 181, 182), and Technology @ Work (189).

2. What is the role of the operating system? (152, 154)

3. What are the advantages of open source software? What are some examples of open source software? (155)

4. What does it mean to edit a project? How does editing differ from formatting? (157)

5. How does a spreadsheet organize data? How are cells identified in a spreadsheet? (160)

6. What kind of information can you find using a reference application? (167)

7. How can you ensure your safety when using mobile payment apps? (168)

8. What are some examples of office productivity apps? What can you accomplish using these apps? (157, 169)

9. Should journalists edit or enhance digital photos? Why or why not? (173)

10. What tasks can you accomplish using mapping apps? (177)

11. How does a personal firewall protect your computer? (179)

12. What happens during the delivery phase of a virus? (180)

13. Why is spam potentially dangerous? What is a phishing scam? (183)

14. How does a search tool locate a file on your computer or mobile device? (184)

15. What is a fragmented disk? How does fragmentation affect a computer's performance? (186)

✵ How To: Your Turn

The How To: Your Turn exercises present general guidelines for fundamental skills when using a computer or mobile device and then require that you determine how to apply these general guidelines to a specific program or situation.

Instructions: You often can complete tasks using technology in multiple ways. Figure out how to perform the tasks described in these exercises by using one or more resources available to you (such as a computer or mobile device, articles on the web or in print, online or program help, user guides, blogs, podcasts, videos, other individuals, trial and error, etc.). Summarize your 'how to' steps, along with the resource(s) used, in the format requested by your instructor (brief report, presentation, discussion, blog post, video, or other means).

❶ Obtain Directions with Mapping Applications and Websites

If you need directions to walk, drive, bike, or even take public transportation to your destination, you can use mapping applications or websites to obtain directions. These applications and websites often provide very accurate directions, but it is important to verify the directions before venturing into unfamiliar areas. If the directions you obtain require using public transportation, you should verify with the transportation provider's website that the routes and time schedules provided by your mapping application still are accurate. The following steps describe how to obtain directions using a mapping application.

a. Search for and install a mapping application or navigate to a mapping website of your choice on your computer or mobile device. Many computers and mobile devices include a mapping application. You also can access websites that provide directions and updated maps. If you are using a mapping application that is installed on your computer or mobile device, make sure the application is updated with the latest maps. Using an application with outdated maps can result in it providing directions that are not accurate.

b. Tap or click the option to obtain directions. Then, if necessary, specify whether you want to obtain driving, biking, walking, or public transportation directions.

c. If you require directions from your current location, mapping applications and websites may be able to use the GPS feature on your mobile device to detect your location automatically. To use this feature, make sure the GPS feature on your mobile device is enabled and then, if necessary, tap or click the button to detect your current location automatically.

d. Enter the address to which you want directions. Make sure you enter the full street address, city, state, and postal code, and then tap or click the button to retrieve the directions.

e. Review the directions and make sure you understand them before beginning your trip.

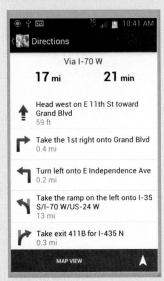

Source: Google Inc.

f. Print the directions and carry them with you during the journey to your destination. If the directions are on a mobile device that you can take with you as you travel to your destination, consider activating the audio feature so that directions can be read aloud as you navigate the route.

g. Upon arriving at your destination, exit the mapping application.

Exercises

1. Research three different mapping applications. Which one would you use, and why?

2. Research three web apps that can provide directions. In your opinion, is it better to use a web app to obtain directions than an application installed on your computer or mobile device? Why or why not?

3. Use a mapping application or web app to obtain directions from your home to your preferred shopping mall. Did the web app or application display directions similar to the route you travel? If not, will you consider traveling the route that the mapping web app or application provided?

❷ View Current Virus Threats

One important way to protect your computer or mobile device from viruses is to be aware of current threats. Several websites exist that not only provide a list of current virus threats but also describe how best to protect your computer or mobile device from these threats. As new virus threats are introduced, it is important to make sure your antivirus program is updated and running properly. The following steps describe how to view a list of current virus threats.

a. Run a browser and then navigate to a search engine of your choice.

How To: Your Turn ☀

b. Perform a search for websites that display current virus threats.

c. Review the search results and visit at least two websites that display current virus threats.

d. View the list of virus threats on each of these websites.

or

a. Run a browser and then navigate to a search engine of your choice.

b. Perform a search for websites created by companies that make antivirus software. Some companies that make antivirus sòftware include Symantec, McAfee, and Microsoft.

c. Navigate to one of these company's websites and search for a link to a webpage displaying current virus threats.

d. Tap or click the link to display current virus threats.

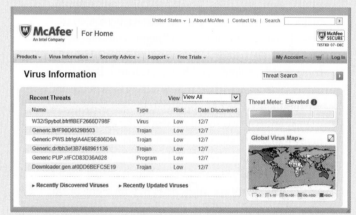

Source: McAfee.com

Exercises

1. Which websites did you access? Compare these websites and determine which you think provided the most helpful information. Why, in your opinion, does the website you chose provide the best information?

2. Has your computer or mobile device ever been infected with a virus? If so, what steps have you taken to remove the virus?

3. Is your computer or mobile device adequately protected from viruses? What steps do you take to keep your computer safe?

❸ Back Up Your Computer

Backing up your computer is an important way to protect your programs, apps, and data from loss. The frequency at which people back up their computers can vary. For instance, if you create and modify a lot of files on your computer, you may choose to back up your computer frequently. If you rarely use

your computer or primarily use your computer for answering email messages and browsing the web, you might not back up your computer as often. The following steps guide you through the process of backing up a computer.

a. Decide which backup program you wish to use. Some operating systems have built-in tools you can use to back up a computer, or you can install a third-party program.

b. Run the program you will use to back up the computer.

c. If necessary, connect the storage device, such as an external hard disk, you will use to store the backup. If you plan to store the backup on an optical disc or another hard disk that already is installed, you will not need to connect an additional storage device.

d. Make sure the storage medium has enough available space for the backed up files. If you are storing the backup on optical discs, make sure you have enough optical discs for the backup.

e. Select the type of backup (full, incremental, differential, or selective) you wish to perform.

f. If you are performing a selective backup, choose the files, programs, and apps you wish to include in the backup.

g. Run the backup. The backup process may take up to several hours, depending on the number of files you are including in the backup.

h. If you are storing the backup on optical discs, the backup program may prompt you to insert new, blank optical discs throughout the backup process.

i. When the backup is complete, store the backup in a safe location. In the event you lose data or information on the computer, you will need to retrieve the backup.

Source: Acronis

Exercises

1. How often do you feel you should back up your computer? Justify your answer.

2. What storage medium do you feel is most appropriate for your backup? Justify your answer.

3. Research at least three programs that you can use to back up your computer. Which programs did you research? Which program or app do you feel is the best? Why?

✳ Internet Research

The Internet Research exercises broaden your understanding of chapter concepts by requiring that you search for information on the web.

Instructions: Use a search engine or another search tool to locate the information requested or answers to questions presented in the exercises. Describe your findings, along with the search term(s) you used and your web source(s), in the format requested by your instructor (brief report, presentation, discussion, blog post, video, or other means).

❶ Making Use of the Web
Travel and Mapping

Pack your bags and grab some great deals on airfare, hotels, rental cars, and resorts just by visiting websites geared toward your travel needs. Some websites compare multiple airlines' fares to cities worldwide and allow you to search for the lowest fares on a particular date or a range of dates, for destinations within a specific price range, or for locations with preferred activities, such as skiing or hiking. Others send alerts when lodging rates or fares drop below a specified price point or give predictions of whether the rates will increase or decrease during the upcoming weeks. The websites also offer reviewers' ratings of hotels, restaurants, and activities.

Getting to a vacation destination can be an adventure in itself, and websites can offer assistance in pointing travelers in the right direction. Some provide interactive maps, display satellite and aerial imagery of the Earth, and recommended restaurants and tourist attractions en route to specific cities.

(a) Visit two travel websites and search for airfares to your favorite vacation destination on your next birthday. Which airlines offer the lowest fares to this location? What hotels or resorts are reviewed favorably? Which aspects of this lodging do the travelers like and dislike? What are the similarities and differences between the two travel websites? Which website is easier to search and locate desired information? Have you used websites to obtain travel information or to make reservations?

(b) Visit a mapping website and obtain the distance from your campus to the Indianapolis Motor Speedway (Speedway, IN), Kennedy Space Center (Merritt Island, FL), or Navy Pier (Chicago, IL). What is the estimated travel time? Locate an aerial or a satellite image of this destination. What features are visible in the picture?

❷ Social Media 🖹

Gaming via social media has seen explosive growth in recent years, with an estimated 235 million people participating in online games each month. Exponential gaming growth has spawned companion businesses that facilitate and manage the gaming experience. Some mobile and desktop apps provide gamers a portal for tracking all their online gaming results in a central location that can be shared with friends and others with similar game interests. These apps integrate with the major instant messaging services, have personalized news feeds, and incorporate a "suggestion" engine for new game discoveries. Many gaming blogs offer game tricks, work-arounds, and hidden features. Beginning gamers can engage their minds during downtime and expand their circle of online friends.

Visit at least two social networks for gamers. How many games are shown? Which topics are featured in community discussions and live chats? Are rewards available? If so, what are they? Which online leagues and tournaments are offered? What are some of the latest news articles about specific games and the gaming industry? Have you participated in gaming social networks? If so, which ones?

❸ Search Sleuth

(1) Who was sitting under an apple tree in Apple's original corporate logo? (2) In what year was the first phone using the Android operating system sold in the United States? (3) Which software developer appeared in the movies *Triumph of the Nerds* and *Aardvark'd: 12 Weeks with Geeks*? (4) Which United States president's speech did Peter Norvig turn into a lighthearted PowerPoint presentation? (5) What is the difference between a serif and sans serif font? Which sans serif font did the German Bauhaus movement develop in 1928? (6) In which year did the United States Department of Revenue first provide tax forms and booklets in Adobe PDF format on its website?

Source: Google Inc.

Internet Research

(7) What company did Bruce Artwick form in 1977, and what game did it license to Microsoft in 1982? (8) Which company coined the term, word processing, in the late 1960s? (9) Microsoft included the Disk Volume Organization Optimizer in its early operating system to defragment which storage medium? (10) Bernd Fix, Atari ST, G Data, and UVK 2000 are names of which category of security tools?

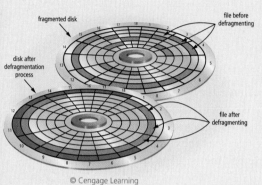

© Cengage Learning

4 Green Computing

When it comes to software recycling, going green may just leave you in the black. Software from that desktop you once cherished, now gathering dust in the corner of your basement, may have some value in its dormant bytes. A niche industry of software brokers now exists that purchases used software and resells it to customers that may not need the latest versions. These customers may have older computers or operating systems that do not support new software revisions. In such cases, vintage software may be a necessity to avoid upgrading to new hardware. Some software recycling companies buy popular used software, such as Microsoft Office, which often is bundled and preinstalled on new computers. These recycling brokers work with organizations that are replacing old hardware with software installed. The brokers first verify that the used software exists and the licensing terms are not violated. They then buy the software and offer it for resale. Recycled software may not be green for the environment, but it can provide some green for your bottom line.

Locate at least two software recycling company websites. Which software titles are available in the inventory? What is the cost of the more popular titles, such as Microsoft Office or Adobe Creative Suite? How much will the companies pay to obtain software? Do they have restrictions on how new the software must be? Are incomplete software packages accepted? How do the companies verify authenticity? Software manufacturers may not update older versions of their products, so recycled software may leave a computer vulnerable to Internet and network security attacks.

Would this security risk dissuade you from purchasing recycled software?

5 Security

Virus hoaxes are widespread and sometimes cause panic among Internet users. Secure IT 4-4 on page 181 gives advice on recognizing and avoiding virus hoaxes. Snopes.com provides further insight on the sources and variations of a wide variety of rumors, deceptions, and folklore.

Visit snopes.com and review the list of the more recent real (indicated by a green dot) and false (indicated by a red dot) rumors circulating on the Internet. Which are the three newest actual warnings, and which are the three latest virus hoaxes? What harm is predicted to occur if a user downloads each of these real or false viruses or views a website laden with malware? What is the origin of the website's name, Snopes?

6 Ethics in Action

As you read in this chapter, a hacker is someone who tries to access a computer or network illegally. Although hacking activity sometimes is a harmless prank, at times it causes extensive damage. Some hackers claim their activities are a form of civil disobedience that forces companies to make their products more secure. Others say their activities allow them to test their skills. Many of these hackers are able to participate in activities and share their knowledge each year at DEF CON, one of the world's largest and continuous-running conferences for hackers. The International Council of E-Commerce Consultants administers professional accreditation to become a Certified Ethical Hacker. Also, community-based hacking projects test researchers' programs and apps under development.

View online websites that provide information about when hackers provide some benefit to the Internet society. In which circumstances are hackers valuable contributors to the computer field? What are the requirements to become a Certified Ethical Hacker? The DefCon Kids event teaches children ages 8 to 16 how to hack hardware, open master locks, break codes, and prevent spying over wireless networks. Should children be taught hacking activities? Will learning these techniques at an early age encourage them to fight cybercrime or entice them to participate in it?

✳ Problem Solving

The Problem Solving exercises extend your knowledge of chapter concepts by seeking solutions to practical problems with technology that you may encounter at home, school, work, or with nonprofit organizations. The Collaboration exercise should be completed with a team.

🔘 Challenge yourself with additional Problem Solving exercises by navigating to this book's Problem Solving resource on Computer Concepts CourseMate.

Instructions: You often can solve problems with technology in multiple ways. Determine a solution to the problems in these exercises by using one or more resources available to you (such as a computer or mobile device, articles on the web or in print, blogs, podcasts, videos, television, user guides, other individuals, electronics or computer stores, etc.). Describe your solution, along with the resource(s) used, in the format requested by your instructor (brief report, presentation, discussion, blog post, video, or other means).

Personal

1. Antivirus Program Not Updating You are attempting to update your antivirus program with the latest virus definitions, but you receive an error message. What steps will you take to resolve this issue?

Source: AVG Technologies

2. Operating System Does Not Load Each time you turn on your computer, the operating system attempts to load for approximately 30 seconds and then the computer restarts. You have tried multiple times to turn your computer off and on, but it keeps restarting when the operating system is trying to load. What are your next steps?

3. Tablet App Malfunctioning When you attempt to run an app on your tablet, the tablet displays an error message stating that the app is unable to run and then returns to the home screen. You have run this app successfully in the past and are unsure of why this problem suddenly is occurring. What are your next steps?

4. News Not Updating Each morning you run an app on your smartphone to view the news for the current day. For the past week, however, you notice that the news displayed in the app is out of date. In fact, the app now is displaying news that is nearly one week old. Why might the app not be updating? What are your next steps?

5. Incompatible App You are using your Android tablet to browse for apps in the Google Play store. You found an app you want to download, but you are unable to download it because a message states it is incompatible with your device. Why might the app be incompatible with your device?

Professional

6. Email Program Freezing Each time you run the email program on your computer and it attempts to download your new email messages, the program freezes and you have to restart the computer. You are able to retrieve your email messages on your mobile device without any issues and do not know why you are having problems with the email program on your computer. What are your next steps?

7. License Agreement You are planning to work from home for several days, but you are unsure of whether you are allowed to install a program you use at work on your home computer. What steps will you take to determine whether you are allowed to install the software on your home computer?

8. Presentation Problems While rehearsing for a presentation you plan to give to some colleagues, you notice that the presentation software automatically is advancing the slides. Instead, you would like the slides to advance when you tap the screen or click your mouse. What steps will you take to fix this problem?

9. Unacceptable File Size Your boss has asked you to design a new company logo using a graphics application installed on your computer. When you save the logo and send it to your boss, she responds that the file size is too large and tells you to find a way to decrease the file size. What might you do to make the image file size smaller?

10. Disc Burning Not Working While attempting to back up some files on your computer on an optical disc, the disc burning software on your computer reports a problem and ejects the disc. When you check the contents of the disc, the files you are trying to back up are not there. What might be wrong?

Collaboration

11. Technology in Entertainment The film department at a local high school is considering developing a movie and has asked for your help. The film teacher would like to incorporate technology wherever possible, in hopes that it would decrease the cost of the movie's production. Form a team of three people to determine what technology can be used to assist in the movie's production. One team member should research the type of technology that can be used during the filming process. Another team member should research the types of hardware and software available for editing footage, and the third team member should research the hardware and software requirements for producing and distributing the media.

The Critical Thinking exercises challenge your assessment and decision-making skills by presenting real-world situations associated with chapter concepts. The Collaboration exercise should be completed with a team.

Critical Thinking ☀

 Challenge yourself with additional Critical Thinking exercises by navigating to this book's Critical Thinking resource on Computer Concepts CourseMate.

Instructions: Evaluate the situations below, using personal experiences and one or more resources available to you (such as articles on the web or in print, blogs, podcasts, videos, television, user guides, other individuals, electronics or computer stores, etc.). Perform the tasks requested in each exercise and share your deliverables in the format requested by your instructor (brief report, presentation, discussion, blog post, video, or other means).

1. Class Discussion

File and Disk Management Tools   You are the director of information technology at a company that hires student interns frequently. The interns tend to have limited experience with using file and disk management tools. As part of your job, you lead workshops that teach the interns the many tasks and functions they can perform using these tools. Choose three categories of tools, such as disk cleanup, PC maintenance, and file compression. Determine whether your computer's operating system includes these tools. Use the web to research popular tools for each category; whether they can be purchased separately or if they are available only as part of an operating system; and the costs for each tool. Choose one program from each category, and read user reviews and articles by industry experts. Describe situations where you would use each type of tool. Share any experiences you have with using the tools.

2. Research and Share

Web and Mobile App Comparison   You recently purchased a new smartphone and want to research mobile apps that also have accompanying web apps. Choose three categories of apps, and find an example for each that has both a free web and mobile version. Read user reviews of each app, and search for articles by industry experts. Research any known safety risks for the apps. If you determine the app is safe and have the appropriate device, and would like to test the mobile app, you can download it to your smartphone or other mobile device. Try accessing the web app on a computer. Using your experience or research, note the differences in functionality between the web and mobile app. Is one or the other easier to use? Why or why not? Compile your findings and then share with the class.

3. Case Study

Farmers' Market   You are the new manager for a group of organic farmers who have a weekly market in season. The farmers' market needs productivity software in order to keep track of vendor and budget information and prepare flyers. You prepare information about productivity software options to present to the board of directors. Use the web to research popular word processing, spreadsheet, and accounting software. Choose three programs from each category. List common features of each, find pricing information, and note any feedback or ratings by users. Which programs would you recommend? Why? Describe the steps involved in developing a project, creating a flyer for the farmers' market as an example. Identify possible uses the farmers' market may have for the spreadsheet and accounting software. Compile your findings.

Source: Google Inc.

Collaboration

4. Educational Program and App Effectiveness   The principal of the local elementary school has recommended that educational applications should play a major role in the learning process. She stated that educational applications enable students to learn at their own pace. Some enable teachers to track an individual student's progress and understanding. Form a three-member team and research the use of educational applications. Each member of your team should choose a different type of application, such as flash cards, testing, or CBT. List the advantages and disadvantages of using that type of application. If possible, download or access a free version of an educational application from each category and spend some time using it. Read user reviews of popular applications, and search for articles by industry experts. Would you recommend using an application for educational purposes? Why or why not? Meet with your team, discuss and compile your findings, and then share with the class.

✳ Beyond the Book

The Beyond the Book exercises expand your understanding of chapter concepts by requiring research.

Access premium content by visiting Computer Concepts CourseMate. If you have a Computer Concepts CourseMate access code, you can reinforce and extend your learning with MindTap Reader, practice tests, video, and other premium content for Discovering Computers. To sign in to Computer Concepts CourseMate at www.cengagebrain.com, you first must create a student account and then register this book, as described at www.cengage.com/ct/studentdownload.

Part 1 Instructions: Use the web or e-book to perform the task identified for each book element below. Describe your findings, along with the search term(s) you used and your web source(s), if appropriate, in the format requested by your instructor (brief report, presentation, discussion, blog post, video, or other means).

1. **Animation** 📱 Review the animation associated with this chapter and then answer the question(s) it poses (154). What search term would you use to learn more about a specific segment of the animation?

2. **Consider This** Select a Consider This in this chapter (153, 156, 158, 164, 167, 174, 179, 182, 185, 187) and find a recent article that elaborates on the topic. What information did you find that was not presented in this book or e-book?

3. **Drag-and-Drop Figures** 📱 Complete the Drag-and-Drop Figure activities associated with this chapter (153, 154, 172, 178, 186). What did you learn from each of these activities?

4. **Ethics & Issues** Select an Ethics & Issues in this chapter (158, 166, 173, 175) and find a recent article that supports one view presented. Does the article change your opinion about the topic? Why or why not?

5. **Facebook & Twitter** Review a recent Discovering Computers Facebook post or Twitter Tweet and read the referenced article(s). What did you learn from the article?

6. **High-Tech Talk** 📱 Locate an article that discusses topics related to 3-D graphics. Would you recommend the article you found? Why or why not?

7. **How To** Select a How To in this chapter (172, 176, 185, 187, 188) and find a recent article that elaborates on the topic. Who would benefit from the content of this article? Why?

8. **Innovative Computing** 📱 Locate two additional facts about Instagram, iTunes U, or Evernote. Do your findings change your opinion about the future of this innovation? Why or why not?

9. **Internet Research** Use the search term in an Internet Research (154, 159, 167, 176, 183, 187) to answer the question posed in the element. What other search term could you use to answer the question?

10. **Mini Features** Locate an article that discusses topics related to one of the mini features in this chapter (169, 177, 180). Do you feel that the article is appropriate for this course? Why or why not?

11. **Secure IT** Select a Secure IT in this chapter (156, 165, 168, 181, 182) and find a recent article about the topic that you find interesting. How can you relate the content of the article to your everyday life?

12. **Technology @ Work** Locate three additional, unique usages of technology in the entertainment industry (189). What makes the use of these technologies unique to the entertainment industry?

13. **Technology Innovators** 📱 Locate two additional facts about Microsoft, Apple, Dan Bricklin, and Adobe Systems. Which Technology Innovator impresses you most? Why?

14. **Third-Party Links** 📱 Visit one of the third-party links identified in this chapter (157, 158, 161, 165, 166, 168, 173, 175, 177, 181, 182, 187, 189) and read the article or watch the video associated with the link. Would you share this link on your online social network account? Why or why not?

Part 2 Instructions: Find specific instructions for the exercises below in the e-book or on Computer Concepts CourseMate. Beside each exercise is a brief description of its online content.

1. 📱 **You Review It** Search for and review a video, podcast, or blog post about the most popular mobile apps that users of mobile devices downloaded this week.

2. 📱 **Windows and Mac** Enhance your understanding and knowledge about using Windows and Mac computers by completing the Creating Documents Using a Text Editor and Creating, Accessing, and Storing Notes Online activities.

3. 📱 **Android, iOS, and Windows Mobile** Enhance your understanding of mobile devices by completing the Organize Your Apps, Widgets, or Tiles and Creating, Accessing, and Storing Notes Online activities.

4. 📱 **Exploring Computer Careers** Read about a career as a game designer, search for related employment ads, and then answer related questions.

5. 📱 **App Adventure** Stay organized by keeping a to-do list of your tasks using apps on your smartphone or tablet.

Digital Safety and Security
Identifying Threats, Issues, and Defenses

5

Users should take precautions to protect their digital content.

"I am careful when browsing the web, use antivirus software, and never open email messages from unknown senders. I use a cloud storage provider to back up my computer and mobile devices. What more do I need to know about digital safety and security?"

True, you may be familiar with some of the material in this chapter, but do you know . . .

How to secure a wireless network?

When an organization can be punished for weak security?

How to tell if your computer or device is functioning as a zombie?

How to use anonymous browsing?

How a digital forensics examiner collects and analyzes cybercrime evidence?

When you might see a CAPTCHA?

How to avoid risks when playing online games?

Which security company's code of conduct expects its employees to raise ethical issues?

How to protect yourself from social engineering scams?

How the federal and local governments use technology?

Why computer vision helps to increase security?

How public key encryption works?

Which retail apps are best suited to your needs?

How to secure a mobile device?

For these answers and to discover much more information essential to this course, read this chapter and visit the associated Computer Concepts CourseMate at www.cengagebrain.com.

✔ Objectives

After completing this chapter, you will be able to:

1 Define the term, digital security risks, and briefly describe the types of cybercriminals

2 Describe various types of Internet and network attacks (malware, botnets, denial of service attacks, back doors, and spoofing) and explain ways to safeguard against these attacks, including firewalls

3 Discuss techniques to prevent unauthorized computer access and use, including access controls, user names, passwords, possessed objects, and biometric devices

4 Explain ways that software manufacturers protect against software piracy

5 Discuss how encryption, digital signatures, and digital certificates work

6 Identify safeguards against hardware theft, vandalism, and failure

7 Explain options available for backing up

8 Identify risks and safeguards associated with wireless communications

9 Recognize issues related to information accuracy, intellectual property rights, codes of conduct, and green computing

10 Discuss issues surrounding information privacy, including electronic profiles, cookies, phishing, spyware and adware, social engineering, privacy laws, employee monitoring, and content filtering

Digital Security Risks

Today, people rely on technology to create, store, and manage their critical information. Thus, it is important that computers and mobile devices, along with the data and programs they store, are accessible and available when needed. It also is crucial that users take measures to protect or safeguard their computers, mobile devices, data, and programs from loss, damage, and misuse. For example, organizations must ensure that sensitive data and information such as credit records, employee and customer data, and purchase information is secure. Home users must ensure that their credit card numbers are secure when they make online purchases.

A **digital security risk** is any event or action that could cause a loss of or damage to computer or mobile device hardware, software, data, information, or processing capability. The more common digital security risks include Internet and network attacks, unauthorized access and use, hardware theft, software theft, information theft, and system failure (Figure 5-1).

While some breaches to digital security are accidental, many are intentional. Some intruders do no damage; they merely access data, information, or programs on the computer or mobile device before signing out. Other intruders indicate some evidence of their presence either by leaving a message or by deliberately altering or damaging data.

Cybercrime

An intentional breach to digital security often involves a deliberate act that is against the law. Any illegal act involving the use of a computer or related devices generally is referred to as a **computer crime**. The term **cybercrime** refers to online or Internet-based illegal acts such as distributing malicious software or committing identity theft. Software used by cybercriminals sometimes is called *crimeware*. Today, combating cybercrime is one of the FBI's top priorities.

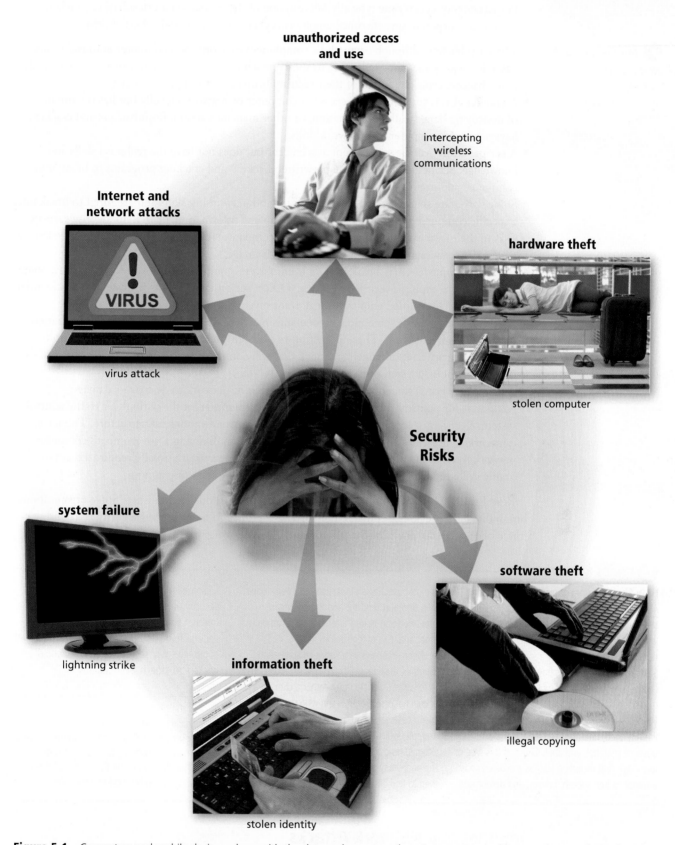

unauthorized access
and use

intercepting
wireless
communications

**Internet and
network attacks**

hardware theft

VIRUS

virus attack

stolen computer

**Security
Risks**

system failure

software theft

lightning strike

illegal copying

information theft

stolen identity

Figure 5-1   Computers and mobile devices, along with the data and programs they store, are exposed to several types of security risks.

Perpetrators of cybercrime typically fall into one of these basic categories: hacker, cracker, script kiddie, corporate spy, unethical employee, cyberextortionist, and cyberterrorist.

Internet Research

What is a white hat hacker?

Search for: white hat hacker

- The term **hacker**, although originally a complimentary word for a computer enthusiast, now has a derogatory meaning and refers to someone who accesses a computer or network illegally. Some hackers claim the intent of their security breaches is to improve security.
- A **cracker** also is someone who accesses a computer or network illegally but has the intent of destroying data, stealing information, or other malicious action. Both hackers and crackers have advanced computer and network skills.
- A **script kiddie** has the same intent as a cracker but does not have the technical skills and knowledge. Script kiddies often use prewritten hacking and cracking programs to break into computers and networks.
- Some corporate spies have excellent computer and networking skills and are hired to break into a specific computer and steal its proprietary data and information, or to help identify security risks in their own organization. Unscrupulous companies hire corporate spies, a practice known as corporate espionage, to gain a competitive advantage.
- Unethical employees may break into their employers' computers for a variety of reasons. Some simply want to exploit a security weakness. Others seek financial gains from selling confidential information. Disgruntled employees may want revenge.
- A **cyberextortionist** is someone who demands payment to stop an attack on an organization's technology infrastructure. These perpetrators threaten to expose confidential information, exploit a security flaw, or launch an attack that will compromise the organization's network — if they are not paid a sum of money.
- A **cyberterrorist** is someone who uses the Internet or network to destroy or damage computers for political reasons. The cyberterrorist might target the nation's air traffic control system, electricity-generating companies, or a telecommunications infrastructure. The term, *cyberwarfare*, describes an attack whose goal ranges from disabling a government's computer network to crippling a country. Cyberterrorism and cyberwarfare usually require a team of highly skilled individuals, millions of dollars, and several years of planning.

Read Ethics & Issues 5-1 to consider how cybercriminals should be punished. Some organizations hire individuals previously convicted of computer crimes to help identify security risks and implement safeguards because these individuals know how criminals attempt to breach security.

✺ ETHICS & ISSUES 5-1

How Should Cybercriminals Be Punished?
A hacker was sentenced to 20 years in jail for stealing credit card information from several large corporations and then selling the information, costing one company approximately $200 million. Legislators have made efforts to deter cybercrime. For example, one country proposed legislation that attempts to specify punishments for cybercrime, such as those involving identity theft, unauthorized access and use, obscene material, and libel. Critics of this type of law claim that including libel as a cybercrime is a threat to free speech, privacy, and democracy.

The proposed legislation received international attention and scrutiny, and the country's supreme court issued a temporary restraining order against the legislation.

Cybercrime laws vary between states and countries, making it difficult to reach a consensus as to what is illegal, and whether a crime is a civil or criminal case. Determining who has jurisdiction over a case can create more legal hassles. For example, which area has jurisdiction: where the victim(s) resides or where the perpetrator lives? The anonymity of the Internet makes it difficult even to find out who has committed the crime.

Some legal experts claim that weak security on the part of corporations using the Internet to conduct business is to blame. The Federal Trade Commission (FTC) has punished companies whose security flaws enabled hackers to breach their systems.

Should the government create new laws specifically aimed at punishing cybercriminals? Why or why not? Should corporations be liable for damages caused by hackers? Why or why not? Who should decide the extent of the true damages caused by a cybercrime? Why?

Internet and Network Attacks

Information transmitted over networks has a higher degree of security risk than information kept on an organization's premises. In an organization, network administrators usually take measures to protect a network from security risks. On the Internet, where no central administrator is present, the security risk is greater. Internet and network attacks that jeopardize security include malware, botnets, denial of service attacks, back doors, and spoofing.

Malware

Recall that **malware**, short for *malicious software*, consists of programs that act without a user's knowledge and deliberately alter the operations of computers and mobile devices. Table 5-1 summarizes common types of malware, all of which have been discussed in previous chapters. Some malware contains characteristics in two or more classes. For example, a single threat could contain elements of a virus, worm, and trojan horse. Some websites maintain lists of known malware.

Malware can deliver its *payload*, or destructive event or prank, on a computer or mobile device in a variety of ways, such as when a user opens an infected file, runs an infected program, connects an unprotected computer or mobile device to a network, or when a certain condition or event occurs, such as the computer's clock changing to a specific date. A common way that computers and mobile devices become infected with viruses and other malware is through users opening infected email attachments (Figure 5-2). Read Secure IT 5-1 on the next page to learn about how malware can affect online gaming.

Table 5-1	Common Types of Malware
Type	**Description**
Virus	A potentially damaging program that affects, or infects, a computer or mobile device negatively by altering the way the computer or device works without the user's knowledge or permission.
Worm	A program that copies itself repeatedly, for example in memory or on a network, using up resources and possibly shutting down the computer, device, or network.
Trojan horse	A program that hides within or looks like a legitimate program. Unlike a virus or worm, a trojan horse does not replicate itself to other computers or devices.
Rootkit	A program that hides in a computer or mobile device and allows someone from a remote location to take full control of the computer or device.
Spyware	A program placed on a computer or mobile device without the user's knowledge that secretly collects information about the user and then communicates the information it collects to some outside source while the user is online.
Adware	A program that displays an online advertisement in a banner or pop-up window on webpages, email messages, or other Internet services.

How a Virus Can Spread via an Email Message

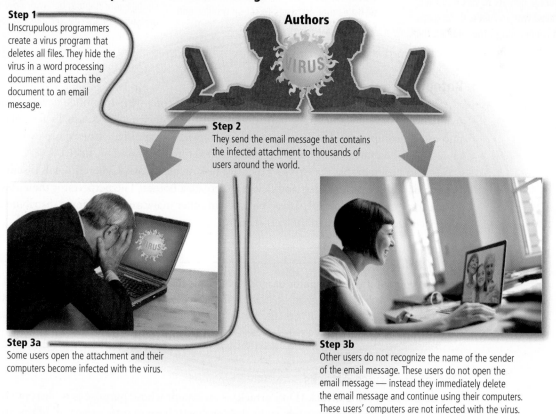

Step 1
Unscrupulous programmers create a virus program that deletes all files. They hide the virus in a word processing document and attach the document to an email message.

Authors

Step 2
They send the email message that contains the infected attachment to thousands of users around the world.

Step 3a
Some users open the attachment and their computers become infected with the virus.

Step 3b
Other users do not recognize the name of the sender of the email message. These users do not open the email message — instead they immediately delete the email message and continue using their computers. These users' computers are not infected with the virus.

Figure 5-2 This figure shows how a virus can spread via an email message.
© Cengage Learning; © iStockphoto / Steve Cukrov; © iStockphoto / Casarsa

CONSIDER THIS

What if you cannot remove malware?
In extreme cases, in order to remove malware from a computer or mobile device, you may need to erase, or reformat, an infected computer's hard disk, or reset a mobile device to its factory settings. For this reason, it is critical you have uninfected (clean) backups of all files. Seek advice from a technology specialist before performing a format or reformat instruction on your media.

Internet Research

What are the latest malware threats?

Search for: malware news

  SECURE IT 5-1

Play It Safe to Avoid Online Gaming Risks

Anyone experiencing the joys of playing games online or playing games with others through online services needs to realize the perils of finding real-life predators lurking behind the scenes. Thieves and hackers take advantage of security holes and vulnerabilities that can turn a gaming session into a nightmare. While gamers often understand general security issues regarding online behavior, they may not be aware of a different set of technology and social risks they may encounter as they interact in the online world.

Viruses, worms, and malware can be hidden in email message attachments, downloaded game files, and instant messaging software. In addition, messages on social networks may encourage gamers to visit fraudulent websites filled with malware. If the game requires a connection to the Internet, then any computer connected to the game's server is subject to security cyberthreats. Thieves can take control of a remote computer that does not have a high level of security protection and use it to control other computers, or they break into the computer and install malware to discover personal information. The Computer Emergency Response Team Coordination Center (CERT/CC) describes many vulnerabilities found in online games and online gaming services used with game consoles and devices.

Malicious users know that the gaming community uses social media intensely, so they also create accounts and attempt to mislead uninformed users into revealing personal information. The thieves may claim to have software updates and free games, when they really are luring users to bogus websites that ask users to set up profiles and accounts.

Gamers should follow these practices to increase their security:

- Before downloading any software, including patches to games, or disclosing any private details, be certain the website or the person making the request is legitimate.
- Exercise extreme caution if the game requires ActiveX or JavaScript to be enabled or if it must be played in administrator mode.
- Use a firewall and make exceptions to allow only trusted individuals to access your computer or mobile device when playing multiplayer online games.
- Do not share personal information with other gamers whom you meet online.

 Have you played online games and followed the advice listed here? How will you change your gaming behavior now that you are aware of specific security threats?

Botnets

A **botnet**, or *zombie army*, is a group of compromised computers or mobile devices connected to a network such as the Internet that are used to attack other networks, usually for nefarious purposes. A compromised computer or device, known as a **zombie**, is one whose owner is unaware the computer or device is being controlled remotely by an outsider.

A *bot* is a program that performs a repetitive task on a network. Cybercriminals install malicious bots on unprotected computers and devices to create a botnet. The perpetrator then uses the botnet to send spam via email, spread viruses and other malware, or commit a distributed denial of service attack (discussed in the next section).

CONSIDER THIS

How can you tell if your computer or mobile device is functioning as a zombie?
Your computer or mobile device may be a zombie if you notice an unusually high disk activity, a slower than normal Internet connection, or connected devices becoming increasingly unresponsive. The chances of your computer or devices becoming part of a botnet greatly increase if they are not running an effective firewall.

Denial of Service Attacks

A **denial of service attack (DoS attack)** is an assault whose purpose is to disrupt computer access to an Internet service such as the web or email. Perpetrators carry out a DoS attack in a variety of ways. For example, they may use an unsuspecting computer to send an influx of confusing data messages or useless traffic to a computer network. The victim computer network slows down considerably and eventually becomes unresponsive or unavailable, blocking legitimate visitors from accessing the network.

A more devastating type of DoS attack is the *distributed DoS attack* (*DDoS attack*) in which a zombie army is used to attack computers or computer networks. DDoS attacks have been able to stop operations temporarily at numerous websites, including powerhouses such as Yahoo!, eBay, Amazon.com, and CNN.com.

The damage caused by a DoS or DDoS attack usually is extensive. During the outage, retailers lose sales from customers, news websites and search engines lose revenue from advertisers, and time-sensitive information may be delayed. Repeated attacks could tarnish reputations, causing even greater losses.

Internet Research

Are DoS attacks still prevalent?

Search for: news of dos attacks

 CONSIDER THIS

Why would someone execute a Dos or DDoS attack?
Perpetrators have a variety of motives for executing a DoS or DDoS attack. Those who disagree with the beliefs or actions of a particular organization claim political anger motivates their attacks. Some perpetrators use the attack as a vehicle for extortion. Others simply want the recognition, even though it is negative.

Back Doors

A **back door** is a program or set of instructions in a program that allows users to bypass security controls when accessing a program, computer, or network. Once perpetrators gain access to unsecure computers, they often install a back door or modify an existing program to include a back door, which allows them to continue to access the computer remotely without the user's knowledge. A rootkit can be a back door. Some worms leave back doors, which have been used to spread other worms or to distribute spam from the unsuspecting victim computers.

Programmers often build back doors into programs during system development. These back doors save development time because the programmer can bypass security controls while writing and testing programs. Similarly, a computer repair technician may install a back door while troubleshooting problems on a computer. If a programmer or computer repair technician fails to remove a back door, a perpetrator could use the back door to gain entry to a computer or network.

Spoofing

Spoofing is a technique intruders use to make their network or Internet transmission appear legitimate to a victim computer or network. Two common types of spoofing schemes are email and IP spoofing.

- *Email spoofing* occurs when the sender's address or other components of an email header are altered so that it appears that the email message originated from a different sender. Email spoofing commonly is used in virus hoaxes, spam, and phishing scams (Figure 5-3).
- *IP spoofing* occurs when an intruder computer fools a network into believing its IP address is associated with a trusted source. Perpetrators of IP spoofing trick their victims into interacting with the phony website. For example, the victim may provide confidential information or download files containing viruses, worms, or other malware.

Figure 5-3 With email spoofing, the components of an email header are altered so that it appears the email message originated from a different sender.
© Cengage Learning

Safeguards against Internet and Network Attacks

Methods that protect computers, mobile devices, and networks from attacks include the following:

- Use antivirus software.
- Be suspicious of unsolicited email attachments.
- Scan removable media for malware before using it.
- Implement firewall solutions.
- Back up regularly.

Secure IT 1-2 on page 23 in Chapter 1 provided some measures you can take to protect your computers and mobile devices from malware. Read Secure IT 5-2 for additional tips to protect home users against Internet and network attacks. The next section discusses firewalls in more depth.

 CONSIDER THIS

How can you determine if your computer or mobile device is vulnerable to an Internet or network attack?

You could use an **online security service**, which is a web app that evaluates your computer or mobile device to check for Internet and email vulnerabilities. The online security service then provides recommendations of how to address the vulnerabilities.

Organizations requiring assistance or information about Internet security breaches can contact or visit the website for the *Computer Emergency Response Team Coordination Center,* or *CERT/CC*, which is a federally funded Internet security research and development center.

 SECURE IT 5-2

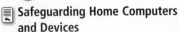

Safeguarding Home Computers and Devices

Sophisticated cybercriminals take advantage of the fact that most home users employ poor security measures. In fact, one study found that home users are victims of 86 percent of all attacks. Instead of resorting to large-scale attacks affecting thousands of users simultaneously, these criminals develop fraud, data theft, and other wealth-generating schemes affecting individual users. In these cases, the users are forced to be reactive in repairing the damage done. The following measures, however, can help home users become proactive by preventing Internet and network attacks.

- **Use routers and firewalls.** These devices can help detect suspicious activities by continuously monitoring activity and blocking

unauthorized entry into the computer. Antivirus software can help thwart attacks that slip by the firewall.

- **Disable macro security settings.** *Macros* are useful to record, save, and then execute a set of keystrokes and instructions repeatedly, and they commonly are found in word processing and spreadsheet files. Macros, however, can be disastrous when hidden in a file and then run without permission. In many office productivity applications, you can change the macro security settings so that macros are executed only with your permission.

- **Address software warnings.** Be wary of tapping or clicking buttons or security bars that seek permission to download or run a program. If you are suspicious of the

authenticity, exit the program or leave the website.

- **Keep software updated.** Major software companies release software patches to repair known vulnerabilities. Many times, home users could have prevented their attacks if they had updated their software with the available patches.

- **Stay informed.** News media and technology websites report current security breaches and threats. Seek out these articles and take preventive measures.

 Which of these techniques do you use on your home computer or mobile devices? What new techniques will you use to help prevent security attacks?

Firewalls

A **firewall** is hardware and/or software that protects a network's resources from intrusion by users on another network such as the Internet (Figure 5-4). All networked and online users should implement a firewall solution.

Organizations use firewalls to protect network resources from outsiders and to restrict employees' access to sensitive data, such as payroll or personnel records. They can implement a firewall solution themselves or outsource their needs to a company specializing in providing firewall protection.

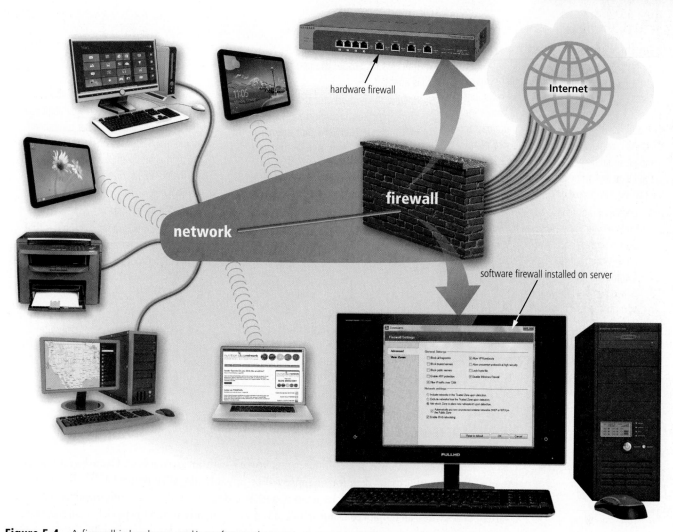

hardware firewall

Internet

firewall

network

software firewall installed on server

Figure 5-4   A firewall is hardware and/or software that protects a network's resources from intrusion by users on another network, such as the Internet.

Large organizations often route all their communications through a proxy server, which typically is a component of the firewall. A *proxy server* is a server outside the organization's network that controls which communications pass in and out of the organization's network. That is, a proxy server carefully screens all incoming and outgoing messages. Proxy servers use a variety of screening techniques. Some check the domain name or IP address of the message for legitimacy. Others require that the messages have digital signatures (discussed later in this chapter).

Home and small/home office users often protect their computers with a personal firewall. As discussed in Chapter 4, a **personal firewall** is a software firewall that detects and protects a personal computer and its data from unauthorized intrusions. Personal firewalls constantly monitor all transmissions to and from the computer and may inform a user of any attempted intrusions. Both Windows and Mac operating systems include firewall capabilities, including monitoring Internet traffic to and from installed applications. Read How To 5-1 on the next page for instructions about setting up a personal firewall.

Some small/home office users purchase a hardware firewall, such as a router or other device that has a built-in firewall, in addition to or instead of a personal firewall. Hardware firewalls stop intrusions before they attempt to affect your computer or network maliciously.

 BTW

AVG, McAfee, and Symantec

Technology Innovators: You should be familiar with AVG, McAfee, and Symantec (security product developers).

HOW TO 5-1

Set Up a Personal Firewall

A personal firewall is a program that helps protect your computer from unauthorized access by blocking certain types of communications. For example, if somebody knows the IP address of your computer and attempts to access it using a browser or other program, the personal firewall can be configured to deny the incoming connection. The following steps describe how to set up a personal firewall.

1. Locate and purchase a personal firewall. You can purchase personal firewalls online and in stores that sell software. Many operating systems include a personal firewall. Computers typically can have only one active personal firewall running at a time. If you purchase a personal firewall, you may need to disable the one that is included with the operating system.

2. If you purchase a personal firewall, follow the instructions to install the program on your computer.

3. Run the personal firewall.

4. If necessary, ensure the personal firewall is enabled.

5. Review the settings for the incoming and outgoing rules. Incoming rules display programs and services that are allowed to access your computer. Outgoing rules display programs and services on your computer that are allowed to communicate with other computers and mobile devices on your network or the Internet.

6. Back up or export your current list of incoming and outgoing rules. If your computer does not function properly after you adjust the rules (in Steps 7 and 8), you will be able to restore the current rules.

7. Adjust your incoming rules to disallow devices, programs, and services you do not want accessing your computer. Be careful adjusting these settings,

as adding or removing rules may hinder a legitimate program's capability to work properly.

8. Adjust your outgoing rules to allow only appropriate programs on your computer to communicate with other computers and mobile devices on your network or the Internet. Examples include a browser, email program, or other communications programs.

9. Save your settings.

10. Test programs on your computer that require Internet access. If any do not function properly, restore the list of rules you backed up or exported in Step 6.

11. Exit the personal firewall.

✸ Which programs on your computer should have access to the Internet? Which programs should not?

Unauthorized Access and Use

Unauthorized access is the use of a computer or network without permission. *Unauthorized use* is the use of a computer or its data for unapproved or possibly illegal activities.

Home and business users can be a target of unauthorized access and use. Unauthorized use includes a variety of activities: an employee using an organization's computer to send personal email messages, an employee using the organization's word processing software to track his or her child's soccer league scores, or a perpetrator gaining access to a bank computer and performing an unauthorized transfer.

Safeguards against Unauthorized Access and Use

Organizations take several measures to help prevent unauthorized access and use. At a minimum, they should have a written *acceptable use policy* (*AUP*) that outlines the activities for which the computer and network may and may not be used. An organization's AUP should specify the acceptable use of technology by employees for personal reasons. Some organizations prohibit such use entirely. Others allow personal use on the employee's own time, such as a lunch hour. Whatever the policy, an organization should document and explain it to employees. The AUP also should

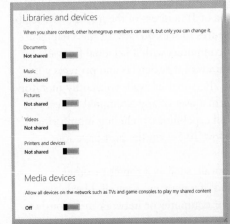

Figure 5-5 To protect files on your local hard disk from hackers and other intruders, turn off file and printer sharing on your Internet connection.
Source: Microsoft

specify the personal activities, if any, that are allowed on company time. For example, can employees check personal email messages or respond to personal text messages during work hours?

To protect your personal computer from unauthorized intrusions, you should disable file and printer sharing in your operating system (Figure 5-5). This security measure attempts to ensure that others cannot access your files or your printer. You also should be sure to use a firewall. The following sections address other techniques for protecting against unauthorized access and use. The technique(s) used should correspond to the degree of risk that is associated with the unauthorized access.

Access Controls

Many organizations use access controls to minimize the chance that a perpetrator intentionally may access or an employee accidentally may access confidential information on a computer, mobile device, or network. An *access control* is a security measure that defines who can access a computer, device, or network; when they can access it; and what actions they can take while accessing it. In addition, the computer, device, or network should maintain an *audit trail* that records in a file both successful and unsuccessful access attempts. An unsuccessful access attempt could result from a user mistyping his or her password, or it could result from a perpetrator trying thousands of passwords.

Organizations should investigate unsuccessful access attempts immediately to ensure they are not intentional breaches of security. They also should review successful access for irregularities, such as use of the computer after normal working hours or from remote computers. The security program can be configured to alert a security administrator whenever suspicious or irregular activities are suspected. In addition, an organization regularly should review users' access privilege levels to determine whether they still are appropriate.

User Names and Passwords

A **user name**, or *user ID* (identification), is a unique combination of characters, such as letters of the alphabet or numbers, that identifies one specific user. A **password** is a private combination of characters associated with the user name that allows access to certain computer resources.

Most operating systems that enable multiple users to share computers and devices or that access a home or business network require users to correctly enter a user name and a password before they can access the data, information, and programs stored on a computer, mobile device, or network. Many systems that maintain financial, personal, and other confidential information also require a user name and password as part of their sign-in procedure (Figure 5-6).

Some systems assign a user name and/or password to each user. For example, a school may use a student ID as a user name. Some websites use your email address as the user name. Information technology (IT) departments may assign passwords so that they have a record in case the employee leaves or forgets the password.

With other systems, users select their own user names and/or passwords. Many users select a combination of their first and last names for their user names. Read Secure IT 1-3 on page 24

Figure 5-6 Many websites that maintain personal and confidential data, such as Citibank's credit card system, require a user to enter a user name (user ID) and password.
Source: Citigroup Inc

in Chapter 1 for tips about creating strong passwords. Once you select a password, change it frequently. Do not disclose it to anyone or write it on a slip of paper kept near the computer, especially taped to the monitor or under the keyboard. Email and telemarketing scams often ask unsuspecting users to disclose their credit card numbers, so be wary if you did not initiate the inquiry or phone call.

 **CONSIDER THIS**

Why do some websites allow me to use my email address as a user name?
No two users can have the same email address; that is, your email address is unique to you. This means you can use your email address and password from one website to validate your identity on another website. Facebook, Google, and Twitter, for example, are three popular websites that provide authentication services to other applications. By using your email address from one of these websites to access other websites, you do not have to create or remember separate user names and passwords for the various websites you visit.

BTW
Microsoft Account
Some computers can be configured so that you can sign in using your Microsoft account. Signing in with your Microsoft account makes additional Windows features available and also enables you to synchronize settings if you sign in to multiple computers.

In addition to a user name and password, some systems ask users to enter one of several pieces of personal information. Such items can include a grandparent's first name, your mother's maiden name, or the name of the elementary school you attended. These items should be facts that you easily remember but are not easy for others to discover about you when using a search engine or examining your profiles on social networking sites. As with a password, if the user's response does not match information on file, the system denies access. Read Secure IT 5-3 to learn about two-step verification, an authentication technique you might encounter with user names and passwords.

Instead of passwords, some organizations use passphrases to authenticate users. A *passphrase* is a private combination of words, often containing mixed capitalization and punctuation, associated with a user name that allows access to certain computer resources. Passphrases, which often can be up to 100 characters in length, are more secure than passwords, yet can be easy to remember because they contain words.

✺ CONSIDER THIS

Why do some websites display distorted characters you must reenter along with your password?

These websites use a CAPTCHA, which stands for Completely Automated Public Turing test to tell Computers and Humans Apart. A *CAPTCHA* is a program developed at Carnegie Mellon University that displays an image containing a series of distorted characters for a user to identify and enter in order to verify that user input is from humans and not computer programs (Figure 5-7). A CAPTCHA is effective in blocking computer-generated attempts to access a website, because it is difficult to write programs for computers to detect distorted characters, while humans generally can recognize them. For visually impaired users or if words are too difficult to read, the CAPTCHA text can be read aloud; you also have the option of generating a new CAPTCHA.

Figure 5-7 To continue with the ticket order process at the Ticketmaster website, the user must enter the characters in the CAPTCHA, which consists of the letters, themssr neillso, in this case.
Source: Carnegie Mellon University

✺ SECURE IT 5-3

Using the Two-Step Verification Process

If you use the same password to access several accounts, you are not alone. More than 10 percent of people think their password is sufficient protection for all their vital online accounts. Cyberthieves are aware of this flawed thinking and take advantage of this practice.

In an attempt to thwart the thieves' actions, financial institutions, universities, and businesses are using a two-step verification process, also known as two-factor authentication. This method requires a mobile phone and a computer. When users sign in to a computer account, they enter a user name and a password. Next, they are prompted to enter another authentication code, which is sent as a text or voice message or via an app on a smartphone. This second code generally is valid for a set time, sometimes only for a few hours. If users do not sign in during this time limit, then they must repeat the process and request another verification code.

One method of circumventing this two-step verification process is to specify one computer as a trusted device. The computer must accept cookies for this designation to be assigned. (Cookies are discussed later in the chapter.) Only limited-use computers in safe areas should be identified as being secure.

A flaw in using the two-step process arises when users lose their mobile phones.

If individuals who own these phones use the two-step process, they would be unable to access their online accounts. Some software developers have created work-arounds; in one instance, a series of images is sent to the computer and one photo from the series is sent to another mobile device. The user must match the photos to authenticate and gain access to the account.

✺ Is the two-step verification process a sufficient practice of adding an extra layer of protection to accounts? Or, is this measure overkill? Is it a better process than requiring users to type a long, complex password? Why or why not?

Possessed Objects

A possessed object is any item that you must carry with you in order to gain access to a computer or computer facility. Examples of possessed objects are badges, cards, smart cards, and keys. The card you use in an ATM (automated teller machine), for example, is a possessed object that allows access to your bank account.

Possessed objects often are used in combination with PINs. A **PIN** (*personal identification number*) is a numeric password, either assigned by a company or selected by a user. PINs provide an additional level of security. An ATM card typically requires a four-digit PIN. Most debit cards and some credit cards use PINs. If someone steals these cards, the thief must enter the user's PIN to access the account. PINs are passwords. Select them carefully and protect them as you do any other password. For example, do not use the same four digits, sequential digits, or dates others could easily determine, such as birth dates.

Biometric Devices

A **biometric device** authenticates a person's identity by translating a personal characteristic, such as a fingerprint, into a digital code that is compared with a digital code stored in a computer verifying a physical or behavioral characteristic. If the digital code in the computer does not match the personal characteristic code, the computer denies access to the individual.

Biometric devices grant access to programs, computers, or rooms using computer analysis of some biometric identifier. Examples of biometric devices and systems include fingerprint readers, face recognition systems, hand geometry systems, voice verification systems, signature verification systems, iris recognition systems, and retinal scanners.

Figure 5-8 A fingerprint reader.
© Flynavyjp / Dreamstime.com

Fingerprint Reader   A **fingerprint reader**, or scanner, captures curves and indentations of a fingerprint (Figure 5-8). Organizations use fingerprint readers to secure doors, computers, and software. With the cost of fingerprint readers often less than $100, some home and small business users install fingerprint readers to authenticate users before they can access a personal computer. The reader also can be set up to perform different functions for different fingers; for example, one finger starts a program and another finger shuts down the computer. External fingerprint readers usually plug into a USB port. Some newer laptops have a fingerprint reader built into their keyboards, which allows users to sign in to programs and websites via their fingerprint instead of entering a user name and password.

BTW
Face Recognition
Innovative Computing: You should be familiar with the FBI's face recognition technology project.

Face Recognition System   A *face recognition system* captures a live face image and compares it with a stored image to determine if the person is a legitimate user. Some buildings use face recognition systems to secure access to rooms. Law enforcement, surveillance systems, and airports use face recognition to protect the public. Some mobile devices use face recognition systems to unlock the device. Face recognition programs are becoming more sophisticated and can recognize people with or without glasses, makeup, or jewelry, and with new hairstyles.

Hand Geometry System   A *hand geometry system* measures the shape and size of a person's hand (Figure 5-9). Because hand geometry systems can be expensive, they often are used in larger companies to track workers' time and attendance or as security devices. Colleges use hand geometry systems to verify students' identities. Daycare centers and hospital nurseries use them to identify parents who pick up their children.

Voice Verification System   A *voice verification system* compares a person's live speech with their stored voice pattern. Larger organizations sometimes use voice verification systems as time and attendance devices. Many companies also use this technology for access to sensitive files and networks. Some financial services use voice verification systems to secure phone banking transactions.

Figure 5-9 A hand geometry system verifies identity based on the shape and size of a person's hand.
Courtesy of Ingersoll Rand Security Technologies

Signature Verification System A *signature verification system* recognizes the shape of your handwritten signature, as well as measures the pressure exerted and the motion used to write the signature. Signature verification systems use a specialized pen and tablet. Signature verification systems often are used to reduce fraud in financial institutions.

 CONSIDER THIS

Do retailers use a signature verification system for credit card purchases?
No. With a credit card purchase, users sign their name on a signature capture pad using a stylus attached to the device. Software then transmits the signature to a central computer, where it is stored. Thus, the retailers use these systems simply to record your signature.

Iris Recognition System High security areas use iris recognition systems. The camera in an *iris recognition system* uses iris recognition technology to read patterns in the iris of the eye (Figure 5-10). These patterns are as unique as a fingerprint. Iris recognition systems are quite expensive and are used by government security organizations, the military, and financial institutions that deal with highly sensitive data. Some organizations use retinal scanners, which work similarly but instead scan patterns of blood vessels in the back of the retina.

Figure 5-10 An iris recognition system.
© Robert F. Balazik / Shutterstock.com; AP Photo / Canadian Press, Adrian Wyld; © Cengage Learning

 CONSIDER THIS

How popular are biometric devices?
Biometric devices are gaining popularity as a security precaution because they are a virtually foolproof method of identification and authentication. For example, some grocery stores, retail stores, and gas stations use *biometric payment*, where the customer's fingerprint is read by a fingerprint reader that is linked to a payment method such as a checking account or credit card. Users can forget their user names and passwords. Possessed objects can be lost, copied, duplicated, or stolen. Personal characteristics, by contrast, are unique and cannot be forgotten or misplaced.

Biometric devices do have disadvantages. If you cut your finger, a fingerprint reader might reject you as a legitimate user. Hand geometry readers can transmit germs. If you are nervous, a signature might not match the one on file. If you have a sore throat, a voice recognition system might reject you. Many people are uncomfortable with the thought of using an iris scanner.

Digital Forensics

Digital forensics, also called *cyberforensics*, is the discovery, collection, and analysis of evidence found on computers and networks. Digital forensics involves the examination of media, programs, data and log files on computers, mobile devices, servers, and networks. Many areas use digital forensics, including law enforcement, criminal prosecutors, military intelligence, insurance agencies, and information security departments in the private sector.

A digital forensics examiner must have knowledge of the law, technical experience with many types of hardware and software products, superior communication skills, familiarity with corporate structures and policies, a willingness to learn and update skills, and a knack for problem solving. For more information about digital forensics, read Mini Feature 5-1 (available in the e-book).

NOW YOU KNOW

Be sure you understand the material presented in the sections titled Digital Security Risks, Internet and Network Attacks, and Unauthorized Access and Use, as it relates to the chapter objectives.
You now should know . . .

- How cybercriminals' backgrounds and intent vary (Objective 1)

- How you can protect your computers and devices from malware, botnets, DoS attacks, back doors, and spoofing (Objective 2)

- Why you should use a firewall (Objective 2)

- How you can prevent unauthorized users from accessing your home or office computers and devices (Objective 3)

Quiz Yourself Online: Check your knowledge of related content by navigating to this book's Quiz Yourself resource on Computer Concepts CourseMate and then tapping or clicking Objectives 1–3.

Software Theft

Software theft occurs when someone steals software media, intentionally erases programs, illegally registers and/or activates a program, or illegally copies a program.
- Physically stealing software: A perpetrator physically steals the media that contains the software, or steals the hardware that contains the media that contains the software. For example, an unscrupulous library patron might steal a game CD/DVD.
- Intentionally erasing software: A perpetrator erases the media that contains the software. For example, a programmer who is terminated from a company may retaliate by removing or disabling the programs he or she has written from company computers.
- Illegal registration/activation: A perpetrator illegally obtains registration numbers and/ or activation codes. A program called a *keygen*, short for key generator, creates software registration numbers and sometimes activation codes. Some unscrupulous individuals create and post keygens so that users can install software without legally purchasing it.
- Illegal copying: A perpetrator copies software from manufacturers. **Software piracy**, often referred to simply as **piracy**, is the unauthorized and illegal duplication of copyrighted software. Piracy is the most common form of software theft.

Safeguards against Software Theft

To protect software media from being stolen, owners should keep original software boxes and media or the online confirmation of purchased software in a secure location, out of sight of prying eyes. All computer users should back up their files and disks regularly, in the event of theft. When some companies terminate a programmer or if the programmer quits, they escort the employee off the premises immediately. These companies believe that allowing terminated employees to remain on the premises gives them time to sabotage files and other network procedures.

Many manufacturers incorporate an activation process into their programs to ensure the software is not installed on more computers than legally licensed. During the **product activation**, which is conducted either online or by phone, users provide the software product's identification number to associate the software with the computer or mobile device on which the software is installed. Usually, the software can be run a preset number of times, has limited functionality, or does not function until you activate it.

To further protect themselves from software piracy, software manufacturers issue users license agreements. As discussed in Chapter 4, a **license agreement** is the right to use software. That is, you do not own the software. The most common type of license included with software purchased by individual users is a *single-user license agreement*, also called an *end-user license agreement (EULA)*. The license agreement provides specific conditions for use of the software, which a user must accept before using the software. These terms usually are displayed when you install the software. Use of the software constitutes acceptance of the terms on the user's part. Figure 5-11 on the next page identifies the conditions of a typical single-user license agreement.

 BTW
BSA
To promote understanding of software piracy, a number of major worldwide software companies formed the *Business Software Alliance (BSA)*. The BSA operates a website and antipiracy hotlines around the world.

 Internet Research
What are the penalties for piracy?
Search for: piracy penalties

Typical Conditions of a Single-User License Agreement

You can...

- Install the software on only one computer. (Some license agreements allow users to install the software on one desktop and one laptop.)
- Make one copy of the software as a backup.
- Give or sell the software to another individual, but only if the software is removed from the user's computer first.

You cannot...

- Install the software on a network, such as a school computer lab.
- Give copies to friends and colleagues, while continuing to use the software.
- Export the software.
- Rent or lease the software.

Figure 5-11 A user must accept the terms of a license agreement before using the software.
© Cengage Learning

To support multiple users' access of software, most manufacturers sell network versions or site licenses of their software, which usually costs less than buying individual stand-alone copies of the software for each computer. A *network license* is a legal agreement that allows multiple users to access the software on the server simultaneously. The network license fee usually is based on the number of users or the number of computers attached to the network. A *site license* is a legal agreement that permits users to install the software on multiple computers — usually at a volume discount.

 CONSIDER THIS

Can you install software on work computers or work-issued smartphones?
Many organizations and businesses have strict written policies governing the installation and use of software and enforce their rules by checking networked or online computers or mobile devices periodically to ensure that all software is licensed properly. If you are not completely familiar with your school's or employer's policies governing installation of software, check with the information technology department or your school's technology coordinator.

Information Theft

Information theft occurs when someone steals personal or confidential information. Both business and home users can fall victim to information theft. An unethical company executive may steal or buy stolen information to learn about a competitor. A corrupt individual may steal credit card numbers to make fraudulent purchases. Information theft often is linked to other types of cybercrime. For example, an individual first might gain unauthorized access to a computer and then steal credit card numbers stored in a firm's accounting department.

Safeguards against Information Theft

Most organizations will attempt to prevent information theft by implementing the user identification and authentication controls discussed earlier in this chapter. These controls are best suited for protecting information on computers located on an organization's premises. To further protect information on the Internet and networks, organizations and individuals use a variety of encryption techniques.

Encryption

Encryption is the process of converting data that is readable by humans into encoded characters to prevent unauthorized access. You treat encrypted data just like any other data. That is, you can store it or send it in an email message. To read the data, the recipient must **decrypt**, or decode it. For example, users may specify that an email application encrypt a message before sending it securely. The recipient's email application would need to decrypt the message in order for the recipient to be able to read it.

In the encryption process, the unencrypted, readable data is called *plaintext*. The encrypted (scrambled) data is called *ciphertext*. An *encryption algorithm*, or *cypher*, is a set of steps that can convert readable plaintext into unreadable ciphertext. Table 5-2 shows examples of some simple encryption algorithms. Encryption programs typically use more than one encryption algorithm, along with an encryption key. An *encryption key* is a set of characters that the originator of the data uses to encrypt the plaintext and the recipient of the data uses to decrypt the ciphertext.

 BTW

Encryption Algorithms
High-Tech Talk: Most secure encryption uses complex encryption algorithms.

Table 5-2 Simple Encryption Algorithms

Name	Algorithm	Plaintext	Ciphertext	Explanation
Transposition	Switch the order of characters	SOFTWARE	OSTFAWER	Adjacent characters swapped
Substitution	Replace characters with other characters	INFORMATION	WLDIMXQUWIL	Each letter replaced with another
Expansion	Insert characters between existing characters	USER	UYSYEYRY	Letter Y inserted after each character
Compaction	Remove characters and store elsewhere	ACTIVATION	ACIVTIN	Every third letter removed (T, A, O)

✳ CONSIDER THIS

What is the Caesar cipher?

The *Caesar cipher* is a substitution encryption algorithm that replaces each character in the plaintext with a different letter by shifting the alphabet a certain number of positions. For example, the plaintext word, computer, would become dpnqvufs when the alphabet shifts one position. The Caesar cipher is named after Julius Caesar because it is believed he used it in his private correspondence.

Two basic types of encryption are private key and public key. With *private key encryption*, also called *symmetric key encryption*, both the originator and the recipient use the same secret key to encrypt and decrypt the data. *Public key encryption*, also called *asymmetric key encryption*, uses two encryption keys: a public key and a private key (Figure 5-12). Public key encryption software generates both the private key and the public key. A message encrypted with a public key can be decrypted only with the corresponding private key, and vice versa. The public key is made known to message originators and recipients. For example, public keys may be posted on a secure webpage or a public-key server, or they may be emailed. The private key, by contrast, should be kept confidential.

An Example of Public Key Encryption

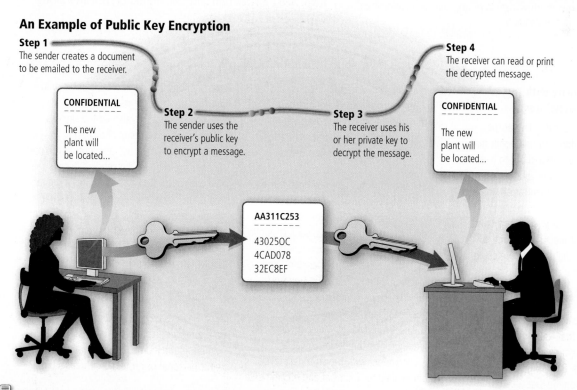

Step 1
The sender creates a document to be emailed to the receiver.

Step 2
The sender uses the receiver's public key to encrypt a message.

Step 3
The receiver uses his or her private key to decrypt the message.

Step 4
The receiver can read or print the decrypted message.

CONFIDENTIAL
The new plant will be located...

CONFIDENTIAL
The new plant will be located...

AA311C253
430250C
4CAD078
32EC8EF

Figure 5-12 This figure shows an example of public key encryption.
© Cengage Learning

Some operating systems and email programs allow you to encrypt the contents of files and messages that are stored on your computer. You also can purchase an encryption program to encrypt files. Many browsers use encryption when sending private information, such as credit card numbers, over the Internet.

Mobile users today often access their company networks through a virtual private network. When a mobile user connects to a main office using a standard Internet connection, a *virtual private network* (*VPN*) provides the mobile user with a secure connection to the company network server, as if the user has a private line. VPNs help ensure that data is safe from being intercepted by unauthorized people by encrypting data as it transmits from a laptop, smartphone, or other mobile device.

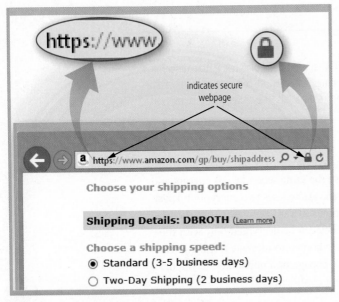

Figure 5-13 Web addresses of secure sites, such as the Amazon.com checkout, often begin with https instead of http. Browsers also often display a lock symbol in the window.

Source: Amazon.com; Microsoft

Digital Signatures and Certificates

A **digital signature** is an encrypted code that a person, website, or organization attaches to an electronic message to verify the identity of the message sender. Digital signatures often are used to ensure that an impostor is not participating in an Internet transaction. That is, digital signatures can help to prevent email forgery. A digital signature also can verify that the content of a message has not changed.

A **digital certificate** is a notice that guarantees a user or a website is legitimate. E-commerce applications commonly use digital certificates. Browsers often display a warning message if a website does not have a valid digital certificate. Read Secure IT 5-4 to learn about ways digital certificates and signatures verify authenticity.

A website that uses encryption techniques to secure its data is known as a **secure site** (Figure 5-13). Web addresses of secure sites often begin with https instead of http. Secure sites typically use digital certificates along with security protocols.

✵ SECURE IT 5-4

Verifying Authenticity with Digital Certificates and Signatures

When you are in the security line at the airport, a security administration agent may compare a government-issued photo ID to your boarding pass to verify your identity. When you receive a document as an email attachment or download a file posted online, however, it is difficult for you to verify who actually created that file. At this point, a digital certificate or digital signature could identify and verify the sender's and document's authenticity.

Online *certificate authority* (CA) providers issue digital certificates. Each CA is a trusted third party that takes responsibility for verifying the sender's identity before issuing a certificate. Every digital certificate has identical components because it is generated using a standard, called X.509. The International Telecommunication Union coordinates this standard along with all telecommunications regulations in effect since 1865 with the invention of the telegraph.

Digital certificates typically have these components: version number, serial number, certificate algorithm identifier, issuer name, validity period, subject name, subject public key information, issuer unique identifier, subject unique identifier, extensions, and certification authority's digital signature.

Individuals and companies can purchase digital certificates from one of more than 35 online CA providers. The cost varies depending upon the desired level of data encryption, with the strongest levels recommended for financial and e-commerce transactions. The certificates can be valid for a maximum of two years.

Digital signatures also tie the signer's identity to the contents of a specific document, but they use an algorithm to detect changes to the file. The sender encrypts the file with a private key and creates a digital signature. Then, the receiver decrypts the same file with a public key and uses the same algorithm to open the document. A symbol, such as a green check mark, often is used to indicate the document is authentic; a different symbol, such as a yellow triangle, would indicate the document has been altered.

✷ Have you ever received a document with a digital certificate or a digital signature? When might you need to generate one for your personal or professional transactions?

Hardware Theft, Vandalism, and Failure

Users rely on computers and mobile devices to create, store, and manage important information. As discussed in Chapter 3, you should take measures to protect computers and devices from theft, vandalism, and failure.

Hardware theft is the act of stealing digital equipment. Hardware vandalism involves defacing or destroying digital equipment. Hardware can fail for a variety of reasons: aging hardware, natural or man-made disasters, or random events such as electrical power problems, and even errors in programs or apps. Figure 5-14 summarizes the techniques you can use to safeguard hardware from theft, vandalism, and failure.

Hardware Theft and Vandalism Safeguards
- Physical access controls (i.e., locked doors and windows)
- Alarm system
- Physical security devices (i.e., cables and locks)
- Device-tracking app

Hardware Failure Safeguards
- Surge protector
- Uninterruptible power supply (UPS)
- Duplicate components or duplicate computers
- Fault-tolerant computer

🔧 BTW

📄 LoJack
Technology Innovator: You should be familiar with the device-tracking app, LoJack.

Figure 5-14
Summary of safeguards against hardware theft, vandalism, and failure.
© Cengage Learning; © iStockphoto / Norebbo

Backing Up — The Ultimate Safeguard

To protect against data loss caused by hardware/software/information theft or system failure, users should back up computer and mobile device files regularly. As previously described, a **backup** is a duplicate of a file, program, or media that can be used if the original is lost, damaged, or destroyed. And, to **back up** a file means to make a copy of it. In the case of system failure or the discovery of corrupted files, you **restore** the files by copying the backed up files to their original location on the computer or mobile device.

If you choose to back up locally, be sure to use high-quality media. A good choice for a home user might be optical discs or an external hard disk. Keep your backup media in a fireproof and heatproof safe or vault, or offsite. *Off-site* means in a location separate from where you typically store or use your computer or mobile device. Keeping backup copies off-site minimizes the chance that a single disaster, such as a fire, would destroy both the original and the backup media. An off-site location can be a safe deposit box at a bank, a briefcase, or cloud storage (Figure 5-15). Recall that cloud storage is an Internet service that provides storage to computer users.

Figure 5-15 Cloud storage, such as Carbonite shown here, is a popular method for off-site backups.
Source: Carbonite, Inc.

Backup programs are available from many sources. Most operating systems include a backup program. Backup devices, such as external disk drives, also include backup programs. Numerous standalone backup tools exist. Cloud storage providers include backup services.

Business and home users can perform four types of backup: full, differential, incremental, or selective. A fifth type, continuous data protection, typically is used only by large enterprises. Table 5-3 on the next page summarizes the purpose, advantages, and disadvantages of each of these backup methods.

Some users implement a three-generation backup policy to preserve three copies of important files. The *grandparent* is the oldest copy of the file. The *parent* is the second oldest copy of the file. The *child* is the most recent copy of the file.

Table 5-3 **Various Backup Methods**

Type of Backup	Description	Advantages	Disadvantages
Full backup	Copies all of the files on media in the computer	Fastest recovery method. All files are saved.	Longest backup time.
Differential backup	Copies only the files that have changed since the last full backup	Fast backup method. Requires minimal storage space to back up.	Recovery is time-consuming because the last full backup plus the differential backup are needed.
Incremental backup	Copies only the files that have changed since the last full or incremental backup	Fastest backup method. Requires minimal storage space to back up. Only most recent changes saved.	Recovery is most time-consuming because the last full backup and all incremental backups since the last full backup are needed.
Selective backup	Users choose which folders and files to include in a backup	Fast backup method. Provides great flexibility.	Difficult to manage individual file backups. Least manageable of all the backup methods.
Continuous data protection (CDP)	All data is backed up whenever a change is made	The only real-time backup. Very fast recovery of data.	Very expensive and requires a great amount of storage.

 MINI FEATURE 5-2

Disaster Recovery

A **disaster recovery plan** is a written plan that describes the steps an organization would take to restore its computer operations in the event of a disaster. A disaster can be natural or man-made (hackers, viruses, etc.). Each company and each department or division within an organization usually has its own disaster recovery plan. The following scenario illustrates how an organization might implement a disaster recovery plan.

Rosewood Associates is a consulting firm that helps clients use social media for marketing and customer outreach. Last week, a fire broke out in the office suite above Rosewood. The heat and smoke, along with water from the sprinkler system, caused extensive damage. As a result, Rosewood must replace all computers, servers, and storage devices. Also, the company lost all of the data that was not backed up.

Rosewood currently backs up its systems daily to an internal server and weekly to a remote cloud server. Because the internal server was damaged, the company lost several days of data. Rosewood does not have a plan for replacing hardware. Thus, they will lose several additional days of productivity while purchasing, installing, and configuring new hardware.

To minimize the chance of this type of loss in the future, the company hired you as a consultant to help create a disaster recovery plan. You first discuss the types of disasters that can strike, as shown in the table. You then explain that the goal of a disaster recovery plan is to prevent, detect, and correct system threats, and to restore the most critical systems first.

A disaster recovery plan typically contains these four components: emergency plan, backup plan, recovery plan, and test plan.

Emergency Plan: An emergency plan specifies the steps Rosewood will take as soon as a disaster strikes. The emergency plan is organized by type of disaster, such as fire, flood, or earthquake, and includes:

1. Names and phone numbers of people and organizations to notify (company management, fire and police department, clients, etc.)

2. Computer equipment procedures, such as equipment or power shutoff, and file removal; these procedures should be followed only if it is safe for an employee to do so

Considerations for Disaster Recovery

Disaster Type	What to Do First	What Might Occur	What to Include in the Plan
Natural (earthquake, hurricane, tornado, etc.)	Shut off power. Evacuate, if necessary. Pay attention to advisories. Do not use telephone lines if lightning occurs	Power outage. Phone lines down. Structural damage to building. Road closings, transportation interruptions. Flooding. Equipment damage	Generator. Satellite phone, list of employee phone numbers. Alternate worksite. Action to be taken if employees are not able to come to work/leave the office. Wet/dry vacuums. Make and model numbers and vendor information to get replacements
Man-made (hazardous material spill, terrorist attacks, fire, hackers, malware, etc.)	Notify authorities (fire departments, etc.) of immediate threat. Attempt to suppress fire or contain spill, if safe to do so. Evacuate, if necessary	Data loss. Dangerous conditions for employees. Criminal activity, such as data hacking and identity theft. Equipment damage	Backup data at protected site. Protective equipment and an evacuation plan. Contact law enforcement. Make and model numbers and vendor information to obtain replacements

3. Employee evacuation procedures

4. Return procedures (who can enter the facility and what actions they are to perform)

Backup Plan: The backup plan specifies how Rosewood will use backup files and equipment to resume computer operations, and includes:

1. The location of backup data, supplies, and equipment

2. Who is responsible for gathering backup resources and transporting them to an alternate computer facility

3. The methods by which the data that is backed up on cloud storage will be restored

4. A schedule indicating the order and approximate time each application should be up and running

Recovery Plan: The recovery plan specifies the actions Rosewood will take to restore full computer operations. As with the emergency plan, the recovery plan differs for each type of disaster. You recommend that Rosewood set up planning committees. Each committee would be responsible for different forms of recovery, such as replacing hardware or software.

Test Plan: The test plan includes simulating various levels of disasters and recording Rosewood's ability to recover. You run a test in which the employees follow the steps in the disaster recovery plan. The test uncovers a few needed recovery actions that are not specified in the plan, so you modify the plan. A few days later, you run another test without giving the employees any advance notice so that they can test the plan again.

✺ For what kind of natural and man-made disasters should a company plan? What roles can cloud storage providers play in helping to recover from a disaster? How involved should employees be in developing and testing disaster recovery plans?

© iStockphoto / Hans Laubel;
© iStockphoto / William Sen;
© Gewoldi / Photos.com

Wireless Security

Billions of home and business users have laptops, smartphones, and other mobile devices to access the Internet, send email and instant messages, chat online, or share network connections — all wirelessly. Home users set up wireless home networks. Mobile users access wireless networks in hot spots at airports, hotels, shopping malls, bookstores, restaurants, and coffee shops. Schools have wireless networks so that students can access the school network using their mobile computers and devices as they move from building to building (Figure 5-16).

Although wireless access provides many conveniences to users, it also poses additional security risks. Some perpetrators connect to other's wireless networks to gain free Internet access; others may try to access an organization's confidential data. Read Ethics & Issues 5-2 to consider issues associated with unsecured wireless networks.

Figure 5-16 Wireless access points or routers around campus allow students to access the school network wirelessly from their classrooms, the library, dorms, and other campus locations.
© Robert Kneschke / Shutterstock.com; © iStockphoto / Christopher Futcher; © Natalia Siverina / Shutterstock.com; © Jupiterimages / Photos.com; © Natalia Siverina / Shutterstock.com; © Bonnie Kamin / PhotoEdit; © Cengage Learning

 **ETHICS & ISSUES 5-2**

Would You Connect to an Unsecured Wireless Network?

If you turn on your laptop and notice that you can connect to a nearby home or business's wireless network and access the Internet for free, you may find yourself in an ethical dilemma. Because they do not know how to secure a wireless network, many home and business users leave their networks open for use by anybody in their signal's range. One study found that 25 percent of wireless connections are unsecured, leaving them susceptible to hackers.

Criminals sometimes use unsecured wireless networks to cover up technology-related crimes. Others may steal connections to avoid the costs of Internet service. In other cases, a user's laptop or mobile device may connect automatically to an open wireless network, without the user's authorization or knowledge.

The Electronic Communications Privacy Act (ECPA) states that it is not illegal "to intercept or access an electronic communication made through an electronic communication system that is configured so that such electronic communication is readily accessible to the general public." It is unclear whether this law refers to an unsecured home network or whether it pertains only to public hot spots, such as restaurants or libraries. Some lawmakers even support punishing those who leave their networks unsecured.

Would you use your neighbor's unsecured wireless home network without permission? Why or why not? What would you do if you found out that someone was using your wireless home network? How should legal authorities address such abuse? How should violators be punished? Should those leaving their networks unsecured be punished, too? Why or why not?

To access a wireless network, the individual must be in range of the wireless network. Some intruders intercept and monitor communications as they transmit through the air. Others connect to a network through an unsecured wireless access point (WAP) or combination router/WAP (Figure 5-12). Read How To 5-2 for instructions about ways to secure a wireless network, in addition to using firewalls.

 BTW

Wi-Fi Signal Blockers
Innovative Computing:
You should be familiar
with unique Wi-Fi signal
blocking innovations.

 CONSIDER THIS

Can you detect if someone is accessing your wireless home network?
If you notice the speed of your wireless connection is slower than normal, it may be a sign that someone else is accessing your network. You also may notice indicator lights on your wireless router flashing rapidly when you are not connected to your wireless network. Most wireless routers have a built-in utility that allows you to view the computers currently connected to your network. If you notice a computer that does not belong to you, consult your wireless router's documentation to determine how to remove it from the network.

 HOW TO 5-2

Secure Your Wireless Network

When you set up a wireless network, it is important to secure the network so that only your computers and mobile devices can connect to it. Unsecured wireless networks can be seen and accessed by neighbors and others nearby, which may make it easier for them to connect to and access the data on the computers and mobile devices on your network. The following list provides suggestions for securing your wireless network.

- Immediately upon connecting your wireless access point and/or router, change the password required to access administrative features. If the password remains at its default setting, others may possibly be able to connect to and configure your wireless network settings.

- Change the *SSID* (service set identifier), which is a network name, from the default to something that uniquely identifies your network, especially if you live in close proximity to other wireless networks.

- Do not broadcast the SSID. This will make it more difficult for others to detect your wireless network. When you want to

connect a computer or mobile device to your wireless network, it will be necessary to enter the SSID manually.

- Enable an encryption method such as WPA2 (Wi-Fi Protected Access 2), and specify a password or passphrase that is difficult for others to guess. Passwords and passphrases that are more than eight characters, contain uppercase and lowercase letters, numbers, and special characters are the most secure.

- Enable and configure the MAC (Media Access Control) address control feature. A *MAC address* is a unique hardware identifier for your computer or device. The *MAC address control* feature specifies the computers and mobile devices that can connect to your network. If a computer or device is not specified, it will not be able to connect.

- Choose a secure location for your wireless router so that unauthorized people cannot access it. Someone who has physical access to a wireless router can restore factory defaults and erase your settings.

⚒ In addition to safeguarding the data and information on your computers from others, why else might it be a good idea to secure your wireless network?

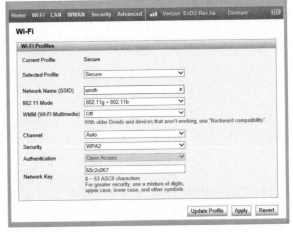

Source: Verizon Wireless

 MINI FEATURE 5-3

Mobile Security

According to some estimates, 113 mobile phones are lost or stolen in the United States every minute. Symantec, one the world's leading online security companies, projects that only one-half of these phones eventually will be returned to their owners. Chances are that the people who find the missing phones likely will have viewed much of the content on the devices in a quest to find the owners and possibly to gain access to private information. Given the amount of storage and the variety of personal and business data stored, the

consequences of losing a smartphone or mobile device are significant.

The goal, therefore, for mobile device users is to make their data as secure as possible. Follow these steps to protect sensitive and personal data and to fight mobile cybercrime.

- **Avoid clicking unsafe links.** Nearly 40 percent of Americans are likely to click an unknown link, which often leads them to malicious websites. If you receive a text message from someone you do not know or an invitation to click a link, resist the urge to fulfill the request. Your financial institution never will send you a message requesting you to enter your account user name and password. Malicious links can inject malware on the mobile device to steal personal information or to create *toll fraud*, which secretly contacts wireless messaging services that impose steep fees on a monthly bill.

- **Be extra cautious locating and downloading apps.** Any device that connects to the Internet is susceptible to mobile malware. Cyberthieves target apps on widely used phones and tablets. Popular games are likely candidates to house malware, and it often is difficult to distinguish the legitimate apps from the fake apps. Obtain mobile device apps from well-known stores, and before downloading anything, read the descriptions and reviews. Look for misspellings and awkward sentence structure, which could be clues that the app is fake. If something looks awry, do not download. Scrutinize the number and types of permissions the app is requesting. If the list seems unreasonable in length or in the personal information needed, deny permission and uninstall the app.

- **Turn off GPS tracking.** GPS technology can track the mobile device's location as long as it is transmitting and receiving signals to and from satellites. This feature is helpful to obtain directions from your current location, view local news and weather reports, find a lost device, summon emergency personnel, and locate missing children. Serious privacy concerns can arise, however, when the technology is used in malicious ways, such as to stalk individuals or trace their whereabouts. Unless you want to allow others to follow your locations throughout the day, disable the GPS tracking feature until needed.

- **Use mobile security software.** Enable the password feature on a mobile device as the first step in stopping prying eyes from viewing contents. More protection is necessary, however, to stop viruses and spyware and to safeguard personal and business data. Mobile security apps can allow you to lock your mobile device and SIM card remotely, erase the memory, and activate the GPS function. Other apps prevent cyberthieves from hijacking your phone and taking pictures, making recordings, placing calls to fee-imposed businesses, and sending infected messages to all individuals in your contact list. Look for security software that can back up data to an online account, set off a screeching alarm on the lost or stolen mobile device, offer live customer service, and provide theft, spam, virus, and malware protection.

✸ As the number of smartphones and mobile devices in use increases, the possibility of security breaches and lost devices increases proportionally. How can manufacturers and wireless carriers emphasize the importance of mobile security and convince users to take the precautions suggested above? What mobile security safeguards have you taken to protect your smartphone or mobile device? What steps will you take after reading this mini feature?

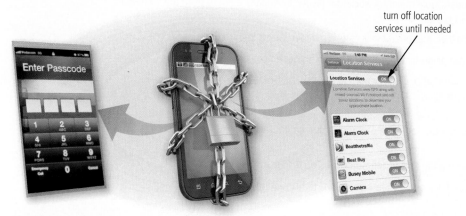

turn off location services until needed

© iStockphoto / Henk Badenhorst; © iStockphoto / Marcello Bortolino; © Cengage Learning

---

✓ NOW YOU KNOW

Be sure you understand the material presented in the sections titled Software Theft; Information Theft; Hardware Theft, Vandalism, and Failure; Backing Up – The Ultimate Safeguard; and Wireless Security as it relates to the chapter objectives. *You now should know . . .*

- What actions you are allowed according to a software license agreement (Objective 4)
- Why you would want to use encryption, digital signatures, or digital certificates (Objective 5)
- How you can protect your hardware from theft, vandalism, and failure (Objective 6)
- Which backup method is most suited to your needs (Objective 7)
- How you can protect your wireless communications (Objective 8)

 Quiz Yourself Online: Check your knowledge of related content by navigating to this book's Quiz Yourself resource on Computer Concepts CourseMate and then tapping or clicking Objectives 4–8.

Ethics and Society

As with any powerful technology, computers and mobile devices can be used for both good and bad intentions. The standards that determine whether an action is good or bad are known as ethics.

Computer ethics are the moral guidelines that govern the use of computers, mobile devices, and information systems. Frequently discussed areas of computer ethics are unauthorized use of computers, mobile devices, and networks; software theft (piracy); information accuracy; intellectual property rights; codes of conduct; green computing; and information privacy. The questionnaire in Figure 5-17 raises issues in each of these areas.

Previous sections in this chapter discussed unauthorized use of computers, mobile devices and networks, and software theft (piracy). The following sections discuss issues related to information accuracy, intellectual property rights, codes of conduct, green computing, and information privacy.

Your Thoughts?

	Ethical	Unethical
1. An organization requires employees to wear badges that track their whereabouts while at work.	☐	☐
2. A supervisor reads an employee's email message.	☐	☐
3. An employee uses his computer at work to send email messages to a friend.	☐	☐
4. An employee sends an email message to several coworkers and blind copies his supervisor.	☐	☐
5. An employee forwards an email message to a third party without permission from the sender.	☐	☐
6. An employee uses her computer at work to complete a homework assignment for school.	☐	☐
7. The vice president of your Student Government Association (SGA) downloads a photo from the web and uses it in a flyer recruiting SGA members.	☐	☐
8. A student copies text from the web and uses it in a research paper for his English Composition class.	☐	☐
9. An employee sends political campaign material to individuals on her employer's mailing list.	☐	☐
10. As an employee in the registration office, you have access to student grades. You look up grades for your friends, so that they do not have to wait for grades to be posted online.	☐	☐
11. An employee makes a copy of software and installs it on her home computer. No one uses her home computer while she is at work, and she uses her home computer only to finish projects from work.	☐	☐
12. An employee who has been laid off installs a computer virus on his employer's computer.	☐	☐
13. A person designing a webpage finds one on the web similar to his requirements, copies it, modifies it, and publishes it as his own webpage.	☐	☐
14. A student researches using only the web to write a report.	☐	☐
15. In a society in which all transactions occur online (a cashless society), the government tracks every transaction you make and automatically deducts taxes from your bank account.	☐	☐
16. Someone copies a well-known novel to the web and encourages others to read it.	☐	☐
17. A person accesses an organization's network and reports to the organization any vulnerabilities discovered.	☐	☐
18. Your friend uses a neighbor's wireless network to connect to the Internet and check email.	☐	☐
19. A company uses recycled paper to print a 50-page employee benefits manual that is distributed to 425 employees.	☐	☐
20. An employee is fired based on the content of posts on his or her social networking site.	☐	☐

Figure 5-17   Indicate whether you think the situation described is ethical or unethical. Be prepared to discuss your answers.
© Cengage Learning

Information Accuracy

Information accuracy is a concern today because many users access information maintained by other people or companies, such as on the Internet. Do not assume that because the information is on the web that it is correct. As discussed in Chapter 2, users should evaluate the value of a webpage before relying on its content. Be aware that the organization providing access to the information may not be the creator of the information.

In addition to concerns about the accuracy of computer input, some individuals and organizations raise questions about the ethics of using computers to alter output, primarily graphic output such as a retouched photo. With graphics equipment and software, users easily can digitize photos and then add, change (Figure 5-18), or remove images.

Figure 5-18 This digitally edited photo shows a fruit that looks like an apple on the outside and an orange on the inside.
© Giuliano20 / Dreamstime.com

Intellectual Property Rights

Intellectual property (IP) refers to unique and original works such as ideas, inventions, art, writings, processes, company and product names, and logos. *Intellectual property rights* are the rights to which creators are entitled for their work. Certain issues arise surrounding IP today because many of these works are available digitally and easily can be redistributed or altered without the creator's permission.

A *copyright* gives authors, artists, and other creators of original work exclusive rights to duplicate, publish, and sell their materials. A copyright protects any tangible form of expression.

A common infringement of copyright is piracy, where people illegally copy software, movies, and music. Many areas are not clear-cut with respect to the law, because copyright law gives the public fair use to copyrighted material. The issues surround the phrase, fair use, which allows use for educational and critical purposes. This vague definition is subject to widespread interpretation and raises many questions:

- Should individuals be able to download contents of your website, modify it, and then put it on the web again as their own?
- Should a faculty member have the right to print material from the web and distribute it to all members of the class for teaching purposes only?
- Should someone be able to scan photos or pages from a book, publish them on the web, and allow others to download them?
- Should someone be able to put the lyrics of a song on the web?
- Should students be able to take term papers they have written and post them on the web, making it tempting for other students to download and submit them as their own work?

These issues with copyright law led to the development of *digital rights management* (DRM), a strategy designed to prevent illegal distribution of movies, music, and other digital content. Read Ethics & Issues 5-3 on the next page to consider liability issues related to copyrighted material.

Internet Research

What is meant by fair use?

Search for: fair use definition

Who Is Liable for Unauthorized Postings of Copyrighted Streaming Materials?

Websites that host user content, such as blogs and social media sites, specify guidelines about what users can and cannot post, including streaming content and links. For example, you cannot stream or post copyrighted digital content, such as music, movies, or book chapters. If a user violates these terms, is the host liable? For example, if a blogger uses a blogging platform to post copyrighted material, is the blogging platform liable?

Several proposed laws attempt to protect copyrighted material from online distribution.

For example, the United States Congress introduced the Stop Online Piracy Act (SOPA), which placed the responsibility on the hosting site to monitor all user-posted content, including links and even comments made about an article. If violations occur, this type of legislation enables judges to block access to websites and requires that advertisers, search engines, and payment services cease conducting business with the website. The movie and music businesses support this type of legislation, saying that it protects intellectual property. Opponents fear that it would shut down an entire domain, such as a blogging

website, because of content posted by a single blogger. For this reason, several websites participated in a large-scale blackout in protest of SOPA. Soon after, Congress abandoned it.

How can the government balance copyright protection with free speech? What types of websites would be affected by a law such as SOPA? Should websites that enable users to post content be liable for the content? Why or why not? Can the government require search engines to remove links to a website if it violates copyright laws? Why or why not?

Codes of Conduct

A **code of conduct** is a written guideline that helps determine whether a specification is ethical/unethical or allowed/not allowed. An IT code of conduct focuses on acceptable use of technology. Employers and schools often specify standards for the ethical use of technology in an IT code of conduct and then distribute these standards to employees and students (Figure 5-19). You also may find codes of conduct online that define acceptable forms of communications for websites where users post commentary or other communications such as blogs, wikis, discussion forums, and so on.

Sample IT Code of Conduct

1. Technology may not be used to harm other people.
2. Employees may not meddle in others' files.
3. Employees may use technology only for purposes in which they have been authorized.
4. Technology may not be used to steal.
5. Technology may not be used to bear false witness.
6. Employees may not copy or use software illegally.
7. Employees may not use others' technology resources without authorization.
8. Employees may not use others' intellectual property as their own.
9. Employees shall consider the social impact of programs and systems they design.
10. Employees always should use technology in a way that demonstrates consideration and respect for fellow humans.

Figure 5-19 Sample IT code of conduct employers may distribute to employees.
© Cengage Learning; © iStockphoto / Oleksiy Mark

Green Computing

People use, and often waste, resources such as electricity and paper while using technology. Recall from Chapter 1 that **green computing** involves reducing the electricity and environmental waste while using computers, mobile devices, and related technologies. Figure 5-20 summarizes measures users can take to contribute to green computing.

Personal computers, display devices, printers, and other devices should comply with guidelines of the ENERGY STAR program. The United States Department of Energy (DOE) and the United States Environmental Protection Agency (EPA) developed the *ENERGY STAR program* to help reduce the amount of electricity used by computers and related devices. This program encourages manufacturers to create energy-efficient devices. For example, many devices switch

Internet Research

Where can I recycle outdated electronics?

Search for: recycle old electronics

to sleep or power save mode after a specified number of inactive minutes or hours. Computers and devices that meet the ENERGY STAR guidelines display an ENERGY STAR label (shown in Figure 5-20).

Enterprise data centers and computer facilities consume large amounts of electricity from computer hardware and associated devices and utilities such as air conditioning, coolers, lighting, etc. Organizations can implement a variety of measures to reduce electrical waste:

- Consolidate servers by using virtualization.
- Purchase high-efficiency equipment.
- Use sleep modes and other power management features for computers and devices.
- Buy computers and devices with low power consumption processors and power supplies.
- When possible, use outside air to cool the data center or computer facility.

Some organizations continually review their *power usage effectiveness* (PUE), which is a ratio that measures how much power enters the computer facility or data center against the amount of power required to run the computers and devices.

Green Computing Tips

1. Conserve Energy
   a. Use computers and devices that comply with the ENERGY STAR program.
   b. Do not leave a computer or device running overnight.
   c. Turn off the monitor, printer, and other devices when not in use.

2. Reduce Environmental Waste
   a. Use paperless methods to communicate.
   b. Recycle paper and buy recycled paper.
   c. Recycle toner and ink cartridges, computers, mobile devices, printers, and other devices.
   d. Telecommute.
   e. Use videoconferencing and VoIP for meetings.

Figure 5-20 A list of suggestions to make computing healthy for the environment.

US Environmental Protection Agency, ENERGY STAR program; © Roman Sotola / Shutterstock.com; © Cengage Learning

 CONSIDER THIS

Should you save out-of-date computers and devices?
Users should not store obsolete computers and devices in their basement, storage room, attic, warehouse, or any other location. Computers, monitors, and other equipment contain toxic materials and potentially dangerous elements including lead, mercury, and flame retardants. In a landfill, these materials release into the environment. Recycling and refurbishing old equipment are much safer alternatives for the environment. Manufacturers can use the millions of pounds of recycled raw materials to make products such as outdoor furniture and automotive parts. Before recycling, refurbishing, or discarding your old computer, be sure to erase, remove, or destroy its hard disk so that the information it stored remains private.

Information Privacy

Information privacy refers to the right of individuals and companies to deny or restrict the collection, use, and dissemination of information about them. Organizations often use huge databases to store records such as employee records, medical records, financial records, and more. Much of the data is personal and confidential and should be accessible only to authorized users. Many individuals and organizations, however, question whether this data really is private. That is, some companies and individuals collect and use this information without your authorization. Websites often collect data about you, so that they can customize advertisements and send you personalized email messages. Some employers monitor your computer usage and email messages.

Figure 5-21 lists measures you can take to make your personal data more private. The following sections address techniques companies and employers use to collect your personal data.

Electronic Profiles

When you fill out a printed form, such as a magazine subscription or contest entry, or an online form to sign up for a service, create a social networking profile, or register a product warranty, the merchant that receives the form usually stores the information you provide in a database. Likewise, every time you click an advertisement on the web or perform a search online, your information and preferences enter a database. Some merchants may sell or share the contents of their databases with national marketing firms and Internet advertising firms. By combining this data with information from public records such as driver's licenses and vehicle registrations, these firms can create an electronic profile of individuals. Electronic profiles may include personal details such as your age, address, phone number, marital status, number and ages of dependents, interests, and spending habits.

How to Safeguard Personal Information

1. Fill in only necessary information on rebate, warranty, and registration forms.

2. Do not preprint your phone number or Social Security number on personal checks.

3. Have an unlisted or unpublished phone number.

4. If you have Caller ID, find out how to block your number from displaying on the receiver's system.

5. Do not write your phone number on charge or credit receipts.

6. Ask merchants not to write credit card numbers, phone numbers, Social Security numbers, and driver's license numbers on the back of your personal checks.

7. Purchase goods with cash, rather than credit or checks.

8. Avoid shopping club and buyer cards.

9. If merchants ask personal questions, find out why they want to know before releasing the information.

10. Inform merchants that you do not want them to distribute your personal information.

11. Request, in writing, to be removed from mailing lists.

12. Obtain your credit report once a year from each of the three major credit reporting agencies (Equifax, Experian, and TransUnion) and correct any errors.

13. Request a free copy of your medical records once a year from the Medical Information Bureau.

14. Limit the amount of information you provide to websites. Fill in only required information.

15. Install a cookie manager to filter cookies.

16. Clear your history file when you are finished browsing.

17. Set up a free email account. Use this email address for merchant forms.

18. Turn off file and printer sharing on your Internet connection.

19. Install a personal firewall.

20. Sign up for email filtering through your ISP or use an anti-spam program.

21. Do not reply to spam for any reason.

22. Surf the web anonymously or through an anonymous website.

Figure 5-21 Techniques to keep personal data private.
© iStockphoto / Norebbo; © Cengage Learning

Direct marketing supporters claim that using information in this way lowers overall selling costs, which lowers product prices. Critics contend that the information in an electronic profile reveals more about an individual than anyone has a right to know. They argue that companies should inform people if they plan to provide personal information to others, and people should have the right to deny such use. Many websites allow people to specify whether they want their personal information shared or preferences retained (Figure 5-22).

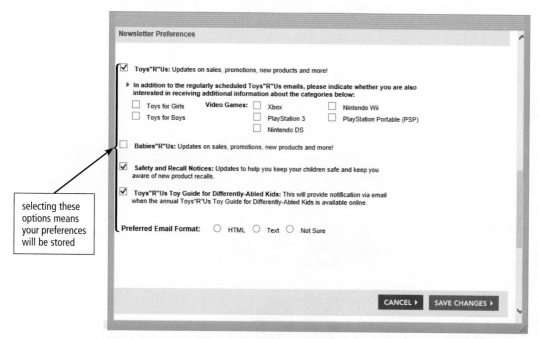

selecting these options means your preferences will be stored

Figure 5-22 Many companies, such as Toys"R"Us shown here, allow users to specify whether they want the company to retain their preferences.
Source: Geoffrey, LLC

Cookies

A **cookie** is a small text file that a web server stores on your computer. Cookie files typically contain data about you, such as your user name, postal code, or viewing preferences. Websites use cookies for a variety of purposes:

• Most websites that allow for personalization use cookies to track user preferences. These cookies may obtain their values when a user fills in an online form requesting personal information. Some websites, for example, store user names in cookies in order to display a personalized greeting that welcomes the user, by name, back to the website. Other websites allow users to customize their viewing experience with preferences such as local news headlines, the local weather forecast, or stock quotes.

• Some websites use cookies to store user names and/or passwords, so that users do not need to enter this information every time they sign in to the website.

• Online shopping sites generally use a *session cookie* to keep track of items in a user's shopping cart. This way, users can start an order during one web session and finish it on another day in another session. Session cookies usually expire after a certain time, such as a week or a month.

• Some websites use cookies to track how often users visit a site and the webpages they visit while at the website.

• Websites may use cookies to target advertisements. These websites store a user's interests and browsing habits in the cookie.

 CONSIDER THIS

Do websites ever sell information stored in cookies?
Some websites sell or trade information stored in your cookies to advertisers — a practice many believe to be unethical. If you do not want personal information distributed, you should limit the amount of information you provide to a website or adjust how your browser handles cookies. You can set your browser to accept cookies automatically, prompt if you want to accept a cookie, or disable all cookie use. Keep in mind if you disable cookie use, you may not be able to use some e-commerce websites. As an alternative, you can purchase software that selectively blocks cookies. Read How To 5-3 on the next page for instructions about cookies and other settings you can adjust in your browser.

Many commercial websites send a cookie to your browser; your computer's hard disk then stores the cookie. The next time you visit the website, your browser retrieves the cookie from your hard disk and sends the data in the cookie to the website. Figure 5-23 illustrates how websites work with cookies. A website can read data only from its own cookie file stored on your hard disk. That is, it cannot access or view any other data on your hard disk — including another cookie file.

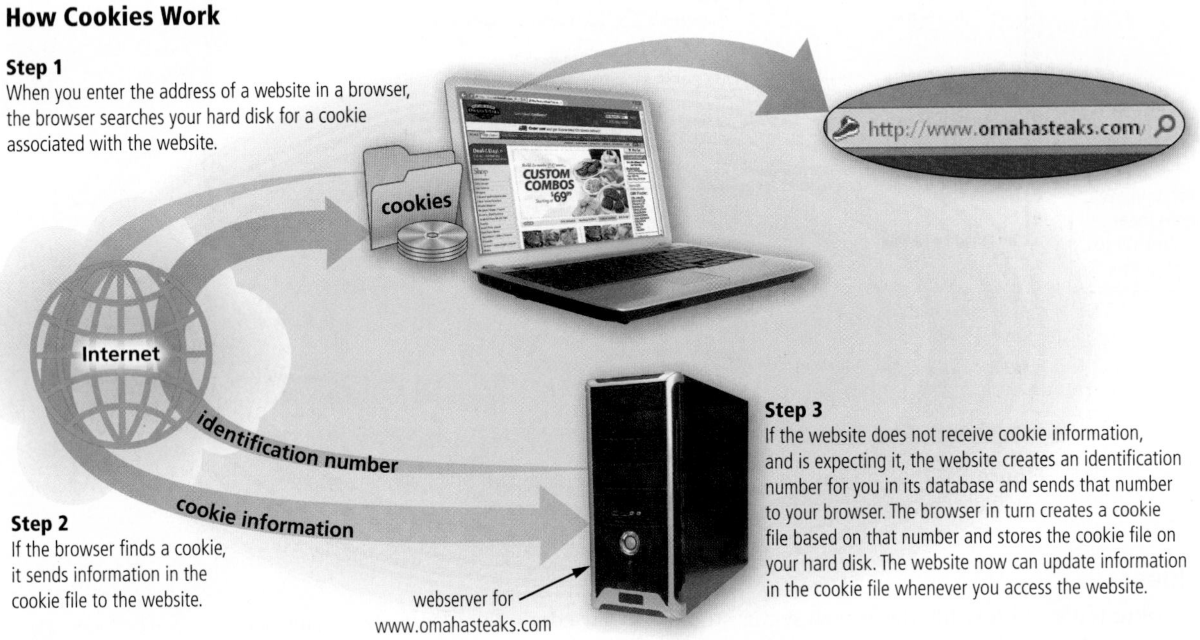

How Cookies Work

Step 1
When you enter the address of a website in a browser, the browser searches your hard disk for a cookie associated with the website.

cookies

http://www.omahasteaks.com

Internet

identification number

cookie information

Step 2
If the browser finds a cookie, it sends information in the cookie file to the website.

webserver for
www.omahasteaks.com

Step 3
If the website does not receive cookie information, and is expecting it, the website creates an identification number for you in its database and sends that number to your browser. The browser in turn creates a cookie file based on that number and stores the cookie file on your hard disk. The website now can update information in the cookie file whenever you access the website.

Figure 5-23 This figure shows how cookies work.
© Alex Staroseltsev / Shutterstock.com; Source: Omaha Steaks International, Inc; © iStockphoto / Norman Chan; © Cengage Learning

---

🌐 HOW TO 5-3

Secure Your Browser

Configuring the security settings in your browser can help ensure that others cannot determine the websites you have visited, your browsing habits, or any personally identifiable or confidential information you might have entered on websites. The settings for securing your browser typically are found in the browser's Settings or Preferences dialog box. The following list provides suggestions for securing a browser.

- **Clear your browsing history often.** Your *browsing history* is a list of all websites you have visited over a period of time. By default, some browsers save your browsing history for 20 days or more. Configuring your browser to clear your browsing history often will help prevent others from seeing the websites you have visited.

- **Enable private browsing.** During *private browsing*, your browser does not keep track of the websites you are visiting. Websites you visit during a private browsing session will not store files on your computer, nor will they appear in your browsing history after you end the browsing session.

- **Turn off location sharing.** *Location sharing* gives websites access to your current location. While this can be particularly useful on websites that display the weather in your current location, this information also could be misused by dishonest individuals.

- **Never store passwords.** Many browsers have the capability of storing your passwords so that you do not have to enter them each time you visit the same websites. Others with access to your computer, however, will be able to access

these secure websites using your account information with relative ease.

- **Clear cookies regularly.** Websites may store cookies and other files on your computer. These files not only take up space, but they also may be used to track your browsing habits. Regularly clear cookies and other data that websites place on your computer.

- **Avoid phishing websites.** Phishing websites often look remarkably similar to real websites and trick visitors into entering confidential information that could be used in an identity theft scam. Many browsers have a built-in feature to help identify phishing websites. Enable this feature and be cautious on websites labeled as unsafe.

☀ What security settings do you currently have enabled on your browser?

Phishing

Recall from Chapter 4 that **phishing** is a scam in which a perpetrator sends an official looking email message that attempts to obtain your personal and/or financial information. These messages look legitimate and request that you update credit card numbers, Social Security numbers, bank account numbers, passwords, or other private information. Read How To 5-4 for instructions about protecting yourself from phishing scams.

Clickjacking is yet another similar scam. With *clickjacking*, an object that can be clicked on a website, such as a button, image, or link, contains a malicious program. When a user clicks the disguised object, a variety of nefarious events may occur. For example, the user may be redirected to a phony website that requests personal information, or a virus may download to the computer. Browsers typically include clickjacking protection.

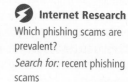

Internet Research

Which phishing scams are prevalent?

Search for: recent phishing scams

 HOW TO 5-4

Protect against a Phishing Scam

Phishing scams can be perpetrated via email messages, websites, and even on the phone. The following guidelines will help protect you against a phishing scam.

Phone Scams

- If you receive a phone call from someone claiming to be from a company with which you do business, record his or her name and the time of the call. Do not disclose personal or financial information to the caller. If the caller is offering a product or service and is requesting a payment, call the company back at the number you have on file, and ask to be transferred to the person who called you initially.

- Whenever possible, enter your payment information on secure websites instead of reading credit card numbers or bank account information on the phone. You never know whether the caller is recording your payment information to use later for malicious purposes.

Email Scams

- If you receive an email message from someone requesting you to verify online account or financial information, do not reply with this information.

- Never tap or click links in email messages, even if the message appears to be from someone you know. Nor should you copy and paste the link from the email message to a browser. Instead, type the link's web address into a browser's address bar manually, and make sure you type it correctly. If you are visiting your financial institution's website, make sure the web address you enter matches the web address you have on file for them.

- Do not reply to email messages asking you for financial assistance — even if the email message appears to originate from someone you know. If you receive this type of email message from someone you know, call the person to verify the message's authenticity.

Website Scams

- When visiting a website, such as your financial institution's website, that will require you to enter confidential information, be sure to type the web address correctly. Typing it incorrectly may take you to a phishing website where the information you enter can be collected by an unknown party.

- Make sure websites requiring your confidential information use the https:// protocol.

- Websites with misspellings, poor grammar, or formatting problems may indicate a phishing website. Do not enter personal or financial information on a website that looks suspicious.

- Enable the *phishing filter* in your browser that can warn or block you from potentially fraudulent or suspicious websites.

✳ Have you experienced a phishing scam? If so, how did it attempt to trick you into providing personal or financial information? How did you respond?

Spyware and Adware

Recall from Chapter 4 that **spyware** is a program placed on a computer or mobile device without the user's knowledge that secretly collects information about the user and then communicates the information it collects to some outside source while the user is online. Some vendors or employers use spyware to collect information about program usage or employees. Internet advertising firms often collect information about users' web browsing habits. Spyware can enter your computer when you install a new program, through malware, or through a graphic on a webpage or in an email message.

Adware is a program that displays an online advertisement in a banner or pop-up window on webpages, email messages, or other Internet services. Adware on mobile phones is known as *madware*, for mobile adware. Sometimes, spyware is hidden in adware.

To remove spyware and adware, you can obtain spyware removers, adware removers, or malware removers that can detect and delete spyware and adware. Some operating systems and browsers include spyware and adware removers. Read Secure IT 5-5 on the next page for tips about the types of websites that might contain spyware or other malware.

Risky Business: Websites to Avoid

Browsing various websites can be a risky practice if you are unaware of the dangers that could be lurking. Specific types of websites are more likely to contain malware, spam, and links to malicious sites. They include websites with .com and .info top-level domains (TLDs) and some country code TLDs (ccTLDs). Scammers are hopeful that users browsing the web will make a typing error and arrive at their websites in error. For example, if a person carelessly types .com and omits the letter, o, the top-level domain becomes .cm, which is the ccTLD for Cameroon, one of the most prolific TLDs for malware.

According to a report by online security firm Symantec, nearly 20 percent of websites categorized as "blogs / web communications" contain malware. Other dangerous categories are "hosting / personal hosted sites; business / economy; shopping; education / reference; technology; computer and Internet; entertainment and music; automotive; and health and medicine."

Symantec reports that social media sites, especially Facebook, are popular websites for online criminals due to the millions of subscribers, many of whom share personal information freely and believe they are operating in a safe environment. For example, cybercriminals created a Dislike button and a stalking app, which claimed to allow users to view names of individuals who had been viewing their profile. In reality, the Dislike button and stalking apps were rogue applications with deceitful intentions such as capturing personal information, sending or posting spam messages, or tricking users into agreeing to charges for phone or online services.

The cybercriminals obtain their website registration from companies with low fees, minimal registration documentation requirements, and volume discounts. These companies often respond to complaints slowly, if at all.

☀ Do you visit websites that fall in the categories of websites more likely to contain malware? If so, what precautions will you take the next time you view these websites?

Social Engineering

As related to the use of technology, **social engineering** is defined as gaining unauthorized access to or obtaining confidential information by taking advantage of the trusting human nature of some victims and the naivety of others. Some social engineers trick their victims into revealing confidential information such as user names and passwords on the phone, in person, or on the Internet. Techniques they use include pretending to be an administrator or other authoritative figure, feigning an emergency situation, or impersonating an acquaintance. Social engineers also obtain information from users who do not destroy or conceal information properly. These perpetrators sift through company dumpsters, watch or film people dialing phone numbers or using ATMs, and snoop around computers or mobile devices looking for openly displayed confidential information.

To protect yourself from social engineering scams, follow these tips:

- Verify the identity of any person or organization requesting personal or confidential information.
- When relaying personal or confidential information, ensure that only authorized people can hear your conversation.
- When personal or confidential information appears on a computer or mobile device, ensure that only authorized people can see your screen.
- Shred all sensitive or confidential documents.
- After using a public computer, clear the cache in its browser.
- Avoid using public computers to conduct banking or other sensitive transactions.

Privacy Laws

The concern about privacy has led to the enactment of federal and state laws regarding the storage and disclosure of personal data, some of which are shown in Table 5-4. Common points in some of these laws are as follows:

1. Information collected and stored about individuals should be limited to what is necessary to carry out the function of the business or government agency collecting the data.
2. Once collected, provisions should be made to protect the data so that only those employees within the organization who need access to it to perform their job duties have access to it.

3. Personal information should be released outside the organization collecting the data only when the person has agreed to its disclosure.
4. When information is collected about an individual, the individual should know that the data is being collected and have the opportunity to determine the accuracy of the data.

Table 5-4   Major U.S. Government Laws Concerning Privacy

Law	Purpose
Children's Internet Protection Act	Protects minors from inappropriate content when accessing the Internet in schools and libraries
Children's Online Privacy Protection Act (COPPA)	Requires websites to protect personal information of children under 13 years of age
Computer Abuse Amendments Act	Outlaws transmission of harmful computer code such as viruses
Digital Millennium Copyright Act (DMCA)	Makes it illegal to circumvent antipiracy schemes in commercial software; outlaws sale of devices that copy software illegally
Electronic Communications Privacy Act (ECPA)	Provides the same right of privacy protection of the postal delivery service and telephone companies to various forms of electronic communications, such as voice mail, email, and mobile phones
Financial Modernization Act	Protects consumers from disclosure of their personal financial information and requires institutions to alert customers of information disclosure policies
Freedom of Information Act (FOIA)	Enables public access to most government records
HIPAA (Health Insurance Portability and Accountability Act)	Protects individuals against the wrongful disclosure of their health information
PATRIOT (Provide Appropriate Tools Required to Intercept and Obstruct Terrorism)	Gives law enforcement the right to monitor people's activities, including web and email habits
Privacy Act	Forbids federal agencies from allowing information to be used for a reason other than that for which it was collected

Employee Monitoring

Employee monitoring involves the use of computers, mobile devices, or cameras to observe, record, and review an employee's use of a technology, including communications such as email messages, keyboard activity (used to measure productivity), and websites visited. Many programs exist that easily allow employers to monitor employees. Further, it is legal for employers to use these programs.

BTW

Computer Vision
Innovative Computing:
You should be familiar
with computer vision and
how it helps to increase
security.

✳ CONSIDER THIS ──────────────

Do employers have the right to read employee email messages?
Actual policies vary widely. Some organizations declare that they will review email messages regularly, and others state that email messages are private. In some states, if a company does not have a formal email policy, it can read email messages without employee notification.

Content Filtering

One of the more controversial issues that surround the Internet is its widespread availability of objectionable material, such as prejudiced literature, violence, and obscene pictures. Some believe that such materials should be banned. Others believe that the materials should be filtered, that is, restricted.

Content filtering is the process of restricting access to certain material. Many businesses use content filtering to limit employees' web access. These businesses argue that employees are unproductive when visiting inappropriate or objectionable websites. Some schools, libraries, and parents use content filtering to restrict access to minors. Content filtering opponents argue that banning any materials violates constitutional guarantees of free speech and personal rights. Read Ethics & Issues 5-4 to consider whether content filtering violates first amendment rights.

Web filtering software is a program that restricts access to specified websites. Some also filter sites that use specific words (Figure 5-24). Others allow you to filter email messages, chat rooms, and programs. Many Internet security programs include a firewall, antivirus program, and filtering capabilities combined. Browsers also often include content filtering capabilities.

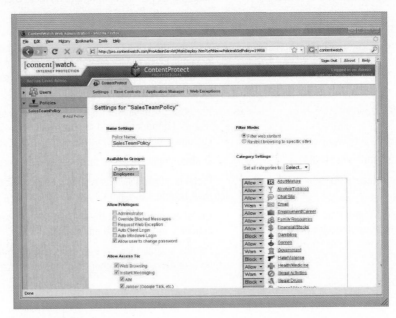

Figure 5-24   Web filtering software restricts access to specified websites.
Courtesy of ContentWatch, Inc.

✴ ETHICS & ISSUES 5-4

Does Content Filtering in a Public Library Violate First Amendment Rights?
Among the resources libraries offer are Internet-enabled computers, which allow patrons to read the news, perform research, and more. The use of content filtering software on library computers controls the type of information a patron can access. Free speech advocates argue that this violates the First Amendment because it restricts library patrons from viewing certain websites and content.

The Children's Internet Protection Act (CIPA) requires that schools and libraries use content filtering software in order to receive certain federal funds. Proponents of CIPA claim it is necessary to protect children. CIPA does allow libraries to turn off the filters, if requested by an adult patron. Some libraries use content filtering software on computers used only by children.

Critics of content filtering software argue that the programs do not always work as intended. They can overfilter content, blocking information or education websites based on a single word; conversely, they can under filter content, which could result in access to webpages with inappropriate media.

Libraries typically have a policy stating acceptable use of the Internet, which outlines appropriate content. In addition, existing copyright laws apply to downloading and viewing content. Libraries' policies also should state whether they use content filtering software, so that the patrons are aware that their search results may not reflect the entire scope of content available on the Internet.

Is it fair for a government to require that libraries use content filtering software? Why or why not? Is content on the Internet covered under free speech? Why or why not?

 **NOW YOU KNOW**

Be sure you understand the material presented in the sections titled Ethics and Society, and Information Privacy as it relates to the chapter objectives.
You now should know . . .

- What issues you might encounter with respect to information accuracy, intellectual property, codes of conduct, and green computing (Objective 9)

- How you can make your personal data more private (Objective 10)

- Why your computer might have a cookie (Objective 10)

> Quiz Yourself Online: Check your knowledge of related content by navigating to this book's Quiz Yourself resource on Computer Concepts CourseMate and then tapping or clicking Objectives 9–10.

Chapter Summary

This chapter presented a variety of digital security risks. You learned about cybercrime and cybercriminals. The chapter discussed risks and safeguards associated with Internet and network attacks, unauthorized access and use, software theft, information theft, and hardware theft, vandalism, and failure. It presented various backup strategies and methods of securing wireless communications. You learned about ethical issues in society and various ways to protect the privacy of personal information.

Test your knowledge of chapter material by accessing the Study Guide, Flash Cards, and Practice Test apps that run on your smartphone, tablet, laptop, or desktop.

TECHNOLOGY @ WORK

National and Local Security

Since 2001, the federal government, local governments, businesses, and individuals have been implementing aggressive new security measures because of the increase in terrorist activity. A security threat can exist anywhere, and it is nearly impossible for humans alone to protect the country. As a result, technology now assists governments, law enforcement officials, business owners, and other individuals with monitoring and maintaining security.

Advancements in computer vision enable computers to monitor indoor and outdoor areas that might be subject to a high volume of criminal activity. For example, some cities are installing cameras in problematic areas. A program analyzes the output from the camera and can determine whether two or more people in close proximity to one another might be engaged in a physical confrontation. If the computer detects suspicious behavior, it automatically notifies local law enforcement.

Computers also use facial recognition to identify individuals who do not belong in a particular area. For example, one theme park takes a picture of individuals they escort out of and ban from the park. As visitors walk from their cars to the park, surveillance cameras positioned in strategic locations scan visitors' faces and compare them with the database containing images of those who are banned from the park. If the computer finds a match, it alerts a security officer who then can investigate the situation. Thousands of people visit theme parks each day, and computers make it easier to perform the otherwise impossible task of identifying those who might be trespassing.

The federal government, particularly the Department of Homeland Security, uses a computerized No Fly List to track individuals who are not authorized to travel on commercial flights within the United States. When an individual makes a reservation, a

computer compares his or her name to the names on the No Fly List. If the computer finds a match, the individual must prove that he or she is not the person on the list before being allowed to board an aircraft.

Whether you are walking outside, visiting an attraction, or traveling, the chances are good that computers are, in some way, ensuring your safety.

In what other ways do computers and technology play a role in national and local security?

STUDENT ASSIGNMENTS

Study Guide

The Study Guide exercise reinforces material you should know for the chapter exam. You will find answers to items with the icon only in the e-book.

⬛ **Access the Study Guide app** that runs on your smartphone, tablet, laptop, or desktop by navigating to this book's Apps resource on Computer Concepts CourseMate.

Instructions: Answer the questions below using the format that helps you remember best or that is required by your instructor. Possible formats may include one or more of these options: write the answers; create a document that contains the answers; record answers as audio or video using a webcam, smartphone, or portable media player; post answers on a blog, wiki, or website; or highlight answers in the book/e-book.

1. Define the terms, digital security risk and cybercrime.

2. Differentiate among hackers, crackers, script kiddies, cyberextortionists, and cyberterrorists. Identify issues with punishing cybercriminals.

3. List common types of malware. A(n) _____ is the destructive event malware delivers.

4. Identify risks and safety measures when gaming.

5. Define these terms: botnet, zombie, and bot.

6. Describe the damages caused by DoS and DDoS attacks.

7. A(n) _____ allows users to bypass security controls.

8. Define the term, spoofing. List ways to protect against Internet and network attacks.

9. Explain how macros can be a security risk.

10. Define the terms, firewall and proxy server. List steps to set up a firewall.

11. 🗐 Name the contributions of AVG, McAfee, and Symantec, with respect to security.

12. Give examples of unauthorized use of a computer or network.

13. Identify what an AUP should specify.

14. Explain how an organization uses access controls and audit trails.

15. Differentiate among user names, passwords, and passphrases.

16. Explain the two-step verification process.

17. Describe the purpose of a CAPTCHA.

18. PIN stands for_____.

19. Define the term, biometric device. List disadvantages of biometric devices.

20. Describe how companies use the following recognition or verification systems: face, hand, voice, signature, and iris.

21. 🗐 Name the security contributions of the FBI's face recognition technology project.

22. Define the term, digital forensics. Name areas in which digital forensics are used.

23. Define the terms, keygen and software piracy. Identify methods to prevent software theft.

24. Explain the process of product activation.

25. Describe the following license agreement types: end-user, network, and site. 🗐 List conditions provided in a license agreement.

26. Give examples of information theft.

27. Describe the functions of an encryption algorithm and an encryption key. Differentiate between private and public key encryption.

28. Unencrypted data is called _____ ; encrypted data is called _____.

29. Describe the purpose of a VPN.

30. Define these terms: digital signature, digital certificate, and secure site.

31. Explain how to verify a digital certificate or signature's authenticity.

32. Describe what occurs during hardware theft or vandalism.🗐 Name the hardware security contributions of LoJack.

33. Define the terms, back up and restore.

34. List the five types of backups. Describe the three-generation backup policy.

35. Identify the components of a disaster recovery plan.

36. Describe security risks associated with wireless access.

37. Identify ways to secure your wireless network.

38. List guidelines to protect your mobile device data.

39. Describe information accuracy, intellectual property rights, and codes of conduct.

40. List measures users can take to contribute to green computing.

41. Define the term, copyright. Identify issues surrounding streaming copyrighted materials.

42. Explain how companies, websites, and employers might infringe on your right to information privacy.

43. Describe how the following techniques are used to collect personal data: electronic profiles, cookies, phishing, and spyware and adware.

44. List methods for securing your browser. How can you protect against phishing scams?

45. 🗐 List some federal and state privacy laws that affect the storage and disclosure of data.

46. Identify methods to protect yourself from social engineering scams.

47. Describe what a company might track when monitoring employees.

48. Identify issues surrounding content filtering.

49. Give examples of how various agencies and businesses use computers to ensure security.

You should be able to define the Primary Terms and be familiar with the Secondary Terms listed below.

Key Terms

Access the Flash Cards app that runs on your smartphone, tablet, laptop, or desktop by navigating to this book's Apps resource on Computer Concepts CourseMate. **View definitions** for each term by navigating to this book's Key Terms resource on Computer Concepts CourseMate. **Listen to definitions** for each term on your portable media player by navigating to this book's Audio Study Tools resource on Computer Concepts CourseMate.

Primary Terms (shown in **bold-black** characters in the chapter)

adware (231)
back door (207)
back up (219)
backup (219)
biometric device (213)
botnet (206)
code of conduct (226)
computer crime (202)
computer ethics (224)
content filtering (234)
cookie (229)
cracker (204)
cybercrime (202)

cyberextortionist (204)
cyberterrorist (204)
decrypt (216)
denial of service attack
   (DoS attack) (206)
digital certificate (218)
digital forensics (214)
digital security risk (202)
digital signature (218)
disaster recovery plan (220)
employee monitoring (233)
encryption (216)
fingerprint reader (213)

firewall (208)
green computing (226)
hacker (204)
information privacy (227)
information theft (216)
license agreement (215)
malware (205)
online security service (208)
password (211)
personal firewall (209)
phishing (231)
PIN (213)
piracy (215)

product activation (215)
restore (219)
script kiddie (204)
secure site (218)
social engineering (232)
software piracy (215)
software theft (215)
spoofing (207)
spyware (231)
user name (211)
web filtering software (234)
zombie (206)

Secondary Terms (shown in *italic* characters in the chapter)

acceptable use policy (AUP) (210)
access control (211)
adware (205)
asymmetric key encryption (217)
audit trail (211)
biometric payment (214)
bot (206)
browsing history (230)
Business Software Alliance (BSA)
   (215)
Caesar cipher (217)
CAPTCHA (212)
CERT/CC (208)
certificate authority (218)
child (219)
ciphertext (216)
clickjacking (231)
Computer Emergency Response Team
   Coordination Center (208)
continuous data protection (CDP) (220)
copyright (225)

crimeware (202)
cyberforensics (214)
cyberwarfare (204)
cypher (216)
differential backup (220)
digital rights management (225)
distributed DoS attack (DDoS
   attack) (207)
email spoofing (207)
encryption algorithm (216)
encryption key (216)
end-user license agreement (EULA)
   (215)
ENERGY STAR program (226)
face recognition system (213)
full backup (220)
grandparent (219)
hand geometry system (213)
incremental backup (220)
intellectual property (IP) (225)
intellectual property rights (225)

IP spoofing (207)
iris recognition system (214)
keygen (215)
location sharing (230)
MAC address (222)
MAC address control (222)
macros (208)
madware (231)
malicious software (205)
network license (216)
off-site (219)
parent (219)
passphrase (212)
payload (205)
personal identification number (213)
phishing filter (231)
plaintext (216)
power usage effectiveness (227)
private browsing (230)
private key encryption (217)
proxy server (209)

public key encryption (217)
rootkit (205)
selective backup (220)
session cookie (229)
signature verification system (214)
single-user license agreement (215)
site license (216)
spyware (205)
SSID (222)
symmetric key encryption (217)
toll fraud (223)
trojan horse (205)
unauthorized access (210)
unauthorized use (210)
user ID (211)
virtual private network (VPN) (218)
virus (205)
voice verification system (213)
worm (205)
zombie army (206)

hand geometry system (213)

Courtesy of Ingersoll Rand Security Technologies

Checkpoint

The Checkpoint exercises test your knowledge of the chapter concepts. The page number containing the answer appears in parentheses after each exercise. The Consider This exercises challenge your understanding of chapter concepts.

Complete the Checkpoint exercises interactively by navigating to this book's Checkpoint resource on Computer Concepts CourseMate. **Access the Test Prep app** that runs on your smartphone, tablet, laptop, or desktop by navigating to this book's Apps resource on Computer Concepts CourseMate. After successfully completing the self-assessment through the Test Prep app, **take the Practice Test** by navigating to this book's Practice Test resource on Computer Concepts Coursemate.

True/False   Mark T for True and F for False.

_____ 1. Any illegal act involving the use of a computer or related devices generally is referred to as crimeware. (202)

_____ 2. Some malware contains elements of a virus, worm, and trojan horse. (205)

_____ 3. A rootkit displays an online advertisement in a banner or pop-up window on webpages, email, or other Internet services. (205)

_____ 4. An audit trail records in a file both successful and unsuccessful access attempts. (211)

_____ 5. It is good practice to change your password frequently. (211)

_____ 6. A typical license agreement allows you to rent or lease the software. (216)

_____ 7. Unencrypted, readable data is called ciphertext. (216)

_____ 8. Private key encryption also is called asymmetric key encryption. (217)

_____ 9. VPNs encrypt data to help ensure that the data is safe from being intercepted by unauthorized people. (218)

_____ 10. Although wireless access provides many conveniences to users, it also poses additional security risks. (221)

_____ 11. It is impossible to detect if someone is accessing your wireless home network. (222)

_____ 12. Before recycling, refurbishing, or discarding your old computer, you should erase, remove, or destroy its hard disk so that the information it stored remains private. (227)

Multiple Choice   Select the best answer.

1. A _____ is someone who demands payment to stop an attack on an organization's technology infrastructure. (204)
   a. cyberterrorist
   b. script kiddie
   c. cracker
   d. cyberextortionist

2. _____ is a type of malware that is placed on a computer without the user's knowledge that secretly collects information about the user. (205)
   a. A rootkit
   b. Spyware
   c. A trojan horse
   d. Adware

3. An employee using an organization's computer to send personal email messages might be an example of _____. (210)
   a. cybercrime
   b. hardware vandalism
   c. intellectual property rights violation
   d. unauthorized access and use

4. A _____ is a private combination of words, often up to 100 characters in length and containing mixed capitalization and punctuation, associated with a user name that allows access to certain computer resources. (212)
   a. passphrase
   b. private key
   c. public key
   d. encryption algorithm

5. A(n) _____ encryption algorithm inserts characters between existing characters. (217)
   a. expansion
   b. transposition
   c. compaction
   d. substitution

6. A(n) _____ is a set of characters that the originator of the data uses to encrypt the text and the recipient of the data uses to decrypt the text. (217)
   a. cipher
   b. plaintext
   c. public key
   d. encryption key

7. A(n) _____ backup method is the only real-time back up, providing very fast recovery of data. (220)
   a. selective
   b. full
   c. incremental
   d. continuous data protection

8. Online shopping websites generally use a _____ to keep track of items in a user's shopping cart. (229)
   a. phishing filter
   b. session cookie
   c. location sharing algorithm
   d. keygen

Checkpoint

Matching   Match the terms with their definitions.

_____ 1. digital security risk (202)

_____ 2. bot (206)

_____ 3. zombie (206)

_____ 4. denial of service attack (206)

_____ 5. spoofing (207)

_____ 6. back door (207)

_____ 7. access control (211)

_____ 8. cyberforensics (214)

_____ 9. digital certificate (218)

_____ 10. digital rights management (225)

a. compromised computer or device whose owner is unaware the computer or device is being controlled remotely by an outsider

b. technique intruders use to make their network or Internet transmission appear legitimate to a victim computer or network

c. program that performs a repetitive task on a network

d. program or set of instructions in a program that allows users to bypass security controls when accessing a program, computer, or network

e. notice that guarantees a user or website is legitimate

f. strategy designed to prevent illegal distribution of movies, music, and other digital content

g. an assault whose purpose is to disrupt computer access to an Internet service such as the web or email

h. any event or action that could cause a loss of or damage to computer or mobile device hardware, software, data, information, or processing capability

i. security measure that defines who can access a computer, device, or network, when they can access it, and what actions they can take while accessing it

j. the discovery, collection, and analysis of evidence found on computers and networks

Short Answer   Write a brief answer to each of the following questions.

1. What is cyberwarfare? (204) Differentiate among the various categories of cybercriminals. (204)

2. Differentiate among denial of service attacks, back doors, and spoofing. (206–207) What are methods to protect computers, mobile devices, and networks from attacks? (208)

3. How does a biometric device work? (213) Explain how a biometric payment is made. (214)

4. List five backup methods and how they differ. (220) What are the four components contained in a disaster recovery plan? (220)

5. What is private browsing? (230) List ways you can secure your browser. (230)

☀ Consider This   Answer the following questions in the format specified by your instructor.

1. Answer the critical thinking questions posed at the end of these elements in this chapter: Ethics & Issues (204, 221, 226, 234), How To (210, 222, 230, 231), Mini Features (220, 222), Secure IT (206, 208, 212, 218, 232), and Technology @ Work (235).

2. What are some common digital security risks? (202)

3. How does malware deliver its payload? (205)

4. Why would a programmer or computer repair technician build a back door? (207)

5. Are passphrases more secure than passwords? Why or why not? (212)

6. How are fingerprint readers used with personal computers? (213)

7. What conditions are found in a typical single-user license agreement? (215)

8. 📄 What security protocols do secure sites use? (218)

9. What should you include in a disaster recovery plan for natural disasters? What should you include for man-made disasters? (220)

10. Is it ethical to access an unsecured wireless network without permission? Why or why not? (221)

11. How can mobile security apps protect your mobile device data? (223)

12. What are some questions that arise surrounding fair use with respect to copyrighted material? (225)

13. What role does the ENERGY STAR program play in green computing? (228)

14. For what purposes do websites use cookies? (229)

15. What is click jacking? (230)

✱ How To: Your Turn

The How To: Your Turn exercises present general guidelines for fundamental skills when using a computer or mobile device and then require that you determine how to apply these general guidelines to a specific program or situation.

Instructions: You often can complete tasks using technology in multiple ways. Figure out how to perform the tasks described in these exercises by using one or more resources available to you (such as a computer or mobile device, articles on the web or in print, online or program help, user guides, blogs, podcasts, videos, other individuals, trial and error, etc.). Summarize your 'how to' steps, along with the resource(s) used, in the format requested by your instructor (brief report, presentation, discussion, blog post, video, or other means).

1 Update Virus Definitions

In addition to installing an antivirus program on your computer or mobile device to keep it safe from viruses, it also is necessary to keep the virus definitions updated so that the antivirus program can search for and detect new viruses on your computer or mobile device. New virus definitions can be released as often as once per day, depending on the number of new viruses that are created. Antivirus programs either can search for and install new virus definitions automatically at specified intervals, or you can update the virus signatures manually. The following steps describe how to update the virus definitions for an antivirus program.

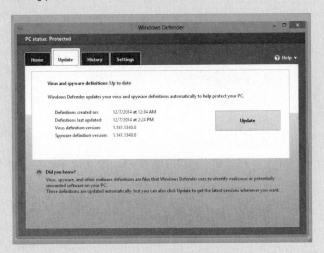

Source: Microsoft

Update Virus Definitions Manually

a. If necessary, establish an Internet connection so that you will be able to update the virus definitions.
b. Run an antivirus program.
c. Tap or click the button to check for updated virus definitions.
d. If new virus definitions are available for the antivirus program, tap or click the link to download the definitions to the computer or mobile device.
e. When the update is complete, tap or click the button to scan the computer or mobile device for viruses.

Configure Automatic Updates for Virus Definitions

a. If necessary, establish an Internet connection so that you will be able to update the virus definitions.
b. Run an antivirus program.
c. Tap or click the option to update virus definitions automatically.
d. Tap or click the option to display the virus definition update schedule.
e. To provide the maximum protection from viruses, configure the antivirus program to update definitions as frequently as possible.
f. After configuring the update schedule, tap or click the button to update virus definitions manually.
g. When the update is complete, tap or click the button to scan the computer or mobile device for viruses.

Exercises

1. What antivirus program, if any, currently is installed on your computer? Is it scheduled to update virus definitions automatically?
2. In addition to downloading and installing virus definitions from within the antivirus program, are other ways available to obtain the latest virus definitions?
3. In addition to keeping the antivirus program's virus definitions current, what other ways can you protect a computer or mobile device from viruses?

2 Determine Whether a Computer or Mobile Device Is Secured Properly

Several steps are required to secure a computer or mobile device properly. In addition to installing antivirus software and updating the virus definitions regularly, you also should install and configure a firewall, keep the operating system up to date, and be careful not to open suspicious email messages, visit unsecure webpages, or download untrusted files while using the Internet. The following steps guide you through the process of making sure your computer or mobile device is secured properly by verifying antivirus software is installed and running, a firewall is enabled and configured, and the operating system is up to date.

Verify Antivirus Software

a. Use the search tool in the operating system or scan the programs on the computer or mobile device for antivirus software.

How To: Your Turn ✳

b. If you are unable to locate antivirus software on the computer or mobile device, obtain an antivirus program and install it.

c. Run the antivirus program.

d. Verify the virus definitions in the antivirus program are up to date. More information about updating virus definitions can be found in How To: Your Turn Exercise 5-1.

Verify the Firewall

a. Use the search tool in the operating system or scan the programs, apps, and settings on the computer or mobile device to access and configure the firewall.

b. If you are unable to locate a firewall on the computer or mobile device, obtain a firewall program and install it.

c. Run the firewall program.

d. View the firewall settings and verify the firewall is turned on.

e. View the list of programs, apps, and features allowed through the firewall. If you do not recognize or use one or more of the programs, apps, or features, remove them from the list of allowed programs, apps, and features.

Verify Operating System Updates

a. If necessary, establish an Internet connection.

b. Navigate to the area of the operating system where you can access the button, link, or command to search for operating system updates. For example, in Microsoft Windows, you would display the settings for Windows Update.

c. Tap or click the button, link, or command to check for updates.

d. If no updates are available, your operating system is up to date. If the operating system locates additional updates, download and install the updates. **NOTE: If the computer or mobile device you are using does not belong to you, check with its owner before downloading and installing updates for the operating system.**

Exercises

1. Before you began this exercise, was your computer or mobile device secured properly? How did you know your computer or mobile device was secured properly? If it was not, what actions did you need to perform to secure it?

2. Which programs, apps, and features do you think are safe to allow through your firewall? Which programs, apps, and features do you feel are not safe to allow through your firewall?

3. What additional ways can you properly secure your computer?

❸ Configure a Browser's Cookie Settings

As discussed in this chapter, cookies can be used for a variety of reasons. Websites can install cookies on your computer or mobile device that can store information on your computer or mobile device, or track your browsing habits. You can configure a browser's settings to disallow websites from storing and accessing cookies on your computer or mobile device. The following steps guide you through the process of configuring a browser's cookie settings.

a. Run the browser.

b. Display the browser's settings.

c. Navigate to the settings that configure the browser's cookie settings. These settings often are found in the Privacy category.

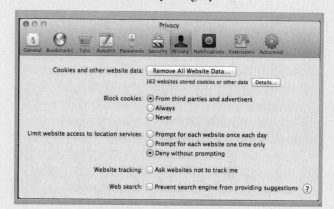

Source: Apple, Inc.

d. Configure how the browser handles first-party cookies and third-party cookies. Some users choose to reject all cookies. To function properly, however, some websites require that you accept their cookies.

e. Save the changes to the settings.

f. Restart the browser.

Exercises

1. What is the difference between first-party cookies and third-party cookies?

2. Configure the browser to deny all first-party and third-party cookies and then navigate to five websites you visit most frequently. Do the websites display any differently now that you are denying all cookies? Describe your browsing experience while the browser is configured to deny all cookies.

3. What security risks are associated with cookies?

❋ Internet Research

The Internet Research exercises broaden your understanding of chapter concepts by requiring that you search for information on the web.

Instructions: Use a search engine or another search tool to locate the information requested or answers to questions presented in the exercises. Describe your findings, along with the search term(s) you used and your web source(s), in the format requested by your instructor (brief report, presentation, discussion, blog post, video, or other means).

❶ Making Use of the Web
News, Weather, and Sports

When a major news, weather, or sports story breaks, more than 40 percent of people turn to the Internet to learn the latest details. They view video and photos from eyewitnesses and fans, read analyses from investigators and coaches, and comment on stories. Apps on tablets, smartphones, and other mobile devices are changing the delivery of the day's top stories, as both younger and older consumers are abandoning the traditional print newspaper. Men and college-educated people are the heaviest users of mobile news websites, and they are likely to read in-depth investigations and analyses. Social networking sites also are a major source of information for many people.

(a) Visit two news websites or apps and locate one national event covered in both sources. Compare the coverage of the two stories. What information is provided in addition to the text, such as video, graphics, or links to related articles? Which story offers a better analysis? Which source is easier to navigate and read? Then, using another website or app, locate and read today's top international news story. What did you learn by reading the story? Were you aware of this event prior to reading the online story? Does the coverage include videos and photos to increase your comprehension?

(b) Visit a weather website or app and obtain the five-day forecast for your hometown. Include details about information that supplements the current and forecast conditions, such as a pollen or air quality index, storm tracking, travel advisories, or season summaries.

(c) Visit a sports website or app and read the first story reported. Describe the coverage of this event. Which sources are quoted in the story? Which links are included to other stories? Describe the features provided on this website, such as the ability to chat, customize the page for your favorite teams, or share the content with media sharing sites.

❷ Social Media 📖

Sharing photos on your social media sites of yesterday's visit to the nature center might be at the top of today's to-do list, but these images might be just the clue cyberthieves need to access your account. Facebook, in particular, is one website that scammers and advertisers use to gather information regarding your whereabouts and your personal life. Their malicious attacks begin with a visit to your timeline or other record of your activities. Searching for keywords on your page, they send targeted messages appearing to originate from trusted friends. If you open their attachments or tap or click their links, you have given these unscrupulous individuals access to your account. In addition, you may think you have crafted a password no one could guess. With your page open for others to view, however, the thieves scour the contents in hopes of locating starting clues, such as children's names, anniversary dates, and pet breeds, which could be hints to cracking your password.

In the Help section of a social network site you use, search for information about changing your profile's security and privacy settings. What steps can you take to mitigate the chance of becoming the victim of a hack? For example, can you adjust the connection settings to restrict who can see stories, send friend requests and messages, or search for you by name or contact information? Can you hide certain posts or block people from posting on your page? Can you report posts if they violate the website's terms?

Source: AccuWeather, Inc.

Internet Research ✳

❸ Search Sleuth

(1) reCAPTCHA is helping to digitize old editions of which newspaper and books? (2) Which U.S. president signed into law the Electronic Signatures in Global and National Commerce (ESIGN) Act, which legalizes and enforces digital signatures, in 2000? (3) What is the name of the teenage hacker group that allegedly stole passwords and data from phone companies in the early 1990s? (4) According to the McAfee website, what are the three newest virus threats? (5) The person behind "Project Rivolta" carried out DDoS attacks on the websites of Yahoo!, CNN, eBay, Dell, and Amazon in 2000. What was his Internet alias? (6) The CERT Program is located in the Software Engineering Institute at which university? (7) Ancient Babylonians used which method to record secure business transactions? (8) What animal is the mascot for the Business Software Alliance's Play it Cyber Safe campaign? (9) What percent of Americans recognized the ENERGY STAR label when the first National Awareness survey was conducted in 2000? (10) The Internet Crime Complaint Center (IC3) is a partnership between which two organizations?

Source: Carnegie Mellon University

❹ Green Computing

Energy-conserving features on your smartphone, mobile device, and computer may add a level of security to your data. Battery-operated devices may shut down (or power off), go into sleep mode, or hibernate after a period of inactivity to extend the battery charge. The power-off mode is more secure because you normally need to press a button to turn on the device. In sleep and hibernate modes, however, the device is placed in a low power-consumption state. The data remains in memory, so the device is vulnerable to the possibility of someone accessing the device remotely over a network. To enhance security, a password sometimes is required to wake the device from its sleep.

You often can specify in a settings menu which of these three modes you prefer. View the Help information for your smartphone, mobile device, or computer to read about setting the sleep and display settings. Which time options are available for turning off the display and putting the computer to sleep? Which power settings can you change? How can you restore the default settings?

❺ Security

Digital certificates and signatures detect a sender's identity and verify a document's authenticity. Secure IT 5-4 on page 218 gives details about how these certificates are issued and how encryption and algorithms identify the documents. Visit websites of at least two companies that issue digital certificates. Compare products offered, prices, and certificate features. What length of time is needed to issue a certificate? What is a green address bar, and when is one issued? What business or organization validation is required? Then, visit websites of at least two companies that provide digital signatures. Compare signing and sending requirements, types of supported signatures, and available security features. Which documents are required to obtain a digital signature? When would a business need a Class 2 rather than a Class 3 digital signature?

❻ Ethics in Action

Retailers are using technology to sell their goods, unbeknownst to most shoppers. Some stores have purchased mannequins equipped with a camera in one eye to record video as input for face recognition software that can identify shoppers' age, race, and gender. The camera also is used to measure the amount of time shoppers view displays and also to search for shoplifters. In another instance, radio frequency identification (RFID) tags placed on such items as prescriptions, computer hardware, and clothing help retailers track inventory, reduce labor costs, and keep shelves stocked. Also, some malls have installed technology that monitors mobile phone signals to track shoppers' activities as they move from store to store. Privacy experts claim these security techniques invade shoppers' privacy because information about specific shoppers' habits and whereabouts are recorded. They claim law enforcement officials, lawyers, marketers, as well as thieves, could use this detailed electronic data to track people at all times of the day.

Visit websites that discuss using spy mannequins, RFID tags, and phone tracking in retail stores and malls. What are the benefits for stores to purchase this technology? What security and privacy issues arise from their use?

✻ Problem Solving

The Problem Solving exercises extend your knowledge of chapter concepts by seeking solutions to practical problems with technology that you may encounter at home, school, work, or with nonprofit organizations. The Collaboration exercise should be completed with a team.

> 💻 Challenge yourself with additional Problem Solving exercises by navigating to this book's Problem Solving resource on Computer Concepts CourseMate.

Instructions: You often can solve problems with technology in multiple ways. Determine a solution to the problems in these exercises by using one or more resources available to you (such as a computer or mobile device, articles on the web or in print, blogs, podcasts, videos, television, user guides, other individuals, electronics or computer stores, etc.). Describe your solution, along with the resource(s) used, in the format requested by your instructor (brief report, presentation, discussion, blog post, video, or other means).

Personal

1. **No Browsing History**   While using the browser on your tablet, you realize that it is not keeping a history of websites you have visited. What might be wrong, and what is the first step you will take to correct this problem?

2. **Windows Updates Will Not Install**   Microsoft Windows is notifying you that updates are available for your computer. You are able to download the updates to the computer, but you receive an error message each time you attempt to install the updates. What are your next steps?

3. **Suspicious File Attachment**   You receive an email message that appears to be from someone you know. When you click to open the attachment, nothing happens. You attempt to open the attachment two more times without any success. Several minutes later, your computer is running slower and you are having trouble running apps. What might be wrong?

4. **Antivirus Software Outdated**   After starting your computer and signing in to the operating system, a message is displayed stating that your virus definitions are out of date and need to be updated. What are your next steps?

5. **Laptop's Physical Security**
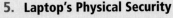
You plan to start taking your laptop to school so that you can record notes in class. You want to make sure, however, that your computer is safe if you ever step away from it for a brief period of time. What steps can you take to ensure the physical security of your laptop?

© iStockphoto / Stephen Krow

Professional

6. **Corporate Firewall Interference**   You installed a new browser on your work computer because you no longer wish to use the default browser provided with the operating system. When you run the new browser, an error message appears stating that a user name and password are required to configure the firewall and allow this program to access the Internet. Why has this happened?

7. **Problems with CAPTCHA**   You are signing up for an account on a website and encounter a CAPTCHA. You attempt to type the characters you see on the screen, but an error message appears stating that you have entered the incorrect characters. You try two more times and get the same result. You are typing the characters to the best of your ability but think you still might be misreading at least one of the characters. What are your next steps?

8. **Unclear Acceptable Use Policy**   You read your company's acceptable use policy, but it is not clear about whether you are able to use the computer in your office to visit news websites on your lunch break. How can you determine whether this type of activity is allowed?

9. **Potential Password Breach**   While signing in to your office computer one morning, you suspect that one of your coworkers was looking over your shoulder when you entered your password. You use the same password to access highly sensitive information, and you fear you may lose your job if someone else accesses your account. What are your next steps?

10. **Connecting Corporate Email**   You want to access your corporate email on your tablet, but your information technology department has asked you first to describe the security measures you take to protect your tablet from unauthorized use. How will you respond?

Collaboration

11. **Technology in National and Local Security**   National and local security agencies often use technology to protect citizens. For example, computers are used to maintain a list of individuals not cleared to board a commercial aircraft. Form a team of three people to create a list of the various ways technology helps to keep the public safe. One team member should research how local agencies, such as police departments, use technology to ensure security. Another team member should research ways national security agencies use technology to protect the public from threats, and the last team member should research ways that private businesses use technology to enhance security. Compile these findings into a report and submit it to your instructor.

The Critical Thinking exercises challenge your assessment and decision-making skills by presenting real-world situations associated with chapter concepts. The Collaboration exercise should be completed with a team.

Critical Thinking

Challenge yourself with additional Critical Thinking exercises by navigating to this book's Critical Thinking resource on Computer Concepts CourseMate.

Instructions: Evaluate the situations below, using personal experiences and one or more resources available to you (such as articles on the web or in print, blogs, podcasts, videos, television, user guides, other individuals, electronics or computer stores, etc.). Perform the tasks requested in each exercise and share your deliverables in the format requested by your instructor (brief report, presentation, discussion, blog post, video, or other means).

1. Class Discussion

Online Gaming Safety   You and your friend frequently play a popular online role-playing game. Your friend's computer had a virus recently, which was traced back to a malware-infected website. Your friend tells you that she visited the website after clicking a link while playing the game. What risks are involved when playing online games? Use the web to find articles about incidents of malware infections associated with online gaming. Research tips for increasing security when playing online games. Did you find other threats and security tips in addition to the ones mentioned in this chapter? Have you ever downloaded updates to a game? If so, how did you ensure the updates were safe? Locate a list of games that are known to cause malware infections. Share your findings and any online gaming security problems you have experienced with the class.

2. Research and Share

Ensuring Safety and Security Online   You work in the information technology department for a large enterprise. An increasing number of users are contacting the help desk complaining about slow computer performance. Help desk representatives frequently attribute the decreased performance to malware. Although the help desk has installed security software on each computer, users also must practice safe computing. Your manager asked you to prepare information that teaches employees how to guard

against malware and other security threats. Include information such as how to determine if a website is safe, how to identify spoofing schemes, guidelines for downloading programs from the Internet, email attachment safety, and how to avoid phishing scams. Create a list of how organizations use common safeguards to protect other users on the network, such as firewalls, proxy servers, user names and passwords, access controls, and audit trails. Compile your findings.

3. Case Study

Farmers' Market   You are the new manager for a group of organic farmers who have a weekly market in season. The market's board of directors asked you to develop a disaster recovery plan for its main office. The main office consists of a small storefront with two back rooms: one room is the office, with all of the electronic equipment and paper files; the other is for storage of nonelectronic equipment. The staff members — you, an administrative assistant, and an IT specialist — work in the office. The electronic equipment in the office includes two desktops, a laptop, an external hard disk for backups, a wireless router, and two printers. In addition, each staff member has a smartphone. Choose either a natural or man-made disaster. Create a disaster recovery plan that outlines emergency strategies, backup procedures, recovery steps, and a test plan. Assign staff members roles for each phase of the disaster recovery plan. Compile your findings.

Collaboration

4. **Implementing Biometric Security**   You are the chief technology officer of a large company. You have been reading an article about computer security. The article discussed several examples of security breaches, including thieves breaking into an office and stealing expensive equipment, and a recently terminated employee gaining access to the office after hours and corrupting data. Because of these incidents, your company would like to start using biometric devices to increase its security. Form a three-member team and research the use of biometric devices to protect equipment and data. Each member of your team should choose a different type of biometric device, such as fingerprint readers, face recognition systems, and retinal scanners. Find products for each device type, and research costs and user reviews. Search for articles by industry experts. Would you recommend using the biometric device for security purposes? Why or why not? Meet with your team, discuss and compile your findings, and then share with the class.

✸ Beyond the Book

The Beyond the Book exercises expand your understanding of chapter concepts by requiring research.

ⓧ **Access premium content** by visiting Computer Concepts CourseMate. If you have a Computer Concepts CourseMate access code, you can reinforce and extend your learning with MindTap Reader, practice tests, video, and other premium content for Discovering Computers. To sign in to Computer Concepts CourseMate at www.cengagebrain.com, you first must create a student account and then register this book, as described at www.cengage.com/ct/studentdownload.

Part 1 Instructions: Use the web or e-book to perform the task identified for each book element below. Describe your findings, along with the search term(s) you used and your web source(s), if appropriate, in the format requested by your instructor (brief report, presentation, discussion, blog post, video, or other means).

1. **Animation** 📖 Review the animation associated with this chapter and then answer the question(s) it poses (217). What search term would you use to learn more about a specific segment of the animation?

2. **Consider This** Select a Consider This in this chapter (206, 207, 208, 211, 212, 214, 216, 217, 222, 227, 230, 233) and find a recent article that elaborates on the topic. What information did you find that was not presented in this book or e-book?

3. **Drag-and-Drop Figures** 📖 Complete the Drag-and-Drop Figure activities associated with this chapter (205, 217, 220, 230, 232). What did you learn from each of these activities?

4. **Ethics & Issues** Select an Ethics & Issues in this chapter (204, 221, 226, 234) and find a recent article that supports one view presented. Does the article change your opinion about the topic? Why or why not?

5. **Facebook & Twitter** Review a recent Discovering Computers Facebook post or Twitter Tweet and read the referenced article(s). What did you learn from the article?

6. **High-Tech Talk** 📖 Locate an article that discusses topics related to complex encryption algorithms. Would you recommend the article you found? Why or why not?

7. **How To** Select a How To in this chapter (210, 222, 230, 231) and find a recent article that elaborates on the topic. Who would benefit from the content of this article? Why?

8. **Innovative Computing** 📖 Locate two additional facts about unique Wi-Fi signal blocking innovations, computer vision, or the FBI's face recognition technology project. Do your findings change your opinion about the future of this innovation? Why or why not?

9. **Internet Research** Use the search term in an Internet Research (204, 206, 207, 215, 225, 226, 230) to answer the question posed in the element. What other search term could you use to answer the question?

10. **Mini Features** Locate an article that discusses topics related to one of the mini features in this chapter (214, 220, 222). Do you feel that the article is appropriate for this course? Why or why not?

11. **Secure IT** Select a Secure IT in this chapter (206, 208, 212, 218, 232) and find a recent article about the topic that you find interesting. How can you relate the content of the article to your everyday life?

12. **Technology @ Work** Locate three additional, unique usages of technology in the national and local security industry (235). What makes the use of these technologies unique to the national and local security industry?

13. **Technology Innovators** 📖 Locate two additional facts about AVG, McAfee, Symantec, and LoJack. Which Technology Innovator impresses you most? Why?

14. **Third-Party Links** 📖 Visit one of the third-party links identified in this chapter (204, 206, 208, 209, 212, 218, 219, 221, 226, 232, 235) and read the article or watch the video associated with the link. Would you share this link on your online social network account? Why or why not?

Part 2 Instructions: Find specific instructions for the exercises below in the e-book or on Computer Concepts CourseMate. Beside each exercise is a brief description of its online content.

1. 📖 **You Review It** Search for and review a video, podcast, or blog post about recent malware or virus outbreaks, or other tips to keep your computer or mobile device safe.

2. 📖 **Windows and Mac** Enhance your understanding and knowledge about using Windows and Mac computers by completing the Check Your Security Programs Status and Clear Your Browsing History activities.

3. 📖 **Android, iOS, and Windows Mobile** Enhance your understanding of mobile devices by completing the Set a Lock Screen on Your Device and Set Bluetooth-enabled devices to Non-discoverable activities.

4. 📖 **Exploring Computer Careers** Read about a career as a digital forensics examiner, search for related employment ads, and then answer related questions.

5. 📖 **App Adventure** Find and compare products you might purchase using retail apps on your smartphone or tablet.

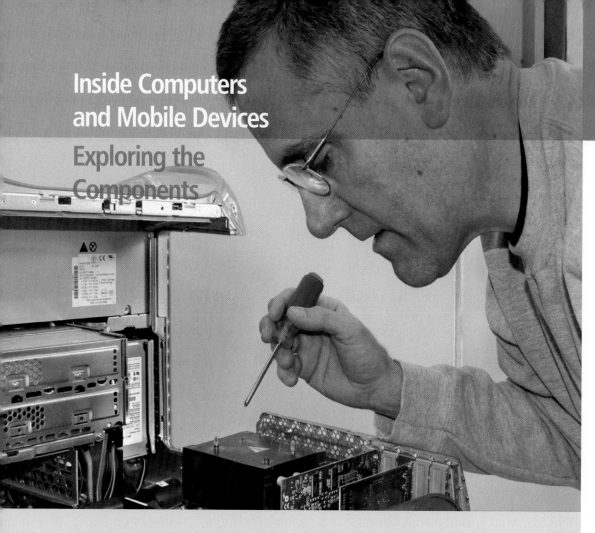

Inside Computers and Mobile Devices

Exploring the Components

6

Computers and mobile devices contain a variety of components.

"I bought my laptop a couple of years ago, and it appears to be working well. Although at times it runs a little slow and generates a lot of heat, I really have not had problems with it. So why do I need to learn about hardware inside the laptop?"

True, you may be familiar with some of the material in this chapter, but do you know . . .

How to install memory?

How to select the right processor?

What efforts are being made to ensure technology products are made with fair trade practices?

How you can secure your computers and mobile devices?

Why computers use Unicode?

How to clean a computer or mobile device?

Where you would find a heat sink?

What Moore's Law predicted?

Which cloud computing services you have used?

How the publishing industry uses technology?

Which media sharing apps are best suited to your needs?

How to conserve battery life on mobile computers and devices?

When you might need an antistatic wristband?

For these answers and to discover much more information essential to this course, read this chapter and visit the associated Computer Concepts CourseMate at www.cengagebrain.com.

✔ Objectives

After completing this chapter, you will be able to:

1 Describe the various computer and mobile device cases and the contents they protect
2 Describe multi-core processors, the components of a processor, and the four steps in a machine cycle
3 Identify characteristics of various personal computer processors on the market today, and describe the ways processors are cooled
4 Explain the advantages and services of cloud computing
5 Define a bit, and describe how a series of bits represents data
6 Explain how program and application instructions transfer in and out of memory
7 Differentiate among the various types of memory: RAM, cache, ROM, flash memory, and CMOS
8 Describe the purpose of adapter cards, USB adapters, and ExpressCard modules
9 Explain the function of a bus
10 Explain the purpose of a power supply and batteries
11 Understand how to care for computers and mobile devices

Inside the Case

Whether you are a home user or a business user, you most likely will purchase a new computer or mobile device, or upgrade an existing computer at some time in the future. Thus, you should understand the purpose of each component in a computer or mobile device. As Chapter 1 discussed, computers and mobile devices include components that are used for input, processing, output, storage, and communications. Many of these components are inside the case that contains and protects the electronics of the computer or mobile device from damage. These cases, which are made of metal or plastic, are available in a variety of shapes and sizes (Figure 6-1).

- Recall that the term, *system unit* or *chassis*, refers to the case on a desktop that contains and protects the motherboard, hard disk drive, memory, and other electronic components. Some desktops have a tower system unit that is a device separate from the monitor. Others that house the monitor and the system unit in the same case are called an all-in-one desktop. Peripheral devices normally occupy space outside the system unit and communicate with the system unit using wired or wireless technology.
- On most laptops, including ultrathin laptops, the keyboard and pointing device often occupy the area on top of the case, and the display attaches to the case by hinges.
- With a slate tablet, which typically does not include a physical keyboard, the case is behind the display. Keyboard options for slate tablets include an on-screen keyboard, a wireless keyboard, or a keyboard that attaches to the slate via a clip or other mechanism. On a convertible tablet, by contrast, the case is positioned below a keyboard, providing functionality similar to a laptop. The difference is that the display attaches to the case with a swivel-type hinge, enabling the user to rotate the display and fold it down over the keyboard to look like a slate tablet.
- Like a slate tablet, the case on a smartphone often is behind the display.
- The case on portable media players, digital cameras, and handheld game devices typically consumes the entire device and houses the display and input devices.
- With game consoles, the input and output devices, such as controllers and a television, reside outside the case.

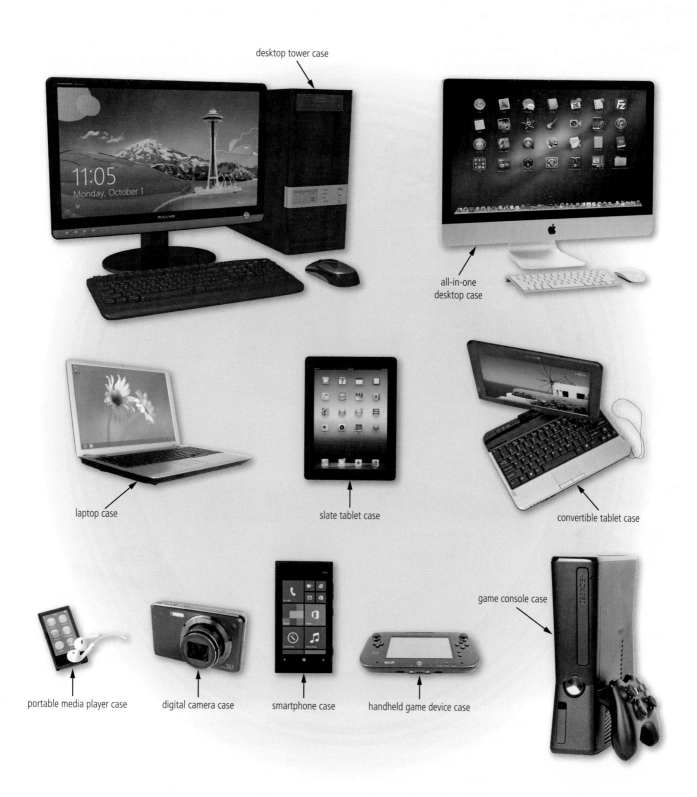

desktop tower case

all-in-one
desktop case

laptop case

slate tablet case

convertible tablet case

game console case

portable media player case   digital camera case   smartphone case   handheld game device case

Figure 6-1   Cases for computers and mobile devices are available in a variety of shapes and sizes.
© iStockphoto / Oleksiy Mark; © iStockphoto / Skip Odonnell; © Alex Staroseltsev / Shutterstock.com; © iStockphoto / franckreporter; Courtesy of Fujitsu Technology Solutions;
© iStockphoto / Frank Rotthaus; © neelsky / Shutterstock.com; © iStockphoto / andres balcazar; © iStockphoto / TommL; © iStockphoto / doram

Internet Research

Which laptops are the most popular?

Search for: laptop market share

At some point, you might have to open the case on a desktop or access panels on a laptop to replace or install a new electronic component, or hire a professional to assist with this task. For this reason, you should be familiar with the electronic components inside the case, some of which are shown in Figure 6-2 and discussed in this chapter. Read Secure IT 6-1 for tips related to protecting your computers and mobile devices from theft.

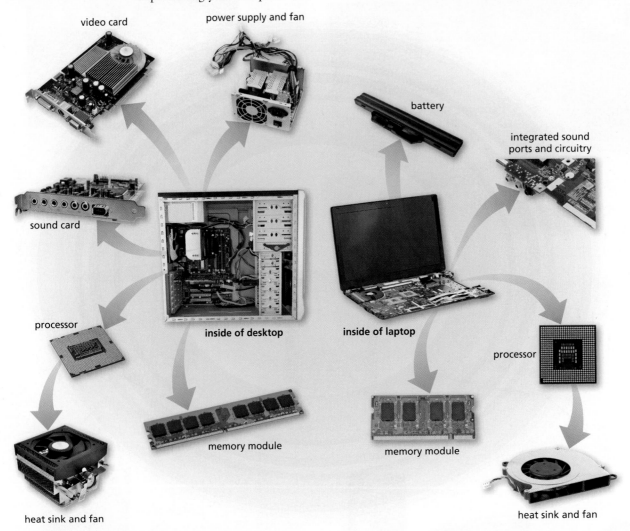

Figure 6-2 This figure shows typical components in a higher-end desktop and laptop. Many basic desktops have integrated video and sound capability, similar to the laptop image shown here.

© Raw Group / Shutterstock.com; © iStockphoto / Maisarau; © iStockphoto / RAW_group; © iStockphoto / RAW_group; © iStockphoto / RAW_group; © iStockphoto / Алексей Никончук; © iStockphoto / PeterPal; © Jiri Pavlik / Shutterstock.com; © saiko3p / Shutterstock.com; © vetkit / Shutterstock.com; © WimL / Shutterstock.com; © iStockphoto / Smith Chetanachan; © iStockphoto / vetkit; © iStockphoto / Tatiana Popova

The Motherboard

The **motherboard**, sometimes called a *system board*, is the main circuit board of the computer. Many electronic components, such as the processor and memory, attach to the motherboard; others are built into it. Figure 6-3 shows photos of current desktop and laptop motherboards.

On personal computers, the circuitry for the processor, memory, and other components reside on a computer chip(s). A computer **chip** is a small piece of semiconducting material, usually silicon, on which integrated circuits are etched. An *integrated circuit* contains many microscopic pathways capable of carrying electrical current. Each integrated circuit can contain millions of elements such as resistors, capacitors, and transistors. A *transistor*, for example, can act as an electronic switch that opens or closes the circuit for electrical charges. Today's computer chips contain millions or billions of transistors.

Most chips are no bigger than one-half-inch square. Manufacturers package chips so that the chips can be attached to a circuit board, such as a motherboard.

✸ SECURE IT 6-1

📄 Securing Computers and Mobile Devices

Millions of smartphones, mobile devices, and computers are stolen in the United States every year, according to some security experts, and only a small percent of these devices are recovered. Many devices can help deter potential thieves and also help trace and recover stolen goods. The following products may be useful in securing and tracking hardware.

- **Clamps, cables, and locks:** Lock kits include mounting plates, glue, cables, and padlocks to protect desktops, monitors, laptops, and peripheral devices.

- **Ultrasonic sensors:** Thieves do not need to remove a computer from an office building or school to commit their crimes; instead, they can open the case on a desktop or server on site and then remove a hard disk or other expensive component. To prevent such tampering, hardware manufacturers have developed an alarm system to install in the case. If the computer is moved or the case is opened,

an ear-piercing alarm sounds and a security company is alerted.

- **Tracking software:** Many smartphones and mobile devices have mapping software that shows the approximate location of devices and computers. The owner can issue commands remotely to have the device play a sound, lock the screen, display a message, or erase all personal information.

- **Asset tags:** Metal security plates affixed to hardware contain unique bar codes that are registered to the owner and stored in a security company's database. If a lost or stolen device is recovered, the finder can call the phone number on the tag, and the company will notify the owner.

- **Personal safes:** Protective cases that are approximately the size of a cereal box can store a smartphone, keys, tablet,

and other valuables. The attached security cable can be secured to a stationary object, such as a chair or table. Some personal safes have built-in electronic locks; others can be secured with a combination lock. The safe can be useful in a hotel room, at the gym, or on campus.

✳ Have you seen any of these security devices at school or at businesses? What other measures can organizations take to prevent security breaches?

Courtesy of SentrySafe

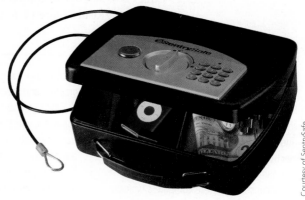

Figure 6-3   A desktop motherboard and a laptop motherboard.
Courtesy of GIGABYTE; © iStockphoto / RAW_group

Processors

The **processor**, also called the **central processing unit** (**CPU**), interprets and carries out the basic instructions that operate a computer. The processor significantly impacts overall computing power and manages most of a computer's operations. On larger computers, such as mainframes and supercomputers, the various functions performed by the processor extend over many separate chips and often multiple circuit boards. On a personal computer, all functions of the processor usually are on a single chip. Some computer and chip manufacturers use the term *microprocessor* to refer to a personal computer processor chip.

Most processor chip manufacturers now offer multi-core processors. A processor core, or simply core, contains the circuitry necessary to execute instructions. The operating system views each processor core as a separate processor. A **multi-core processor** is a single chip with two or more separate processor cores. Multi-core processors are used in all sizes of computers. Read Ethics & Issues 6-1 to consider whether mass-produced computers are better than custom-built computers. Read Secure IT 6-2 to learn how chips can help to identify and secure animals.

⚙ ETHICS & ISSUES 6-1

Are Mass-Produced Computers Better than Custom Built?

Before buying a new desktop computer, you should consider many factors, such as price and service packages. If you visit a computer or electronics store, you will find mass-produced computers designed to meet the needs of many consumers. These computers typically provide only a few customization options, such as the processor type or hard disk size. If you want more options, you may consider building your own computer or purchasing a custom-built computer. A custom-built computer often contains components from several manufacturers. For example, you can customize a computer's video and sound capabilities to use a higher-end video card if you play a lot of computer games or frequently work with graphics and media software.

When you purchase a custom-built computer, you may choose its components from a variety of manufacturers. This means the quality and performance of custom-built computers can vary greatly based on the customer's budget or needs. If you can research and select a top brand for each component, however, you can create a high-quality computer.

Typically, mass-produced computers offer service packages that include over-the-phone technical support and warranties on replacement components. A vendor of a custom-built computer may or may not provide the same types of support.

Custom-built computers also often do not include recovery media, such as an optical disc, which will restore the computer in the event it fails. Custom-built computers instead rely on the media provided by each component's manufacturer when drivers need to be reinstalled.

Would you purchase a mass-produced or custom-built computer? Why? Should vendors be required to provide service for computer components that are used in custom-built computers? Why or why not? What level of service should vendors of custom-built computers provide?

⚙ SECURE IT 6-2

Chip Implants Secure Animals' Identity

Millions of dogs and cats are lost each year, and the search for them is traumatic for their owners. The animals' safe return home may be based on data stored on a chip that veterinarians have implanted under the skin, usually at the neck or shoulder blades.

The chip — sometimes called a microchip because it is so small (about the size of a grain of rice) — has a unique number that is registered to the owner's name and address. It contains an antenna and transponder encased in a glass tube. The antenna receives low-frequency radio waves when a scanning device passes over the chip, and the transponder sends a signal with the chip's number back to the scanner.

Shelters and animal control centers routinely scan runaway pets for chips in an attempt to reunite animals with their owners. Most shelters require pets to have the implant before the animals are adopted or before a once-lost pet is returned to its owner. Some veterinarians also scan new pets for chips to ensure the animal does not belong to someone else.

Microchips also are implanted or attached externally in other animals, including horses, elephants, cows, birds, fish, lizards, and snakes. Breeders, farmers, and animal associations implant the chips to deter thieves. Chips also can monitor an animal's temperature, so that a farmer can prevent the spread of disease by identifying and removing an ill animal from a herd. Researchers, including those at the U.S. Fish and Wildlife Service, also use this technology to track migration of wild animals and fish and to study how these species interact with their environment.

⚙ Do you have or know anyone who has a pet that has been implanted with a chip? Why might some people oppose mandatory animal chipping? Do you think people someday might choose to have a chip implanted to eliminate the need to carry identification? Why or why not?

⊛ **CONSIDER THIS** ──────────────────────────────

Are multi-core processors better than single-core processors?
Each processor core on a multi-core processor generally runs at a slower speed than a single-core processor, but multi-core processors typically increase overall performance. For example, although a dual-core processor does not double the processing speed of a single-core processor, it can approach those speeds. The performance increase is especially noticeable when users are running multiple programs simultaneously such as antivirus software, spyware remover, email program, instant messaging, media player, and photo editing software. Multi-core processors also are more energy efficient than separate multiple processors, requiring lower levels of power consumption and emitting less heat inside the case.

Processors contain a control unit and an arithmetic logic unit (ALU). These two components work together to perform processing operations. Figure 6-4 illustrates how other devices connected to the computer communicate with the processor to carry out a task. When a user runs an application, for example, its instructions transfer from a storage device to memory. Data needed by programs and applications enters memory from either an input device or a storage device. The control unit interprets and executes instructions in memory, and the arithmetic logic unit performs calculations on the data in memory. Resulting information is stored in memory, from which it can be sent to an output device or a storage device for future access, as needed.

🔁 **Internet Research**
What is Moore's Law?
Search for: moores law

The Control Unit

The **control unit** is the component of the processor that directs and coordinates most of the operations in the computer. The control unit has a role much like a traffic officer: it interprets each instruction issued by a program or an application and then initiates the appropriate action to carry out the instruction. Types of internal components that the control unit directs include the arithmetic logic unit, registers, and buses, each discussed in this chapter.

The Arithmetic Logic Unit

The **arithmetic logic unit** (*ALU*), another component of the processor, performs arithmetic, comparison, and other operations.

Arithmetic operations include basic calculations such as addition, subtraction, multiplication, and division. *Comparison operations* involve comparing one data item with another to determine whether the first item is greater than, equal to, or less than the other item. Depending on the result of the comparison, different actions may occur. For example, to determine if an employee should receive overtime pay, software instructs the ALU to compare the number of hours an employee worked during the week with the regular time hours allowed (e.g., 40 hours). If the hours worked exceed 40, for example, software instructs the ALU to perform calculations that compute the overtime wage.

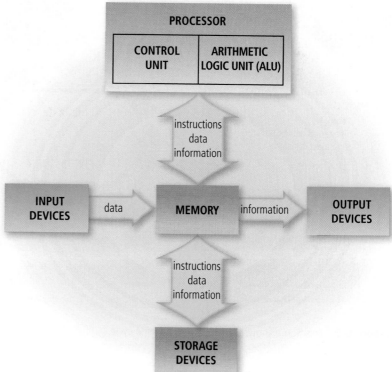

Figure 6-4   Most devices connected to the computer communicate with the processor to carry out a task.
© Cengage Learning

Machine Cycle

For every instruction, a processor repeats a set of four basic operations, which comprise a *machine cycle* (Figure 6-5): (1) fetching, (2) decoding, (3) executing, and, if necessary, (4) storing.

- *Fetching* is the process of obtaining a program or an application instruction or data item from memory.
- *Decoding* refers to the process of translating the instruction into signals the computer can execute.
- *Executing* is the process of carrying out the commands.
- *Storing*, in this context, means writing the result to memory (not to a storage medium).

In some computers, the processor fetches, decodes, executes, and stores only one instruction at a time. With others, the processor fetches a second instruction before the first instruction completes its machine cycle, resulting in faster processing. Some use multiple processors simultaneously to increase processing times.

The Steps in a Machine Cycle

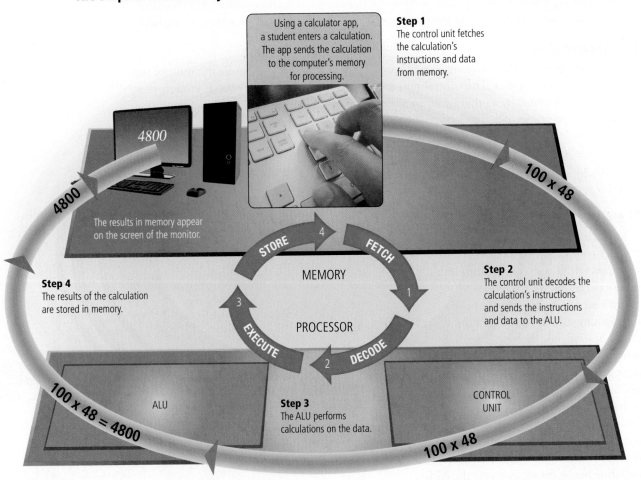

Using a calculator app, a student enters a calculation. The app sends the calculation to the computer's memory for processing.

Step 1
The control unit fetches the calculation's instructions and data from memory.

The results in memory appear on the screen of the monitor.

Step 4
The results of the calculation are stored in memory.

Step 2
The control unit decodes the calculation's instructions and sends the instructions and data to the ALU.

Step 3
The ALU performs calculations on the data.

Figure 6-5 This figure shows the steps in a machine cycle.

Registers

A processor contains small, high-speed storage locations, called *registers*, that temporarily hold data and instructions. Registers are part of the processor, not part of memory or a permanent storage device. Processors have many different types of registers, each with a specific storage function. Register functions include storing the location from where an instruction was fetched, storing an instruction while the control unit decodes it, storing data while the ALU calculates it, and storing the results of a calculation.

The System Clock

The processor relies on a small quartz crystal circuit called the **system clock** to control the timing of all computer operations. Just as your heart beats at a regular rate to keep your body functioning, the system clock generates regular electronic pulses, or ticks, that set the operating pace of components of the system unit.

Each tick equates to a *clock cycle*. Processors today typically are *superscalar*, which means they can execute more than one instruction per clock cycle.

The pace of the system clock, called the **clock speed**, is measured by the number of ticks per second. Current personal computer processors have clock speeds in the gigahertz range. Giga is a prefix that stands for billion, and a *hertz* is one cycle per second. Thus, one **gigahertz (GHz)** equals one billion ticks of the system clock per second. A computer that operates at 3 GHz has 3 billion (giga) clock cycles in one second (hertz).

The faster the clock speed, the more instructions the processor can execute per second. The speed of the system clock is just one factor that influences a computer's performance. Other factors, such as the type of processor chip, amount of cache, memory access time, bus width, and bus clock speed, are discussed later in this chapter.

 Internet Research
What are the fastest processor clock speeds?
Search for: fastest processor

 BTW
System Clock and Peripheral Devices
The speed of the system clock has no effect on peripheral devices such as a printer or disk drive.

⚜ CONSIDER THIS

Does the system clock also keep track of the current date and time?
No, a separate battery-backed chip, called the *real-time clock*, keeps track of the date and time in a computer. The battery continues to run the real-time clock even when the computer is off.

Personal Computer and Mobile Device Processors

The leading manufacturers of personal computer processor chips are Intel and AMD. AMD manufactures *Intel-compatible processors*, which have an internal design similar to Intel processors, perform the same functions, and can be as powerful, but often are less expensive. These manufacturers often identify their processor chips by a model name or model number. Read How To 6-1 for items to consider when selecting a processor for a computer.

BTW
Intel and AMD
Technology Innovators: You should be familiar with Intel, Gordon Moore, and AMD.

 **HOW TO 6-1**

Select the Right Processor

When you are shopping for a new computer, it is important to select one with a processor that will meet your needs. For example, some processors are designed for home users, some are designed for power users, and others are designed for mobile users. Performing basic research before you shop for a new computer can help you select the most appropriate processor. The following steps describe how to select the right processor.

1. **Determine your needs.** Think about how you will use your computer and the programs and applications you plan to run. If you will be using your computer for basic tasks such as web browsing or checking email, you may require a less

expensive processor than a user who will be running many programs and applications simultaneously.

2. **Determine your current processor.** If you are replacing your existing computer with a new computer, determine the processor in your existing computer so that you can make sure the new processor is better and faster than the one in use currently.

3. **Research processor models.** While shopping for computers in your price range, pay attention to the types of processors they include. Visit the processor manufacturer's website and verify that the processor will meet your computing needs adequately. It is not always necessary to

purchase the most expensive computer with the fastest processor.

⚜ What type of processor is in your current computer? If you were to upgrade your processor, which one would you choose? Why?

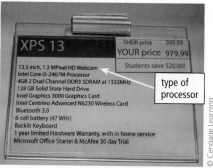

In the past, chip manufacturers listed a processor's clock speed in marketing literature and advertisements. As previously mentioned, though, clock speed is only one factor that impacts processing speed in today's computers. To help consumers evaluate various processors, manufacturers such as Intel and AMD now use a numbering scheme that more accurately reflects the processing speed of their chips.

Processor chips include technologies to improve processing performance (for example, to improve performance of media and 3-D graphics). Some also include technology to track computer hardware and software, diagnose and resolve computer problems, and secure computers from outside threats. Processors for mobile computers also include technology to optimize and extend battery life and integrate wireless capabilities. Smaller mobile devices often use more compact processors that consume less power, yet offer high performance. Read Secure IT 6-3 for tips about recycling computers and mobile devices.

BTW
Nvidia and Qualcomm
Technology Innovators:
You should be familiar
with Nvidia, maker
of high-performance
graphics processors, and
Qualcomm, maker of
chips for mobile devices.

SECURE IT 6-3

Recycling Computers and Mobile Devices

Unwrapping a new smartphone or computer and turning it on for the first time often evokes feelings of excitement. American consumers upgrade to new smartphones every 21 months on average, more often than any other country in the world, so an enormous amount of equipment in working condition is abandoned when the new products are activated. The U.S. Environmental Protection Agency (EPA) estimates that more than 80 percent of mobile phones find a final resting place in municipal landfills, despite many state laws that prohibit the disposal of electronics in the household garbage. These older devices can find a new home,

however, with electronics recycling, or **eCycling**, options that include the following:

- **Wireless carriers and big box retailers:** Stores that sell electronics often accept donations or offer buy-back programs. Many of these companies participate in the Sustainable Materials Management (SMM) Electronics Challenge, which promotes responsible electronics recycling by using third-party certified recyclers.

- **Not-for-profit organizations:** Civic and community organizations sponsor recycling events and then distribute the devices to people serving in the military, victims of natural disasters, and less fortunate citizens.

- **Secondary market:** Amazon, eBay, and other websites list thousands of used devices for sale.

- **EPA:** The EPA's website lists several resources to locate electronics donation and recycling centers in communities.

eCycling can help conserve natural resources because precious metals, glass, and solid waste are removed before the shell is taken to landfills. The EPA states that 35,000 pounds of copper, 772 pounds of silver, 75 pounds of gold, and 33 pounds of palladium are recovered from every 1 million recycled mobile phones.

 How have you disposed of or recycled your computers and mobile devices? How might you encourage your friends to eCycle or your school to offer eCycling events?

CONSIDER THIS

Can you upgrade an existing computer's processor?
You might be able to upgrade a processor to increase the computer's performance. Be certain the processor you buy is compatible with your computer's motherboard; otherwise, you will have to replace the motherboard, too. Replacing a processor is a fairly simple process, whereas replacing a motherboard is much more complicated.

BTW
Mobile Device Cooling
Mobile devices often use
low-voltage processors,
which have such low
power demands that
they do not require
additional cooling.

Processor Cooling

Processor chips for laptops, desktops, and servers can generate quite a bit of heat, which could cause the chip to malfunction or fail. Although the power supply on some computers contains a main fan to generate airflow, today's personal computer processors often require additional cooling. Some computer cases locate additional fans near certain components, such as a processor, to provide additional cooling. Heat sinks, liquid cooling technologies, and cooling mats often are used to help further dissipate processor heat.

A *heat sink* is a small ceramic or metal component with fins on its surface that absorbs and disperses heat produced by electrical components, such as a processor. Many heat sinks have fans to help distribute air dissipated by the heat sink. Some heat sinks are packaged as part of a processor chip. Others are installed on the top or the side of the chip (Figure 6-6).

Some computers use liquid cooling technology to reduce the temperature of a processor. *Liquid cooling technology* uses a continuous flow of fluid(s), such as water and glycol, in a process that transfers the heated fluid away from the processor to a radiator-type grill, which cools the liquid, and then returns the cooled fluid to the processor.

Laptop users often use a cooling pad to help further reduce the heat generated by their computer. A *cooling pad* rests below a laptop and protects the computer from overheating and also the user's lap from excessive heat (Figure 6-7). Some cooling pads contain a small fan to transfer heat away from the laptop. These types of cooling pads often draw power from a USB port. Instead of using power, other pads absorb heat through a conductive material inside the pad.

heat sink fan

heat sink

processor

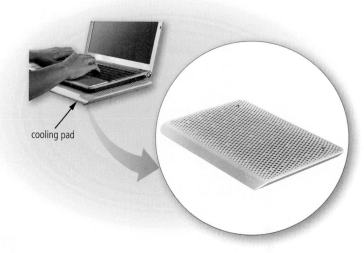

cooling pad

Figure 6-6 This photo shows a heat sink being attached to the top of a processor to prevent the chip from overheating.
© Claudio Bravo / Shutterstock.com

Figure 6-7 A laptop cooling pad helps reduce heat generated by a laptop.
Courtesy of Targus Group International, Inc; Courtesy of Targus Group International, Inc.

 **NOW YOU KNOW**

Be sure you understand the material presented in the sections titled Inside the Case and Processors as it relates to the chapter objectives.
You now should know . . .

- Why you should protect the contents of computers and mobile devices (Objective 1)
- How processors in computers and mobile devices operate (Objective 2)
- Which processors might be best suited to your needs, and how to keep processors and other components from overheating (Objective 3)

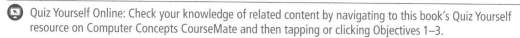 Quiz Yourself Online: Check your knowledge of related content by navigating to this book's Quiz Yourself resource on Computer Concepts CourseMate and then tapping or clicking Objectives 1–3.

Cloud Computing

Recall that cloud computing refers to an environment of servers that house and provide access to resources users access via the Internet. Home and business users choose cloud computing for a variety of reasons:

- **Accessibility:** Data and/or applications are available worldwide from any computer or device with an Internet connection.
- **Cost savings:** The expense of software and high-end hardware, such as fast processors and high-capacity memory and storage devices, shifts away from the user.
- **Space savings:** Floor space required for servers, storages devices, and other hardware shifts away from the user.
- **Scalability:** Provides the flexibility to increase or decrease computing requirements as needed.

Cloud computing consists of a front end and a back end, connected to each other through a network. The front end includes the hardware and software with which a user interacts to access the cloud. For example, a user might access a resource on the cloud through a browser on a laptop. The back end consists of the servers and storage devices that manage and store the resources accessed by users.

 **Internet Research**

Which companies offer cloud computing services?
Search for: cloud computing providers

MINI FEATURE 6-1

Cloud Computing

Cloud computing allows companies to outsource, or contract to third-party providers, elements of their information technology infrastructure. They pay only for the computing power, storage, bandwidth, and access to applications that they actually use. As a result, companies need not make large investments in equipment, or the staff to support it. Read Secure IT 6-4 for issues related to cloud computing security.

Consumers and organizations rely on cloud computing services to manage IT infrastructure (Infrastructure as a Service), provide applications (Software as a Service), access online data (Data as a Service), and create applications using web-based development platforms (Platform as a Service).

Infrastructure as a Service

Infrastructure as a Service (*IaaS*) uses software to emulate hardware capabilities, enabling companies to scale, or adjust up or down, storage, processing power, or bandwidth as needed. For example, retailers may need to increase these capabilities to accommodate additional traffic to their websites during busy holiday shopping seasons. When the season ends, retailers easily can reduce these settings.

Two special cases of IaaS are Storage as a Service and Desktop as a Service:

- Storage as a Service: Cloud storage providers offer file management services such as storing files online, system backup, and archiving earlier versions of files. Cloud storage is especially useful to tablet and smartphone users, because it enables them to access their files on all of their devices.

- Desktop as a Service: Some companies specify the applications, security settings, and computing resources available to employees on their desktop computers. These images, or configurations, provide a common desktop work environment available to employees across an entire organization. Because the desktop and its applications appear to be installed on the user's own computer, Desktop as a Service also is known as *virtual desktop*.

Software as a Service

Software as a Service (*SaaS*) describes a computing environment where an Internet server hosts and deploys applications. Editing documents or photos, sending email messages, and managing finances are common consumer tasks of SaaS applications. A pioneering provider of SaaS applications for companies is Salesforce, which offers customer relationship management (CRM) software. Salesforce users subscribe to modules to handle tasks such as sales and marketing campaigns and customer services.

SaaS application running in browser

© Tom Wang / Shutterstock.com / © Studio 101 / Alamy;
© Cengage Learning

Data as a Service

Government agencies, companies, and social media sites make data available for developers to incorporate in applications or to use when making business decisions and plans. *Data as a Service* (*DaaS*) allows users and applications to access a company's data. *Mashups* are applications that incorporate data from multiple providers into a new application. Displaying homes or crime statistics on a map are examples of mashups that require data from real estate, police records, and mapping providers.

Platform as a Service

Application developers need to maintain computers running specific hardware, operating systems, development tools, databases, and other software. *Platform as a Service* (*PaaS*) allows developers to create, test, and run their solutions on a cloud platform without having to purchase or configure the underlying hardware and software.

⚙ Cloud computing services are based on a "pay as you go" model. How are cloud services different from desktop or mobile applications? What services are customers paying for from a SaaS provider? Under what circumstances might it be advantageous to purchase an external hard disk to store your files on it, rather than storing them on a third-party server on the cloud?

SECURE IT 6-4

Security Threats in Cloud Storage

A growing number of consumers and businesses are moving their data to the cloud, but concerns about using online storage services remain. While the cloud offers a tremendous amount of storage space at a relatively low cost, the security of this data and the reliability of cloud companies trigger concerns.

Foremost is the worry about data security. The Cloud Security Alliance (CSA) warns of hackers who register for the service with a credit card or for a free trial period and then unleash malware in an attempt to gain access to passwords. Because the registration and validation procedure for accessing the cloud

is relatively anonymous, authorities can have difficulty locating the abusers.

Another concern arises when transferring data between a network and the cloud. When the data is traveling to or from a computer and the storage service, it is subject to interception. To minimize risk, security experts emphasize that a browser's web address must begin with https, and the data should be encrypted and authenticated.

Law enforcement's access to the data raises another security issue. Email messages stored on a private server belong to the company or individual who owns the computer, so law enforcement officials must obtain a search warrant to read a particular

user's messages. In contrast, law enforcement officials can access email messages stored on the cloud by requesting the information from the company that owns the cloud service. The user might not be notified of the search until up to 90 days after the search occurred; moreover, the search may occur without limitations and may include continuous monitoring of an individual's email communications.

✳ Do you have concerns about the security of your data stored on the cloud? What types of information and personal data would you store? Should law enforcement officials be able to access your data without your consent? Why or why not?

Data Representation

To understand how a computer processes data, you should know how a computer represents data. People communicate through speech by combining words into sentences. Human speech is **analog** because it uses continuous (wave form) signals that vary in strength and quality. Most computers are **digital**. They recognize only two discrete states: on and off. This is because computers are electronic devices powered by electricity, which also has only two states: on and off.

Bits and Bytes

The two digits, 0 and 1, easily can represent these two states (Figure 6-8). The digit 0 represents the electronic state of off (absence of an electronic charge). The digit 1 represents the electronic state of on (presence of an electronic charge).

When people count, they use the digits in the decimal system (0 through 9). The computer, by contrast, uses a binary system because it recognizes only two states. The **binary system** is a number system that has just two unique digits, 0 and 1, called bits. A **bit** (short for *binary digit*) is the smallest unit of data the computer can process. By itself, a bit is not very informative.

When 8 bits are grouped together as a unit, they form a **byte**. A byte provides enough different combinations of 0s and 1s to represent 256 different characters. These characters include numbers, uppercase and lowercase letters of the alphabet, punctuation marks, and other keyboard symbols, such as an asterisk (*), ampersand (&), and dollar sign ($).

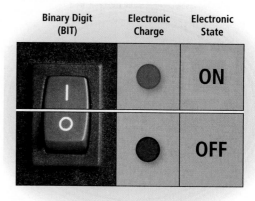

Figure 6-8 The circuitry in a computer or mobile device represents the on or the off states electronically by the presence or absence of an electronic charge.
© iStockphoto / rjmiz; © Cengage Learning

Coding Schemes

The combinations of 0s and 1s that represent uppercase and lowercase letters, numbers, and special symbols are defined by patterns called a coding scheme. Coding schemes map a set of *alphanumeric characters* (letters and numbers) and special symbols to a sequence of numeric values that a computer can process. *ASCII* (pronounced ASK-ee), which stands for American Standard Code for Information Interchange, is the most widely used coding scheme to represent a set of characters. In the ASCII coding scheme, the alphabetic character E is represented as 01000101; the symbolic character '*' is represented as 00101010; the numeric character 6 is represented as 00110110 (Figure 6-9 on the next page). For a detailed discussion of coding schemes and

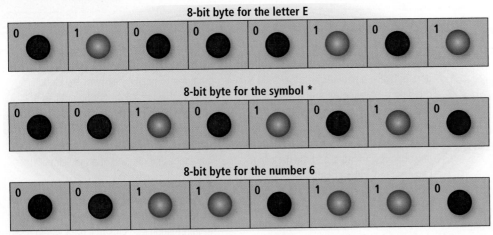

8-bit byte for the letter E

| 0 | 1 | 0 | 0 | 0 | 1 | 0 | 1 |

8-bit byte for the symbol *

| 0 | 0 | 1 | 0 | 1 | 0 | 1 | 0 |

8-bit byte for the number 6

| 0 | 0 | 1 | 1 | 0 | 1 | 1 | 0 |

Figure 6-9 Eight bits grouped together as a unit are called a byte. A byte represents a single character in the computer or mobile device.
© Cengage Learning

number systems, read Mini Feature 6-2 (available in the e-book).

When you press a key on a keyboard, a chip in the keyboard converts the key's electronic signal into a special code, called a scan code, that is sent to the electronic circuitry in the computer. Then, the electronic circuitry in the computer converts the scan code into its ASCII binary form and stores it as a byte value in its memory for processing. When processing is finished, the computer converts the byte into a human-recognizable number, letter of the alphabet, or special character that is displayed on a screen or is printed (Figure 6-10). All of these conversions take place so quickly that you do not realize they are occurring.

How a Letter Is Converted to Binary Form and Back

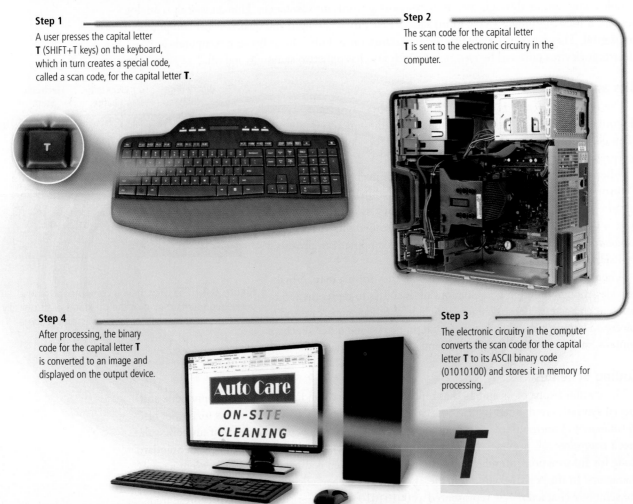

Step 1
A user presses the capital letter **T** (SHIFT+T keys) on the keyboard, which in turn creates a special code, called a scan code, for the capital letter **T**.

Step 2
The scan code for the capital letter **T** is sent to the electronic circuitry in the computer.

Step 4
After processing, the binary code for the capital letter **T** is converted to an image and displayed on the output device.

Step 3
The electronic circuitry in the computer converts the scan code for the capital letter **T** to its ASCII binary code (01010100) and stores it in memory for processing.

Auto Care
ON-SITE CLEANING

Figure 6-10 This figure shows how a letter is converted to binary form and back.
© Chiyacat / Shutterstock.com; © Kitch Bain / Shutterstock.com; © Cengage Learning; Source: Microsoft; © iStockphoto/sweetym

Why are coding schemes necessary?
Computers rely on logic circuits, which are controlled by electronic switches whose state can be either on or off. Each switch's on/off state is represented by one bit, whose value is either 0 or 1. Coding schemes translate real-world data into a form that computers can process easily.

Memory

Memory consists of electronic components that store instructions waiting to be executed by the processor, data needed by those instructions, and the results of processing the data (information). Memory usually consists of one or more chips on the motherboard or some other circuit board in the computer. Memory stores three basic categories of items:

1. The operating system and other programs that control or maintain the computer and its devices
2. Applications that carry out a specific task, such as word processing
3. The data being processed by the applications and the resulting information

This role of memory to store both data and programs is known as the *stored program concept*.

Bytes and Addressable Memory

A byte (character) is the basic storage unit in memory. When an application's instructions and data are transferred to memory from storage devices, the instructions and data exist as bytes. Each byte resides temporarily in a location in memory that has an *address*. Simply put, an address is a unique number that identifies the location of a byte in memory. To access data or instructions in memory, the computer references the addresses that contain bytes of data. The photo in Figure 6-11 shows how seats in a stadium are similar to addresses in memory: (1) a seat, which is identified by a unique seat number, holds one person at a time, and a location in memory, which is identified by a unique address, holds a single byte; and (2) both a seat, identified by a seat number, and a byte, identified by an address, can be empty.

Manufacturers state the size of memory in terms of the number of bytes it has available for storage. Common sizes for memory are in the gigabyte and terabyte range. A *gigabyte* (*GB*) equals approximately 1 billion bytes. A *terabyte* (*TB*) is equal to approximately 1 trillion bytes.

Figure 6-11   Seats in a stadium are similar to addresses in memory: a seat holds one person at a time, and a location in memory holds a single byte; and both a seat and a byte can be empty.
© Getty Images

Types of Memory

Computers and mobile devices contain two types of memory: volatile and nonvolatile. When the computer's power is turned off, *volatile memory* loses its contents. *Nonvolatile memory*, by contrast, does not lose its contents when power is removed from the computer. Thus, volatile memory is temporary and nonvolatile memory is permanent. RAM is the most common type of volatile memory. Examples of nonvolatile memory include ROM, flash memory, and CMOS. The following sections discuss these types of memory.

RAM

Users typically are referring to RAM when discussing computer and mobile device memory. **RAM** (*random access memory*), also called *main memory*, consists of memory chips that can be read from and written to by the processor and other devices. When you turn on power to a computer or mobile device, certain operating system files (such as the files that determine how the desktop or home screen appears) load into RAM from a storage device such as a hard disk. These files remain in RAM as long as the computer or mobile device has continuous power. As additional applications and data are requested, they also load into RAM from storage.

The processor interprets and executes a program or application's instructions while the program or application is in RAM. During this time, the contents of RAM may change (Figure 6-12). RAM can accommodate multiple programs and applications simultaneously.

How Program Instructions Transfer in and out of RAM

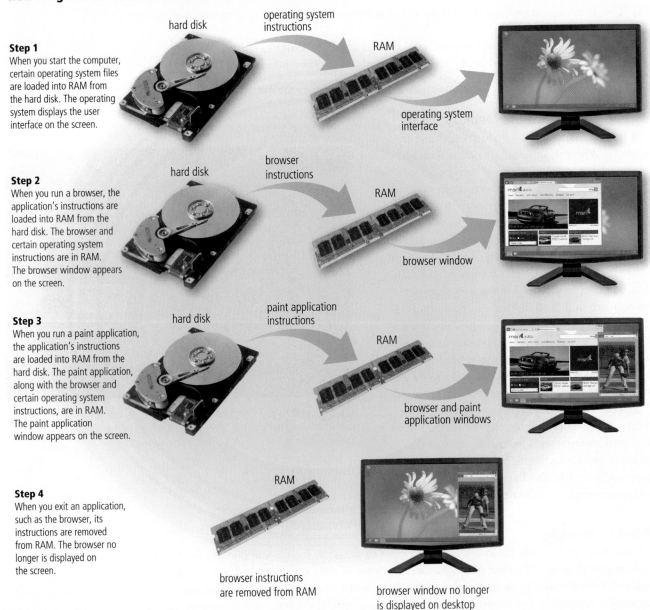

Step 1
When you start the computer, certain operating system files are loaded into RAM from the hard disk. The operating system displays the user interface on the screen.

hard disk | operating system instructions | RAM | operating system interface

Step 2
When you run a browser, the application's instructions are loaded into RAM from the hard disk. The browser and certain operating system instructions are in RAM. The browser window appears on the screen.

hard disk | browser instructions | RAM | browser window

Step 3
When you run a paint application, the application's instructions are loaded into RAM from the hard disk. The paint application, along with the browser and certain operating system instructions, are in RAM. The paint application window appears on the screen.

hard disk | paint application instructions | RAM | browser and paint application windows

Step 4
When you exit an application, such as the browser, its instructions are removed from RAM. The browser no longer is displayed on the screen.

RAM | browser instructions are removed from RAM | browser window no longer is displayed on desktop

Figure 6-12   This figure shows how program and application instructions transfer in and out of RAM.

Most RAM is *volatile*, which means it loses its contents when the power is removed from the computer. For this reason, you must save any data, instructions, and information you may need in the future. Saving is the process of copying data, instructions, and information from RAM to a storage device such as a hard disk.

Types of Ram   Two common types of RAM are dynamic RAM and static RAM:

- *Dynamic RAM* (*DRAM* pronounced DEE-ram) chips must be reenergized constantly or they lose their contents. Many variations of DRAM chips exist, most of which are faster than the basic DRAM (Table 6-1).
- *Static RAM* (*SRAM* pronounced ESS-ram) chips are faster and more reliable than any variation of DRAM chips. These chips do not have to be reenergized as often as DRAM chips; hence, the term, static. SRAM chips, however, are much more expensive than DRAM chips. Special applications such as cache use SRAM chips. A later section in this chapter discusses cache.

Table 6-1   Common DRAM Variations

Name	Comments
SDRAM (Synchronous DRAM)	• Synchronized to the system clock • Much faster than DRAM
DDR SDRAM (Double Data Rate SDRAM)	• Transfers data twice, instead of once, for each clock cycle • Faster than SDRAM
DDR2	• Second generation of DDR • Faster than DDR
DDR3	• Third generation of DDR • Designed for computers with multi-core processors • Faster than DDR2
DDR4	• Fourth generation of DDR • Faster than DDR3
RDRAM (Rambus DRAM)	• Much faster than SDRAM

Memory Modules   RAM chips usually reside on a **memory module**, which is a small circuit board. **Memory slots** on the motherboard hold memory modules.

Two types of memory modules are SIMMs and DIMMs (Figure 6-13). A *SIMM* (*single inline memory module*) has pins on opposite sides of the circuit board that connect together to form a single set of contacts. With a *DIMM* (*dual inline memory module*), by contrast, the pins on opposite sides of the circuit board do not connect and, thus, form two sets of contacts. Read How To 6-2 on the next page for instructions about determining memory requirements and installing memory modules.

⚙ BTW
RAM
High-Tech Talk: How is data written to and stored in DRAM? Transistors and a capacitor create a memory cell, which represents a single bit of data.

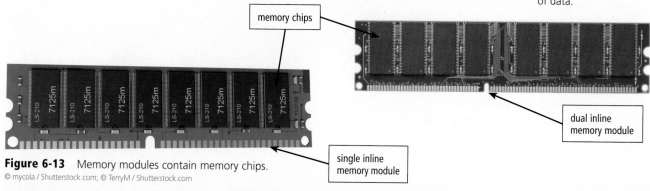

memory chips

dual inline memory module

single inline memory module

Figure 6-13   Memory modules contain memory chips.
© mycola / Shutterstock.com; © TerryM / Shutterstock.com

⭐ HOW TO 6-2

Determine Memory Requirements and Install Memory Modules

If you are shopping for a new computer or looking to upgrade your existing computer, be sure that it will have sufficient memory. When a computer has insufficient memory, its performance can slow significantly. On the other hand, it would be an unnecessary expense to purchase a computer with more memory than you will ever use. The following steps describe how to determine memory requirements and install memory modules.

1. If you are upgrading the memory in your existing computer, determine the following:
   a. Amount of memory currently installed
   b. Amount of memory the computer can support
   c. Type of memory modules currently installed
   d. Whether memory modules must be installed in pairs
   e. Number of available slots for memory modules

2. Determine the amount of memory your computer requires by checking the memory requirements for the operating system and programs and applications you plan to run. You can find the system requirements, which will specify the memory requirements, on product packaging or on a software manufacturer's website. If you are planning to upgrade your computer and the amount of memory you require exceeds the amount of memory your computer currently can support, you may need to purchase a new computer. If you are purchasing a new computer, view the computer's specifications to make sure it has sufficient memory. Some online vendors offer a web app that will check the configuration on your computer to determine the memory modules that are compatible and offer options to you for purchase.

3. Once you have determined your memory requirements, you are ready to purchase the memory modules. Memory modules are available for purchase in many computer and electronic stores, directly from computer manufacturers, and on various websites. When you are purchasing memory modules, keep the following in mind:
   a. Many types of memory modules are available. Purchase a type, size, and speed that is compatible with your computer.
   b. If your computer requires that you install memory in pairs, be sure to purchase two memory modules that are the same type, size, and speed.
   c. Do not purchase more memory modules than you have slots available. You may need to remove existing memory modules to make room for new memory modules.

If you are upgrading your existing computer, your next step is to install the new memory modules. The following steps describe how to install new memory modules.

1. Turn off and unplug your computer from the power source. If you are using a laptop, remove its battery.

2. Wear an antistatic wristband to protect the computer from static electricity.

3. Remove or open the computer case. If you are upgrading a laptop, you may be able to locate the slots for the memory modules through an access panel.

4. If necessary, remove any existing memory modules you no longer need. If clips are holding the memory module in place, you may need to pull the clips away from the memory module before removing it. Remove the memory modules by lifting them out by the side edges.

5. Remove the new memory modules from the packaging.

6. Slowly and carefully insert the memory modules into the slots on your computer's motherboard. Be sure they are facing the correct way as you insert them. The memory modules should "click" in place once they are inserted completely.

7. Close the computer case or any access panel you have opened.

8. Plug in the computer and turn it on.

9. Check the system information in the operating system to make sure it is recognizing the new amount of memory installed.

✺ How much memory would be appropriate for your computer based on your current computing needs?

dual inline memory module

memory slot

© iStockphoto / gabyjalbert

Cache

Most of today's computers improve their processing times with **cache** (pronounced cash), which is a temporary storage area. Two common types of cache are memory cache and disk cache. This chapter discusses memory cache. Chapter 8 discusses disk cache.

Memory cache helps speed the processes of the computer because it stores frequently used instructions and data. Most personal computers today have two types of memory cache: Level 1 (L1) cache and Level 2 (L2) cache. Some also have Level 3 (L3) cache.

- *L1 cache* is built directly on the processor chip. L1 cache usually has a very small capacity.
- *L2 cache* is slightly slower than L1 cache but has a much larger capacity. Current processors include *advanced transfer cache* (*ATC*), a type of L2 cache built directly on the processor chip. Processors that use ATC perform at much faster rates than those that do not use it.
- *L3 cache* is a cache on the motherboard that is separate from the processor chip. L3 cache exists only on computers that use L2 advanced transfer cache.

When the processor needs an instruction or data, it searches memory in this order: L1 cache, then L2 cache, then L3 cache (if it exists), then RAM — with a greater delay in processing for each level of memory it must search (Figure 6-14). If the instruction or data is not found in memory, then it must search a slower speed storage medium, such as a hard disk or optical disc.

BTW
L2 Cache
When discussing cache, most users are referring to L2 cache.

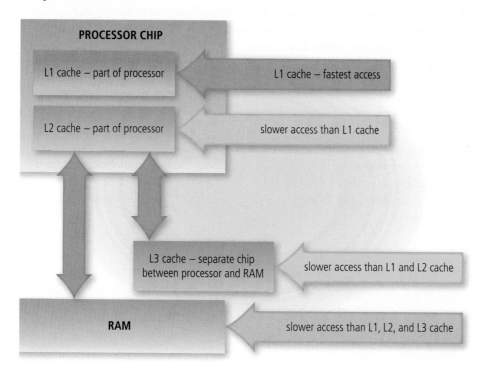

PROCESSOR CHIP

L1 cache – part of processor ← L1 cache – fastest access

L2 cache – part of processor ← slower access than L1 cache

L3 cache – separate chip between processor and RAM ← slower access than L1 and L2 cache

RAM ← slower access than L1, L2, and L3 cache

Figure 6-14 Memory cache helps speed processing times when the processor requests data, instructions, or information.
© Cengage Learning

ROM

Read-only memory (**ROM** pronounced rahm) refers to memory chips storing permanent data and instructions. The data on most ROM chips cannot be modified — hence, the name read-only. ROM is nonvolatile, which means its contents are not lost when power is removed from the computer. In addition to computers and mobile devices, many peripheral devices contain ROM chips. For example, ROM chips in printers contain data for fonts.

Manufacturers of ROM chips often record data, instructions, or information on the chips when they manufacture the chips. These ROM chips, called **firmware**, contain permanently written data, instructions, or information such as a computer or mobile device's start-up instructions. Read Ethics & Issues 6-2 on the next page to consider issues related to the manufacture of computer and mobile device components.

✸ **ETHICS & ISSUES 6-2**

Should Companies Reveal Which Products They Manufacture Using Fair Trade Practices?

Despite the increased cost, many coffee and tea drinkers gladly purchase fair trade products. Fair trade labels indicate that the workers who pick the coffee beans or tea leaves work in humane conditions and receive fair pay for their labor.

With respect to technology, several cases of unfair labor practices exist. Some technology manufacturers use products or components that are made in areas of extreme poverty. In these cases, factory owners coerce workers, including children,

to work long hours in unsafe or unsanitary conditions for little pay. In another example, mining for the raw materials needed to manufacture technology components may occur in areas where military conflict exists. Those involved in the military conflict may use the revenue from mining this material, sometimes called conflict minerals, to fund the soldiers and continue the discord.

Recently, the U.S. passed the Wall Street Reform and Consumer Protection Act. Under this act, manufacturers must review their supply sources and provide disclosure if the materials were mined in areas of conflict. These manufacturers, however, are not punished if they continue to use conflict

minerals. By contrast, some companies make efforts to obtain materials from ethical sources. One major technology company recently joined the Fair Labor Association, which provides workplace standards for the environment and treatment of workers at all stages of product development.

Would you pay more for a fair trade smartphone or laptop? Why or why not? Are companies responsible for the source of the materials used in their products? Why or why not? Should the government require companies to comply with fair trade policies? Why or why not?

Flash Memory

Flash memory is a type of nonvolatile memory that can be erased electronically and rewritten. Most computers use flash memory to hold their start-up instructions because it allows the computer to update its contents easily. For example, when the computer changes from standard time to daylight savings time, the contents of a flash memory chip (and the real-time clock chip) change to reflect the new time.

Flash memory chips also store data and programs on many mobile devices and peripheral devices, such as smartphones, portable media players, printers, digital cameras, automotive devices, and digital voice recorders. When you enter names and addresses in a smartphone, for example, a flash memory chip stores the data. Some portable media players store music on flash memory chips; others store music on tiny hard disks or memory cards. Memory cards contain flash memory on a removable device instead of a chip. Read Secure IT 6-5 for tips about protecting data on a smartphone. Read Ethics & Issues 6-3 to consider an issue related to repair technicians and your data.

✸ **SECURE IT 6-5**

Wiping Mobile Phone Memory

If you ever have lent your smartphone to someone, left it sitting on your desk at school or work, or placed it in your car's center console at valet parking, you might have provided someone access without your consent to all your personal information stored on that device. A thief can plug a small device, called a *Cellular Seizure Investigation (CSI) stick*, into the phone and then download sensitive data in seconds.

While this unscrupulous activity seems alarming, a similar action occurs every day when smartphone users recycle or sell their devices without wiping all their personal records from memory. A person

buying or acquiring the phone then can access the sensitive data left in memory. Some recyclers claim that 95 percent of the mobile phones they receive are not completely cleaned.

Deleting all information from a mobile phone's memory is a relatively simple process, but it is not a universal procedure. Each device has its own set of steps described in the owner's manual or online. In general, users must locate their device's settings area on a menu and then look for a reset command. Most electronics manufacturers post instructions for this process on their websites. Mobile phone retailers often can offer help in clearing personal data; if you

resort to this measure, be certain to watch the sales associate perform this action. If your mobile phone has a SIM or memory card, remove and destroy it if you are not going to transfer it to another phone. Employees who use their phone to access email messages on corporate servers sometimes are required to enter a passcode on the phone so that if it is lost or stolen, the data can be wiped remotely.

✸ Have you ever wiped the memory of your mobile phone? What action would you take if you received or bought a used mobile phone and then discovered the previous owner's personal information stored in memory?

ETHICS & ISSUES 6-3

Should Repair Technicians Be Required to Hold a Private Investigator License?

In one state, computer repair technicians are required by law to obtain a private investigator license if they review or analyze data on computers that they repair. The interpretation is that the technician is performing an investigation, in a sense, when business managers and parents hire them to analyze the computer usage habits of employees or children. Technicians who violate this requirement, along with customers who hire technicians in violation, are subject to fines and jail time.

To obtain a private investigator license, a technician must obtain a criminal justice degree or serve as an apprentice for a private investigator. This process takes up to three years and is costly. Many smaller computer repair companies claim that, if enforced, this law will put them out of business. Larger companies are not as vulnerable because they sometimes have employees, or can afford to hire employees, with private investigator licenses.

After technicians filed several lawsuits, the state government amended the law to require licenses only for those investigating data. That is, a technician who performs hardware maintenance and repair does not need a license under the revised law. Some technicians claim that the law still is too broad, as during the course of routine repairs or maintenance, technicians often unintentionally uncover personal data.

Should states require computer repair technicians to have a private investigator license? Why or why not? Should the government consider a different type of certification for computer repair technicians who must review or analyze customer data? If so, what should be required for the certification?

CMOS

Some RAM chips, flash memory chips, and other memory chips use complementary metal-oxide semiconductor (*CMOS* pronounced SEE-moss) technology because it provides high speeds and consumes little power. CMOS technology uses battery power to retain information even when the power to the computer is off. Battery-backed CMOS memory chips, for example, can keep the calendar, date, and time current even when the computer is off. The flash memory chips that store a computer's start-up information often use CMOS technology.

Memory Access Times

Access time is the amount of time it takes the processor to read data, instructions, and information from memory. A computer's access time directly affects how fast the computer processes data. Accessing data in memory can be more than 200,000 times faster than accessing data on a hard disk because of the mechanical motion of the hard disk.

Today's manufacturers use a variety of terminology to state access times (Table 6-2). Some use fractions of a second, which for memory occurs in nanoseconds. A *nanosecond* (abbreviated *ns*) is one billionth of a second. A nanosecond is extremely fast (Figure 6-15). In fact, electricity travels about one foot in a nanosecond.

10 million operations = 1 blink

Table 6-2   Access Time Terminology

Term	Abbreviation	Speed
Millisecond	ms	One-thousandth of a second
Microsecond	μs	One-millionth of a second
Nanosecond	ns	One-billionth of a second
Picosecond	ps	One-trillionth of a second

Figure 6-15 It takes about one-tenth of a second to blink your eye, in which time a computer can perform some operations 10 million times.
© iStockphoto / drbimages; © iStockphoto / drbimages

CONSIDER THIS

What if a manufacturer states access times in megahertz instead of fractions of a second?

Some manufacturers state access times in MHz; for example, 800 MHz DDR2 SDRAM. If a manufacturer states access time in megahertz, you can convert it to nanoseconds by dividing 1 billion ns by the megahertz number. For example, 800 MHz equals approximately 1.25 ns (1,000,000,000/800,000,000). The higher the megahertz, the faster the access time; conversely, the lower the nanoseconds, the faster the access time.

While access times of memory greatly affect overall computer performance, manufacturers and retailers often list a computer's memory in terms of its size, not its access time. For example, an advertisement might describe a computer as having 8 GB of RAM.

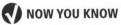 **NOW YOU KNOW**

Be sure you understand the material presented in the sections titled Cloud Computing, Data Representation, and Memory, as it relates to the chapter objectives.
You now should know . . .

- Which cloud computing service is best suited to your needs (Objective 4)
- How your computers and mobile devices represent data (Objective 5)
- How memory on your computer or mobile device works with your programs and applications (Objective 6)
- When you are using RAM, cache, ROM, flash memory, and CMOS (Objective 7)

Quiz Yourself Online: Check your knowledge of related content by navigating to this book's Quiz Yourself resource on Computer Concepts CourseMate and then tapping or clicking Objectives 4–7.

Adapters

Although the circuitry in many of today's computers integrates all the necessary functionality, some require additional capabilities in the form of adapters. Desktops and servers use adapter cards; mobile computers use USB adapters and ExpressCard modules. Read How To 6-3 to learn about ports you might consider including in a computer or mobile device that can eliminate the need for adapters.

 HOW TO 6-3

Determine Which Ports You Need on a Computer or Mobile Device

When purchasing a computer or mobile device, it is important to make sure it has the correct ports so that it can connect your peripheral devices. The following list will help identify the ports you need on a computer or mobile device.

- **Display Devices:** If you plan to connect your computer or mobile device to a display device such as a monitor or projector, make sure your computer or mobile device has a port that is compatible with the display device. For example, if you plan to connect

a laptop to a monitor that has an HDMI port, your computer or mobile device should have a port capable of HDMI output.

- **Networking:** If you plan to connect your computer or mobile device to a wired computer network, it should have an Ethernet port to which you can connect network cables.

- **Audio:** If you plan to connect your computer or mobile device to an audio output device such as speakers, headphones, or earbuds, your computer or mobile device should have a port for audio output.

- **Other Input, Output, and Storage Devices:** If you plan to connect other devices such as a keyboard, mouse, external hard disk, or printer, look at the cable that connects this device to the computer, and make sure your computer has a port that will accept the connector on the cable. In many cases, these devices will connect to your computer using a USB connection. Make sure your computer has a sufficient number of USB ports to support the devices you want to connect. If you are unable to connect a computer with enough USB ports, you can purchase a USB hub.

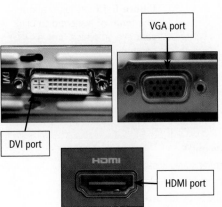

DVI port

VGA port

HDMI port

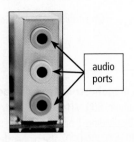

audio ports

Ethernet port

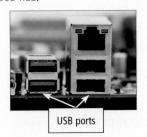

USB ports

In addition to the devices discussed above, what other devices might you connect to your computer or mobile device?

Adapter Cards

An **adapter card**, sometimes called an *expansion card* or *adapter board*, is a circuit board that enhances the functions of a component of a desktop or server system unit and/or provides connections to peripheral devices. An **expansion slot** is a socket on a desktop or server motherboard that can hold an adapter card. Figure 6-16 shows a variety of adapter cards in expansion slots on a desktop motherboard.

Two popular adapter cards are sound cards and video cards. A *sound card* enhances the sound-generating capabilities of a personal computer by allowing sound to be input through a microphone and output through external speakers or headphones. A *video card*, also called a *graphics card*, converts computer output into a video signal that travels through a cable to the monitor, which displays an image on the screen. Table 6-3 identifies the purpose of some adapter cards. Sometimes, all functionality is built in the adapter card. With others, a cable connects the adapter card to a device, such as a digital video camera, outside the computer.

Today's computers support **Plug and Play** technology, which means the computer automatically can recognize peripheral devices as you install them. Plug and Play support means you can plug in a device and then immediately begin using it.

USB Adapters and ExpressCard Modules

Because of their smaller form factors, mobile computers typically do not have expansion slots. Adapters for mobile computers are in the form of a removable flash memory device. Two popular adapters for mobile computers are USB adapters and ExpressCard modules. A **USB adapter**, which is a dongle that plugs into a USB port, enhances functions of a mobile computer and/or provides connections to peripheral devices (Figure 6-17). An *ExpressCard module* is a removable device, about 75 mm long (approximately 3 inches) and 34 mm wide (approximately 1.3 inches) or L-shaped with a width of 54 mm (approximately 2 inches), that fits in an ExpressCard slot (Figure 6-18). USB adapters and ExpressCard modules can be used to add memory, communications, multimedia, security, and storage capabilities to mobile computers. Read Ethics & Issues 6-4 on the next page to consider whether manufacturers should eliminate proprietary connectors.

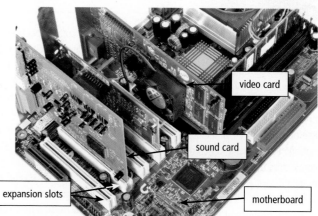

Figure 6-16 Cards inserted in expansion slots on a desktop motherboard.
© Olga Lipatova / Shutterstock.com

Table 6-3   Adapter Cards

Type	Purpose
Bluetooth	Enables Bluetooth connectivity
MIDI	Connects to musical instruments
Modem	Connects to transmission media, such as cable television lines or phone lines
Network	Provides network connections, such as to an Ethernet port
Sound	Connects to speakers or a microphone
TV tuner	Allows viewing of digital television broadcasts on a monitor
USB	Connects to high-speed USB ports
Video	Provides enhanced graphics capabilities, such as accelerated processing or the ability to connect a second monitor
Video capture	Connects to a video camera

Figure 6-17 A USB adapter inserts into a USB port on a computer or mobile device.
© vetkit / Shutterstock.com; © vetkit / Shutterstock.com

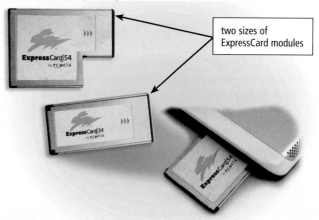

Figure 6-18 ExpressCard modules, which are available in two sizes, fit in an ExpressCard slot.
Courtesy of USB Implementers Forum Inc; Courtesy of USB Implementers Forum Inc; Courtesy of USB Implementers Forum Inc; © Cengage Learning

Should Manufacturers Eliminate Proprietary Connectors?

If you need to replace the cable that connects your mobile device to a USB port, you might have a choice of many makes, models, and prices. Some devices, however, require the use of proprietary connectors, limiting your options to those manufacturers who make connectors that match the port on your mobile device.

When Apple released the iPhone 5 in 2012, for example, it required the use of a proprietary connector that was incompatible with connectors used with prior iPhone models. Critics argue that requiring customers to purchase proprietary connectors unnecessarily increases the cost of purchasing or upgrading a mobile device.

The International Electronics Commission (IEC) is working to make micro USB the universal connector standard for charging mobile devices. This type of universal standard has several advantages. It will save customers money because they will not have to purchase a new connector with their new phone, even if it is a different brand of phone. A universal standard connector also will enable users with different phone models to share connectors. The environment will benefit because fewer outdated or incompatible cords will be discarded into landfills. Further, the manufacturing process will generate less waste because fewer cords will be required.

Should customers pressure manufacturers to use a universal connector standard? Why or why not? Would you consider the connector type when purchasing a new phone? Why or why not?

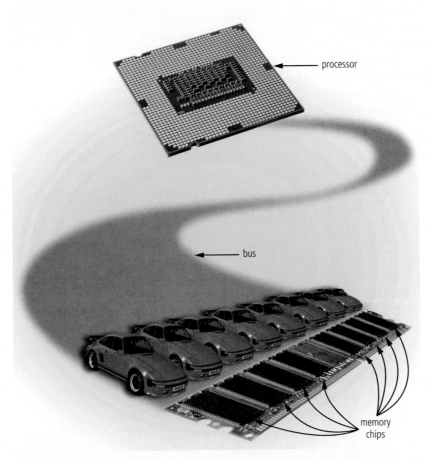

Figure 6-19 Just as vehicles travel on a highway, bits travel on a bus. Buses are used to transfer bits from input devices to memory, from memory to the processor, from the processor to memory, and from memory to output or storage devices.

Courtesy of Intel Corporation; © Cengage Learning

Unlike adapter cards that require you to open the system unit and install the card on the motherboard, you can change a removable flash memory device without having to open the system unit or restart the computer. This feature, called *hot plugging*, allows you to insert and remove a device while the computer is running.

Buses

As explained earlier in this chapter, a computer processes and stores data as a series of electronic bits. These bits transfer internally within the circuitry of the computer along electrical channels. Each channel, called a **bus**, allows the various devices both inside and attached to the system unit to communicate with each other. Just as vehicles travel on a highway to move from one destination to another, bits travel on a bus (Figure 6-19).

Buses are used to transfer bits from input devices to memory, from memory to the processor, from the processor to memory, and from memory to output or storage devices. Buses consist of a data bus and an address bus. The *data bus* is used to transfer actual data, and the *address bus* is used to transfer information about where the data should reside in memory.

Bus Width

The size of a bus, called the *bus width*, determines the number of bits that the computer can transmit at one time. For example, a 32-bit bus can transmit 32 bits (4 bytes) at a time. On a 64-bit bus, bits transmit from one location to another 64 bits (8 bytes) at a time. The larger the number of bits handled by the bus, the faster the computer transfers data. Using the highway analogy again, assume that one lane on a highway can carry one bit. A 32-bit bus is like a 32-lane highway. A 64-bit bus is like a 64-lane highway.

If a number in memory occupies 8 bytes, or 64 bits, the computer must transmit it in two separate steps when using a 32-bit bus: once for the first 32 bits and once for the second 32 bits. Using a 64-bit bus, the computer can transmit the number in a single step, transferring all 64 bits at once. The wider the bus, the fewer number of transfer steps required and the faster the transfer of data. Most personal computers today use a 64-bit bus.

In conjunction with the bus width, many computer professionals refer to a computer's word size. **Word size** is the number of bits the processor can interpret and execute at a given time. That is, a 64-bit processor can manipulate 64 bits at a time. Computers with a larger word size can process more data in the same amount of time than computers with a smaller word size. In most computers, the word size is the same as the bus width.

 BTW

Cyborg Technology
Innovative Computing:
You should be familiar with this cyborg technology, which operates at several hundred hertz.

 CONSIDER THIS ————————————————————————————————————

How is bus speed measured?
Every bus also has a clock speed. Just like the processor, manufacturers state the clock speed for a bus in hertz. The higher the bus clock speed, the faster the transmission of data, which results in programs running faster.

Types of Buses

A computer has a system bus, possibly a backside bus, and an expansion bus.

- A *system bus*, also called the *front side bus* (*FSB*), is part of the motherboard and connects the processor to main memory.
- A *backside bus* (*BSB*) connects the processor to cache.
- An *expansion bus* allows the processor to communicate with peripheral devices.

When computer professionals use the term, bus, by itself, they usually are referring to the system bus.

Power Supply and Batteries

Many personal computers plug in standard wall outlets, which supply an alternating current (AC) of 115 to 120 volts. This type of power is unsuitable for use with a computer or mobile device, which requires a direct current (DC) ranging from 5 to more than 15 volts. The **power supply** or laptop AC adapter converts the wall outlet AC power into DC power (Figure 6-20). Different motherboards and computers require different wattages on the power supply. If a power supply is not providing the necessary power, the computer will not function properly.

Built into the power supply is a fan that keeps the power supply cool. Some have variable speed fans that change speed or stop running, depending on temperature in the case. Many newer computers have additional fans near certain components in the system unit such as the processor, hard disk, and ports. Some users install more fans to help dissipate heat generated by the components of the computer.

Some external peripheral devices, such as a cable modem, speakers, or a printer, have an AC adapter, which is an external power supply. One end of the AC adapter plugs in the wall outlet and the other end attaches to the peripheral. The AC adapter converts the AC power into the DC power that the peripheral requires, and also often charges the battery in a mobile computer or device.

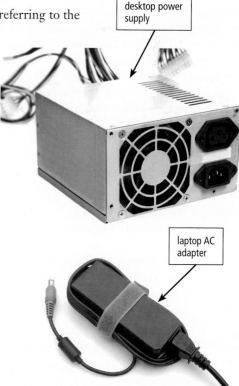

desktop power supply

laptop AC adapter

Figure 6-20 Examples of desktop power supply and laptop AC adapter.
© robootb / Shutterstock.com; © iStockphoto / Freer Law

CONSIDER THIS

How many fans are in a desktop case?
Most have at least three fans: one in the power supply, one in the case, and one on the processor heat sink. In addition, you also might find a fan on a video card or other adapter card. While some computers contain fans that are designed to be quiet or operate in quiet mode, others allow you to turn off noisy fans until they are needed. You also can purchase programs that slow or stop the fan until the temperature reaches a certain level.

laptop battery

smartphone battery

Mobile computers and devices can run using either a power supply or batteries. The batteries typically are rechargeable lithium-ion batteries (Figure 6-21). Read How To 6-4 for tips on conserving battery life of mobile computers and devices. Some mobile devices and computers, such as some ultrathin laptops, do not have removable batteries.

Figure 6-21 Rechargeable batteries for mobile computers and devices.
© Thejipen / Dreamstime.com; © Anaken2012 / Dreamstime.com

 HOW TO 6-4

Conserve Battery Life of Mobile Computers and Devices

As consumers rely on mobile computers and devices more and more every day, it is increasingly important for the battery life on these devices to support high usage demands. Unfortunately, battery life on these devices often is not sufficient for many users to make it throughout the day with moderate activity on their devices. For this reason, it is important to conserve battery life so that a mobile computer or device can remain functional until it is possible to connect it to a battery charger. The following list contains suggestions for conserving battery life on mobile computers and devices:

• When you first obtain a new mobile computer or device or purchase a new battery for your computer or mobile device, charge the battery completely. Most new mobile computers and devices will indicate

how long to charge the battery before its first use.

• Charge the battery only when it is drained completely. Many batteries on computers and mobile devices can be charged only a certain number of times before they fail completely. For this reason, you should charge batteries only when absolutely necessary.

• When you charge your mobile computer or device, try not to unplug the battery charger until the battery is charged completely.

• Use the battery charger supplied with the mobile computer or device. Connecting inexpensive battery chargers from other vendors may damage the battery.

• If you are using a laptop or tablet, disable Wi-Fi and Bluetooth unless you are using them.

• Adjust the display's brightness. Brighter displays consume more battery life, so

keep the display as dim as you can without having to strain your eyes.

• Download and install an app that will inform you which other apps are running and consuming battery life. If an app does not need to run, you should exit it so that the app does not consume your battery.

• Avoid turning your mobile computer or device on and off multiple times per day. The power-saving features on mobile computers and devices often require less power than turning on your computer or mobile device from a powered-off state.

• Turn off automatic app update capabilities on your phone or mobile device, so that your device is not constantly checking for new apps and downloading them to your device.

 What other ways can you think of to conserve the battery life on your mobile computer or device?

 Internet Research

How effective are solar chargers?
Search for: portable solar charger reviews

 CONSIDER THIS

How often do batteries for mobile computers and devices need to be replaced?
Battery life depends on usage. While some may last several years, you may need to replace a battery much sooner than that. When the battery no longer can hold a charge, you should replace it with a battery made by, or recommended by, the manufacturer of the computer or device.

 **MINI FEATURE 6-3**

Proper Care for Computers and Mobile Devices

Taking proper care of computers and mobile devices not only will help prolong their life, but also keep them running optimally. Caring for a computer or mobile device requires both that the hardware be kept in good condition and that the programs, apps, and data on the device are maintained properly.

Hardware Maintenance

Before performing any of the following steps to care for your computer or mobile device, turn off and unplug the device from its power source. If the computer or mobile device has a removable battery, you also should remove the battery. All hardware maintenance should be performed in an area that is clean and free from clutter.

- Use a damp cloth to gently clean the screen. Do not use any special cleaners to clean the display, as they may damage the display. Water is sufficient to remove dust and most dirt. Read How To 6-5 on the next page for additional ways to protect screens and replace them if necessary.

- If the computer or mobile device has a keyboard, use a can of compressed air to free the keyboard from any dirt and debris that might interfere with the operation of the keys or pose a risk of getting inside the computer. When using compressed air, hold the can upright, and not at an angle, when dispensing the air. Holding the can at an angle can cause the can to dispense a very cold liquid instead of air, which can damage components in your computer or mobile device.

- When you insert media such as an optical disc, be sure the media is clean. Inserting dirty media can damage a computer or mobile device's internal components.

- If you are transporting a laptop, be sure to store it in a case with plenty of padding. If you are using a mobile device, such as a tablet or smartphone, protect it with a case. A case will better protect the device in the event you drop it and may make it easier for you to grip the device while using it.

- If the computer or mobile device has an air vent where a fan removes heat from the computer or mobile device, make sure the vent is free of dust and debris. A blocked vent can prohibit heat from escaping, which ultimately can cause the computer or mobile device to overheat. If the air vent is dirty, contact a trained professional to have it cleaned properly. Improperly cleaning an air vent can result in more debris entering the computer or mobile device.

Software Maintenance

Maintaining the software on your computers and mobile devices can help them run optimally. While no specific recommendation exists for the frequency with which you should perform the following actions, you should do so if you begin to notice a decline in your computer or mobile device's performance.

- Uninstall programs and remove apps you no longer need on your computer or mobile device. These programs and apps may consume a significant amount of space on your storage medium and decrease the performance of your computer or mobile device. More information about uninstalling programs and removing apps can be found in How To 4-3 on page 185.

- If you are using a desktop or laptop, defragment the computer's hard disk should you notice a decline in the computer's performance. More information about defragmenting your computer's hard disk can be found in How To 4-4 on page 187.

- Install programs and apps only from reputable software manufacturers. In addition, make sure you are installing the program or app from the original installation media, the software manufacturer's website, or from your mobile device's app store or marketplace. You also should read reviews for programs and apps before you download and/or install them to make sure the program or app will meet your needs.

☀ In addition to the methods mentioned in this mini feature, what other ways can you care for your computer or mobile device?

CONSIDER THIS

How does an antistatic wristband work?

When working with electronic components, such as a motherboard, you should wear an antistatic wristband. An *antistatic wristband* is a bracelet designed to protect electronics from an electrostatic discharge by preventing a buildup of static electricity on a user. The wristband has an attached clip that you connect to any bare metal surface, which acts as a ground.

 HOW TO 6-5

Protect and Replace Screens

One way to protect the screen on your mobile device is to use a screen protector. A *screen protector* is a thin plastic film that adheres to the screen of your device. While screen protectors may not protect the screen if you drop your device or an object impacts it with excessive force, it will protect the screen from minor scratches obtained through normal use. Screen protectors often can be purchased from the same place you bought your mobile device and also are available online. If you cannot find a screen protector that is the exact same size as the screen on your mobile device, you can purchase a larger one and then trim it to fit your screen.

In the event the screen on your mobile device breaks, the following steps will guide you through the process of replacing it. Even if your device continues to work with a broken screen, you still should replace it as soon as possible to avoid injury. **NOTE: Screen replacement should be attempted only by advanced users. If you are uncomfortable following these steps, seek help from a trained**

professional. In addition, the exact steps to replace a broken screen can vary with each device. If the steps for your device vary from the steps listed below, follow the instructions from your device's manufacturer.

1. Back up the data on your mobile device before starting a screen replacement. While a successful screen replacement should not threaten the data, it is a good idea to keep a backup in case a problem arises unexpectedly.

2. Turn off the mobile device and disconnect it from all power sources. If the device uses a removable battery, remove it.

3. Protect your hands and eyes before beginning glass replacement.

4. If possible, carefully remove all pieces of broken glass. Consider using compressed air to remove any dust.

5. Remove the display assembly. Refer to your device's documentation for information about removing the display. You may need a small, nonmagnetic screwdriver and/or metal or plastic tool to remove

the assembly. If the display assembly is connected to the mobile device with a cable, carefully disconnect the cable.

6. Unpack the new screen and connect it to the mobile device, connecting any necessary cables.

7. Reassemble the mobile device, reconnect the power source and/or the battery, and turn on the device.

 Why might you replace a cracked screen instead of replacing the entire mobile device?

© Andrey Arkusha / Shutterstock.com

 BTW

Robot
Innovative Computing: You should be familiar with one type of humanoid robot, which is powered with a rechargeable lithium-ion battery.

 NOW YOU KNOW

Be sure you understand the material presented in the sections titled Adapters, Buses, and Power Supply and Batteries, as it relates to the chapter objectives.
You now should know . . .

- When you would use an adapter card, a USB adapter, and an ExpressCard module (Objective 8)

- How your computer uses buses (Objective 9)

- Why your computers and mobile devices need power supplies or batteries (Objective 10)

- How to care for your computers and mobile devices (Objective 11)

Quiz Yourself Online: Check your knowledge of related content by navigating to this book's Quiz Yourself resource on Computer Concepts CourseMate and then tapping or clicking Objectives 8–11.

Chapter Summary

This chapter presented the various components inside computers and mobile devices. It discussed types of processors, steps in a machine cycle, and processor cooling methods. You learned about advantages and services of cloud computing. The chapter discussed how memory stores data and described various types of memory. You learned about adapters, buses, power supplies and batteries, and ways to care for computers and mobile devices.

Test your knowledge of chapter material by accessing the Study Guide, Flash Cards, and Practice Test apps that run on your smartphone, tablet, laptop, or desktop.

TECHNOLOGY @ WORK

Publishing

Today, virtually any material that you read exists in electronic form. In publishing's early years, and before computers existed, authors and writers recorded content using a typewriter, which then would be duplicated and bound into a publication. When word processors were introduced, writers not only could type their work, but also were able to apply basic formatting and check their spelling. While typewriters and word processors performed their tasks adequately, they pale in comparison to the extent to which today's computers and mobile devices have improved the publishing process.

Before computers and other related technological advances, publishing a book would be a very long process. After the authors wrote a manuscript, it was converted into a form that was ready to print; the printing process then could take several weeks to complete. Today, authors can use programs and apps to write material in a format that will require minimal, if any, conversion before it is ready to print.

Many book, magazine, and newspaper publishers are turning away from the print medium and encouraging consumers to read content electronically. In fact, some publishers are turning exclusively to publishing in electronic form and abandoning the print medium altogether. As mentioned previously in this book, you can read book content or magazine and newspaper articles either on the web or using an e-book reader. Content on the web usually is available free or for a fee. For example, some newspapers allow people to read articles for free, while others may charge a digital subscription fee. If you are using an e-book reader, you often have to pay to download and read content, although some items are available for free.

Programs and apps, including web apps, also are enabling individuals to publish content themselves. Individuals easily can publish content to a blog on the web, or they can use an app to create and publish an e-book for others to purchase and download.

Many libraries also are taking advantage of advances in technology by enabling users to check out books electronically. Similar to a print book, library patrons can reserve an e-book on their computer or mobile device. When the e-book is available, it will download to the user's computer or mobile device automatically. When the e-book is due or when the user decides to return the book, it will remove itself from the user's computer or mobile device. While many people believe that libraries can check out unlimited copies of the same e-book simultaneously, this is not true. Libraries are able to check out simultaneously only the number of copies, or licenses, of the e-book they purchase. For example, if a library purchases two licenses of an e-book, only two copies of that e-book can be checked out simultaneously. If a third user wants to check out this e-book, he or she must wait for one copy to be returned. Read Ethics & Issues 3-3 on page 124 for a related discussion.

Technology has greatly improved the publishing industry. Not only is content published more quickly and in an easily accessible form, but it also now is less prone to errors because the development process is much more streamlined.

✹ In what other ways do computers and technology play a role in the publishing industry?

© geophoto / Alamy

STUDENT ASSIGNMENTS

Study Guide

The Study Guide exercise reinforces material you should know for the chapter exam. You will find answers to items with the 🖥 icon only in the e-book.

💻 Access the Study Guide app that runs on your smartphone, tablet, laptop, or desktop by navigating to this book's Apps resource on Computer Concepts CourseMate.

Instructions: Answer the questions below using the format that helps you remember best or that is required by your instructor. Possible formats may include one or more of these options: write the answers; create a document that contains the answers; record answers as audio or video using a webcam, smartphone, or portable media player; post answers on a blog, wiki, or website; or highlight answers in the book/e-book.

1. Describe the hardware referred to by the terms, system unit and chassis.

2. Name the typical location of the case for a laptop, slate tablet, smartphone, portable media player, and game console.

3. List products for securing and tracking hardware and how each is used.

4. Define the terms, motherboard and chip. Describe how a chip can be used to locate a lost animal.

5. Describe the purpose of the processor and how multi- and single-core processors differ.

6. 🖥 List some processor chip manufacturers.

7. List reasons a user might build or purchase a custom-built computer.

8. Explain the role of the control unit and ALU in performing computer operations.

9. Describe what happens during each step in the machine cycle.

10. Define these terms: register, system clock, and clock speed. Describe how clock speed is measured.

11. List considerations when choosing a processor. 🖥 Name the contributions of Intel, Gordon Moore, and AMD, with respect to processor chips.

12. 🖥 Name the contributions of Nvidia and Qualcomm, with respect to processors and chips.

13. Describe eCycling options.

14. List options for cooling a processor, and describe how each works.

15. Explain why a home or business user might choose cloud computing. Describe services offered with cloud computing.

16. List security threats in cloud storage. 🖥 Explain the security efforts of the CSA.

17. Differentiate between the terms, analog and digital.

18. Define the terms, bit and byte. Describe the binary system and the ASCII coding scheme.

19. Explain if a company is responsible for using computer components manufactured using fair trade practices.

20. List categories of items stored in memory. Explain how manufacturers state memory size.

21. Differentiate between volatile and nonvolatile memory. List an example of each.

22. Describe how RAM works. List two types of RAM.

23. Define the terms, memory module and memory slot. List two types of memory modules.

24. Explain how to determine memory requirements, and list the steps to install memory modules.

25. Describe how a computer uses cache. Differentiate among L1, L2, and L3 cache.

26. Describe what is stored in ROM. Define the term, firmware.

27. Identify uses for flash memory.

28. List actions you should take when recycling or selling a used mobile device.

29. Explain why a computer repair technician might be expected to hold a private investigator license.

30. Describe CMOS technology and its possible uses.

31. Define the term, access time. List different methods used to state access time.

32. Identify the port options for computers and mobile devices. Explain the function of each type.

33. Describe the purpose of an adapter card and the role of an expansion slot. List types of adapter cards.

34. Explain Plug and Play technology.

35. Describe USB adapters and ExpressCard modules, and list the functions of each.

36. Explain the advantages of using a universal standard connector.

37. Define the term, hot plugging.

38. Identify the role of a bus. Differentiate between a data bus and an address bus.

39. Describe how bus width and word size affect and are used to measure computer speed.

40. 🖥 Define cyborg technology.

41. List types of buses and describe the purpose of each.

42. Explain how a power supply converts AC current into DC current.

43. List methods to conserve battery life on a mobile computer and device.

44. Identify guidelines for caring for a computer or mobile device.

45. Explain how to maintain hardware and software on your computer or mobile device.

46. List steps and precautions to take when replacing the screen on a mobile device.

47. Identify how technology is used in the publishing industry.

Key Terms

You should be able to define the Primary Terms and be familiar with the Secondary Terms listed below.

Access the Flash Cards app that runs on your smartphone, tablet, laptop, or desktop by navigating to this book's Apps resource on Computer Concepts CourseMate. View definitions for each term by navigating to this book's Key Terms resource on Computer Concepts CourseMate. Listen to definitions for each term on your portable media player by navigating to this book's Audio Study Tools resource on Computer Concepts CourseMate.

Primary Terms (shown in **bold-black** characters in the chapter)

access time (267)
adapter card (269)
analog (259)
arithmetic logic unit (253)
binary system (259)
bit (259)
bus (270)
byte (259)
cache (265)

central processing unit (CPU) (252)
chip (250)
clock speed (255)
control unit (253)
digital (259)
eCycling (256)
expansion slot (269)
firmware (265)

flash memory (266)
gigahertz (GHz) (255)
memory (261)
memory cache (265)
memory module (263)
memory slots (263)
motherboard (250)
multi-core processor (252)

Plug and Play (269)
power supply (271)
processor (252)
RAM (262)
read-only memory (ROM) (265)
system clock (255)
USB adapter (269)
word size (271)

Secondary Terms (shown in *italic* characters in the chapter)

adapter board (269)
address (261)
address bus (270)
advanced transfer cache (ATC) (265)
alphanumeric characters (259)
ALU (253)
antistatic wristband (274)
arithmetic operations (253)
ASCII (259)
backside bus (BSB) (271)
binary digit (259)
bus width (270)
Cellular Seizure Investigation (CSI) stick (266)
chassis (248)
clock cycle (255)
CMOS (267)
comparison operations (253)
cooling pad (257)
Data as a Service (DaaS) (258)

data bus (270)
DDR SDRAM (263)
DDR2 (263)
DDR3 (263)
DDR4 (263)
decoding (254)
DIMM (dual inline memory module) (263)
dynamic RAM (DRAM) (263)
executing (254)
expansion bus (271)
expansion card (269)
ExpressCard module (269)
fetching (254)
front side bus (FSB) (271)
gigabyte (GB) (261)
graphics card (269)
heat sink (256)
hertz (255)
hot plugging (270)

Infrastructure as a Service (IaaS) (258)
integrated circuit (250)
Intel-compatible processors (255)
L1 cache (265)
L2 cache (265)
L3 cache (265)
liquid cooling technology (256)
machine cycle (254)
main memory (262)
mashups (258)
microprocessor (252)
nanosecond (ns) (267)
nonvolatile memory (261)
Platform as a Service (PaaS) (258)
random access memory (262)
RDRAM (263)
real-time clock (255)
registers (254)
screen protector (274)

SDRAM (263)
SIMM (single inline memory module) (263)
Software as a Service (SaaS) (258)
sound card (269)
static RAM (SRAM) (263)
stored program concept (261)
storing (254)
superscalar (255)
system board (250)
system bus (271)
system unit (248)
terabyte (TB) (261)
transistor (250)
video card (269)
virtual desktop (258)
volatile (263)
volatile memory (261)

motherboard (250)

Checkpoint

The Checkpoint exercises test your knowledge of the chapter concepts. The page number containing the answer appears in parentheses after each exercise. The Consider This exercises challenge your understanding of chapter concepts.

Complete the Checkpoint exercises interactively by navigating to this book's Checkpoint resource on Computer Concepts CourseMate. **Access the Test Prep app** that runs on your smartphone, tablet, laptop, or desktop by navigating to this book's Apps resource on Computer Concepts CourseMate. After successfully completing the self-assessment through the Test Prep app, **take the Practice Test** by navigating to this book's Practice Test resource on Computer Concepts CourseMate.

True/False   Mark T for True and F for False.

_____ 1. A slate tablet typically does not include a physical keyboard. (248)

_____ 2. On a personal computer, all functions of the processor usually are on a single chip. (252)

_____ 3. A dual-core processor doubles the processing speed of a single-core processor. (253)

_____ 4. In general, multi-core processors are less energy efficient than separate multiple processors. (253)

_____ 5. The speed of the system clock affects the speed of peripheral devices, such as a printer or disk drive. (255)

_____ 6. Today's personal computer processors do not require additional cooling. (256)

_____ 7. In the binary system, the digit 1 represents the electronic state of on (presence of an electronic charge). (259)

_____ 8. Common sizes for memory are in the bit and byte range. (261)

_____ 9. The processor interprets and executes a program or application's instructions while the program or application is in nonvolatile memory. (262)

_____ 10. You can change a removable flash memory device without having to open the system unit or restart the computer. (270)

_____ 11. As with processors, manufacturers state the clock speed for a bus in hertz. (271)

_____ 12. The power supply converts the wall outlet DC power into AC power. (271)

Multiple Choice   Select the best answer.

1. The _____ is the main circuit board of the computer. (250)
   a. ALU
   b. CPU
   c. motherboard
   d. system chassis

2. A _____ is a single chip with two or more separate processor cores. (252)
   a. transistor
   b. multi-core processor
   c. resistor
   d. capacitor

3. _____ include basic calculations such as addition, subtraction, multiplication, and division. (253)
   a. Arithmetic operations
   b. Comparison operations
   c. Machine cycles
   d. Transistors

4. In the machine cycle, the _____ operation obtains a program or application instruction or data item from memory. (254)
   a. fetching
   b. decoding
   c. executing
   d. storing

5. A processor contains small, high-speed storage locations, called _____, that temporarily hold data and instructions. (254)
   a. capacitors
   b. back ends
   c. registers
   d. mashups

6. A _____ is a small ceramic or metal component with fins on its surface that absorbs and disperses heat produced by electrical components, such as a processor. (256)
   a. cooling pad
   b. liquid glycol chiller
   c. heat sink
   d. radiator

7. An aspect of cloud computing that describes a computing environment where an Internet server hosts and deploys applications is known as _____. (258)
   a. Data as a Service (DaaS)
   b. Infrastructure as a Service (IaaS)
   c. Software as a Service (SaaS)
   d. Platform as a Service (PaaS)

8. A(n) _____ is a circuit board that enhances the functions of a component of a desktop or server system unit and/or provides connections to peripheral devices. (269)
   a. expansion slot
   b. USB adapter
   c. front side bus
   d. adapter card

Checkpoint

Matching   Match the terms with their definitions.

_____ 1. motherboard (250)

_____ 2. chip (250)

_____ 3. microprocessor (252)

_____ 4. registers (254)

_____ 5. superscalar (255)

_____ 6. mashups (258)

_____ 7. ASCII (259)

_____ 8. address (261)

_____ 9. firmware (265)

_____ 10. bus width (270)

a. small, high-speed storage locations contained in a processor

b. term used to describe processors that can execute more than one instruction per clock cycle

c. widely used coding scheme to represent a set of characters

d. the main circuit board of the computer

e. term used by some computer manufacturers to refer to a personal computer chip

f. ROM chips that contain permanently written data, instructions, or information

g. determines the number of bits that the computer can transmit at one time

h. a unique number that identifies the location of a byte in memory

i. small piece of semiconducting materials, usually silicon, on which integrated circuits are etched

j. applications that incorporate data from multiple providers into a new application

Short Answer   Write a brief answer to each of the following questions.

1. What are the two components contained in the processor? (253) Differentiate between arithmetic operations and comparison operations. (253)

2. What is clock speed? (255) Describe how clock speed affects the processor. (255)

3. What should you consider when selecting a processor? (255) What eCycling options are available? (256)

4. List some reasons that home and businesses choose cloud computing. (257) In reference to cloud computing, describe the front end and back end. (257)

5. Differentiate between volatile and nonvolatile memory. (261) Differentiate between RAM and ROM. (262, 265)

✳ Consider This   Answer the following questions in the format specified by your instructor.

1. Answer the critical thinking questions posed at the end of these elements in this chapter: Ethics & Issues (252, 261, 267, 270), How To (255, 264, 268, 272, 274), Mini Features (258, 273), Secure IT (250, 252, 256, 259, 266), and Technology @ Work (275).

2. Where is the typical location of the case on a laptop, tablet, portable media player, and game console? (248)

3. How does tracking software help secure hardware? (250)

4. What are the advantages and disadvantages of custom-built and mass-produced computers? (252)

5. What does the term superscalar mean, with regards to the clock cycle? (255)

6. 📄 How do processors for home users, power users, and mobile users differ? (255)

7. How does a cooling pad reduce the heat generated by a computer? (257)

8. What advantages does Infrastructure as a Service offer? (258)

9. What are some security concerns regarding cloud storage? (259)

10. 📄 How do coding schemes and number systems represent data? (259)

11. How do L1, L2, and L3 cache differ? (265)

12. How do computers use flash memory? (266)

13. What is the function of an adapter card? What does Plug and Play do? (269)

14. Should a universal connector standard be adopted? Why or why not? (270)

15. How does bus width measure a computer's processing speed? (270)

✳ How To: Your Turn

The How To: Your Turn exercises present general guidelines for fundamental skills when using a computer or mobile device and then require that you determine how to apply these general guidelines to a specific program or situation.

Instructions: You often can complete tasks using technology in multiple ways. Figure out how to perform the tasks described in these exercises by using one or more resources available to you (such as a computer or mobile device, articles on the web or in print, online or program help, user guides, blogs, podcasts, videos, other individuals, trial and error, etc.). Summarize your 'how to' steps, along with the resource(s) used, in the format requested by your instructor (brief report, presentation, discussion, blog post, video, or other means).

1 Locate a Lost Mobile Computer or Device

Mobile computers and devices sometimes contain a feature that can help you locate it in the event you lose it. If the device does not contain this feature, you may be able to download and install an app that can help you track its location. The following steps guide you through the process of locating a lost mobile computer or device.

a. Before you lose or misplace a mobile computer or device, enable the feature that allows you to track its location remotely.
b. Make sure the GPS feature on your device is enabled. If GPS is not enabled, the device might be more difficult to locate.
c. If you lose your smartphone, try calling it to see if someone answers. He or she may have located your misplaced phone. If nobody answers, send it a text message inquiring about the phone's location.
d. If you lose a device, you can run an app or navigate to a website that will enable you to track the device's location. The device's location typically will be displayed on a map and include the approximate address.
e. If the device is in an unfamiliar location, use a service such as Google Maps to obtain driving directions to the location.
f. If the device is in a location other than where you originally lost it, exercise extreme caution while trying to retrieve your device. You might consider contacting a local law enforcement agency to accompany you while trying to retrieve your device.

Exercises

1. What privacy concerns might arise as a result of keeping the GPS feature on a device enabled?
2. What steps might you take to locate a lost device if the device does not have a built-in feature or app to locate it?

2 Run Diagnostic Tools and Check for Hardware Errors

If your computer is not functioning properly and you believe the problem is related to the computer's hardware, you can run diagnostic tools to check for hardware errors. If the diagnostic tool identifies a hardware error, you then can communicate information about the error to technical support personnel so that they either can correct the problem or suggest replacing the problematic hardware. The following steps guide you through the process of running diagnostic tools and checking for hardware errors.

Obtain Diagnostic Tools

Your computer may have included diagnostic tools you can use to check for hardware errors. If it did not include diagnostic tools, follow these steps to download diagnostic tools from the computer manufacturer's website:

a. Navigate to the computer manufacturer's website.
b. Tap or click the necessary links to display information about the computer.
c. Tap or click the link to display a page containing drivers and/or downloads for the computer's model.
d. Browse for a diagnostic tool that you can download to your computer.
e. Some diagnostic tools can run within the operating system, and some require that you copy them to an optical disc or USB flash drive so that you can start the computer from this media and run the diagnostic tools. If necessary, copy the diagnostic tools to an optical disc or USB flash drive.

Run the Diagnostic Tools

a. Run the program containing the diagnostic tools. If you copied the diagnostic tools to an optical disc or USB flash drive, restart the computer with the optical disc or USB flash drive inserted, and be sure to select the option to boot (start) from that device.
b. Select the option to scan all computer hardware for errors.
c. Begin the scan. Please note that because the program is scanning all hardware, it may take some time to complete. Some specific tests during the scan will require input from you, so watch the computer closely while the scan is in progress.

How To: Your Turn ✳

d. When the scan is complete, note any errors and, if desired, report them to the computer manufacturer's technical support team.

e. When the scan is complete, if necessary, restart the computer.

Exercises

1. What might cause you to use diagnostic tools to scan a computer for hardware errors?

2. After scanning your computer for hardware errors, were any found?

3 **Determine How Much Memory Is Being Used on Your Computer**

If your computer is running slowly, it could be running low on memory. A number of factors can contribute to a computer's slow performance, but checking the memory usage is fast and easy. If a computer's memory is almost all used, you may be able to determine which applications are using the most memory. Exiting these applications may make more memory available and increase a computer's performance. If you require these applications, you may need to add more memory to the computer to increase performance. The following steps guide you through the process of determining how much memory is being used on a computer.

a. Restart the computer.

b. Sign in to the operating system.

c. Navigate to the operating system's Task Manager or Activity Monitor. (*Hint:* In Windows 8, you can access the Task Manager by pressing **CTRL+ALT+DELETE** on the keyboard. In OS X, you can access the Activity Monitor by performing a search.)

d. Tap or click the option to view memory usage.

e. Tap or click the option to show the list of running processes. This list will show you how much memory each process is using. This list also includes the programs and apps currently running. If you notice that a program or app is consuming a high amount of memory, consider exiting the program or app to make the memory available.

f. When you are finished, exit the Activity Monitor or Task Manager.

Source: Microsoft

Exercises

1. How much memory is installed on your computer? How much currently is being used?

2. Which three processes are using the largest amount of memory on your computer?

4 **Check Your Computer's Hardware Configuration**

If you are experiencing a problem with hardware component on your computer, you can check the computer's hardware configuration to determine the manufacturer's name and model number for the hardware in question. With this information, you then can search for ways to correct the problem. Alternatively, if you reinstall the operating system on the computer, you may check the computer's hardware configuration to make sure the operating system is recognizing correctly all hardware connected to the computer. The following steps guide you through the process of checking a computer's hardware configuration.

a. If you are using a Mac, display the Apple menu and then select the option to display information about the computer. If you are running Windows, display the Control Panel.

b. Navigate to the area that displays information about the hardware and devices currently connected to the computer. (*Hint:* In Windows, display the Device Manager. On a Mac, display the System Report.)

c. Tap or click the categories of hardware devices to see details related to those types of devices.

d. If you are familiar with the hardware devices on the computer, verify that the operating system is recognizing these devices correctly.

e. If you notice a problem with the operating system detecting any of these devices, you might need to run the installation software and/or install the drivers for the hardware device so that the operating system can communicate with the device. If necessary, contact the computer manufacturer's technical support for assistance.

Exercises

1. List at least three hardware devices listed in the System Report or in the Device Manager.

2. In addition to the reasons mentioned above, what are some other reasons why you might want to check the hardware configuration on a computer?

✳ Internet Research

The Internet Research exercises broaden your understanding of chapter concepts by requiring that you search for information on the web.

Instructions: Use a search engine or another search tool to locate the information requested or answers to questions presented in the exercises. Describe your findings, along with the search term(s) you used and your web source(s), in the format requested by your instructor (brief report, presentation, discussion, blog post, video, or other means).

❶ Making Use of the Web

Research and Educational   Navigating the Internet to locate information for school assignments and personal projects can be a daunting task. Researchers need to locate reliable resources and then evaluate the available information. General reference websites, which include online encyclopedias, libraries, and reference collections, are excellent sources of comprehensive, accurate, and organized facts on specific topics. History and literary buffs can appreciate the websites that translate text, contain thousands of free books to download, and provide literary analyses. Answers to perplexing science questions and math problems are available on several educational websites that include practice tests, conversion tables, and current news articles.

(a) Visit two general reference websites or apps and locate information about one of the key terms in this chapter. Compare the information provided in these two sources. Which source is more comprehensive? Do the articles provide additional resources, such as video, graphics, or links to related articles? Is one article easier to navigate and read than the other? Why or why not?

(b) Visit a history website or app and locate any free resources that you can download to your computer or mobile device. What materials are available to download? What is the focus of this resource? For which classes would you find the contents useful? Are you able to browse and search the collections?

(c) Visit a math or science website or app, such as HowStuffWorks, and browse its contents. Which general topics are available? Are practice tests, games, and exercises offered? What types of current news articles are displayed? How often are they updated? Are previous stories archived so that you can research these events?

❷ Social Media

Companies review the conversations, comments, complaints, and feedback on their social media pages to obtain valuable information that ultimately enhances developing or improving products and services. In some cases, companies have asked consumers to view videos of product demonstrations, Tweet their immediate impressions, and suggest improvements. Small companies with limited marketing and advertising budgets, in particular, increasingly view social media as an inexpensive means of building relationships with and among customers. Social media users interact with others who have similar interests and exchange information about their experiences. In general, companies have found that customers are eager to provide feedback and recommend improvements.

View at least two travel websites, such as those for airlines or cruise ships. Which social media are featured? Choose one of the websites and review the content. What topics are being discussed? In which ways is the company encouraging participation, such as by sponsoring contests or providing opportunities for fans to upload photos and videos? Can travelers create an account to share advice, rate and review hotels, and discuss travel experiences?

❸ Search Sleuth

(1) Should a right-handed person wear an antistatic wristband on the left or right wrist? (2) Who proposed the first lithium batteries, and at which company did he work during the 1970s? (3) What term did the firm, NetCentric, attempt to trademark in 1997? (4) What are the two moving parts in most liquid cooling systems? (5) In which city is the Intel Museum located? (6) What did Robert Noyce invent in 1959? How many patents

Internet Research ✳

were awarded to him? (7) What is fabricated in a cleanroom? (8) How many HD movies can be stored in one zettabyte (ZB)? (9) Which Sesame Street character did Qualcomm feature during its International CES keynote presentation introducing Snapdragon processors? (10) Which company manufactured the processors used in the Transformers thrill ride at Universal Studios, California?

4 Green Computing

If you panic when your laptop's battery power almost is depleted, you may have a solution as long as the weather forecast calls for sunshine. Solar chargers are available for a variety of mobile devices, but locating the proper device and determining its usefulness is challenging. For example, some solar cells require 30 minutes of complete sunshine exposure to provide 20 minutes of mobile phone talk time and perhaps one week of the exposure to charge a device fully. Some chargers snap on the back of smartphones and mobile devices; others have panels and connect to devices via USB or other cables. Solar chargers are popular with international travelers who do not want to worry about having the correct electricity converter or with people who spend time outside, such as campers, hikers, runners, and bikers. Some of these outdoor-minded people have expressed concern, however, that their solar chargers do not have enough cells to generate sufficient power that meets or exceeds the power requirements of their feature-laden devices.

Locate solar chargers that are made specifically for your smartphone, mobile device, or laptop. Then, locate portable charging kits that can charge a variety of devices. Compare prices, features, charging times, number of panels, wattage, guarantees, weight, and dimensions. Which of the chargers do you prefer? Why?

5 Security

Nearly one-half of mobile phone users under the age of 25 have lost or had their mobile phone stolen at least once. The odds are not much better for people between the ages of 35 to 54, because 30 percent of those individuals have suffered from a lost or stolen phone. Secure IT 6-1 on page 251 describes categories of products that can help secure

and track hardware. Which apps are available for your smartphone to erase data remotely? Which location-tracking apps allow you to take a photo of the thief and then send an email message that contains the image to you automatically? If your device is lost and you file a police report, you will need the device's serial number. Locate that number now and write it on a piece of paper. Also, locate the phone's 15-digit International Mobile Equipment Identity (IMEI) number and record that number. Store the document with these two numbers in a secure location. In addition, research the latest developments with the U.S. Federal Communications Commission's joint initiatives with mobile service providers and law enforcement to create a centralized database of lost and stolen mobile phones. Has Congress introduced legislation to criminalize tampering with hardware identifiers on mobile devices?

6 Ethics in Action

At airports and other points of entry into the U.S, the Department of Homeland Security (DHS) may search and seize laptops, cameras, mobile phones, and storage media from people arriving into the country without "reasonable suspicion." The DHS Office for Civil Rights and Civil Liberties has concluded that the policies for these searches comply with the First Amendment and Fourth Amendment and, therefore, do not violate civil rights. Travelers can refuse to give passwords to access the devices, but these individuals can be detained or their computers and devices can be confiscated if they do not comply with the requests. Opponents have argued that the storage media in the laptops and mobile phones is like memories stored in the brain and is not a physical object. They claim that the government should be able to inspect the hardware but not the contents of storage media without a warrant.

Locate articles that discuss lawsuits challenging the border agents' power to conduct digital searches without reasonable suspicion of illegal activity. Why do the plaintiffs believe these searches violate civil liberties? Why does the government believe the searches help combat terrorism and criminal activity? Approximately how many travelers are subjected to secondary searches daily, and of that number, how many face searches of their electronic devices?

✷ Problem Solving

The Problem Solving exercises extend your knowledge of chapter concepts by seeking solutions to practical problems with technology that you may encounter at home, school, work, or with nonprofit organizations. The Collaboration exercise should be completed with a team.

🔘 Challenge yourself with additional Problem Solving exercises by navigating to this book's Problem Solving resource on Computer Concepts CourseMate.

Instructions: You often can solve problems with technology in multiple ways. Determine a solution to the problems in these exercises by using one or more resources available to you (such as a computer or mobile device, articles on the web or in print, blogs, podcasts, videos, television, user guides, other individuals, electronics or computer stores, etc.). Describe your solution, along with the resource(s) used, in the format requested by your instructor (brief report, presentation, discussion, blog post, video, or other means).

Personal

1. **No Matching Port**   Your uncle has given you a new monitor for your computer. When you attempt to connect it, you notice that none of the ports on the back of your computer is able to accept the connector at the end of the monitor's cable. What are your next steps?

2. **Incompatible Power Adapter**   While using your laptop, you notice the battery life is running low. When you plug in the AC adapter that was included with the laptop, an error message is displayed stating that the AC adapter is incompatible. You unplug the AC adapter and plug it back in, but the same message keeps appearing. Why might this be happening?

3. **Nonworking Fan**   Each time you turn on your computer, you hear the noise generated by the fans in the system unit. Recently, however, you turned on the computer and noticed that the noise was not as loud and that the fan in the back of the system unit was not spinning. What are your next steps?

© Suwan_bjp / Shutterstock.com

4. **Protecting Computer Hardware**   Your roommate recently informed you that thieves are looking for unattended desktops and laptops and stealing the memory inside the computer. What measures can you take to make sure nobody is able to access the inside of your laptop?

5. **Low Battery Life**   You have had your smartphone for more than one year and notice that your battery is losing its charge more quickly than normal. What are some ways you can conserve battery life so that your smartphone does not lose its charge as quickly?

Professional

6. **Installing Memory**   You have installed an additional 8 GB of memory in your office laptop so that you will have a total of 16 GB. When you turn on your laptop and view the hardware configuration, the extra memory is not recognized. Why might this be happening?

7. **Selecting the Right Processor**   Your boss has given you permission to purchase a new processor for your aging desktop computer, but many models are available. What steps will you take to make sure you purchase the processor that is best for you?

8. **Computer Possibly Overheating**   Each time you turn on your office computer, an error message is displayed stating that the temperature inside the computer recently has been out of range. Why might this be happening?

9. **Internet Access Unavailable**   You are using a cloud storage provider to save files you want to use both at work and at home, so that you do not have to carry a USB flash drive back and forth with your files. When you arrive at work, you notice that your Internet connection is unavailable and you are unable to access the files stored in the cloud. What steps can you take to prevent this in the future?

10. **System Password**   You started working at a company to replace someone who has just been terminated. When you turn on your computer, which previously was used by the terminated employee, the computer immediately asks for a system password. You do not know the password but need to access the computer so that you can start working. What are your next steps?

Collaboration

11. **Technology in Publishing**   You have been hired to select employees for the IT department in a start-up publishing company. Before you can begin hiring employees, you must familiarize yourself with the technology requirements in the publishing industry. Form a team of three people to compose a plan for creating the IT department. One team member should research the hardware requirements for people working in the publishing industry. Another team member should research the types of software used in this industry, and the third team member should compile a list of interview questions to ask each candidate.

The Critical Thinking exercises challenge your assessment and decision-making skills by presenting real-world situations associated with chapter concepts. The Collaboration exercise should be completed with a team.

Critical Thinking ✳

Challenge yourself with additional Critical Thinking exercises by navigating to this book's Critical Thinking resource on Computer Concepts CourseMate.

Instructions: Evaluate the situations below, using personal experiences and one or more resources available to you (such as articles on the web or in print, blogs, podcasts, videos, television, user guides, other individuals, electronics or computer stores, etc.). Perform the tasks requested in each exercise and share your deliverables in the format requested by your instructor (brief report, presentation, discussion, blog post, video, or other means).

1. Class Discussion

Cloud Storage   The owner of the motorcycle repair shop where you work as a part-time office manager is seeking alternatives to using a network server to store and back up files. She asks you to investigate the feasibility of using cloud storage, rather than purchasing additional storage for the company's computers and network servers. Analyze the advantages and disadvantages of using cloud storage. Include in your discussion security concerns, costs, and a comparison between two different cloud storage offerings. Which company offers the better arrangement? Why? Explore one other area of cloud computing, such as Software as a Service (SaaS), and determine how the service might benefit the shop. Find three providers of the cloud service and compare prices, user reviews, and features. Compile your findings. List the risks and benefits of using the cloud for storage and other services.

2. Research and Share

Upgrading Memory   You are an IT consultant at a bank. An analyst at the bank is complaining that her laptop is performing slowly. You determine that the analyst's memory is insufficient for the complex calculations and reports she is running. Search the web to learn more about current memory modules available to increase memory capacity. Evaluate the differences among various options, including type, size, speed, and price. Find articles from industry experts that list methods and recommendations for upgrading a laptop's memory. Also determine how to add memory to a laptop, obtaining answers to the following questions: How can you determine the type and correct amount

of memory to add? Why should you not purchase more memory than your computer can support? How do you determine the available slots for memory modules? What safety measures should you take when upgrading memory? Is it better to upgrade the memory or purchase a new laptop?

© iStockphoto / PeterPal

3. Case Study

Farmers' Market   You are the new manager for a group of organic farmers who have a weekly market in season. You recently purchased replacement smartphones for yourself and another employee, along with an upgraded tablet that the staff can use. Because you are discarding the outdated devices, the market's board of directors is concerned about both data security and the effect on the environment. The board asked you to prepare information they can use in a press release to educate the market's customers about keeping data secure when discarding a device; they also are interesting in discussing eCycling options. Determine the possible steps needed to wipe the memory and storage media in the devices. What kind of data is important to delete? Why? What are the risks of not wiping the memory and storage media in a device before you discard it? Research eCycling, and find locations in your area to eCycle or donate an outdated device. List three benefits of eCycling. Do any eCycling options include memory or storage media removal as a service? Compile your findings.

Collaboration

4. **Mobile Device Batteries**   You work in the IT department for a large publishing company that just purchased new tablets for all employees. The department manager asked you to prepare information about how to conserve the battery life of the tablets. Form a three-member team. Each member of your team should choose a different type of tablet. Find information about the battery life for each device type, including recommendations for use by the manufacturer and user reviews of the device and its chargers. Research apps that track battery life. Search for articles by industry experts that give tips on conserving the battery life of a tablet. Meet with your team, and discuss and compile your findings. Which tablet would you recommend? Why? How does the charger affect the battery life? What did you learn about battery conservation? What apps would you recommend? Why? Share your findings with the class.

✸ Beyond the Book

The Beyond the Book exercises expand your understanding of chapter concepts by requiring research.

🖥 **Access premium content** by visiting Computer Concepts CourseMate. If you have a Computer Concepts CourseMate access code, you can reinforce and extend your learning with MindTap Reader, practice tests, video, and other premium content for Discovering Computers. To sign in to Computer Concepts CourseMate at www.cengagebrain.com, you first must create a student account and then register this book, as described at www.cengage.com/ct/studentdownload.

Part 1 Instructions: Use the web or e-book to perform the task identified for each book element below. Describe your findings, along with the search term(s) you used and your web source(s), if appropriate, in the format requested by your instructor (brief report, presentation, discussion, blog post, video, or other means).

1. **Animations** 📖 Review the animation associated with this chapter and then answer the question(s) it poses (254). What search term would you use to learn more about a specific segment of the animation?

2. **Consider This** Select a Consider This in this chapter (253, 255, 256, 261, 267, 271, 272, 274) and find a recent article that elaborates on the topic. What information did you find that was not presented in this book or e-book?

3. **Drag-and-Drop Figures** 📖 Complete the Drag-and-Drop Figure activities associated with this chapter (253, 254, 257, 260, 263, 267, 269). What did you learn from each of these activities?

4. **Ethics & Issues** Select an Ethics & Issues in this chapter (252, 266, 267, 270) and find a recent article that supports one view presented. Does the article change your opinion about the topic? Why or why not?

5. **Facebook & Twitter** Review a recent Discovering Computers Facebook post or Twitter Tweet and read the referenced article(s). What did you learn from the article?

6. **High-Tech Talk** 📖 Locate an article that discusses topics related to random access memory (RAM). Would you recommend the article you found? Why or why not?

7. **How To** Select a How To in this chapter (255, 264, 268, 272, 274) and find a recent article that elaborates on the topic. Who would benefit from the content of this article? Why?

8. **Innovative Computing** 📖 Locate two additional facts about humanoid robot or the cyborg surgeon. Do your findings change your opinion about the future of this innovation? Why or why not?

9. **Internet Research** Use the search term in an Internet Research (250, 253, 255, 257, 272) to answer the question posed in the element. What other search term could you use to answer the question?

10. **Mini Features** Locate an article that discusses topics related to one of the mini features in this chapter (258, 260, 273). Do you feel that the article is appropriate for this course? Why or why not?

11. **Secure IT** Select a Secure IT in this chapter (251, 252, 256, 259, 266) and find a recent article about the topic that you find interesting. How can you relate the content of the article to your everyday life?

12. **Technology @ Work** Locate three additional, unique usages of technology in the publishing industry (275). What makes the use of these technologies unique to the publishing industry?

13. **Technology Innovators** 📖 Locate two additional facts about Intel, Gordon Moore, AMD, Nvidia, and Qualcomm. Which Technology Innovator impresses you most? Why?

14. **Third-Party Links** 📖 Visit one of the third-party links identified in this chapter (251, 252, 255, 256, 259, 266, 267, 270, 275) and read the article or watch the video associated with the link. Would you share this link on your online social network account? Why or why not?

Part 2 Instructions: Find specific instructions for the exercises below in the e-book or on Computer Concepts CourseMate. Beside each exercise is a brief description of its online content.

1. 📖 **You Review It** Search for and review a video, podcast, or blog post about current models and features of tablets and smartphones.

2. 📖 **Windows and Mac** Enhance your understanding and knowledge about using Windows and Mac computers by completing the Number System Conversion and Scan My Computer's Memory activities.

3. 📖 **Android, iOS, and Windows Phone** Enhance your understanding of mobile devices by completing the Set the Brightness and Using the Accelerometer activities.

4. 📖 **Exploring Computer Careers** Read about a career as a computer repair technician, search for related employment ads, and then answer related questions.

5. 📖 **App Adventure** Post photos and videos online using media sharing apps on your smartphone or tablet.

Input and Output

Examining Popular Devices

7

Users interact with a variety of input and output devices every day.

"After work or school, I video chat with my friends and discuss our gaming strategies. I print photos from my digital camera on my ink-jet printer. I have a wireless surround sound system that works with my laptop and phone. What other input and output devices could I need?"

True, you may be familiar with some of the material in this chapter, but do you know . . .

How to prevent unauthorized use of a webcam?

How to generate a QR code?

Why you would use a satellite speaker?

How you can protect yourself from hardware radiation?

When you should calibrate a touch screen?

How 3-D printing works?

What is meant by the term, printer hacking?

How the military uses motion input?

How the IDEA affects technology purchases in the education industry?

Which travel apps would fit your lifestyle best?

Which technology company was founded on a farm in Apples, Switzerland?

How to improve the quality of scanned documents?

How computers are used in space exploration?

Which assistive technologies are designed for input and output?

For these answers and to discover much more information essential to this course, read this chapter and visit the associated Computer Concepts CourseMate at www.cengagebrain.com.

✔ Objectives

After completing this chapter, you will be able to:

1 Differentiate among various types of keyboards: standard, compact, on-screen, virtual, ergonomic, gaming, and wireless

2 Describe characteristics of various pointing devices: mouse, touchpad, pointing stick, and trackball

3 Describe various uses of touch screens

4 Describe various types of pen input: stylus, digital pen, and graphics tablet

5 Describe various uses of motion input, voice input, and video input

6 Differentiate among various scanners and reading devices: optical scanners, optical readers, bar code readers, RFID readers, magstripe readers, MICR readers, and data collection devices

7 Explain the characteristics of various displays

8 Summarize the various types of printers: ink-jet printers, photo printers, laser printers, all-in-one printers, thermal printers, mobile printers, label printers, plotters and large-format printers, and impact printers

9 Identify the purpose and features of speakers, headphones and earbuds, data projectors, interactive whiteboards, and force-feedback game controllers and tactile output

10 Identify various assistive technology input and output methods

What Is Input?

Input is any data and instructions entered into the memory of a computer. As shown in Figure 7-1, people have a variety of options for entering data and instructions into a computer.

As discussed in Chapter 1, *data* is a collection of unprocessed items, including text, numbers, images, audio, and video. Once data is in memory, a computer or mobile device interprets and executes instructions to process the data into information. Instructions that a computer or mobile device processes can be in the form of software (programs and apps), commands, and user responses.

- *Software* is a series of related instructions, organized for a common purpose, that tells a computer or mobile device what tasks to perform and how to perform them. When software developers write programs or apps, they usually enter the instructions into the computer or mobile device by using a keyboard, mouse, or other input method. The software developer then stores the program in a file that a user can execute (run). When a user runs a program or app, the computer or mobile device loads the program or app from a storage medium into memory. Thus, a program or app is entered into a computer's or mobile device's memory.

- A *command* is an instruction that causes a program or app to perform a specific action. Programs and apps respond to commands that a user issues. Users issue commands by touching an area on a screen, pressing keys on the keyboard, clicking a mouse button to control a pointer on the screen, or speaking into a microphone.

- A *user response* is an instruction a user issues by responding to a message displayed by a program or app. A response to the message instructs the program or app to perform certain actions. For example, if you respond with a reply of 'Yes' when a program asks the question, Do you want to save the changes you made to this file?, the program will save the changes you made. If you respond with a reply of 'No', the program will not save your changes before exiting.

Commonly used input methods include the keyboard, pointing devices, touch screens, pen input, motion input, voice input, video input, and scanners and reading devices. This chapter discusses each of these input methods.

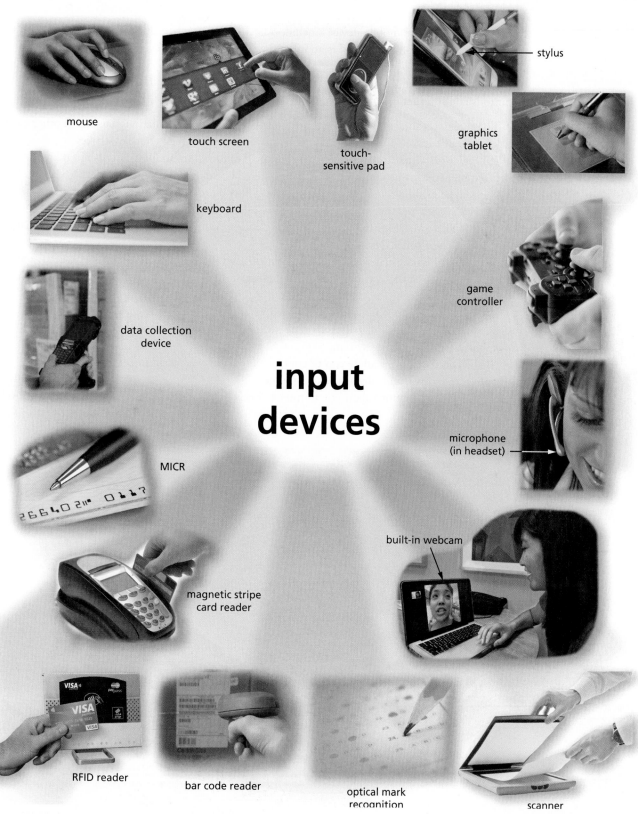

mouse

touch screen

touch-sensitive pad

stylus

graphics tablet

keyboard

game controller

data collection device

input devices

microphone (in headset)

MICR

built-in webcam

magnetic stripe card reader

RFID reader

bar code reader

optical mark recognition

scanner

Figure 7-1 Users can enter data and instructions into computers and mobile devices in a variety of ways.

Keyboards

Most computers and mobile devices include a keyboard or keyboarding capabilities. As discussed in previous chapters, a **keyboard** is an input device that contains keys you press to enter data and instructions into a computer or mobile device. Nearly all keyboards have a typing area, function keys, toggle keys, and arrow keys (Figure 7-2). Many also include media control buttons and Internet control buttons.

- The typing area includes letters of the alphabet, numbers, punctuation marks, and other basic keys. Read Secure IT 7-1 to learn about software that can track your keystrokes.
- *Function keys*, which are labeled with the letter F followed by a number, are special keys programmed to issue commands to a computer. The command associated with a function key may vary, depending on the program with which you are interacting.
- A *toggle key* is a key that switches between two states each time a user presses the key. CAPS LOCK and NUM LOCK are examples of toggle keys. Many keyboards have status lights that light up when you activate a toggle key.
- Users can press the arrow keys and sometimes other directional keys such as PAGE UP and PAGE DOWN on the keyboard to move the insertion point in an application left, right, up, or down.
- A *keyboard shortcut* is one or more keyboard keys that you press to perform an operating system or application-related task. Some keyboard shortcuts are unique to a particular application or operating system.
- Media control buttons allow you to control a media player program, access the computer's optical disc drive, and adjust speaker volume.
- Internet control buttons allow you to run an email application, run a browser, and search the web.

BTW

Insertion Point
The *insertion point,* also known as a *cursor* in some applications, is a symbol on the screen, usually a blinking vertical bar, that indicates where the next character you type will appear.

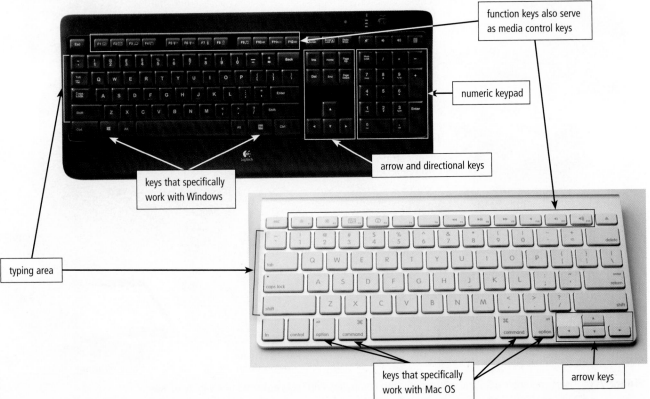

function keys also serve as media control keys

numeric keypad

arrow and directional keys

keys that specifically work with Windows

typing area

keys that specifically work with Mac OS

arrow keys

Figure 7-2   On a standard keyboard, you type using keys in the typing area and on the numeric keypad. Some of the keys on standard keyboards differ, depending on the operating system with which they are designed to work.
Courtesy of Logitech; © iStockphoto / Jill Fromer

SECURE IT 7-1

Keyboard Monitoring

Few programs have both criminal and beneficial purposes, but *keyboard monitoring software,* also called *keylogging software,* fits these objectives. This software runs undetected and stores every keystroke in a file for later retrieval.

When used for malicious purposes, criminals use the program on both public and private computers to capture user names, passwords, credit card numbers, and other sensitive data and then use this data to access financial accounts and private networks. When used in a positive light, employers can measure the efficiency of data entry personnel. This software also can verify that employees are not releasing company secrets, are not viewing personal or inappropriate content on work computers, and are not engaging in activities that could subject the company to harassment, hacking, or other similar charges. Employers sometimes use the software to troubleshoot technical problems and to back up their networks. Parents, likewise, can verify their children are using the home computer safely and are not visiting inappropriate websites. This software also can monitor activity in chat rooms and other similar locations.

Many keylogging programs are available, and they perform a variety of functions. Some simply record keystrokes in a hidden file stored on the hard disk that can be accessed by supplying the correct password. More sophisticated programs record software used, websites visited, and periodic screen shots and then transmit this data to a remote computer.

It can be difficult to locate keylogging software on a computer, but taking these steps may help detect the programs:

- **Run detection software regularly.** Several antivirus and spyware detection programs check for known keylogging programs.

- **Review hard disk files.** Regularly look at the most recent files and note any that are updated continually. These files might be the keylogging software's logs.

- **Check running programs.** Periodically examine which software is loaded from the computer's hard disk into memory when you start the computer and which are running while you are using the computer. If you are uncertain of any program names, perform a search to learn the software's function and if it is a known keylogging program.

Do you know anyone who has installed keylogging software? Is keylogging software an invasion of privacy? Should employers inform employees if the software is installed? Why or why not?

Some keyboards also include USB ports on one side or in the back so that you can plug a USB device directly in the keyboard instead of in the computer or mobile device. Others may include a fingerprint reader or a pointing device.

Types of Keyboards

Desktops include a standard keyboard. Standard keyboards typically have from 101 to 105 keys, which include function keys along the top and a numeric keypad on the right (shown in the top keyboard in Figure 7-2).

As discussed in previous chapters, you have a variety of keyboard options for mobile computers and devices (Figure 7-3). These devices often use a *compact keyboard,* which is smaller than a standard keyboard and usually does not include the numeric keypad. Typically, the keys on a compact keyboard serve two or three purposes in order to provide the same functionality as standard keyboards. Some compact keyboards are built into the computer or mobile device and/or are permanently attached with hinges, a sliding mechanism, or some other technique. Other compact keyboards are separate devices that communicate wirelessly or attach to the computer or device with a clip or other mechanism. Some users prefer to work with on-screen or virtual keyboards instead of a physical keyboard. Others, however, prefer to use a standard keyboard with their mobile devices because these keyboards provide added functionality and tactile comfort.

built-in laptop keyboard

clip-on tablet keyboard

on-screen keyboards

Figure 7-3 Users have a variety of keyboard options for mobile computers and devices.
Source: Microsoft; © iStockphoto / EricVega; © iStockphoto / pictafolio; © iStockphoto / Mutlu Kurtbas

 CONSIDER THIS

What is the rationale for the arrangement of keys in the typing area?
The keys originally were arranged to reduce the frequency of key jams on old mechanical typewriters. Called a *QWERTY keyboard,* the six first letters on the top row of letter keys spell QWERTY.

Figure 7-4 An ergonomic keyboard.
© iStockphoto / peng wu

An *ergonomic keyboard* has a design that reduces the chance of repetitive strain injuries (RSIs) of wrist and hand (Figure 7-4). Recall that the goal of ergonomics is to incorporate comfort, efficiency, and safety in the design of the workplace. Even keyboards that are not ergonomically designed attempt to offer a user more comfort by including a wrist rest.

A *gaming keyboard* is a keyboard designed specifically for users who enjoy playing games on the computer. Gaming keyboards typically include programmable keys so that gamers can customize the keyboard to the game being played. The keys on gaming keyboards light up so that the keys are visible in all lighting conditions. Some have small displays that show important game statistics, such as time or targets remaining.

 Internet Research

How prevalent are RSIs?

Search for: RSI statistics

CONSIDER THIS

Why use a wireless keyboard?
Although some keyboards connect via a cable to a USB port on the computer, many users choose a wireless keyboard to eliminate the clutter of a cord and/or to free USB ports for other uses. A *wireless keyboard* is a battery-powered device that transmits data to the computer or mobile device using wireless technology. For example, Bluetooth keyboards are especially popular with tablets because they do not require a USB port and are easy to pair with the devices. Many vendors offer tablet cases with a built-in Bluetooth keyboard so that you easily can transport a keyboard with the tablet.

BTW

Logitech
Technology Innovator: You should be familiar with Logitech (manufacturer of a variety of input and other devices).

Pointing Devices

In a graphical user interface, a **pointer** is a small symbol on the screen whose location and shape change as a user moves a pointing device. A pointing device can select text, graphics, and other objects such as buttons, icons, links, and menu commands. The following pages discuss a variety of pointing devices.

Mouse

A **mouse** is a pointing device that fits under the palm of your hand comfortably. As you move a mouse, the pointer on the screen also moves. The bottom of a mouse is flat and contains a mechanism that detects movement of the mouse. Desktop users have an optical mouse or a touch mouse, both of which can be placed on nearly all types of flat surfaces (Figure 7-5).

An *optical mouse* uses optical sensors that emit and sense light to detect the mouse's movement. Similarly, a *laser mouse* uses laser sensors that emit and sense light to detect the mouse's

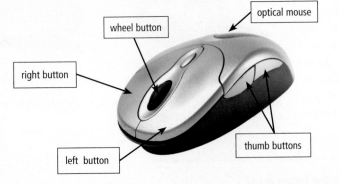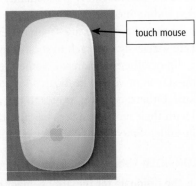

Figure 7-5 An optical mouse has buttons. A touch mouse often has no buttons.
© Anton Derevschuk / Shutterstock.com; © iStockphoto / Jill Fromer

movement. Some mouse devices use a combination of both technologies. The top and sides of an optical or laser mouse may have one to four buttons; some may also have a small wheel. Some are more sensitive than others for users requiring more precision, such as graphic artists, engineers, or game players.

A *touch mouse* is a touch-sensitive mouse that recognizes touch gestures, in addition to detecting movement of the mouse and traditional click and scroll operations. For example, you press a location on a touch mouse to simulate a click, sweep your thumb on the mouse to scroll pages, or slide multiple fingers across the mouse to zoom.

As with keyboards, you can purchase an ergonomic mouse to help reduce the chance of RSIs or to reduce pain and discomfort associated with RSIs.

BTW
Douglas Engelbart
Technology Innovator:
You should be familiar with Douglas Engelbart (creator of the mouse).

✺ CONSIDER THIS

Why use a wireless mouse?
Similar to keyboard, many users choose a wireless mouse to eliminate the clutter of a cord and/or to free USB ports for other uses. A *wireless mouse* is a battery-powered device that transmits data using wireless technology. A wireless mouse typically transmits data to a receiver that plugs in a USB port or uses Bluetooth technology to pair with the device.

Internet Research
What are mouse gestures?
Search for: mouse gestures

Touchpad

A **touchpad** is a small, flat, rectangular pointing device that is sensitive to pressure and motion (Figure 7-6). Touchpads are found most often on laptops and convertible tablets. Desktop users who prefer the convenience of a touchpad can purchase a separate touchpad, which usually connects wirelessly with the computer.

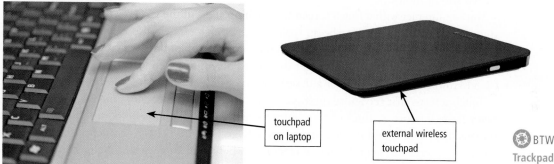

touchpad on laptop

external wireless touchpad

BTW
Trackpad
Apple uses the term, *trackpad*, to refer to the touchpad on its laptops.

Figure 7-6 Laptop users often use the touchpad to control movement of the pointer. You also can purchase an external wireless touchpad for use with desktops and tablets.
© Andrew Donehue / Shutterstock.com; Courtesy of Logitech

To move the pointer using a touchpad, slide your fingertip across the surface of the pad. Some touchpads have one or more buttons around the edge of the pad that work like mouse buttons; others have no buttons. On most touchpads, you also can tap the pad's surface to imitate mouse operations, such as clicking. Some touchpads also recognize touch gestures such as swipe, pinch, and stretch motions.

Pointing Stick

A **pointing stick** is a pressure-sensitive pointing device shaped like a pencil eraser that is positioned between keys on a mobile computer keyboard (Figure 7-7). To move the pointer using a pointing stick, you push the pointing stick with a finger. The pointer on the screen moves in the direction you push the pointing stick.

pointing stick

Figure 7-7 Some laptops include a pointing stick to allow a user to control the movement of the pointer.
© David / Shutterstock.com

Trackball

A **trackball** is a stationary pointing device with a ball on its top or side (Figure 7-8). The ball in most trackballs is about the size of a Ping-Pong ball.

To move the pointer using a trackball, you rotate the ball with your thumb, fingers, or the palm of your hand. In addition to the ball, a trackball usually has one or more buttons that work like mouse buttons.

Figure 7-8 Shown here is a trackball mouse, which is a single device that provides the functionality of both a trackball and a mouse.
© iStockphtoo / peng wu

 CONSIDER THIS

Why use a trackball instead of a mouse?

For users who have limited desk space, a trackball is a good alternative to a mouse because the device is stationary. Keep in mind, however, that a trackball requires frequent cleaning because it picks up oils from fingers and dust from the environment.

Touch Screens

A **touch screen** is a touch-sensitive display device. Touch screens are convenient because they do not require a separate device for input. They also are becoming more popular as computers and mobile devices become smaller, leaving less room to connect external input devices, such as a keyboard or mouse.

You can interact with a touch screen by touching areas of the screen with your finger or a stylus to make selections or to begin typing. Many touch screens also respond to gestures. A *gesture* is a motion you make on a touch screen with the tip of one or more fingers or your hand. For example, you can slide your finger to drag an object or pinch your fingers to zoom out. (Read How To 1-1 on page 5 for a description of widely used touch screen gestures.)

Touch screens that recognize multiple points of contact at the same time are known as *multi-touch*. Because gestures often require the use of multiple fingers (points of contact), touch screens that support gestures are multi-touch. Read How To 7-1 for instructions about calibrating a touch screen to help the device recognize where your fingers are touching the screen. Read Secure IT 7-2 to learn how gestures may replace passwords.

 HOW TO 7-1

Calibrate a Touch Screen

If you own a device with a touch screen, you may need to calibrate the touch screen at one time or another. The calibration process helps the device determine exactly where one or more fingers are touching the screen. When you purchase a new device with a touch screen, you often will be directed through a calibration process when you turn on the device for the first time. It also may be necessary to calibrate the touch screen if the computer or mobile device is registering your touch in a location other than where you actually touched the screen. The following steps describe the process for calibrating a touch screen:

1. Before calibrating the touch screen, clean the touch screen so that it is free of debris, such as dust and dirt.

2. Access your device's touch screen settings. If your device does not have a feature to calibrate its touch screen, you may have to refer to your device's documentation to reset the device. If resetting the device is necessary, back up your data before performing the reset operation.

3. Choose the option to calibrate the touch screen. The calibration process may require that you touch the screen in various locations, such as the center of the screen and the screen's extreme outer edges. You also may need to perform other actions such as swiping, dragging, and sliding.

4. When the calibration process is complete, verify the touch screen is working properly. If not, you may need to contact your device's manufacturer.

 What are some reasons why a touch screen may need to be calibrated?

To provide calibration samples, tap the crosshair each time that it appears on the screen.

Right-click anywhere on the screen to return to the last calibration point. Press the Esc button to close the tool. Do not change your screen orientation until you have completed the calibration process.

Source: Microsoft

SECURE IT 7-2

Using Finger Swipes and Fingerprints as Passwords

Drawing straight lines and circles and swiping a tablet or smartphone are fast and innovative methods of securing devices with touch screens. Each person generally has a unique touch gesture, with variations attributed to the distances between fingertips, various tracks used to pinch, and swiping speeds. Some studies have indicated that gestures people find fun to draw are more secure than text passwords because hackers can guess the combinations of characters traditionally used as passwords but cannot determine the components of creative gestures.

Fingerprints are among the biometric identifiers used to authenticate a person's identity. Fingerprint readers capture the curves and indentations of a person's fingertip, and the software stores a template of this pattern. Security issues can arise if this template is stolen, duplicated, and then used to bypass the security of the system it was meant to protect. In one study, a forged fingerprint gained access to a security system one-third of the times it was tested.

Most biometric devices are used in lieu of a password, but security experts recommend that access to accounts should be granted with this hardware and two other components: an object, such as a

mobile phone, ID card, or security token; and knowledge, such as a password, PIN, or response to a question. Some studies suggest, however, that users have a false sense of security when they use a text password in conjunction with a fingerprint reader because they tend to create weaker passwords.

✺ Have you used a fingerprint reader at work, with a computer, or at an amusement park? Would using a biometric device make you feel more secure than using a password alone? If you were to create a fun gesture (suitable for all audiences) for a touch device, which gesture would you draw? What action would it represent?

 MINI FEATURE 7-1

Touch Input

Many new computers and devices are using touch as a primary method of input. In fact, newer operating systems are optimizing their user interfaces for touch input. Devices that utilize touch input include monitors for desktops and screens on laptops and tablets, smartphones, portable media players, digital cameras, tablets, kiosks, and navigation systems.

Desktop Monitors and Screens on Laptops and Tablets

© iStockphoto / urbancow

© iStockphoto / Anatoliy Babiy

An increasing number of desktop monitors and screens on laptops and tablets support touch input. These touch-enabled monitors and screens allow users to interact with the operating system without a keyboard or pointing device. Instead of using a mouse to click an object on the screen, users simply can tap or double-tap the item they otherwise would have clicked. For example, users can tap or double-tap an icon to run a program or an application, slide their finger to scroll, or use their finger to drag items across the screen.

Smartphones

Smartphones are becoming more functional, lighter weight, and now often do not include a physical keyboard. Touch input can help smartphone manufacturers achieve all these goals. The gestures you might perform on a

smartphone that supports touch input include tapping to run an app, sliding or swiping to scroll, and pinching and stretching to zoom. The absence of a physical keyboard makes it more difficult to type without looking at the screen, so it is not advisable to use a smartphone when performing actions that require undivided attention. Read Ethics & Issues 7-1 on the next page to consider issues related to using a phone while driving.

Portable Media Players

Portable media players widely use touch as the primary method of input so that the size of the screen on the device is maximized. That is, space on the device does not have to be dedicated to other controls, such as buttons or click wheels. Users slide and swipe to browse their music libraries on their portable media players and then tap to select the song they want to play. While songs are playing, users can tap the screen to display controls so that they can pause or stop the song, navigate to another song, or adjust the volume.

Digital Cameras

As digital cameras start to include built-in features to browse and edit photos without requiring a computer, touch input helps digital camera users perform these functions with greater accuracy. For example, you can perform gestures such as swiping left and right on the screen to browse your photos, tapping the screen to identify the area on which you wish to focus when taking a picture, pinching and stretching to zoom while viewing photos, tapping areas of photos to remove red-eye, and dragging borders of photos to crop them.

Kiosks

Touch input also is used on devices where a keyboard and pointing device might not endure its high

✺ **BTW**
Biometrics: Personalized Security
High-Tech Talk: Biometric technology, including finger-scan technology, uses enrollment and matching to authenticate a user's identity.

volume of use. Kiosks, such as those at an airport allowing you to check in for a flight, can be used by hundreds of people per day. Because kiosks are designed to help you perform a specific function as quickly as possible, touch input is ideal for their user-friendly interfaces. Users typically interact with kiosks by tapping various areas of the screen to select options (shown in Figure 3-13 on page 115). If typing is required, an on-screen keyboard is displayed so that users can enter information, such as their name or a confirmation number. Kiosks requiring sensitive or a significant amount of input also might include a separate keyboard and pointing device. For example, ATMs with touch screens often have a separate keypad to enter your PIN so that others are not able to see what you are typing.

Navigation Systems

Navigation systems in cars and other vehicles use touch input because typing on a separate keyboard is not practical while operating a vehicle. Navigation

© iStockphoto / Rafal Olechowski

system users can perform actions such as tapping to enter a destination address, dragging to display different areas of the map, or pinching and stretching to zoom. Operating a navigation system with touch input requires you to take your eyes off the road to interact with the device, so you should operate a navigation system only while your vehicle is parked or stopped. To reduce the chances of driver distraction, some built-in navigation systems reduce functionality while the vehicle is in motion.

✳ Do you find it is easier to use touch input instead of using a keyboard or mouse? Does your answer depend on the type of device you are using or the task you are trying to accomplish?

✳ **ETHICS & ISSUES 7-1**

Should It Be Legal to Use a Mobile Device while Driving?

As you are driving, you receive a text message from a friend. Is it safe to read the text message? Is it legal? Should you respond to it? A few minutes later, your sister calls. Do you answer the call? Millions of Americans acknowledge that they talk on their mobile phones while driving. Today's newer vehicles include sophisticated hands-free systems that use Bluetooth and other technologies to connect mobile devices to the vehicle's sound system.

The debate about mobile phone safety while driving elicits different points of view from vehicle insurance companies, consumer

safety groups, and the telecommunications industry. In some states, it is illegal to send text messages while driving. Other states have outlawed the use of mobile phones or they require drivers to use hands-free devices while driving.

Critics say that using a hands-free device gives people a false sense of security. Others claim that drivers can be just as easily distracted if they are discussing business or emotional matters. A recent study stated that talking on a phone while driving affects drivers' response times as much as if they had consumed alcohol. One study reported that 62 percent of teenage drivers use mobile phones

while driving, and 24 percent of them do not believe their phone use is a safety issue. One phone company created a mobile app that automatically responds to incoming text messages if the vehicle is traveling in excess of 25 mph, informing the message sender that you are driving and will respond later.

Do you think the government should be able to establish rules about mobile device usage while driving? Why or why not? Do you believe you are distracted if you talk on the phone while driving? Why or why not? Do you believe hands-free devices are safe? Why or why not?

✳ **CONSIDER THIS**

What is the purpose of a touch-sensitive pad?

Portable media players that do not have touch screens typically have a touch-sensitive pad. A *touch-sensitive pad* is an input device that contains buttons and/or wheels you operate with a thumb or other finger. Using the touch-sensitive pad, you can scroll through and play music; view photos; watch videos or movies; navigate through song, photo, or movie lists; display a menu; adjust volume; customize settings; and perform other actions. For example, users can rotate a portable media player's touch-sensitive pad to browse through the device's playlists and press the pad's buttons to play or pause media (Figure 7-9).

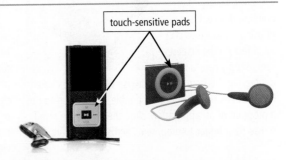
touch-sensitive pads

Figure 7-9 You use your thumb or finger to rotate or press buttons on a touch-sensitive pad, which commonly is found on portable media players.
© iStockphoto / Jorge Juan Pérez Suárez; © iStockphoto / Lusoimages

Pen Input

With **pen input**, you touch a stylus or digital pen on a flat surface to write, draw, or make selections.

Stylus

A **stylus** is a small metal or plastic device that looks like a tiny ink pen but uses pressure instead of ink (Figure 7-10). Nearly all tablets and mobile devices, some laptop screens, and a few desktop monitors have touch screens that support pen input, in addition to touch input, and thus include a stylus. The stylus included with these devices may include buttons you can press to simulate clicking a mouse.

To capture a handwritten signature, a user writes his or her name on a **signature capture pad** with a stylus that is attached to the device. Software then transmits the signature to a central computer, where the signature is stored. Retailers use signature capture pads to record purchasers' signatures. Signature capture pads often work with POS terminals and include a magnetic stripe card reader, discussed later in the chapter.

Figure 7-10 You use a stylus to write, draw, or make selections on a touch screen that supports pen input.
© iStockphoto / Petar Chernaev; © iStockphoto / pictafolio; © iStockphoto / tirc83

Digital Pen

A **digital pen**, which is slightly larger than a stylus, is an input device that captures and converts a user's handwriting or drawings into a digital format, which users can upload (transfer) to a computer or mobile device. Some require the user to write or draw on special paper or a tablet; others can write or draw on any surface (Figure 7-11).

Once uploaded, *handwriting recognition software* on the computer or mobile device translates the handwritten letters and symbols created on the screen into typed text or objects that the computer or device can process. For this reason, digital pens most often are used for taking notes. Some are battery operated or USB powered; others use wireless technology such as Bluetooth.

Figure 7-11 Users take notes with a digital pen and then upload the notes to a computer or mobile device, where software translates the notes to typed text.
Courtesy of LiveScribe

Graphics Tablet

To use pen input on a computer that does not have a touch screen, you can attach a graphics tablet to the computer. A **graphics tablet,** also called a *digitizer,* is an electronic plastic board that detects and converts movements of a stylus or digital pen into digital signals that are sent to the computer (Figure 7-12). Each location on the graphics tablet corresponds to a specific location on the screen. Architects, mapmakers, designers, and artists, for example, use graphics tablets to create images, sketches, or designs.

pen

graphics tablet

Figure 7-12 Architects use a graphics tablet to create blueprints.
© iStockphoto / small_frog

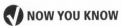 **NOW YOU KNOW** ──────────────────────────

Be sure you understand the material presented in the sections titled What is Input?, Keyboards, Pointing Devices, Touch Screens, and Pen Input, as it relates to the chapter objectives.
You now should know . . .

- Which type of keyboard is best suited to your needs (Objective 1)
- When you would use a mouse, touchpad, pointing stick, and trackball (Objective 2)
- What devices use touch screens (Objective 3)
- When you might use a stylus, digital pen, and graphics tablet (Objective 4)

Quiz Yourself Online: Check your knowledge of related content by navigating to this book's Quiz Yourself resource on Computer Concepts CourseMate and then tapping or clicking Objectives 1–4.

Motion Input

Internet Research

What are other uses of gesture recognition?

Search for: gesture recognition uses

Many of today's computers, mobile devices, and game devices support motion input. With *motion input,* sometimes called *gesture recognition,* users can guide on-screen elements using air gestures. *Air gestures* involve moving your body or a handheld input device through the air. With motion input, a device containing a camera detects your gesture and then converts it to a digital signal that is sent to a computer, mobile, or game device. For example, gamers can swing their arm or a controller to simulate rolling a bowling ball down a lane toward the pins.

 MINI FEATURE 7-2 ──────────────────────────────

📖 Motion Input

Until a few years ago, the idea of controlling a computer by waving your hands was seen only in Hollywood science fiction movies. Today, the entertainment industry (such as for gaming and animating movies), the military, and the medical field have found uses for motion input.

Entertainment

Motion-sensing devices communicate with a game console or a personal computer using wired or wireless technology. The console or computer translates a player's natural gestures, facial movements, and full-body motion into input. Although these devices originally were intended for gaming, developers are working on adapting them or using similar technology outside of the gaming and entertainment industry.

Motion-sensing game controllers enable a user to guide on-screen elements by moving a handheld input device through the air. Examples include handheld devices that enable gamers to use sweeping arm movements to simulate sports activities such as a tennis swing, balance boards that judge stability and motion when holding yoga poses, and remote control attachments, such as a steering wheel used to guide a car along a race course.

Some controllers track peripheral motion within a specific area. With these devices, users can move their finger to draw or move their whole body to dance or exercise. Some use a device that can track small finger gestures, enabling users to be more precise in their movements.

Facial motion capture converts people's facial movements into digital format while they talk, smile, and more. Animators, for example, use the digital data to simulate facial movements to create realistic gaming avatars, or computer-generated characters in movies. Facial movements, however, are more subtle and difficult to detect. Thus, the technology used for capturing facial motions requires more precision and a higher resolution than that required by gaming devices.

Military

Military uses of motion input include training, such as flight simulation or weapon usage. To ensure safety, trainees maneuver a helicopter or other device using motion input from a remote location. Motion input also aids in physical rehabilitation for wounded soldiers by providing a method for conducting physical therapy exercises outside of a military hospital. Another use of motion input is to assist in recovery from post-traumatic stress disorder. Sufferers of this ailment can use avatars and simulators to work through scenarios in a comfortable environment.

Medical Field

The medical field also uses motion input for training. For example, surgeons can practice new technologies in a simulated environment. Using motion input that enhances movements, surgeons also can operate less invasively. Surgeons even operate remotely, enabling experts to manipulate surgical devices and share their expertise to save lives around the world.

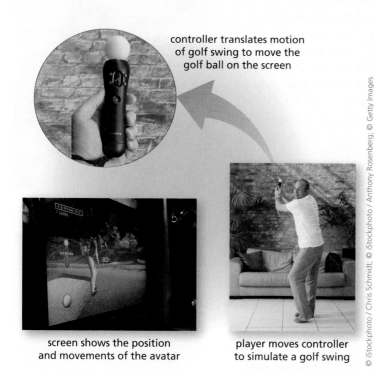

controller translates motion of golf swing to move the golf ball on the screen

screen shows the position and movements of the avatar

player moves controller to simulate a golf swing

© iStockphoto / Chris Schmidt; © iStockphoto / Anthony Rosenberg; © Getty Images

❋ Have you used a motion-sensing device or game controller? What were your impressions? What security issues surround military use of motion input? What issues might the medical field encounter when using motion input?

Voice Input

Voice input is the process of entering input by speaking into a microphone. The microphone may be built in the computer or device, in a headset, or an external peripheral device that sits on top of a desk or other surface. Some external microphones have a cable that attaches to a port on a computer; others communicate using wireless technology, such as Bluetooth.

Uses of voice input include instant messaging that supports voice conversations, chat rooms that support voice chats, video calls, videoconferencing, VoIP, and voice recognition. Recall that VoIP enables users to speak to other users via their Internet connection. **Voice recognition,**

 Internet Research

How accurate is voice recognition?

Search for: voice recognition accuracy

also called *speech recognition*, is the computer or mobile device's capability of distinguishing spoken words. Some computers and mobile devices make use of built-in and third-party voice recognition applications, which have a natural language interface (Figure 7-13). A *voice recognition application* allows users to dictate text and enter instructions by speaking into a microphone.

On mobile devices, these applications allow users to speak simple, task-based instructions to the device, such as setting an alarm, entering a calendar appointment, or making a call. Some mobile devices have a dictation feature, which recognizes a user's spoken words and enters them into email messages, text messages, or other applications that support typed text entry.

Figure 7-13 With Siri, you can speak instructions and commands to the smartphone and its apps. As shown here, the user asks Siri about the weather, to which Siri replies by speaking a message and displaying the forecast.
© iStockphoto / alexander kirch

Audio Input

Voice input is part of a larger category of input called audio input. *Audio input* is the process of entering any sound into the computer such as speech, music, and sound effects. To enter high-quality sound into computer, the computer uses a sound card or integrated sound capability. Users enter sound into computers and mobile devices via devices such as microphones, CD/DVD/Blu-ray Disc players, or radios, each of which plugs in a port on the computer or device.

Some users also record live music and other sound effects into a computer by connecting external music devices such as an electronic keyboard (Figure 7-14), guitar, drums, harmonica, and microphones to a computer. *Music production software* allows users to record, compose, mix, and edit music and sounds. For example, music production software enables you to change the speed, add notes, or rearrange the score to produce an entirely new arrangement.

Figure 7-14 This sound engineer uses a computer to mix music.
© iStockphoto / Chris Schmidt

✳ **CONSIDER THIS**

How do external music devices connect to a computer?
External music devices typically connect to USB, FireWire, and MIDI ports. When purchasing a music device, check its specifications for the type(s) of ports to which it connects.

Video Input

Video input is the process of capturing full-motion images and storing them on a computer or mobile device's storage medium, such as a hard disk or optical disc. A **digital video (DV) camera** records video as digital signals, which you can transfer directly to a computer or mobile device with the appropriate connection.

 **MINI FEATURE 7-3**

Digital Video Technology

Everywhere you look, people are capturing videos using DV cameras and mobile devices with built-in digital cameras. Using **DV technology**, you can input, edit, manage, publish, and share your videos. You can enhance digital videos by adding scrolling titles and transitions, cutting out or adding scenes, and adding background music and voice-over narration. The following sections outline the steps involved in the process of using DV technology.

Step 1: Select a DV Camera

DV cameras range from inexpensive consumer versions to high-end DV camera models that support Blu-ray or HDV standards. Many mobile devices allow you to record digital video that you later can transmit to your computer or email from the device. When selecting a DV camera, consider features such as zoom, sound quality, editing capabilities, and resolution.

Step 2: Record a Video

With most DV cameras, you have a choice of recording programs that include different combinations of camera settings. These programs enable you to adjust the exposure and other functions to match the recording environment. You also have the ability to select special digital effects, such as fade, wipe, and black and white.

Step 3: Transfer and Manage Videos

You can connect most video cameras and mobile devices to a computer using a USB port. With many devices, you can transfer the videos to a media sharing or social networking site. Before doing this, however, consider the frame rate and video file format. The *frame rate* of a video refers to the number of frames per second (fps). A smaller frame rate results in a smaller file size for the video, but playback of the video will not be as smooth as one recorded with a higher frame rate. A video file format holds the video information in a manner specified by a vendor.

Step 4: Edit a Video

When editing, you first split the video into smaller pieces, or scenes, that you can manipulate easily. Most video editing software automatically splits the video into scenes. After splitting, you should delete, or prune, unwanted scenes or portions of scenes. You can crop, or resize, scenes, and add logos, special effects, or titles. Special effects include warping, changing from color to black and white, morphing, or zoom motion. Morphing transforms one video image into another image over the course of several frames of video.

The next step is to add audio effects, including voice-over narration and background music. Using many video editing programs, you can add additional tracks, or layers, of sound to a video in addition to the sound that the video camera or mobile device recorded. In the final step, you use video editing software to combine the scenes into a complete video by ordering scenes and adding transition effects. Transitions include fades, wipes, blurs, bursts, ruptures, and erosions.

Step 5: Distribute a Video

Some mobile devices allow you to upload video directly to video sharing and social networking sites, as well as to send a video message. You can save digital video to media such as a DVD or Blu-ray Disc and package it for individual distribution or sale.

✷ Have you used a DV camera? If so, for what purpose? Does your mobile device have a DV camera? Have you ever posted a video to a video sharing or social media site? If so, were you pleased with the quality of the uploaded video? Why or why not?

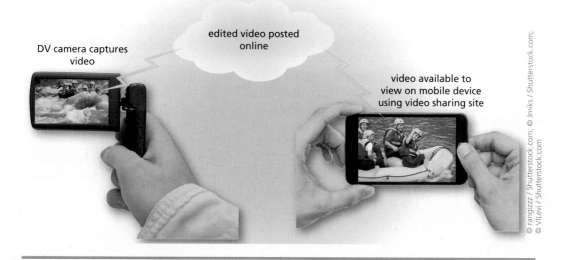

DV camera captures video

edited video posted online

video available to view on mobile device using video sharing site

© rangizzz / Shutterstock.com; © Jmiks / Shutterstock.com; © ViLevi / Shutterstock.com

Figure 7-15 During a video call, users see one another as they communicate.
© iStockphoto / Anatoliy Babiy

Webcams

A **webcam** is a type of DV camera that enables you to capture video and still images, and usually audio input, for viewing or manipulation on a computer or mobile device. Using a webcam, you can send email messages with video attachments, add live images to instant messages, broadcast live images over the Internet, conduct videoconferences, and make video calls. During a **video call**, all parties see one another as they communicate over the Internet (Figure 7-15).

You can configure some webcams to display their output on a webpage. This use of a webcam attracts website visitors by showing images that change regularly. Home or small business users might use webcams to show a work in progress, weather and traffic information, or employees at work; they also might use it as a security system. Some websites have live webcams that display still pictures and update the displayed image at a specified time or time intervals, such as every 15 seconds. A *streaming cam* has the illusion of moving images because it sends a continual stream of still images.

Many laptops, tablets, and smartphones have built-in webcams. You also can purchase a separate external webcam, which usually sits on top of a desktop monitor. Read How To 7-2 for instructions about setting up and using a webcam. Read Secure IT 7-3 to learn about security issues related to using webcams.

 HOW TO 7-2

Set Up and Use a Webcam

As mentioned previously in this book, webcams are used to record and/or send live video to others. Before you can record and send video to others, you must have a webcam set up on your computer or mobile device. Some computers and mobile devices have built-in webcams; others require you to set up a separate webcam. The following steps describe how to set up and use a webcam:

Setting Up a Webcam

1. If the webcam included software, install the software on your computer or mobile device before connecting the webcam.

2. Connect the webcam to your computer or mobile device either when the software prompts you or after you have installed the necessary software. If no software accompanied your webcam, connect the webcam to the computer or mobile device.

3. When the computer or mobile device acknowledges that a webcam has been connected, you are ready to begin using it.

© Yuganov Konstantin / Shutterstock.com

Using a Webcam

1. Run the app that will use the webcam.

2. Display the app's settings and make sure the app recognizes the webcam.

3. If you are using the webcam to record a video, record a short clip and then replay it to make sure the webcam properly captured audio and video. If you are using the webcam for a videoconference, place a call to somebody using the videoconferencing app and make sure he or she is able to see and hear you.

4. If you experience problems with the webcam capturing audio or video, try the following:

   a. Run the program that came with the webcam and see if a troubleshooter can identify and correct the problem you are experiencing.

   b. Disconnect the webcam from the computer or mobile device, restart the computer or mobile device, and then reconnect the webcam.

   c. Disconnect the webcam, uninstall the program(s) included with the webcam, restart the computer or mobile device, and then follow the previous steps to set up and use the webcam.

   d. If you continue experiencing problems after attempting these steps, contact the technical support team for the webcam's manufacturer.

✹ What are some reasons why you might need a webcam on your computer or mobile device?

✷ SECURE IT 7-3

Webcam Security

Sales of home security systems are on the rise due to their low costs and easy setup. These systems use cameras to monitor activity, and some send a message via mobile phone to alert a user of movement and entrance or exit into the dwelling and send the webcam's live feed of the scene.

This use of webcams serves a practical use in a private setting. Similarly, webcams in public areas, such as shopping malls, parking lots, and school cafeterias, help with surveillance measures and record everyday activity.

Webcam use, however, is criticized when the live feeds are used in a manner without the recorded parties' consent. In some situations, for example, criminals hacked into home computers and streamed live video

feeds, school administrators took 66,000 pictures and screen captures of students using school-distributed laptops at home, and rent-to-own stores rented laptops with spyware that captured photos of customers in their homes.

If you have a webcam, follow these measures to prevent its unauthorized use:

- **Unplug the webcam.** This obvious suggestion offers the most secure solution. If the webcam is not connected to the computer, it cannot reveal what is occurring in front of the lens.

- **Cover the lens.** Place a piece of black electrical tape over the lens. This solution is ideal for tablets and laptops equipped with cameras.

- **Register the hardware.** Hardware manufacturers continually update their firmware to fix issues. If you register your product, the companies can notify you of known security holes and offer updates to download.

- **Use a strong password.** When connecting a webcam to a network, create a strong password that hackers would have difficulty guessing. Read Secure IT 1-3 on page 24 for tips about creating strong passwords.

✷ If you have a webcam, what actions will you take to protect your privacy after reading this? Should you be warned of webcam use when you are in a public area? If so, how can these warnings be given?

Videoconference

A **videoconference** is a meeting between two or more geographically separated people who use a network or the Internet to transmit audio and video data (Figure 7-16). To participate in a videoconference using a computer, you need videoconferencing software or access to a video-conferencing web app, along with a microphone, speakers, and a video camera attached to or built into a computer. As you speak, members of the meeting hear your voice on their speakers. Any image in front of the video camera, such as a person's face, appears in a window on each participant's screen.

Scanners and Reading Devices

Figure 7-16 To save on travel expenses, many large businesses use videoconferencing.
© Comstock / Photos.com

Some input devices save users time by capturing data directly from a *source document*, which is the original form of the data. Examples of source documents include time cards, order forms, invoices, paychecks, advertisements, brochures, photos, inventory tags, or any other document that contains data to be processed.

Devices that can capture data directly from a source document include optical scanners, optical readers, bar code readers, RFID (radio frequency identification) readers, magnetic stripe card readers, and MICR (magnetic-ink character recognition) readers.

Optical Scanners

An optical scanner, usually called a **scanner**, is a light-sensing input device that reads printed text and graphics and then translates the results into a form the computer can process. A flatbed scanner works in a manner similar to a copy machine except it creates a file of the document in memory instead of a paper copy (Figure 7-17). Once you scan a picture or document, you can display the scanned object on the screen, modify its appearance, store it on a storage medium, print it, attach it to an email message, include it in another document, or post it on a website or photo community for everyone to see.

The quality of a scanner is measured by its resolution, that is, the number of bits it stores in a pixel and the number of pixels per inch. The higher each number, the better the quality, but the more expensive the scanner.

Many scanners include *OCR* (optical character recognition) *software*, which can read and convert text documents into electronic files. OCR software converts a scanned image into a text file that can be edited, for example, with a word processing application.

How a Flatbed Scanner Works

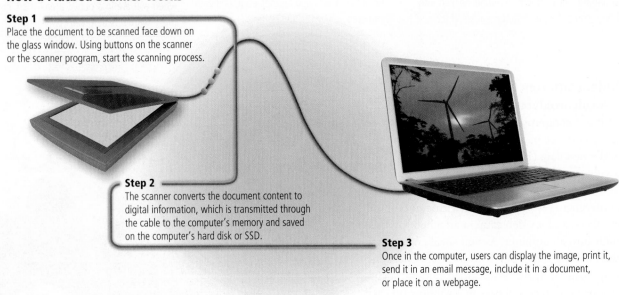

Step 1
Place the document to be scanned face down on the glass window. Using buttons on the scanner or the scanner program, start the scanning process.

Step 2
The scanner converts the document content to digital information, which is transmitted through the cable to the computer's memory and saved on the computer's hard disk or SSD.

Step 3
Once in the computer, users can display the image, print it, send it in an email message, include it in a document, or place it on a webpage.

 Figure 7-17 This figure shows how a flatbed scanner works.
© Cengage Learning; © Mile Atanasov / Shutterstock.com; © Alex Staroseltsev / Shutterstock.com

❋ CONSIDER THIS ────────────────────────

How can you improve the quality of scanned documents?
Place a blank sheet of paper behind translucent papers, newspapers, and other transparent types of paper. If the original is crooked, draw a line on the back at the bottom of the image. Use that mark to align the original on the scanner. Use photo editing software to fix imperfections in images.

Optical Readers

An optical reader is a device that uses a light source to read characters, marks, and codes and then converts them into digital data that a computer can process. Two technologies used by optical readers are optical character recognition (OCR) and optical mark recognition (OMR).

• Most **OCR devices** include a small optical scanner for reading characters and sophisticated software to analyze what is read. OCR devices range from large machines that can read thousands of documents per minute to handheld wands that read one document at a time. OCR devices read printed characters in a special font.

- **OMR devices** read hand-drawn marks, such as small circles or rectangles. A person places these marks on a form, such as a test, survey, or questionnaire answer sheet (shown in Figure 7-1 on page 289).

Bar Code Readers

A **bar code reader**, also called a *bar code scanner*, is an optical reader that uses laser beams to read bar codes (Figure 7-18). A **bar code** is an identification code that consists of either a set of vertical lines and spaces of different widths or a two-dimensional pattern of dots, squares, and other images. The bar code represents data that identifies the manufacturer and the item.

Manufacturers print a bar code either on a product's package or on a label that is affixed to a product, such as groceries, books, clothing, vehicles, mail, and packages. Each industry uses its own type of bar code. The United States Postal Service (USPS) uses a POSTNET bar code. Retail and grocery stores use the *UPC* (*Universal Product Code*) bar code.

A **QR code** (quick response code) is known as a 2-D bar code because it stores information in both a vertical and horizontal direction. The information it stores can correspond to a web address or other information, such as bank account or credit card information. QR codes can be read with a QR bar code reader or a QR code reader app on a smartphone or other mobile device. Read How To 7-3 for instructions about scanning and generating QR codes.

Figure 7-18 A bar code reader uses laser beams to read bar codes on products such as groceries.
Gilles Rolle / REA / Redux

 Internet Research

What are current uses of QR codes?

Search for: qr code uses

  **HOW TO 7-3**

Work with QR Codes

QR codes initially were used in the automotive industry to track vehicles during the production process. Today, QR codes often are used in publications and advertisements to direct users to a website, to download a file, or to an app store or marketplace to download an app. Exercise caution when scanning QR codes because they may direct your mobile computer or device to a malicious website or file. For example, avoid scanning QR codes appearing on homemade flyers.

Scanning QR Codes

When you encounter a QR code that you want to scan, you should use an app capable of reading QR codes. The following steps describe how to scan QR codes:

1. Download and install an app that can read QR codes.

2. When you see a QR code you want to scan, run the app on your mobile

computer or device. If necessary, select the option to scan a QR code.

3. Hold the device still and point its camera toward the QR code to scan it.

4. Once your device scans the QR code, it will direct your device to the appropriate location.

Generating QR Codes

If you want to generate a QR code to make it easier for others to navigate to a particular location or perform an action, you should use a QR code generator. The following steps describe how to generate QR codes:

1. Download, install, and run an app capable of generating QR codes or locate a website that has a QR code generator.

2. Enter the information, such as a web address, that you want the QR code to contain, and then tap or click the button to generate the QR code.

3. Copy the generated QR code and then paste it in the desired location.

4. Scan the QR code to make sure it directs you to the intended location.

✸ What are some reasons why you might want to generate a QR code? Other than web addresses, what additional types of information can a QR code represent?

© Cengage Learning

RFID Readers

RFID (radio frequency identification) is a technology that uses radio signals to communicate with a tag placed in or attached to an object, an animal, or a person. RFID tags, which contain a memory chip and an antenna, are available in many shapes and sizes. An **RFID reader** reads information on the tag via radio waves. RFID readers can be handheld devices or mounted in a stationary object, such as a doorway.

Many retailers see RFID as an alternative to bar code identification because it does not require direct contact or line-of-site transmission. Each product in a store would contain a tag that identifies the product. As consumers remove products from the store shelves and walk through a checkout area, an RFID reader reads the tag(s) and communicates with a computer that calculates the amount due and updates inventory.

Other uses of RFID include tracking times of runners in a marathon; tracking location of people, airline baggage, and misplaced or stolen goods; checking lift tickets of skiers; managing inventory; gauging temperature and pressure of tires on a vehicle; checking out library books; providing access to rooms or buildings (Figure 7-19); managing purchases; and tracking payment as vehicles pass through booths on tollway systems.

Figure 7-19 RFID readers read information stored in an RFID tag. In this figure, the RFID tag is embedded in the electronic key, which communicates with the security system.
© iStockphoto / Ignard Karel Maria ten Have

Magstripe Readers

A **magstripe reader**, short for *magnetic stripe card reader*, reads the magnetic stripe on the back of credit cards, entertainment cards, bank cards, identification cards, and other similar cards. The stripe contains information identifying you and the card issuer (Figure 7-20). Some information stored in the stripe includes your name, account number, the card's expiration date, and a country code. When a consumer swipes a credit card through a magstripe reader (shown in Figure 7-1 on page 289), it reads the information stored on the magnetic stripe on the card.

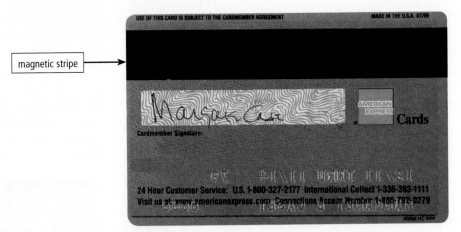

magnetic stripe

Figure 7-20 A magstripe reader reads information encoded on the stripe on the back of a credit card.
©Spencer Grant / Photo Edit

 **CONSIDER THIS**

Why are some magnetic stripes not readable by a magstripe reader?
If the magstripe reader rejects the card, it is possible that the magnetic stripe is scratched, dirty, or erased. Exposure to a magnet or magnetic field can erase the contents of a card's magnetic stripe.

MICR Readers

MICR (magnetic-ink character recognition) *devices* read text printed with magnetized ink. An MICR reader converts MICR characters into a form the computer can process. The banking industry almost exclusively uses MICR for check processing. Each check in your checkbook has precoded MICR characters beginning at the lower-left edge (Figure 7-21).

When a bank receives a check for payment, it uses an MICR inscriber to print the amount of the check in MICR characters in the lower-right corner. The check then is sorted or routed to the customer's bank, along with thousands of others. Each check is inserted in an MICR reader, which sends the check information — including the amount of the check — to a computer for processing.

Figure 7-21   The MICR characters preprinted on the check represent the bank routing number, customer account number, and check number. The amount of the check in the lower-right corner is added after the check is cashed.
© Cengage Learning

Data Collection Devices

Instead of reading or scanning data from a source document, a *data collection device* obtains data directly at the location where the transaction or event takes place. For example, employees use bar code readers, handheld computers, or other mobile devices to collect data wirelessly (Figure 7-22). These types of data collection devices are used in restaurants, grocery stores, factories, warehouses, the outdoors, or other locations where heat, humidity, and cleanliness are not easy to control. For example, factories and retail stores use data collection devices to take inventory and order products.

Figure 7-22   An employee at a hardware store uses this data collection device to scan items, which wirelessly transmits information about the scanned item to the store's inventory system.
Courtesy of Intermec Technologies

Data collection devices and many mobile computers and devices have the capability of wirelessly transmitting data over a network or the Internet. Increasingly more users today send data wirelessly to central office computers using these devices.

🕐 NOW YOU KNOW

Be sure you understand the material presented in the sections titled Motion Input, Voice Input, Video Input, and Scanners and Reading Devices, as it relates to the chapter objectives.
You now should know . . .

- Which type of motion, voice, and video input are best suited to your needs (Objective 5)

- Why you would use optical scanners and readers, bar code readers, RFID readers, magstripe readers, MICR readers, and data collection devices (Objective 6)

🖱 Quiz Yourself Online: Check your knowledge of related content by navigating to this book's Quiz Yourself resource on Computer Concepts CourseMate and then tapping or clicking Objectives 5–6.

What Is Output?

Output is data that has been processed into a useful form. Recall that computers process data (input) into information (output). The form of output varies, depending on the hardware and software being used and the requirements of the user. Users view or watch output on a screen, print it, or hear it through speakers, headphones, or earbuds. While working with a computer or mobile device, a user encounters four basic types of output: text, graphics, audio, and video (Figure 7-23). Very often, a single form of output, such as a webpage, includes more than one of these types of output.

Text

Graphics

Audio

Video

Figure 7-23 Four types of output are text, graphics, audio, and video.

- **Text:** Examples of output that primarily contain text are text messages, instant messages, memos, letters, press releases, reports, classified advertisements, envelopes, and mailing labels. On the web, users read blogs, news and magazine articles, books, television show transcripts, stock quotes, speeches, and lectures.
- **Graphics:** Many forms of output include graphics to enhance visual appeal and convey information. Business letters have logos. Reports include charts. Newsletters use drawings, clip art, and photos. Users print high-quality photos taken with a digital camera. Many websites use animation.
- **Audio:** Users download their favorite songs and listen to the music. Software such as games, encyclopedias, and simulations often include musical accompaniments and audio clips, such as narrations and speeches. On the web, users listen to radio broadcasts, audio clips, podcasts, sporting events, news, music, and concerts. They also use VoIP.
- **Video:** As with audio, software and websites often include video clips and video blogs. Users watch news reports, movies, sporting events, weather conditions, and live performances on a computer or mobile device. They attach a video camera to a computer or mobile device to watch video or programs.

Common methods of output include displays, printers, speakers, headphones and earbuds, data projectors, interactive whiteboards, and force-feedback game controllers and tactile output. The following sections discuss each of these output devices.

Displays

A *display device*, or simply **display**, is an output device that visually conveys text, graphics, and video information. Sometimes called *soft copy*, information on a display exists electronically and appears for a temporary period. Displays consist of a screen and the components that produce the information on the screen. Most current displays are a type of *flat-panel display*, which means they have a shallow depth and a flat screen. Figure 7-24 shows displays for a variety of computers and mobile devices.

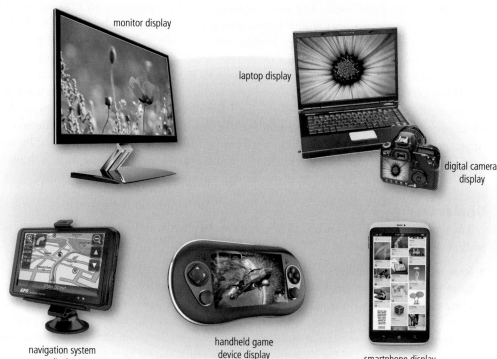

Figure 7-24 A variety of displays.

Desktops often use a monitor as their display. A **monitor** is a display that is packaged as a separate peripheral device. Some monitors have a tilt-and-swivel base, which allows you to adjust the angle of the screen to minimize neck strain and reduce glare from overhead lighting. With some, you also can rotate the screen. Adjustable monitor stands allow you to adjust the height of the monitor. Monitor controls enable you to adjust the brightness, contrast, positioning, height, and width of images. Some have touch screens, integrated speakers, and/or a built-in webcam. Today's monitors have a small footprint; that is, they do not take up much desk space. For additional space savings, some monitors are wall mountable.

Most mobile computers and devices integrate the display and other components into the case. Size of these displays varies depending on the mobile computer or device. Some mobile computers and many mobile devices have touch screens. Traditional laptops have a display that attaches with a hinge to the case. Tablets are available with two types of displays: one that attaches with a hinge and one built into the top of the case. Some smartphone and digital camera displays also attach with a hinge to the device. On other smartphones and most portable media players, digital cameras, and handheld game consoles, the display is built into the case. Newer vehicles integrate a display in the dashboard, enabling drivers to control audio, video, navigation, temperature, and other settings.

⚙ **BTW**

Measuring Displays
You measure the screen on a monitor, laptop, tablet, smartphone, or other mobile device the same way you measure a television; that is, you measure diagonally from one corner to the other.

Display Technologies

Many desktop monitors, along with the screens on mobile computers and devices, use some type of LCD technology. A *liquid crystal display* (**LCD**) sandwiches a liquid compound between two sheets of material that presents sharp, flicker-free images on a screen when illuminated. The light source, called the *backlight*, often uses either CCFL (cold cathode fluorescent lamp) or *LED* (light-emitting diode) technology.

A display that uses LED for the backlight often is called an *LED display* or an LED LCD display. LED displays consume less power, last longer, and are thinner, lighter, and brighter than a display that uses CCFL technology, but they also may be more expensive. Screens in laptops and mobile devices often use LED backlight technology.

LCD displays typically produce color using *active-matrix*, or *TFT* (thin-film transistor), technology, which uses a separate transistor to apply charges to each liquid crystal cell and, thus, displays high-quality color that is viewable from all angles. Several types of active matrix displays, or panels, are available, with some providing higher quality than others.

Instead of LCD or traditional LED, some displays use OLED technology. *OLED* (organic LED) uses organic molecules that are self-illuminating and, thus, do not require a backlight. OLED displays consume less power and produce an even brighter, easier-to-read display than LCD or LED displays, but they can have a shorter life span. OLEDs also can be fabricated on thin, flexible surfaces.

Many mobile computers and devices use either AMOLED or Retina Display technology. An *AMOLED* (active-matrix OLED) screen uses both active-matrix and OLED technologies, combining the benefits of high-quality viewing from all angles with lower power consumption. Variations of AMOLED provide different levels of viewing quality. *Retina Display*, developed by Apple, produces vibrant colors and supports viewing from all angles because the LCD technology is built into the screen instead of behind it and contains more pixels per inch of display. Recall that a *pixel* (short for picture element) is a single point in an electronic image.

🔍 **Internet Research**

What is in-plane switching (IPS)?

Search for: ips display

Display Quality

The quality of a display depends primarily on its resolution, response time, brightness, dot pitch, and contrast ratio.

- **Resolution** is the number of horizontal and vertical pixels in a display. For example, a monitor or screen that has a 1600 × 900 resolution displays up to 1600 pixels per horizontal row and 900 pixels per vertical row, for a total of 1,440,000 pixels to create a screen image. A higher resolution uses a greater number of pixels and, thus, provides a smoother, sharper, and clearer image. As the resolution increases, however, some items on the screen appear smaller.

  Displays are optimized for a specific resolution, called the *native resolution*. Although you can change the resolution to any setting, for best results, use the monitor or screen's native resolution setting.

- *Response time* of a display refers to the time in milliseconds (ms) that it takes to turn a pixel on or off. Response times of displays range from 2 to 16 ms. The lower the number, the faster the response time.
- Brightness of a display is measured in nits. A *nit* is a unit of visible light intensity equal to one candela (formerly called candlepower) per square meter. The *candela* is the standard unit of luminous intensity. Displays today range from 250 to 550 nits. The higher the nits, the brighter the images.
- *Dot pitch*, sometimes called *pixel pitch*, is the distance in millimeters between pixels on a display. Text created with a smaller dot pitch is easier to read. Advertisements normally specify a display's dot pitch or pixel pitch. Average dot pitch on a display should be .30 mm or lower. The lower the number, the sharper the image.
- *Contrast ratio* describes the difference in light intensity between the brightest white and darkest black that can be produced on a display. Contrast ratios today range from 500:1 to 2000:1. Higher contrast ratios represent colors better.

Graphics Chips, Ports, and Flat-Panel Monitors A cable on a monitor plugs in a port on the computer, which enables communications from a graphics chip. This chip, called the *graphics processing unit (GPU)*, controls the manipulation and display of graphics on a display device. The GPU either is integrated on the motherboard or resides on a video card in a slot on the motherboard.

Today's monitors use a digital signal to produce a picture. To display the highest quality images, the monitor should plug in a DVI port, an HDMI port, or a DisplayPort.

- A *DVI (Digital Video Interface) port* enables digital signals to transmit directly to a monitor.
- An *HDMI (High-Definition Media Interface) port* combines DVI with high-definition (HD) television and video. Some ultrathin laptops have mini-HDMI ports that require the use of an adapter when connecting to a standard-size HDMI display.
- A *DisplayPort* is an alternative to DVI that also supports HDMI.

Over the years, several video standards have been developed to define the resolution, aspect ratio, number of colors, and other display properties. The *aspect ratio* defines a display's width relative to its height. A 2:1 aspect ratio, for example, means the display is twice as wide as it is tall. The aspect ratio for a *widescreen monitor* is 16:9 or 16:10. Some displays support multiple video standards. For a display to show images as defined by a video standard, both the display and GPU must support the same video standard.

DTVs and Smart TVs

Home users sometimes use a digital television (DTV) as a display. Gamers also use a television as their output device. They plug one end of a cable in the game console and the other end in the video port on the television.

HDTV (*high-definition television*) is the most advanced form of digital television, working with digital broadcast signals, transmitting digital sound, supporting wide screens, and providing high resolutions. A *Smart TV* is an Internet-enabled HDTV from which you can browse the web, stream video from online media services, listen to Internet radio, communicate with others on social media sites, play online games, and more — all while watching a television show (Figure 7-25). Using a Smart TV, you can stream content from the TV to other Internet-enabled devices, such as a tablet or smartphone, and use cloud storage services to share content.

Figure 7-25 Smart TVs enable you to connect to the Internet and/or watch television shows.
Courtesy of LG Electronics USA Inc.

DTVs often use LCD, LED, or plasma technology. A *plasma display* uses gas plasma technology, which sandwiches a layer of gas between two glass plates. When voltage is applied, the gas releases ultraviolet (UV) light. This UV light causes the pixels on the screen to glow and form an image. Read Ethics & Issues 7-2 to consider the effects of radiation from monitors and other devices.

 ETHICS & ISSUES 7-2

 Should We Be Concerned with Hardware Radiation?

When you work on a computer or talk on a mobile phone, could you be at risk from harmful radiation? Every electronic device emits some level of radiation. While the amounts for computers and mobile devices are not considered harmful in low doses, some critics argue that constant exposure, such as sitting in an office all day or wearing a Bluetooth headset for several hours at a time, can cause levels of radiation that, over time, may cause cancer or other health concerns. In addition to the computer itself, peripheral devices, such as

printers, along with the wireless or cordless methods to connect the devices, emit radiation. Research is inconclusive about safe levels and long-term risks. Most agree that it is not the level from any one device, but rather the cumulative effect from long-term exposure (several hours a day over many years) to multiple devices simultaneously that causes harm.

You can protect yourself and minimize your risks. Replace older equipment, such as CRT (cathode-ray tube) monitors, with devices that meet current emission standards. Sit back from your monitor as far as possible, and place a barrier between your computer and

your lap. Move other electronic sources, such as hard disks and printers, as far away as possible. Minimize your wireless connections, such as a wireless keyboard or a wireless mouse. Remove your Bluetooth headset when not in use, and frequently switch the headset from one ear to the other.

Do you consider computers and mobile devices to be harmful to your health? Why or why not? Would you change your electronic device usage or rearrange your computer work area to minimize your risk? Why or why not? What modifications can you make?

 NOW YOU KNOW

Be sure you understand the material presented in the sections titled What is Output? and Displays, as it relates to the chapter objectives.
You now should know . . .

- What to consider when purchasing computers and devices with various displays (Objective 7)

Quiz Yourself Online: Check your knowledge of related content by navigating to this book's Quiz Yourself resource on Computer Concepts CourseMate and then tapping or clicking Objective 7.

Printers

A **printer** is an output device that produces text and graphics on a physical medium such as paper. Printed information (hard copy) exists physically and is a more permanent form of output than that presented on a display (soft copy).

A hard copy, also called a *printout*, is either in portrait or landscape orientation. A printout in *portrait orientation* is taller than it is wide, with information printed across the shorter width of the paper. A printout in *landscape orientation* is wider than it is tall, with information printed across the widest part of the paper. Letters, reports, and books typically use portrait orientation. Spreadsheets, slide shows, and graphics often use landscape orientation.

 CONSIDER THIS

Can you print documents and photos from a mobile computer and device without physically connecting to the printer with a cable?

Yes. Many printers contain memory card slots, so that you can remove the memory card from a camera, insert it in the printer, and print photos directly from the card. You also can connect a printer to a wireless network so that devices with a Wi-Fi connection can print wirelessly. With *Bluetooth printing*, a computer or other device transmits output to a printer via radio waves. The computer or other device and the printer do not have to be aligned with each other; rather, they need to be within an approximate 30-foot range. Read Secure 7-4 for techniques to secure networked printers.

 BTW

HP
Technology Innovator: You should be familiar with HP (manufacturer of printers and other technology products).

SECURE IT 7-4

Securing Network Printers

Have you sent a file to a printer and then become distracted and forgot to retrieve it from the print tray? Or, have you seen a classmate's handout on the printer and read part of its contents? Document snooping and theft are among the more common printer security breaches. Another common threat is *printer hacking*, where an individual from within the organization or outside the building can print a document without permission if the network is connected to the Internet.

In many offices, any employee who can view the printer's IP address (unique set of numbers that identifies the printer) can use it to gain access to the printer by changing settings and redirecting printouts to

that location. Outsiders, too, can access the company network through the Internet and use the printer. If the printer has a hard disk to spool documents, criminals can access documents retained on that storage device, which might contain confidential company or product information.

Steps that organizations can take to secure their printers include the following:

- Place printers in a secure room, not out in the open.
- If the printer has a hard disk, destroy it before disposing of the printer at the end of its useful life.
- Encrypt documents before sending them to the printer using a secured network.

- Restrict users through the use of sign-in procedures, passwords, and types of documents they are allowed to print.
- Use a printer program to track and report the types of jobs, and keep a record of the users who sent them.
- Unplug the printer when it is not in use, or do not connect it to a network.
- Update the printer with the latest firmware.

⁂ Have you ever read a classmate's or an employee's document that mistakenly was left on the printer tray, or have you attempted to retrieve a document and found it missing? If so, what action did you take? What measures does your school or company take to secure a printer?

To meet the range of printing needs from home users to enterprise users, many different types and styles of printers exist with varying speeds, capabilities, and printing methods. Figure 7-26 presents a list of questions to help you determine the printer best suited to your needs.

Nonimpact Printers

A **nonimpact printer** forms characters and graphics on a piece of paper without actually contacting the paper. Some spray ink, while others use heat or pressure to create images.

Commonly used nonimpact printers are ink-jet printers, photo printers, laser printers, all-in-one printers, thermal printers, mobile printers, label printers, plotters, and large-format printers.

Ink-Jet Printers

An **ink-jet printer** is a type of nonimpact printer that forms characters and graphics by spraying tiny drops of liquid ink onto a piece of paper. Ink-jet printers have become a popular type of color printer for use in the home.

1. What is my budget?
2. How fast must my printer print?
3. Do I need a color printer?
4. What is the cost per page for printing?
5. Do I need multiple copies of documents?
6. Will I print graphics?
7. Do I want to print photos?
8. Do I want to print directly from a memory card?
9. What types of paper does the printer use?
10. What sizes of paper does the printer accept?
11. Do I want to print on both sides of the paper?
12. How much paper can the printer tray hold?
13. Will the printer work with my computer and software?
14. How much do supplies such as ink, toner, and paper cost?
15. Can the printer print on envelopes?
16. How many envelopes can the printer print at a time?
17. How much do I print now, and how much will I be printing in a year or two?
18. Will the printer be connected to a network?
19. Do I want wireless printing capability?

Figure 7-26 Questions to consider before purchasing a printer.
© Cengage Learning

Ink-jet printers produce text and graphics in both black-and-white and color on a variety of paper types and sizes (Figure 7-27). These printers normally use individual sheets of paper stored in one or two removable or stationary trays. Most ink-jet printers can print lab-quality photos. Ink-jet printers also print on other materials, such as envelopes, labels, index cards, greeting card paper (card stock), transparencies, and iron-on T-shirt transfers. Many ink-jet printers include software for creating greeting cards, banners, business cards, and letterhead.

The speed of an ink-jet printer is measured by the number of pages per minute (ppm) it can print. Graphics and colors print at a slower rate than text.

Figure 7-27 Ink-jet printers are a popular type of color printer used at home and in the office.
© iStockphoto / Greg Nicholas; JurgaR / iStockphoto; Courtesy of Xerox Corporation; JurgaR / iStockphoto; Courtesy of Xerox Corporation

 CONSIDER THIS

How does resolution affect print quality?

As with many other input and output devices, one factor that determines the quality of an ink-jet printer is its resolution. Printer resolution is measured by the number of *dots per inch* (*dpi*) a printer can print. With an ink-jet printer, a dot is a drop of ink. A higher dpi means the print quality is higher because the drops of ink are smaller and more drops fit in an area.

The difference in quality becomes noticeable when the size of the printed image increases. That is, a wallet-sized image printed at 1200 dpi may look similar in quality to one printed at 2400 dpi. When you increase the size of the image, to 8 × 10 for example, the printout of the 1200 dpi resolution may look grainier than the one printed using a 2400 dpi resolution.

Ink Cartridges The printhead mechanism in an ink-jet printer contains ink-filled cartridges. Each cartridge has fifty to several hundred small ink holes, or nozzles. The steps in Figure 7-28 illustrate how a drop of ink appears on a page. The ink propels through any combination of the nozzles to form a character or image on the paper.

When the cartridge runs out of ink, you simply replace the cartridge. Most ink-jet printers use two or more ink cartridges, one containing black ink and the other(s) containing colors. Some color cartridges contain a variety of ink colors; others contain only a single color. Consider the

 **Internet Research**

How much do ink cartridges cost?

Search for: ink cartridge cost comparison

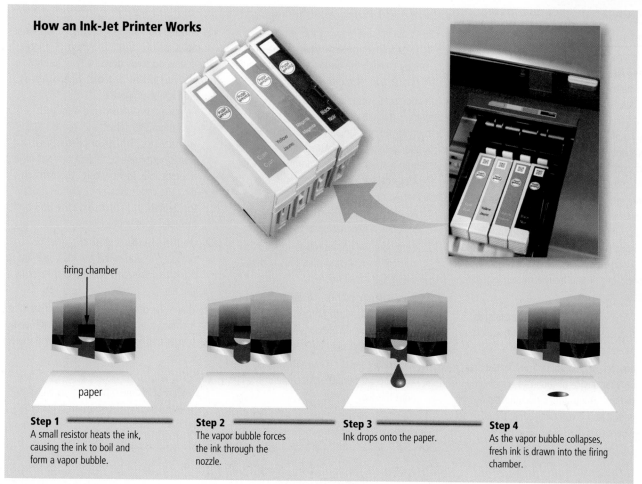

How an Ink-Jet Printer Works

firing chamber

paper

Step 1
A small resistor heats the ink, causing the ink to boil and form a vapor bubble.

Step 2
The vapor bubble forces the ink through the nozzle.

Step 3
Ink drops onto the paper.

Step 4
As the vapor bubble collapses, fresh ink is drawn into the firing chamber.

Figure 7-28 This figure shows how an ink-jet printer works.
© Boyan Dimitrov / Shutterstock.com; © Almaamor / Dreamstime.com; © Cengage Learning

number of ink cartridges a printer requires, along with the cost of the cartridges, when purchasing a printer. To reduce the expense of purchasing cartridges, some users opt to purchase refilled cartridges or have empty cartridges refilled by a third-party vendor.

Photo Printers

A **photo printer** is a color printer that produces lab-quality photos (Figure 7-29). Some photo printers print just one or two sizes of photos, for example, 3 × 5 inches and 4 × 6 inches. Others print up to 8 × 10 or even larger. Some even print panoramic photos. Generally, the more sizes the printer prints, the more expensive the printer.

Many photo printers use ink-jet technology. With models that can print letter-sized documents, users connect the photo printer to their computer and use it for all their printing needs. For a few hundred dollars, this type of photo printer is ideal for the home or small business user.

Most photo printers are PictBridge enabled, so that you can print photos without a computer. *PictBridge* is a standard technology that

Figure 7-29 A photo printer.
© iStockphoto / Tamás Ambrits

allows you to print photos directly from a digital camera by connecting a cable from the digital camera to a USB port on the printer. Photo printers also usually have a built-in card slot(s) so that the printer can print digital photos directly from a memory card. Read How To 7-4 on the next page for instructions about printing from a smartphone or tablet.

HOW TO 7-4

Print from a Smartphone or Tablet

As smartphones and tablets become more widely used and packed with features, you may need to print items stored on these devices. For example, you may capture a great photo while spending time with your family and want to print the photo to place on your desk, or you may take notes on your tablet and want to print a hard copy. You have several options available to print from a smartphone or tablet. The method you use will depend primarily on the type of mobile device and printer you are using. If your printer supports printing from a mobile device, the following steps will guide you through the process of printing from a smartphone or tablet:

1. Verify your mobile device or tablet is connected to the same network as the printer.
2. If necessary, download and install an app on your device or tablet to enable you to print. The printer's documentation will inform you if you need an app and, if so, where to obtain it.

3. When you are viewing the item that you want to print on your smartphone or tablet, select the option to print on your printer and then retrieve the printout.

In addition to using an app or built-in features on your mobile device or computer to print, you may be able to configure your printer so that you can attach files and send them to a specified email address. The following steps describe how to use this feature on supported printers:

1. Access your printer's settings and make sure the printer is connected to your network.
2. Configure the option to set up an email address for receiving print jobs and write down that email address.
3. On your computer or mobile device, send the file you want to print as an attachment to an email message addressed to the email address determined in Step 2.
4. When the printer receives the email message with the file attachment, it will print the file.

If your mobile device or printer does not support wireless printing, you also can print

by transferring the file from your smartphone or tablet to your desktop, laptop, or printer. The following steps describe how to print from a smartphone or tablet when wireless printing is not supported:

1. Remove the memory card from your smartphone or tablet and insert it into your desktop, laptop, or printer. *Note:* If your smartphone or tablet does not have a removable memory card, you can connect the smartphone or tablet to a desktop, laptop, or printer using the USB cable included with your device.
2. On the desktop, laptop, or printer, navigate to and select the file you want to print, and then select the option to print the file.
3. When the printer stops, safely remove the memory card from the desktop, laptop, or printer and insert it in your smartphone or tablet.

✷ What are some other reasons why you might want to print from a smartphone or tablet?

Figure 7-30 A laser printer.
Courtesy of Xerox Corporation

🔵 **Internet Research**

How much does toner for a laser printer cost?

Search for: laser printer toner cost comparison

Laser Printers

A **laser printer** is a high-speed, high-quality nonimpact printer (Figure 7-30). Laser printers are available in both black-and-white and color models. A laser printer for personal computers ordinarily uses individual 8½ × 11-inch sheets of paper stored in one or more removable trays that slide in the printer case.

Laser printers print text and graphics in high-quality resolutions. While laser printers usually cost more than ink-jet printers, many models are available at affordable prices for the home user. Laser printers usually print at faster speeds than ink-jet printers.

Depending on the quality, speed, and type of laser printer, the cost ranges from a few hundred to a few thousand dollars for the home and small office user, and several hundred thousand dollars for the enterprise user. Read Ethics & Issues 7-3 to consider whether schools should charge for printed output.

When printing a document, laser printers process and store the entire page before they actually print it. For this reason, laser printers sometimes are called page printers. Storing a page before printing requires that the laser printer has a certain amount of memory in the device. The more memory in the printer, the faster it usually can print.

Operating in a manner similar to a copy machine, a laser printer creates images using a laser beam and powdered ink, called *toner*. The laser beam produces an image on a drum inside the printer. The light of the laser alters the electrical charge on the drum wherever it hits. When this occurs, the toner sticks to the drum and then transfers to the paper through a combination of pressure and heat (Figure 7-31). When the toner runs out, you replace the toner cartridge.

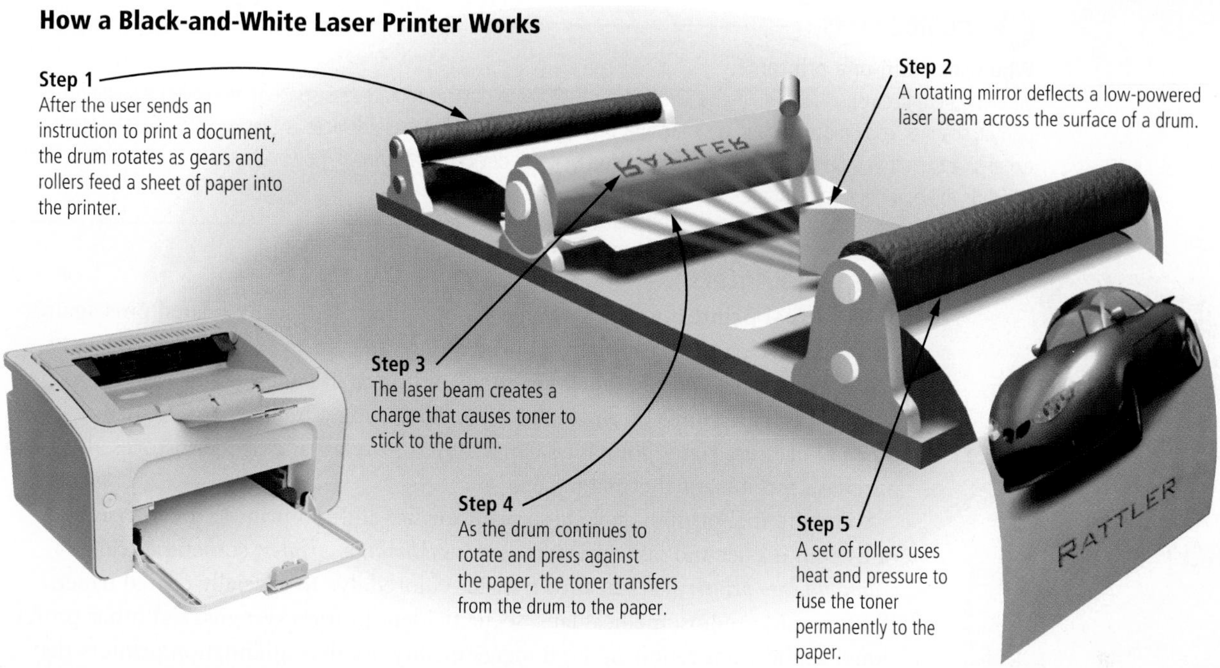

How a Black-and-White Laser Printer Works

Step 1
After the user sends an instruction to print a document, the drum rotates as gears and rollers feed a sheet of paper into the printer.

Step 2
A rotating mirror deflects a low-powered laser beam across the surface of a drum.

Step 3
The laser beam creates a charge that causes toner to stick to the drum.

Step 4
As the drum continues to rotate and press against the paper, the toner transfers from the drum to the paper.

Step 5
A set of rollers uses heat and pressure to fuse the toner permanently to the paper.

Figure 7-31 This figure shows how a black-and-white laser printer works.
© Cengage Learning; © Serg64 / Shutterstock.com

☀ ETHICS & ISSUES 7-3

Should Educational Institutions Charge Students Printing Fees?

After you enroll in a school and pay your tuition, you may have to purchase additional items, such as textbooks and supplies. Should you also be required to pay fees to print assignments for class, or should your tuition include costs associated with printing required assignments? Due to budgetary concerns and to curb excessive or wasteful printing, some colleges and schools require students to pay printing costs. One school's website states that on average 14,000 sheets of paper are recycled in the IT center each week, many of which students sent to the printer but then never picked up.

Printing methods and charges vary, depending on the school. Some include a flat-rate printing charge to all students and then allow unlimited printing. Other schools allot students a per semester quota, after which the school charges per page. Some require students to pay per page using the spending account associated with their student ID. One school, when instituting a printing fee, placed information on its website about how to save search results and other electronic information to encourage students to use less paper. When an instructor requires students to turn in a printed assignment, in most cases the associated printing fee is the student's responsibility.

Should schools charge additional printing fees? Why or why not? How might a printing fee impact the environment? Should instructors consider the school's printing policy when assigning printed papers? Why or why not?

All-in-One Printers

An **all-in-one printer**, also called a *multifunction printer* (MFP), is a single device that looks like a printer or a copy machine but provides the functionality of a printer, scanner, copy machine, and perhaps a fax machine (Figure 7-32). Some use color ink-jet printer technology, while others use laser technology.

Figure 7-32 An all-in-one printer.
Courtesy of Epson America, Inc.

Who uses all-in-one printers?
Small/home office users have all-in-one printers because these devices require less space than having a separate printer, scanner, copy machine, and fax machine. Another advantage of these devices is they are significantly less expensive than if you purchase each device separately. If the device breaks down, however, you lose all four functions, which is the primary disadvantage.

Thermal Printers

A **thermal printer** generates images by pushing electrically heated pins against heat-sensitive paper. Basic thermal printers are inexpensive, but the print quality is low, the images tend to fade over time, and thermal paper can be expensive. Self-service gas pumps often print gas receipts using a built-in, lower-quality thermal printer. Many point-of-sale terminals in retail and grocery stores also print purchase receipts on thermal paper.

Some thermal printers have high print quality and can print at much faster rates than ink-jet and laser printers. A *dye-sublimation printer*, sometimes called a *digital photo printer*, uses heat to transfer colored dye to specially coated paper. Photography studios, medical labs, security identification systems, and other professional applications requiring high image quality use dye-sublimation printers that can cost thousands of dollars (Figure 7-33). Dye-sublimation printers for the home or small business user, by contrast, typically are much slower and less expensive than their professional counterparts. Some are small enough for the mobile user to carry in a briefcase.

Figure 7-33 A dye-sublimation printer.
Courtesy of Mitsubishi Electric Visual Solutions America, Inc.

Mobile Printers

A **mobile printer** is a small, lightweight, battery-powered printer that allows a mobile user to print from a laptop, smartphone, or other mobile device while traveling (Figure 7-34). Barely wider than the paper on which they print, mobile printers fit easily in a briefcase alongside a laptop.

Figure 7-34 A mobile printer is small enough to fit in a backpack.
Courtesy of Brother International Corporation

Mobile printers mainly use ink-jet or thermal technology. Many connect to a USB port. Others have a built-in wireless port through which they communicate with the computer wirelessly.

Label Printers

A **label printer** is a small printer that prints on an adhesive-type material that can be placed on a variety of items such as envelopes, packages, optical discs, photos, and file folders (Figure 7-35). Most label printers also print bar codes. Label printers typically use thermal technology.

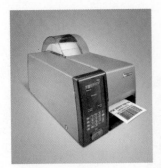

Figure 7-35 A label printer.
Courtesy of Intermec Technologies

Plotters and Large-Format Printers

Plotters are sophisticated printers used to produce high-quality drawings such as blueprints, maps, and circuit diagrams. These printers are used in specialized fields such as engineering and drafting and usually are very costly. Current plotters use a row of charged wires (called styli) to draw an electrostatic pattern on specially coated paper and then fuse toner to the pattern. The printed image consists of a series of very small dots, which provides high-quality output.

Using ink-jet printer technology, but on a much larger scale, a **large-format printer** creates photo-realistic-quality color prints. Graphic artists use these high-cost, high-performance printers for signs, posters, and other professional quality displays (Figure 7-36).

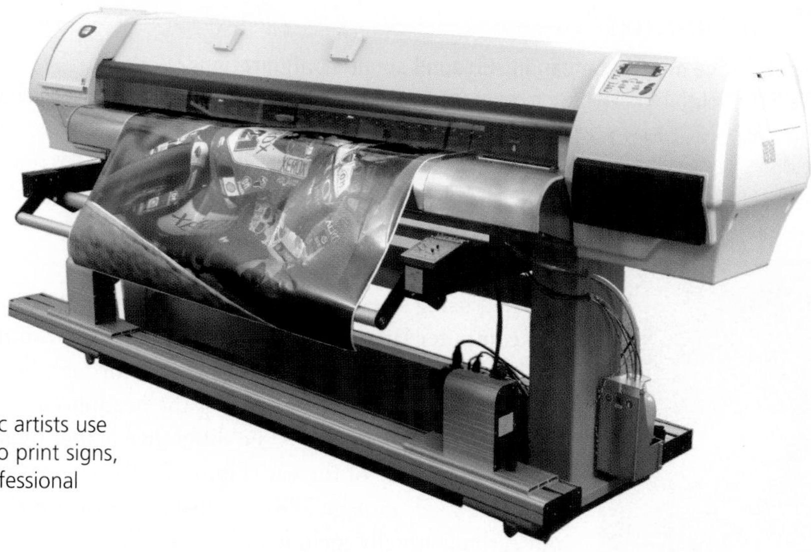

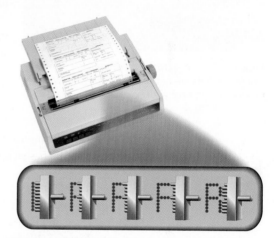

Figure 7-36 Graphic artists use large-format printers to print signs, posters, and other professional quality displays.
Courtesy of Xerox Corporation

🔵 **BTW**
3-D Printing
Innovative Computing:
You should be familiar
with 3-D Printing.

Impact Printers

An **impact printer** forms characters and graphics on a piece of paper by striking a mechanism against an inked ribbon that physically contacts the paper. Impact printers characteristically are noisy because of this striking activity (Figure 7-37). Impact printers are ideal for printing multipart forms because they easily print through many layers of paper. Factories, warehouses, and retail counters may use impact printers because these printers withstand dusty environments, vibrations, and extreme temperatures.

Other Output Devices

In addition to displays and printers, other output devices are available for specific uses and applications. These include speakers, headphones and earbuds, data projectors, interactive whiteboards, and force-feedback game controllers and tactile output.

Figure 7-37 An impact printer produces printed images when tiny pins strike an inked ribbon.
Courtesy of Oki Data Americas, Inc.; © Cengage Learning

Speakers

Most personal computers and mobile devices have a small internal speaker that usually emits only low-quality sound. Thus, many users attach surround sound **speakers** or speaker systems to their computers, game consoles, and mobile devices to generate higher-quality sounds for playing games, interacting with multimedia presentations, listening to music, and viewing movies (Figure 7-38).

Most surround sound computer speaker systems include one or two center speakers and two or more *satellite speakers* that are positioned so that sound emits from all directions. Speakers typically have tone and volume controls, allowing users to adjust settings. To boost the low bass sounds, surround sound speaker systems also include a *subwoofer*.

In some configurations, a cable connects the speakers or the subwoofer to a port on the computer or device. With wireless speakers, however, a transmitter connects to a port on the computer, which wirelessly communicates with the speakers.

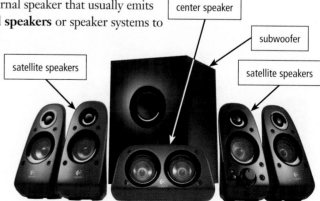

center speaker

subwoofer

satellite speakers

satellite speakers

Figure 7-38 Users often attach high-quality surround sound speaker systems to their computers, game consoles, and mobile devices.
Courtesy of Logitech

 **CONSIDER THIS**

What do the numbers mean in surround sound configurations?
The first number refers to the number of speakers, and the second number refers to the number of subwoofers. For example, a 2.1 speaker system contains two speakers and one subwoofer. A 5.1 speaker system has five speakers (i.e., four satellite speakers, one center speaker) and one subwoofer. A 7.2 speaker system has seven speakers (i.e., four satellite speakers, two side speakers, one center speaker) and two subwoofers.

Figure 7-39 In a crowded environment where speakers are not practical, users can wear headphones to hear audio output.
© Terrie L. Zeller / Shutterstock.com

Headphones and Earbuds

When using speakers, anyone in listening distance can hear the output. In a computer laboratory or other crowded environment, speakers might not be practical. Instead, users can listen through headphones or earbuds so that only the individual wearing the headphones or earbuds hears the sound from the computer. The difference is that **headphones** cover or are placed outside of the ear (Figure 7-39), whereas **earbuds** (shown in Figure 7-23 on page 308) rest inside the ear canal. Both headphones and earbuds usually include noise-cancelling technology to reduce the interference of sounds from the surrounding environment.

A *headset* is a device that functions as both headphones and a microphone (shown in Figure 7-1 on page 289). Computer and smartphone users wear a headset to free their hands for typing and other activities while talking or listening to audio output. Many headsets communicate wirelessly with the computer or mobile device.

As an alternative to headphones, earbuds, or headsets, you can listen to audio from mobile devices, such as a portable media player or smartphone, through speakers in a vehicle or on a stereo system at home or work. Or, you can purchase speakers specifically designed to play audio from the device.

Data Projectors

A **data projector** is a device that takes the text and images displaying on a computer or mobile device screen and projects the images on a larger screen so that an audience can see the image clearly (Figure 7-40). For example, many classrooms use data projectors so that all students easily can see an instructor's presentation on the screen.

Some data projectors are large devices that attach to a ceiling or wall in an auditorium. Others, designed for the mobile user, are small portable devices that can be transported easily. Two types of smaller, lower-cost units are LCD projectors and DLP projectors.

- An *LCD projector*, which uses liquid crystal display technology, attaches directly to a computer or mobile device and uses its own light source to display the information shown on the computer screen. Because LCD projectors tend to produce lower-quality images, users often prefer DLP projectors for their sharper, brighter images.
- A *digital light processing (DLP) projector* uses tiny mirrors to reflect light, which produces crisp, bright, colorful images that remain in focus and can be seen clearly, even in a well-lit room. Some newer televisions use DLP instead of LCD or plasma technology.

data projector

Figure 7-40 A data projector projects an image from a computer or mobile device screen on a larger screen so that an audience easily can see the image.
© iStockphoto / poba; © iStockphoto / Michal Szwedo

Interactive Whiteboards

An **interactive whiteboard** is a touch-sensitive device, resembling a dry-erase board, that displays the image on a connected computer screen, usually via a projector. A presenter controls the program by clicking a remote control, touching the whiteboard, drawing on or erasing the whiteboard with a special digital pen and eraser, or writing on a special tablet. Notes written on the interactive whiteboard can be saved directly on the computer and/or printed. Interactive whiteboards are used frequently in classrooms as a teaching tool (Figure 7-41), during meetings as a collaboration tool, and to enhance delivery of presentations.

Figure 7-41 Teachers and students can write directly on an interactive whiteboard, or they can write on a slate that communicates wirelessly with the whiteboard.
© Bob Daemmrich / Alamy

Force-Feedback Game Controllers and Tactile Output

Joysticks, wheels, gamepads, and motion-sensing game controllers are input devices used to control movements and actions of a player or object in computer games, simulations, and video games. These devices also function as output devices when they include *force feedback*, which is a technology that sends resistance to the device in response to actions of the user (Figure 7-42). For example, as you use the simulation software to drive from a smooth road onto a gravel alley, the steering wheel trembles or vibrates, making the driving experience as realistic as possible. These devices also are used in practical training applications, such as in the military and aviation.

Some input devices, such as a mouse, and mobile devices, such as a smartphone, include *tactile output* that provides the user with a physical response from the device. For example, users may sense a bumping feeling on their hand while scrolling through a smartphone's contact list.

Figure 7-42 Gaming devices often use force feedback, giving the user a realistic experience.
© Vetkit / Dreamstime.com; © shutswis / Shutterstock.com; © Robseguin / Dreamstime.com

Assistive Technology Input and Output

The ever-increasing presence of computers in everyone's lives has generated an awareness of the need to address computing requirements for those who have or may develop physical limitations. The **Americans with Disabilities Act (ADA)** requires any company with 15 or more employees to make reasonable attempts to accommodate the needs of physically challenged workers. Read Ethics & Issues 7-4 on the next page to consider who should pay for assistive technologies.

Besides voice recognition, which is ideal for blind or visually impaired users, several other input options are available. Users with limited hand mobility who want to use a keyboard can

Internet Research

What are new developments related to assistive technologies?

Search for: assistive technology devices

use an on-screen keyboard or a keyboard with larger keys. Users with limited hand movement can use a head-mounted pointer to control the pointer or insertion point (Figure 7-43). To simulate the functions of a mouse button, a user works with switches that control the pointer. The switch might be a hand pad, a foot pedal, a receptor that detects facial motions, or a pneumatic instrument controlled by puffs of air.

For users with mobility, hearing, or vision disabilities, many different types of output options are available. Hearing-impaired users, for example, can instruct programs to display words instead of sounds. Visually impaired users can change screen settings, such as increasing the size or changing the color of the text to make the words easier to read. Instead of using a monitor, blind users can work with voice output. That is, the computer speaks out loud the information that appears on the screen. Another alternative is a Braille printer, which prints information on paper in Braille (Figure 7-44).

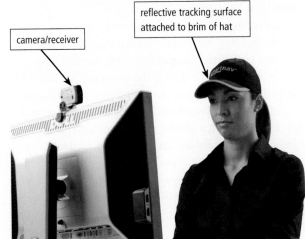

Figure 7-43 A camera/receiver mounted on the monitor tracks the position of the head-mounted pointer, which is the reflective material on the brim of the hat. As the user moves her head, the pointer on the screen also moves.
Courtesy of NaturalPoint, Inc.

Figure 7-44 A Braille printer.
Courtesy of Enabling Technologies;
© Don Farrall / Getty Images

✸ ETHICS & ISSUES 7-4

📄 Who Should Pay for Assistive Technologies?

Public institutions, such as schools and libraries, are required to have doors, restroom facilities, and ramps that can accommodate visitors or students who require wheelchairs or other devices to enter and move about the building. Should the same accommodations be made to those who need assistive technologies? Assistive technologies include devices such as a mouse you can operate with your foot or keyboards, printers, and display devices that use Braille. Many sources are available to fund assistive technologies,

including health insurance and government programs such as Medicare, Medicaid, or Social Security. In addition, private or non-profit groups may provide grants or donations.

Many libraries offer digital versions of books, including digital Braille and audio, for those with visual impairments or dyslexia. Patrons must fill out a request that includes recommendations from a doctor. The Individuals with Disabilities Education Act (IDEA) requires that public schools provide free and appropriate education for all students. Because technology is an

increasingly important part of a student's education, schools are required to purchase or acquire funding for adaptive technologies for students who need them. If a student's parents provide an assistive technology that a student uses at school, the school must pay to repair and service the device.

Should parents of children who need assistive technology devices be required to provide funding or partial funding? Why or why not? What resources should public libraries provide to patrons with disabilities?

⏻ NOW YOU KNOW

Be sure you understand the material presented in the sections Printers, Other Output Devices, and Assistive Technology Input and Output, as it relates to the chapter objectives.
You now should know . . .

- Which type of printer might be suited to your needs (Objective 8)

- When you would use speakers, headphones, earbuds, data projectors, interactive whiteboards, and game controllers (Objective 9)

- Which types of assistive technology options are available (Objective 10)

Quiz Yourself Online: Check your knowledge of related content by navigating to this book's Quiz Yourself resource on Computer Concepts CourseMate and then tapping or clicking Objectives 8–10.

⏻ Chapter Summary

This chapter presented a variety of options for input and output. Input options included the keyboard, mouse and other pointing devices, touch screens, pen input, motion input, voice input, video input, and scanners and reading devices. Output options included displays, printers, speakers, headphones and earbuds, data projectors, interactive whiteboards, and force-feedback game controllers and tactile output. The chapter also presented several assistive technology options for input and output.

Test your knowledge of chapter material by accessing the Study Guide, Flash Cards, and Practice Test apps that run on your smartphone, tablet, laptop, or desktop.

⏻ TECHNOLOGY @ WORK

Space Exploration

Watching the television closely, you hear the announcer count the seconds until the space-craft lifts off from its launchpad: "Three, two, one, and we have liftoff." The engines ignite and the glow from the burning fuel illumi-nates the sky as it begins its journey toward space. As you sit back and watch, mesmer-ized by our ability to launch a spacecraft of such considerable size and weight into space, hundreds of individuals and computers are working behind the scenes to ensure a safe mission.

Because space exploration is filled with risk, it is extremely important that all decisions be made with precision and that personnel are alerted to problems before the problems become too serious. For instance, space vehicles contain a huge amount of sensors that measure environmental variables such as temperature, velocity, position, and altitude. If the sensors return readings outside an acceptable range, computers correct any problems or notify mission managers as necessary. Employees work around

the clock monitoring the output from the spacecraft's sensors while it is in flight and communicating to astronauts any actions required to ensure a continued safe mission.

In addition to keeping the spacecraft safe while in orbit, computers also help guide the spacecraft into and out of orbit. To reach the International Space Station, for example, spacecraft can be launched safely only during specified launch time frames. Once the spacecraft is launched, it must travel in a precise direction at an exact velocity to ensure a successful mission. As the mission nears completion and a capsule containing the astronauts reenters the atmosphere, onboard computers position the capsule precisely so that the extreme

temperatures at the reentry interface do not cause catastrophic damage. Furthermore, these onboard computers help to ensure that the capsule touches down in a safe location. With billions of dollars spent on space travel, computers play a vital role in guaranteeing the safety of the space vehicle, the astronauts, and those of us on Earth.

☀ How else might computers and technology be used in space exploration?

Courtesy of NASA

Study Guide

The Study Guide exercise reinforces material you should know for the chapter exam. You will find answers to items with the ▤ icon only in the e-book.

⊙ **Access the Study Guide app** that runs on your smartphone, tablet, laptop, or desktop by navigating to this book's Apps resource on Computer Concepts CourseMate.

Instructions: Answer the questions below using the format that helps you remember best or that is required by your instructor. Possible formats may include one or more of these options: write the answers; create a document that contains the answers; record answers as audio or video using a webcam, smartphone, or portable media player; post answers on a blog, wiki, or website; or highlight answers in the book/e-book.

1. Define these terms: data, software, and command. Give an example of a user response.

2. List features that are common to most keyboards.

3. Describe how a keyboard shortcut functions.

4. Explain the criminal and beneficial purposes of keyboard monitoring software.

5. Differentiate among compact, ergonomic, gaming, and wireless keyboards.

6. Define the term, pointer. Name objects a pointing device can select.

7. List different mouse types.

8. Describe the following input devices: touchpad, pointing stick, and trackball.

9. Explain how to interact with a touch screen. Outline steps for calibrating a touch screen.

10. Describe security issues surrounding using finger swipes and fingerprints as passwords.

11. ▤ Define the terms, enrollment and matching, with respect to finger-scan technology.

12. Describe how desktop monitors, smartphones, portable media players, digital cameras, kiosks, and navigation systems use touch input.

13. Explain issues surrounding using a mobile device while driving.

14. List methods and devices for using pen input. Define the term, digitizer.

15. Define the term, motion input. Describe how the entertainment industry, military, and medical field use motion input.

16. Name hardware and devices used for voice and audio input.

17. ▤ Name types of voice recognition applications.

18. Outline steps involved in using DV technology.

19. List steps for setting up and using a webcam. Describe webcam security issues.

20. Explain what occurs during a videoconference and the technology needed.

21. Describe types of scanners and reading devices. Explain how to work with QR codes.

22. Explain why a retailer would use RFID technology and how a bank uses MICR technology.

23. Give examples of data collection devices and describe how they are used.

24. Define the term, output. List types of output.

25. ▤ Describe the contributions of Ursula Burns, with regard to document management.

26. Define the terms, display and monitor. Describe different types of monitors.

27. Differentiate among LCD, LED, OLED, and AMOLED technologies.

28. Describe how display quality is determined. Define these terms: native resolution, nit, and candela.

29. Explain the purpose of the GPU.

30. List and describe port types for monitors.

31. ▤ Describe video standards used to define display properties.

32. Describe the technologies used by HDTV. Explain the capabilities of a Smart TV.

33. Explain safety issues surrounding hardware radiation.

34. Describe orientation options for printouts.

35. Explain what is needed for to print using Bluetooth.

36. ▤ Describe the contributions of HP, with respect to printers and other technology products.

37. Explain how an ink-jet printer works.

38. Explain how resolution affects printer quality.

39. Outline steps for printing from a smartphone or tablet.

40. Explain how a photo printer uses PictBridge. Compare the price and quality of laser printers to ink-jet printers.

41. Explain issues surrounding whether an institution should charge students printing fees.

42. Describe the following printer types: all-in-one, thermal, mobile, label, plotter, and impact.

43. Explain how computers and mobile devices use speakers, such as satellite speakers, to emit sound.

44. Differentiate between headphones and earbuds.

45. Define the term, data projector. Differentiate between LCD and DLP projector technology.

46. Describe uses of interactive whiteboards and force-feedback game controllers. Define the term, tactile output.

47. List types of assistive technologies for input and output.

48. Explain issues surrounding payment for assistive technologies.

49. Explain how the space exploration field uses technology.

You should be able to define the Primary Terms and be familiar with the Secondary Terms listed below.

Key Terms

Access the Flash Cards app that runs on your smartphone, tablet, laptop, or desktop by navigating to this book's Apps resource on Computer Concepts CourseMate. **View definitions** for each term by navigating to this book's Key Terms resource on Computer Concepts CourseMate. **Listen to definitions** for each term on your portable media player by navigating to this book's Audio Study Tools resource on Computer Concepts CourseMate.

Primary Terms (shown in **bold-black** characters in the chapter)

all-in-one printer (317)
Americans with
  Disabilities Act
  (ADA) (321)
bar code (305)
bar code reader (305)
data projector (320)
digital pen (297)
digital video (DV)
  camera (300)
display (309)
DV technology (301)
earbuds (320)
graphics tablet (298)

HDTV (311)
headphones (320)
impact printer (319)
ink-jet printer (313)
input (288)
interactive whiteboard (321)
keyboard (290)
label printer (318)
large-format printer (318)
laser printer (316)
LCD (310)
magstripe reader (306)
mobile printer (318)
monitor (310)

mouse (292)
nonimpact printer (313)
OCR devices (304)
OMR devices (305)
output (308)
pen input (297)
photo printer (315)
plotters (318)
pointer (292)
pointing stick (293)
printer (312)
QR code (305)
resolution (310)
RFID (306)

RFID reader (306)
scanner (304)
signature capture
  pad (297)
speakers (319)
stylus (297)
thermal printer (318)
touch screen (294)
touchpad (293)
trackball (294)
video call (302)
videoconference (303)
voice recognition (299)
webcam (302)

Secondary Terms (shown in *italic* characters in the chapter)

active-matrix (310)
air gestures (298)
AMOLED (310)
aspect ratio (311)
audio input (300)
backlight (310)
bar code scanner (305)
Bluetooth printing (312)
candela (311)
command (288)
compact keyboard (291)
contrast ratio (311)
cursor (290)
data (288)
data collection device (307)
digital light processing (DLP)
  projector (320)
digital photo printer (318)
digitizer (298)
display device (309)
DisplayPort (311)
dot pitch (311)
dots per inch (dpi) (314)
DVI (Digital Video Interface)
  port (311)
dye-sublimation printer (318)
ergonomic keyboard (292)

flat-panel display (309)
force feedback (321)
frame rate (301)
function keys (290)
gaming keyboard (292)
gesture (294)
gesture recognition (298)
graphics processing unit
  (GPU) (311)
handwriting recognition
  software (297)
HDMI (High-Definition Media
  Interface) port (311)
headset (320)
high-definition television (311)
insertion point (290)
keyboard monitoring software (291)
keyboard shortcut (290)
keylogging software (291)
landscape orientation (312)
laser mouse (292)
LCD projector (320)
LED display (310)
liquid crystal display (310)
magnetic stripe card reader (306)
MICR devices (307)
motion input (298)

multifunction printer (317)
multi-touch (294)
music production software (300)
native resolution (310)
nit (311)
OCR software (304)
OLED (310)
optical mouse (292)
PictBridge (315)
pixel (310)
pixel pitch (311)
plasma display (312)
portrait orientation (312)
printer backing (313)
printout (312)
QWERTY keyboard (291)
response time (311)
Retina Display (310)
satellite speakers (319)
Smart TV (311)
soft copy (309)
software (288)
source document (303)
speech recognition (300)
streaming cam (302)
subwoofer (319)
tactile output (321)

TFT (310)
toggle key (290)
toner (316)
touch mouse (293)
touch-sensitive pad (296)
trackpad (293)
UPC (Universal Product
  Code) (305)
user response (288)
video input (300)
voice input (299)
voice recognition application (300)
widescreen monitor (311)
wireless keyboard (292)
wireless mouse (293)

Courtesy of Epson America, Inc.

all-in-one printer (317)

Checkpoint

The Checkpoint exercises test your knowledge of the chapter concepts. The page number containing the answer appears in parentheses after each exercise. The Consider This exercises challenge your understanding of chapter concepts.

Complete the Checkpoint exercises interactively by navigating to this book's Checkpoint resource on Computer Concepts CourseMate. **Access the Test Prep app** that runs on your smartphone, tablet, laptop, or desktop by navigating to this book's Apps resource on Computer Concepts CourseMate. After successfully completing the self-assessment through the Test Prep app, **take the Practice Test** by navigating to this book's Practice Test resource on Computer Concepts CourseMate.

True/False   Mark T for True and F for False.

_____ 1. CAPS LOCK and NUM LOCK are two examples of toggle keys. (290)

_____ 2. Kiosks are designed to endure a high volume of use and can be used by hundreds of people per day. (296)

_____ 3. Motion input is utilized by the military for flight simulation and weapon training. (299)

_____ 4. A smaller frame rate results in a smaller file size for a video, as well as a smoother playback. (301)

_____ 5. Optical character recognition (OCR) and optical mark recognition (OMR) are two technologies used by optical readers. (304)

_____ 6. It is important to exercise caution when using QR codes because they may direct your mobile computer or device to a malicious website or file. (305)

_____ 7. A data collection device reads and scans data from a source document. (307)

_____ 8. Most current displays use CRT technology. (309)

_____ 9. Contrast ratio defines a display's width relative to its height. (311)

_____ 10. Every electronic device emits some level of radiation. (312)

_____ 11. Printer resolution is measured by the number of pixels per inch a printer can print. (314)

_____ 12. The Individuals with Disabilities Education Act (IDEA) requires any company with 50 or more employees to make reasonable attempts to accommodate the needs of physically challenged workers. (321)

Multiple Choice   Select the best answer.

1. A _____ is an instruction a user issues by responding to a message displayed by a program or app. (288)
   a. command
   b. user response
   c. keyboard shortcut
   d. function

2. Which of the following is *not* an example of a pointing device? (294)
   a. touchpad
   b. trackball
   c. touch screen
   d. pointing stick

3. Another name for a graphics tablet is a(n) _____. (298)
   a. digitizer
   b. interactive whiteboard
   c. grablet
   d. digital drawing board

4. Air gestures are used in _____. (298)
   a. motion input
   b. voice input
   c. touch input
   d. OCR

5. The United States Postal Service uses the _____ bar code. (305)
   a. UPC   c. POSTNET
   b. MAILTIME   d. FWC

6. LCD displays typically produce color using _____ technology, which uses a separate transistor to supply charges to each liquid crystal cell. (310)
   a. passive-matrix
   b. OLED
   c. Retina Display
   d. active-matrix

7. _____ orientation refers to a printout that is wider than it is tall. (312)
   a. Cinematic
   b. Portrait
   c. Landscape
   d. Widescreen

8. How many subwoofers would a 7.2 speaker system contain? (320)
   a. 1   c. 7
   b. 2   d. 9

Checkpoint

Matching   Match the terms with their definitions.

_____ 1. input (288)

_____ 2. keyboard shortcut (290)

_____ 3. pointing stick (293)

_____ 4. touch-sensitive pad (296)

_____ 5. voice recognition (299)

_____ 6. scanner (304)

_____ 7. resolution (310)

_____ 8. graphics processing unit (311)

_____ 9. headset (320)

_____ 10. interactive whiteboard (321)

a. the number of horizontal and vertical pixels in a display

b. pressure-sensitive pointing device shaped like a pencil eraser that is positioned between keys on a mobile computer keyboard

c. input device that contains buttons and/or wheels you operate with a thumb or other finger

d. device that functions as both headphones and a microphone

e. touch-sensitive device that displays the image on a connected computer screen, usually via projector

f. chip that controls the manipulation and display of graphics on a display device

g. any data and instructions entered into the memory of a computer

h. computer or mobile device's capability of distinguishing spoken words

i. light-sensing input device that reads printed text and graphics and then translates the result into a form the computer can process

j. one or more keyboard keys that you press to perform an operating system or application-related task

Short Answer   Write a brief answer to each of the following questions.

1. Define keyboard monitoring software. (291) List steps you can take to detect it. (291)

2. Define motion input. (298) Name three disciplines in which motion input is being used. (298)

3. Define DV technology. (301) List the steps involved in using DV technology. (301)

4. What is a streaming cam? (302) List steps you can take to prevent unauthorized webcam use. (303)

5. Define printer hacking. (313) List steps you can take to secure printers. (313)

✳ Consider This   Answer the following questions in the format specified by your instructor.

1. Answer the critical thinking questions posed at the end of these elements in this chapter: Ethics & Issues (296, 312, 317, 322), How To (294, 302, 305, 316), Mini Features (295, 298, 301), Secure IT (291, 295, 303, 313), and Technology @ Work (323).

2. What are some examples of data?

3. What happens when you press a toggle key?

4. How could you use keyboard monitoring software for legitimate purposes?

5. What steps do you follow to calibrate a touch screen? 📄 How are operating systems incorporating touch screen technology?

6. What are the steps involved in using DV technology? 📄 What should you consider when purchasing a DV camera?

7. What steps should you take to secure a webcam?

8. For what purpose could you use a QR code?

9. How do LCD, LED, and OLED technologies differ?

10. What does resolution measure?

11. Should you be concerned about the effects of long-term hardware radiation? Why or why not?

12. Why is it necessary to secure a network printer?

13. What type of business uses a high-quality dye-sublimation printer?

14. How do gaming devices use force-feedback technology?

15. Should schools and companies be required to pay for assistive technologies? Why or why not?

✸ How To: Your Turn

The How To: Your Turn exercises present general guidelines for fundamental skills when using a computer or mobile device and then require that you determine how to apply these general guidelines to a specific program or situation.

Instructions: You often can complete tasks using technology in multiple ways. Figure out how to perform the tasks described in these exercises by using one or more resources available to you (such as a computer or mobile device, articles on the web or in print, online or program help, user guides, blogs, podcasts, videos, other individuals, trial and error, etc.). Summarize your 'how to' steps, along with the resource(s) used, in the format requested by your instructor (brief report, presentation, discussion, blog post, video, or other means).

❶ Transfer Movies to a Computer

Whether you record movies on a DV camera, smartphone, tablet, or other device, you eventually may want to transfer the movies to a computer so that you can edit them, send them to others, or post them online. The following steps guide you through the process of transferring movies to a computer.

a. Connect the device or media containing the movie to the computer.

b. When the computer recognizes the device or media containing the movie(s) to transfer, open a window on the computer containing the contents of the connected device or media.

c. Locate the movie or movies you want to transfer to the computer.

d. Transfer the movie to a folder on the computer using one of the following methods:

- Drag the movie from the device or media to an appropriate location on the computer.
- Run the software that came with your camera and use its features to import the movie from the device or media.

e. Play the movie on the computer to make sure it has transferred correctly. If you notice any problems with the movie you import, try copying or importing the movie again.

f. Once you have verified the movie has transferred properly and it plays without issue, if desired, delete the movie from your device or media.

g. Properly remove the device or media from your computer.

Exercises

1. What apps can you use to import and organize your movies?
2. In addition to storing movies on your computer, where else might you store them to protect them from loss?

❷ Record and Edit a Movie

Once you have finished recording a movie, you may want to edit it before sharing it others. For example, you might want to remove portions of the movie, add special effects, or play an audio track instead of the audio recorded with the movie. The following steps guide you through the process of recording and editing a movie.

Record a Movie

a. Verify your camera's battery is charged and that the device has sufficient space available to store the movie you are about to record.

b. If you plan to record the movie from one location, consider placing the camera on a stable surface so that it does not move.

c. If you intend to record outside where it is windy, shield the camera from the wind.

d. Start the recording.

e. If you plan to move the camera during recording, do so with slow, smooth movements.

f. Stop the recording.

Edit a Movie

a. Use the steps presented in Exercise 1 to transfer the movie to a computer.

b. Make a copy of the movie so that you can revert to the original if you make a mistake.

c. Run a video editing program on your computer and open the movie.

d. To trim a movie — that is, remove portions from the beginning and/or end of the movie — tap or click the command to trim the movie. Select the new starting and ending position for the movie.

e. To add a special effect to the movie, select the location in the movie where you want to add the special effect, and then tap or click the command corresponding to the special effect you want to add.

f. To add music that will play while the movie is playing, tap or click the command to add a separate audio track to the movie. Next, navigate to and select the music file you want to add. Finally, select the starting and ending locations in the movie for the music.

g. Preview the movie.

h. Save your changes.

i. Exit the video editing program.

Exercises

1. What reasons might you want to trim a movie?
2. What type of device do you use to record movies? Why?

How To: Your Turn ✳

③ Save as or Print to a PDF File

In an effort to conserve paper, people today think twice before printing a hard copy of a document. Instead of printing a hard copy of a document, many applications have a built-in feature enabling you to print soft copies in various formats, such as PDF. If you have Adobe Acrobat installed on your computer, you can print to a PDF file from just about any application. When you save in or print to a PDF file (both saving in or printing to PDF produce the same results), anyone with an app capable of reading PDFs will be able the view the file without opening it in the same program with which it was created. Several free apps you can use to view PDF files are available. The following steps guide you through the process of printing to a PDF file.

a.   Verify the app from which you want to print has a built-in feature to save files in or print files to PDF format. If this feature is not available, search for and install an app that enables you to save files to or print files in PDF format.

b.   Open the file you want to save in or print to PDF format.

c.   If you want to save the file in PDF format, display the app's Save As dialog box and see if PDF is one of the available file types.

d.   If you want to print the file to a PDF, display the screen to print the file and select the appropriate printer to print the file to PDF.

Source: Microsoft

e.   Tap or click the button to save or print the file.

f.   Specify a file name and save location for the PDF file.

Exercises

1.   What are some applications you can use to view PDF files?

2.   In addition to saving paper, what are some other reasons why you might save or print to a PDF?

④ Obtain and Set a Ringtone

Today's smartphones include a variety of ringtones from which you can choose, but you may decide to download or record and set a custom ringtone. For example, you might want a specific ringtone to identify calls from specific friends. Many ringtones are available for free, while others are available for purchase from your device's app store. The following steps guide you through the process of setting a ringtone using the built-in features on your phone.

a.   If necessary, download or transfer to your phone the audio file you want to use as your ringtone.

b.   Display your phone's settings.

c.   Navigate to the option to set your ringtone.

d.   Select the desired audio file to use as your ringtone.

e.   Some phones allow you to set ringtones for specific contacts. To do this, display the contact's information, select the option to edit it, and then select the new ringtone for the contact.

You also can install third-party apps to obtain and set ringtones on your phone. The following steps guide you through the process of obtaining and setting a ringtone using a third-party app.

a.   Search your device's app store or marketplace for apps that provide ringtones.

b.   Because some ringtone apps can contain malware, search the web for reviews and information about the ringtone app(s) you are planning to download. If any of your research indicates that an app may be unsafe, consider a different app.

c.   Download and install the ringtone app of your choice. Please note that some apps are free to download and some are not. If you do not want to pay for one of these apps, download a safe, free ringtone app.

d.   Run the app.

e.   Locate and select the desired ringtone you want to use.

Exercises

1.   What are some apps you can use to download and install ringtones?

2.   Would you pay to download and install custom ringtones on your phone? Why or why not?

✸ Internet Research

The Internet Research exercises broaden your understanding of chapter concepts by requiring that you search for information on the web.

Instructions: Use a search engine or another search tool to locate the information requested or answers to questions presented in the exercises. Describe your findings, along with the search term(s) you used and your web source(s), in the format requested by your instructor (brief report, presentation, discussion, blog post, video, or other means).

1 Making Use of the Web
Business, Governmental, and Organizational

Accessing the latest business-critical information is essential to understanding the global economy. Politics and governmental regulations play an important role in shaping the policies that guide business decisions. A variety of websites gives useful information and insights into the world of organizations and global markets.

(a) Visit two business websites or download business apps and locate information about one of the companies that manufactures an input or output product described in this chapter. What is the latest news about the company? Locate two governmental websites to see if this company has been the target of governmental regulation or legal challenges. If it is a public company, what is its financial state, and what position are investors taking on buying or selling its stock?

(b) Review workplace policies that have drawn criticism, such as banning telecommuting, imposing dress codes, or not allowing employees at call centers to eat at their office desks. What arguments do employers and the employees make on these issues? Do the articles provide additional resources, such as videos or links to related articles?

(c) Visit the Library of Congress website or download its app and browse its contents. Which collections are highlighted? What resources and programs are available, including podcasts and webcasts? What content is being collected for the National Digital Information Infrastructure and Preservation Program?

2 Social Media 📑

Aspiring musicians have turned to social media to break into the music business and to promote their material. Musical artists are urged to develop accounts on Facebook, Twitter, YouTube, MySpace, and other social media sites to interact and stay connected with their fans. They can post information about concerts and album releases and sell concert tickets. They also can add music that fans can listen to, download at no charge, or purchase. Some social media sites sponsor contests for bands to showcase their talents and vie for fans' votes to play live at a local venue. Others are crowd-funding websites where bands can ask fans to pledge a specific amount of money to support the artists' creative efforts.

View at least two websites that allow listeners to recommend music and share playlists. What similarities and differences do these websites have? Locate one of your favorite artists on a social media site and describe the content displayed. For example, are concerts and new releases being promoted? Then, listen to music channels and describe the types of music available. Which new artists and songs did you hear?

Source: USA.gov

Internet Research

3 Search Sleuth

(1) Which automobile company developed a QR code measuring 1,711 square feet? (2) According to the Smart Card Alliance, what is the maximum distance at which a contactless smart card operates? (3) Who are the current MIDI Manufacturers Association (MMA) executive board members, and what companies do they represent? (4) How is the term, disability, defined in the Americans with Disabilities Act? (5) Which television network was the first to broadcast a high-definition signal in 1997? (6) What product did HP develop in 2004 based on the efforts of engineer Daryl Anderson? (7) Which country has imposed a maximum limit of 100 decibels produced on all portable media players sold? (8) Which countries have adopted the ENERGY STAR program? (9) What is the function of a Bayer filter in a digital camera? (10) When Tom Cranston, Fred Longstaff, and Kenyton Taylor invented the trackball in 1952, which object did they use as the ball?

© iStockphoto / peng wu

4 Green Computing

The U.S. Environmental Protection Agency (EPA) introduced the ENERGY STAR program in 1992 in an effort to urge consumers to purchase energy-efficient products. The first ENERGY STAR-qualified products were computers and monitors, and printers were added the following year. Four years later, the EPA partnered with the U.S. Department of Energy. These agencies state that consumers can reduce their energy bills by one-third by switching to energy-efficient household products and undertaking remodeling projects that improve home comfort while decreasing greenhouse gas emissions.

Examine several televisions, washers, dryers, refrigerators, appliances, mobile phones, computers, or monitors in your home, school, or dormitory to see if they have ENERGY STAR logos. Look up these models on the ENERGY STAR website and assess their energy efficiency. Read about common energy-draining problems found in homes and possible solutions. Then, assess your home's energy efficiency. What improvements can you make to help protect the environment? Which settings can you adjust on your display to save energy? What changes can you make to your software to conserve electricity?

5 Security

Issued in 2013, Executive Order 13636, *Improving Critical Infrastructure Cybersecurity*, directs government agencies to increase sharing classified computer security information with private companies that provide or support the country's critical infrastructure. These companies likely are targets of cyberattacks and provide services such as air traffic control, natural gas supplies, water treatment, power plants, and finance. Under the order, federal agencies must comply with and routinely assess privacy standards and civil liberties protections. The government must share information regarding the cyberthreats, such as malicious code found on networks, but not contents of personal email messages. The private companies are urged to adopt the security incentives and increase their security systems, but participation is voluntary.

Locate Executive Order 13636 and read its contents. Then, research news articles describing lawmakers' and businesses' support and criticism of this order. What components of this order were proposed to increase the nation's cybersecurity? What positions do the Internet Security Alliance and The Internet Association take on this matter? What efforts has Congress made to pass legislation addressing computer security?

6 Ethics in Action

"Netomania" is not a recognized disorder, but this popular name for Internet Addiction Disorder (IAD) may be affecting approximately 12 percent of U.S. Internet users who spend many hours gaming, social networking, and shopping. People may be addicted when they spend up to 10 hours a day online, they occasionally binge for extended Internet sessions, and they suffer withdrawal symptoms when they have not been online for some time. Some researchers, however, believe the Internet problem is just a symptom of other psychiatric abnormalities, such as bipolar disorder.

Locate articles that discuss IAD. What are specific signs and symptoms of Internet addiction? To which types of websites are males more likely to become addicted? To which types of websites are females more likely to become addicted? Which risk factors may lead to Internet addiction? Which self-help tips may help break Internet addiction? Which organizations are opposed to classifying IAD as an addition? Why do they claim this behavior is a compulsion and not an addiction or a specific disorder? What are the components of the Internet Addiction Test, and which countries have validated this test?

✳ Problem Solving

The Problem Solving exercises extend your knowledge of chapter concepts by seeking solutions to practical problems with technology that you may encounter at home, school, work, or with nonprofit organizations. The Collaboration exercise should be completed with a team.

💻 Challenge yourself with additional Problem Solving exercises by navigating to this book's Problem Solving resource on Computer Concepts CourseMate.

Instructions: You often can solve problems with technology in multiple ways. Determine a solution to the problems in these exercises by using one or more resources available to you (such as a computer or mobile device, articles on the web or in print, blogs, podcasts, videos, television, user guides, other individuals, electronics or computer stores, etc.). Describe your solution, along with the resource(s) used, in the format requested by your instructor (brief report, presentation, discussion, blog post, video, or other means).

Personal

1. **Input Device Not Recognized**   You connected a new touchpad to your computer using a USB connection, but the computer is not recognizing the new device. What are your next steps?

2. **Wrong Paper Tray**   You are trying to print a photo on your photo printer. Each time you print the photo, the printer prints it on regular paper instead of the paper loaded in the photo tray. What can you do to resolve this issue?

3. **Touch Gestures Not Working**   You are using the stretch touch gesture to zoom in on your mobile device. Each time you perform the gesture, however, instead of zooming, one of your fingers appears to be dragging an item around the screen. What might be the problem?

© Andrew Donehue / Shutterstock.com

4. **Dim Screen**   While using your laptop, the screen suddenly becomes dim. You set the brightness to its highest setting before it dimmed and wonder why it suddenly changed. After resetting the brightness to its highest setting, you continue working. What might have caused the screen to dim?

5. **Malfunctioning Earbud**   While listening to music on your portable media player, one side of your earbuds suddenly stops working. What might have caused this?

Professional

6. **Printer Problem**   You are attempting to print on your wireless printer from your laptop, but each time you tap or click the Print button, you receive an error message that the printer is not connected. What are your next steps?

7. **Voice Input Issues**   You are using voice input with speech recognition software on your computer; however, the software does not appear to be recognizing what you are saying. What steps can you take to correct this problem?

8. **Fingerprints Not Recognized**   To increase security, your company now requires employees to sign in to their computers using a fingerprint reader instead of entering a user name and password. This past weekend, you cut the finger you use to sign in, and your computer now does not recognize your fingerprint. As a result, you are unable to access your computer. What are your next steps?

9. **Access Denied**   Your company uses security badges with embedded RFID tags to authenticate the rooms to which employees have access. This badge also grants employees access to the company's parking lot. When arriving at work one morning, you wave your badge in front of the RFID reader, but the gate that allows access to the parking lot does not open. In addition, a red light blinks on the RFID reader. What are your next steps?

10. **Monitors Reversed**   You have two monitors set up on your desk at work: the monitor on the left is your primary monitor and displays the taskbar and the applications you are currently using, and you typically use the monitor on the right to display an email program. When you arrive at work and sign in to your Windows account, you realize that the monitor on the right is now the primary monitor. What might have happened?

Collaboration

11. **Technology in Space Exploration**   The space tourism industry is gaining worldwide attention. Many more people might express interest in experiencing space travel if prices become more reasonable and safety concerns are minimized. Technology helps ensure safety by helping the space vehicles to fly with great precision, but human intervention also is necessary. Form a team of three people and determine how computer output can provide enough information to ensure a safe experience. One team member should research current space exploration and data returned from space vehicles that proves useful. Another team member should research how space vehicles collect this data and present it in a useful form, and the other team member should think of additional ways that computer output can assist in space exploration. Write a brief report summarizing your findings.

The Critical Thinking exercises challenge your assessment and decision-making skills by presenting real-world situations associated with chapter concepts. The Collaboration exercise should be completed with a team.

Critical Thinking

 Challenge yourself with additional Critical Thinking exercises by navigating to this book's Critical Thinking resource on Computer Concepts CourseMate.

Instructions: Evaluate the situations below, using personal experiences and one or more resources available to you (such as articles on the web or in print, blogs, podcasts, videos, television, user guides, other individuals, electronics or computer stores, etc.). Perform the tasks requested in each exercise and share your deliverables in the format requested by your instructor (brief report, presentation, discussion, blog post, video, or other means).

1. Class Discussion

Bar Codes versus RFID   You work as an efficiency analyst at one of the largest retail companies in the world, with multiple stores in every state, as well as in many other countries. For the past 25 years, the company has used bar code readers at checkout counters that scan the bar code on products to determine from a database the price to charge customers and to keep a record of inventory. The company is considering replacing the bar codes and bar code readers with RFID. Analyze and discuss the impact such a change would have on the company, its suppliers, and its customers. Include in your discussion any security risks. Find two examples of RFID readers and compare prices, user reviews, and features. Are handheld options for RFID readers available for store clerks to use on the store floor or for customer checkout? Compile your findings. List advantages and disadvantages of implementing RFID. Include information about reliability and costs.

to / Ignard Karel Maria ten Have

2. Research and Share

Carpal Tunnel Syndrome   While attending college for the past two years, you have worked part-time as a data entry clerk. Recently, you began to feel a pain in your right wrist. Your doctor diagnosed the problem as carpal tunnel syndrome, which is the most well-known of a series of musculoskeletal disorders that fall under the umbrella of repetitive strain injuries (RSIs). Your doctor made several recommendations to relieve the pain. You want to learn more about this debilitating injury. Use the web to investigate carpal tunnel syndrome. Research the carpal tunnel syndrome warning signs and risk factors. Find suggestions about proper workstation ergonomics to avoid carpal tunnel syndrome. Evaluate the differences among various treatment options. Does insurance typically cover treatment? Include in your discussion the average length of time of recovery. How should you change your workspace to help heal and prevent further damage? Should the company's insurance pay for changes to your workspace? Why or why not?

3. Case Study

Farmers' Market   You are the new manager for a group of organic farmers who have a weekly market in season. You recently hired a part-time employee who is visually impaired. The market's board of directors has asked you to assess your current input and output devices and make recommendations for assistive technologies. The new employee will need to input data and review on-screen and printed information in order to ensure accuracy and to identify trends. Use the web to find information about assistive input devices, such as voice recognition and larger keyboards. Research output devices, such as large screen monitors and Braille printers. In addition to devices, research assistive software that you can install on existing computers and devices shared by others. Find reviews from users of these assistive devices. Research costs for implementation, and find information about any grants your company can apply for as a nonprofit to ease the costs. Compile your findings.

Collaboration

4. Printer Comparison   You work for a local real estate agency as an IT consultant. The agency needs a new, networked printer it can use to print high-quality, custom color brochures for the homes it is showing. Each brochure is printed double-sided on glossy paper, and the agency prints an average of 200 per week. Figure 7-26 on page 313 lists several questions to consider when choosing a printer. Form a three-member team. Divide the questions among your team. Each team member should answer each question according to what the employer needs. Then, each team member should use the web to research at least two printers that meet the requirements. Meet with your team, and discuss and compile your findings. Share information about the printers you researched, describe their features, and evaluate their advantages and disadvantages. Identify any additional questions you might have for the employer, such as needs for wireless printing and printing from mobile devices. Which printer you would recommend? Why?

✳ Beyond the Book

The Beyond the Book exercises expand your understanding of chapter concepts by requiring research.

💻 **Access premium content** by visiting Computer Concepts CourseMate. If you have a Computer Concepts CourseMate access code, you can reinforce and extend your learning with MindTap Reader, practice tests, video, and other premium content for Discovering Computers. To sign in to Computer Concepts CourseMate at www.cengagebrain.com, you first must create a student account and then register this book, as described at www.cengage.com/ct/studentdownload.

Part 1 Instructions: Use the web or e-book to perform the task identified for each book element below. Describe your findings, along with the search term(s) you used and your web source(s), if appropriate, in the format requested by your instructor (brief report, presentation, discussion, blog post, video, or other means).

1. **Animation** 📱 Review the animation associated with this chapter and then answer the question(s) it poses (301). What search term would you use to learn more about a specific segment of the animation?

2. **Consider This** Select a Consider This in this chapter (291, 292, 293, 294, 296, 300, 304, 306, 312, 314, 318, 320) and find a recent article that elaborates on the topic. What information did you find that was not presented in this book or e-book?

3. **Drag-and-Drop Figures** 📱 Complete the Drag-and-Drop Figure activities associated with this chapter (290, 304, 315, 317). What did you learn from each of these activities?

4. **Ethics & Issues** Select an Ethics & Issues in this chapter (296, 312, 317, 322) and find a recent article that supports one view presented. Does the article change your opinion about the topic? Why or why not?

5. **Facebook & Twitter** Review a recent Discovering Computers Facebook post or Twitter Tweet and read the referenced article(s). What did you learn from the article?

6. **High-Tech Talk** 📱 Locate topics related to how biometric technology, including finger-scan technology, uses enrollment and matching. Would you recommend the article you found? Why or why not?

7. **How To** Select a How To in this chapter (294, 302, 305, 316) and find a recent article that elaborates on the topic. Who would benefit from the content of this article? Why?

8. **Innovative Computing** 📱 Locate two additional facts about 3-D printing or assistive technology programs. Do your findings change your opinion about the future of this innovation? Why or why not?

9. **Internet Research** Use the search term in an Internet Research (292, 293, 297, 298, 299, 305, 310, 314, 316, 320, 321) to answer the question posed in the element. What other search term could you use to answer the question?

10. **Mini Features** Locate an article that discusses topics related to one of the mini features in this chapter (295, 298, 301). Do you feel that the article is appropriate for this course? Why or why not?

11. **Secure IT** Select a Secure IT in this chapter (291, 295, 303, 313) and find a recent article about the topic that you find interesting. How can you relate the content of the article to your everyday life?

12. **Technology @ Work** Locate three additional, unique usages of technology in the space exploration industry (323). What makes the use of these technologies unique to the space exploration industry?

13. **Technology Innovators** 📱 Locate two additional facts about Logitech, Douglas Engelbart, Ursula Burns, and HP. Which Technology Innovator impresses you most? Why?

14. **Third-Party Links** 📱 Visit one of the third-party links identified in this chapter (291, 294, 295, 296, 298, 301, 303, 304, 305, 312, 313, 315, 317, 322, 323) and read the article or watch the video associated with the link. Would you share this link on your online social network account? Why or why not?

Part 2 Instructions: Find specific instructions for the exercises below in the e-book or on Computer Concepts CourseMate. Beside each exercise is a brief description of its online content.

1. 📱 **You Review It** Search for and review a video, podcast, or blog post about current models and features of digital cameras and product reviews.

2. 📱 **Windows and Mac** Enhance your understanding and knowledge about using Windows and Mac computers by completing the Taking Screen Shots and Setting Screen Password activities.

3. 📱 **Android, iOS, and Windows Phone** Enhance your understanding of mobile devices by completing the Taking Screen Shots and Search by Voice activities.

4. 📱 **Exploring Computer Careers** Read about a career as a graphic designer, search for related employment ads, and then answer related questions.

5. 📱 **App Adventure** Plan your next trip using travel apps on your smartphone or tablet.

8

Digital Storage
Preserving on Media and in the Cloud

Users have a variety of storage options available.

"I use cloud storage for all my homework files. I transfer my digital photos from an SD card to my laptop's hard drive, which has plenty of extra space for my music. Weekly, I back up files from my computer to an external hard drive. What other types of storage could I need?"

True, you may be familiar with some of the material in this chapter, but do you know . . .

How to recover a file you accidentally delete?

How to replace a hard disk or SSD?

Which type of backup plan best meets your needs?

Why various RAID levels exist and the purpose of each?

What prompted the Sarbanes-Oxley Act?

Why you would use a geotag?

How RECAPTCHAs are used to digitize newspapers and books?

Where you might see an SSD?

How to protect your credit card?

How the manufacturing industry relies on computers, mobile devices, and related technologies?

Which reference apps are most suited to your needs?

How to fix a scratch on an optical disc?

Which online retailer started its shipping operations in a garage?

Why you might need a card reader/writer?

For these answers and to discover much more information essential to this course, read this chapter and visit the associated Computer Concepts CourseMate at www.cengagebrain.com.

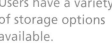

© Andresr / Shutterstock.com

✔ Objectives

After completing this chapter, you will be able to:

1 Differentiate between storage and memory
2 Describe the characteristics of internal hard disks
3 Identify uses of external hard disks and RAID
4 Describe the benefits of solid-state drives
5 Differentiate among various types of memory cards and USB flash drives
6 Discuss the benefits and uses of cloud storage
7 Describe characteristics of and differentiate among types of optical discs
8 Explain types of enterprise storage: RAID, NAS, SAN, and tape
9 Identify uses of magnetic stripe cards, smart cards, RFID tags, and microfilm and microfiche

Storage

A storage medium, also called *secondary storage*, is the physical material on which a computer keeps data, information, programs, and applications. Examples of storage media include internal hard disks, external hard disks, solid-state drives (SSDs), memory cards, USB flash drives, optical discs, network attached storage devices, magnetic stripe cards, smart cards, RFID tags, and microfilm. Cloud storage is another storage option, in which the actual online storage media used is transparent to the user. Figure 8-1 shows a variety of storage options.

BTW

Hard Drives
The term, *internal hard drive*, sometimes is used to refer collectively to hard disks and SSDs inside a computer. Similarly, the term, *external hard drive*, may be used to refer globally to external hard disks and external SSDs.

In addition to programs and apps, users store a variety of data and information on storage media in their computers and mobile devices or on cloud storage. For example, many users store digital photos, appointments, schedules, contacts, email messages and other correspondence, and tax records. A home user also might store budgets, bank statements, a household inventory, records of stock purchases, homework assignments, recipes, music, home movies, and videos. In addition or instead, a business user stores reports, financial records, travel records, customer orders and invoices, vendor payments, payroll records, inventory records, presentations, quotations, and contracts. Business and power users store diagrams, drawings, blueprints, designs, marketing literature, corporate newsletters, and product catalogs.

A **storage device** is the hardware that records and/or retrieves items to and from storage media. **Writing** is the process of transferring data, instructions, and information from memory to a storage medium. **Reading** is the process of transferring these items from a storage medium into memory. When storage devices write on storage media, they are creating output. Similarly, when storage devices read from storage media, they function as a source of input. Nevertheless, they are categorized as storage devices, not as input or output devices.

Storage Capacity

Capacity is the number of bytes (characters) a storage medium can hold. Table 8-1 on page 338 identifies the terms manufacturers may use to define the capacity of storage media. For example, a storage medium with a capacity of 750 GB can hold approximately 750 billion bytes.

 CONSIDER THIS ⎯⎯⎯⎯⎯⎯⎯⎯⎯⎯⎯⎯⎯⎯⎯⎯⎯⎯⎯⎯⎯⎯⎯⎯⎯

What can a gigabyte store?
The total number of items that can be stored in a gigabyte will vary, depending on resolution and a variety of other factors. As a general guide, though, a gigabyte can hold approximately 500,000 pages of text, 600 average-resolution photos, 250 average-length songs, 4 hours of low-resolution video, or 15 minutes of high-definition video.

internal hard disk

external hard disk

solid-state drive

memory cards

microfilm

USB flash drive

RFID tag

cloud storage

smart card

storage

magnetic stripe card

network attached storage device

optical discs

Figure 8-1   A variety of storage options.

Storage requirements among users vary greatly. Home users, small/home office users, and mobile users typically have much smaller storage requirements than enterprise users. For example, a home user may need 1 to 2 TB (trillions of bytes) of storage, while enterprises may require 20 to 40 PB (quadrillions of bytes) of storage.

Table 8-1	Terms Used to Define Storage	
Storage Term	**Approximate Number of Bytes**	**Exact Number of Bytes**
Kilobyte (KB)	1 thousand	2^{10} or 1,024
Megabyte (MB)	1 million	2^{20} or 1,048,576
Gigabyte (GB)	1 billion	2^{30} or 1,073,741,824
Terabyte (TB)	1 trillion	2^{40} or 1,099,511,627,776
Petabyte (PB)	1 quadrillion	2^{50} or 1,125,899,906,842,624
Exabyte (EB)	1 quintillion	2^{60} or 1,152,921,504,606,846,976
Zettabyte (ZB)	1 sextillion	2^{70} or 1,180,591,620,717,411,303,424
Yottabyte (YB)	1 septillion	2^{80} or 1,208,925,819,614,629,174,706,176

 Internet Research

What is the largest storage capacity available today?

Search for: largest storage medium bytes

BTW

DNA Storage
Innovative Computing: You should be familiar with the innovation of DNA as long-term storage.

Storage versus Memory

Items on a storage medium remain intact even when you turn off a computer or mobile device. Thus, a storage medium is nonvolatile. Most memory (i.e., RAM), by contrast, holds data and instructions temporarily and, thus, is volatile. Figure 8-2 illustrates this concept of volatility.

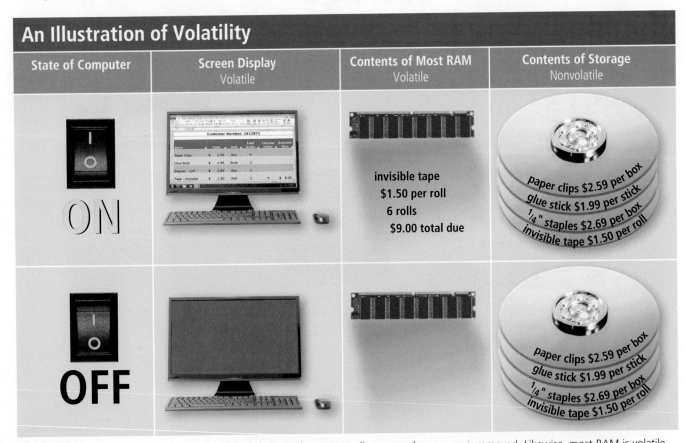

Figure 8-2 A screen display is considered volatile because its contents disappear when power is removed. Likewise, most RAM is volatile. That is, their contents are erased when power is removed from a computer or mobile device. Storage, by contrast, is nonvolatile. Its contents remain when power is off.

✲ CONSIDER THIS

How do storage and memory interact?

When you turn on a computer or mobile device, it locates the operating system on its storage medium and loads the operating system into its memory (specifically, RAM). When you issue a command to run an application, such as a browser, the operating system locates the application on a storage medium and loads it into memory (RAM). When you are finished using the application, the operating system removes it from RAM, but the application remains on the storage medium.

A storage medium is similar to a filing cabinet that holds file folders, and memory is similar to the top of your desk. When you want to work with a file, you remove it from the filing cabinet (storage medium) and place it on your desk (memory). When you are finished with the file, you remove it from your desk (memory) and return it to the filing cabinet (storage medium).

Storage Access Times

The speed of storage devices and memory is defined by access time. **Access time** measures (1) the amount of time it takes a storage device to locate an item on a storage medium or (2) the time required to deliver an item from memory to the processor. The access time of storage devices is slow, compared with the access time of memory. Memory (chips) accesses items in billionths of a second (nanoseconds). Storage devices, by contrast, access items in thousandths of a second (milliseconds) or millionths of a second (microseconds).

Instead of, or in addition to, access time, some manufacturers state a storage device's transfer rate because it affects access time. *Transfer rate* is the speed with which data, instructions, and information transfer to and from a device. Transfer rates for storage are stated in *KBps* (kilobytes per second), *MBps* (megabytes per second), and *GBps* (gigabytes per second).

Numerous types of storage media and storage devices exist to meet a variety of users' needs. Figure 8-3 shows how different types of storage media and memory compare in terms of transfer rates and uses. This chapter discusses these and other storage media.

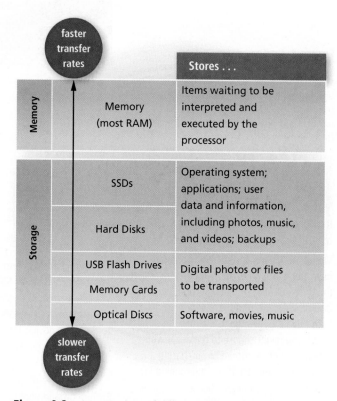

Figure 8-3 A comparison of different types of storage media and memory in terms of relative speed and uses. Memory is faster than storage but is expensive and not practical for all storage requirements. Storage is less expensive but is slower than memory.
© Cengage Learning

Hard Disks

A **hard disk**, also called a *hard disk drive* (*HDD*), is a storage device that contains one or more inflexible, circular platters that use magnetic particles to store data, instructions, and information. Depending on how the magnetic particles are aligned, they represent either a 0 bit or a 1 bit. Recall from Chapter 7 that a bit (binary digit) is the smallest unit of data a computer can process. Thus, the alignment of the magnetic particles represents the data.

Desktops and laptops often contain at least one hard disk. The entire hard disk is enclosed in an airtight, sealed case to protect it from contamination. A hard disk that is mounted inside the computer's case sometimes is called a *fixed disk* because it is not portable (Figure 8-4 on the next page). Some people use a second hard disk to duplicate the contents of the first hard disk, in case the first is damaged or destroyed. Read How To 8-1 on the next page for instructions about replacing internal hard drives (hard disks or SSDs) and adding a second one. Read How To 8-2 on page 341 for instructions about transferring files from one internal hard drive to another.

BTW

Al Shugart
Technology Innovator:
You should be familiar
with Al Shugart (storage
pioneer).

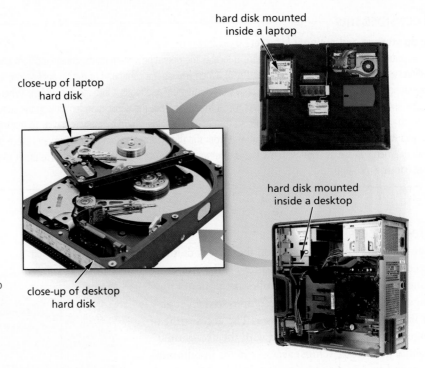

hard disk mounted inside a laptop

close-up of laptop hard disk

hard disk mounted inside a desktop

close-up of desktop hard disk

Figure 8-4 The hard disk in a personal computer is enclosed inside an airtight, sealed case. In these photos of the desktop and laptop hard disks, the top plate is removed for illustration purposes. The laptop hard disk is much smaller than the desktop hard disk.
© Kitch Bain / Shutterstock.com; © ludodesign / Fotolia;
© Oleksiy Maksymenko Photography / Alamy

 HOW TO 8-1

Replace an Internal Hard Drive or Add a Second One

Various situations arise where you might need to replace an existing internal hard drive (hard disk or SSD) or add a second one (hard disk or SSD). For example, if your existing hard drive is beginning to malfunction or has failed, you might choose to replace it with a new hard drive instead of purchasing a brand-new computer. If you are running low on disk space, you might choose to replace your existing hard drive with a new, larger hard disk, or you might add a second hard disk to your computer. If you are planning to add a second internal hard drive to your computer, review your computer's documentation to be certain it can support multiple internal hard drives.

The following steps describe how to replace an internal hard drive or add a second one. Many users seek the services of a professional for this task. The following instructions are designed to present the general steps required and are not meant to serve as a substitute for any documentation provided by the manufacturer of your computer or internal hard drive. If you choose to perform these tasks yourself, be sure to wear an antistatic wristband while accessing components inside the computer to protect it from static electricity.

Removing an Existing Internal Hard Drive (Hard Disk or SSD)

If you are replacing an internal hard drive, the first step is to remove the existing one:

1. Before removing the internal hard drive, back up any necessary data. If you plan to dispose of the internal hard drive, you also should erase its contents.
2. Turn off and unplug the computer. If you are removing the internal hard drive from a mobile computer with a removable battery, remove the battery.
3. Open the computer cover or access panel to gain access to the internal hard drive.
4. If the internal hard drive is secured with one or more screws, remove the screws with a nonmagnetic screwdriver.
5. Unseat the internal hard drive from its location and carefully unplug the cables that are connected to it.

Installing an Internal Hard Drive (Hard Disk or SSD)

If you are replacing an internal hard drive or adding a second one, the following steps guide you through the process of installing the new internal hard drive in a computer. Before installing a new internal hard drive, make sure you purchase one that is compatible with your computer.

1. Place the new internal hard drive in the correct location.
2. Connect the cables and, if necessary, tighten the screws to secure the internal hard drive in place.
3. Replace the computer cover, reconnect the power, and, if necessary, replace the battery.
4. Turn on the computer. If you are replacing your existing internal hard drive, because most new ones do not have an operating system installed, insert your operating system's installation media to begin the installation process. If you are adding a second internal hard drive, after you turn on your computer and the operating system finishes loading, be certain it recognizes your second internal hard drive. If it does not, you may need to contact the manufacturer of the internal hard drive.

✴ Would you benefit from replacing your internal hard drive or adding a second one? Why or why not?

HOW TO 8-2

Transfer Files from One Internal Hard Drive to Another

If you are replacing an existing internal hard drive (hard disk or SSD), you may want to transfer the files from one internal hard drive to another one. The following list describes ways to transfer files from one internal hard drive to another.

- Connect the new internal hard drive as a second internal hard drive in your computer (more information about installing a second internal hard drive can be found in How To 8-1). When the operating system finishes loading, use the file manager in the operating system to drag the files you want to transfer from the original internal hard drive to the second one.
- Use a docking station or an external enclosure to connect the second internal hard drive to the computer that contains the original internal hard drive. (An enclosure is a case that contains the

same adapters found on a motherboard with which to connect the internal hard drive. The enclosure usually connects to a computer through a USB port.) Use the file manager in the operating system to move or copy files from the original internal hard drive to the new one.

Courtesy of Xigmatek

- Move or copy the files you want to transfer from the original internal hard drive to a separate storage device, such as a USB flash drive, or to a cloud storage provider. Next, connect the second internal hard drive and then move or copy the files from the storage device or cloud storage provider to the second internal hard drive.
- Install and run a program designed to transfer files from an old internal hard drive to a new one. Some programs not only will transfer files but also may transfer programs and settings.

⚛ If you are purchasing a new internal hard drive, what types of files might you want to transfer from your existing internal hard drive? What types of files would you not transfer? Why?

Characteristics of a Hard Disk

The storage capacity of hard disks varies and is determined by the number of platters the hard disk contains, the composition of the magnetic coating on the platters, whether it uses longitudinal or perpendicular recording, and its density.

- A *platter* is made of aluminum, glass, or ceramic and has a thin coating of alloy material that allows items to be recorded magnetically on its surface.
- *Longitudinal recording* aligns the magnetic particles horizontally around the surface of the disk. With *perpendicular recording*, by contrast, hard disks align the magnetic particles vertically, or perpendicular to the disk's surface, making much greater storage capacities possible (Figure 8-5).
- *Density* is the number of bits in an area on a storage medium. A higher density means more storage capacity.

⚛ **BTW**

Traditional Hard Disks
Magnetic hard disks sometimes are called traditional hard disks.

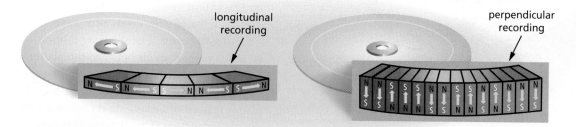

Figure 8-5   Magnetic particles are aligned horizontally in longitudinal recording and vertically in perpendicular recording.

© Cengage Learning

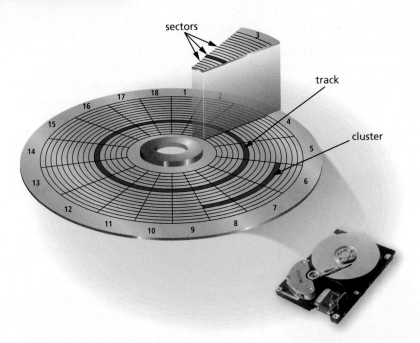

Figure 8-6   Tracks form circles on the surface of a hard disk. The disk's storage locations are divided into wedge-shaped sections, which break the tracks into small arcs called sectors. Several sectors form a cluster.
© Cengage Learning; © Gilmanshin / Shutterstock.com

Hard disks are read/write storage media. That is, you can read from and write on a hard disk any number of times. Before any data can be read from or written on a hard disk, however, the disk must be formatted. *Formatting* is the process of dividing the disk into tracks and sectors (Figure 8-6) so that the operating system can store and locate data and information on the disk. A *track* is a narrow recording band that forms a full circle on the surface of the disk. The disk's storage locations consist of wedge-shaped sections, which break the tracks into small arcs called *sectors*. On a hard disk, a sector typically stores up to 512 bytes of data. Sometimes, a sector has a flaw and cannot store data. When you format a disk, the operating system marks these bad sectors as unusable.

On desktops, the platters most often have a form factor (size) of approximately 3.5 inches in diameter. On laptops, mobile devices, and some servers, the form factor is 2.5 inches or less. A typical hard disk has multiple platters stacked on top of one another. Each platter has two read/write heads, one for each side. A **read/write head** is the mechanism that reads items and writes items in the drive as it barely touches the disk's recording surface. A head actuator on the hard disk attaches to arms that move the read/write heads to the proper location on the platter (Figure 8-7).

While the computer is running, the platters in the hard disk rotate at a high rate of speed. This spinning, which usually is 5,400 to 15,000 *revolutions per minute* (*rpm*), allows nearly instant access to all tracks and sectors on the platters. The platters may continue to spin until power is removed from the computer, or more commonly today, the platters stop spinning or slow down after a specified time to save power. The spinning motion creates a cushion of air between the platter and its read/write head. This cushion ensures that the read/write head floats above the platter instead of making direct contact with the platter surface. The distance between the read/write head and the platter is about two-millionths of one inch.

How a Hard Disk Works

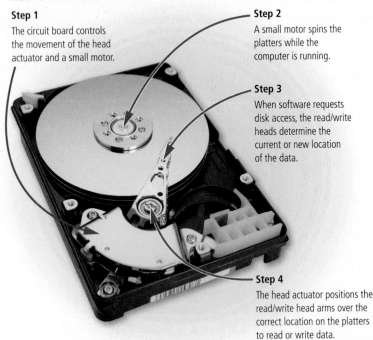

Step 1
The circuit board controls the movement of the head actuator and a small motor.

Step 2
A small motor spins the platters while the computer is running.

Step 3
When software requests disk access, the read/write heads determine the current or new location of the data.

Step 4
The head actuator positions the read/write head arms over the correct location on the platters to read or write data.

Figure 8-7   This figure shows how a hard disk works.
© Alias Studiot Oy / Shutterstock.com; © Cengage Learning

✳ **CONSIDER THIS**

What happens if dust touches the surface of a platter on a hard disk?

Because of the close clearance between the read/write head and the platter on a hard disk, dust, dirt, hair, smoke, or any other contaminant could cause a disk to crash (Figure 8-8). A *head crash* occurs when a read/write head touches the surface of a platter, usually resulting in a loss of data or sometimes loss of the entire disk.

Although current internal hard disks are built to withstand shocks and are sealed tightly to keep out contaminants, head crashes occasionally still do occur. Thus, it is crucial that you back up a hard disk regularly.

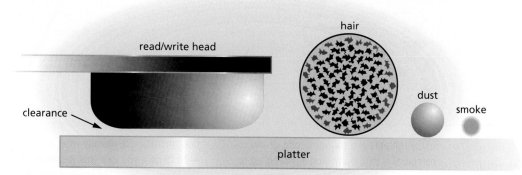

Figure 8-8 The clearance between a hard disk read/write head and the platter is about two-millionths of an inch. Any contaminant could render the disk unusable.
© Cengage Learning

 Internet Research

Can you recover data after a disk crash?

Search for: disk crash recovery

Disk Cache

Hard disks improve their access time by using disk cache. *Disk cache*, sometimes called a buffer, consists of a memory chip(s) on a hard disk that stores frequently accessed data, instructions, and information. Disk cache and memory cache (discussed in Chapter 6) work in a similar fashion. When a processor requests data, instructions, or information from the hard disk, the hard disk first checks its disk cache — before moving any mechanical parts to access the platters. If the requested item is in disk cache, the hard disk sends it to the processor. If the hard disk does not find the requested item in the disk cache, then the processor must wait for the hard disk to locate and transfer the item from the disk to the processor. The larger the disk cache, the faster the hard disk.

RAID

Some personal computer manufacturers provide a hard disk configuration that connects multiple smaller disks into a single unit that acts like a single large hard disk. A group of two or more integrated hard disks is called a **RAID** (redundant array of independent disks). RAID is an ideal storage solution in situations where uninterrupted access to the data is critical (Figure 8-9). Because enterprises often use RAID, the characteristics of these devices are discussed in more depth in the enterprise storage section of this chapter.

 Internet Research

How much does RAID cost for the home user?

Search for: RAID home storage

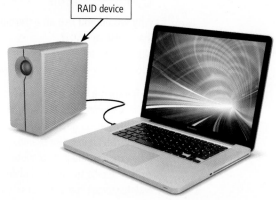

RAID device

Figure 8-9 An example of RAID for the home or small business user.
Courtesy of LaCie

External Hard Disks

An **external hard disk** is a separate freestanding storage device that connects with a cable to a USB port or other port on a computer or mobile device (Figure 8-10 on the next page). Sizes and storage capacities of external hard disks vary, with some having greater capacities than internal hard disks. Smaller external hard disks are portable and enable mobile users to transport photos and other files from one computer to another easily. As with an internal hard disk, an entire external hard disk is enclosed in an

 BTW

Seagate
Technology Innovator:
You should be familiar with storage solutions of Seagate.

airtight, sealed case. External hard disk units can include multiple hard disks that you can use for different purposes, if desired. Read How To 8-3 for instructions about encrypting files or disks to protect data.

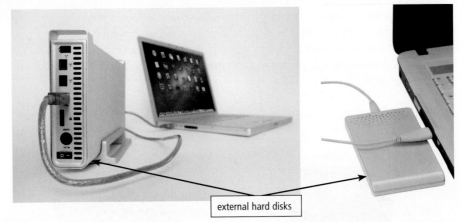

Figure 8-10 Examples of external hard disks.
© Joachim Wendler / Shutterstock.com;
© iStockphoto / Yury Minaev;
Source: Apple Inc

external hard disks

 HOW TO 8-3

 Encrypt a File or Files

If a hard disk or SSD falls into the wrong hands, the person with the media might be able to access its data. When you connect a hard disk or SSD to another computer, the data on it may be unprotected and subject to unrestricted access. Encrypting a file or files on the media will help ensure that unauthorized people will not be able to view its files. (Read pages 216 through 218 for details about encryption.) While encrypted files offer greater security, an operating system may require more time to open and access encrypted files. Your operating system may provide a feature allowing you to encrypt individual files or the

entire contents of a storage device, or you can install a third-party program designed to encrypt files. The following steps describe how to encrypt files:

1. Run the program or access the feature you will use to encrypt the file, files, or entire hard disk or SSD.

2. Select the file, files, or drive you want to encrypt.

3. If necessary, specify a password you will use to decrypt the file or files when you want to access them.

4. Before you begin the encryption process, review the program or operating system's

documentation to identify what you will need to do if you lose your password. If this process seems too cumbersome or you anticipate great risk if you lose access to your encrypted files, you might reconsider encrypting your files.

5. Start the encryption process. Depending on the number of files you are encrypting, this process may take several minutes or more to complete.

 What types of files would you encrypt on media in or attached to your computer or mobile device?

 CONSIDER THIS

Why would you use an external hard drive (hard disk or SSD) instead of a second internal hard drive (hard disk or SSD)?

Although the transfer rate of external hard drives usually is slower than that of internal hard drives, external hard drives do offer many advantages over internal hard drives:

- Transport a large number of files.
- Back up important files or an entire internal hard drive (most external hard drive models include backup software).
- Easily store large audio and video files.
- Secure your data; for example, at the end of a work session, you can relocate or lock up an external hard drive, leaving no data in a computer.
- Add storage space to a mobile computer, such as a laptop or tablet.
- Add storage space to a desktop without having to open the case or connect to a network.

Maintaining Data Stored on a Hard Disk

Most manufacturers guarantee their hard disks to last approximately three to five years. Many last much longer with proper care. To prevent the loss of items stored on a hard disk, you regularly should perform preventive maintenance such as defragmenting or scanning the disk for errors. Read How To 4-4 on page 187 for instructions about defragmenting a hard disk. Read Secure IT 8-1 for ways to recover deleted files.

SECURE IT 8-1

Restoring Deleted Files or Erased Media

Accidents happen. Perhaps you mistakenly deleted what you thought were unused or unwanted files from a hard disk or other storage medium and then realized you really did need a particular photo or document. Or, perhaps a virus deleted files without your knowledge. Help is available to assist with these misfortunes in an attempt to recover a deleted file.

In some cases, the file actually is not deleted from storage media when you issue the command to delete the file. Instead, as shown in the figure, its file name merely is deleted from the file directory, and the path or direct access to the file is lost. The key to successful recovery is to act quickly to avoid compromising access to data. Do not save any files or install any software on the disk or other storage medium until you recover the file. Some computers permanently delete files when shutting down or the computer may write data to the area where the file once resided, so the longer you wait, the less likely you will be able to recover the file you deleted accidentally.

- **Recycle Bin/Trash Recovery:** Both Windows and Mac operating systems have a location to store discarded files.

Often, files remain in these recycle or trash bins until a user manually instructs the operating system to delete them. Look in the recycle or trash bins for a desired file. If you locate it, a restore command may move the file back to its original location. If you empty the recycle or trash bin, your chances of recovering a desired file are diminished greatly.

- **Freeware:** Several free recovery programs are available to download. It is best to

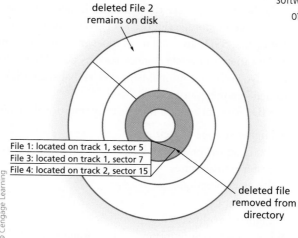

deleted File 2 remains on disk

File 1: located on track 1, sector 5
File 3: located on track 1, sector 7
File 4: located on track 2, sector 15

deleted file removed from directory

© Cengage Learning

save this software on a storage medium other than where the deleted files are located. Many of these programs also can recover files on memory cards and USB flash drives, and they also may help repair damaged hard drives. Bear in mind, however, that recovery success rates are low.

- **Commercial data recovery:** Expert data recovery software is available at retail stores, and it offers the greatest chances of retrieving desired files. The best software can recover a variety of data files from USB flash drives, memory cards, CDs and DVDs, and damaged sectors on internal and external hard disks.

✹ Have you mistakenly deleted files from a hard disk or other storage medium? If so, were you able to retrieve the lost data? What precautions can you take to avoid losing critical files?

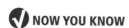 **NOW YOU KNOW**

Be sure you understand the material presented in the sections titled Storage and Hard Disks, as it relates to the chapter objectives.

You now should know . . .

- When you would use storage and when you use memory (Objective 1)
- What type of internal hard disk you would find in a desktop or laptop (Objective 2)
- Why you would use an external hard disk or RAID (Objective 3)

⊡ Quiz Yourself Online: Check your knowledge of related content by navigating to this book's Quiz Yourself resource on Computer Concepts CourseMate and then tapping or clicking Objectives 1–3.

Flash Memory Storage

As discussed in Chapter 6, flash memory is a type of nonvolatile memory that can be erased electronically and rewritten. Flash memory chips are a type of *solid-state media*, which means they consist entirely of electronic components, such as integrated circuits, and contain no moving parts. The lack of moving parts makes flash memory storage more durable and shock resistant than other types of media, such as magnetic hard disks or optical discs.

Types of flash memory storage include solid-state drives, memory cards, and USB flash drives. Read Secure IT 8-2 on the next page to learn how security screening equipment affects media.

Protecting Storage Media Near Security Screening Equipment

If you are concerned about placing your laptop, mobile phone, and digital camera on the conveyor belt and through the X-ray machines at airports, electronics experts claim you should relax. Repeated studies find that airport security scanners do not damage memory cards, optical discs, and other magnetic media. In all cases, however, it is wise

to back up the files on these devices before arriving at the airport.

Unfortunately, however, the same positive results are not always true of film, negatives, and recorded media. Radiation and magnetic fields emanating from the scanning equipment and systems that detect explosives can fog undeveloped film and negatives. In general, videotape and audiotape should not be affected, but Sony issues a caution

to international travelers because scanning equipment varies widely throughout the world. If you are transporting audiotapes, videotapes, or medical X-rays, experts recommend placing them in carry-on luggage and asking security personnel to inspect items by hand.

 Have your electronics been X-rayed at airport security checkpoints? If so, have they been affected by the scanning equipment?

SSDs

 BTW

SSD Access Times
You do not need to defragment an SSD because the location of the stored data has no impact on its access times.

An **SSD** (**solid-state drive**) is a flash memory storage device that contains its own processor to manage its storage (Figure 8-11). With available form factors of 3.5 inches, 2.5 inches, and 1.8 inches, SSDs are used in all types of computers, including servers, desktops, laptops, tablets, and a variety of mobile devices, such as portable media players and DV cameras. Some computers have both a traditional hard disk and also an SSD. External SSDs also are available, as mentioned in a previous section.

SSDs have several advantages over traditional (magnetic) hard disks, including the following:

- Higher storage capacities
- Faster access times (can be more than 80 times faster)
- Faster transfer rates
- Quieter operation
- More durable
- Lighter weight
- Less power consumption (leads to longer battery life)
- Less heat generation
- Longer life (more than 10 times longer)

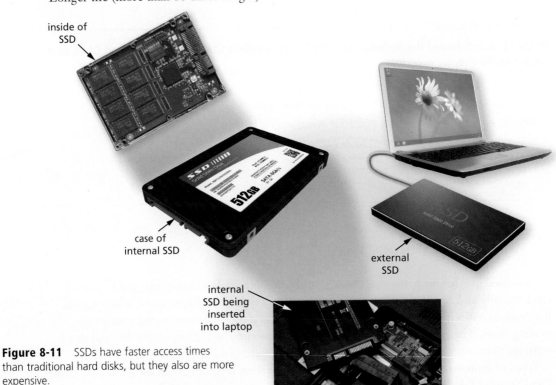

Figure 8-11 SSDs have faster access times than traditional hard disks, but they also are more expensive.

The disadvantages of SSDs are that data recovery in the event of failure can be more difficult than for traditional hard disks, and their cost is higher per gigabyte. In order to keep the price of a laptop affordable, laptops with SSDs usually have a lower storage capacity than laptops with a traditional hard disk. Read Ethics & Issues 8-1 to consider whether governments should be able to search the content of media and confiscate computers and mobile devices.

 Internet Research

How does the capacity and cost of SSDs compare to that of traditional hard disks?

Search for: ssd vs traditional hard disk

 ETHICS & ISSUES 8-1

Is Government Search and Seizure of Computers Ethical?

In the interest of national security, the Department of Homeland Security may search and seize any computer or mobile device belonging to anyone arriving in the United States. Authorities can conduct the sometimes random searches without a warrant or even a reason. Additionally, the government has taken computers from schools and libraries in a similar manner. Authorities might confiscate computers and mobile devices for an off-site inspection for any amount of time.

The Fourth Amendment protects against unreasonable search and seizure. Yet sometimes, authorities do not return the devices and provide little or no reason for the seizure. At airports and other points of entry to the country, the government considers computers and mobile devices to be containers, just as a piece of luggage is a container. Authorities, therefore, can search and seize computers without reasonable suspicion, as they can with luggage.

Opponents claim that users may be unaware of some of the contents of a hard disk or SSD. Users also may not realize that the media on the computer or mobile device contains Internet search history, deleted email messages and documents, and drafts of email messages or documents that they never sent or saved. Opponents also claim that the government should be able to inspect the hardware but not the contents of memory or a hard disk. Librarians and school administrators have stated that the government is invading the privacy of patrons and students.

Is government search and seizure of computers without a warrant ethical? Why or why not? Do you believe a government employee should have the power to inspect the data on your mobile computer or device? Why or why not? If memories or thoughts could someday be deciphered by a computer at a security checkpoint, should the government be allowed to scan them? Why or why not?

Memory Cards

Memory cards enable mobile users easily to transport digital photos, music, videos, or other files to and from mobile devices and computers or other devices. As mentioned in Chapter 1, a **memory card** is a removable flash memory storage device, usually no bigger than 1.5 inches in height or width, that you insert in and remove from a slot in a computer, mobile device, or card reader/writer (Figure 8-12).

Figure 8-12 Many types of computers and devices have slots for memory cards.

© iStockphoto / Tomasz Zajaczkowski; Courtesy of Epson America Inc; © Future Publishing / Getty Images; © Verisakeet / Fotolia; © Thejipen / Dreamstime.com; © iStockphoto / Brian Balster; © Cengage Learning

BTW
SanDisk
Technology Innovator:
You should be familiar
with the flash memory
products of SanDisk.

Common types of memory cards include **CF (CompactFlash)**, **SDHC (Secure Digital High Capacity)**, **SDXC (Secure Digital Expanded Capacity)**, **miniSD**, **microSD**, **microSDHC**, **microSDXC**, **xD Picture Card**, **Memory Stick PRO Duo**, and **M2 (Memory Stick Micro)**. Capacities of memory cards vary. A slot on a computer or device often accepts multiple types of cards. For example, an SD slot will accept an SDHC and SDXC card. To read a mini or micro card in a computer, you insert it in an adapter that fits in a standard-sized slot on the computer or device (shown in Figure 8-1 on page 337).

If your computer or printer does not have a built-in card slot, you can purchase a *card reader/ writer*, which is a device that reads from and writes on memory cards. Card reader/writers usually connect to the USB port on a computer. The type of card determines the type of card reader/writer needed. Some accept multiple types of cards; others accept one type. Figure 8-13 shows how one type of memory card works with a card reader/writer.

How SD Cards Work

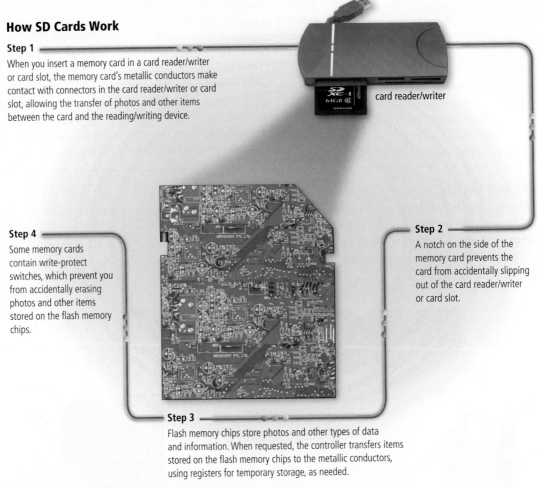

Step 1
When you insert a memory card in a card reader/writer or card slot, the memory card's metallic conductors make contact with connectors in the card reader/writer or card slot, allowing the transfer of photos and other items between the card and the reading/writing device.

card reader/writer

Step 2
A notch on the side of the memory card prevents the card from accidentally slipping out of the card reader/writer or card slot.

Step 4
Some memory cards contain write-protect switches, which prevent you from accidentally erasing photos and other items stored on the flash memory chips.

Step 3
Flash memory chips store photos and other types of data and information. When requested, the controller transfers items stored on the flash memory chips to the metallic conductors, using registers for temporary storage, as needed.

Figure 8-13 This figure shows how an SD card works.
© iStockphoto / Hugo Oswaldo Lara Gámez; Courtesy of Kingston Technology Company Inc.; © Cengage Learning

 CONSIDER THIS

What is the life span of a memory card?
Depending on the card, manufacturers claim their media can last from 10 to 100 years with proper care, including the following:

 **Internet Research**

Which memory cards are best?

Search for: memory card reviews

- Do not bend the card.
- Avoid dropping the card.
- Keep cards away from direct sunlight.
- Do not expose cards to extreme temperatures.
- Do not remove the card while data is transferring to or from it.

📃 Media Sharing

Sharing photos, video, and music with friends and family can be fun and easy to do. The latest online services offer a host of tools for sharing media. Simple instructions make posting, viewing, listening, and downloading easy to perform.

For useful starting points when researching locations to share media files, ask yourself the following questions:

- **Where do my original files need to reside?** Can I upload from my computer, mobile device, or camera? Can I send via email?

- **What is the cost?** Is the service free, or must I pay a monthly or annual fee? What happens to my files if I miss a payment or cancel my account?

- **Can I annotate my media?** Does the service allow me to add notes, tags, and locations?

- **How do I access and share the files safely?** Is the service password protected? Can I use Facebook, Twitter, blogs, and email to share the files?

- **What privacy rights are available?** Can I determine who is able to view or hear the files and see my profile? Does the website have a privacy settings section? Can I enable and disable a *geotag*, which is geographical data that can pinpoint the location on a map where a photo was taken?

- **Are online reviews of the services available?** What experiences have other people had using the websites? Are they generally pleased or displeased with the service's reliability and ease of use?

- **What help and website support are available?** Does the service have an extensive Help section? Are FAQs, tutorials, and user forums posted?

Photos

Some photo sharing websites have millions of images to view and possibly download. When deciding which websites to use, consider the following factors:

- **Services:** Many services allow the owner and guests to print the images. They also offer photo-customizing products. Others have photo contests.

- **Tools:** Owners can create webpages and keep photos organized by using albums, titles, and tags. They also can join forums and groups to share common experiences.

- **Features:** It is efficient if you can upload many files simultaneously in one batch. Many websites allow visitors to write comments on uploaded photos.

- **Storage space:** Some services offer unlimited storage, while others may limit members to a maximum number of stored photos, limit the size of each photo, or limit the total storage space.

Video

With video recording available on most smartphones and cameras, virtually anyone who owns these devices can produce videos to distribute. The following features are found on popular video sharing websites:

- **Video creation:** Editing tools allow special effects, editing, titles, and descriptions.

- **Audience interaction:** On-screen and keyboard controls allow viewers to play, pause, fast-forward, and stop files. Audience members can rate the videos and browse specific categories.

- **Features:** Most services accept files saved in a wide variety of file formats, but the maximum file size may be restricted or a total limit per week may be imposed.

- **Genre:** Some websites accept a wide variety of content, while others require original work.

© iStockphoto / Baris Simsek

© Maximus256 / Shutterstock.com

Music

Online social networks and personal radio stations are popular sources of music. Some of these services are for listening only, while others sell songs to download. The following features are found on music sharing websites:

- **Playlists:** Musicians and listeners can organize the songs and albums into specific categories, such as by artist or genre. In a playlist, each song can be played sequentially or shuffled to play in random order.

- **Compatibility:** Some file types will not play on specific mobile devices, so check permissible formats before attempting to upload or download songs.

- **Features:** Services show the album cover, list artist information, and provide song previews.

- **Titles:** Musicians use music hosting websites as a convenient method of distributing their works.

© Dmitrydesign / Shutterstock.com

Protecting Your Rights to Files You Share

When you post your files on many media sharing sites, you should be able to determine who is able to access the files. Creative Commons is a nonprofit organization that gives the owner of a creative work a license granting permission for others to use a file in a specific way. For example, someone can use the work commercially or modify the file. When posting and downloading media files, it is important to ensure you are not infringing on copyright protection. Read Ethics & Issues 8-2 on the next page to consider additional issues related to posting photos of others.

✸ Have you used photo, video, or music sharing websites? If so, which ones, and how did you decide the services to use? If not, would you like to try uploading or viewing at least one of these websites?

Should You Be Required to Obtain Permission before Posting Photos of Others?

Your friends or followers on social media sites instantly can view photos you post. If others are included in the photo and you post it without their permission, they might feel you have violated their privacy. Tagging people in a photo may create a link to their social media profiles, exposing their identity. Depending on your privacy settings, your friends' contacts can view a photo you post and/or share the photo without your permission.

You can use Facebook's privacy settings to approve all photos in which you are tagged.

The person posting the photo still can upload the photo, but your tag will not appear on the photo until you approve it. Facebook also allows you to report a photo as abusive if you feel it portrays you negatively or if the person who posted it refuses to remove it upon request.

People may not want photos of themselves posted for a variety reasons. They may have professional contacts as friends on their social networking site and do not want to show themselves in a personal setting. Others are not concerned with personal photos of themselves being posted but do not want their children's photos shared online. Or, they simply may find the photo unflattering.

Before you post a photo of others or tag people in a posted photo, consider whether they would approve the photo. If you are unsure, consider contacting the other parties before posting the photo.

Is it ever acceptable to post photos of others without permission? Why or why not? Has someone posted or tagged you in a photo that you did not want others to see? How did you handle the situation? If asked to remove a photo or tag, would you respect the person's feelings and honor the request? What restrictions and policies should social media sites have about posting photos of others?

Figure 8-14 A close-up of the flash memory and circuitry inside a USB flash drive.
© cheyennezj / Shutterstock.com; © photonic 15 / Alamy; © Cengage Learning

USB Flash Drives

As mentioned in Chapter 1, a **USB flash drive**, sometimes called a *thumb drive*, is a flash memory storage device that plugs in a USB port on a computer or mobile device (Figure 8-14). USB flash drives are convenient for mobile users because they are small and lightweight enough to be transported on a keychain or in a pocket. With a USB flash drive, users easily transfer documents, photos, music, and videos from one computer to another. Storage capacities of USB flash drives vary. Read How to 8-4 for instructions about safely removing a USB flash drive and other media.

Safely Remove Media

If you are using a USB flash drive or other removable storage media with your computer or mobile device, you should not remove the device or media while it is in use. Disconnecting a USB flash drive while it is in use, for example, may cause damage to the files stored on the device. Although you might not be actively accessing files on the USB flash drive, the operating system still might be accessing the device. Operating systems typically provide an option to safely remove or eject the device or media and then will notify you when the device or media no longer is in use and can be removed safely. The following steps describe

how to remove or eject removable storage media safely:

1. If necessary, close any files or exit any programs that are opened or running on the media.

2. Open the window displaying all the drives and media connected to your computer or mobile device.

3. Tap or click to select the drive or media you want to remove safely.

4. Tap or click the command to safely remove or eject the removable storage media. If you are unable to locate this command, you may need to press and hold or right-click the icon representing the device or media to display a shortcut

menu and then tap or click the command to remove or eject the device or media safely.

5. When the notification appears stating that the device or media is safe to remove or eject, disconnect or remove it from your computer. If a notification does not appear, you can disconnect or remove the device or media once it no longer appears in your operating system as connected to your computer.

✻ Should you follow the above steps before disconnecting devices such as digital cameras and portable media players from your computer? Why or why not?

Cloud Storage

Some users choose cloud storage instead of storing data locally on a hard disk, SSD, or other media. As discussed in previous chapters, **cloud storage** is an Internet service that provides storage to computer or mobile device users.

Cloud storage is available for home and business users, with various degrees of storage services available. Cloud storage fee arrangements vary, depending on the user's storage requirements. Read Ethics & Issues 8-3 to consider issues related to data stored on the cloud.

 **Internet Research**

Which cloud storage providers are the best?

Search for: cloud storage reviews

 CONSIDER THIS

What are some advantages of cloud storage?

Users subscribe to cloud storage for a variety of reasons:

- To access files on the Internet from any computer or device that has Internet access
- To store large audio, video, and graphics files on the Internet instantaneously, instead of spending time downloading to a local hard disk or other media
- To allow others to access their files on the Internet so that others can listen to an audio file, watch a video clip, or view a photo — instead of sending the file to them via an email message
- To view time-critical data and images immediately while away from the main office or location; for example, doctors can view X-ray images from another hospital, home, or office, or while on vacation
- To store off-site backups of data
- To provide data center functions, relieving enterprises of this task

 BTW

Amazon and Jeff Bezos
Technology Innovator:
You should be familiar with Amazon and its founder, Jeff Bezos.

 ETHICS & ISSUES 8-3

 Who Is Responsible for Data Left on the Cloud?

Businesses often contract with cloud storage providers to host their data storage needs. In many cases, these businesses use cloud storage providers to store their sensitive customer data. This data could include contact information, credit card numbers, and ordering history. Ownership of cloud data becomes an issue when a cloud storage provider or the business using the cloud services ceases its operations, if the business fails to pay its storage fees to the cloud storage provider, or when a contract between the cloud storage provider and the business terminates.

Many feel that it is the responsibility of the business owner to remove and destroy company data before a contract expires. Supporters of this argument believe that cloud storage providers should not be accessing or processing confidential data. Others contend that if a business fails to remove and destroy its data before its cloud storage contract expires, a trustworthy cloud storage provider should remove the data permanently.

Ownership of data should be included in any contract between a business and cloud storage provider. Contracts also should specify what occurs to the data in a variety of scenarios, including if either party ceases its operations.

If a business ceases its operations, who should remove its data from cloud storage? Why? Should a business be responsible for backing up the data it stores on the cloud? Why or why not? If a customer fails to remove its data before a contract ends, should a cloud storage provider be required to return or provide access to the data, or should it be allowed to dispose of or sell the data? Why or why not?

MINI FEATURE 8-2

What Can You Do with Cloud Storage?

Cloud storage provides access to your files across many devices. Amazon Cloud Drive, iCloud, Box, Dropbox, Google Drive, and SkyDrive are among the many options that consumers consider for cloud storage. These and other cloud storage providers enable you to synchronize files, write documents, back up your computer or mobile device, share project work, stream music, post photos, and play games online. Many offer

a limited amount of free storage and make additional storage available for a fee.

Synchronize Files

Dropbox, Google Drive, and SkyDrive place a folder on your computer with contents you can synchronize across multiple devices. Other providers allow you to upload files for storage online, and download them via a web app or mobile app. Many cloud storage providers retain previous versions of your files, in case you need to revert to an earlier one.

Write Documents

Google Drive and SkyDrive provide apps to edit documents online and store them on the cloud. Third-party tools such as Evernote, a note taking application, store notes as files in your Dropbox account.

Back Up Your Computer

Some companies, such as Carbonite, automatically copy a computer or mobile device's files to the cloud, freeing users of performing backups themselves. This provides an added level of security, as files are stored safely on a remote server.

Stream Music

You can play music and videos stored offline (i.e., on your computer or mobile devices) in places without Internet access. Many people also store media files online, so as not to use up the limited internal storage available on mobile devices. Some music services support streaming music stored on the cloud to Android, iOS, and other devices.

Post Photos

Several options are available for uploading photos from a smartphone or tablet to the cloud or publishing photos to media sharing sites and online social networks.

Play Games

Internet-connected game consoles enable you to save games in progress. Because game information is stored on the cloud, you can continue playing where you left off, regardless of whether you are using your own or another's game console.

Evaluating Providers

With so many providers offering free and paid cloud storage services, it is important to compare features to take advantage of the capabilities that each offers. Criteria to consider include the amount of free storage offered, the cost to purchase more if needed, and the maximum file size that each service allows you to upload. Keep the files you use most on the service on which you have the most storage space; use services that support streaming to store and play media files. Photos, songs, and videos take longer to upload than smaller text or webpage files, so it is important to select a provider whose servers have sufficient bandwidth to support large file transfers.

It also is important to read a cloud storage provider's privacy policy and terms of agreement to which you must consent before using it. Some cloud storage providers may not guarantee the protection of the files you upload, so you still should keep a backup of the files you stored on the cloud.

✳ What are advantages of storing your files on the cloud? When does it make sense to use physical storage media, such as a USB flash drive, to store your files? Storing files on the cloud encourages collaboration and sharing. How can you share files stored on the cloud with your team members? Many cloud storage providers offer several gigabytes of free storage to their users. Visit a cloud storage provider's website. What additional services does it offer its customers for a fee? Look online for promotional deals from cloud storage providers. What is the largest amount of free storage you can find? Who is the provider? Do you see any drawbacks? Are you concerned about the security of your files when stored on the cloud? What information, if any, would you not store in the cloud?

Enjoy your music, anywhere

Play or download your music from the cloud with Amazon Cloud Player, available on the web, Kindle Fire, iPhone, iPad, iPod touch, Android phone or tablet, Sonos, Roku, or Samsung Smart TV. Browse and search your library, create and manage playlists, stream your music from the cloud, or download it for offline playback. Launch Cloud Player for web, or learn more about music on your Kindle Fire or about the app for Sonos, Roku, Samsung Smart TV, Android, or iPhone, iPad and iPod touch.

© Cengage Learning; Amazon.com, Inc.

Optical Discs

An **optical disc** is a type of storage medium that consists of a flat, round, portable disc made of metal, plastic, and lacquer that is written and read by a laser. Optical discs used in computers typically are 4.75 inches in diameter and less than one-twentieth of an inch thick. Game consoles and mobile devices, however, may use a *mini disc* that has a diameter of 3 inches or less; mini discs also work in standard-sized optical disc drives. Three widely used types of optical discs are CDs (compact discs), DVDs (digital versatile discs and sometimes digital video discs), and Blu-ray Discs.

On some computers, you push a button to slide out a tray, insert the disc, and then push the same button to close the tray; others are slot loaded, which means you insert the disc in a narrow opening on the drive (Figure 8-15). When you insert the disc, the operating system automatically may run a program, play music, or start a video on the disc. Desktops and traditional laptops usually have an optical disc drive. Ultrathin laptops, tablets, and mobile devices typically do not have an optical disc drive.

Many different formats of optical discs exist today. Some are read only, meaning users cannot write (save) on the media. Others are read/write, which allows users to save on the disc just as they save on a hard disk. With most discs, you can read and/or write on one side only. Manufacturers usually place a silk-screened label on the top layer of these single-sided discs. You insert a single-sided disc in the drive with the label side up. Some drives use *LightScribe technology*, which means it can etch labels directly on the specially coated discs (as opposed to placing an adhesive label on the disc).

Figure 8-15 An optical disc in a disc drive.
© ra2studio / Shutterstock.com

Characteristics of Optical Discs

Optical discs store items by using microscopic pits (indentations) and lands (flat areas) that are in the middle layer of the disc (Figure 8-16). A high-powered laser light creates the pits. A lower-powered laser light reads items from the disc by reflecting light through the bottom of

How a Laser Reads Data on an Optical Disc

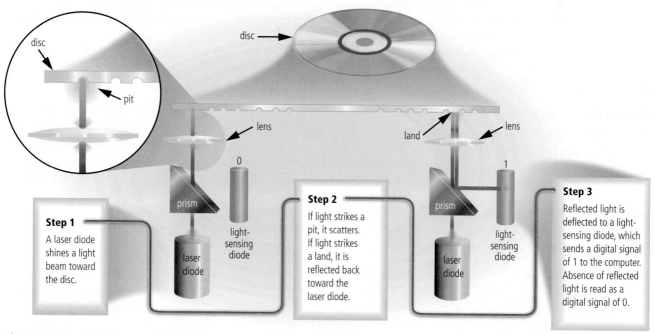

Figure 8-16 This figure shows how a laser reads data on an optical disc.
© Cengage Learning

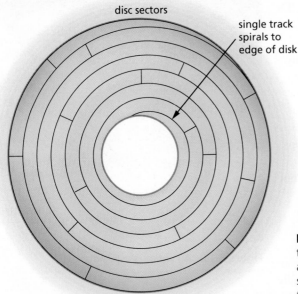

disc sectors

single track
spirals to
edge of disk

the disc. The reflected light is converted into a series of bits the computer can process. A land causes light to reflect, which is read as binary digit 1. Pits absorb the light; this absence of light is read as binary digit 0.

Optical discs commonly store items in a single track that spirals from the center of the disc to the edge of the disc. As with a hard disk, this single track is divided into evenly sized sectors on which items are stored (Figure 8-17).

Figure 8-17 An optical disc typically stores data, instructions, and information in a single track that spirals from the center of the disc to the edge of the disc.
© Cengage Learning

 CONSIDER THIS

What is the life span of an optical disc?
Manufacturers claim that a properly cared for high-quality optical disc will last 5 years but could last up to 100 years. Tips for proper care of optical discs include the following:

- Never bend a disc; it may break.
- Do not expose discs to extreme temperatures or humidity. The ideal temperature range for disc storage is 50 to 70 degrees Fahrenheit.
- Stacking discs, touching the underside of discs, or exposing them to any type of contaminant may scratch a disc. Read How To 8-5 for instructions about cleaning and fixing scratches on a disc.
- Place an optical disc in its protective case, called a *jewel case*, when you are finished using it, and store it in an upright (vertical) position.

 HOW TO 8-5

Clean an Optical Disc and Fix Scratches

If you are having trouble accessing programs and files on an optical disc, such as a CD or DVD, you may need to clean the disc or fix scratches on its surface. To avoid the risk of not being able to access a disc because it is dirty, you should clean a disc when you first notice dirt on its surface. The following steps describe how to clean or fix scratches on an optical disc:

Cleaning an Optical Disc

1. While holding the disc by its edges, use compressed air to blow excess dust off of its surface. Hold the can of compressed air upright while using it.

2. Use a soft, nonabrasive cloth to gently wipe debris off of the disc's surface.

Wipe the disc from the center out to its edges.

3. If any dirt remains on the disc, dip a soft cloth or cotton ball in isopropyl alcohol (or a cleaner designed for optical discs) and then gently wipe the soiled areas.

4. Use a soft cloth to dry the disc's surface or allow it to air dry. You never should insert a wet disc in a computer.

Fixing Scratches on an Optical Disc

1. Complete the previous Steps 1–4 to clean the disc. If it still contains scratches, follow the remaining steps.

2. As with any maintenance you perform, risks are associated with attempting to fix scratches on an optical disc. For this reason,

if possible, you should back up the data on the disc before attempting to fix a scratch.

3. Place a very small amount of rubbing compound (available at a hardware store) on a soft, nonabrasive cloth and rub the compound on the disc from its center outward at the location of the scratch. If rubbing compound is not available, place a small amount of toothpaste (not a gel) on the scratched area and rub from the inside of the disc outward.

4. Test the disc. If you still are experiencing problems because of the scratch(es), consider having a professional remove the scratch.

 What other household products can be used to clean or fix scratches on an optical disc?

CDs

CDs are available in three basic formats: read-only, recordable, and rewritable.

- A **CD-ROM** (CD-read-only memory) is a type of optical disc that users can read but not write on (record) or erase — hence, the name read-only. Manufacturers write the contents of standard CD-ROMs and distribute them to consumers. A standard CD-ROM is called a *single-session disc* because manufacturers write all items on the disc at one time. Software manufacturers sometimes distribute their programs using CD-ROMs. The term, *photo CD*, sometimes is used to refer to CDs that contain only photos.
- A **CD-R** (CD-recordable) is an optical disc on which users can write once, but not erase, their own items, such as text, graphics, and audio. Because a CD-R can be written on only one time, the format of these discs sometimes is called *WORM* (write once, read many). Some CD-Rs are *multisession*, which means you can write on part of the disc at one time and another part at a later time — if the disc has free space.
- A **CD-RW** (CD-rewritable) is an erasable multisession disc users can write on multiple times. CD-RW overcomes the major disadvantage of CD-R because it allows users to write and rewrite data, instructions, and information on the CD-RW disc multiple times — instead of just once. Reliability of the disc tends to drop, however, with each successive rewrite.

A popular use of CD-RW and CD-R discs is to create audio CDs. For example, you can record your own music and save it on a CD, purchase and download songs from the web, or rearrange tracks on a purchased music CD.

 CONSIDER THIS

Can all CD drives read all CD formats?
A CD-ROM drive or a CD player may be able to read only CD-ROMs and sometimes CD-Rs. Because audio CDs and CD-ROMs use the same laser technology, you may be able to use a CD-ROM drive to listen to an audio CD while using the computer.

Most CD-R drives can read audio CDs, CD-ROMs, CD-Rs, and sometimes CD-RWs. Most CD-RW drives can read audio CDs, CD-ROMs, CD-Rs, and CD-RWs. To write on a CD-R disc, you must have a CD-R drive. Similarly, to write on a CD-RW disc, you must have a CD-RW drive.

DVDs

DVD quality far surpasses that of CDs because items are stored in a slightly different manner, which enables DVDs to have greater storage capacities and higher resolutions than CDs. The first storage technique involves making the disc denser by packing the pits closer together. The second involves using two layers of pits. This technique doubles the capacity of the disc because the lower layer of pits is semitransparent, which allows the laser to read through it to the upper layer. Finally, some DVDs are double-sided. A more expensive DVD format is **Blu-ray**, which has a higher capacity and better quality than standard DVDs, especially for high-definition audio and video.

As with CDs, DVDs are available in three basic formats: read-only, recordable, and rewritable.

- A **DVD-ROM** (DVD-read-only memory) is a high-capacity optical disc that users can read but not write on or erase. Manufacturers write the contents of DVD-ROMs and distribute them to consumers. DVD-ROMs store movies, music, music videos, huge databases, and complex software.
- **DVD-R** and **DVD+R** are competing DVD-recordable WORM formats, on which users can write once but not erase their own items, including video, audio, photos, graphics, and text.
- **DVD-RW**, **DVD+RW**, and **DVD+RAM** are competing DVD-rewritable formats that users can write on multiple times.

 BTW
Burning and Ripping
The process of writing on an optical disc is called *burning*. The process of copying audio and/or video data from a purchased disc and saving it on your own media is called *ripping*.

 BTW
DVD/CD-RW
Some drives, called *DVD/CD-RW drives*, are combination drives that read and write on DVD and CD media. Current computers that include optical drives often use these combination drives.

CONSIDER THIS

Can all DVD drives read all DVD formats?

No. In addition to DVD-ROMs, most DVD-ROM drives also can read audio CDs, CD-ROMs, CD-Rs, and CD-RWs. Recordable and rewritable DVD drives usually can read a variety of DVD and CD media. Blu-ray Disc (BD) drives and players are backward compatible with DVD and CD formats. Before investing in equipment, check to be sure it is compatible with the media on which you intend to record.

 CONSIDER THIS

How do drives connect to a computer?

A *controller*, previously called a disk controller, consists of a special-purpose chip and electronic circuits that control the transfer of data, instructions, and information from a drive to and from the system bus and other components in the computer. The controller may be part of a drive, may be on the motherboard, or may be a separate adapter card inside the computer.

In personal computer advertisements, vendors usually state the type of interface supported by the controller. In addition to USB, which can function as an interface for an external hard drive, four other types of interfaces for use in personal computers are EIDE, SCSI, SAS, and SATA.

- *EIDE* (Enhanced Integrated Drive Electronics) is an interface that uses parallel signals to transfer data, instructions, and information. EIDE interfaces provide connections for hard disks, RAID, SSDs, optical disc drives, and tape drives.
- Like EIDE, *SCSI* (Small Computer System Interface) also uses parallel signals, but can support up to 8 or 15 peripheral devices. Supported devices include hard disks, RAID, SSDs, optical disc drives, tape drives, printers, scanners, network cards, and more.
- *SAS* (*serial-attached SCSI*) is a type of SCSI that uses serial signals to transfer data, instructions, and information. Advantages of SAS over parallel SCSI include thinner, longer cables; reduced interference; lower cost; support for many more connected devices at once; and faster speeds. SAS interfaces support connections to hard disks, RAID, SSDs, optical disc drives, printers, scanners, digital cameras, and other devices.
- *SATA* (Serial Advanced Technology Attachment) uses serial signals to transfer data, instructions, and information. The primary advantage of SATA interfaces is their cables are thinner, longer, more flexible, and less susceptible to interference than cables that use parallel signals. SATA interfaces support connections to hard disks, RAID, SSDs, and optical disc drives. External drives can use the *eSATA* (external SATA) interface, which is much faster than USB.

 BTW
Serial versus Parallel
With serial transfers, data is sent one bit at a time. Parallel transfers, by contrast, send several bits at once.

 MINI FEATURE 8-3

Backup Plans

Data loss or corruption can cause many issues. A user who accidentally misplaces a mobile device may lose contact information. A small business owner whose hard disk is infected with a virus may lose financial data, making billing and tax preparation difficult. A power user whose office floods and ruins a desktop not only may lose work completed on complex projects but also may need to replace expensive software. The best method for protecting against data loss from these types of unforeseen circumstances is to back up data.

A *backup plan* specifies a regular schedule for copying and storing important data, information, apps, and programs. Organizations should state their backup plans clearly, document them in writing, and follow them consistently. Home and small business users can use a calendar app or other reminder to back up their computers or mobile devices. Backup plans should weigh the time and expense of performing a backup against the value of the data, information, apps, and programs. For example, a small business may perform one type of backup daily, while a home user may find that monthly backups are sufficient.

As briefly discussed in Chapter 5, business and home users can perform four types of backup: full, differential, incremental, or selective. Typically, only large enterprises uses a fifth type, continuous data protection.

- A *full backup*, sometimes called an *archival backup*, provides the best protection against data loss because it copies all program and data files. Generally, users should perform a full backup at regular intervals, such as at the end of each week and at the end of the month.

- Between full backups, you can perform differential or incremental backups. A *differential backup* copies only the files that have changed since the last full backup. An *incremental backup* copies only the files that have changed since the last full or last incremental backup.

- A *selective backup*, sometimes called a *partial backup*, allows the user to choose specific files to back up, regardless of whether or not the files have changed since the last incremental backup.

Backup software enables you to schedule backups, select the appropriate backup type, and choose the storage media for the backup. Traditional storage media includes CDs or DVDs, external hard drives, or removable SSDs, including USB flash drives or memory cards. Whichever storage media you choose, it should be stored separately from the device you are backing up to ensure it is available in case of theft or disaster. When choosing storage media, consider price and reliability. A USB flash drive may be inexpensive, but it also could be corrupted or lost easily. Increasingly, home and business users are contracting the services of cloud storage providers to back up their data. Cloud storage may be more expensive, but your data will be in a remote location and accessible from anywhere at any time.

Many smartphones and other mobile devices include services that sync data to a computer or to a cloud service. To sync data to a computer, the mobile device

October					
MONDAY	**TUESDAY**	**WEDNESDAY**	**THURSDAY**	**FRIDAY**	**SAT/SUN**
28 DAILY INCREMENTAL BACKUP	**29** DAILY INCREMENTAL BACKUP	**30** END OF MONTH FULL BACKUP	**1** DAILY INCREMENTAL BACKUP	**2** WEEKLY FULL BACKUP	**3/4**
5 DAILY INCREMENTAL BACKUP	**6** DAILY INCREMENTAL BACKUP	**7** DAILY INCREMENTAL BACKUP	**8** DAILY INCREMENTAL BACKUP	**9** WEEKLY FULL BACKUP	**10/11**
12 DAILY INCREMENTAL BACKUP	**13** DAILY INCREMENTAL BACKUP	**14** DAILY INCREMENTAL BACKUP	**15** DAILY INCREMENTAL BACKUP	**16** WEEKLY FULL BACKUP	**17/18**
19 DAILY INCREMENTAL BACKUP	**20** DAILY INCREMENTAL BACKUP	**21** DAILY INCREMENTAL BACKUP	**22** DAILY INCREMENTAL BACKUP	**23** WEEKLY FULL BACKUP	**24/25**
26 DAILY INCREMENTAL BACKUP	**27** DAILY INCREMENTAL BACKUP	**28** DAILY INCREMENTAL BACKUP	**29** DAILY INCREMENTAL BACKUP	**30** END OF MONTH FULL BACKUP	**31/1**

© Cengage Learning

either requires cables to connect via a USB port or uses wireless methods such as Bluetooth. Many mobile apps sync data to web apps automatically, which means you may not need to schedule a procedure to back up items on a mobile device, such as contacts, calendars, email messages, notes, and apps. For additional protection, however, some users still back up certain mobile data for easy retrieval if the device is lost or corrupted.

✳ Do you have a backup plan for your mobile device and/or computer? Why or why not? How often do you think you need to back up your devices? Why? What storage media is best suited for your backup needs? Why?

✔ NOW YOU KNOW

Be sure you understand the material presented in the sections titled Flash Memory Storage, Cloud Storage, and Optical Discs, as it relates to the chapter objectives.
You now should know . . .

- Why you would use an SSD (Objective 4)
- Whether you should use a memory card or a USB flash drive (Objective 5)
- Why you would use cloud storage (Objective 6)
- Which optical disc format is best suited to your needs (Objective 7)

⬛ Quiz Yourself Online: Check your knowledge of related content by navigating to this book's Quiz Yourself resource on Computer Concepts CourseMate and then tapping or clicking Objectives 4–7.

Enterprise Storage

Enterprise hardware allows large organizations to manage and store data and information using devices intended for heavy use, maximum efficiency, and maximum availability. The availability of hardware to users is a measure of how often it is online. Highly available hardware is accessible 24 hours a day, 365 days a year. To meet these needs, enterprise hardware often includes levels of *redundancy*, which means that if one component fails or malfunctions, another can assume its tasks.

Some organizations manage an enterprise storage system in-house. Others elect to off-load all (or at least the backup) storage management to an outside organization or a cloud storage provider, a practice known as *outsourcing*.

Enterprises use a combination of storage techniques to meet their large-scale needs, including some of the previously discussed methods, along with RAID, network attached storage, storage area networks, and tape. Enterprise storage often uses *Fibre Channel* (*FC*) technology as the interface that connects the devices to the network because FC technology has much faster transmission rates than SCSI and other previously discussed interfaces.

RAID

For applications that depend on reliable data access, users must have the data available when they attempt to access it. Some manufacturers provide a type of hard disk system that connects several smaller disks into a single unit that acts like a single large hard disk. As mentioned earlier in this chapter, a group of two or more integrated hard disks is called a RAID (Figure 8-18). Although RAID can be more expensive than traditional hard disks, it is more reliable. Computers and enterprise storage devices often use RAID.

RAID duplicates data, instructions, and information to improve data reliability. RAID implements this duplication in different ways, depending on the storage design, or level, being used. The simplest RAID storage design is *level 1*, called *mirroring*, which writes data on two disks at the same time to duplicate the data (Figure 8-19a). A level 1 configuration enhances storage reliability because, if a disk should fail, a duplicate of the requested item is available elsewhere within the array of disks.

Figure 8-18 Shown here is a rack-mounted RAID chassis, including many integrated hard disks.
© stavklem / Shutterstock.com

BTW
RAID Levels
High-Tech Talk:
RAID levels are not hierarchical. That is, higher levels are not necessarily better than lower levels. RAID levels optimize capacity, reliability, performance, and availability of data.

Other RAID levels use a technique called *striping*, which splits data, instructions, and information across multiple disks in the array (Figure 8-19b). Striping improves disk access times, but does not offer data duplication. For this reason, some RAID levels combine both mirroring and striping.

(a)

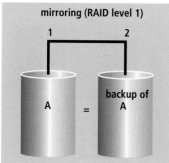

(b)

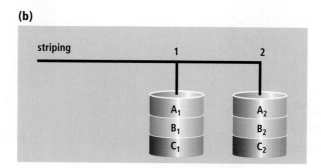

 Figure 8-19   In RAID level 1, called mirroring, a backup disk exists for each disk. Other RAID levels use striping; that is, portions of each disc are placed on multiple disks.
© Cengage Learning

NAS and SAN

Network attached storage (NAS) is a server that is placed on a network with the sole purpose of providing storage to users, computers, and devices attached to the network (Figure 8-20). A network attached storage server, often called a *storage appliance*, has its own IP address, usually does not have a keyboard or display, and contains at least one hard disk, often configured in a RAID. Administrators quickly can add storage to an existing network by connecting a network attached storage server to a network.

A **storage area network (SAN)** is a high-speed network with the sole purpose of providing storage to other attached servers (Figure 8-21 on the next page). In fact, a storage area network includes only storage devices. High-speed fiber-optic cable usually connects other networks and servers to the storage area network, so that the networks and servers have fast access to large storage capacities. A storage area network can connect to networks and other servers that are miles away using high-speed network connections.

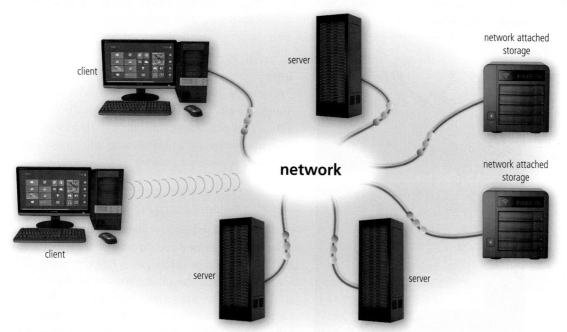

Figure 8-20   An example of how network attached storage connects on a network.
© iStockphoto / luismmolina; © lucadp / Shutterstock.com; © Cengage Learning; © Oleksiy Mark / Shutterstock.com; Source: Microsoft

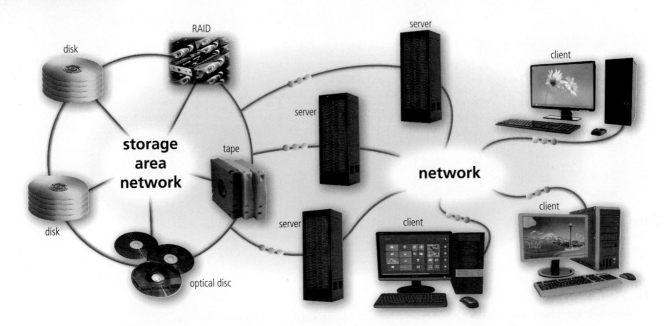

Figure 8-21 A storage area network provides centralized storage for servers and networks.

© Cengage Learning; © stavklem / Shutterstock.com; © iStockphoto / luismmolina; © Cengage Learning; © bigmagic / Shutterstock.com; © Oleksiy Mark / Shutterstock.com; © iStockphoto / sweetym; © iStockphoto / 123render; Source: Microsoft

Both network attached storage and storage area network solutions offer easy management of storage, fast access to storage, sharing of storage, and isolation of storage from other servers. Isolating the storage enables the other servers to concentrate on performing a specific task, rather than consuming resources involved in the tasks related to storage. Both storage solutions include disk, optical disc, and tape types of storage.

✳ CONSIDER THIS

Which do enterprises typically use, network attached storage or storage area networks?

Enterprises sometimes choose to implement both network attached storage and storage area network solutions. A network attached storage server is better suited for adding storage to an existing network, such as a department's file server. A company typically implements a storage area network solution as central storage for an entire enterprise.

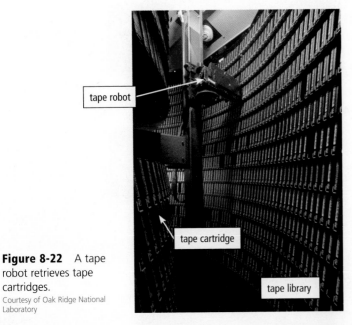

Figure 8-22 A tape robot retrieves tape cartridges.

Courtesy of Oak Ridge National Laboratory

Tape

One of the first storage media used with enterprise computers was tape. **Tape** is a magnetically coated ribbon of plastic that is capable of storing large amounts of data and information at a low cost. Tape no longer is used as a primary method of storage. Instead, businesses use tape most often for long-term storage and backup.

Comparable to a cassette recorder, a *tape drive* reads from and writes on a magnetic tape. Although older computers used reel-to-reel tape drives, today's tape drives use tape cartridges. A *tape cartridge* is a small, rectangular, plastic housing for tape. Enterprises often use a *tape library*, where individual tape cartridges are mounted in a separate cabinet. Often, a tape robot automatically retrieves tape cartridges (Figure 8-22), which are identified by location or bar code.

CONSIDER THIS

Is tape as fast as other storage techniques?

No. Tape storage requires *sequential access*, which refers to reading or writing data consecutively. In much the same way you would find a specific song on a cassette tape or videotape, you must forward or rewind to a specific position to access a specific piece of data. On a tape, for example, to access items ordered A, B, C, and D, you must pass through items A, B, and C sequentially before you can access item D.

Hard drives, flash memory storage, and optical discs all use direct access. *Direct access*, also called *random access*, means that the device can locate a particular data item or file immediately, without having to move consecutively through items stored in front of the desired data item or file. When writing or reading specific data, direct access is much faster than sequential access.

 BTW
Digitizing Media
Innovative Computing: You should be familiar with the innovation of using RECAPTCHAs to digitize newspapers and books.

Other Types of Storage

In addition to the previously discussed types of storage, other options are available for specific uses and applications. These include magnetic stripe cards, smart cards, RFID tags, and microfilm and microfiche. Read Secure IT 8-3 for tips about storage.

 SECURE IT 8-3

Realize Digital Content Is Permanent

"Your digital activity is public and permanent," warns The Institute for Responsible Online and Cell-Phone Communication (IROC2). This nonprofit organization urges all users of digital equipment to act responsibly and safely and emphasizes, "You cannot undo your digital mistake!"

While people may think their email messages, photos, videos, and text messages are private, everything online has the potential to be archived, forwarded, and captured as a screen shot. This digital footprint never truly can be deleted because everything you do on the Internet, including conducting searches and viewing photos, is saved in databases

and backed up on servers in multiple locations worldwide.

Potential and current employers, college admissions officers, professional organizations, and officials scour online websites in search of information that could affect employment or acceptance decisions. In some studies, 75 percent of companies have policies to conduct online research of applicants, and 33 percent of employers searching the Internet found online content that resulted in eliminating an applicant from consideration for a position. In several cases, employees have lost their jobs when objectionable comments and photos are discovered on social media, professional, and personal

websites. (Read Ethics & Issues 1-2 on page 22 for additional information.)

Parents and teachers are urged to talk with their children and students about the consequences of their digital interactions and about becoming a highly regarded digital citizen. The bottom line is never to write anything online, including in email messages, that one day could become detrimental.

✳ Have you seen or received material from friends or coworkers that could be construed as objectionable by some people? If so, did you mention this potentially offensive content to the sender? After reading this information, are you less apt to share material knowing that it is online permanently? Why or why not?

Magnetic Stripe Cards

A **magnetic stripe card** is a credit card, entertainment card, bank card, or other similar card with a stripe that contains information identifying you and the card (Figure 8-23). The card issuer, such as a financial organization, encodes information in the stripe. The information in the stripe often includes your name, account number, and the card's expiration date. When you swipe the card through a magstripe reader, discussed in the previous chapter, it reads information stored on the stripe.

magnetic stripe

Figure 8-23 The magnetic stripe on the back of credit cards and other ID cards contain information that identifies you and the card.

© iStockphoto / Ryan Warnick

Smart Cards

A **smart card**, which is an alternative to a magnetic stripe card, stores data on an integrated circuit embedded in the card (Figure 8-24). Two types of smart cards are contact and contactless. When you insert a contact smart card in a specialized card reader, the information on the smart card is read and, if necessary, updated. Contactless smart cards communicate with a reader using a radio frequency, which means the user simply places the card near the reader.

Internet Research

Which credit cards are smart cards?

Search for: credit card chips

✳ CONSIDER THIS

What are some uses of smart cards?

Uses of smart cards include storing medical records, vaccination data, and other health care and identification information; tracking information, such as employee attendance or customer purchases; storing a prepaid amount of money, such as for student purchases on campus or fares for public transportation; and authenticating users, such as for Internet purchases or building access. In addition, a smart card can double as an ID card or credit card. Read Secure IT 8-4 for tips about protecting your credit cards.

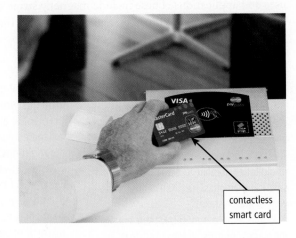

contact smart card

contactless smart card

Figure 8-24 Examples of contact and contactless smart cards and their readers.
© iStockphoto / oytun karadayi; © iStockphoto / alexander kirch

✳ SECURE IT 8-4

Using Credit Cards Safely

Consumers in the United States own more than 600 million credit cards, and the average cardholder has more than 3 cards available to use. With this widespread use, the potential for theft is high.

The newest smart cards have embedded RFID tags that allow vendors to obtain the account number without physically touching the card. While this technology is convenient for both the merchant and consumer, it also enables thieves with remote scanners to capture the card's information without the owner's knowledge.

Thieves also use a handheld device to swipe the card and then obtain and store account details. This action, called *skimming*, is prevalent at gas stations, restaurants, and lounges, where unscrupulous employees sell the information to criminals who then spend your money or steal your identity.

Follow the tips below to help keep your credit card account safe:

Do

- Use a card with added security features, such as a photo.
- Draw a line through blank areas on restaurant charge slips. If you have left a cash tip on the table, write the words, On Table, in the slip's tip amount section.
- Cover the keypad when entering a PIN.
- Save charge receipts and check them against monthly statements or online postings.
- Keep a record in a safe place of all your credit card numbers, expiration dates, and toll-free numbers to call if you need to report a lost or stolen card.
- Purchase an RFID-proof wallet to shield smart cards from remote readers.
- Shred new credit account mail solicitations.
- Look for skimmers, which can capture a credit card number. (Read Secure IT 3-2 on page 114 for information about skimmers.)

Do Not

- Reveal your account number during a phone call unless you have initiated the call.
- Write your PIN on the card or on the protective envelope.
- Sign a blank charge slip.
- Carry extra cards, especially when traveling to unfamiliar locations.
- Let your card out of sight. While you may not be able to follow this advice at a restaurant when you hand the card to a server, you can be observant of employees' behaviors.

✳ Do you know anyone who has been a victim of credit card theft? What steps will you take to use credit cards more safely after reading this information?

RFID Tags

Recall that RFID is a technology that uses radio signals to communicate with a tag placed in or attached to an object, an animal, or a person. The **RFID tag** consists of an antenna and a memory chip that contains the information to be transmitted via radio waves (Figure 8-25). An RFID reader reads the radio signals and transfers the information to a computer or computing device.

RFID tags are either passive or active. An active RFID tag contains a battery that runs the chip's circuitry and broadcasts a signal to the RFID reader. A passive RFID tag does not contain a battery and, thus, cannot send a signal until the reader activates the tag's antenna by sending out electromagnetic waves. Because passive RFID tags contain no battery, these can be small enough to be embedded in skin.

Figure 8-25 An RFID reader reads radio signals from an RFID tag.
© iStockphoto / © Jaap Hart;
© Amy Evenstad / Photos.com;
Rolf Vennenbernd/dpa /Landov

 CONSIDER THIS

How do RFID tags differ from contactless smart cards?

The physical size of the chip and storage capacities in an RFID tag typically are much smaller than the chips in contactless smart cards. The chips in RFID tags usually are read only, whereas the chips in contactless smart cards can function as a processor. Also, RFID tags often are not as secure as contactless smart cards. Thus, credit cards that contain RFID tags, called RFID-enabled credit cards, may not be as secure as those that use contactless technology.

Microfilm and Microfiche

Microfilm and microfiche store microscopic images of documents on roll or sheet film. **Microfilm** is a 100- to 215-foot roll of film. **Microfiche** is a small sheet of film, usually about 4 × 6 inches. A *computer output microfilm recorder* is the device that records the images on the film. The stored images are so small that you can read them only with a microfilm or microfiche reader (Figure 8-26).

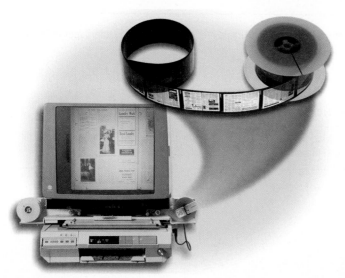

Figure 8-26 Images on microfilm can be read only with a microfilm reader.
© Bill Aron /Photo Edit; © Cengage Learning

The use of microfilm and microfiche provides a number of advantages. They greatly reduce the amount of paper that firms must handle. They are inexpensive and have the longest life of any storage media. To save on physical storage space and to make access easier, however, some organizations have invested in special scanners that convert existing microfilm and microfiche to digital files. Read Ethics & Issues 8-4 to consider storage requirements for public companies.

 ETHICS & ISSUES 8-4

How Much Data Should Companies Be Required to Keep?

Over a decade ago, after a string of corporate scandals, lawmakers enacted the *Sarbanes-Oxley Act*. The law provides a myriad of financial reporting requirements and guidelines for public companies. A main focus of the law is the retention of business records. Because of the law, companies have been confronted with massive new data storage requirements for these records. For example, under this law, a company must retain all of its email messages just as it would other business records. Deleting stored email messages constitutes a destruction of evidence infraction. Employees can face penalties of up to 20 years in prison for altering or destroying records or documents. IT departments must not only understand this complex law, but they also must ensure accuracy of financial data, determine policies for record retention, and provide storage capacity to hold all of the data.

Supporters of the law state that it is essential to avoid corporate scandals caused by lack of accuracy in financial reporting. They also say that consumer confidence has increased because the financial statements are more transparent. Further, the financial costs for complying with the law have decreased since companies have implemented plans. Opponents claim that the law is overreaching and costs too much for the added benefits. In addition, opponents blame the law for a decline in the number of IPOs (initial public offerings), as well as the transfer of several large companies to foreign countries.

Is the Sarbanes-Oxley Act an unfair burden on companies? Why or why not? Does this law impact internal communications in an organization? Why or why not? Are such laws necessary in order to protect the public? Why or why not?

 CONSIDER THIS

Who uses microfilm and microfiche?

Microfilm and microfiche use is widespread, with many organizations allowing you to search through and view microfilm images online. Libraries use these media to store back issues of newspapers, magazines, and genealogy records. Enterprises may use microfilm and microfiche to archive inactive files. Some financial organizations use them to store transactions and canceled checks. The U.S. Army uses them to store personnel records.

 NOW YOU KNOW

Be sure you understand the material presented in the sections titled Enterprise Storage and Other Types of Storage, as it relates to the chapter objectives.
You now should know . . .

- When you might use RAID, network attached storage, storage area network, and tape (Objective 8)
- Where you would use a magnetic stripe card, smart card, and microfilm and microfiche (Objective 9)

 Quiz Yourself Online: Check your knowledge of related content by navigating to this book's Quiz Yourself resource on Computer Concepts CourseMate and then tapping or clicking Objectives 8–9.

Chapter Summary

This chapter presented a variety of storage options. You learned about storage capacity and storage access times. The chapter discussed characteristics of hard disks, RAID, and external hard drives. It discussed various types of flash memory storage, including SSDs, memory cards, and USB flash drives. It presented advantages and various uses of cloud storage. Next, the chapter discussed characteristics of optical discs. Enterprise storage options were presented. You also learned about magnetic stripe cards, smart cards, RFID tags, and microfilm and microfiche.

Test your knowledge of chapter material by accessing the Study Guide, Flash Cards, and Practice Test apps that run on your smartphone, tablet, laptop, or desktop.

TECHNOLOGY @ WORK

Manufacturing

Manufacturing plays a crucial role in today's society. To keep up with our growing population's increasing demand for various products, organizations explore ways to streamline manufacturing processes while simultaneously minimizing costs. These organizations often find that using technology in the manufacturing process requires fewer people-hours, and products and parts are manufactured with greater accuracy and less waste.

Automakers, for example, manufacture cars on an assembly line. In the early years of car manufacturing, people were involved at all stages of the manufacturing process. It was not uncommon to find hundreds or thousands of individuals working along the line. Although the assembly line allowed individuals to manufacture cars as quickly as they could, companies soon realized that computer-aided manufacturing (CAM) would increase output and decrease labor costs. In fact, CAM proved to be most effective when used in conjunction with computer-aided design (CAD). CAD designs an item, such as a car, to manufacture; CAM then manufactures the car according to the original design. Computers also determine the exact amount of material necessary to build the car, as well as the expected output.

Communications during the assembly process is critical. Computers automatically communicate with each other along the assembly line and provide alerts when factors arise that can interrupt the process. For example, running out of hinges that attach the door to the car's body will halt the line until someone replenishes the hinges. Computers, however, often alert individuals to low supplies before they run out and the assembly halts. Failure to detect the missing hinges might result in the machinery attempting to manufacture the car without hinges. This could result in damage to the door and/or the car's body further along the assembly line.

Today, technology assists with manufacturing many types of items. Although some might argue that computers perform jobs that people once held, their introduction has helped to meet society's increased demand for products and desire for low prices.

How else might computers and technology be used in manufacturing?

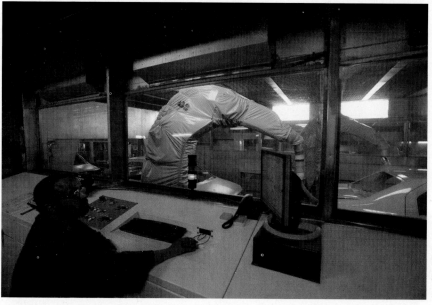

Associated Press

Study Guide

The Study Guide exercise reinforces material you should know for the chapter exam. You will find answers to items with the 📄 icon only in the e-book.

Access the Study Guide app that runs on your smartphone, tablet, laptop, or desktop by navigating to this book's Apps resource on Computer Concepts CourseMate.

Instructions: Answer the questions below using the format that helps you remember best or that is required by your instructor. Possible formats may include one or more of these options: write the answers; create a document that contains the answers; record answers as audio or video using a webcam, smartphone, or portable media player; post answers on a blog, wiki, or website; or highlight answers in the book/e-book.

1. Define the term, secondary storage. List types of storage media.

2. Differentiate between writing and reading data to storage media.

3. _____ refers to the number of bytes a storage medium can hold. Identify terms manufacturers use to determine this.

4. Differentiate between storage and memory and describe how they interact.

5. Explain what access time measures and how transfer rates are stated.

6. List characteristics of a hard disk.

7. List steps for installing an internal hard drive. Describe how to transfer files from one internal hard drive to another.

8. Define the term, read/write head.

9. 📄 Describe the contributions of Al Shugart, with respect to storage.

10. Describe how disk cache improves hard disk access time.

11. RAID is an acronym for _____.

12. 📄 List sizes and storage capacities of different external hard disks.

13. Explain how to encrypt files.

14. 📄 Describe the contributions of Seagate, with respect to storage solutions.

15. Explain how you can restore deleted files and erased media.

16. List how to protect storage media from security screening equipment.

17. Define the term, SSD. List devices that use SSDs.

18. List advantages and disadvantages of SSDs versus magnetic hard disks.

19. Explain the ethical issues surrounding government search and seizure of computers.

20. Describe memory cards and their uses. 📄 List types of memory cards.

21. Identify questions to ask before deciding how to share media files. 📄 List examples of photo, video, and music sharing websites.

22. Explain the ethical issues surrounding posting photos of others on Facebook. 📄 Describe Facebook's privacy settings.

23. Explain how to eject removable storage media safely.

24. List advantages of cloud storage.

25. 📄 Describe the contributions of Amazon and Jeff Bezos.

26. Explain the ethical issues surrounding ownership of cloud data.

27. Name uses of cloud storage. Explain criteria for evaluating cloud storage providers.

28. Define the term, optical disc. 📄 List formats of optical discs.

29. Optical discs store items by using microscopic indentations called _____, and flat areas called _____.

30. List steps for cleaning and fixing scratches on optical discs.

31. Differentiate among CD-ROM, CD-R, and CD-RW discs.

32. Describe the storage techniques that make DVD storage higher capacity than CD storage.

33. Explain the role of a controller for transferring data from a drive to the computer components.

34. List and describe interfaces for use in personal computers.

35. Describe the four types of backup used by business and home users. 📄 Explain how enterprises use continuous data protection.

36. Explain how to back up smartphones and other mobile devices.

37. Define the terms, redundancy and outsourcing, as they relate to enterprise computing.

38. Enterprise storage devices often use _____, which duplicates data to improve its reliability.

39. Describe how RAID uses mirroring and striping. 📄 Explain how RAID levels optimize computing.

40. Differentiate between a NAS and an SAN.

41. Explain how enterprise computers use tape for storage.

42. Differentiate between sequential and direct access.

43. Explain the implications of the permanence of digital content.

44. Define the terms, magnetic stripe card and smart card. Describe the uses of each.

45. List tips for using credit cards safely.

46. Differentiate between active and passive RFID tags.

47. Explain how microfilm and microfiche are used and the advantages of using these technologies.

48. Explain the ethical issues surrounding the Sarbanes-Oxley Act.

49. Describe how technology is used in the manufacturing industry.

You should be able to define the Primary Terms and be familiar with the Secondary Terms listed below.

Key Terms

Access the Flash Cards app that runs on your smartphone, tablet, laptop, or desktop by navigating to this book's Apps resource on Computer Concepts CourseMate. View definitions for each term by navigating to this book's Key Terms resource on Computer Concepts CourseMate. Listen to definitions for each term on your portable media player by navigating to this book's Audio Study Tools resource on Computer Concepts CourseMate.

Primary Terms   (shown in **bold-black** characters in the chapter)

access time (339)
Blu-Ray (355)
capacity (336)
CD-R (355)
CD-ROM (355)
CD-RW (355)
CF (CompactFlash) (348)
cloud storage (351)
DVD-R (355)
DVD-ROM (355)
DVD-RW (355)
DVD+R (355)

DVD+RAM (355)
DVD+RW (355)
external hard disk (343)
hard disk (339)
M2 (Memory Stick Micro) (348)
magnetic stripe card (361)
memory card (347)
Memory Stick PRO Duo (348)
microfiche (363)
microfilm (363)
microSD (348)

microSDHC (348)
microSDXC (348)
miniSD (348)
network attached storage (NAS) (359)
optical disc (352)
RAID (343)
read/write head (342)
reading (336)
RFID tag (363)
SDHC (Secure Digital High Capacity) (348)

SDXC (Secure Digital Expanded Capacity) (348)
smart card (362)
SSD (solid-state drive) (346)
storage area network (SAN) (359)
storage device (336)
tape (360)
USB flash drive (350)
writing (336)
xD Picture Card (348)

Secondary Terms   (shown in *italic* characters in the chapter)

archival backup (357)
backup plan (356)
burning (355)
card reader/writer (348)
computer-output microfilm recorder (363)
controller (356)
density (341)
differential backup (357)
direct access (361)
disk cache (343)
DVD/CD-RW drives (355)
EIDE (356)
eSATA (356)
exabyte (EB) (338)
external hard drive (336)
Fibre Channel (FC) (358)
fixed disk (339)
formatting (342)

full backup (357)
GBps (339)
geotag (349)
gigabyte (GB) (338)
hard disk drive (HDD) (339)
head crash (343)
incremental backup (357)
internal hard drive (336)
jewel case (354)
KBps (339)
kilobyte (KB) (338)
level 1 (358)
LightScribe technology (353)
longitudinal recording (341)
MBps (339)
megabyte (MB) (338)
mini disc (352)
mirroring (358)
multisession (355)

outsourcing (358)
partial backup (357)
perpendicular recording (341)
petabyte (PB) (338)
photo CD (355)
platter (341)
random access (361)
redundancy (358)
revolutions per minute (rpm) (342)
ripping (355)
Sarbanes-Oxley Act (364)
SAS (serial-attached SCSI) (356)
SATA (356)
SCSI (356)
secondary storage (336)
sectors (342)
selective backup (357)
sequential access (361)
single-session disc (355)

skimming (362)
solid-state media (345)
storage appliance (359)
striping (358)
tape cartridge (360)
tape drive (360)
tape library (360)
terabyte (TB) (338)
thumb drive (350)
track (342)
transfer rate (339)
WORM (355)
yottabyte (YB) (338)
zettabyte (ZB) (338)

external hard disk (343)

Checkpoint

The Checkpoint exercises test your knowledge of the chapter concepts. The page number containing the answer appears in parentheses after each exercise. The Consider This exercises challenge your understanding of chapter concepts.

Complete the Checkpoint exercises interactively by navigating to this book's Checkpoint resource on Computer Concepts CourseMate. **Access the Test Prep app** that runs on your smartphone, tablet, laptop, or desktop by navigating to this book's Apps resource on Computer Concepts CourseMate. After successfully completing the self-assessment through the Test Prep app, **take the Practice Test** by navigating to this book's Practice Test resource on Computer Concepts CourseMate.

True/False Mark T for True and F for False.

_____ 1. Storage devices can be categorized as input or output devices. (336)

_____ 2. A storage medium is volatile; that is, items stored on it remain intact even when you turn off a computer or mobile device. (338)

_____ 3. Compared with the access time of memory, the access time of storage devices is slow. (339)

_____ 4. Because of current standards, head crashes no longer occur. (343)

_____ 5. While encrypted files offer greater security than unencrypted files, an operating system may require more time to open and access encrypted files. (344)

_____ 6. The transfer rate of external hard drives usually is slower than that of internal hard drives. (344)

_____ 7. Solid-state media is more durable and shock resistant than other types of media, such as magnetic hard disks or optical discs, because it contains no moving parts. (345)

_____ 8. Like a hard disk, you regularly should defragment an SSD to increase access times. (346)

_____ 9. When you are finished using a USB flash drive, simply remove it from the USB port. (350)

_____ 10. Mini discs require a separate mini disc drive; that is, they do not work in standard-sized optical disc drives. (353)

_____ 11. With serial transfers, data is sent one bit at a time. (356)

_____ 12. An active RFID tag contains a battery than runs the chip's circuitry and broadcasts a signal to the RFID reader; because they are so small, they can be embedded in skin. (363)

Multiple Choice Select the best answer.

1. _____ measures the amount of time it takes a storage device to locate an item on a storage medium and/or the time required to deliver an item from memory to the processor. (339)
   a. Rpm(s)
   b. Transfer time
   c. Access time
   d. Clock speed

2. A(n) _____ is a storage device that contains one or more inflexible, circular platters that use magnetic particles to store data, instructions, and information. (339)
   a. hard disk
   b. SSD
   c. USB flash drive
   d. optical disc

3. A hard disk's storage locations consist of wedge-shaped sections, which break the tracks into small arcs called _____. (342)
   a. sectors
   b. formats
   c. segments
   d. platters

4. _____, sometimes called a buffer, consists of a memory chip(s) on a hard disk that stores frequently accessed items, such as data, instructions, and information. (343)
   a. RAID
   b. SSD
   c. A mini disc
   d. Disk cache

5. A disc on which you can write multiple times sometimes is called a _____ disc. (355)
   a. single-session
   b. CD-ROM
   c. multisession
   d. WORM

6. The process of copying audio and/or video data from a purchased disc and saving it on your own media is called _____. (355)
   a. ripping
   b. burning
   c. tearing
   d. formatting

7. A selective backup sometimes is called a(n) _____ backup. (357)
   a. differential
   b. incremental
   c. partial
   d. archival

8. Enterprise storage often uses _____ technology as the interface that connects the devices to the network because it has much faster transmission rates than SCSI. (358)
   a. SAS
   b. serial transfer
   c. Fibre Channel
   d. SATA

Checkpoint

Matching Match the terms with their definitions.

_____ 1. writing (336)

_____ 2. reading (336)

_____ 3. capacity (336)

_____ 4. density (341)

_____ 5. perpendicular recording (341)

_____ 6. longitudinal recording (341)

_____ 7. solid-state media (345)

_____ 8. controller (356)

_____ 9. mirroring (358)

_____ 10. random access (361)

a. storage method in which the magnetic particles are aligned horizontally around a disk's surface

b. the number of bits in an area on a storage medium

c. the number of bytes a storage medium can hold

d. special-purpose chip and electronic circuits that control the transfer of data, instructions, and information from a drive to and from the system bus and other components in the computer

e. flash memory chip type that consists entirely of electronic components, such as integrated circuits, and contains no moving parts

f. the simplest RAID storage design, which writes data on two disks at the same time to duplicate the data

g. process of transferring data, instructions, and information from memory to a storage medium

h. storage method in which the magnetic particles are aligned vertically to a disk's surface, making much greater storage capacities possible

i. storage technique in which a device is able to locate a particular data item or file immediately, without having to move consecutively through items stored in front of the desired item or file

j. process of transferring data, instructions, and information from a storage medium into memory

Short Answer Write a brief answer to each of the following questions.

1. Differentiate between volatile and nonvolatile memory. (338) Is a screen display volatile or nonvolatile? (338)

2. How does the access time of storage compare with the access time of memory? (339) At what speeds do they access items? (339)

3. How does the transfer rate of external hard drives compare to that of internal hard drives? (344) List some advantages of external hard drives. (344)

4. What is the life span of a memory card? (348) List ways to care for a memory card. (348)

5. Describe differences between microfilm and microfiche. (363) What are some advantages of using microfilm and microfiche for storage? (364)

☀ Consider This Answer the following questions in the format specified by your instructor.

1. Answer the critical thinking questions posed at the end of these elements in this chapter: Ethics & Issues (347, 350, 351, 364), How To (340, 341, 344, 350, 354), Mini Features (349, 351, 356), Secure IT (345, 346, 361, 362), and Technology @ Work (365).

2. What does access time measure? (339)

3. 🖥 What is the range of the storage capacities of hard disks? (341)

4. How does disk cache affect a hard disk's speed? (343)

5. What should you do if you accidentally delete a file or erase media? (345)

6. What are some disadvantages of SSDs? (347)

7. How can you determine the best place to share your media files? (349)

8. 🖥 Which Facebook privacy settings allow you to control whether others post photos of you? (350)

9. How is cloud storage used to share projects in a work environment? (352)

10. How do optical discs store items? (353)

11. What are the differences among a CD-ROM, a CD-R, and a CD-RW? (355)

12. 🖥 What are some types and features of backup software? (357)

13. What does redundancy mean with respect to enterprise storage? (358)

14. Which is faster: sequential or direct access? Why? (361)

15. Are email messages considered business records? Why or why not? (364)

✸ How To: Your Turn

The How To: Your Turn exercises present general guidelines for fundamental skills when using a computer or mobile device and then require that you determine how to apply these general guidelines to a specific program or situation.

Instructions: You often can complete tasks using technology in multiple ways. Figure out how to perform the tasks described in these exercises by using one or more resources available to you (such as a computer or mobile device, articles on the web or in print, online or program help, user guides, blogs, podcasts, videos, other individuals, trial and error, etc.). Summarize your 'how to' steps, along with the resource(s) used, in the format requested by your instructor (brief report, presentation, discussion, blog post, video, or other means).

❶ Organize Files on a Storage Device Using Folders

Organizing the files on a storage device not only can improve your computer's performance, but it also can make your files easy to locate. If you are accustomed to saving files to your desktop or to a folder on your storage device, you should consider organizing the files by storing them in appropriate folders. The following steps guide you through the process of using folders to organize files on a storage device.

a. Review the types of files you currently store on your device.

b. Current operating systems such as Windows and Mac OS include locations for storing different types of files such as documents, music files, video files, and photos. Within these locations, however, you should create additional folders to further organize these file types. The method you use to organize each file type might vary.

1. Create folders to store your documents by the type of content they contain. For example, you might create separate folders to store files related to academics, finances, and entertainment. Then, consider whether you should create folders within these folders. For instance, you might create additional folders within the Academics folder to organize your files by subject.

2. Create folders to store your music by genre. Within each genre, create additional folders to sort your music by artist. If you have many songs for a particular artist, consider creating folders within the artist's folder to store the songs by album.

3. Create folders to store your photos and videos either by date, event, or a combination of the two. For example, you could have a folder for a particular year, and then within that folder, create additional folders for all events that occurred within that year.

c. Although the desktop seems to be a convenient location to store files, it quickly can become cluttered. The only files you should store on the desktop are the ones you will need in the immediate future. If will not need a file again for at least several days, consider storing it in one of the folders mentioned previously.

d. Review the files on your storage device periodically and delete the ones you no longer need. Delete only the files you have placed on your storage device; be careful not to delete files that any programs or the operating system may need to run.

Exercises

1. Review the files and folders on your storage device. In your opinion, do you feel they are organized effectively? Why or why not?

2. How are the files and folders on your storage device organized?

3. When you take photos on a digital camera, the camera often generates a file name consisting of a generic prefix and sequential number. What are some ways to identify the photos easily on your digital camera's memory card?

❷ Copy Individual Files to Another Storage Device, and Copy Files to Cloud Storage

If you save a file on your computer or mobile device and later will need to access it on another device, you likely will have to copy the file to another storage device or to the cloud so that you can access the file on the other device. The following steps guide you through the process of copying files to another storage device or to the cloud.

Copying Files to Another Storage Device

a. Navigate to the location containing the file you want to copy. If the file is on an external storage device or memory card, connect the storage device to your computer or insert the flash memory card into your computer's card reader. Next, navigate to the location containing the file you want to copy.

b. Navigate to the location to which you want to copy the file. If the location to which you want to

How To: Your Turn ✳

copy the file is on an external storage device or on a memory card, connect the external storage device to your computer or insert the flash memory card into your computer's card reader. Next, navigate to the location to which you want to copy the file.

c. Drag the file you want to copy to the destination location. After you drag the file, make sure the file exists both in the source and destination location.

Copying a File to the Cloud

a. If necessary, sign up for an account with an online service that can store your files. Some online services store only photos and videos, while other services store all types of files, such as documents and other media files.

© iStockphoto / Aaltazar

b. Sign in to the online service and navigate to the page where you can upload files.
c. Tap or click the button or link to upload a file.
d. Navigate to and then tap or click the file you want to upload.
e. Tap or click the button or link to upload the file.

Exercises

1. What types of files might you want to copy to the cloud? Why would you copy files to the cloud instead of copying them to an external storage device?
2. What are at least three online services that allow you to store files? Are they free, or do they charge a fee? How much space do they provide? How do you obtain more storage space?
3. What steps would you take to copy a file from the cloud to your computer or mobile device?

❸ Manage Space on a Storage Device

As you use your computer or mobile device, chances are that you are storing more files and installing additional programs and apps. At some point, you might require additional space or need to improve performance on your storage device. While purchasing an additional storage device might seem like the best option, ways may be available to help you manage the space on your existing storage device so that an additional purchase is not necessary. The following steps guide you through the process of managing space on a storage device.

a. Review the files on your storage device and identify unused files you might be able to delete. Be careful not to remove files that the operating system, programs, or apps require to run properly.
b. View the list of programs and apps you have installed on your computer or mobile device. If you no longer need a program or app, uninstall it.
c. If you have files you may need in the future but not immediately, consider compressing them or copying them to an external storage device or to cloud storage. Verify the files have copied properly and then remove the files from your primary storage device.
d. Defragment the storage device. If the storage device has not been defragmented recently, this process might improve performance significantly.
e. Search for and use any other tools that might be available in your operating system to maximize available space or improve performance. Note that some programs that claim to increase free space by compressing the files on your hard disk may slow your computer's performance.
f. If the above options do not increase performance enough or create sufficient free space, you might need to purchase an additional storage device.

Exercises

1. What files on your storage device might you consider deleting to save space? Why?
2. Does your computer or mobile device contain any programs or apps that you no longer need? How can you uninstall programs and apps from your computer or mobile device?
3. How does defragmentation help increase performance on your computer?

✸ Internet Research

The Internet Research exercises broaden your understanding of chapter concepts by requiring that you search for information on the web.

Instructions: Use a search engine or another search tool to locate the information requested or answers to questions presented in the exercises. Describe your findings, along with the search term(s) you used and your web source(s), in the format requested by your instructor (brief report, presentation, discussion, blog post, video, or other means).

1 Making Use of the Web
Environment and Science

Protecting the Earth's fragile ecosystem is a task ecologists and conservationists undertake daily. Their environmental websites seek to educate and often persuade citizens to become aware of issues. The information helps consumers to make environmentally responsible purchasing decisions and urges people to become involved in solving global environmental problems. Scientists, likewise, work to research issues on Earth. Their efforts extend beyond investigating this planet to exploring the great frontier of space. Their science websites contain information about current studies, conferences, and breakthroughs in such areas as biology, earth and ocean sciences, physics, and chemistry.

(a) Visit two environmental or science websites or apps and locate recent news stories or blog entries. What issues are being discussed? Are volunteer opportunities available? What media materials are available to view and download? Are links to news stories or research articles shown? What projects or campaigns are proposed?

(b) Visit a space or astronomy website, such as NASA, and browse its contents or download related apps. Which general topics are available for students? What types of current news articles are displayed? Are additional resources, such as videos and photos, available? Are social media accounts listed to interact with scientists, astronauts, and researchers?

2 Social Media 📄

Digital footprints tracking your Internet activity are relatively easy to find. Maintaining online anonymity is difficult to achieve once you have established social media accounts with your actual name. While deleting a social media account is a fairly easy process, deleting all remnants of information relating to the account can be a more difficult task. Just because you no longer can sign in to the account does not mean your posts, photos, and personal information do not exist somewhere on a website.

If you desire to remove an Internet presence for security or personal reasons, begin by searching for your name or account user names. Remove your profiles from any social media account that is displayed in the search results. Each of the social media websites has a process to close an account, generally through the account's settings page. Next, contact the websites listed in the search results and ask that your name be removed. Many companies have a form to complete and submit. A third place to hunt for your information is on websites listing public records and people searches. Again, attempt to contact these companies and request that your personal information be removed. As a last resort, some services will perform these tasks for a fee.

Use a search engine to locate instances of your name or user names. Did the search results list these names? If so, which social media sites or companies have records of your name? Then, search for your name on at least two websites that have public records or people databases. Did you see your name on these websites? If so, do you want the details, such as a phone number or address, available for anyone to see? If not, attempt to remove this data and write a report of the steps you took and your success in deleting the personal information.

Source: NASA.gov

Internet Research ☀

❸ Search Sleuth

(1) Which technology innovator appeared on *Dancing with the Stars* in 2009? (2) In which city is the Storage Networking Industry Association's Technology Center located? (3) What company introduced using a hard disk for accounting projects in 1956? (4) Which country requires every citizen to carry a smart card for health insurance purposes? (5) Which nonprofit organization facilitates USB standards and testing? (6) What is the maximum length a USB cable can be before signal strength and voltage decline? (7) Which musician released a special edition of the album, *The Fame Monster*, on a USB flash drive? (8) Which flash memory storage manufacturer has a factory in China that is the size of five football fields, yet employs only 400 workers at that facility? (9) Which symbol is the logo for ExpressCard technology? (10) Which company invented flash memory?

© iStockphoto / Oleksiy Mark

❹ Green Computing

Signing up for paperless billing and electing to receive e-receipts at the grocery store are popular methods consumers use in an effort they believe helps save trees and benefits the environment. Indeed, for more than 30 years the notions of conserving paper and moving toward a paperless office have resonated among environmentally conscious citizens. According to some estimates, however, global consumption of paper has increased 50 percent since 1980.

Some researchers believe the overall paper conservation efforts actually can do more harm to the environment than good when the manufacturing and disposal processes are considered. Greenhouse gas emissions, fossil fuel use, water consumption, and solid waste are part of the products' life cycles. In one example, Apple states that one iPad accounts for 287 pounds of carbon emissions. In contrast, one print book accounts for only 8.85 pounds of carbon dioxide emissions.

Locate articles discussing the paper usage of countries worldwide. Which countries are the largest consumers of paper? Then, locate articles comparing the ecological effects of manufacturing and eCycling e-readers and printed materials. In general, how much energy is required to manufacture mobile devices?

How have sustainable forestry practices helped address environmental concerns? What steps can consumers take to make wise paper choices and use recycled materials when purchasing electronics?

❺ Security

Permanently destroying files on storage media is recommended when donating or selling a computer. Federal laws have imposed strict requirements and penalties for data security, particularly regarding health and insurance records and credit transactions. Secure IT 8-1 on page 345 describes methods for restoring deleted files or erased media, but often companies and individuals truly desire that the data never can be recovered. Sensitive medical and financial information, in particular, should be erased so that savvy criminals and digital forensics examiners cannot recover deleted files. The U.S. Department of Defense and the National Security Agency set standards for sanitizing magnetic media and specify that *degaussing*, or demagnetizing, is the preferred method in lieu of permanently destroying the storage medium. What types of degaussers are available? How do they wipe a drive's contents? How are Gauss and Oersted ratings applied? What length of time is required to degauss a drive? Some companies offer degaussing services. What procedures do they use to ensure secure practices?

❻ Ethics in Action

Although millions of users have stored their data and files on the cloud without incident, Apple cofounder Steve Wozniak is an outspoken critic of using this technology for storing sensitive data. He claims that "horrible problems" will occur with cloud computing in the near future. He also criticizes the terms of service with which cloud computing users must comply.

Locate articles discussing Wozniak's comments about using cloud computing. Why does he criticize the cloud services his company uses? Do you share his concerns about storing data on the cloud? When have iCloud accounts been hacked? What is Wozniak's opinion of Siri, the digital personal assistant available on Apple products, prior to when his company bought the program in 2010? What is his current opinion of Siri?

✳ Problem Solving

The Problem Solving exercises extend your knowledge of chapter concepts by seeking solutions to practical problems with technology that you may encounter at home, school, work, or with nonprofit organizations. The Collaboration exercise should be completed with a team.

💻 Challenge yourself with additional Problem Solving exercises by navigating to this book's Problem Solving resource on Computer Concepts CourseMate.

Instructions: You often can solve problems with technology in multiple ways. Determine a solution to the problems in these exercises by using one or more resources available to you (such as a computer or mobile device, articles on the web or in print, blogs, podcasts, videos, television, user guides, other individuals, electronics or computer stores, etc.). Describe your solution, along with the resource(s) used, in the format requested by your instructor (brief report, presentation, discussion, blog post, video, or other means).

Personal

1. **Unrecognized Storage Device** You have connected an external storage device to your new MacBook Pro, but the operating system is not recognizing the device's contents. Instead, it asks whether you want to format the device. Why might this be happening?

2. **Second Hard Disk Connection** While installing a second hard disk in your computer, you realize that your computer does not include a cable to connect the hard disk to the motherboard. How can you determine what type of cable to purchase?

3. **Incompatible Memory Card** While attempting to copy files from your digital camera to your laptop, you realize that the memory card from your camera does not fit in the memory card slot on your laptop. What other steps can you take to copy the pictures from the camera to the laptop?

4. **Error Copying Files** You are copying files to your external storage device, but halfway through copying one of your files, an error message is displayed and the copy process ends immediately. What are your next steps?

5. **Increase Smartphone Storage** You want to increase the amount of storage space on your smartphone by purchasing an additional memory card. How can you determine if your smartphone can support a memory card and which type of memory card to purchase?

Professional

6. **Inaccessible Files** Your company requires you to store your files on a remote server so that you can access the files from any location within the company. When you sign in to another computer using your account, you cannot see your files. What might be causing this?

7. **Encrypted Storage Device** You have purchased an external storage device so that you can back up files on your office computer. The IT department in your company informs you that you must make sure the data on the device is encrypted. What are your next steps?

8. **Alternative to Tape Storage** Your company still uses tape storage to back up important files, but your manager has asked you to begin researching alternatives to the aging technology. What steps will you take to research current storage technologies that are suitable to store company backups?

9. **Faulty RFID Card** You use an RFID card to obtain access to your office. When you attempt to scan your card, the RFID reader acts like it does not recognize your card is nearby. What are your next steps?

10. **Hard Disk Failure** Your computer displays a message during the boot process stating that a hard disk error has occurred, and you are unable to run the operating system. What are your next steps?

Collaboration

11. **Technology in Manufacturing** Today, technology is used in the manufacturing of nearly every type of item. Your instructor would like everyone to realize the importance of technology in today's society and requests that each person select an item and determine how technology might have been used to assist in the manufacturing process of that item. Form a team of three people. Each team member should locate one item that he or she believes was manufactured with the help of technology. Then, team members should research exactly how the technology was used and then record their findings. Finally, the three team members should compare their research to discover similarities and differences and then compile their findings into a brief report.

The Critical Thinking exercises challenge your assessment and decision-making skills by presenting real-world situations associated with chapter concepts. The Collaboration exercise should be completed with a team.

Critical Thinking ☀

 Challenge yourself with additional Critical Thinking exercises by navigating to this book's Critical Thinking resource on Computer Concepts CourseMate.

Instructions: Evaluate the situations below, using personal experiences and one or more resources available to you (such as articles on the web or in print, blogs, podcasts, videos, television, user guides, other individuals, electronics or computer stores, etc.). Perform the tasks requested in each exercise and share your deliverables in the format requested by your instructor (brief report, presentation, discussion, blog post, video, or other means).

1. Class Discussion

Increasing Storage Capacity   You are the office manager at a local boutique. The store needs to increase its storage capacity, and so decides to buy an external hard drive. Your boss asks you to research access times and storage capacities of various external hard drives. Use the web to learn more about available hard drive options. What other factors should you evaluate when determining the appropriate hard drive to purchase? Analyze the advantages and disadvantages of using external hard drives for storage. Include in your discussion backup plans, costs, and alternate options. Recommend two hard drives to your boss. Include user reviews and any information by industry experts in your comparison between the two different hard drives. Which is the best option? Why? Compile your findings.

2. Research and Share

Permanently Removing Data   Many companies and government agencies make extensive efforts to protect the data and information stored on their computers and mobile devices. When a computer or device reaches the end of its useful life, it either is recycled or discarded. Although the obsolete computer or device does not perform well, if at all, the data on the computer or device often is intact. Companies and government agencies should take precautionary measures to remove the data and information so that someone else cannot recover it and use it for malicious purposes. Use the web to find ways to destroy data before discarding computers and devices. What methods are used? What reasons are given, if any? Locate software you can use to wipe a computer's hard drive, or the data from a mobile device. Which programs would you recommend? Why? How does wiping a hard drive differ from erasing data from a mobile device?

3. Case Study

Farmers' Market   You are the new manager for a group of organic farmers who have a weekly market in season. The board of directors has asked you to create a backup plan for the market's computers and devices. Use the web to find industry experts' recommendations for backing up data. Write a sample backup plan and schedule for the board, and include types of backups you will use. Include the different computers and device types the market uses: multiple laptops, a desktop, and a tablet, as well as several smartphones. Describe each backup type you propose and why you recommend it. Is any special software required to back up the different devices? The board asked you to present reasons for using cloud storage as part of your backup plan. Research the benefits of using cloud storage over other backup methods. Why would you choose cloud storage? What are the cost differences? Compare three cloud storage providers, ordering them by cost and storage capacity.

Collaboration

4. **Computers in Telemarketing**   Your team is performing IT research for a magazine-subscription telemarketing company. The company's 150 telemarketers must make a minimum of 100 calls a day. If telemarketers do not meet the minimum number, they must finish the calls from home. The company must decide on the type of storage device to provide the telemarketers so that they can take the necessary data home. Management has narrowed the choice to three storage options: rewritable optical discs, cloud storage, or USB flash drives. Form a three-member team and assign an option to each member. Each team member should evaluate the advantages and disadvantages. Include features such as capacity, access time, durability of media, ease of transporting between home and office, and cost. Meet with your team, and discuss and compile your findings. Which method would you recommend? Why? What are the advantages of each? Share your findings with the class.

Courtesy of Kingston Technology Company Inc.

✳ Beyond the Book

The Beyond the Book exercises expand your understanding of chapter concepts by requiring research.

🔘 **Access premium content** by visiting Computer Concepts CourseMate. If you have a Computer Concepts CourseMate access code, you can reinforce and extend your learning with MindTap Reader, practice tests, video, and other premium content for Discovering Computers. To sign in to Computer Concepts CourseMate at www.cengagebrain.com, you first must create a student account and then register this book, as described at www.cengage.com/ct/studentdownload.

Part 1 Instructions: Use the web or e-book to perform the task identified for each book element below. Describe your findings, along with the search term(s) you used and your web source(s), if appropriate, in the format requested by your instructor (brief report, presentation, discussion, blog post, video, or other means).

1. **Animations** 📱 Review the animations associated with this chapter and then answer the question(s) they pose (342, 359). What search term would you use to learn more about a specific segment of the animation?

2. **Consider This** Select a Consider This in this chapter (336, 339, 343, 344, 348, 351, 354, 355, 356, 360, 361, 362, 363, 364) and find a recent article that elaborates on the topic. What information did you find that was not presented in this book or e-book?

3. **Drag-and-Drop Figures** 📱 Complete the Drag-and-Drop Figure activities associated with this chapter (338, 342). What did you learn from each of these activities?

4. **Ethics & Issues** Select an Ethics & Issues in this chapter (347, 350, 351, 364) and find a recent article that supports one view presented. Does the article change your opinion about the topic? Why or why not?

5. **Facebook & Twitter** Review a recent Discovering Computers Facebook post or Twitter Tweet and read the referenced article(s). What did you learn from the article?

6. **High-Tech Talk** 📱 Locate an article that discusses topics related to RAID levels. Would you recommend the article you found? Why or why not?

7. **How To** Select a How To in this chapter (340, 341, 344, 350, 354) and find a recent article that elaborates on the topic. Who would benefit from the content of this article? Why?

8. **Innovative Computing** 📱 Locate two additional facts about DNA as long-term storage or the use of RECAPTCHAs to digitize newspapers and books. Do your findings change your opinion about the future of this innovation? Why or why not?

9. **Internet Research** Use the search term in an Internet Research (338, 343, 347, 348, 351, 362) to answer the question posed in the element. What other search term could you use to answer the question?

10. **Mini Features** Locate an article that discusses topics related to one of the mini features in this chapter (349, 351, 356). Do you feel that the article is appropriate for this course? Why or why not?

11. **Secure IT** Select a Secure IT in this chapter (345, 346, 361, 362) and find a recent article about the topic that you find interesting. How can you relate the content of the article to your everyday life?

12. **Technology @ Work** Locate three additional, unique usages of technology in the manufacturing industry (365). What makes the use of these technologies unique to the manufacturing industry?

13. **Technology Innovators** 📱 Locate two additional facts about Al Shugart, Seagate, SanDisk, and Amazon and its founder, Jeff Bezos. Which Technology Innovator impresses you most? Why?

14. **Third-Party Links** 📱 Visit one of the third-party links identified in this chapter (343, 344, 345, 346, 348, 349, 351, 361, 362, 364, 365) and read the article or watch the video associated with the link. Would you share this link on your online social network account? Why or why not?

Part 2 Instructions: Find specific instructions for the exercises below in the e-book or on Computer Concepts CourseMate. Beside each exercise is a brief description of its online content.

1. 📱 **You Review It** Search for and review a video, podcast, or blog post about current developments in cloud computing.

2. 📱 **Windows and Mac** Enhance your understanding and knowledge about using Windows and Mac computers by completing the Install a Cloud Storage App and Empty Recycle Bin activities.

3. 📱 **Android, iOS, and Windows Phone** Enhance your understanding of mobile devices by completing the Install a Cloud Storage App and Determine Your Device's Capacity activities.

4. 📱 **Exploring Computer Careers** Read about a career as a storage administrator, search for related employment ads, and then answer related questions.

5. 📱 **App Adventure** Find the information you need using reference apps on your smartphone or tablet.

Operating Systems
Managing, Coordinating, and Monitoring Resources

9

Users work with a variety of operating systems on their computers and mobile devices.

"My laptop is running slower than when I bought it, but it seems to be working properly. I install my operating system updates regularly. I added a printer using my operating system's configuration options. Aside from knowing where my files are stored, why do I need to learn about operating systems?"

True, you may be familiar with some of the material in this chapter, but do you know . . .

How to set up a virtual machine?

Whether you need to create an administrator account on your computer?

Who developed an operating system when he was a 21-year-old computer science student in Finland?

What you would find on the Charms bar?

Why you would use Boot Camp?

Which video apps are most suited to your needs?

Where you would find the Launchpad?

Whether you should choose open source or closed source software?

How the textile industry relies on computers, mobile devices, and related technologies?

How benchmarks help measure performance?

What is meant by the term, Live USB?

What causes a computer to start thrashing?

What you can do if your phone runs low on memory?

If employees are required to disclose personal text messages on company-issued devices?

For these answers and to discover much more information essential to this course, read this chapter and visit the associated Computer Concepts CourseMate at www.cengagebrain.com.

✔ Objectives

After completing this chapter, you will be able to:

1 Define an operating system

2 Describe the start-up process and shutdown options on computers and mobile devices

3 Explain how an operating system provides a user interface, manages programs, manages memory, and coordinates tasks

4 Describe how an operating system enables users to configure devices, establish an Internet connection, and monitor performance

5 Identify file management and other tools included with an operating system, along with ways to update operating system software

6 Explain how an operating system enables users to control a network or administer security

7 Summarize the features of several desktop operating systems: Windows, OS X, UNIX, Linux, and Chrome OS

8 Briefly describe various server operating systems: Windows Server, OS X Server, UNIX, and Linux

9 Summarize the features and uses of several mobile operating systems: Google Android, Apple iOS, and Windows Phone

Operating Systems

When you purchase a computer or mobile device, it usually has an operating system and other tools installed. As previously discussed, the operating system and related tools collectively are known as system software because they consist of the programs that control or maintain the operations of the computer and its devices. An **operating system (OS)** is a set of programs that coordinate all the activities among computer or mobile device hardware. Other tools, which were discussed in Chapter 4, enable you to perform maintenance-type tasks usually related to managing devices, media, and programs used by computers and mobile devices.

Most operating systems perform similar functions that include starting and shutting down a computer or mobile device, providing a user interface, managing programs, managing memory, coordinating tasks, configuring devices, establishing an Internet connection, monitoring performance, providing file management and other device or media-related tasks, and updating operating system software. Some operating systems also allow users to control a network and administer security (Figure 9-1).

Although an operating system can run from an external drive, in most cases, an operating system resides inside a computer or mobile device. For example, it is installed on a hard disk or SSD in a laptop or desktop. On mobile devices, the operating system may reside on firmware in the device. *Firmware* consists of ROM chips or flash memory chips that store permanent instructions.

Different sizes of computers typically use different operating systems because the operating systems generally are written to run on a specific type of computer. For example, a supercomputer does not use the same operating system as a laptop or desktop. Even the same types of computers, such as laptops, may not use the same operating system. Some, however, can run multiple operating systems.

When purchasing a program or an application, you must ensure that it works with the operating system installed on your computer or mobile device. The operating system that a computer uses sometimes is called the *platform*. With purchased applications, its specifications will identify the required platform(s), or the operating system(s), on which it will run.

A *cross-platform application* is an application that runs the same on multiple operating systems.

administer security

start and shut down the computer

provide a user interface

control a network

manage programs

update automatically

operating system functions

manage memory

provide file management and other tools

coordinate tasks and configure devices

establish an Internet connection

monitor performance

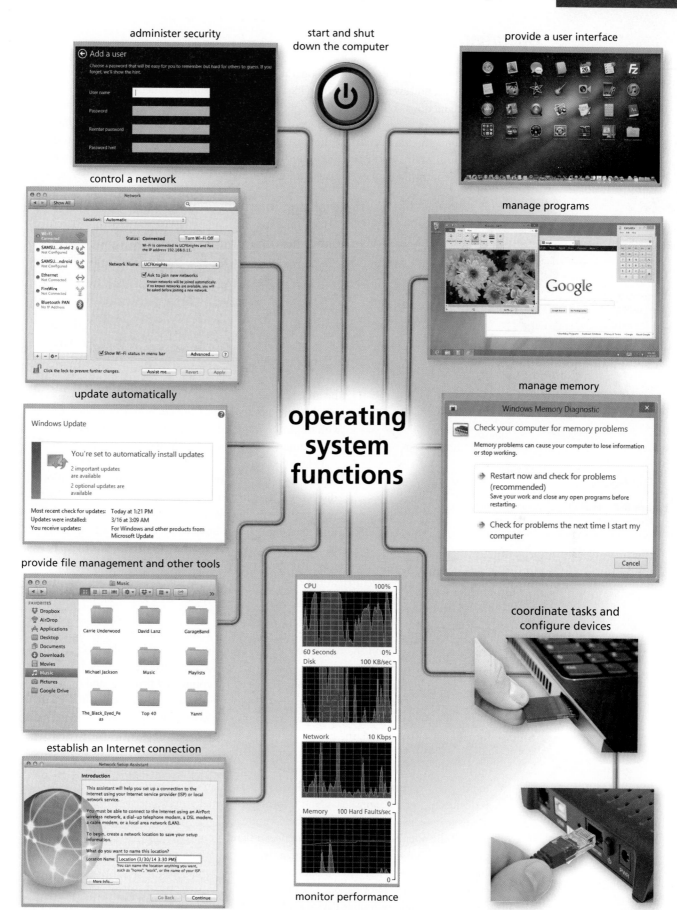

Figure 9-1   Most operating systems perform similar functions, a variety of which are illustrated above.

Operating System Functions

Every computer and mobile device has an operating system. Regardless of the size of the computer or device, however, most operating systems provide similar functions. The following sections discuss functions common to most operating systems. These functions include starting and shutting down computers and mobile devices, providing a user interface, managing programs, managing memory, coordinating tasks, configuring devices, establishing an Internet connection, monitoring performance, providing file and disk management, updating operating system software, controlling a network, and administering security.

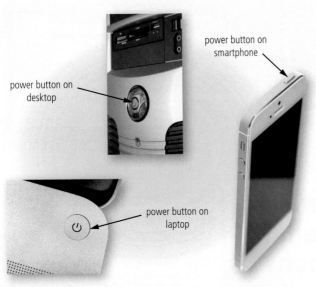

power button on smartphone

power button on desktop

power button on laptop

Figure 9-2   Examples of power buttons on computers and mobile devices.
© Olinchuk / Shutterstock.com; © iStockphoto / kizilkayaphotos; © iStockphoto / Nikada

Starting Computers and Mobile Devices

If a computer or mobile device is off, you press a power button to turn it on (Figure 9-2). If it is on, you may need to restart the computer or mobile device for a variety of reasons. For example, you might install a new program or app, update existing software, or experience network or Internet connectivity problems. Alternatively, you might notice that the performance of the computer or device is sluggish, or it may stop responding altogether. The method you use to restart a computer or device differs, depending on the situation and also the hardware. You may be able to use operating system instructions or press keys on the keyboard to restart the computer or device. Or, you might be required to respond to on-screen prompts. Sometimes, the computer or device restarts automatically.

When you start or restart a computer, a series of messages may appear on the screen. The actual information displayed varies depending on the make and type of the computer or mobile device and the equipment installed. The start-up process, however, is similar for large and small computers, as described in the following steps.

Step 1: When you turn on the computer or mobile device, the power supply or battery sends an electrical current to circuitry in the computer or mobile device.

Step 2: The charge of electricity causes the processor chip to reset itself and finds the firmware that contains start-up instructions.

Step 3: The start-up process executes a series of tests to check the various components. These tests vary depending on the type of computer or devices and can include checking the buses, system clock, adapter cards, RAM chips, mouse, keyboard, and drives. It also includes making sure that any peripheral devices are connected properly and operating correctly. If any problems are identified, the computer or device may beep, display error messages, or cease operating — depending on the severity of the problem.

Step 4: If the tests are successful, the kernel of the operating system and other frequently used instructions load from the computer or mobile device's internal storage media to its memory (RAM). The *kernel* is the core of an operating system that manages memory and devices, maintains the internal clock, runs programs, and assigns the resources, such as devices, programs, apps, data, and information. The kernel is *memory resident*, which means it remains in memory while the computer or mobile device is running. Other parts of the operating system are *nonresident*; that is, nonresident instructions remain on a storage medium until they are needed, at which time they transfer into memory (RAM).

Step 5: The operating system in memory takes control of the computer or mobile device and loads system configuration information. The operating system may verify that the person attempting to use the computer or mobile device is a legitimate user. Finally, the user interface appears on the screen, and any start-up applications, such as antivirus software, run.

CONSIDER THIS

What is meant by the term, booting a computer?

The process of starting or restarting a computer or mobile device is called *booting*. Some people use the term *cold boot* to refer to the process of starting a computer or mobile device from a state when it is powered off completely. Similarly, *warm boot* refers to the process of restarting a computer or mobile device while it remains powered on.

A warm boot generally is faster than a cold boot because it skips some of the operating system start-up instructions that are included as part of a cold boot. If you suspect a hardware problem, it is recommended that you use a cold boot to start a computer or device because this process detects and checks connected hardware devices. If a program or app stops working, a warm boot often is sufficient to restart the device because this process clears memory.

A **boot drive** is the drive from which your personal computer starts, which typically is an internal hard drive, such as a hard disk or SSD. Sometimes, an internal hard drive becomes damaged and the computer cannot boot from it, or you may want to preview another operating system without installing it. In these cases, you can start the computer from a *boot disk*, which is removable media, such as a CD or USB flash drive, that contains only the necessary operating system files required to start the computer.

When you purchase a computer, it may include recovery media in the form of a CD. If it does not, the operating system usually provides a means to create one. When the word, live, is used with a type of media, such as *Live USB* or *Live CD*, this usually means the media can be used to start the computer.

Recovery Media
In situations when a boot disk is required to restart a computer or device that will not start from its boot drive, the boot disk often is referred to as *recovery media*.

Shutting Down Computers and Mobile Devices

Some users choose to leave their computers or mobile devices running continually and never turn them off. Computers and devices that are left on always are available, and users can run back up or other similar programs while the computer or device is not being used. These users also do not need to wait for the boot process, which can be time consuming on older computers. Other users choose to shut down their computers and mobile devices regularly. These users might be concerned with security, want to reduce energy costs, or prefer to clear memory often. To turn off a computer or mobile device, you may be required to use operating system commands, press keyboard key(s), push a power button, or a combination of these methods.

Power options include shutting down (powering off) the computer or mobile device, placing it in sleep mode, or placing it in hibernate mode. Both sleep mode and hibernate mode are designed to save time when you resume work on the computer or device. *Sleep mode* saves any open documents and running programs or apps to memory, turns off all unneeded functions, and then places the computer in a low-power state. If, for some reason, power is removed from a computer or device that is in sleep mode, any unsaved work could be lost. *Hibernate mode*, by contrast, saves any open documents and running programs or apps to an internal hard drive before removing power from the computer or device.

The function of the power button on a computer or mobile device varies, and users typically are able to configure its default behavior. For example, quickly pressing the power button (or closing the lid) on a laptop may place the computer or mobile device in sleep mode. Pressing and holding down the power button may remove all power from the computer or mobile device.

 Internet Research
When should I turn off a computer or use sleep mode?
Search for: shut down or sleep computer

Providing a User Interface

You interact with an operating system through its user interface. That is, a **user interface (UI)** controls how you enter data and instructions and how information is displayed on the screen. Two types of operating system user interfaces are graphical and command line. Operating system user interfaces often use a combination of these techniques to define how a user interacts with a computer or mobile device.

Graphical User Interface Most users today work with a graphical user interface. With a *graphical user interface (GUI)*, you interact with menus and visual images by touching, pointing, tapping, or clicking buttons and other objects to issue commands (Figure 9-3 on the next page). Many current GUI operating systems incorporate features similar to those of a browser, such as links and navigation buttons (i.e., Back button and Forward button) when navigating the computer or mobile device's storage media to locate files.

Figure 9-3 Examples of operating system user interfaces on a variety of computers and mobile devices.
© iStockphoto / Erik Khalitov; © iStockphoto / Hocus Focus Studio; Source: Microsoft; © iStockphoto / Gergana Valcheva

A graphical user interface designed for touch input sometimes is called a *touch user interface*. Some operating systems for desktops and laptops and many operating systems for mobile devices have a touch user interface.

CONSIDER THIS

What is a natural user interface?
With a **natural user interface** (**NUI**), users interact with the software through ordinary, intuitive behavior. NUIs are implemented in a variety of ways: touch screens (touch input), gesture recognition (motion input), speech recognition (voice input), and virtual reality (simulations).

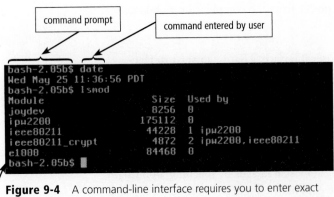

Figure 9-4 A command-line interface requires you to enter exact spelling, grammar, and punctuation.
© Cengage Learning

command prompt

Command-Line Interface To configure devices, manage system resources, automate system management tasks, and troubleshoot network connections, network administrators and other technical users work with a command-line interface. In a *command-line interface*, a user types commands represented by short keywords or abbreviations (such as dir to view a list of files) or presses special keys on the keyboard (such as function keys or key combinations) to enter data and instructions (Figure 9-4).

Some people consider command-line interfaces difficult to use because they require exact spelling, form, and punctuation. Minor errors, such as a missing period, generate an error message. Command-line interfaces, however, give a user more control to manage detailed settings. When working with a command-line interface, the set of commands used to control actions is called the *command language*.

Managing Programs

How an operating system handles programs directly affects your productivity. An operating system can be single tasking or multitasking:

- A single tasking operating system allows only one program or app to run at a time. For example, if you are using a browser and want to check email messages, you must exit the browser before you can run the email program. Operating systems on embedded computers and some mobile devices use a single tasking operating system.
- Most operating systems today are multitasking. A *multitasking* operating system allows two or more programs or apps to reside in memory at the same time. Using the example just cited, if you are working with a multitasking operating system, you do not have to exit the browser to run the email program. Both programs can run concurrently.

When a computer is running multiple programs concurrently, one program is in the foreground and the others are in the background (Figure 9-5). The one in the *foreground* is the active program, that is, the one you currently are using. The other programs running but not in use are in the *background*. The foreground program typically is displayed on the screen, and the background programs are hidden partially or completely behind the foreground program. A multitasking operating system's user interface easily allows you to switch between foreground and background programs.

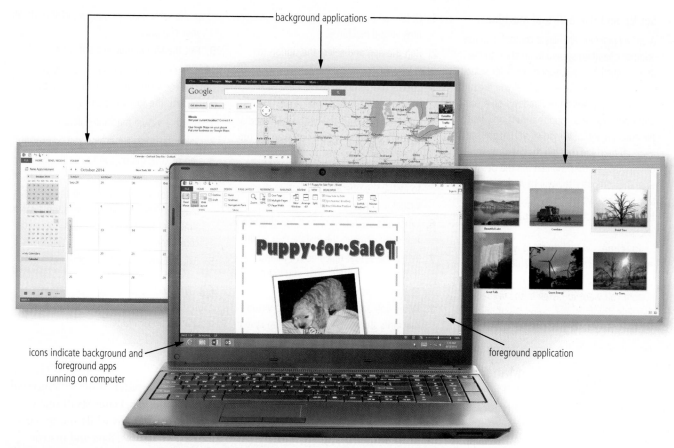

Figure 9-5 The foreground application, Microsoft Word, is displayed on the screen. The other applications (Microsoft Outlook, Google Maps in Internet Explorer, and File Explorer) are in the background.

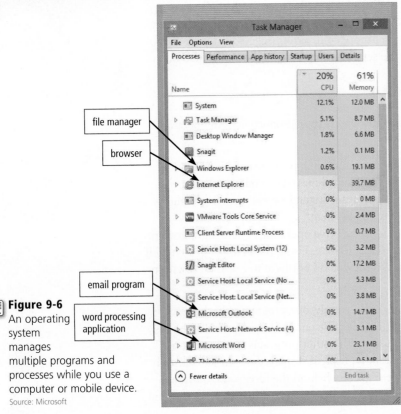

file manager

browser

email program

word processing application

 Figure 9-6
An operating system manages multiple programs and processes while you use a computer or mobile device.
Source: Microsoft

In addition to managing applications, an operating system manages other processes. These processes include programs or routines that provide support to other programs or hardware. Some are memory resident. Others run as they are required. Figure 9-6 shows a list of some processes running on a Windows computer; notice the list contains the applications running in Figure 9-5 on the previous page, as well as other programs and processes.

Some operating systems support a single user; others support thousands of users running multiple programs. A *multiuser* operating system enables two or more users to run programs simultaneously. Networks, servers, and supercomputers allow hundreds to thousands of users to connect at the same time and, thus, use multiuser operating systems. Read How To 9-1 to learn how to run multiple operating systems on a single computer.

HOW TO 9-1

Set Up and Use a Virtual Machine

A *virtual machine* enables a computer to run another operating system in addition to the one installed. Various reasons exist for using a virtual machine. For example, if you are running the latest version of Windows on a computer but require an app that runs only in a previous version of Windows, you might set up a virtual machine running the previous version of Windows so that you can run the desired app. The computer still will have the latest version of Windows installed, but you easily will be able to switch to the previous version when necessary.

To set up a virtual machine, you will need software that can set up a virtual machine, as well as installation media for the operating system you want to install in the virtual machine. The following steps describe how to set up a virtual machine:

1. Obtain and install an app that creates and runs virtual machines.
2. Run the app and select the option to create a new virtual machine.
3. Specify the settings for the new virtual machine.
4. If necessary, insert the installation media for the operating system you want to run in the virtual machine.
5. Run the virtual machine. Follow the steps to install the operating system in the virtual machine.
6. When the operating system has finished installing, remove the installation media.
7. While the virtual machine is running, if desired, install any apps you want to run.
8. When you are finished using the virtual machine, shut down the operating system

in the same manner you would shut down your computer.

9. Exit the virtual machine software.

After you set up the virtual machine, you can use the virtual machine any time by performing the following steps:

1. Run the virtual machine software.
2. Select the virtual machine you want to run.
3. Tap or click the button to run the virtual machine.
4. When you are finished using the virtual machine, shut down the operating system similar to how you would shut down your computer.
5. Exit the virtual machine software.

✸ What are some other reasons that might require you to set up and use a virtual machine on a computer?

Managing Memory

The purpose of memory management is to optimize the use of a computer or device's internal memory, i.e., RAM. As Chapter 6 discussed, RAM (random access memory) consists of one or more chips on the motherboard that hold items such as data and instructions while the processor interprets and executes them. The operating system allocates, or assigns, data and instructions to an area of memory while they are being processed. Then, it carefully monitors the contents of memory. Finally, the operating system releases these items from being monitored in memory when the processor no longer requires them.

If several programs or apps are running simultaneously, your computer or mobile device may use up its available RAM. For example, assume an operating system requires 2 GB of RAM to run, an antivirus program — 256 MB, a browser — 512 MB, a productivity software suite — 1 GB, and a photo editing program — 512 MB. With all these programs running simultaneously, the total RAM required would be 4.352 GB (2048 MB + 256 MB + 512 MB + 1024 MB + 512 MB) (Figure 9-7). If the computer has only 4 GB of RAM, the operating system may have to use virtual memory in order to run all of the applications at the same time. When a computer or mobile device runs low on available RAM, this often results in the computer or mobile device running sluggishly.

Applications Using RAM

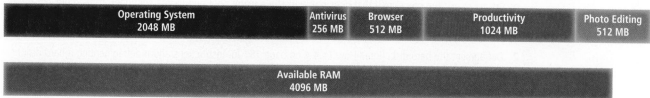

| Operating System 2048 MB | Antivirus 256 MB | Browser 512 MB | Productivity 1024 MB | Photo Editing 512 MB |

| Available RAM 4096 MB |

Figure 9-7   Many applications running at the same time may exhaust a computer's or device's available RAM.
© Cengage Learning

With **virtual memory**, the operating system allocates a portion of a storage medium, such as the hard disk or a USB flash drive, to function as additional RAM (Figure 9-8). As you interact with a program, part of it may be in physical RAM, while the rest of the program is on the hard disk as virtual memory. Because virtual memory is slower than RAM, users may notice the computer slowing down while it uses virtual memory.

How a Computer Might Use Virtual Memory

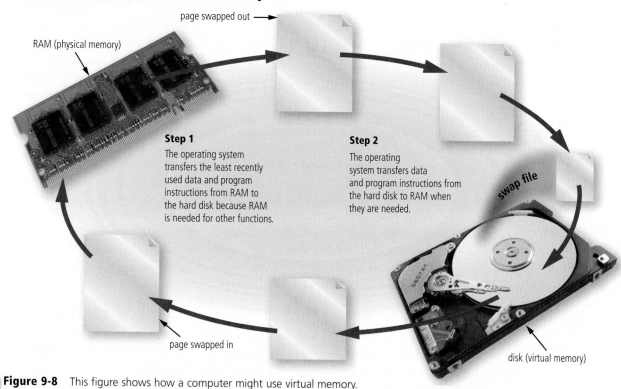

page swapped out

RAM (physical memory)

Step 1
The operating system transfers the least recently used data and program instructions from RAM to the hard disk because RAM is needed for other functions.

Step 2
The operating system transfers data and program instructions from the hard disk to RAM when they are needed.

swap file

page swapped in

disk (virtual memory)

Figure 9-8   This figure shows how a computer might use virtual memory.
© TungCheung / Shutterstock.com; © kastianz / Shutterstock.com; © Cengage Learning

The area of the hard disk used for virtual memory is called a *swap file* because it swaps (exchanges) data, information, and instructions between memory and storage. A *page* is the amount of data and program instructions that can swap at a given time. The technique of swapping items between memory and storage, called *paging*, is a time-consuming process for the computer. When an operating system spends much of its time paging, instead of executing application software, it is said to be *thrashing*.

✸ CONSIDER THIS

What happens if an application stops responding or the computer appears to run sluggishly?

If an application, such as a browser, has stopped responding, the operating system may be thrashing. When this occurs, try to exit the program. If that does not work, try a warm boot and then a cold boot. To help prevent future occurrences of thrashing, you might consider the following:

1. Remove unnecessary files and uninstall seldom used programs and apps.
 2. Defragment the hard disk. (Read How To 4-4 on page 187 for instructions about defragmenting a hard disk.)
3. Purchase and install additional RAM. (Read How To 6-2 on page 264 for instructions about installing memory modules.)

✸ CONSIDER THIS

What if my smartphone runs out of memory?

If your smartphone or other mobile device displays a message that it is running low on memory, try the following:

1. Exit unnecessary applications that are running.
2. Restart the smartphone or mobile device.
3. Uninstall seldom used applications.
4. Remove unnecessary files (you may want to copy them to a computer or memory card first).
5. If your smartphone supports the use of an external memory card, specify that applications, photos, videos, or downloaded files should be saved on a memory card instead of the smartphone's internal memory.

Coordinating Tasks

The operating system determines the order in which tasks are processed. A task, or job, is an operation the processor manages. Tasks include receiving data from an input device, processing instructions, sending information to an output device, and transferring items from storage to memory and from memory to storage.

Sometimes, a device already may be busy processing one task when it receives a request to perform a second task. For example, if a printer is printing a document when the operating system sends it a request to print another document, the printer must store the second document in memory until the first document has completed printing.

While waiting for devices to become idle, the operating system places items in buffers. A *buffer* is a segment of memory or storage in which items are placed while waiting to be transferred from an input device or to an output device.

An operating system commonly uses buffers with printed documents. This process, called *spooling*, sends documents to be printed to a buffer instead of sending them immediately to the printer. If a printer does not have its own internal memory or if its memory is full, the operating system's buffer holds the documents waiting to print while the printer prints from the buffer at its own rate of speed. By spooling documents to a buffer, the computer or mobile device's processor can continue interpreting and executing instructions while the printer prints. This allows users to perform other activities on the computer while a printer is printing. Multiple documents line up in a **queue** (pronounced Q) in the buffer. A program, called a *print spooler*, intercepts documents to be printed from the operating system and places them in the queue (Figure 9-9).

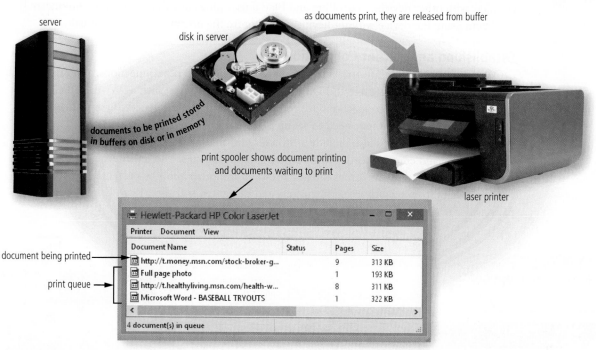

server

disk in server

as documents print, they are released from buffer

documents to be printed stored in buffers on disk or in memory

print spooler shows document printing and documents waiting to print

laser printer

document being printed

print queue

Document Name	Status	Pages	Size
http://t.money.msn.com/stock-broker-g...		9	313 KB
Full page photo		1	193 KB
http://t.healthyliving.msn.com/health-w...		8	311 KB
Microsoft Word - BASEBALL TRYOUTS		1	322 KB

Hewlett-Packard HP Color LaserJet

Printer   Document   View

4 document(s) in queue

Figure 9-9 Spooling increases both processor and printer efficiency by placing documents to be printed in a buffer or on disk before they are printed. This figure shows three documents in the queue with one document printing.
© iStockphoto / luismmolina; © iStockphoto / Lee Rogers; © Kitch Bain / Shutterstock.com; © Cengage Learning

Configuring Devices

A **driver**, short for *device driver*, is a small program that tells the operating system how to communicate with a specific device. Each device connected to a computer, such as a mouse, keyboard, monitor, printer, card reader/writer, digital camera, webcam, portable media player, smartphone, or tablet, has its own specialized set of commands and, thus, requires its own specific driver. When you start a computer or connect a device via a USB port, the operating system loads a device's driver. Drivers must be installed for each connected device in order for the device to function properly. Read How To 9-2 for instructions about finding the latest drivers for devices.

 HOW TO 9-2

Find the Latest Drivers for Devices

Device manufacturers sometimes release updated driver versions either to correct problems with previous drivers, enhance a device's functionality, or increase compatibility with new operating system versions. The following steps describe how to find the latest drivers for devices:

1. Search for and navigate to the device manufacturer's website.

2. Tap or click the link on the website to display the webpage containing technical support information.

3. Select or enter the device's model number to display support information for the device.

4. Browse the device's support information and then tap or click the link or button to download the most current driver. Manufacturers often create different versions of drivers for different operating systems, so make sure you download the driver that is compatible with the operating system you currently are using.

5. When the download is complete, follow the instructions that accompanied the driver to install it.

What might you do if you are unable to locate your device's driver on the manufacturer's website?

If you attach a new device, such as a portable media player or smartphone, to a computer, its driver must be installed before you can use the device. Today, most devices and operating systems support Plug and Play. As discussed in Chapter 6, *Plug and Play* means the operating system automatically configures new devices as you install them. Specifically, it assists you in the device's installation by loading the necessary drivers automatically from the device and checking for conflicts with other devices. With Plug and Play, a user plugs in a device and then immediately can begin using the device without having to configure the operating system manually.

Establishing an Internet Connection

Operating systems typically provide a means to establish Internet connections. You can establish wired connections, such as cable and DSL, or wireless connections, such as Wi-Fi, mobile broadband, and satellite. Some connections are configured automatically as soon as you connect to the Internet. With others, you may need to set up a connection manually (Figure 9-10).

Some operating systems also include a browser and an email program, enabling you to begin using the web and communicating with others as soon as you set up an Internet connection. Operating systems also sometimes include firewalls and other tools to protect computers and mobile devices from unauthorized intrusions and unwanted software. Read Ethics & Issues 9-1 to consider whether operating systems should include antivirus programs.

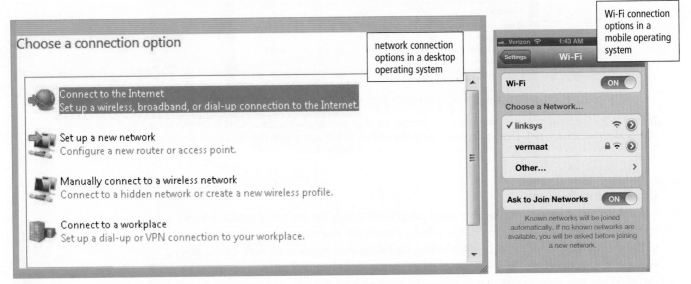

Figure 9-10 Shown here are Internet connection options for desktop and mobile operating systems.
Source: Microsoft; Source: Apple Inc.

⚙ ETHICS & ISSUES 9-1

Should Operating Systems for Computers and Mobile Devices Include Virus Protection?

Security experts recommend using antivirus software. Users who want protection from viruses can choose from one of several antivirus programs for their computers and mobile devices. They can search for and download a free program or app from a software provider's website. They also can choose from many reputable vendors, such as Norton and McAfee, who sell subscriptions to their antivirus software.

OEMs (original equipment manufacturers) often include and profit from installing trial versions of antivirus software on their computers. When one software vendor announced that its operating system would

include a full antivirus program, how did this impact OEMs? Those who distributed computers running that operating system were required to disable the built-in antivirus software so that they could install trial versions of subscription-based antivirus products.

Critics argue that an operating system with built-in antivirus software intrudes on the open market by removing the need for separate antivirus software. Vendors who specialize in antivirus products claim that their products are more effective than those included with an operating system. They also argue that their technical support and features such as online backup storage make their products more desirable. Supporters claim that operating system developers have

full access to the operating system code as they develop antivirus software, making built-in antivirus programs more secure than those written by third-party vendors. Supporters also state that if a user does not purchase a subscription to the installed trial version of an antivirus program, they will not be defenseless when the trial ends because they can use another antivirus program that is compatible with the operating system.

Should OEMs be able to install antivirus programs to run alongside capabilities built into a computer or mobile device's operating system? Why or why not? Would you rely on a built-in antivirus program, or would you prefer an independent program? Why?

Monitoring Performance

Operating systems typically include a performance monitor. A **performance monitor** is a program that assesses and reports information about various computer resources and devices (Figure 9-11). For example, users can monitor the processor, disks, network, and memory usage.

The information in performance reports helps users and administrators identify a problem with resources so that they can try to resolve any issues. If a computer is running extremely slow, for example, the performance monitor may determine that the computer's memory is being used to its maximum. Thus, you might consider installing additional memory in the computer.

⚙ BTW
Benchmarking
High-Tech Talk: A benchmark is a set of conditions used to measure the performance of hardware or software.

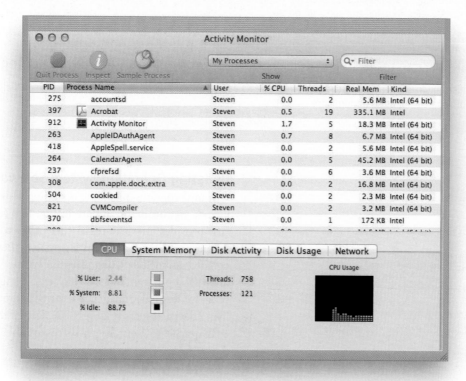

Figure 9-11 The Activity Monitor in this figure is tracking CPU (processor) usage.
Source: Apple Inc.

 NOW YOU KNOW

Be sure you understand the material presented in the section titled Operating Systems and the first nine sections in Operating System Functions, as it relates to the chapter objectives.
You now should know . . .

- The purpose of an operating system (Objective 1)

- What processes are occurring when you start up or shut down your computers or mobile devices (Objective 2)

- How an operating system enables you to interact with the user interface, manage programs, manage memory, coordinate tasks, configure devices, establish an Internet connection, and monitor performance (Objectives 3 and 4)

🖳 Quiz Yourself Online: Check your knowledge of related content by navigating to this book's Quiz Yourself resource on Computer Concepts CourseMate and then tapping or clicking Objectives 1–4.

Providing File and Disk Management

Operating systems often provide users with a variety of tools related to managing a computer, its devices, or its programs. These file and disk management tools were discussed in Chapter 4 and are summarized in Table 9-1 on the next page.

Table 9-1 File and Disk Management Tools

Tool	Function
File Manager	Performs functions related to displaying files; organizing files in folders; and copying, renaming, deleting, moving, and sorting files
Search	Attempts to locate a file on your computer or mobile device based on specified criteria
Image Viewer	Displays, copies, and prints the contents of a graphics file
Uninstaller	Removes a program or app, as well as any associated entries in the system files
Disk Cleanup	Searches for and removes unnecessary files
Disk Defragmenter	Reorganizes the files and unused space on a computer's hard disk so that the operating system accesses data more quickly and programs and apps run faster
Screen Saver	Causes a display's screen to show a moving image or blank screen if no keyboard or mouse activity occurs for a specified time
File Compression	Shrinks the size of a file(s)
PC Maintenance	Identifies and fixes operating system problems, detects and repairs disk problems, and includes the capability of improving a computer's performance
Backup and Restore	Copies selected files or the contents of an entire storage medium to another storage location

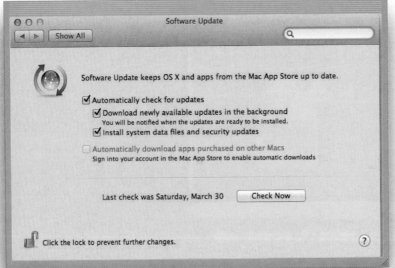

Updating Operating System Software

Many programs, including operating systems, include an **automatic update** feature that regularly provides new features or corrections to the program. With an operating system, these updates can include fixing program errors, improving program functionality, expanding program features, enhancing security, and modifying device drivers (Figure 9-12). Read Ethics & Issues 9-2 to consider who is responsible for operating system security flaws.

Figure 9-12 An operating system usually includes a means to download and install important updates.
Source: Apple Inc.

 ETHICS & ISSUES 9-2

Should Operating System Manufacturers Be Liable for Breaches Due to Security Flaws?

If you purchase a household device with a warranty, you can hold the manufacturer responsible for replacing and fixing it. Some argue that the same product liability laws that protect consumers in other industries should apply to software. Users' devices and data are vulnerable due to security flaws in operating systems for computers and mobile devices. A flaw in an operating system can affect the performance of the computer or mobile device and subject data to corruption or unauthorized use. A user may not even be aware when a computer or mobile device is corrupted.

Hackers look for ways to break into a computer or mobile device using flaws in the operating system. An operating system is complex software that includes millions of lines of code. Developers write code as securely as possible, but with the volume of code, mistakes are bound to occur. Users sometimes are unaware of their own role in infecting their own computer or mobile device. Perhaps a hacker took advantage of a user with an unsecured Wi-Fi connection, or the user did not install the latest updates to the operating system.

Some argue that making software manufacturers responsible for flaws will inhibit innovation. If a company spends more time looking for potential security flaws, it has less time to spend enhancing the software. In addition, some of the same features that enhance an operating system, such as web integration, increase the software's vulnerability.

Has your computer or mobile device become infected with malware due to a flaw in the operating system? How did you know? What responsibility does a software manufacturer have for preventing and fixing operating system flaws? Should users expect their software to be perfect? Why or why not?

Many software makers provide free downloadable updates, sometimes called a *service pack*, to users who have registered and/or activated their software. With operating systems, the automatic update feature can be configured to alert users when an update is available or to download and install the update automatically. Users without an Internet connection usually can order the updates on an optical disc for a minimal shipping fee. Read Secure IT 9-1 for issues related to automatic updates.

 BTW
Bugs
An error in a program sometimes is called a *bug*.

 **SECURE IT 9-1**

Automatic Updates — Safe or Not?

Software manufacturers recommend you download and install all available updates when they become available. In most cases, you have the choice either to allow the software to update automatically or to assess and then decide whether to install each update individually.

The automatic update option occasionally has caused problems. In one case, people preparing their income tax returns were unable to print forms when Microsoft issued an automatic update one week before the filing deadline. In another situation, an automatic update was installed on all computers — even those with this feature disabled. Microsoft claimed that the update was harmless and was for the benefit of its customers. Only later did some users realize that this secret update caused serious problems. One problem, ironically, was that updates no longer could be installed on the affected computers. Customers were furious about the issues, especially because Microsoft made the changes without informing the computer owners. One consequence of the ensuing outrage was that many people turned off the automatic update feature, fearing that future updates might cause even more damage.

✻ Is the automatic update feature enabled or disabled on your computer? Should software companies be able to send automatic updates to your computer without your knowledge? Why or why not?

Controlling a Network

Some operating systems are designed to work with a server on a network. These multiuser operating systems allow multiple users to share a printer, Internet access, files, and programs.

Some operating systems have network features built into them. In other cases, the operating system for the network is a set of programs that are separate from the operating system on the client computers or mobile devices that access the network. When not connected to the network, the client computers use their own operating system. When connected to the network, the operating system on the network may assume some of the operating system functions on the client computers or mobile devices.

The *network administrator*, the person overseeing network operations, uses the server operating system to add and remove users, computers, and other devices to and from the network. The network administrator also uses the operating system on the network to configure the network, install software, and administer network security. Read Secure IT 9-2 for security tools sometimes included in operating systems.

 BTW
 Sun
Technology Innovator: You should be familiar with products and services of Sun.

 BTW
Technology Careers
For additional information about careers in technology, see the Technology Careers appendix (available in the e-book).

 SECURE IT 9-2

Using and Evaluating an Operating System's Built-In Security Tools

Maintaining a secure computer is a never-ending task. Software updates fix bugs and enhance performance. Security software must run constantly to protect against new viruses and malware and spyware attacks. Operating systems can include the following security tools:

- **Firewall:** Security experts recommend using a firewall and configuring it to turn on or off automatically.
- **Automatic updating:** Security updates are issued at least once daily, and other updates are generated on an as-needed basis. Many people enjoy the convenience offered by allowing these fixes to install automatically instead of continually checking for new files to download. Users can view the update history to see when specific updates were installed. If an update caused a problem to occur, a user can uninstall these new files.
- **Antivirus software:** You always should run exactly one antivirus program on a computer. Some users mistakenly think they should install and run more than one antivirus program simultaneously for more protection. If they install multiple programs, however, the programs could conflict with each other and slow overall performance.
- **Spyware and malware detection software:** Sophisticated malware and spyware threats are emerging at an unparalleled rate, so comprehensive spyware and malware detection software is mandatory to fend off attacks on the computer.

The operating system generally is scheduled to scan and update when the computer is idle, such as in the middle of the night. Overall, the security tools should run constantly and quietly in the background to ensure a safe computing experience.

✻ Does your operating system have a firewall and protection against spyware and malware? Do updates occur automatically or manually? Which operating systems are more susceptible to malware attacks? Why?

Administering Security

Network administrators, as well as owners of computers, typically have an *administrator account* that enables them to access all files and programs, install programs, and specify settings that affect all users on a computer, mobile device, or network. Settings include creating user accounts and establishing permissions. These *permissions* define who can access certain resources and when they can access those resources. Read Secure IT 9-3 to learn more about administrator accounts.

Figure 9-13 Most multiuser operating systems allow each user to sign in, which is the process of entering a user name and a password into the computer. Single-user operating systems often use a password to lock an entire device or computer.
Source: Microsoft

For each user, the network administrator or computer owner establishes a user account. A user account enables a user to **sign in** to, or access resources on, a network or computer (Figure 9-13). Each user account typically consists of a user name and password. Recall that a **user name**, or user ID, is a unique combination of characters, such as letters of the alphabet and/or numbers, that identifies a specific user.

A **password** is a private combination of characters associated with the user name that allows access to certain computer, mobile device, or network resources. Some operating systems allow the network administrator to assign passwords to files and commands, restricting access to only authorized users. Mobile device owners often assign a password to the entire device, restricting all access until the correct password is entered. Read Secure IT 1-3 on page 24 for tips on creating strong passwords.

To prevent unauthorized users from accessing computer resources, keep your password confidential. After entering a user name and/or password, the operating system compares the user's entry with the authorized user name(s) and password(s). If the entry matches the user name and/or password stored in a file, the operating system grants the user access. If the entry does not match, the operating system denies access to the user.

The operating system on a network records successful and unsuccessful sign-in attempts in a file. This allows the network administrator to review who is using or attempting to use the computer. The administrators also use these files to monitor computer usage. Read How To 9-3 for instructions about adding user accounts.

 BTW

Passwords
While users type a password, most computers and mobile devices hide the actual password characters by displaying some other characters, such as asterisks (*) or dots.

 CONSIDER THIS

What are some alternatives to passwords?
Many computers and mobile devices offer alternatives to setting and entering a password in order to gain access. Alternatives to passwords include specifying passcodes containing only numeric characters, swiping or touching areas of the screen in a specified order or pattern, or fingerprint or facial recognition.

 SECURE IT 9-3

Differing Functions in Administrator and Standard User Accounts

When you purchase a new computer or install a new operating system, you are required to establish an administrator account that gives unrestricted permission to install hardware and software, change security settings, and access all files. Administrators then can establish standard user accounts requiring the administrator's permission to make changes affecting other users or altering the security settings. Users, therefore, can run the same software that an administrator can run, but they cannot install or uninstall software and hardware or delete operating system files.

Security experts recommend every administrator create at least one standard user account, even if only one person will use the computer. The administrator should use the administrator account on a limited basis because the operating system is susceptible to spyware and malware attacks in this setting. In contrast, the administrator should sign in to the user account for daily activities, such as checking email or browsing the web. Microsoft claims that 92 percent of threats are blocked when using a standard account because administrator accounts typically are more vulnerable.

🌼 Do you have both an administrative and a standard user account on your computer? If so, do you use the standard user account for everyday tasks? Why or why not?

HOW TO 9-3

Add Users to an Operating System

If you share your computer with others, you can add more user accounts to the operating system. When users sign in to their accounts, they can customize their settings and store files in locations that may not be accessible to other users on the computer. The following steps describe how to add users to an operating system:

1. Sign in to a user account that has administrative privileges; that is, the user account should have the capability to perform functions such as adding users.
2. Display the operating system settings.
3. Tap or click the option to display user accounts.

4. Tap or click the option to add a new user account.
5. Specify the options for the new user account:
   - Enter a name to identify the user account.
   - Specify a default password for the user account.
   - Select the type of user account (administrative, standard, etc.). You should create user accounts with administrative access only if you want the user to be able to perform tasks such as change computer settings; add or remove programs; and add, modify, or remove a user account.

   - If necessary, set parental controls for the user account.
6. Save the settings for the new user account.
7. Sign out of the existing user account.
8. Sign in to the newly created user account and make sure everything works as intended.

✸ If you have two roommates sharing your computer, would you create additional user accounts? Why or why not? If you would create user accounts, what would you set as the user account name, and what type of account would you create? Why?

✸ CONSIDER THIS

Do operating systems encrypt data and files?

To protect sensitive data and information further as it travels over a network, the operating system may encrypt it. Recall that *encryption* is the process of encoding data and information into an unreadable form. Administrators can specify that data be encrypted as it travels over a network to prevent unauthorized users from reading the data. When an authorized user attempts to read the data, it is automatically decrypted, or converted back into a readable form.

Types of Operating Systems

Many of the first operating systems were device dependent and proprietary. A *device-dependent* program is one that runs only on a specific type or make of computer or mobile device. *Proprietary software* is privately owned and limited to a specific vendor or computer or device model. Some operating systems still are device dependent. The trend today, however, is toward *device-independent* operating systems that run on computers and mobile devices provided by a variety of manufacturers. The advantage of device-independent operating systems is you can retain existing applications and data files even if you change computer or mobile device models or vendors.

When you purchase a new computer or mobile device, it typically has an operating system preinstalled. As new versions of the operating system are released, users often upgrade their existing computers and mobile devices to incorporate features of the new versions. Some upgrades are free; some offer an upgrade price that is less than the cost of purchasing the entire operating system.

New versions of an operating system usually are *backward compatible*, which means they recognize and work with applications written for an earlier version of the operating system (or platform). The application, by contrast, may or may not be *upward compatible*, meaning it may or may not run on new versions of the operating system.

The three basic categories of operating systems on computers and mobile devices are desktop, server, and mobile. Table 9-2 lists examples in each of these categories, which are discussed on the following pages.

Table 9-2	Examples of Operating Systems by Category
Category	**Name**
Desktop	Windows
	OS X
	UNIX
	Linux
	Chrome OS
Server	Windows Server
	Mac OS X Server
	UNIX
	Linux
Mobile	Google Android
	Apple iOS
	Windows Phone

Internet Research

What is the most widely used desktop operating system?

Search for: desktop os market share

Desktop Operating Systems

A **desktop operating system**, sometimes called a *stand-alone operating system*, is a complete operating system that works on desktops, laptops, and some tablets. Desktop operating systems sometimes are called *client operating systems* because they also work in conjunction with a server operating system. Client operating systems can operate with or without a network.

Examples of the more widely used desktop operating systems are Windows, Mac OS, UNIX, Linux, and Chrome OS.

Windows

In the mid-1980s, Microsoft developed its first version of Windows, which provided a graphical user interface. Since then, Microsoft continually has updated its Windows operating system, incorporating innovative features and functions with each subsequent version. In addition to basic capabilities, Windows 8 offers these features:

 BTW

Networking
Some desktop operating systems include networking capabilities, allowing the home and small business user to set up a small network.

- Start screen interface with tiles
- Includes the desktop interface
- Support for input via touch, mouse, and keyboard
- Email app, calendar app, and browser (*Internet Explorer*) included
- Photos, files, and settings can sync with *SkyDrive*, Microsoft's cloud server
- Enhanced security through an antivirus program, firewall, and automatic updates
- Windows Store offers additional applications for purchase

 MINI FEATURE 9-1

Windows

BTW

PC
The term, PC, sometimes is used to describe a computer that runs a Windows operating system.

The following screens show the components of the Windows 8 interface. The Windows operating system simplifies the process of working with documents and apps by organizing the manner in which you interact with the computer.

The Windows 8 interface begins with the Start screen, as shown in the figure below.

When you run an app in Windows, it may appear in an on-screen work area app, called the *desktop*, shown in the figure on the facing page. Many Office and Windows programs, such as Paint, contain common elements.

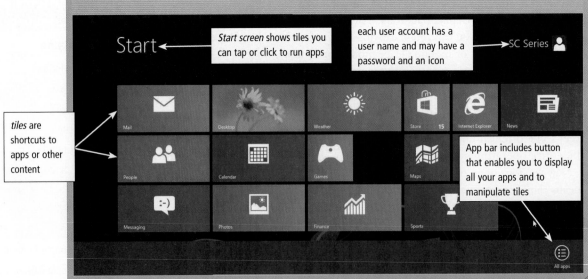

Source: Microsoft

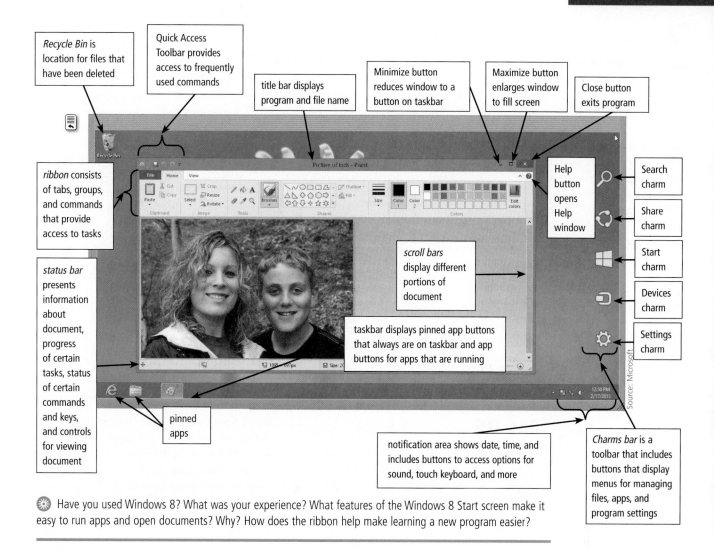

Recycle Bin is location for files that have been deleted

Quick Access Toolbar provides access to frequently used commands

title bar displays program and file name

Minimize button reduces window to a button on taskbar

Maximize button enlarges window to fill screen

Close button exits program

ribbon consists of tabs, groups, and commands that provide access to tasks

Help button opens Help window

Search charm

Share charm

Start charm

Devices charm

Settings charm

status bar presents information about document, progress of certain tasks, status of certain commands and keys, and controls for viewing document

scroll bars display different portions of document

taskbar displays pinned app buttons that always are on taskbar and app buttons for apps that are running

pinned apps

notification area shows date, time, and includes buttons to access options for sound, touch keyboard, and more

Charms bar is a toolbar that includes buttons that display menus for managing files, apps, and program settings

Source: Microsoft

Have you used Windows 8? What was your experience? What features of the Windows 8 Start screen make it easy to run apps and open documents? Why? How does the ribbon help make learning a new program easier?

Mac OS

Since it was released in 1984 with Macintosh computers, Apple's *Macintosh operating system* (*Mac OS*) has earned a reputation for its ease of use and has been the model for most of the new GUIs developed for non-Macintosh systems. The latest version, **OS X**, is a multitasking operating system available for computers manufactured by Apple. Features of the latest version of OS X include the following:

- Mail, calendars, contacts, and other items sync with *iCloud*, Apple's cloud server
- Communicate and play games with users of mobile devices running Apple's mobile operating system (iOS)
- Built-in Facebook and Twitter support allows you to post a status, comments, or files from any app
- Browser (*Safari*)
- Open multiple desktops at once
- Dictated words convert to text
- Support for Braille displays
- Mac App Store provides access to additional apps and software updates

Read How To 9-4 on the next page for instructions about installing the Windows operating system on a Mac computer.

HOW TO 9-4

Use Boot Camp to Install the Windows Operating System on a Mac

If you are using an Apple computer such as an iMac or MacBook Pro, you may encounter instances where you need to run apps in the Windows operating system. Newer versions of Mac OS enable you to install Windows on a computer using a program called *Boot Camp*. The following steps describe how to use Boot Camp to install the Windows operating system on a Mac:

1. Obtain the installation media for the version of Windows you want to install.

2. Use the operating system's search feature to locate the Boot Camp Assistant application. (*Hint:* Use the search text, boot camp.)

3. Click the search result for the Boot Camp Assistant application.

4. When the Boot Camp Assistant runs, read the introduction and then click the Continue button.

5. Next, you create a *partition* which is a section of storage or memory reserved for a specific program or application. Partitions enable a single drive to be treated as multiple drives. Follow the remaining steps to create a Windows partition and install Windows:

   • Specify the amount of disk space to use for the Windows partition. The partition should be large enough to store all operating system files, apps you want to run in Windows, and any files you want to store using Windows.

   • Complete the steps described in the Windows installation process.

6. When the installation is complete and Windows starts, if necessary, enter your user name and password to sign in to Windows.

If you want to switch between Mac OS and Windows, press and hold the option key on the keyboard while turning on or restarting the computer. When the list of operating systems is displayed, select the operating system you want to run.

What apps might someone want to run in Windows that are unavailable in the Mac OS? How does Boot Camp differ from a virtual machine?

MINI FEATURE 9-2

Mac OS

The following screens show the components of the OS X user interface. Mac OS is installed on Apple computers such as iMacs, MacBook Pros, MacBook Airs, Mac Pros, and Mac minis. The user interface contains components such as the Dock, icons, and windows.

The OS X interface begins with the desktop. Many OS X programs and apps contain common elements, as shown in the desktop figure below.

You can use the *Launchpad* to view, organize, and run apps, as shown in the figure below.

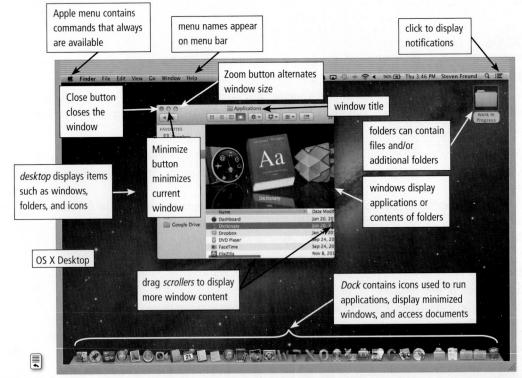

Apple menu contains commands that always are available

menu names appear on menu bar

click to display notifications

Zoom button alternates window size

Close button closes the window

window title

folders can contain files and/or additional folders

Minimize button minimizes current window

desktop displays items such as windows, folders, and icons

windows display applications or contents of folders

OS X Desktop

drag *scrollers* to display more window content

Dock contains icons used to run applications, display minimized windows, and access documents

Source: Apple Inc.

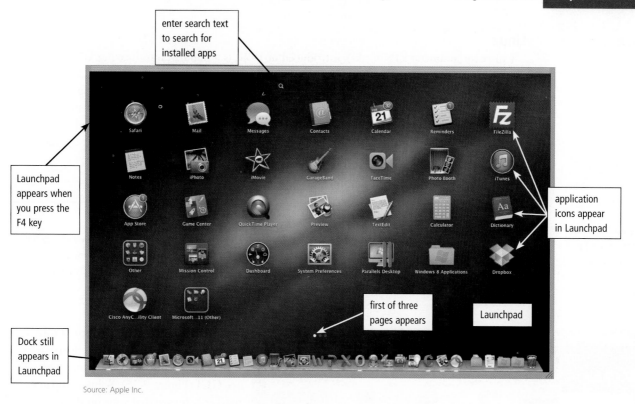

enter search text to search for installed apps

Launchpad appears when you press the F4 key

application icons appear in Launchpad

first of three pages appears

Launchpad

Dock still appears in Launchpad

Source: Apple Inc.

How is the user interface in OS X similar to the Windows user interface? How is it different?

UNIX

UNIX (pronounced YOU-nix) is a multitasking operating system developed in the early 1970s by scientists at Bell Laboratories. Bell Labs (a subsidiary of AT&T) was prohibited from actively promoting UNIX in the commercial marketplace because of federal regulations. Bell Labs instead licensed UNIX for a low fee to numerous colleges and universities, where UNIX obtained a wide following. UNIX was implemented on many different types of computers. In the 1980s, the source code for UNIX was licensed to many hardware and software companies to customize for their devices and applications. As a result, several versions of this operating system exist, each with slightly different features or capabilities.

Today, a version of UNIX is available for most computers of all sizes. Although some versions of UNIX have a command-line interface, most versions of UNIX offer a graphical user interface (Figure 9-14). Power users often work with UNIX because of its flexibility and capabilities. An industry standards organization, *The Open Group*, now owns UNIX as a trademark.

BTW
OS X
OS X is a UNIX-based operating system.

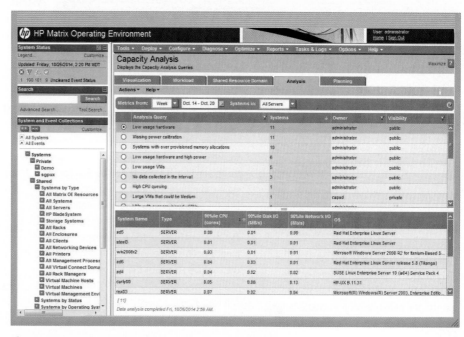

Figure 9-14 One version of the UNIX operating system.
Courtesy of Hewlett-Packard Company

Linux

Linux (pronounced LINN-uks), introduced in 1991, is a popular, multitasking UNIX-based operating system that runs on a variety of personal computers, servers, and devices. In addition to the basic operating system, Linux also includes many free tools and programming languages.

Linux is not proprietary software like the operating systems discussed thus far. Instead, Linux is *open source software*, which means its code is provided for use, modification, and redistribution. Many programmers have donated time to modify and redistribute Linux to make it the most popular UNIX-based operating system.

✹ CONSIDER THIS

Why use open source software?

Open source software has no restrictions from the copyright holder regarding modification of the software's internal instructions and redistribution of the software. Promoters of open source software state two main advantages: users who modify the software share their improvements with others, and customers can personalize the software to meet their needs. Read Ethics & Issues 9-3 to consider whether open or closed source programs are better.

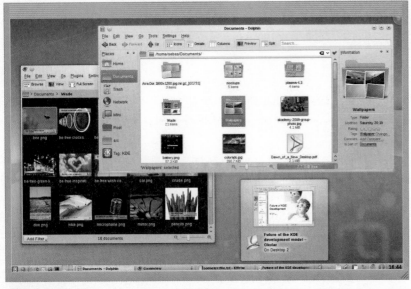

Figure 9-15 A GUI distribution of Linux.
Courtesy of KDE

Linux is available in a variety of forms, known as distributions. Some distributions of Linux are command line. Others are GUI (Figure 9-15). Some companies market software that runs on their own distribution of Linux. Many application programs, tools, and plug-ins have Linux distributions.

Users obtain versions of Linux in a variety of ways. Some download it free from a provider's website and create media to install it on a computer, or they create a Live CD or Live USB from which to preview it. Others purchase optical discs from vendors who may bundle their own software with the operating system or download it from their websites. Some retailers will preinstall Linux on a new computer on request.

✹ ETHICS & ISSUES 9-3

Are Open Source or Closed Source Operating Systems Better?

One feature that separates Linux from other operating systems is that its source code, along with any changes, remains public. Closed source operating systems, where developers refuse to share some or all of the code, may hinder third-party software developers who create programs and apps for the operating system.

Supporters of open source, such as the GNU Project, maintain that open source software enables developers to examine, correct, and enhance code to create better programs. Communities of open source programmers can make changes immediately, which they claim results in higher-quality software. For example, proponents of open source software use Linux, which is known for its speed and stability. Of the 500 fastest supercomputers, 90 percent use variants of Linux. Companies and nonprofit organizations can distribute and sell their versions of Linux. This enables those without the expertise to modify open source software to benefit from the creative efforts of the Linux community.

Fear of viruses and other security concerns can lead some to question about whether open source software is worthwhile.

Dishonest and anonymous developers can use open source software to create programs that may be malware. Proponents of closed source software also argue that companies and developers should be able to control, and profit from, the operating systems they create.

Are the security concerns about open source software legitimate? Why or why not? What might be some of the advantages and disadvantages of open source versus closed source operating systems? Does the open source model lead to higher-quality software? Why or why not?

Chrome OS

Chrome OS, introduced by Google, is a Linux-based operating system designed to work primarily with web apps (Figure 9-16). Apps are available through the Chrome Web Store, and data is stored on Google Drive. The only apps typically installed on the computer are the Chrome browser, a media player, and a file manager. A specialized laptop that runs Chrome OS is called a *Chromebook*, and a specialized desktop that runs Chrome OS is called a *Chromebox*. Chromebooks and Chromeboxes typically use SSDs for internal storage. Users also can run Chrome OS as a virtual machine.

Because computers running Chrome OS work mostly with web apps, they do not require as much internal storage capacity as other desktop

Figure 9-16 Chrome OS is a Linux-based operating system by Google.
Courtesy of Volha Kryvets; Source: Google Inc.

operating systems discussed in this section. Their start-up and shutdown time also is considerably less than other desktop operating systems because Chrome OS uses a streamlined start-up procedure.

 **NOW YOU KNOW**

Be sure you understand the material presented in the last four sections in Operating System Functions and the sections titled Types of Operating Systems and Desktop Operating Systems, as it relates to the chapter objectives. *You now should know . . .*

- How to update your operating system and tools (Objective 5)
- How you can use an operating system to control a network or administer security (Objective 6)
- Which desktop operating system is best suited to your needs (Objective 7)

 Quiz Yourself Online: Check your knowledge of related content by navigating to this book's Quiz Yourself resource on Computer Concepts CourseMate and then tapping or clicking Objectives 5–7.

Server Operating Systems

A **server operating system** is a multiuser operating system that organizes and coordinates how multiple users access and share resources on a network. Client computers on a network rely on server(s) for access to resources.

Many of the desktop operating systems discussed in the previous section function as clients and work in conjunction with a server operating system. Although desktop operating systems may include networking capability, server operating systems are designed specifically to support all sizes of networks, including medium- to large-sized businesses and web servers. Server operating systems can handle high numbers of transactions, support large-scale messaging and communications, and have enhanced security and backup capabilities.

Many also support virtualization. Recall that *virtualization* is the practice of sharing or pooling computing resources, such as servers or storage devices. Through virtualization, for example, server operating systems can separate a physical server into several virtual servers. Each virtual server then can perform independent, separate functions.

Examples of server operating systems include the following:

- **Windows Server:** Developed by Microsoft, Windows Server enables organizations to manage applications and websites on-site and/or on the cloud.
- **OS X Server:** Developed by Apple, OS X Server enables organizations to collaborate, share files, host websites and mail servers, and more on Mac computers and iOS devices.

 BTW

Multipurpose OS
Operating systems, such as UNIX and Linux, that function as both desktop and server operating systems sometimes are called *multipurpose operating systems.*

 **Internet Research**

What is the most widely used server operating system?
Search for: server os market share

- **UNIX:** Capable of handling a high volume of transactions in a multiuser environment and working with multiple processors, UNIX often is used on web servers.
- **Linux:** Because it provides a secure, stable multiuser environment, Linux often is used on web servers and on supercomputers.

Mobile Operating Systems

Internet Research

What is the most widely used mobile operating system?

Search for: mobile os market share

The operating system on mobile devices and many consumer electronics is called a **mobile operating system** and resides on firmware. Mobile operating systems typically include or support the following: calendar and contact management, text messaging, email, touch screens, accelerometer (so that you can rotate the display), digital cameras, media players, speech recognition, GPS navigation, a variety of third-party apps, a browser, and wireless connectivity such as cellular, Wi-Fi, and Bluetooth. Read Ethics & Issues 9-4 to consider the privacy of text messages.

 ETHICS & ISSUES 9-4

Should Text Messages Sent by Employees Be Private?

When an employer asks a worker to disclose text messages sent on a company-issued mobile phone, is the employee required legally to reveal all texts, even personal ones? Companies provide employees with mobile devices, such as smartphones, to be used for work communications. Employers typically create acceptable use policies. These policies address ownership of electronic communications, including email messages, voice mail messages, and text messages. Regardless of the policy, employees may believe they have the rights of privacy and

self-expression when they use a company-issued mobile device for personal use. With email and voice mail, a company typically archives the messages on its own servers. Often, however, a company must request to access text messages from the mobile device's service provider.

The U.S. Supreme Court ruled that an employer can read workers' text messages if the employer has reason to believe the text messages violate workplace rules. The Court held that employees can purchase their own mobile devices for personal use. Critics state that employees have a reasonable expectation of privacy. Supporters of the

decision argue that employers own the devices because they provide the devices and pay for the service for the employee. They claim, therefore, that employers have a right to view the content of all text messages.

Should text messages sent by employees be private? Why or why not? How can employers impose policies regarding text messages sent on company-issued mobile devices? Should employers demand that mobile device service providers offer the option to disclose all employee text message communications? Why or why not?

 MINI FEATURE 9-3

Mobile Operating Systems

Whether on a desktop or mobile device, an operating system has the same role. It manages operations and provides a user interface. Because of this shared role, many similarities exist between the functions of desktop and mobile operating systems. From a user's perspective, the operating systems enable you to work with apps and to monitor and maintain the functions of the computer or device. Typical functions included in mobile operating systems include the following:

- Main areas, such as a desktop or home screen, enable you to access and organize apps.
- Methods exist to return to the main area quickly.
- Organize the app icons or tiles in the main areas easily by moving them to pages or folders or by adding them to menus.
- Manage system functions, such as battery power and Internet connections.

- Control security settings.

Whether you are purchasing a computer or mobile device, the choice of an operating system plays an important role.

Historically, the two types of operating systems have had different uses and capabilities. The differences are due in part to the disparity in screen size, keyboards, and processing power. Because of convergence, as well as the increased reliance on mobile devices for communications and productivity, the use and function of mobile and desktop operating systems are becoming more similar. The prevalence of web apps and cloud storage services enables users to access the same programs and files they work with on their desktop from a mobile device. Developers now are creating operating systems that share code and have common features, regardless of whether they are installed on a computer or mobile device. Features such as tiles and icons, typically used in mobile devices, make the transition between using a mobile device and computer

BTW

Android Releases
Google names its Android releases alphabetically after sweet treats, such as Gingerbread, Honeycomb, Ice Cream Sandwich, Jelly Bean, and Key Lime Pie.

easier. For example, mobile devices include capabilities that allow users to take advantage of the touch screen displays.

Many differences exist in the way a user interacts with a mobile operating system.

- A desktop operating system may use menus, windows, and bars to run apps and to access features within apps. On a desktop, you can run multiple programs simultaneously and seamlessly due to the large screen and the use of pointing devices. This feature makes desktops more relevant than mobile operating systems to productivity and multitasking.

- A mobile operating system typically has one program running at a time, although others may be running in the background. Quick movements and gestures are often all that you need to perform tasks on a mobile device. Mobile operating systems use technologies such as cellular, Bluetooth, Wi-Fi, GPS, and NFC to communicate with other devices and to connect to the Internet. Mobile devices also typically include cameras, video cameras, voice recorders, and sometimes speech recognition.

✻ What similarities have you noticed between mobile and desktop operating systems? What differences have you noticed between mobile and desktop operating systems? What features work better with a mobile versus a desktop operating system? Why? Is the convergence trend beneficial or should each device type take advantage of its strengths? Why?

Sources: Google Inc.; Apple Inc.

Android

Android is an open source, Linux-based mobile operating system designed by Google for smartphones and tablets (Figure 9-17). A variety of manufacturers produce devices that run the Android operating system, adding their own interface elements and bundled software. As a result, an Android smartphone manufactured by Samsung may have different user interface features from one manufactured by Google.

Features unique to recent versions of the Android operating system include the following:

- *Google Play* app store provides access to apps, songs, books, and movies.
- *Google Drive* provides access to email, contacts, calendar, photos, files, and more.
- Face recognition can unlock the device.

Figure 9-17 An Android phone and tablet.
© iStockphoto / Petko Danov; © iStockphoto / Gergana Valcheva

iOS tablet

iOS phone

Figure 9-18 An iOS tablet and phone.
© iStockphoto / Hocus Focus Studio

Figure 9-19 A Windows Phone.
© iStockphoto / TommL

- Share contacts and other information by touching two devices together (using NFC technology).
- Speech output assists users with vision impairments.

iOS

iOS (originally called iPhone OS), developed by Apple, is a proprietary mobile operating system specifically made for Apple's mobile devices (Figure 9-18). Supported devices include the iPhone, iPod Touch, and iPad. Features unique to recent versions of the iOS operating system include the following:

- *Siri*, a voice recognition app, enables you to speak instructions or questions to which it takes actions or responds with speech output.
- *Passbook* app provides a centralized location for coupons, boarding passes, loyalty cards, and mobile payment accounts in a single, easily accessible location.
- iCloud enables you to sync mail, calendars, contacts, and other items.
- *iTunes Store* provides access to music, books, podcasts, ringtones, and movies.
- Integrates with iPod to play music, video, and other media.
- Mac App Store provides access to additional apps and software updates.

Windows Phone

Windows Phone, developed by Microsoft, is a proprietary mobile operating system that runs on some smartphones (Figure 9-19). Features unique to recent versions of the Windows Phone operating system include the following:

- Sync photos, files, and settings with SkyDrive.
- Use your phone as a remote control for your TV.
- Access a global catalog of music, videos, or podcasts, or listen to iTunes music.
- *Windows Phone Store* provides access to additional apps and software updates.
- *Wallet* app provides a centralized location for coupons, credit cards, loyalty cards, and memberships in a single, easily accessible location.

 BTW
Steve Ballmer
Technology Innovator: You should be familiar with Steve Ballmer.

 BTW
Monitor Health Status
Innovative Computing: You should be familiar with how mobile devices and software can be used to monitor health status.

 CONSIDER THIS

Do other mobile operating systems exist?
Yes. Several other mobile operating systems exist, although they are not as widely used as Android, iOS, and Windows Phone. For example, the *Blackberry operating system* is a proprietary mobile operating system that runs on Blackberry smartphones and Blackberry tablets. *Firefox OS* is a Linux-based open source operating system that runs on smartphones and tablets developed by Mozilla. Several phones also run a version of Linux.

 **CONSIDER THIS**

Do embedded computers use mobile operating systems?
Typically, an embedded computer uses an *embedded operating system*, sometimes called a *real-time operating system* (RTOS). Examples of products that use embedded operating systems include digital cameras, ATMs, digital photo frames, HDTV receivers, fuel pumps, ticket machines, process controllers, robotics, and automobile components. Embedded operating systems often perform a single task, usually without requiring input from a user. Several embedded operating systems are available, each intended for various uses.

NOW YOU KNOW

Be sure you understand the material presented in the sections titled Server Operating Systems and Mobile Operating Systems, as it relates to the chapter objectives.
You now should know . . .

- When you might use a server operating system (Objective 8)

- Which mobile operating system you would prefer to use (Objective 9)

Quiz Yourself Online: Check your knowledge of related content by navigating to this book's Quiz Yourself resource on Computer Concepts CourseMate and then tapping or clicking Objectives 8–9.

Chapter Summary

This chapter discussed the functions common to most operating systems: starting and shutting down computers and mobile devices, providing a user interface, managing programs, managing memory, coordinating tasks, configuring devices, establishing an Internet connection, monitoring performance, providing file and disk management, updating operating system software, controlling a network, and administering security. It also presented a variety of desktop operating systems, server operating systems, and mobile operating systems.

Test your knowledge of chapter material by accessing the Study Guide, Flash Cards, and Practice Test apps that run on your smartphone, tablet, laptop, or desktop.

 TECHNOLOGY @ WORK

Textile Industry

While preparing to attend a wedding, you realize the shirt you planned to wear has a stain that will be impossible to remove before the event. You write down the size of the stained shirt, stop at a department store on your way to the wedding, purchase a new shirt of the same color and size, and quickly change shirts. As expected, the new shirt fits perfectly.

Technology assists in many aspects of the textile industry. In the past, people made fabrics and clothing articles by hand. Today, technology is speeding up and improving accuracy of the process for tasks such as designing clothing, creating patterns, and embroidering designs on garments. Similar to how the construction and automotive industries use computer-aided design (CAD) to design buildings and cars, the textile industry also uses CAD to design and produce fabrics and clothing. Recall that CAD software is a type of application that assists professional designers in creating engineering, architectural, and scientific designs and models.

CAD use in the textile industry begins with the design of clothing. While fashion designers often start with a vision of

how they would like the finished product to appear, computers assist by showing illustrations of how certain fabrics appear on bodies of different shapes and sizes, how various designs and colors look together, and the amount of material required to manufacture the items.

Once the design phase is complete and the designer makes his or her final selections, an automated manufacturing process minimizes human intervention. In addition, technology also reduces manufacturing time and decreases costs by minimizing the amount of waste generated by human error.

Technology not only assists with the design and manufacture of fabrics and clothing, but also with creating solar textiles. A solar textile is a fabric or cloth that contains a solar material that is designed to absorb sunlight and then convert the sunlight to usable energy, resulting in decreased electricity costs. Using 3-D modeling software, architects and others create designs with solar textiles, which are more flexible than traditional solar panels. In the future, you might see more solar textiles embedded in roofs and walls or being used as curtains.

The textile industry, which once relied solely on individuals to design and

manufacture textiles, has made a tremendous transformation during the past decade and might play an even larger role as we continue to discover natural energy sources.

How else might computers and technology be used in the textile industry?

MARC ROMANELLI / Alamy

Study Guide

The Study Guide exercise reinforces material you should know for the chapter exam. You will find answers to items with the icon only in the e-book.

Access the Study Guide app that runs on your smartphone, tablet, laptop, or desktop by navigating to this book's Apps resource on Computer Concepts CourseMate.

Instructions: Answer the questions below using the format that helps you remember best or that is required by your instructor. Possible formats may include one or more of these options: write the answers; create a document that contains the answers; record answers as audio or video using a webcam, smartphone, or portable media player; post answers on a blog, wiki, or website; or highlight answers in the book/e-book.

1. Define the term, operating system. List the functions of an operating system.

2. Define the term, firmware. Name another term for an operating system.

3. List methods to restart a computer or device.

4. Identify the five steps in the start-up process.

5. The _____ is the core of an operating system. Differentiate between resident and nonresident, with respect to memory.

6. The process of starting or restarting a computer or mobile device is called _____.

7. List reasons why users might shut down computers or mobile devices regularly. Describe what occurs when a computer is placed in sleep mode.

8. Define the term, user interface. Differentiate between a GUI and a command-line interface.

9. Define the terms foreground and background in a multitasking operating system.

10. List steps for setting up a virtual machine. Identify reasons to use a virtual machine.

11. Describe how a computer manages memory. Define the term, virtual memory.

12. The technique of swapping items between memory and storage is called _____.

13. If an application has stopped responding, the operating system may be _____.

14. List actions you should take if a mobile device displays a message that it is running low on memory.

15. Explain how a computer coordinates tasks. Define these terms: buffer, spooling, and queue.

16. Describe the role of a driver. Explain how to find the latest drivers for a device.

17. Explain the issues surrounding an operating system's inclusion of virus protection software.

18. Describe the role of a performance monitor.

19. Explain how a benchmark measures the performance of hardware or software.

20. List file and disk management tools, and describe the function of each.

21. Identify changes that may be made to an operating system during an automatic update. List security concerns regarding automatic updates.

22. An error in a program is sometimes called a(n) _____.

23. Explain issues surrounding responsibility for operating system security flaws.

24. Describe the role of a network administrator.

25. Describe the contributions of Sun, with respect to networks.

26. List and describe security tools used by operating systems.

27. Differentiate between administrator and user accounts on a network.

28. List alternatives to using passwords.

29. List steps to add users to an operating system.

30. Differentiate between device-dependent and device-independent programs.

31. Define these terms: proprietary software, backward compatible, and upward compatible.

32. List two other names for a desktop operating system.

33. Define the term, desktop, with respect to Windows and Mac OS.

34. The term, _____, sometimes is used to describe a computer that runs a Windows operating system.

35. Identify features of OS X. Define the term, Launchpad.

36. List steps for using Boot Camp to install the Windows operating system on a Mac.

37. Describe the contributions Steve Wozniak has made to develop the company, Apple.

38. Explain why power users often work with UNIX.

39. Define the term, open source software.

40. Explain the issues surrounding open versus closed operating systems.

41. Identify features of Chrome OS.

42. Describe a server operating system. List examples of server operating systems.

43. Identify common features of mobile operating systems.

44. Explain issues surrounding ownership of text messages sent using company-issued devices.

45. List differences and similarities between how a user interacts with mobile versus desktop operating systems.

46. Differentiate between the features of the Android, iOS, and Windows Phone mobile operating systems.

47. Describe how embedded computers use operating systems.

48. Explain how the textile industry uses technology.

You should be able to define the Primary Terms and be familiar with the Secondary Terms listed below.

Key Terms

Access the Flash Cards app that runs on your smartphone, tablet, laptop, or desktop by navigating to this book's Apps resource on Computer Concepts CourseMate. View definitions for each term by navigating to this book's Key Terms resource on Computer Concepts CourseMate. Listen to definitions for each term on your portable media player by navigating to this book's Audio Study Tools resource on Computer Concepts CourseMate.

Primary Terms   (shown in **bold-black** characters in the chapter)

Android (401)
automatic update (390)
boot drive (381)
Chrome OS (399)
desktop operating
  system (394)
driver (387)

iOS (402)
Linux (398)
mobile operating system
  (400)
natural user interface (NUI)
  (382)
operating system (OS) (378)

OS X (395)
password (392)
performance
  monitor (389)
queue (386)
server operating
  system (399)

sign in (392)
UNIX (397)
user interface (UI) (381)
user name (392)
virtual memory (385)
Windows Phone (402)

Secondary Terms   (shown in *italic* characters in the chapter)

administrator account (392)
background (383)
Backup and Restore (390)
backward compatible (393)
Blackberry operating system (402)
Boot Camp (396)
boot disk (381)
booting (381)
buffer (386)
bug (391)
Charms bar (395)
Chromebook (399)
Chromebox (399)
client operating systems (394)
cold boot (381)
command language (383)
command-line interface (382)
cross-platform application (378)
desktop (394, 396)
device driver (387)
device-dependent (393)
device-independent (393)
Disk Cleanup (390)

Disk Defragmenter (390)
Dock (396)
embedded operating system (402)
encryption (393)
File Compression (390)
File Manager (390)
Firefox OS (402)
firmware (378)
foreground (383)
Google Drive (401)
Google Play (401)
graphical user interface (GUI) (381)
hibernate mode (381)
iCloud (395)
Image Viewer (390)
Internet Explorer (394)
iTunes Store (402)
kernel (380)
Launchpad (396)
Live CD (381)
Live USB (381)
Macintosh operating system
  (MAC OS) (395)

memory resident (380)
multipurpose operating systems (399)
multitasking (383)
multiuser (384)
network administrator (392)
nonresident (380)
open source software (398)
page (386)
paging (386)
partition (396)
Passbook (402)
PC Maintenance (390)
permissions (392)
platform (378)
Plug and Play (387)
print spooler (386)
proprietary software (393)
real-time operating system (402)
recovery media (381)
Recycle Bin (395)
ribbon (395)
Safari (395)
Screen Saver (390)

scroll bars (395)
scrollers (396)
Search (390)
service pack (391)
Siri (402)
Sky Drive (394)
sleep mode (381)
spooling (386)
stand-alone operating system (394)
Start screen (394)
status bar (395)
swap file (386)
The Open Group (397)
thrashing (386)
tiles (394)
touch user interface (382)
Uninstaller (390)
upward compatible (393)
virtual machine (384)
virtualization (399)
Wallet (402)
warm boot (381)
Windows Phone Store (402)

© iStockphoto / TommL

Windows Phone (402)

Checkpoint

The Checkpoint exercises test your knowledge of the chapter concepts. The page number containing the answer appears in parentheses after each exercise. The Consider This exercises challenge your understanding of chapter concepts.

Complete the Checkpoint exercises interactively by navigating to this book's Checkpoint resource on Computer Concepts CourseMate. **Access the Test Prep app** that runs on your smartphone, tablet, laptop, or desktop by navigating to this book's Apps resource on Computer Concepts CourseMate. After successfully completing the self-assessment through the Test Prep app, **take the Practice Test** by navigating to this book's Practice Test resource on Computer Concepts CourseMate.

True/False   Mark T for True and F for False.

_____ 1. Operating systems provide vastly different functions, depending on the size of the computer or mobile device. (380)

_____ 2. The kernel is nonresident, which means it remains in memory while the computer or mobile device is running. (380)

_____ 3. Most users today work with a command-line interface. (381)

_____ 4. A user interface controls how you enter data and instructions and how information is displayed on the screen. (381)

_____ 5. Most operating systems today are multitasking. (383)

_____ 6. If the operating system is thrashing, you first should try to exit the program before attempting to reboot the computer. (386)

_____ 7. Each device connected to a computer requires its own specific driver. (387)

_____ 8. An administrator should use the administrator account on a limited basis because the operating system is susceptible to spyware and malware attacks in this setting. (392)

_____ 9. Many of the first operating systems were device dependent and proprietary. (393)

_____ 10. Client operating systems cannot operate without a network. (394)

_____ 11. Linux is proprietary software. (398)

_____ 12. Operating systems that function as both desktop and server operating systems sometimes are called multipurpose operating systems. (399)

Multiple Choice   Select the best answer.

1. A _____ application is an application that runs the same on multiple operating systems. (378)
   a. cross-platform
   b. stand-alone
   c. device driver
   d. multitasking

2. The _____ is the core of an operating system that manages memory and devices, maintains the internal clock, runs programs, and assigns the resources. (380)
   a. firmware
   b. driver
   c. platform
   d. kernel

3. Placing a computer in _____ mode saves any open documents and running programs or apps to an internal hard drive before removing power from the computer or device. (381)
   a. sleep
   b. hibernate
   c. kernel
   d. NUI

4. In a _____, a user types commands represented by short keywords or abbreviations or presses special keys on the keyboard to enter data and instructions. (382)
   a. NUI
   b. GUI
   c. command-line interface
   d. touch interface

5. The technique of swapping items between memory and storage is called _____. (385)
   a. thrashing
   b. paging
   c. spooling
   d. buffering

6. With _____, the operating system allocates a portion of a storage medium to function as additional RAM. (386)
   a. live USB
   b. a natural user interface
   c. virtual memory
   d. spooling

7. In Windows, the _____ consist(s) of tabs, groups, and commands that provide access to tasks. (395)
   a. tiles
   b. status bar
   c. charms
   d. ribbon

8. A _____ is a multiuser operating system that organizes and coordinates how multiple users access and share resources on a network. (399)
   a. stand-alone operating system
   b. server operating system
   c. virtual machine
   d. multipurpose operating system

Checkpoint

Matching
Match the terms with their definitions.

_____ 1. firmware (378)

_____ 2. cold boot (381)

_____ 3. warm boot (381)

_____ 4. command language (383)

_____ 5. buffer (386)

_____ 6. driver (387)

_____ 7. proprietary software (393)

_____ 8. device-independent (393)

_____ 9. tile (394)

_____ 10. partition (396)

a. process of restarting a computer or mobile device while it remains powered on

b. small program that tells the operating system how to communicate with a specific device

c. Windows term for a shortcut to an app or other content

d. software that is privately owned and limited to a specific vendor or computer or device model

e. ROM chips or flash memory chips that store permanent instructions

f. operating system that runs on computers and mobile devices provided by a variety of manufacturers

g. section of storage or memory reserved for a specific program or application

h. process of starting a computer or mobile device from a state when it is powered off completely

i. segment of memory or storage in which items are placed while waiting to be transferred from an input device or to an output device

j. set of commands used to control actions performed in a command-line interface

Short Answer
Write a brief answer to each of the following questions.

1. What is a platform? (378) What is a cross-platform application? (378)

2. Describe the process of starting a computer. (380) Differentiate between memory resident and nonresident. (380)

3. How does the operating system coordinate tasks? (386) What is a buffer? (386)

4. What is a service pack? (391) How do users without an Internet connection obtain updates? (391)

5. What are permissions? (392) List alternatives to passwords. (392)

✳ Consider This
Answer the following questions in the format specified by your instructor.

1. Answer the critical thinking questions posed at the end of these elements in this chapter: Ethics & Issues (388, 390, 398, 400), How To (384, 387, 393, 396), Mini Features (394, 396, 400), Secure IT (391, 392), and Technology @ Work (403).

2. Why might you restart a computer or mobile device? (380)

3. What is the difference between a cold and warm boot? (381)

4. What is the role of virtual memory? What does it mean when an operating system is thrashing? (385)

5. In a multiuser operating system, are tasks processed on a first-come, first-served basis? Why or why not? (386)

6. Should an operating system include virus protection? Why or why not? (388)

7. Do the security risks associated with automatic updates outweigh the advantages? Why or why not? (391)

8. How does a network administrator establish permissions and user accounts? (392)

9. What is the advantage of device-independent operating systems? 📋 What is an example of a device-independent operating system? (393)

10. What features are available on the Windows 8 Charms bar? What features are available on the OS X Dock? (395, 397)

11. Do open source operating systems have advantages over closed source operating systems? Why or why not? (398)

12. Why do computers running Chrome OS require less internal storage capacity than those running other desktop operating systems? (399)

13. How do server operating systems use virtualization? (399)

14. Does a company have a right to view text messages sent using a company phone? Why or why not? (400)

15. What are the similarities and differences between desktop and mobile operating systems? (400)

✴ How To: Your Turn

The How To: Your Turn exercises present general guidelines for fundamental skills when using a computer or mobile device and then require that you determine how to apply these general guidelines to a specific program or situation.

Instructions: You often can complete tasks using technology in multiple ways. Figure out how to perform the tasks described in these exercises by using one or more resources available to you (such as a computer or mobile device, articles on the web or in print, online or program help, user guides, blogs, podcasts, videos, other individuals, trial and error, etc.). Summarize your 'how to' steps, along with the resource(s) used, in the format requested by your instructor (brief report, presentation, discussion, blog post, video, or other means).

❶ Determine Your Operating System Version

Companies such as Microsoft, Apple, and Google release new versions of operating systems periodically. Software and drivers sometimes are designed for specific operating system versions, which means you may need to determine your operating system version so that you can obtain the proper software. The following steps describe how to determine your operating system version.

a. If necessary, turn on your computer or mobile device and, if necessary, sign in to the operating system. Some operating systems will display the version when they run. If the operating system version is not displayed, continue following these steps.

b. If you are using a Mac, click the command on the Apple menu to display information about the Mac to determine the operating system version. If you are running an operating system other than Mac OS, continue following these steps.

c. Display the control panel or settings for your computer or mobile device.

d. Navigate to and then tap or click the command to display system information about the computer or device, and then locate the operating system version.

Source: Apple Inc.

Exercises

1. What operating system are you running?
2. What are some other reasons why you might need to know the operating system version on your computer or mobile device?
3. What might happen if you attempt to install a program or app that is not designed for your operating system version?

❷ Search for Files on a Computer

Advances in technology enable users to store a large number of files, such as documents, photos, videos, and music, on their computers. Users store contacts, appointments, email messages, and other information on mobile devices to retrieve at a later time. With all the information you can store on computers and mobile devices, it sometimes can be difficult to locate an item you need to access. Today's operating systems contain a search tool that provides an easy way to locate files stored on a computer or mobile device. To search for an item on a computer or mobile device, you should know information about the item for which you are searching. The following steps guide you through the process of searching a computer or mobile device.

a. If necessary, run the search tool on your computer or mobile device. If you are using a mobile device such as a smartphone or tablet, you may be able to access the search tool by pressing a search button on the phone or tablet.

b. If you remember all or part of the name of the file for which you are searching, enter all or part of the file name in the search box.

Source: Apple Inc.

c. Tap or click the search button to display the search results. Depending upon the number of files and folders on your computer or mobile device, it may take several minutes for search results to appear.

d. If no search results are displayed, consider searching again and entering less information in the search box.

e. When you locate the file for which you are searching, you can open it either by tapping, double-tapping, or double-clicking the file. The method you should use to open the file will depend on the operating system you are using.

How To: Your Turn

Exercises

1. Have you used the search tool on your computer? If so, what files were you attempting to locate? If not, do you think the search tool will be helpful to you?
2. Have you used the search tool on a mobile device? What were you attempting to locate?
3. In addition to searching for files, what other items might the search tool locate?

❸ Personalize Your Operating Environment

When you purchase a new computer or mobile device, the first task you might want to complete is to personalize the operating environment to suit your tastes. For example, you might want to have your favorite sports team's logo as your desktop background, a screen saver consisting of a slide show containing pictures of your recent vacation, or specific sounds that play when certain events occur. The following steps guide you through the process of personalizing your operating environment.

a. If necessary, sign in to your operating system.

b. Display your operating system's control panel, settings, or system preferences.

c. Tap or click the option to modify the display settings and then navigate to the specific setting to change the desktop background (the desktop background also may be referred to as wallpaper).

d. Tap or click the option to locate the image to use as your desktop background. If you are planning to download an image from the web, you should do so before completing this step. Download only an image that is not protected by copyright.

e. Navigate to the location of the image to use as the desktop background and then select the image to set it as your desktop background.

f. Navigate to the screen saver settings and then select the desired screen saver. If necessary, set the desired preferences for the screen saver.

g. Navigate to the sound settings.

h. Select the event for which you want to assign or change the sound.

i. Select the sound you want to play. If you are not using one of the operating system's prerecorded sounds, navigate to the location of the sound you want to use and then select the sound.

j. If necessary, save the changes and close the control panel, settings, or system preferences.

Exercises

1. What image are you currently using as your desktop background or wallpaper?
2. Do you have a screen saver configured on your computer or mobile device? If so, what does it look like?

❹ Configure Accessibility Settings

Many modern operating systems allow users to configure accessibility settings to make it easier for some individuals to interact with them. Accessibility features can perform functions such as enhancing the contrast between colors on the display device, narrating text that is displayed on the screen, and allowing the user to control the pointer using keys on the keyboard. The following steps guide you through the process of configuring accessibility settings.

a. If necessary, sign in to the operating system.

b. Display your operating systems control panel, settings, or system preferences.

c. Tap or click the command to display accessibility settings.

d. Select the accessibility setting you want to configure, and specify your desired settings.

e. Repeat the previous step for all remaining accessibility settings you want to configure.

f. When you have finished configuring the accessibility settings, save your changes and close the window containing the control panel, settings, or system preferences.

g. If you no longer require the accessibility settings, display your operating system's control panel, settings, or system preferences, display the setting you want to disable, and then disable the setting.

Exercises

1. Accessibility settings are not only for people with impairments; these settings can make it easier for anyone to use a computer. Can you think of any accessibility settings that you might consider using to make it easier to interact with the computer?
2. Which third-party programs can provide additional features for accessibility?

✷ Internet Research

The Internet Research exercises broaden your understanding of chapter concepts by requiring that you search for information on the web.

Instructions: Use a search engine or another search tool to locate the information requested or answers to questions presented in the exercises. Describe your findings, along with the search term(s) you used and your web source(s), in the format requested by your instructor (brief report, presentation, discussion, blog post, video, or other means).

❶ Making Use of the Web

Financial Making wise investments and spending and managing money are among the most important decisions consumers can make. Abundant advice is available on a variety of financial websites. Online banking, portfolio management, tax preparation, personal finance, and small business and commercial services are available along with business news and advice, stock market quotes, and company earnings reports.

(a) Visit two websites that provide information about the stock market. Search for information about Microsoft, Google, and Apple. Write a paragraph about each of these stocks describing the revenues, net incomes, total assets for the previous year, current stock price per share, highest and lowest prices of each stock during the past year, and other relevant investment information.

(b) Visit two financial websites that feature information about technology. Read two stories discussing companies or products that you have read about in this textbook. Do these articles present favorable or unfavorable views? Do the writers predict the corporations or technology show promise as being sound financial investments? What technology trends are discussed in the latest articles?

❷ Social Media 🖺

Operating systems constantly evolve as developers add new features, fix security issues, and modify functions. Computer and mobile device users need to stay abreast of these changes, especially when the updates affect performance and safety. Many blogs feature content about operating systems. Their posts cover industry news, photos, product reviews, previews of forthcoming software and hardware, and management changes.

Search online for a blog that tracks features or updates to a mobile, desktop, or other operating system that you use or would like to know more about. Report the web address of the blog, along with a summary of the most recent blog post.

❸ Search Sleuth

(1) Which bird is the logo for Linux? What is its name? (2) Who are two individuals who published the requirements for virtualization in 1974? (3) What company supplies the CUDA (Compute Unified Device Architecture) drivers for their graphic processing units? (4) According to BitDefender, what percent of people use the same password for their email and online social network accounts? (5) What are common names for a UNIX administrator account? (6) On which day of the week does Microsoft typically provide automated updates? What is the nickname for this day? How often do these updates typically occur? (7) Which company did Andy Rubin, Chris White, Nick Sears, and Rich Miner cofound? (8) What is the name of the operating system for Radio Shack's TRS-80 introduced in 1980? What was the data storage mechanism for this computer? (9) In a Windows/DOS system, the command-line interface to list files is dir. What is the equivalent command for UNIX or Linux? (10) In what year was the first Chromebook available for sale in the United States?

CNBC.COM

» More From Technology: Trends

TECHNOLOGY | COMPANIES | TRENDS | DATA | MONEY & STARTUPS | GADGETS & GAMING

3-D Printers and the Cool Stuff They Make

Three-dimensional printing is gaining traction in both the business realm and among consumers, but there is still some confusion about how these machines work and what exactly the printers can build.

While lots of attention has been focused on 3-D printers and printing off weapons, the fact is the machines are capable of fabricating a variety of products—from gadgets and clothing to human tissue. One 3-D printing company even printed off a concrete house.

In 3-D printing, also known as additive manufacturing, a product is created layer by layer. The printer uses a blueprint of a digital model to make the item one layer at a time. Printers have been designed to use different materials—including plastic, ceramic, silver, steel, concrete and even stem cells—to make products.

Here's a look at how four companies are using the technology to create the future.

» Read less

David Paul Morris | Bloomberg | Getty Images

Recommend 62   Twitter 57   +1 1   LinkedIn 3   Share

MORE FROM TECHNOLOGY: TRENDS

Source: CNBC LLC

Internet Research

4 Green Computing

Operating systems consume power as they perform functions to coordinate activities among computer hardware resources. The power supply provides the current to run all these internal devices. Computer manufacturers rarely specify the amount of power each component uses, but, in general, the following list provides a range of the amount of watts consumed.

- Motherboard: 50 to 75 watts
- Processor: 50 to 100 watts
- RAM: 5 to 15 watts per module
- Hard drive: 15 to 30 watts
- Cooling fan: 3 to 5 watts
- Optical disc drive: 15 to 35 watts

Power supplies become overloaded when users add a second hard drive and upgrade their video cards and processors. Operating systems can help monitor computer energy use and suggest methods for reducing electricity through efficient power management. Experts claim monitoring systems can save each computer user at least $60 per year in electricity costs. Suggestions include not using a screen saver, turning down a monitor's brightness level, and using a high-performance power setting that balances processing power with laptop and tablet battery life.

Locate websites and articles that provide information about power management. Which methods are effective in reducing power consumption, especially for laptops and tablets? Which sleep state setting provides significant power savings? Which power management settings are recommended for balanced, power saver, and high performance?

5 Security

The use of antivirus and spyware and malware detection software is discussed in Secure IT 9-2 on page 391. An operating system should include this security software to fend off intrusions. Major companies that provide this software often include information on their websites about recently discovered virus threats and hoaxes. They also track scheduled virus payload strikes and map global and regional virus attacks.

Visit at least two virus protection websites to obtain virus information. When were the latest active threats discovered and updated? What are their names and risk levels? When is the next virus payload strike scheduled? What type of malware is spreading via mobile device use? Which virus removal tools and resources are available?

6 Ethics in Action

Several vehicle insurers are promising drivers insurance premium discounts up to 30 percent if they voluntarily install a data recorder in their vehicles' diagnostic ports to track their driving and then exercise good driving behavior. The device records speed, time of day, and the number of quick stops. Privacy experts predict more insurance companies will offer this monitoring system and that it eventually will become mandatory. These critics fear that negative data will be used against poor drivers, but the insurance companies claim that policy rates will not increase if customers drive aggressively by stopping and then accelerating quickly or if they drive at night, which is when accidents are more likely to occur. Some drivers have expressed concerns that the monitoring devices will track actual routes driven, but the insurance companies say the recorders do not have a GPS and, therefore, cannot pinpoint the vehicle's location.

Parents, similarly, are using devices to oversee their teenagers' driving habits in an effort to promote safe driving. These monitors are equipped with a GPS. Low-cost models store the data for retrieval at a later time; high-end devices require monthly subscriptions to transmit data whenever the vehicles are in motion and to notify parents via email or text message when the vehicle has exceeded a specific speed limit or traveled beyond a geographical boundary. Studies have shown that teens are more careful drivers when they know their driving actions are being recorded, so some insurance companies offer reduced policy rates if the tracking device is installed permanently in the vehicle.

Locate websites and articles that provide information about vehicle monitoring devices. How are insurance companies promoting the use of this hardware? Are policyholders with these devices seeing reductions in their insurance premiums? Which studies have shown a correlation between permanently installing monitors and safer driving? Could the data transmitted be compromised and sent to criminals who could, in turn, track drivers' whereabouts?

✺ Problem Solving

The Problem Solving exercises extend your knowledge of chapter concepts by seeking solutions to practical problems with technology that you may encounter at home, school, work, or with nonprofit organizations. The Collaboration exercise should be completed with a team.

💻 Challenge yourself with additional Problem Solving exercises by navigating to this book's Problem Solving resource on Computer Concepts CourseMate.

Instructions: You often can solve problems with technology in multiple ways. Determine a solution to the problems in these exercises by using one or more resources available to you (such as a computer or mobile device, articles on the web or in print, blogs, podcasts, videos, television, user guides, other individuals, electronics or computer stores, etc.). Describe your solution, along with the resource(s) used, in the format requested by your instructor (brief report, presentation, discussion, blog post, video, or other means).

Personal

1. **Difficulty Signing in to Operating System**   You are attempting to sign in to your mobile device, but you receive an error message stating that you have entered an invalid password. What are your next steps?

2. **Missing Customization Settings**   When you sign in to your operating system, your customized desktop background does not appear. Instead, the operating system displays the default desktop background. What might have happened?

3. **Incompatible Program**   You have upgraded to the latest version of an operating system on your computer. After the upgrade, you realize that programs that used to run without issue now are having problems. What are your next steps?

4. **Computer Stops Responding**   While using your computer with multiple programs running, the computer suddenly stops responding and you are unable to tap, click, or type anything. What are your next steps?

Source: Apple Inc.

5. **Software Update Issues**   You have heard that new software updates are available for your operating system, but when the operating system checks for updates, it shows that no updates are available. Why might this be the case?

Professional

6. **Virtual Machine Error**   You use virtual machines on your office computer so that you can run and test software in multiple operating system versions. When you attempt to run one of the virtual machines, you receive an error message that the virtual machine already is running. You are certain that the virtual machine is not running. What steps can you take to correct the problem?

7. **Memory Requirements**   Your boss has asked you to start pricing new laptops so that you can replace your current, aging laptop. How can you determine how much memory (RAM) you will need on the new laptop?

8. **Device Connection Problem**   You have connected a peripheral device to your computer that is supposed to support Plug and Play, but you receive an error message in your operating system stating that a driver for the device cannot be found. What are your next steps?

9. **Mobile Device Operating System Upgrade**   A notification appears on your mobile phone stating that an operating system upgrade has been downloaded and is ready to install. Your company has provided the mobile phone to you for work-related business, and you are hesitant to install the upgrade. What are your next steps?

10. **Slow System Performance**   Your office computer has been running slow lately, and you are attempting to determine the cause. What steps can you take to determine what might be slowing your computer's performance?

Collaboration

11. **Technology in the Textile Industry**   Many businesses in the textile industry are using advancements in technology to aid in designing and manufacturing textiles. Department stores and companies selling clothing online also use technology to show consumers how various articles of clothing will fit or how they will match other garments. Form a team of three people to report on ways they see technology changing the textile industry. Each team member should visit local malls and websites and record at least three ways that technology has improved the industry. Compile the findings and then submit a brief report to your instructor.

The Critical Thinking exercises challenge your assessment and decision-making skills by presenting real-world situations associated with chapter concepts. The Collaboration exercise should be completed with a team.

Critical Thinking

 Challenge yourself with additional Critical Thinking exercises by navigating to this book's Critical Thinking resource on Computer Concepts CourseMate.

Instructions: Evaluate the situations below, using personal experiences and one or more resources available to you (such as articles on the web or in print, blogs, podcasts, videos, television, user guides, other individuals, electronics or computer stores, etc.). Perform the tasks requested in each exercise and share your deliverables in the format requested by your instructor (brief report, presentation, discussion, blog post, video, or other means).

1. Class Discussion
Using Operating System Tools   You are the office manager at a social media consulting business. The office recently upgraded and replaced several computers. You now are running the latest version of Windows on all of your computers. Your boss asks you to explore the various tools that are included with the operating system and to evaluate any additional needs you might have. Use the web to learn more about the following Windows operating system tools: firewalls, automatic updates, and software that scans for viruses, spyware, and other malware. Read reviews by industry experts and users. Analyze the advantages and disadvantages of using built-in operating system tools. Do any built-in operating system tools present security concerns? If so, what would you recommend? Explore alternatives for each of the tools, and determine whether you should disable the Windows tool and if any risks exist. Compile your findings.

2. Research and Share
Complete Security Solutions   Your neighbor started a new construction business. He would like to hire you to set up his new computers. His business will use the Internet to communicate with clients via email, store backups of data, and access cloud-based accounting software. The office will include two networked computers, which will share a printer and an Internet connection. In addition, he will use a tablet so that he can access the cloud-based accounting software using Wi-Fi. Because of security concerns with using the Internet, he first would like you to install a program(s)

designed to protect his computers from various security threats. What types of security threats exist on the Internet relevant that could impact his business? What types of security measures should he use? Evaluate two programs that provide a comprehensive security solution. What are the programs' functions? What is their cost? Do the services charge subscription fees in order to receive automatic updates? Which would you recommend? Why?

3. Case Study
Farmers' Market   You are the new manager for a group of organic farmers who have a weekly market in season. The board of directors has asked you to recommend options for mobile operating systems for the new smartphones they would like to purchase. Select two mobile operating systems to explore (such as Android, iOS, and Windows Phone). Use the web to find industry experts' recommendations and user reviews for each operating system. Include the different device types for which each is available. Examine differences in security, features, speed, and reliability. What security concerns exist? What security features enable you to protect the smartphone and its data? Which mobile operating system offers the best features? Which is considered faster and/or more reliable? Your office computers run the Mac OS X operating system. Do compatibility issues exist with any of the mobile operating systems? If so, what are the issues? Can you find solutions that would enable you to sync data? Compile your findings.

Collaboration

4. **Desktop Operating Systems**   You are an analyst for a large manufacturer of laundry soaps. The company currently uses an early version of the Windows operating system on its 5,000 desktop computers. This year, the company plans to upgrade the operating system and, if necessary, its desktops. The company asks your team to compare the latest versions of the Windows, Mac OS, and Linux operating systems. Form a three-member team and assign each member an operating system. Each member should use the web to develop a feature/benefit analysis and answer the following questions. What is the initial cost of the operating system per computer? What are the memory and storage requirements? Will the operating system require the company to purchase new computers? Which is best at protecting against viruses, spam, and spyware? Which provide support to touch input? As a team, compile your findings and share your recommendation with the class.

Beyond the Book

The Beyond the Book exercises expand your understanding of chapter concepts by requiring research.

Access premium content by visiting Computer Concepts CourseMate. If you have a Computer Concepts CourseMate access code, you can reinforce and extend your learning with MindTap Reader, practice tests, video, and other premium content for Discovering Computers. To sign in to Computer Concepts CourseMate at www.cengagebrain.com, you first must create a student account and then register this book, as described at www.cengage.com/ct/studentdownload.

Part 1 Instructions: Use the web or e-book to perform the task identified for each book element below. Describe your findings, along with the search term(s) you used and your web source(s), if appropriate, in the format requested by your instructor (brief report, presentation, discussion, blog post, video, or other means).

1. **Animation** 📖 Review the animation associated with this chapter and then answer the question(s) it poses (386). What search term would you use to learn more about a specific segment of the animation?

2. **Consider This** Select a Consider This in this chapter (381, 382, 386, 392, 393, 398, 402) and find a recent article that elaborates on the topic. What information did you find that was not presented in this book or e-book?

3. **Drag-and-Drop Figures** 📖 Complete the Drag-and-Drop Figure activities associated with this chapter (384, 385, 390, 393, 395, 396). What did you learn from each of these activities?

4. **Ethics & Issues** Select an Ethics & Issues in this chapter (388, 390, 398, 400) and find a recent article that supports one view presented. Does the article change your opinion about the topic? Why or why not?

5. **Facebook & Twitter** Review a recent Discovering Computers Facebook post or Twitter Tweet and read the referenced article(s). What did you learn from the article?

6. **High-Tech Talk** 📖 Locate an article that discusses topics related to using a benchmark. Would you recommend the article you found? Why or why not?

7. **How To** Select a How To in this chapter (384, 387, 393, 396) and find a recent article that elaborates on the topic. Who would benefit from the content of this article? Why?

8. **Innovative Computing** 📖 Locate two additional facts about Linux powering the Internet of Things or how mobile devices and software can be used to monitor health status. Do your findings change your opinion about the future of this innovation? Why or why not?

9. **Internet Research** Use the search term in an Internet Research (382, 394, 399, 400) to answer the question posed in the element. What other search term could you use to answer the question?

10. **Mini Features** Locate an article that discusses topics related to one of the mini features in this chapter (394, 396, 400). Do you feel that the article is appropriate for this course? Why or why not?

11. **Secure IT** Select a Secure IT in this chapter (391, 392) and find a recent article about the topic that you find interesting. How can you relate the content of the article to your everyday life?

12. **Technology @ Work** Locate three additional, unique usages of technology in the textile industry (403). What makes the use of these technologies unique to the textile industry?

13. **Technology Innovators** 📖 Locate two additional facts about Sun, Steve Wozniak, Linus Torvalds, and Steve Ballmer. Which Technology Innovator impresses you most? Why?

14. **Third-Party Links** 📖 Visit one of the third-party links identified in this chapter (388, 390, 391, 392, 395, 398, 400, 402, 403) and read the article or watch the video associated with the link. Would you share this link on your online social network account? Why or why not?

Part 2 Instructions: Find specific instructions for the exercises below in the e-book or on Computer Concepts CourseMate. Beside each exercise is a brief description of its online content.

1. 📖 **You Review It** Search for and review a video, podcast, or blog post about news about Windows, Mac, or Linux operating systems.

2. 📖 **Windows and Mac** Enhance your understanding and knowledge about using Windows and Mac computers by completing the Set Screen Saver and Check for Operating System Updates activities.

3. 📖 **Android, iOS, and Windows Phone** Enhance your understanding of mobile devices by completing the Set Wallpaper and Set Screen Timeout activities.

4. 📖 **Exploring Computer Careers** Read about a career as a systems programmer, search for related employment ads, and then answer related questions.

5. 📖 **App Adventure** Stream Internet-hosted audio and video on your smart phone or tablet.

Communications and Networks
Sending and Receiving Digital Content

10

Users interact with a variety of communications media.

"I use my smartphone to send text messages, listen to voice mail messages, and navigate using a GPS app. At home, I have a broadband Internet connection, and I also access the Internet wirelessly at local hot spots and on campus. What more do I need to learn about communications and networks?"

True, you may be familiar with some of the material in this chapter, but do you know . . .

How to use your smartphone as a mobile hot spot?

How you can strengthen a wireless signal?

Why 802.11 is significant?

What to consider when planning a home network?

How DSL differs from cable Internet service?

Where you would find a geocache?

How to determine if an intruder is accessing your home network?

Whether you should be concerned about radiation from mobile phones and Wi-Fi devices?

How agriculture relies on computers, mobile devices, and related technologies?

Which mapping apps are best suited to your needs?

When you would use a BAN?

How GPS works?

How RFID toll collection works?

Who promised to eat his words if his prediction of the Internet's collapse was wrong?

For these answers and to discover much more information essential to this course, read this chapter and visit the associated Computer Concepts CourseMate at www.cengagebrain.com.

© 9Stockphoto / Nadya Lukic; © iStockphoto / SpaceManKris; © Artem Loskutnikov / Shutterstock.com; © Neyro / Shutterstock.com; © Fotolia; © iko / Shutterstock.com

✔ Objectives

After completing this chapter, you will be able to:

1 Discuss the purpose of components required for successful communications (sending device, communications device, transmission media, and receiving device) and identify various sending and receiving devices

2 Differentiate among LANs, MANs, WANs, and PANs

3 Differentiate between client/server and peer-to-peer networks

4 Differentiate among a star network, bus network, and ring network

5 Describe various network communications standards and protocols: Ethernet, token ring, TCP/IP, Wi-Fi, Bluetooth, UWB, IrDA, RFID, NFC, and WiMAX

6 Explain the purpose of communications software

7 Describe various types of communications lines: cable, DSL, ISDN, FTTP, T-carrier, and ATM

8 Describe commonly used communications devices: broadband modems, wireless modems, wireless access points, routers, network cards, and hubs and switches

9 Discuss ways to set up and configure a home network

10 Differentiate among physical transmission media: twisted-pair cable, coaxial cable, and fiber-optic cable

11 Differentiate among wireless transmission media: infrared, broadcast radio, cellular radio, microwaves, and communications satellite

Communications

Digital communications describes a process in which two or more computers or devices transfer data, instructions, and information. Today, even the smallest computers and devices can communicate directly with one another, with hundreds of computers on a corporate network, or with millions of other computers around the globe — often via the Internet.

Figure 10-1 shows a sample communications system. Some communications involve cables and wires; others are sent wirelessly through the air. For successful communications, you need the following:

- A **sending device** that initiates an instruction to transmit data, instructions, or information
- A communications device that connects the sending device to a communications channel
- Transmission media, or a *communications channel*, on which the data, instructions, or information travel
- A communications device that connects the communications channel to a receiving device
- A **receiving device** that accepts the transmission of data, instructions, or information

As shown in Figure 10-1, all types of computers and mobile devices serve as sending and receiving devices in a communications system. This includes servers, desktops, laptops, smartphones, portable media players, handheld game devices, and GPS receivers. Communications devices, such as modems, wireless access points, and routers, connect transmission media to a sending or receiving device. Transmission media can be wired or wireless.

This chapter presents types of networks, along with various types of communications lines and devices, and transmission media.

Communications System

Figure 10-1 A simplified example of a communications system. Some devices that serve as sending and receiving devices are (a) servers, (b) desktops, (c) laptops, (d) tablets, (e) smartphones and headsets, (f) portable media players, (g) handheld game devices, and (h) GPS receivers in vehicles. Transmission media consist of phone and power lines, cable television and other underground lines, microwave stations, and satellites.

Networks

As discussed in Chapter 1, a **network** is a collection of computers and devices connected together via communications devices and transmission media. A network can be internal to an organization or span the world by connecting to the Internet. Many home and business users create a network to facilitate communications, share hardware, share data and information, share software, and transfer funds (Figure 10-2):

- **Facilitate communications.** Using a network, people communicate efficiently and easily via email, instant messaging, chat rooms, blogs, wikis, online social networks, video calls, online meetings, videoconferencing, VoIP, wireless messaging services, and more. Some of these communications occur within an internal network. Other times, they occur globally over the Internet.

- **Share hardware.** Each computer or device on a network can be provided access to hardware on the network. For example, each computer and mobile device user can access a printer on the network, as they need it. Thus, home and business users create networks to save money on hardware expenses.

- **Share data and information.** Any authorized user can access data and information stored on a network. A large company, for example, might have a database of customer information. Any

Internet Research

How do you physically transfer files without a network connection?

Search for: sneakernet

Figure 10-2 Networks facilitate communications; enable sharing of hardware, data and information, and software; and provide a means for transferring funds.

© Iain Masterton / Alamy; © YanLev / Shutterstock.com; © Sergey Peterman / Shutterstock.com; © Kitch Bain / Shutterstock.com; © Oleksiy Mark / Shutterstock.com; © iStockphoto / 123render; © Cengage Learning authorized employee can access the database using a computer or mobile device connected to the network.

Most businesses use a standard, such as *EDI* (*electronic data interchange*), that defines how business documents transmit across transmission media. For example, businesses use EDI to send bids and proposals, place and track orders, and send invoices.

- **Share software.** Users connected to a network have access to software on the network. To support multiple users' software access, vendors often sell versions of their software designed to run on a network. These network versions usually cost less than buying individual copies of the software for each computer. Recall from Chapter 5 that a *network license* is a legal agreement that allows multiple users to access the software on a server simultaneously. The network license fee usually is based on the number of users or the number of computers attached to the network.
- **Transfer funds.** *Electronic funds transfer* (*EFT*) allows users connected to a network to exchange money from one account to another via transmission media. Both businesses and consumers use EFT. Examples include wire transfers, use of credit cards and debit cards, direct deposit of funds into bank accounts, online banking, and online bill payment.

Instead of using the Internet or investing in and administering an internal network, some companies hire a value-added network provider for network functions. A *value-added network* (*VAN*) provider is a third-party business that provides networking services such as EDI services, secure data and information transfer, storage, or email. Some VANs charge an annual or monthly fee; others charge by the service used.

 CONSIDER THIS

What is an intranet?

Recognizing the efficiency and power of the Internet, many organizations apply Internet and web technologies to their internal networks. An *intranet* (intra means within) is an internal network that uses Internet technologies. Intranets generally make company information accessible to employees and facilitate collaboration within an organization.

One or more servers on an intranet host an organization's internal webpages, applications, email messages, files, and more. Users locate information, access resources, and update content on an intranet using methods similar to those used on the Internet. The difference is that the host name of the intranet server differs from the host name of the company's public web server (recall that the host name of public web servers often is www).

Sometimes a company uses an *extranet*, which allows customers or suppliers to access part of its intranet. Package shipping companies, for example, allow customers to access their intranet via an extranet to print air bills, schedule pickups, and track shipped packages as the packages travel to their destinations.

LANs, MANs, WANs, and PANs

Networks usually are classified as a local area network, metropolitan area network, wide area network, or personal area network. The main difference among these classifications is their area of coverage.

LAN A **local area network** (**LAN**) is a network that connects computers and devices in a limited geographical area such as a home, school, office building (Figure 10-3 on the next page), or closely positioned group of buildings. Each computer or device on the network, called a *node*, often shares resources such as printers, large hard drives, and programs. Often, the nodes are connected via cables.

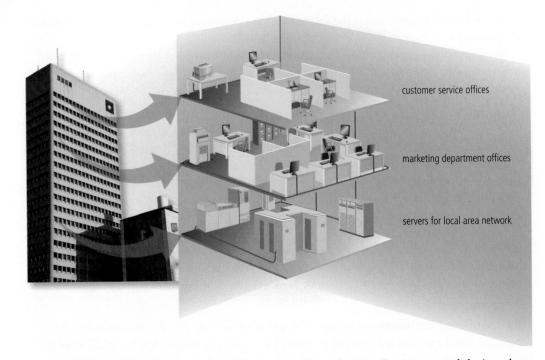

Figure 10-3
Computers and devices on different floors access the same LAN in an office building.
© Xtuv Photography / Shutterstock.com;
© Cengage Learning

customer service offices

marketing department offices

servers for local area network

A **wireless LAN (WLAN)** is a LAN that uses no physical wires. Computers and devices that access a wireless LAN must have built-in wireless capability or the appropriate wireless network card, USB adapter or other wireless device. A WLAN may communicate with a wired LAN for access to its resources, such as software, hardware, and the Internet (Figure 10-4).

wireless access point is center of wireless network

wired network

Internet

high-speed Internet connection

Figure 10-4 Computers and mobile devices on a WLAN may communicate via a wireless access point with a wired LAN to access its hardware, software, Internet connection, and other resources.
© iStockphoto / Stephen Krow; © Oleksiy Mark / Shutterstock.com; © iStockphoto / 123render; © iStockphoto / pictafolio; © iStockphoto / Moncherie; © Natalia Siverina / Shutterstock.com; © Ruslan Kudrin / Shutterstock.com; © Cengage Learning

MAN A *metropolitan area network* (*MAN*) is a high-speed network that connects local area networks in a metropolitan area, such as a city or town, and handles the bulk of communications activity across that region. A MAN typically includes one or more LANs, but covers a smaller geographic area than a WAN.

A MAN usually is managed by a consortium of users or by a single network provider that sells the service to the users. Local and state governments, for example, regulate some MANs. Phone companies, cable television providers, and other organizations provide users with connections to the MAN.

WAN A **wide area network** (**WAN**) is a network that covers a large geographic area (such as a city, country, or the world) using a variety of wired and wireless transmission media (Figure 10-5). A WAN can be one large network or can consist of multiple LANs connected together. The Internet is the world's largest WAN.

PAN A **personal area network** (**PAN**) is a network that connects computers and devices in an individual's workspace using wired and wireless technology. Devices include smartphones, digital cameras, printers, and more. A PAN may connect devices through a router

Figure 10-5 A simplified example of a WAN.

© Maksim Toome / Shutterstock.com; © Paul Matthew Photography / Shutterstock.com; © imging / Shutterstock.com; © Vtls / Shutterstock.com; © iStockphoto / Oleksiy Mark; © iStockphoto / cotesebastien; © Mmaxer / Shutterstock.com; © Cengage Learning

using network cables or directly using special USB cables. PANs also may use Bluetooth or Wi-Fi technology. Read Ethics & Issues 10-1 to consider another type of personal network.

✳ ETHICS & ISSUES 10-1

Would You Use a BAN to Monitor Medical Data?

By inserting or attaching small devices to a body, medical professionals can track vital signs and monitor heart rhythms, breathing rates, and much more. A *body area network* (*BAN*) uses low-powered sensors to collect data. The BAN sends the collected data wirelessly to an Internet-connected device, which relays the data to a medical data server, or in some cases, directly to emergency services. Some devices also automatically can dispense medications based on the data.

Because these devices transmit data in real time, a patient does not have to visit a

medical facility to receive the benefits. Heart patients, diabetics, or those with asthma or other similar conditions can perform regular daily activities while wearing the device. If it collects any unusual data, medical resources can be provided immediately to the patient. These devices also are used for first responders. A fire chief, for example, can monitor firefighters as they battle a fire by checking body temperature and oxygen levels.

The disadvantages of BANs include data validity and security. If a device stops working or its data becomes corrupt, serious health complications could result if the patient is not

monitoring conditions via another technique. For example, devices that administer medication could cause an overdose or underdose if not working properly. Medical data is highly sensitive. An unscrupulous individual could intercept vital signs and other personal data during transfer, violating a patient's confidentiality. Privacy advocates also have concerns about nonmedical uses of BANs.

Should insurance companies be required to pay for BANs? Why or why not? Would you use a BAN for a medical condition? Why or why not?

Network Architectures

The configuration of computers, devices, and media in a network, sometimes called the *network architecture*, is categorized as either client/server or peer-to-peer.

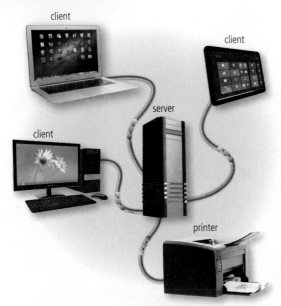

client

client

server

client

printer

Figure 10-6 As illustrated by the communications in this simplified diagram, on a client/server network, one or more computers act as a server, and the client computers and mobile devices access the server(s).

© iStockphoto / Oleksiy Mark; © iStockphoto / Stephen Krow; © Oleksiy Mark / Shutterstock.com; © Mr.Reborn55 / Shutterstock.com; © iStockphoto / luismmolina; © Cengage Learning

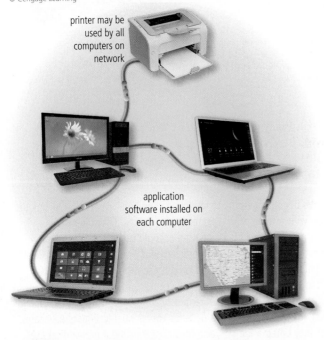

printer may be used by all computers on network

application software installed on each computer

Figure 10-7 As illustrated by the communications in this simplified diagram, each computer on a P2P network shares its hardware and software with other computers on the network.

© Serg64 / Shutterstock.com; © Alex Staroseltsev / Shutterstock.com; © iStockphoto / 123render; © Sergey Peterman / Shutterstock.com; © Oleksiy Mark / Shutterstock.com; Source: Microsoft; © Cengage Learning

Client/Server On a **client/server network**, one or more computers act as a server, and the other computers on the network request services from the server (Figure 10-6). A **server**, sometimes called a *host computer*, controls access to the hardware, software, and other resources on the network and provides a centralized storage area for programs, data, and information. The **clients** are other computers and mobile devices on the network that rely on the server for its resources. For example, a server might store an organization's email messages. Clients on the network, which include any users' connected computers or mobile devices, access email messages on the server.

Although it can connect a smaller number of computers, a client/server network typically provides an efficient means to connect 10 or more computers. Most client/server networks require a person to serve as a network administrator because of the large size of the network.

As discussed in Chapter 3, some servers are dedicated servers that perform a specific task. For example, a network server manages network traffic (activity), and a web server delivers requested webpages to computers or mobile devices.

Peer-to-Peer A *peer-to-peer network* (*P2P*) is a simple, inexpensive network that typically connects fewer than 10 computers. Each computer, called a *peer*, has equal responsibilities and capabilities, sharing hardware (such as a printer), data, or information with other computers on the peer-to-peer network (Figure 10-7). Each computer stores files on its own storage devices. Thus, each computer on the network contains both the operating system and applications. All computers on the network share any peripheral device(s) attached to any computer. For example, one computer may have a laser printer and a scanner, while another has an ink-jet printer and an external hard drive.

P2P networks are ideal for very small businesses and home users. Some operating systems include a P2P networking tool that allows users to set up a peer-to-peer network. Many businesses also see an advantage to using P2P. That is, companies and employees can exchange files using P2P, freeing the company from maintaining a network server for this purpose. Business-to-business e-commerce websites find that P2P easily allows buyers and sellers to share company information such as product databases.

Internet Research

Why have some file sharing networks been shut down?

Search for: file sharing network shutdown

❋ **CONSIDER THIS**

What is P2P file sharing?

P2P file sharing, sometimes called a *file sharing network*, describes an Internet network on which users access each other's hard drives and exchange files directly over the Internet via a file sharing program. As more users connect to the network, each user has access to shared files on other users' hard drives. When users sign off the network, others no longer have access to their hard drives.

Network Topologies

A **network topology** refers to the layout of the computers and devices in a communications network. Three basic network topologies are star, bus, and ring. Most networks, including the Internet, use combinations of these basic topologies. Thus, you should be familiar with the layout of communications in these topologies.

Star Network   On a *star network*, all of the computers and devices (nodes) on the network connect to a central device, thus forming a star (Figure 10-8). All data that transfers from one node to another passes through the central device.

Star networks are fairly easy to install and maintain. Nodes can be added to and removed from the network with little or no disruption to the network.

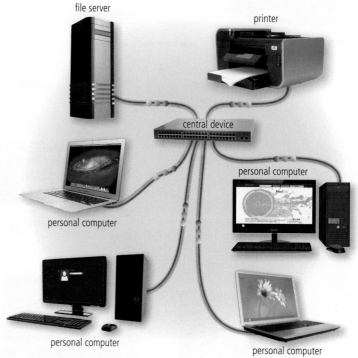

Figure 10-8   A star network contains a single, centralized device through which all computers and devices on the network communicate.
© Natalia Siverina / Shutterstock.com; © Kitch Bain / Shutterstock.com; © iStockphoto / Oleksiy Mark; © Alex Staroseltsev / Shutterstock.com; © iStockphoto / sweetym; © iStockphoto / Stephen Krow; © iStockphoto / luismmolina; © Cengage Learning

 CONSIDER THIS

What happens if a node or the central device fails on a star network?
On a star network, if one node fails, only that node is affected (as long as that node is not providing services to other nodes on the network). The other nodes continue to operate normally. If the central device fails, however, the entire network is inoperable until the device is repaired. Most large star networks, therefore, keep a duplicate of the central devices (hubs or switches) available in case the primary one fails.

 CONSIDER THIS

Does the word, node, have multiple meanings?
Yes. Any computer or device connected to a network that has an IP address often is called a node. A central connection on a network also is known as a node.

BTW
Hub or Switch
Two types of devices that provide a common central connection point for nodes on the network are a hub and a switch, which are discussed later in this chapter.

Bus Network   A *bus network* consists of a single central cable, to which all computers and other devices connect (Figure 10-9). The bus is the physical cable that connects the computers and other devices. The bus in a bus network transmits data, instructions, and information in both directions. When a sending device transmits data, the address of the receiving device is included with the transmission so that the data is routed to the appropriate receiving device.

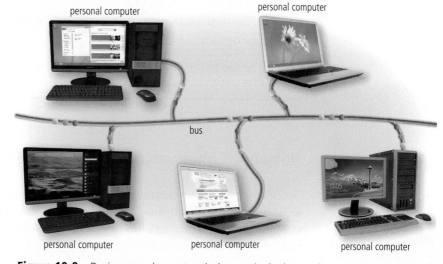

Figure 10-9   Devices on a bus network share a single data path.
© Oleksiy Mark / Shutterstock.com; © Alex Staroseltsev / Shutterstock.com; © Oleksiy Mark / Shutterstock.com; © Alex Staroseltsev / Shutterstock.com; © iStockphoto / 123render; © Cengage Learning

Figure 10-10 On a ring network, all connected devices form a continuous loop.
© Alex Staroseltsev / Shutterstock.com; © Mr.Reborn55 / Shutterstock.com; © Oleksiy Mark / Shutterstock.com;
© iStockphoto / 123render; © iStockphoto / luismmolina; © Alex Staroseltsev / Shutterstock.com; © Cengage Learning

Bus networks are inexpensive and easy to install. One advantage of the bus network is that computers and other devices can be attached and detached at any point on the bus without disturbing the rest of the network. Another advantage is that failure of one device usually does not affect the rest of the bus network. The greatest risk to a bus network is that the bus itself might become inoperable. If that happens, the network remains inoperative until the bus is back in working order.

Ring Network On a ring network, a cable forms a closed loop (ring) with all computers and devices arranged along the ring (Figure 10-10). Data transmitted on a ring network travels from device to device around the entire ring, in one direction.

If a computer or device on a ring network fails, the entire network potentially could stop functioning. A ring network can span a larger distance than a bus network, but it is more difficult to install. The ring topology primarily is used for LANs, but it also is used in WANs.

 NOW YOU KNOW

Be sure you understand the material presented in the sections titled Communications and Networks, as it relates to the chapter objectives.
You now should know . . .

- When you are using a sending device, a communications device, transmission media, and a receiving device (Objective 1)
- When you might use a LAN, MAN, WAN, and PAN (Objective 2)
- Why you would use a client/server or a P2P network (Objective 3)
- How networks are arranged (Objective 4)

Quiz Yourself Online: Check your knowledge of related content by navigating to this book's Quiz Yourself resource on Computer Concepts CourseMate and then tapping or clicking Objectives 1–4.

Network Communications Standards and Protocols

Today's networks connect terminals, devices, and computers from many different manufacturers across many types of networks. For the different devices on various types of networks to be able to communicate, the network must use similar techniques of moving data through the network from one application to another.

To alleviate the problems of incompatibility and ensure that hardware and software components can be integrated into any network, various organizations such as ANSI (American National Standards Institute) and IEEE (Institute of Electrical and Electronics Engineers) propose, develop, and approve network standards. A *network standard* defines guidelines that specify the way computers access the medium to which they are connected, the type(s) of medium used, the speeds used on different types of networks, and the type(s) of physical cable and/or the wireless technology used. Hardware and software manufacturers design their products to meet the guidelines specified in a particular standard, so that their devices can communicate with the network. A standard that outlines characteristics of how two devices communicate on a network is called a *protocol*. Specifically, a protocol may define data format, coding schemes, error handling, and the sequence in which data transfers over a network.

Table 10-1 identifies some of the more widely used network communications standards and protocols for both wired and wireless networks. The following sections discuss each of these standards and protocols.

Table 10-1	Network Communications Standards and Protocols	
Name	**Type**	**Sample Usage**
Ethernet	Standard	LAN
Token ring	Standard	LAN
TCP/IP	Protocol	Internet
Wi-Fi	Standard	Hot spots
Bluetooth	Protocol	Wireless headset
UWB	Standard	Inventory tracking
IrDA	Standard	Remote control
RFID	Protocol	Tollbooth
NFC	Protocol	Mobile phone payment
WiMax	Standard	Hot spots

 CONSIDER THIS

Do network standards and protocols work together?
Network standards and protocols often work together to move data through a network. Some of these standards define how a network is arranged physically, while others specify how messages travel along a network. Thus, as data moves through a network from one program to another, it may use one or more of these standards.

Ethernet

Ethernet is a network standard that specifies no central computer or device on the network (nodes) should control when data can be transmitted. That is, each node attempts to transmit data when it determines the network is available to receive communications. If two computers or devices on an Ethernet network attempt to send data at the same time, a collision will occur. When this happens, the computers or devices resend their messages until data transfer is successful.

Ethernet is based on a bus topology, but Ethernet networks can be wired in a star pattern. The Ethernet standard defines guidelines for the physical configuration of a network, e.g., cabling, network devices, and nodes. Ethernet currently is the most popular network standard for LANs because it is relatively inexpensive and easy to install and maintain. Depending on the transmission media used, Ethernet networks have data transfer rates that range from 10 Mbps for small office/home users to 100 Gbps for enterprise users.

Token Ring

The **token ring** standard specifies that computers and devices on the network share or pass a special signal, called a token, in a unidirectional manner and in a preset order. A *token* is a special series of bits that functions like a ticket. The device with the token can transmit data over the network. Only one token exists per network. This ensures that only one computer transmits data at a time. Although token ring is not as widely used today, many networks use the concept of a token.

BTW
Robert Metcalfe
Technology Innovator: You should be familiar with Robert Metcalfe, Ethernet inventor.

BTW
Data Transfer Rates
Mbps (megabits per second) is one million bits per second, and *Gbps* (gigabits per second) is one billion bits per second.

Token ring is based on a ring topology (although it can use a star topology). The token ring standard defines guidelines for the physical configuration of a network, e.g., cabling, network cards, and devices. Some token ring networks connect up to 72 devices. Other use a special type of wiring that allows up to 260 connections. The data transfer rate on a token ring network ranges from 4 Mbps to 1 Gbps.

TCP/IP

Short for Transmission Control Protocol/Internet Protocol, **TCP/IP** is a network protocol that defines how messages (data) are routed from one end of a network to the other, ensuring the data arrives correctly. TCP/IP describes rules for dividing messages into small pieces, called *packets*; providing addresses for each packet; checking for and detecting errors; sequencing packets; and regulating the flow of messages along the network.

TCP/IP has been adopted as the network standard for Internet communications. Thus, all hosts on the Internet follow the rules defined in this standard. As shown in Figure 10-11, Internet communications also use other standards, such as the Ethernet standard, as data is routed to its destination.

When a computer sends data over the Internet, the data is divided into packets. Each packet contains the data, as well as the recipient (destination), the origin (sender), and the sequence information used to reassemble the data at the destination. Each packet travels along the fastest individual available path to the recipient's computer or mobile device via routers. This technique of breaking a message into individual packets, sending the packets along the best route available, and then reassembling the data is called *packet switching*. Read Secure IT 10-1 for another use of packets.

Example of How Communications Standards Work Together

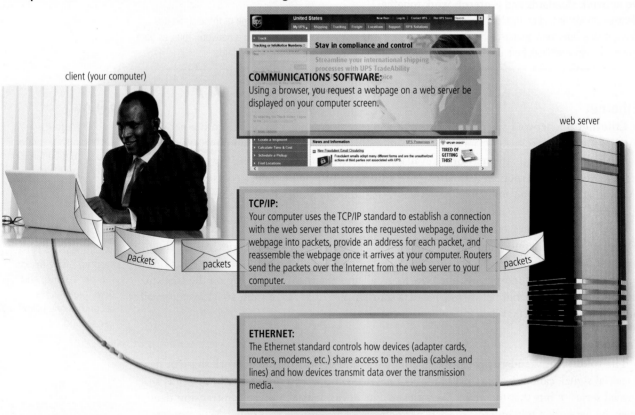

Figure 10-11 Network communications use a variety of standards to ensure that data travels correctly to its destination. Some standards used in Internet communications include TCP/IP and Ethernet.

SECURE IT 10-1

Monitoring Network Traffic

Network monitoring software constantly assesses the status of a network and sends an email or text message usually to the network administrator when it detects a problem. These messages may state that an outage has occurred, the server's available memory space is near capacity, a new user account has been added, or some other critical event has developed.

Monitoring software can measure the amount of network traffic, graph network usage, and show the bandwidth used by each computer. On networks that use the TCP/IP protocol, for example, *packet sniffer* software monitors and logs packet traffic for later analysis. Packet sniffing can detect problems, such as why traffic is flowing slowly.

The software also can play a security role, including identifying unusual or excessive network activity. For example, it can flag one remote computer always connected to the network or someone making repeated attempts to sign in to an account. Hackers use packet sniffers to hijack a computer. They can capture a user's packets and then reassemble a webpage, obtain user names and passwords, and trace photos and videos viewed.

How would you determine if your employer or school has monitoring software? Would you change your computer activities, including browsing certain websites, if you knew the software could track your computer usage?

 CONSIDER THIS

Can IP addresses be used to determine a computer or device's location?

In many cases, you can determine a computer or a device's location from its IP address. For example, if an IP address begins with 132.170, a small amount of research will uncover that the University of Central Florida assigns IP addresses beginning with these numbers; however, additional research would be necessary to determine where the computer or mobile device is located on the network. Certain websites allow visitors to find a location by entering an IP address. Some web apps infer your approximate location from your IP address when GPS is not available in order to provide you with local information or search results.

> **Internet Research**
>
> What does it mean to be Wi-Fi Certified?
>
> *Search for:* wi-fi certified

Wi-Fi

Computers and devices that have the appropriate wireless capability can communicate via radio waves with other computers or devices using **Wi-Fi** (wireless fidelity), which identifies any network based on the 802.11 standards. Developed by IEEE, **802.11** is a series of network standards that specifies how two wireless devices communicate over the air with each other. Common standards include 802.11a, 802.11b, 802.11g, 801.11n, 802.11ac, and 802.11ad, with data transfer rates ranging from 11 Mbps to 7 Gbps. Many devices support multiple standards. For example, a designation of 802.11 b/g/n on a computer or device indicates it supports those three standards (b, g, and n).

Wi-Fi sometimes is referred to as *wireless Ethernet* because it uses techniques similar to the Ethernet standard to specify how physically to configure a wireless network. Thus, Wi-Fi networks easily can be integrated with wired Ethernet networks. When a Wi-Fi network accesses the Internet, it works in conjunction with the TCP/IP network standard.

One popular use of the Wi-Fi network standard is in hot spots that offer mobile users the ability to connect to the Internet with their Wi-Fi enabled wireless computers and devices. Many homes and small businesses also use Wi-Fi to network computers and devices wirelessly. In open or outdoor areas free from interference, the computers or devices should be within 300 feet of a wireless access point or hot spot. In closed areas, the wireless network range is about 100 feet. To obtain communications at the maximum distances, you may need to install extra hardware to extend or strengthen a wireless signal.

Bluetooth

Bluetooth is a network protocol that defines how two Bluetooth devices use short-range radio waves to transmit data. The data transfers between devices at a rate of up to 3 Mbps. To communicate with each other, Bluetooth devices often must be within about 33 feet but can be extended to about 325 feet with additional equipment.

A Bluetooth device contains a small chip that allows it to communicate with other Bluetooth devices. For computers and devices not Bluetooth-enabled, you can purchase a Bluetooth wireless port adapter that will convert an existing USB port into a Bluetooth port. Most current operating systems have built-in Bluetooth support. When connecting two devices using Bluetooth, the originating device sends a code to the connecting device. The codes must match to establish the connection. Devices that share a Bluetooth connection are said to be paired.

> **BTW**
>
> **Bluetooth Inventors**
> Technology Innovators: You should be familiar with the Bluetooth inventors, Sven Mattisson and Jaap Haartsen.

MINI FEATURE 10-1

Bluetooth Technology

Most mobile phones and computers manufactured today are equipped with Bluetooth capability. One of the earliest and most popular uses of Bluetooth is to connect hands-free headsets to a mobile phone. Bluetooth has many additional uses, and device manufacturers are increasingly including Bluetooth technology.

BTW

Bluetooth Future
Innovative Computing: You should be familiar with future Bluetooth uses.

Uses

You can use Bluetooth enabled or enhanced devices in many ways, including the following:

- Connect devices such as mobile phones, portable media players, or GPS devices with vehicle stereos, which use the vehicle's speakers to project sound.
- Use GPS receivers to send directions to a mobile phone or GPS-enabled device.
- Transfer photos wirelessly from a digital camera to a laptop or server.
- Play music on a smartphone through the speakers on a computer or other Bluetooth-enabled device.
- Send signals between video game accessories, video game devices, and a television.
- Establish a PAN (personal area network).
- Allow communications between a computer and devices, such as a keyboard, printer, fax machine, or mobile phone. Connecting these devices enables you to print documents, share calendar appointments, and more.
- Replace wired communications devices such as bar code scanners with wireless devices to enhance portability.
- Transmit data from a medical device, such as a blood glucose monitor, to a mobile phone or other device.
- Change the channel, pause a program, or schedule a recording using a Bluetooth-compatible television and remote control.

- Track objects that include tags or nodes used to send wireless signals read by a real-time location system.

Advantages and Disadvantages

Advantages to using Bluetooth technology include the following:

- If a device has Bluetooth capability, using Bluetooth technology is free.
- Although Bluetooth devices need to be near each other, they do not have to be in the same room, within the same line of sight, or facing each other.
- Bluetooth devices typically have low processing power and use little energy, so using Bluetooth technology will not drain a device's batteries.
- Establishing a wireless Bluetooth connection is easy. With most Bluetooth-enabled devices, you simply tap or click a Bluetooth shortcut or icon to enable Bluetooth. Once enabled, the devices usually immediately recognize a connection. (Before initial use, you may need to pair two Bluetooth devices so that they can communicate with each other. Read How To 3-3 on page 132 for instructions about pairing Bluetooth devices.)
- Bluetooth connections have low security risks. If you want to secure a Bluetooth channel, you would define an identification number for the connection and create a PIN that you can distribute as needed. If the secured computer or device detects an unknown Bluetooth connection, you can choose to accept or reject it.
- Bluetooth technology is standardized globally, meaning that it can be used to connect devices that are not the same make or model.
- Bluetooth connections have little risk of interference with other wireless networks because the strength of the wireless signals is weak and because of frequency hopping, which changes frequency channels periodically.

One negative of Bluetooth technology is its low bandwidth. Because of its slow data transfer speeds, Bluetooth technology is not an ideal solution for replacing a LAN. Most agree that the advantages of Bluetooth technology far outweigh the negatives.

✳ Have you used Bluetooth technology to connect two devices? What devices, and what was your experience? In your opinion, what is the best reason to use Bluetooth? Why? What devices do you think will include Bluetooth technology in the future?

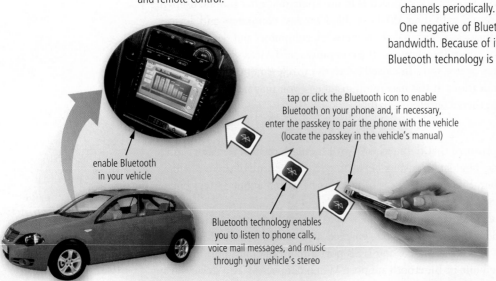

tap or click the Bluetooth icon to enable Bluetooth on your phone and, if necessary, enter the passkey to pair the phone with the vehicle (locate the passkey in the vehicle's manual)

enable Bluetooth in your vehicle

Bluetooth technology enables you to listen to phone calls, voice mail messages, and music through your vehicle's stereo

UWB

UWB, which stands for **ultra-wideband**, is a network standard that specifies how two UWB devices use short-range radio waves to communicate at high speeds with each other. At distances of about 33 feet, the data transfer rate is 110 Mbps. At closer distances, such as about 6.5 feet, the transfer rate is at least 480 Mbps. UWB can transmit signals through doors and other obstacles. Because of its high transfer rates, UWB is best suited for transmission of large files such as video, graphics, and audio. Examples of UWB uses include locating and tracking inventory, equipment, or personnel (especially in remote or dangerous areas).

IrDA

Some devices, such as television remote controls, use the **IrDA** (Infrared Data Association) standard to transmit data wirelessly to each other via infrared (IR) light waves. The devices transfer data at rates from 115 Kbps (thousand bits per second) to 4 Mbps between their IrDA ports. Infrared requires *line-of-sight transmission*; that is, the sending device and the receiving device must be in line with each other so that nothing obstructs the path of the infrared light wave. Because Bluetooth and UWB do not require line-of-sight transmission, these technologies are more widespread than IrDA.

RFID

RFID (*radio frequency identification*) is a protocol that defines how a network uses radio signals to communicate with a tag placed in or attached to an object, an animal, or a person. The tag, called a transponder, consists of an antenna and a memory chip that contains the information to be transmitted via radio waves. Through an antenna, an RFID reader, also called a transceiver, reads the radio signals and transfers the information to a computer or computing device. Read Secure IT 6-2 on page 252 for uses of animal implants. Read Secure IT 10-2 to consider privacy issues related to RFID.

Depending on the type of RFID reader, the distance between the tag and the reader ranges from 5 inches to 300 feet or more. Readers can be handheld or embedded in an object such as a doorway or a tollbooth (Figure 10-12 on the next page).

Internet Research

Are RFID chips safe?

Search for: rfid implant side effects

 SECURE IT 10-2

RFID Tracking Your Every Move

In an effort to increase campus security and safety, one Texas high school district requires students to wear an RFID badge. These identification badges have a tiny embedded chip and a battery to broadcast students' locations constantly when they are on campus. Administrators also use the badges to take attendance and to admit students to the library and cafeteria.

In the retail environment, merchants attach RFID chips to product tags and sew them into clothing. RFID can help locate items in a warehouse and identify items that need to be replenished. For consumers, RFID can supply detailed product information, and

someday allow buyers to bypass check-out lines and take purchases directly from the store, with the item's cost charged to their credit card.

Privacy advocates worry that RFID could destroy a person's anonymity. They fear that with an RFID reader, any individual or organization could track a person's movements and make that information available to marketers or government agencies. Several researchers have shown that current RFID passports can be copied and forged, so they fear that the RFID chip could be copied by a hidden RFID reader and then used for fraudulent purposes, such as stealing a traveler's identity.

Privacy advocates insist that merchants should be forced to disable RFID transmitters as soon as buyers leave a store. They also recommend that RFID-enabled documents, such as passports, be kept in special containers made of material that will not allow the chip to be read until it is removed from the container.

☀ Would you be comfortable wearing a form of identification that included RFID at school or at work? Why or why not? Should buyers be allowed to request that RFID transmitters be disabled after they make a purchase, or should merchants be required to render transmitters inoperative when the product leaves the store? Why or why not?

How Electronic RFID Toll Collection Works

Step 1
Motorist purchases an RFID transponder or RFID tag and attaches it to the vehicle's windshield.

Step 2
As the vehicle approaches the tollbooth, the RFID reader in the tollbooth sends a radio wave that activates the windshield-mounted RFID tag. The activated tag sends vehicle information to the RFID reader.

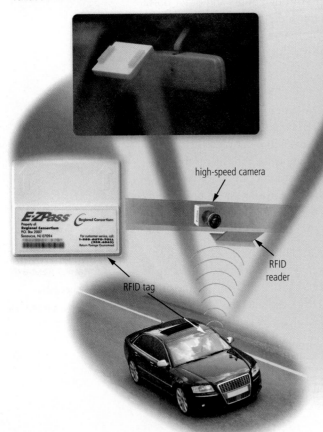

high-speed camera

RFID reader

RFID tag

Step 3
The RFID reader sends the vehicle information to the lane controller. The lane controller, which is part of a local area network, transmits the vehicle information to a central computer that subtracts the toll from the motorist's account. If the vehicle does not have an RFID tag, a high-speed camera takes a picture of the license plate and the computer prints a violation notice, which is mailed to the motorist.

Figure 10-12 This figure shows how electronic RFID toll collection works.
© James Leynse / Corbis; © James Leynse / Corbis; © Vibrant Image Studio / Shutterstock.com; © Getty Images; © iStockphoto / luismmolina; © Cengage Learning

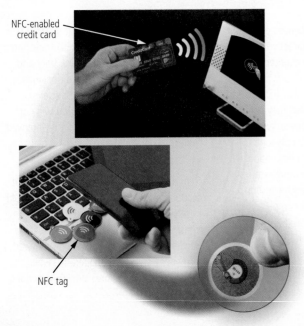

NFC-enabled credit card

NFC tag

Figure 10-13 Some objects, such as credit cards, are NFC enabled. You also can program NFC tags yourself.
© Alexander Kirch / Shutterstock.com; © iStockphoto / Gianni Furlan; © iStockphoto / pierrephoto

NFC

NFC (*near field communications*) is a protocol, based on RFID, that defines how a network uses close-range radio signals to communicate between two devices or objects equipped with NFC technology (Figure 10-13). Examples of NFC-enabled devices include smartphones, digital cameras, televisions, and terminals. Credit cards, tickets, and NFC tags are examples of objects that also use NFC technology. An NFC tag is a chip that can store small amounts of data. NFC tags are in a variety of objects such as posters, ski lift tickets, business cards, stickers, and wristbands.

For successful communications, the devices or objects touch or are placed within an inch or two of each other. For example, you can touch two NFC-enabled phones together to transfer contacts, touch an NFC-enabled phone to an NFC tag to display a map, or hold an NFC-enabled phone near a parking meter to pay for parking. Contactless payment, such as the parking meter example, is a popular use of NFC technology. Other uses of NFC technology include sharing contacts or photos, downloading apps, and gaining access or admittance.

 **CONSIDER THIS**

Can you buy a blank NFC tag?
Yes. Consumers can purchase blank NFC tags at a reasonable cost and easily program them to perform certain actions. For example, you can program an NFC tag to contain your home network user name and password. Visitors to your home can touch their phones to the NFC tag to access your home network without entering the user name and password.

WiMAX

WiMAX (Worldwide Interoperability for Microwave Access), also known as 802.16, is a network standard developed by IEEE that specifies how wireless devices communicate over the air in a wide area. Using the WiMAX standard, computers or devices with the appropriate WiMAX wireless capability communicate via radio waves with other computers or devices through a WiMAX tower. The WiMAX tower, which can cover up to a 30-mile radius, connects to the Internet or to another WiMAX tower.

Two types of WiMAX specifications are fixed wireless and mobile wireless. With fixed wireless WiMAX, a customer accesses the Internet from a desktop at home or other permanent location. Mobile wireless WiMAX, by contrast, enables users to access the WiMAX network with mobile computers and mobile devices, such as smartphones. Fixed wireless WiMAX has data transfer rates up to 40 Mbps, while mobile wireless WiMAX has data transfer rates up to 15 Mbps.

WiMAX, similar to Wi-Fi, connects mobile users to the Internet via hot spots. Many computers and mobile devices have built-in WiMAX capability. Some game consoles also support the WiMAX standard.

 **BTW**
Technology Milestones
For a history of technology milestones, see the Timeline (available in the e-book).

Communications Software

Communications software consists of programs and apps that (1) help users establish a connection to another computer, mobile device, or network; (2) manage the transmission of data, instructions, and information; and (3) provide an interface for users to communicate with one another. The first two often are provided by or included as tools with an operating system or bundled with a communications device. The third is provided by applications such as email, FTP, browser, discussion boards, chat rooms, instant messaging, videoconferencing, and VoIP.

Sometimes, communications devices are preprogrammed to accomplish communications tasks. Some routers, for example, contain firmware for various protocols. Other communications devices require separate communications software to ensure proper transmission of data. Communications software works with the network standards and protocols presented in the previous section to ensure data moves through the network or the Internet correctly.

 MINI FEATURE 10-2

Mobile Communications

Following a visit with your parents for the weekend, you receive a text message from your mom: "was gr8 2 c u!" Soon after, you start a video call with your sister from a coffee shop with free Wi-Fi to make plans for your upcoming visit with her. During the call, you receive an email message from your room-mate that contains directions and a link to the web-site of the restaurant where both of you are meeting friends for dinner. At dinner, you post a Tweet that the food was delicious. When you return home, you chat on Facebook with a classmate about your semester project and then catch up on your friends'

updates. Before going to sleep, you speed-dial your brother and wish him a happy birthday. From text and instant messages to email messages and voice and video calls, mobile devices offer many ways to communicate.

When using mobile devices, it is important to consider the amount of data required for each type of communication. Be sure to subscribe to a data plan that matches the amount of data you actually use each month on average. The data plan enables you to access the Internet through your mobile service provider's network when Wi-Fi is not available. Without a data plan, you must use Wi-Fi or a wired connection to access the Internet on your mobile device.

Some mobile service providers offer an unlimited data plan, providing unlimited data access for your device, while many charge based on the amount of data that you send or receive. If you exceed your data limit in a given month, additional fees apply. Many carriers offer apps that help track data usage. While an unlimited plan may be tempting, the cost may exceed what you would pay if using a limited data plan. You should monitor your data usage to see how much you use on average over a few months, and then decide on the best plan for you. Recognizing that individuals and families own more than one mobile device, some carriers offer a data sharing plan that provides access to a data connection across several phones, smartphones, tablets, laptops, gaming devices, and mobile hot spots. Using Wi-Fi when available to access the Internet is one way to save on data usage charges if you have a limited data plan.

Email is best for sharing longer, detailed messages. For sharing shorter or time-sensitive messages, consider using these forms of immediate communications:

Text/Picture/Video Messaging

Text, picture, and video messages often take the place of phone conversations among many people, who find these messages less intrusive and more efficient than voice conversations. SMS (short message service) text messages are messages of 300 or fewer characters sent from one user to another through a mobile service provider's cell phone tower. With MMS (multimedia message service), users also can send and receive photos, videos, and audio files. Occasional users might subscribe to a text message plan, where they pay their provider a few cents for each message that they send or receive. In contrast, avid users, who post to Instagram photos of every latte they consume, often pay a flat monthly rate to be able to send as many photos or messages as their thumbs can handle. To avoid paying text message fees to carriers, some people opt for free messaging apps and services available via third-party providers. These services send messages over the Internet rather than a provider's network. Many of these "app to app" services are

© iStockphoto / TommL

free when both parties subscribe to the service, or place advertising content alongside the messages.

Instant Messaging

With instant messaging (IM) services, you can send text or multimedia messages in real time to other online users. To access an IM service, you need the service's desktop, web, or mobile app, and an Internet connection on your computer or mobile device. Users with accounts on multiple IM services often use an IM aggregator. IM aggregators are desktop, web, or mobile apps that allow you to sign in, manage buddy lists, and chat on different IM networks simultaneously.

Voice and Video Calling

Some VoIP services such as Skype and FaceTime also provide voice and video calling services over the Internet. These often are much less expensive than making phone calls over a provider's network. It also is possible to make calls from a VoIP program to a mobile or landline phone. Many of these services are available as desktop, web, or mobile apps. Voice and video calling require large amounts of bandwidth. As a result, some carriers prohibit the use of calling services over their networks, requiring users to connect via Wi-Fi in order to make these types of calls.

© Sonica83 / Dreamstime.com

✳ Think about how you use different forms of mobile communications to share information or communicate with your friends as part of your daily routine. For what purposes do you generally send email messages or text messages? After exchanging text messages, when might you make a phone call or use VoIP service to talk in real time? Under what circumstances is each form of communication most efficient?

Communications Lines

A **dedicated line** is a type of always-on physical connection that is established between two communications devices. Businesses often use dedicated lines to connect geographically distant offices. Dedicated lines can be either analog or digital. Digital lines increasingly are connecting home and business users to networks around the globe because they transmit data and information at faster rates than analog lines.

Digital dedicated lines include cable television lines, DSL, ISDN lines, FTTP, T-carrier lines, and ATM. Table 10-2 shows speeds of various dedicated digital lines.

Cable

The cable television (CATV) network provides high-speed Internet connections, called *cable Internet service*. The CATV signal enters a building through a single line, usually a coaxial cable. This cable connects to a modem (discussed in the next section), which typically attaches to your computer via an Ethernet cable. Home and small business users often subscribe to cable Internet service.

DSL

DSL (*Digital Subscriber Line*) transmits on existing standard copper phone wiring. Some DSL installations include a dial tone, providing users with both voice and data communications. These DSL installations often require that filters be installed to reduce noise interference when voice communications share the same line. DSL is a popular digital line alternative for the small business or home user.

ADSL is a popular type of DSL. As shown in Figure 10-14, *ADSL* (*asymmetric digital subscriber line*) is a type of DSL that supports faster transfer rates when receiving data (the *downstream rate*) than when sending data (the *upstream rate*). ADSL is ideal for Internet access because most users download more information from the Internet than they upload.

Table 10-2 Speeds of Various Dedicated Digital Lines	
Type of Line	**Transfer Rates**
Cable	256 Kbps to 52 Mbps
DSL	256 Kbps to 8.45 Mbps
ISDN	Up to 1.54 Mbps
FTTP	5 Mbps to 300 Mbps
Fractional T1	128 Kbps to 768 Kbps
T1	1.544 Mbps
T3	44.736 Mbps
ATM	155 Mbps to 622 Mbps, can reach 10 Gbps

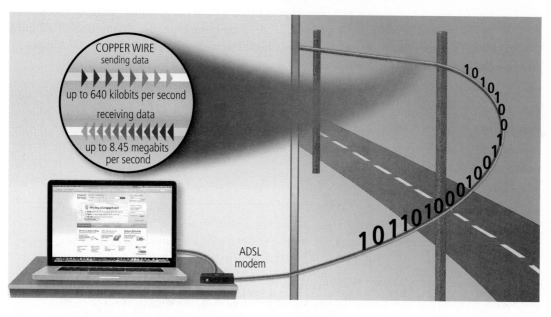

Figure 10-14
ADSL connections transmit data downstream (receiving) at a much faster rate than upstream (sending).
© artjazz / Shutterstock.com;
© Cengage Learning

✳ CONSIDER THIS

Which is a better choice, DSL or cable Internet service?
Each has its own advantages. DSL uses a line that is not shared with other users in the neighborhood. With cable Internet service, by contrast, users might share the node with up to hundreds of other cable Internet users. Simultaneous access by many users can cause the cable Internet service to slow down. Cable Internet service, however, has widespread availability.

ISDN

Not as widely used today as in the past, *ISDN* (Integrated Services Digital Network) is a set of standards for digital transmission of data over standard copper phone lines. With ISDN, the same phone line that could carry only one computer signal now can carry three or more signals at once through the same line, using a technique called *multiplexing*.

FTTP

FTTP, which stands for **Fiber to the Premises**, uses fiber-optic cable to provide extremely high-speed Internet access to a user's physical permanent location.

- *FTTH (Fiber to the Home)* provides home users with Internet access via fiber-optic cable.
- *FTTB (Fiber to the Building)* refers to small businesses that use fiber-optic cables to access the Internet.

With FTTP service, an optical terminal at your location receives the signals and transfers them to a router connected to a computer. As the cost of installing fiber decreases, more homes and businesses are expected to choose FTTP.

T-Carrier

A **T-carrier line** is any of several types of long-distance digital phone lines that carry multiple signals over a single communications line. Whereas a standard phone line carries only one signal, digital T-carrier lines use multiplexing so that multiple signals share the line. T-carrier lines provide very fast data transfer rates. Only medium to large companies usually can afford the investment in T-carrier lines because these lines are so expensive.

The most popular T-carrier line is the *T1 line*. Businesses often use T1 lines to connect to the Internet. Home and small business users purchase *fractional T1*, in which they share a connection to the T1 line with other users. Fractional T1 is slower than a dedicated T1 line, but it also is less expensive. Users who do not have other high-speed Internet access in their areas can opt for fractional T1. With fractional T1 lines, the data transfer rates become slower as additional users are added.

A *T3 line* is equal in speed to 28 T1 lines. T3 lines are quite expensive. Main users of T3 lines include large corporations, phone companies, and ISPs connecting to the Internet backbone. The Internet backbone itself also uses T3 lines.

ATM

ATM (Asynchronous Transfer Mode) is a service that carries voice, data, video, and media at very high speeds. Phone networks, the Internet, and other networks with large amounts of traffic use ATM. Some experts predict that ATM eventually will become the Internet standard for data transmission, replacing T3 lines.

 **NOW YOU KNOW** ———————————————————————————

Be sure you understand the material presented in the sections titled Network Communications Standards and Protocols, Communications Software, and Communications Lines, as it relates to the chapter objectives. *You now should know . . .*

- Which network communications standards and protocols you have used (Objective 5)
- Why you would use communications software (Objective 6)
- Which communications line is best suited to your needs (Objective 7)

 Quiz Yourself Online: Check your knowledge of related content by navigating to this book's Quiz Yourself resource on Computer Concepts CourseMate and then tapping or clicking Objectives 5–7.

 BTW

Transmission Media
Computers process data as digital signals. Data, instructions, and information travel along transmission media in either analog or digital form, depending on the transmission media.

Communications Devices

A **communications device** is any type of hardware capable of transmitting data, instructions, and information between a sending device and a receiving device. At the sending end, a communications device sends the data, instructions, or information from the sending device to transmission media. At the receiving end, a communications device receives the signals from the transmission media.

The following pages describe a variety of communications devices: digital modems, wireless modems, wireless access points, routers, network cards, and hubs and switches. Read Ethics & Issues 10-2 to consider the use of communications in the classroom.

ETHICS & ISSUES 10-2

 Should Mobile Computers and Devices Be Banned from the Classroom?

Many students use mobile computers and devices to communicate with the instructor, take notes, make recordings of lectures, and perform lecture-related research. Other students have found that mobile computers and devices provide endless entertainment, instant messaging, and other activities unrelated to coursework during a lecture. Some instructors and students find these uses of computers during a lecture to be distracting or disrespectful, especially if the computer or device makes sounds when messages are received. Opponents of mobile device usage in the classroom also cite cyberbullying and cheating as concerns. During a test, for example, unethical students could use their device to look up answers to the test questions, send text messages to communicate with others taking the test, or take a photo of a paper test and share the photo with others who have the same class at a different time.

Some instructors, however, are embracing the devices and incorporating them into classroom use. For example, instructors use them to monitor attendance or allow students to use their phones to send responses to quiz questions so that the instructor can gauge understanding of the lecture topic. Some instructors encourage students to use Twitter to communicate by sending questions and comments, which the instructor can display live on an interactive whiteboard.

Are mobile computers and devices too distracting in the classroom? Why? Should instructors, departments, or entire schools be able to ban mobile computers and devices in the classroom? Why or why not? What are proper and improper uses of mobile computers and devices in the classroom? Why? Is the use of mobile computers and devices more of a distraction than taking notes or drawing in a notepad during class? Why or why not?

Digital Modems: Cable, DSL, and ISDN

A *broadband modem*, also called a *digital modem*, is a communications device that sends and receives data and information to and from a digital line. Three types of broadband modems are cable modems, DSL modems, and ISDN modems. These modems typically include built-in Wi-Fi connectivity.

A **cable modem** is a broadband modem that sends and receives digital data over the CATV network. To access the Internet using the CATV service, as shown in Figure 10-15, the CATV provider installs a splitter inside your house. From the splitter, one part of the cable runs to your televisions and the other part connects to the cable modem. Many CATV providers include a cable modem as part of the installation; some offer a rental plan, and others require that you purchase one separately. A cable modem usually is an external device, in which one end of a cable connects to a CATV wall outlet and the other end plugs in a port on a computer.

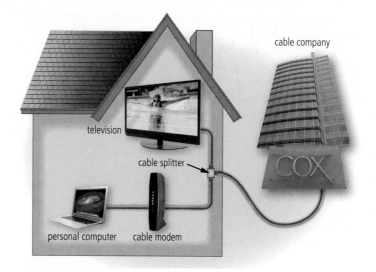

Figure 10-15 A typical cable modem installation.
© tiridifilm / iStockphoto; © image100 / Alamy; © Erik S. Lesser / Landov; © iStockphoto / Stephen Krow; © Pablo Eder / Shutterstock.com; © Cengage Learning

A **DSL modem** is a broadband modem that sends digital data and information from a computer to a DSL line and receives digital data and information from a DSL line. Similarly, an *ISDN modem* is a broadband modem that sends digital data and information from a computer to an ISDN line and receives digital data and information from an ISDN line. DSL and ISDN modems usually are external devices, in which one end connects to the phone line and the other end connects to a port on the computer.

 **BTW**
Cable and DSL
Cable and DSL are more widely used than ISDN.

 CONSIDER THIS

What are dial-up modems?

A *dial-up modem* is a communications device that converts digital signals to analog signals and analog signals to digital signals, so that data can travel along an analog phone line. For example, a dial-up modem connected to a sending computer converts the computer's digital signals into analog signals. The analog signals then can travel over a standard phone line. A dial-up modem connected to a receiving computer converts the analog signals from a standard phone line into digital signals that the computer can process.

A dial-up connection must be reestablished each time the modem is used. With transfer rates of only up to 56 Kbps, dial-up connections also are much slower than broadband connections. For these reasons, dial-up connections are used only in remote areas or where high-speed or wireless options are not available.

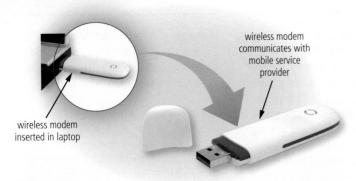

Figure 10-16 Wireless modems allow users to access the Internet wirelessly using a mobile provider's network. Some manufacturers refer to the type of wireless modem shown in this figure as a USB modem.
© iStockphoto / nolimitpictures; © Cengage Learning

Wireless Modems

Some mobile users have a *wireless modem* that uses a mobile phone provider's network to connect to the Internet wirelessly from a computer or mobile device (Figure 10-16). Wireless modems, which have an external or built-in antenna, are available as USB adapters, ExpressCard modules, and other devices.

Some smartphones also can function as a wireless modem, called a *mobile hot spot*, when tethered to a personal computer. Read How To 10-1 for instructions about using your phone as a mobile hot spot.

HOW TO 10-1

Use Your Phone as a Mobile Hot Spot

If you are in a location without a wireless Internet connection, you may be able to access the Internet from your desktop or mobile computer if you enable your smartphone as a mobile hot spot. When you enable a phone as a mobile hot spot, the phone acts as a wireless access point. You then can connect your desktop or mobile computer to the phone and utilize the data plan on your phone to access the Internet. If you have a limited data plan with your mobile service provider, you should be careful not to use your phone as a hot spot too often. While the speed from a mobile hot spot might not be as fast as your home or office network, it should be more than sufficient for performing tasks such as browsing the web or sending and receiving email messages that contain mostly text. The next steps describe how to use your phone as a mobile hot spot:

1. Contact your mobile service provider and determine whether your plan allows for your phone to be used as a mobile hot spot. Using your phone as a mobile hot spot may carry an additional monthly charge.

2. Determine whether your phone has built-in functionality to be used as a mobile hot spot. If not and if supported by your service plan, you may be able to download a separate app that allows your phone to function as a mobile hot spot.

3. Access your phone's settings and enable the mobile hot spot. Your phone should display the SSID and password to access the hot spot. Read How To 5-2 on page 222 for additional information about SSIDs.

4. Connect to the mobile hot spot on a computer or mobile device using the SSID and password displayed in the previous step.

5. When you are finished using the hot spot, disconnect from the wireless network on your computer and disable the hot spot feature on your phone.

☀ How can you determine how much data you are using on your smartphone's data plan?

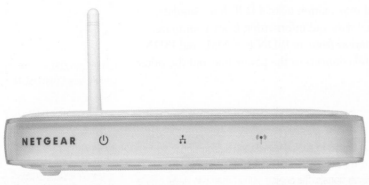

Figure 10-17 Wireless access point.
Copyright 2013 NETGEAR

Wireless Access Points

A *wireless access point* is a central communications device that allows computers and devices to transfer data wirelessly among themselves or to transfer data wirelessly to a wired network using wireless technologies such as Wi-Fi (Figure 10-17). Wireless access points have high-quality internal or external antennas for optimal signals. For the best signal, some manufacturers suggest positioning the wireless access point at the highest possible location and using an amplifier.

A wireless access point either connects to a router via an Ethernet or other cable or is part of a router. Read How To 10-2 for tips to strengthen your wireless signal.

🟤 HOW TO 10-2

Strengthen Your Wireless Signal

If you reside in a large apartment or house and use a wireless network, you may find that you either experience poor network performance or you are unable to access the network in certain locations. These problems may be related to a weak wireless signal in your home. Various options are available to strengthen a wireless signal to increase network performance and ensure you have a wireless connection throughout your home. The following points describe how to strengthen a wireless signal:

- If your wireless router or wireless access point has antennas, make sure the antennas are extended completely.

- If you are able to remove the antenna(s) from your wireless router or wireless access point, consider replacing them with a wireless signal booster. Check

your device's and the wireless signal booster's documentation to determine whether it will work with your device.

- If possible, position the wireless router or wireless access point in a central location of your home and away from appliances or other electronic devices that may degrade the signal.

- Purchase a range extender for your wireless router or wireless access point. Some range extenders are compatible only with specific wireless routers or wireless access points, and others are universal. Make sure the range extender you purchase is compatible with your device. Once installed, follow the range extender's instructions to enable it on your network.

- If you still experience problems with the strength of your wireless signal after following the suggestions above, consider

replacing your wireless router or wireless access point with a newer model.

🌼 What problems may arise if your wireless network's range extends beyond the confines of your house? How can you determine the range of your wireless network?

Routers

A *router* is a communications device that connects multiple computers or other routers together and transmits data to its correct destination on a network. A router can be used on a network of any size. On the largest scale, routers along the Internet backbone forward data packets to their destination using the fastest available path. For smaller business and home networks, a router allows multiple computers and mobile devices to share a single broadband Internet connection, such as through a cable modem or DSL modem (Figure 10-18).

🟢 Internet Research

What is a core router?

Search for: core router definition

cable or DSL modem

router

Figure 10-18 Through a router, home and small business networks can share access to a broadband Internet connection, such as through a cable or DSL modem.

BTW

Hardware Firewall
To prevent unauthorized users from accessing files and computers, many routers are protected by a built-in firewall, called a *hardware firewall*. Some also have built-in antivirus protection.

If the network has a separate router, it connects to the router via a cable. Similarly, if the network has a separate wireless access point, it connects to the router via a cable. Many users, however, opt for routers that provide additional functionality:

- A *wireless router* is a device that performs the functions of a router and also a wireless access point.
- A *broadband router* is a device that performs the functions of a router and also a broadband modem.
- A *broadband wireless router* is a device that performs the functions of a router, a wireless access point, and a cable or DSL modem.
- A *mobile broadband wireless router* is a device that performs the functions of a router, a wireless access point, and a wireless modem (Figure 10-19). Consumers use mobile broadband wireless routers to create a mobile hot spot.

These combination devices eliminate the need for a separate wireless access point and/or modem on a network. These routers also enable you easily to configure and secure the device against unauthorized access.

 CONSIDER THIS

How many connections can a router support?
Although a router may be able to connect more than 200 wired and/or wireless computers and mobile devices, the performance of the router may decline as you add connections. Some mobile service providers limit the number of connections to their mobile broadband wireless routers.

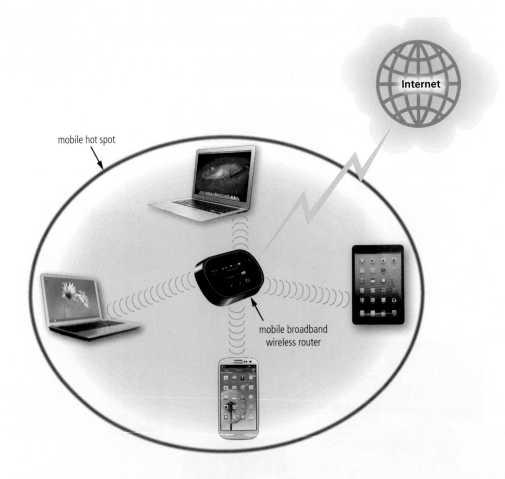

Figure 10-19
Through a mobile broadband wireless router, users can create a mobile hot spot via 3G or 4G mobile broadband Internet service.

Network Cards

A *network card*, sometimes called a *network interface card* (*NIC* pronounced nick), is a communications device that enables a computer or device that does not have built-in networking capability to access a network. The network card coordinates the transmission and receipt of data, instructions, and information to and from the computer or device containing the network card.

Network cards are available in a variety of styles (Figure 10-20). A network card for a desktop is an adapter card that has a port to which a cable connects. A network card for mobile computers and devices is in the form of a USB adapter, ExpressCard module, or other device. A network card follows the guidelines of a particular network communications standard, such as Ethernet or token ring.

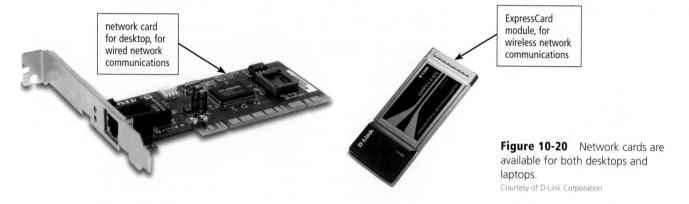

network card for desktop, for wired network communications

ExpressCard module, for wireless network communications

Figure 10-20   Network cards are available for both desktops and laptops.
Courtesy of D-Link Corporation

Hubs and Switches

Today, thousands of computer networks exist, ranging from small networks operated by home users to global networks operated by widespread telecommunications firms. Interconnecting these many types of networks requires various types of communications devices. A *hub* or *switch* is a device that provides a central point for cables in a network (Figure 10-21). Larger networks typically use a hub, while smaller networks use a switch. Some hubs and/or switches include routers. That is, the hub or switch receives data from many directions and then forwards it to one or more destinations.

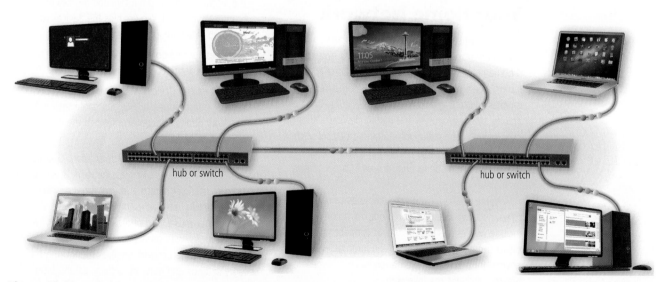

hub or switch

hub or switch

Figure 10-21   A hub or switch is a central point that connects several devices in a network together, as well as connects to other networks, as shown in this simplified diagram.
Courtesy of D-Link Corporation; © iStockphoto / sweetym; © Oleksiy Mark / Shutterstock.com; © Oleksiy Mark / Shutterstock.com; © iStockphoto / Skip ODonnell; © Natalia Siverina / Shutterstock.com; © iStockphoto / Skip ODonnell; © iStockphoto / sweetym; © Alex Staroseltsev / Shutterstock.com; © iStockphoto / sweetym; © Cengage Learning

Home Networks

Internet Research

What is an intelligent home network?

Search for: intelligent home network

Many home users connect multiple computers and devices together in a **home network**. Vendors typically offer home networking packages that include all the necessary hardware and software to network your home using wired or wireless techniques. You no longer need extensive knowledge of networks to set up a home network. For example, desktop operating systems often enable you to connect all computers in your house to a home network easily. Read Secure IT 10-3 to learn how to detect if an intruder is accessing your network.

 SECURE IT 10-3

Detecting an Intruder Accessing Your Wireless Home Network

IP hijacking is one of the largest Internet security threats. This theft of someone's paid Internet access is growing, and catching thieves is a difficult task for law enforcement officials. The cyberthieves tap into home routers or cable modems and can use the connection to commit illegal acts.

Unscrupulous people hijack Internet service in one of two ways. Either the neighbor's network has no security, or the thieves determine the network name and password and then reprogram their modem's settings to duplicate the neighbor's settings. The Electronic Communications Privacy Act and a lack of funding prevent fraud examiners from investigating and prosecuting many IP thieves.

Experts recommend using the following steps to determine if someone is accessing a wireless network without permission:

- **Sign in to the administrative interface.** The modem's user's guide will provide instructions to view wireless clients actively using a wireless access point.

- **Count the number of connected devices.** Each device connected wirelessly to the network should be displayed in a table that shows, at a minimum, the device's name, MAC address, and IP address. (Read How To 5-2 on page 222 for additional information about MAC address controls.) Wireless devices include smartphones, game consoles, DVD players, and other hardware. If the number of devices seems extraordinarily high, use a MAC lookup website, which can help you

to determine the manufacturer of wireless devices in the list.

- **Secure the network.** The router's manufacturer's website should provide instructions about upgrading the security strength. Change the default network name and password, and be certain to use the latest wireless encryption technology. Enable the router's firewall and, if possible, use "stealth mode" to make the network less visible to outsiders. Disable the feature that allows users to administer the router wirelessly, so that changes can be made only when using a physical connection with an Ethernet cable.

☀ If you use a wireless router, have you taken any of these steps to prevent IP theft? Which steps will you now take? Do you know anyone who has had an intruder access his or her network?

 MINI FEATURE 10-3

Planning and Designing Your Home Network

As with any network, a home network's basic purpose is to share resources and connect devices. You can use a home network to share files and folders or to allow multiple devices to share a printer. A home network enables you to use a common Internet connection among many computers and mobile devices. Other uses include connecting entertainment devices such as digital video recorders (DVRs) and televisions to the Internet, and connecting devices in order to play multiplayer games.

A home network can be as simple as using a cable to connect two devices. More complex home networks include wireless technologies that connect several devices to one another and to the Internet. Hardware needed for a wireless, Internet-connected home network includes the following:

- A modem, such as a cable or DSL modem, that connects to an ISP and establishes the Internet connection for the network

- A router, which establishes the connection between the Internet and all computers and devices on the home network and also enables the devices to communicate with each other

- A wireless access point, often included as part of the router, in order to connect wireless devices

- Computers and devices, such as desktops, laptops, tablets, smartphones, televisions, cable set-top boxes, or a VoIP phone, that you connect to the home network

Read How To 10-3 for instructions about creating a home network. Once the wireless network is configured, you can create user names and user groups. Names and groups establish network users, who can share files such as documents, music, and photos, as well as devices such as printers, with others connected to the network.

Maintaining the network involves monitoring the security settings and network activity, establishing connections to new devices as needed, and enhancing the wireless signal if necessary. Wireless home network speeds and ranges vary. The strength of the wireless signal affects the range of the network. When the space between a router and the device is too distant or is obstructed, it weakens or interrupts the device's network connection. To maintain a strong wireless signal, place the wireless access point in a central location. Floors, walls, and metal can obstruct the wireless signals, so place the access point on a shelf or mount it to the wall. To enhance the speed and range of the network, you can replace or add hardware.

Read How To 10-2 on page 437 for instructions about strengthening a wireless signal.

✳ Do you have a home network? What devices are connected to it? Is your network password protected? Why or why not? Is the signal weaker in certain areas in your home? If so, where? Have you tried enhancing the home network signal? Why or why not?

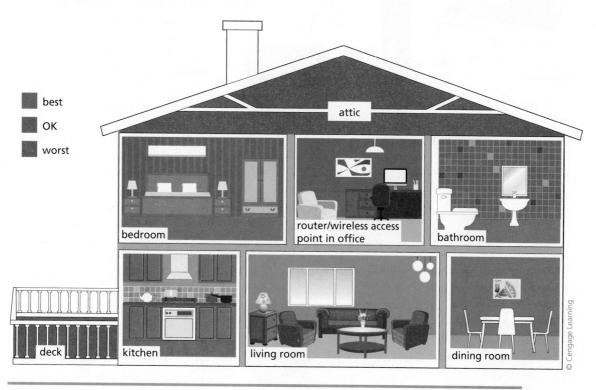

© Cengage Learning

 HOW TO 10-3

📑 Create a Home Network

If you have multiple computers and mobile devices in your home and want to share resources, you can create a home network. The following steps describe how to create a home network:

1. Establish a connection to the Internet. In many cases, your ISP will provide a modem that serves as the connection between the computers and mobile devices in your home and the Internet connection.

2. Most modems allow you to connect only one computer or mobile device and may not have the capability to serve also as a wireless access point. If you intend to use more than one computer or mobile device with your Internet connection, purchase and connect a router with a sufficient number of ports and then connect it to the modem. If you desire wireless access in your home, purchase and connect a wireless router.

3. For computers that will use a wired network connection, connect a network cable from the computer to an available port on the router.

4. Follow the router's instructions to configure it. If you are configuring wireless access, perform the following steps:
   a. Set an SSID to uniquely identify your wireless network.
   b. Select an encryption method and choose an encryption key that will be easy for you to remember but very difficult for others to guess.
   c. Connect the wireless devices to the network by enabling the wireless card if necessary, selecting the SSID of your wireless network, and specifying the proper encryption key. Read How To 5-2 on page 222 for additional information about SSIDs and encryption methods.

5. Test the connection on all devices, whether wired or wireless, that are connected to the network. You can verify that your network is working properly by running a browser and navigating to a webpage.

6. If desired, enable file sharing so that you can share files among the computers and mobile devices on your home network. Operating systems today typically include a feature that allows you to enable sharing with other computers on the same network. For another computer or mobile device to access shared files on your computer, the user will need to know the IP address or name of your computer, as well as the location of the files.

7. For maximum security, disable Internet and network connections when you are not using them.

✳ What are some other benefits of creating a home network? What disadvantages might be associated with creating a home network?

An Example of Sending a Request over the Internet Using a Variety of Transmission Media

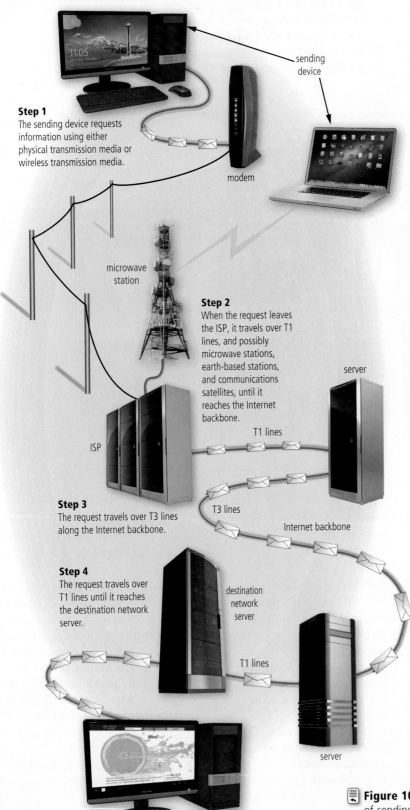

Step 1
The sending device requests information using either physical transmission media or wireless transmission media.

sending device

modem

microwave station

Step 2
When the request leaves the ISP, it travels over T1 lines, and possibly microwave stations, earth-based stations, and communications satellites, until it reaches the Internet backbone.

server

T1 lines

ISP

Step 3
The request travels over T3 lines along the Internet backbone.

T3 lines

Internet backbone

Step 4
The request travels over T1 lines until it reaches the destination network server.

destination network server

T1 lines

server

Transmission Media

Transmission media consist of materials or substances capable of carrying one or more communications signals. When you send data from a computer or mobile device, the signal that carries the data may travel over various transmission media. This is especially true when the transmission spans a long distance. Figure 10-22 illustrates the variety of transmission media, including both physical and wireless, used to complete a data request over the Internet. Although many media and devices are involved, the entire communications process could take less than one second.

Broadband media transmit multiple signals simultaneously. The amount of data, instructions, and information that can travel over transmission media sometimes is called the **bandwidth**. The higher the bandwidth, the more data transmitted. For transmission of text only, a lower bandwidth is acceptable. For transmission of music, graphics, photos, virtual reality images, or 3-D games, however, you need a higher bandwidth. When the bandwidth is too low for the application, you will notice a considerable slowdown in system performance.

Latency is the time it takes a signal to travel from one location to another on a network. Several factors that negatively can affect latency include the distance between the two points, the type of transmission media, and the number of nodes through which the data must travel over the network. For best performance, bandwidth should be high and latency low. Read Ethics & Issues 10-3 to consider whether ISPs should be able to control Internet usage.

Figure 10-22 This figure shows a simplified example of sending a request over the Internet using a variety of transmission media.

⚙ ETHICS & ISSUES 10-3

Should ISPs Be Allowed to Control Your Internet Usage?

People often compare the early days of the Internet and web to a wild frontier. ISPs simply offered customers an Internet connection and exerted no control over how the customer used the connection. This is similar to a phone company, which does not control who a customer calls, the length of a call, or the reason for the call. Online gaming, VoIP, video and audio streaming, and the use of web apps and cloud services led to an increased reliance on the Internet. Because of these increases, ISPs are attempting to regulate and limit their customers' usage.

Controversy surrounds the data caps that ISPs establish. Providers argue that caps are necessary to regulate traffic and ensure equal access to the Internet for all of its users. Critics argue that ISPs use data caps to unfairly increase customer fees. Legislators are attempting to solve this issue. Proposals include standardizing how data transfer rates are measured and involving the Federal Communications Commission (FCC). The FCC would evaluate the data caps to ensure that ISPs intend to regulate traffic instead of make a profit. It would look at whether caps are appropriate for low usage times, such as in the middle of the night, and other related issues.

Should ISPs be allowed to control your Internet usage? Why or why not? Are data caps at peak usage times reasonable? Why or why not? Should the government regulate data caps? Why or why not?

Physical Transmission Media

Physical transmission media use wire, cable, and other tangible materials to send communications signals. These wires and cables typically are used within, underground, or between buildings. Ethernet and token ring LANs often use physical transmission media.

Table 10-3 lists the transfer rates of LANs using various physical transmission media. The following sections discuss each of these types.

Twisted-Pair Cable

One of the more widely used transmission media for network cabling and landline phone systems is twisted-pair cable. **Twisted-pair cable** consists of one or more twisted-pair wires bundled together (Figure 10-23). Each *twisted-pair wire* consists of two separate insulated copper wires that are twisted together. The wires are twisted together to reduce **noise**, which is an electrical disturbance that can degrade communications.

Table 10-3 Transfer Rates for Physical Transmission Media Used in LANs	
Type of Cable and LAN	**Maximum Transfer Rate**
Twisted-Pair Cable	
• 10Base-T (Ethernet)	10 Mbps
• 100Base-T (Fast Ethernet)	100 Mbps
• 1000Base-T (Gigabit Ethernet)	1 Gbps
• Token ring	4 Mbps to 16 Mbps
Coaxial Cable	
• 10Base2 (ThinWire Ethernet)	10 Mbps
• 10Base5 (ThickWire Ethernet)	10 Mbps
Fiber-Optic Cable	
• 10Base-F (Ethernet)	10 Mbps
• 100Base-FX (Fast Ethernet)	100 Mbps
• FDDI (Fiber Distributed Data Interface) token ring	100 Mbps
• Gigabit Ethernet	1 Gbps
• 10-Gigabit Ethernet	10 Gbps
• 40-Gigabit Ethernet	40 Gbps
• 100-Gigabit Ethernet	100 Gbps

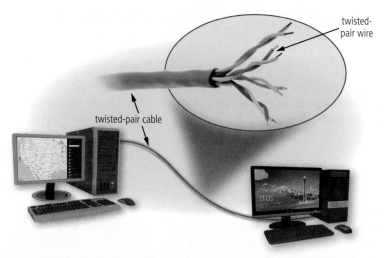

twisted-pair wire

twisted-pair cable

Figure 10-23 A twisted-pair cable consists of one or more twisted-pair wires. Each twisted-pair wire usually is color coded for identification. Landline phone networks and LANs often use twisted-pair cable.

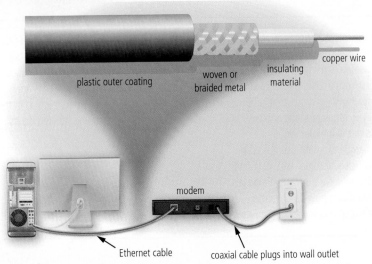

Figure 10-24 On coaxial cable, data travels through a copper wire. This simplified illustration shows a computer connected to a modem, which also is connected to the CATV network through a coaxial cable.
© iStockphoto / THEPALMER; © iStockphoto / Evgeny Karandaev; Courtesy of Zoom Telephonics, Inc.;
© Cengage Learning

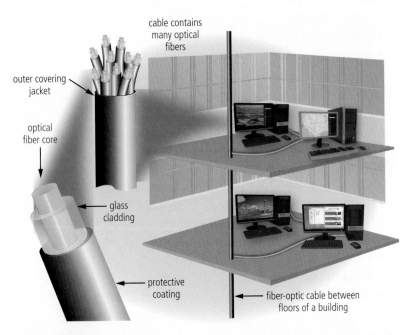

Figure 10-25 A fiber-optic cable consists of hair-thin strands of glass or plastic that carry data as pulses of light, as shown in this simplified example.
© Cengage Learning; © Oleksiy Mark / Shutterstock.com; © iStockphoto /123render; © Oleksiy Mark / Shutterstock.com; © Oleksiy Mark / Shutterstock.com

Coaxial Cable

Coaxial cable, often referred to as *coax* (pronounced KO-ax), consists of a single copper wire surrounded by at least three layers: (1) an insulating material, (2) a woven or braided metal, and (3) a plastic outer coating (Figure 10-24).

CATV network wiring often uses coaxial cable because it can be cabled over longer distances than twisted-pair cable. Most of today's computer networks, however, do not use coaxial cable because other transmission media such as fiber-optic cable transmit signals at faster rates.

Fiber-Optic Cable

The core of a **fiber-optic cable** consists of dozens or hundreds of thin strands of glass or plastic that use light to transmit signals. Each strand, called an *optical fiber*, is as thin as a human hair. Inside the fiber-optic cable, an insulating glass cladding and a protective coating surround each optical fiber (Figure 10-25).

Fiber-optic cables have the following advantages over cables that use wire, such as twisted-pair and coaxial cables:

- Capability of carrying significantly more signals than wire cables
- Faster data transmission
- Less susceptible to noise (interference) from other devices, such as a copy machine
- Better security for signals during transmission because they are less susceptible to noise
- Smaller size (much thinner and lighter weight)

Disadvantages of fiber-optic cable are it costs more than twisted-pair or coaxial cable and can be difficult to install and modify. Despite these limitations, many phone companies replaced original analog phone lines with fiber-optic cables, enabling them to offer fiber Internet access to home and business users. Businesses also use fiber-optic cables in high-traffic networks or as the backbone in a network.

Wireless Transmission Media

Wireless transmission media send communications signals through the air or space. Many users opt for wireless transmission media because it is more convenient than installing cables. In addition to convenience, businesses use wireless transmission media in locations where it is impossible to install cables. Read How To 10-4 for instructions about adding a printer to a wireless network.

HOW TO 10-4

Add a Wireless Printer to a Home/Small Office Network

Adding a wireless printer to a home or small office network has several advantages. For example, multiple computers and mobile devices on the network can use the printer. You also can place the printer anywhere in the home or office, as long as it is within range of the wireless signal. For example, a wireless router can be on the first floor of your house, and a wireless printer can be on the second floor. The following steps describe how to add a wireless printer to a home/small office network:

1. Determine the location to install the wireless printer. This location must have an electrical outlet for the printer and also be within range of the wireless network. You can check the strength of wireless signals in your home or office by walking around with a mobile computer or device while connected to the network and monitoring the signal strength.

2. Be sure to place the printer on a stable surface.

3. Access the printer's settings and navigate to the network settings.

4. Connect to the wireless network in your home or small office. If necessary, specify the encryption key for your network.

5. Enter any remaining required information.

6. Install the printer software on the computer(s) from which you want to print to the wireless printer. During the installation process, you will select the wireless printer that you have connected and configured. If the printer does not appear, return to Step 4 and try connecting the printer to the wireless network again. If the problem persists, consider contacting the printer's manufacturer.

7. Verify the computers are able to print successfully to the wireless printer.

❂ What are some ways to prevent some computers or mobile devices on your network from printing to your wireless printer?

© iStockphoto / btrenkel; © Cengage Learning

Types of wireless transmission media used in communications include infrared, broadcast radio, cellular radio, microwaves, and communications satellites. Table 10-4 lists transfer rates of various wireless transmission media, which are discussed in the following sections.

Infrared

As discussed earlier in the chapter, infrared (IR) is a wireless transmission medium that sends signals using infrared light waves. Mobile computers and devices, such as a mouse, printer, and smartphone, may have an IrDA port that enables the transfer of data from one device to another using infrared light waves.

Broadcast Radio

Broadcast radio is a wireless transmission medium that distributes radio signals through the air over long distances such as between cities, regions, and countries and short distances, such as within an office or home.

For radio transmissions, you need a transmitter to send the broadcast radio signal and a receiver to accept it. To receive the broadcast radio signal, the receiver has an antenna that is located in the range of the signal. Some networks use a transceiver, which both sends and receives signals from wireless devices. Broadcast radio is slower and more susceptible to noise than physical transmission media, but it provides flexibility and portability.

Bluetooth, UWB, Wi-Fi, and WiMAX communications technologies discussed earlier in this chapter use broadcast radio signals. Bluetooth and UWB are alternatives to infrared communications, with the latter designed for high bandwidth transmissions. Hot spots use Wi-Fi, WiMAX, and Bluetooth networks.

Table 10-4	Wireless Transmission Media Transfer Rates	
Medium		**Maximum Transfer Transmission Rate**
Infrared		115 Kbps to 4 Mbps
Broadcast radio	• Bluetooth	1 Mbps to 24 Mbps
	• 802.11b	11 Mbps
	• 802.11a	54 Mbps
	• 802.11g	54 Mbps
	• 802.11n	300 Mbps
	• 802.11ac	500 Mbps to 1 Gbps
	• 802.11ad	up to 7 Gbps
	• UWB	110 Mbps to 480 Mbps
Cellular radio	• 2G	9.6 Kbps to 144 Kbps
	• 3G	144 Kbps to 3.84 Mbps
	• 4G	Up to 100 Mbps
Microwave radio		10 Gbps
Communications satellite		2.56 Tbps

 BTW

Data Transfer Rates
Tbps (terabits per second) is one trillion bits per second.

BTW
Verizon
Technology Innovator:
You should be familiar
with Verizon.

Cellular Radio

Cellular radio is a form of broadcast radio that is in wide use for mobile communications, specifically wireless modems and mobile phones (Figure 10-26). A mobile phone uses high-frequency radio waves to transmit voice and digital data messages. Because only a limited number of radio frequencies exist, mobile service providers reuse frequencies so that they can accommodate the large number of users. Some users install an amplifier or booster to improve the signal strength. Read Secure IT 10-4 to consider issues related to radiation from mobile phones and other devices.

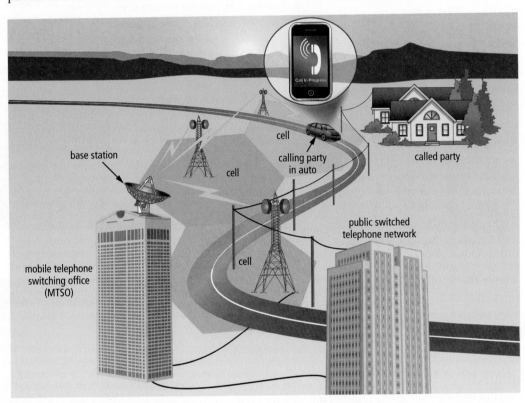

Figure 10-26 As a person with a mobile phone drives from one cell to another, the radio signals transfer from the base station (microwave station) in one cell to a base station in another cell.
© Stuartmile... / Dreamstime.com; © Cengage Learning

SECURE IT 10-4

Radiation from Mobile Phones, Cellular Antennas, and Wi-Fi Devices

Many people are concerned about potential health effects from using mobile phones, living near cellular antennas, and being exposed to Wi-Fi signals that permeate businesses, public areas, and homes. The increased use of wireless technology, particularly among younger users and in schools, is troubling to some parents and educators. It generally is agreed that no study conclusively demonstrates negative health effects from mobile phones, cellular antennas, and Wi-Fi devices, but skeptics claim that the technology is too new. Long-term studies that are under way on humans may not provide results for decades.

Wireless technology uses radio frequency (RF) energy, which is nonionizing and, therefore, does not alter the structure of atoms. It does, however, create heat, but not at levels exceeding Federal Communications Commission limits. Some mobile phone users who suffered rare illnesses have filed lawsuits against mobile phone manufacturers, but the cases usually are lost due to lack of scientific evidence linking the use of the phones to the illnesses. To reduce exposure to possible radiation, use a mobile phone in hands-free mode to keep the device away from your head, and also try to limit the number and length of calls. People with pacemakers might consider keeping the mobile phone as far away as possible from the implant area because the RF energy could interfere with the pacemaker.

While debates rage in communities over placement of cellular antennas, the consideration of health effects on residents is muted because the federal government's Telecommunications Act of 1996 prohibits local governments from considering health effects when making decisions about cellular antenna placement. The law does not apply to Wi-Fi antennas, and some municipalities reject municipal Wi-Fi deployment due to residents' health concerns.

Do you or does anyone you know minimize mobile phone use due to health concerns? Are you concerned about mobile phone, cellular antenna, or Wi-Fi radiation? Would you be apprehensive about living next to a cellular antenna? Why or why not?

Several categories of cellular radio transmissions exist, defining the development of cellular networks. Although the definitions of these categories may vary by mobile service providers, below are some general guidelines:

- 1G (first generation of cellular transmissions)
  - Analog data transfer at speeds up to 14.4 Kbps
- 2G (second generation of cellular transmissions)
  - Digital data transfer at speeds from 9.6 Kbps to 144 Kbps
  - Improved voice transmissions, added data communications, and added SMS (short message service) or text messaging services
  - Standards include *GSM* (Global System for Mobile Communications) and *GPRS* (General Packet Radio Service)
- 3G (third generation of cellular transmissions)
  - Digital data transfer at speeds from 144 Kbps to 3.84 Mbps
  - Improved data transmissions, added MMS (multimedia message services) or picture message services
  - Standards include *UMTS* (Universal Mobile Telecommunications System), CDMA (Code Division Multiple Access), EDGE (Enhanced Data GSM Environment), and EVDO (Evolution Data Optimized)
- 4G (fourth generation of cellular transmissions)
  - Digital data transfer at speeds up to 100 Mbps
  - Improved video transmissions
  - Standards include Long Term Evolution (*LTE*), Ultra Mobile Broadband (*UMB*), and IEEE 802.16 (WiMAX)
- 5G (fifth generation of cellular transmissions)
  - Future generation of cellular transmissions
  - Expected to improve bandwidth
  - Expected to provide artificial intelligence capabilities on wearable devices

Microwaves

Microwaves are radio waves that provide a high-speed signal transmission. Microwave transmission, often called *fixed wireless*, involves sending signals from one microwave station to another (Figure 10-27). A *microwave station* is an earth-based reflective dish that contains the antenna, transceivers, and other equipment necessary for microwave communications. As with infrared, microwaves use line-of-sight transmission. To avoid possible obstructions, such as buildings or mountains, microwave stations often sit on the tops of buildings, towers, or mountains.

Microwave transmission typically is used in environments where installing physical transmission media is difficult or impossible and where line-of-sight transmission is

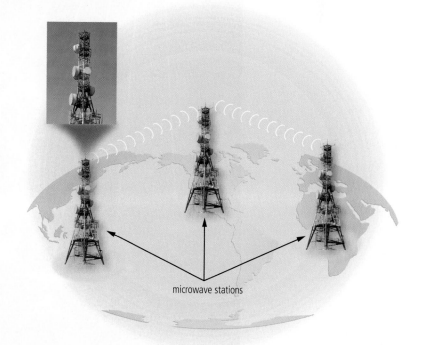

microwave stations

Figure 10-27 A microwave station is a ground-based reflective dish that contains the antenna, transceivers, and other equipment necessary for microwave communications.

© Cengage Learning; © Alfonso de Tomas / Shutterstock.com

available. For example, microwave transmission is used in wide-open areas such as deserts or lakes, between buildings in a close geographic area, or to communicate with a satellite. Current users of microwave transmission include universities, hospitals, city governments, CATV providers, and phone companies. Homes and small businesses that do not have other high-speed Internet connections available in their area also opt for lower-cost fixed wireless plans.

Communications Satellite

A **communications satellite** is a space station that receives microwave signals from an earth-based station, amplifies (strengthens) the signals, and broadcasts the signals back over a wide area to any number of earth-based stations (Figure 10-28). These earth-based stations often are microwave stations. Other devices, such as smartphones and GPS receivers, also can function as earth-based stations. Transmission from an earth-based station to a satellite is an *uplink*. Transmission from a satellite to an earth-based station is a *downlink*.

Applications such as air navigation, television and radio broadcasts, weather forecasting, videoconferencing, paging, GPS, and Internet connections use communications satellites. With

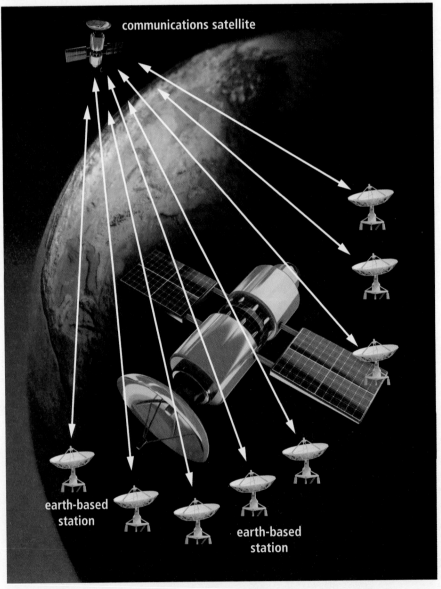

Figure 10-28 Communications satellites are placed about 22,300 miles above the Earth's equator.

© Cengage Learning; © Mmaxer / Shutterstock.com; © Mmaxer / Shutterstock.com; © SSSCCC / Shutterstock.com the proper satellite dish and a satellite modem, consumers can access the Internet using satellite technology. With satellite Internet connections, however, uplink transmissions usually are slower than downlink transmissions. This difference in speeds usually is acceptable to most Internet satellite users because they download much more data than they upload. Although a satellite Internet connection is more expensive than cable Internet or DSL connections, sometimes it is the only high-speed Internet option in remote areas.

GPS   As described previously, a global positioning system (GPS) is a navigation system that consists of one or more earth-based receivers that accept and analyze signals sent by satellites in order to determine the receiver's geographic location (Figure 10-29).

Many mobile devices such as smartphones have GPS capability built into the device or as an add-on feature. Some users carry a handheld GPS receiver; others mount a receiver to an object such as an automobile, a boat, an airplane, farm and construction equipment, or a computer or mobile device. A GPS receiver is a handheld, mountable, or embedded device that contains an antenna, a radio receiver, and a processor. Many include a screen display that shows an individual's location on a map.

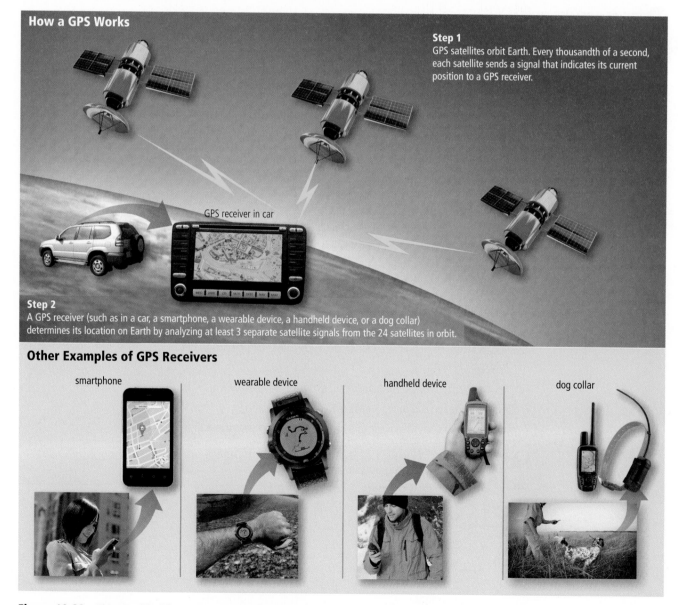

How a GPS Works

Step 1
GPS satellites orbit Earth. Every thousandth of a second, each satellite sends a signal that indicates its current position to a GPS receiver.

GPS receiver in car

Step 2
A GPS receiver (such as in a car, a smartphone, a wearable device, a handheld device, or a dog collar) determines its location on Earth by analyzing at least 3 separate satellite signals from the 24 satellites in orbit.

Other Examples of GPS Receivers

smartphone   wearable device   handheld device   dog collar

Figure 10-29   This simplified figure shows how a GPS works.

CONSIDER THIS

What are uses of GPS?

The first and most used application of GPS technology is to assist people with determining where they are located. The data obtained from a GPS, however, can be applied to a variety of other uses: creating a map, ascertaining the best route between two points, locating a lost person or stolen object, monitoring the movement of a person or object, determining altitude, and calculating speed.

Many vehicles use GPSs to provide drivers with directions or other information, such as alternate traffic routes, automatically call for help if the airbag is deployed, dispatch roadside assistance, unlock the driver's side door if keys are locked in the car, and track the vehicle if it is stolen. Newer GPS receivers also give drivers information about nearby points of interest, such as gas stations, restaurants, and hotels. Hikers and remote campers may carry GPS receivers in case they need emergency help or directions.

Some GPS receivers work in conjunction with a cellular radio network. Parents, for example, can locate a child's whereabouts through a mobile phone equipped with a GPS receiver. Read Ethics & Issue 10-4 to consider whether GPS tracking is ethical.

 ETHICS & ISSUES 10-4

 Should GPS Tracking Be Legal?

Vehicles and smartphones that use GPS enable a driver or phone user to obtain directions, find nearby restaurants or shops, and connect with safety services in the event of an accident or emergency. A third party, such as an employer, also can use GPS to track the whereabouts of a vehicle, phone, and other items. Are any ethical or legal boundaries broken when an employer uses GPS to track an employee?

Employers have legitimate reasons for tracking employees' whereabouts. For example, a shipping company can use GPS to locate the trucks in its fleet to predict when a shipment will arrive. A company can use this data to keep track of its trucks, which are company assets. Managers can analyze GPS data to improve business by determining the best routes, ensuring drivers get enough sleep, and using mileage driven to schedule vehicle maintenance. Employers who issue company vehicles also may use GPS devices to ensure that employees are not driving the vehicle for personal use.

Many people agree that employers have a right to use GPS trackers on company equipment to collect data they can use for business purposes. Some feel that a company should use GPS tracking to discover information about some employees, but not others. Many privacy advocates further recommend that employees should be informed of the tracking devices in advance and that the company's policies should state the purpose of the data collection.

Does an employer have a right to use GPS tracking without informing the employee? Why or why not? What limits, if any, should an employer have when using data collected from GPS tracking? Why?

 NOW YOU KNOW

Be sure you understand the material presented in the sections titled Communications Devices, Home Networks, Transmission Media, Physical Transmission Media, and Wireless Transmission Media, as it relates to the chapter objectives. *You now should know . . .*

- When you would use various communications devices (Objective 8)

- How you can set up and configure a home network (Objective 9)

- Which types of transmission media are best suited to your needs (Objectives 10 and 11)

Quiz Yourself Online: Check your knowledge of related content by navigating to this book's Quiz Yourself resource on Computer Concepts CourseMate and then tapping or clicking Objectives 8–11.

✓ Chapter Summary

This chapter presented a variety of networks and communications technologies. It discussed various types of network architectures, topologies, and standards and protocols. It explained communications software. Several types of communications lines and communications devices were presented. The chapter discussed how to create a home network. It also presented a variety of physical transmission media and wireless transmission media.

Test your knowledge of chapter material by accessing the Study Guide, Flash Cards, and Practice Test apps that run on your smartphone, tablet, laptop, or desktop.

⚙ TECHNOLOGY @ WORK

Agriculture

The world's dependence on the agriculture industry is enormous. The demand to keep food prices affordable encourages those working in this industry to operate as efficiently as possible. Although people have worked in agriculture for more than 10,000 years, advances in technology assist with maintaining and protecting land and crops.

Almost all individuals and organizations in this industry have many acres of land that they must maintain. It is not always feasible for farmers to take frequent trips around the property to perform basic tasks, such as watering soil in the absence of rain. The number of people-hours required to water soil manually on several thousand acres of land might result in businesses spending thousands of dollars in labor and utility costs. If an irrigation system is installed instead, one or more individuals still are responsible for deciding when to water and how long to water. If the irrigation process is automated, sensors detect how much rain has fallen recently, as well as whether the soil is in need of watering. The sensors then send this data to a computer that processes it and decides when and how much to water. Many automated home irrigation systems also are programmable and use rain sensors, which regulates operation of the irrigation system.

In addition to keeping the soil moist and reducing maintenance costs, computers also can use sensors to analyze the condition of crops in the field and determine whether pests or diseases are affecting the crops. If sensors detect pests and/or diseases, computers send a notification to the appropriate individual to take corrective action. In some cases, the discovery of pests might trigger a pesticide to discharge in the affected area automatically.

Until recently, the lack of adequate cellular and wireless network signals in the fields made communications difficult for farmers. Mobile cellular antennas and amplifiers stretch mobile broadband coverage across entire farms, enabling farmers to receive wireless signals up to eight times farther from the cellular tower than they would without the antennas and amplifiers. Wireless access throughout the farm also allows farmers to monitor their farms and communicate with colleagues from remote locations.

The next time you take a bite of a delicious carrot or juicy cucumber, you can appreciate how technology has helped to maintain an ideal environment for these vegetables to grow and protected them from unwanted pests, all for a reasonable price when you purchase them from your local supermarket.

✺ How else might computers and technology be used in the agriculture industry?

eliandric / iStockphoto

Study Guide

The Study Guide exercise reinforces material you should know for the chapter exam. You will find answers to items with the 📖 icon only in the e-book.

🖥 **Access the Study Guide app** that runs on your smartphone, tablet, laptop, or desktop by navigating to this book's Apps resource on Computer Concepts CourseMate.

Instructions: Answer the questions below using the format that helps you remember best or that is required by your instructor. Possible formats may include one or more of these options: write the answers; create a document that contains the answers; record answers as audio or video using a webcam, smartphone, or portable media player; post answers on a blog, wiki, or website; or highlight answers in the book/e-book.

1. List the device types you need for successful communications.

2. A(n) _____ is a collection of computers and devices connected together via communications devices and transmission media.

3. List reasons home and business users create a network. Identify how networks facilitate communications.

4. A(n) _____ is a third-party business that provides networking services, such as EDI.

5. Define the terms, intranet and extranet.

6. Differentiate among LANs, MANs, WANs, and PANs. Explain issues surrounding the use of BANs.

7. Name and describe two types of network architectures. Define the terms, server and client.

8. Explain P2P file sharing. 📖 Name file sharing programs.

9. A network _____ is the layout of the computers and devices in a communications network.

10. Differentiate among star, bus, and ring networks.

11. Define the terms, network standard and protocol.

12. 📖 Describe how the OSI Reference Model works.

13. Define the term, Ethernet. Explain what happens when two devices on an Ethernet attempt to send data at the same time.

14. 📖 Explain the role of Robert Metcalfe, with regard to Ethernet.

15. Describe how a network transmits data using a token.

16. TCP/IP is the network standard for _____ communications. Describe packet sniffer software.

17. Explain whether you can use an IP address to determine a computer or device's location.

18. Describe how Wi-Fi enables users to connect to the Internet.

19. Define the term, Bluetooth.

20. 📖 Explain the role of Sven Mattisson and Jaap Haartsen, with respect to Bluetooth.

21. List uses for Bluetooth devices. Name advantages and disadvantages to using Bluetooth.

22. Differentiate among UWB, IrDA, RFID, and NFC technologies.

23. Explain how RFID chips are used, and list privacy concerns with RFID technology.

24. Define the term, WiMAX. List two types of WiMAX specifications.

25. Name uses of communications software.

26. Describe the following mobile communications: text/picture/video messaging, instant messaging, and voice and video calling. 📖 List services for each.

27. Identify the role of a dedicated line. List types of digital dedicated lines.

28. Explain the advantages of cable Internet services and DSL.

29. Define the term, communications device.

30. Explain issues surrounding mobile computers and devices in the classroom.

31. List two widely used types of broadband modems.

32. Define the term, dial-up modem.

33. List the steps to use your phone as a mobile hot spot.

34. Define the term, wireless access point. Explain how to strengthen your wireless signal.

35. Identify the role of a router. List types of routers that offer additional functionality.

36. Describe the function of a network card.

37. Identify the roles of hubs and switches on a network.

38. 📖 Explain the role of Cisco, with respect to networks.

39. Identify hardware needed to set up a home network. List steps to create a home network.

40. List steps to determine if someone is accessing a wireless network without permission.

41. Define the terms, transmission media, bandwidth, and latency.

42. Explain issues surrounding ISPs setting limits on Internet usage.

43. Name types of physical transmission media. Define the term, noise.

44. Identify advantages and disadvantages of fiber-optic cables.

45. List steps to add a wireless printer to a home/small office network.

46. Name types of wireless transmission media. Differentiate among 1G, 2G, 3G, 4G, and 5G cellular transmissions.

47. Explain how to protect yourself from radiation from mobile phones, cellular antennas, and Wi-Fi devices.

48. List uses of GPS. Explain issues surrounding GPS tracking.

49. Explain how the agriculture industry uses technology.

You should be able to define the Primary Terms and be familiar with the Secondary Terms listed below.

Key Terms

Access the **Flash Cards app** that runs on your smartphone, tablet, laptop, or desktop by navigating to this book's Apps resource on Computer Concepts CourseMate. **View definitions** for each term by navigating to this book's Key Terms resource on Computer Concepts CourseMate. **Listen to definitions** for each term on your portable media player by navigating to this book's Audio Study Tools resource on Computer Concepts CourseMate.

Primary Terms   (shown in **bold-black** characters in the chapter)

802.11 (427)
ATM (434)
bandwidth (442)
Bluetooth (427)
broadband (443)
broadcast radio (445)
cable modem (435)
cellular radio (446)
client/server network (422)
clients (422)
coaxial cable (444)
communications
  device (434)

communications
  satellite (448)
communications
  software (431)
dedicated line (432)
DSL (433)
DSL modem (435)
Ethernet (425)
fiber-optic cable (444)
FTTP (Fiber to the
  Premises) (434)
home network (440)
IrDA (429)

latency (442)
local area network
  (LAN) (419)
microwaves (447)
network (418)
network topology (423)
NFC (430)
noise (443)
personal area network
  (PAN) (421)
receiving device (416)
RFID (429)
sending device (416)

server (422)
T-carrier line (434)
TCP/IP (426)
token ring (425)
transmission media (442)
twisted-pair cable (443)
UWB (ultra-wideband) (429)
wide area network
  (WAN) (421)
Wi-Fi (427)
WiMax (431)
wireless LAN
  (WLAN) (420)

Secondary Terms   (shown in *italic* characters in the chapter)

ADSL (asymmetric digital
  subscriber line) (433)
body area network (BAN) (421)
broadband modem (435)
broadband router (438)
broadband wireless router (438)
bus network (423)
cable Internet service (433)
coax (444)
communications channel (416)
dial-up modem (435)
digital modem (435)
Digital Subscriber Line (433)
downlink (448)
downstream rate (433)
EDI (electronic data
  interchange) (419)
electronic funds transfer (EFT) (419)
extranet (419)

file sharing network (422)
fixed wireless (447)
fractional T1 (434)
FTTB (Fiber to the Building) (434)
FTTH (Fiber to the Home) (434)
Gbps (425)
GPRS (447)
GSM (447)
hardware firewall (438)
host computer (422)
hub (439)
intranet (419)
ISDN (433)
ISDN modem (435)
line-of-sight transmission (429)
LTE (447)
Mbps (425)
metropolitan area network
  (MAN) (421)

microwave station (447)
mobile broadband wireless router (438)
mobile hot spot (436)
multiplexing (433)
near field communications (430)
network architecture (421)
network card (439)
network interface card (NIC) (439)
network license (419)
network standard (425)
node (419)
optical fiber (444)
packet sniffer (427)
packet switching (426)
packets (426)
peer (422)
peer-to-peer network (P2P) (422)
protocol (425)
radio frequency identification (429)

router (437)
star network (423)
switch (439)
T1 line (434)
T3 line (434)
Tbps (444)
token (425)
twisted-pair wire (443)
UMB (447)
UMTS (447)
uplink (448)
upstream rate (433)
value-added network (VAN) (419)
wireless access point (436)
wireless Ethernet (427)
wireless modem (436)
wireless router (438)

© Alfonso de Tomas / Shutterstock.com;
© Cengage Learning

microwave station (447)

Checkpoint

The Checkpoint exercises test your knowledge of the chapter concepts. The page number containing the answer appears in parentheses after each exercise. The Consider This exercises challenge your understanding of chapter concepts.

Complete the Checkpoint exercises interactively by navigating to this book's Checkpoint resource on Computer Concepts CourseMate. **Access the Test Prep app** that runs on your smartphone, tablet, laptop, or desktop by navigating to this book's Apps resource on Computer Concepts CourseMate. After successfully completing the self-assessment through the Test Prep app, **take the Practice Test** by navigating to this book's Practice Test resource on Computer Concepts CourseMate.

True/False   Mark T for True and F for False.

_____ 1. All types of computers and mobile devices serve as sending and receiving devices in a communications system. (416)

_____ 2. On a client/server network, the client controls access to the resources on the network and provides a centralized storage area. (422)

_____ 3. On a P2P network, each computer has equal responsibilities and capabilities. (422)

_____ 4. Wi-Fi networks cannot be integrated with Ethernet networks. (427)

_____ 5. Most current operating systems do not yet have built-in Bluetooth support. (427)

_____ 6. UWB requires line-of-sight transmission, so its technology is not as widespread as IrDA. (429)

_____ 7. For successful communications with NFC devices, the devices or objects must touch or be placed within an inch or two of each other. (430)

_____ 8. DSL transmits on existing standard copper phone wiring. (433)

_____ 9. Phone networks, the Internet, and other networks with large amounts of traffic use DSL. (434)

_____ 10. A broadband modem is a communications device that converts digital signals to analog signals and analog signals to digital signals, so that data can travel along an analog phone line. (435)

_____ 11. Although some routers may be able to connect more than 200 computers and mobile devices, the performance of the router may decline as you add connections. (438)

_____ 12. With satellite Internet connections, uplink transmissions usually are slower than downlink transmissions. (449)

Multiple Choice   Select the best answer.

1. For successful communications, you need all of the following *except* _____. (416)
   a. a sending device
   b. a transponder
   c. a communications channel
   d. transmission media

2. A(n) _____ is an internal network that uses Internet technologies. (419)
   a. router
   b. extranet
   c. intranet
   d. communications channel

3. A _____ is a network that connects computers and devices in a limited geographical area such as a home, school, office building, or closely positioned group of buildings. (419)
   a. LAN
   b. PAN
   c. BAN
   d. WAN

4. A(n) _____ network is a simple, inexpensive network that typically connects fewer than 10 computers. (422)
   a. protocol
   b. WAN
   c. extranet
   d. P2P

5. On a _____ network, all of the computers and devices on the network connect to a central device. (423)
   a. bus
   b. ring
   c. star
   d. token ring

6. Wi-Fi sometimes is referred to as _____. (427)
   a. Bluetooth
   b. UWB
   c. IrDA
   d. wireless Ethernet

7. Which of the following is not a digital dedicated line? (432)
   a. NFC
   b. cable Internet service
   c. FTTP
   d. T-carrier lines

8. A _____ is a central communications device that allows computers and devices to transfer data wireless among themselves or to transfer data wirelessly to a wired network using wireless technologies. (436)
   a. hub
   b. router
   c. switch
   d. wireless access point

Checkpoint

Matching   Match the terms with their definitions.

_____ 1. value-added network (VAN) (419)

_____ 2. node (419)

_____ 3. network topology (423)

_____ 4. protocol (425)

_____ 5. network standard (425)

_____ 6. token (425)

_____ 7. TCP/IP (426)

_____ 8. packet switching (426)

_____ 9. bandwidth (442)

_____ 10. latency (442)

a. standard that outlines characteristics of how two devices communicate on a network

b. guidelines that specify the way computers access the medium to which they are connected, the type(s) of medium used, the speeds used on different types of networks, and the type(s) of physical cable and/or the wireless technology used

c. third-party business that provides networking services such as EDI services, storage, or email

d. technique of breaking a message into individual packets, sending them along the best route available, and then reassembling the data

e. network protocol that defines how messages are routed from one end of a network to the other, ensuring the data arrives correctly

f. the amount of data, instructions, and information that can travel over transmission media

g. layout of computers and devices in a communications network

h. term used to refer to each computer or device on a network

i. the time it takes a signal to travel from one location to another on a network

j. a special series of bits that function like a ticket

Short Answer   Write a brief answer to each of the following questions.

1. List some reasons why users create networks. (418) What are EDI and EFT? (419)

2. What are some network communications standards and protocols? (425) What is a disadvantage of using Bluetooth? (428)

3. List various communications devices. (434) List ways you can try to strengthen your wireless signal. (437)

4. What hardware is necessary for a wireless, Internet-connected home network? (440) What does a user need to know in order for another computer or mobile device to access shared files on a computer? (441)

5. What is IP hijacking? (440) Differentiate between an uplink and a downlink. (448)

✳ Consider This   Answer the following questions in the format specified by your instructor.

1. Answer the critical thinking questions posed at the end of these elements in this chapter: Ethics & Issues (421, 435, 443, 450), How To (436, 437, 440, 445), Mini Features (428, 431, 440), Secure IT (427, 429, 440, 446), and Technology @ Work (451).

2. For what purposes do home and business users create networks? (418)

3. Why might a company use an intranet or extranet? (419)

4. For what purposes do small business and home users use a P2P network? (422)

5. Why do some networks keep a duplicate central device? (423)

6. 📱 How do the network standards developed by IEEE differ from one another? (427)

7. What are some advantages to using Bluetooth technology? (428)

8. Which wireless technology requires line-of-sight transmission? Which do not? (429)

9. How can RFID tracking violate your privacy? (429)

10. Why is ADSL ideal for Internet access? (433)

11. Should instructors allow mobile devices in the classroom? Why or why not? (435)

12. Why might it be necessary to strengthen a wireless signal? How do you accomplish this? (437)

13. What factors negatively affect latency? (442)

14. What advantages do fiber-optic cables have over cables that use wires? (444)

15. Should you be concerned about radiation from mobile phones, cellular antennas, and Wi-Fi devices? Why or why not? (446)

✸ How To: Your Turn

The How To: Your Turn exercises present general guidelines for fundamental skills when using a computer or mobile device and then require that you determine how to apply these general guidelines to a specific program or situation.

Instructions: You often can complete tasks using technology in multiple ways. Figure out how to perform the tasks described in these exercises by using one or more resources available to you (such as a computer or mobile device, articles on the web or in print, online or program help, user guides, blogs, podcasts, videos, other individuals, trial and error, etc.). Summarize your 'how to' steps, along with the resource(s) used, in the format requested by your instructor (brief report, presentation, discussion, blog post, video, or other means).

❶ Evaluate Internet Access Plans

If you are planning to connect to the Internet from your computer or mobile device, you will need to subscribe to an Internet access plan. Cable companies, phone companies, and mobile service providers all offer Internet access plans, so it is important to evaluate the plans in your area to determine which one is best for you. The following steps guide you through the process of evaluating Internet access plans.

a. Create a budget. Internet access plans are available for a monthly fee, so determine how much money you are able to spend for Internet access on a monthly basis.

b. Locate and list the Internet access plans available in your area. To determine Internet access plans that are available, check the local cable or phone company's website and search for available plans. You may have to enter your ZIP code to determine whether certain plans are available in your area. Alternatively, visit a local electronics store and inquire about wireless Internet access plans available in your area.

c. Compare Internet access speeds. Each Internet access plan may offer a different speed, so determine which speed is sufficient for you. If you mainly browse webpages and send or receive email messages, you may not need a plan that offers the fastest transfer rates. If you plan to download files, play online games, and play movies on the Internet, you should consider a plan with fast transfer rates. You also should consider a plan with faster transfer rates if you will have multiple devices accessing the Internet simultaneously in your household. If an ISP offers multiple plans with a variety of transfer rates, it often will let you switch back and forth between plans without penalty so that you can find the one with the transfer rate that is best for you.

d. Check for package deals. If you already have service with an existing CATV or phone provider, they may be able to add Internet access to your current services at a reduced rate. Bundling multiple services can make each service (such as

Internet access) less expensive, but you should be careful not to sign up for services you do not need.

e. Think about how much data you intend to transfer each month. Some Internet access plans limit the amount of data you can upload or download each month. While it can be difficult to determine how much data you will upload or download, you first should purchase a plan that might allow you to transfer more than you think you will need. Monitor your data usage each month and consider downgrading to a plan that provides the amount of data transfer that better represents your use.

f. Determine where you require Internet access. Some ISPs will allow you to use its hot spots for free in locations such as shopping malls, coffeehouses, and airports. Consider the additional locations from where you can access the Internet for free, and determine whether it makes the Internet access plan more desirable.

g. Consider whether a wireless Internet access plan is appropriate. While these plans can cost more and transfer rates often are not as fast, they do provide the flexibility of allowing you to connect to the Internet from almost anywhere. If you often travel and regularly need to access the Internet while away from home, a wireless Internet access plan might be right for you.

Exercises

1. What Internet access plans are available in your area?
2. Prepare a table comparing the Internet access plans in your area. Based on your current Internet usage, which plan appears to be the best? Why?

❷ Locate Hot Spots

If you are using a mobile computer or device and need to access the Internet, you will need to locate a hot spot. Hot spots are available in a variety of locations such as coffeehouses, shopping malls, public libraries, airports, and educational institutions. Once you locate a hot spot, be sure to use it safely. Read Secure IT 1-4 on page 30 for more information about using public Wi-Fi hot spots safely. If you plan

How To: Your Turn ☀

to connect to a wireless hot spot, make sure you are authorized to connect. For example, you should not connect to people's or businesses' hot spots without their knowledge or consent. If you are unsure of whether you are authorized to connect to a hot spot, contact someone representing the residence or business providing the hot spot. The following are guidelines that can assist you in locating a hot spot:

- Turn on your mobile computer or device's Wi-Fi and see whether it automatically detects any wireless networks. If one or more wireless networks are detected, connect to the one with the SSID that accurately describes your location. For example, if you are at a coffeehouse, the SSID of the wireless network might be the coffeehouse's name. If you unsure of which wireless network to connect, contact an employee at the location and inquire. If the wireless network is protected with a password, the employee may be able to provide the password.
- You can check the location's website or app in advance to determine whether it has free Wi-Fi. For example, if you are flying out of your local airport, the airport's website might indicate whether Wi-Fi is available.
- Businesses offering free Wi-Fi sometimes have a decal on a front door or window indicating the location has Wi-Fi. If necessary, contact an employee to determine how to connect to the wireless network.
- Search for and navigate to a website that lists Wi-Fi hot spots in a particular area. These websites sometimes do not provide the most up-to-date information, so do not rely completely on the information you locate.

© DeiMosz / Shutterstock.com

Exercises

1. What public hot spots are available near where you live?
2. Have you connected to a public hot spot before? If so, when? If not, do you have concerns about a public hot spot's security?

❸ Test Your Internet Speed

As discussed in this chapter, cookies can be used for a variety of reasons. Websites can install cookies that can store information on your computer or mobile device or track your browsing habits. You can configure a browser's settings to disallow websites from storing and accessing cookies on your computer or mobile device. The following

steps guide you through the process of testing your Internet speed:

a. Turn off any computers or mobile devices that might be accessing the Internet, except for the computer on which you want to test your broadband speed.
b. If your broadband Internet service is provided through your phone company, do not talk on the phone during the test. If your CATV company provides your broadband Internet service, turn off all devices accessing the cable television. If you have cable boxes or converters, disconnect them from their power source so that they cannot communicate using the Internet connection while you are testing your broadband speed.
c. Run the browser.
d. Search for and navigate to a website that can test your Internet speed.
e. Tap or click the button to start the test. The test may take up to one minute to complete before displaying results.

Source: Speedtest.net

f. Internet speeds sometimes can vary with the time of day or day of the week. Repeat the previous steps to test your Internet speed at various times throughout the day, as well as on weekdays and weekends.
g. If you have any concerns regarding your Internet speed, contact your Internet access provider.

Exercises

1. What is the speed of the Internet connection on the computer or mobile device you currently are using?
2. Test your Internet speed while other computers and mobile devices also are using the Internet connection. How do the results vary from when your other devices are turned off?
3. Do you see differences in the Internet speed when you test it during the day versus at night? If so, what might explain these differences in speed?

✳ Internet Research

The Internet Research exercises broaden your understanding of chapter concepts by requiring that you search for information on the web.

Instructions: Use a search engine or another search tool to locate the information requested or answers to questions presented in the exercises. Describe your findings, along with the search term(s) you used and your web source(s), in the format requested by your instructor (brief report, presentation, discussion, blog post, video, or other means).

❶ Making Use of the Web

Blogs and Wikis Writers can publish their views and share their interests using blogs, as you learned in Chapter 2. The blogosphere began as an easy way for individuals to express their opinions on the web. Today, this communications vehicle has become a powerful tool for individuals, groups, and corporations to promote their ideas and to advertise their products. Individuals easily may set up a blog free or for a fee, and they do not need to have knowledge of web design or programming.

Wikis are collaborative websites. As discussed in Chapter 2, users can develop, modify, and delete content on these public or private websites. This information can include articles, documents, photos, and videos.

(a) Visit two blogging websites. What steps are required to start a blog? Does the website have monthly fees? Do storage limitations exist? What options are available to customize the design? Can products or services be sold or advertised? If you were to set up a blog, which topics would you cover? Could you assign your own domain name to your blog?

(b) Visit two reference wikis. Which subjects are featured? Which organizations host the websites? How are the wikis funded? Are they public or private? Who may edit the content? What procedure is used to add, modify, or delete information?

❷ Social Media 🔖

Using social media can be an excellent opportunity to unite with people who share similar interests. In some cases, local groups form for members to improve themselves and their communities. Dog owners, runners, photographers, entrepreneurs, parents, and travelers are among the thousands of groups with members who met online. In addition, at least five percent of singles in the United States subscribe to at least one of the 1,400 dating websites. Online dating can offer a safe opportunity to meet a variety of people if some practical advice is followed. Reputable dating services keep information confidential and have many members. Some have niche dating demographics, such as age, professions, religion, cultural interests, or geographical regions, and members can search for matches with desired criteria.

Search at least two online dating websites for information about these services. How many members do they have? What is the cost to join? What are the monthly membership fees? What claims do their privacy statements make about not disclosing personal information? What policies are in place to report members who have acted inappropriately?

❸ Search Sleuth

(1) What IEEE document number establishes standards for wireless local networks (WLAN)? In what year was the standard first released? (2) One defining trait of coax cable is characteristic impedance. What is characteristic impedance and how is it typically used in CATV networks? (3) Which computer company used a token ring network in the 1980s and eventually was sold to HP in 1989? (4) The term, datagram, is associated with what type of network? (5) What are the three frequency bands used for wireless LAN? (6) According to the Bluetooth standard, how

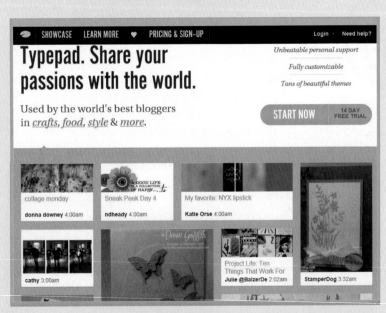

Source: Typepad, Inc.

STUDENT ASSIGNMENTS

© Fotolia

many devices does that network protocol support? (7) Which company developed the first commercial modem for computers? In what year was it sold? What was this modem's data rate? (8) What device did Dennis C. Hayes invent in 1977? (9) What type of wireless network does not rely on routers or access points? (10) What is the origin of the Bluetooth name?

4 Green Computing

Facebook and Google are among the companies building server farms outside the United States. Facebook's facility in northern Sweden will consume the same amount of energy that 16,000 homes would use in one year, and it will cover the area of three football fields. The brisk outside air, which averages 36.5 degrees (2 degrees Celsius), will cool the plant. Google's plans are to place its data centers on barges at sea. Machines will harness the energy from ocean waves and convert it to electricity, which will run the servers and cool the farms. Google can add more wave energy converting machines when electricity demand increases.

Locate websites and articles that provide information about Facebook's and Google's data center plans. How do their server farms lower electricity costs and manage power? Why did they decide to place the server farms in these specific locations? What are possible ecological or environmental changes that might occur when the data centers are running?

5 Security

The Social Media exercise on the previous page discusses online dating websites. According to some of these dating services, 20 percent of people currently in committed relationships met online. While using these dating websites may result in a positive experience, the Better Business Bureau and other consumer-oriented organizations receive thousands of complaints each year about these services. Security experts caution online dating members to follow safe practices, including the following:

- Compose a profile carefully, and be certain it reflects the image you want to portray. Do not post your full name, phone number, or home or work location.
- Use the service's messaging system before sending email or text messages or having a phone conversation.

- When arranging a first date, meet in a safe location, such as a restaurant during a busy time of the day. Share your plans with a friend, and keep a mobile phone handy.
- Trust your instincts. If you feel uncomfortable or threatened, leave the location and call a friend.

Visit at least two websites providing advice for online dating members. What guidance is provided in addition to the four safe practices above? What behaviors may signal potentially dangerous situations? Where can members verify other members' reputations? How can members report fraud and inappropriate behavior?

6 Ethics in Action

Consumers may be unaware of how they become targeted to receive marketing messages. For example, when they conduct online searches to locate details about a specific new vehicle they would like to purchase, they soon may receive unsolicited advertisements for other vehicles. When people visit some websites, their IP address, browser software, operating system, date, time, and viewing habits are tracked and recorded along with their wish lists and purchase histories. These details are collected and shared among advertisers without the computer users' consent.

The Center for Digital Democracy (CDD) estimates interactive marketing and advertising will become a $106 billion industry by 2016. The CDD states that these targeted advertisements and user profiles can constitute an invasion of privacy and can be harmful to one's health, especially when unhealthy foods and beverages are marketed to children. This organization helped to pass the Children's Online Privacy Protection Act (COPPA) in 1998 and is working to enact new laws to protect online privacy.

Visit the CDD website and other websites discussing online ads and privacy concerns. How are the CDD and other organizations working to protect consumers from being exploited by digital advertisers? What concerns do they express about how Facebook "likes" reveal personal details to marketers? What steps can users take to avoid sharing personal data with marketers? Have you received advertisements for cars, vacation destinations, political parties, nonprofit organizations, or other products or groups after visiting particular websites?

✷ Problem Solving

The Problem Solving exercises extend your knowledge of chapter concepts by seeking solutions to practical problems with technology that you may encounter at home, school, work, or with nonprofit organizations. The Collaboration exercise should be completed with a team.

🖥 Challenge yourself with additional Problem Solving exercises by navigating to this book's Problem Solving resource on Computer Concepts CourseMate.

Instructions: You often can solve problems with technology in multiple ways. Determine a solution to the problems in these exercises by using one or more resources available to you (such as a computer or mobile device, articles on the web or in print, blogs, podcasts, videos, television, user guides, other individuals, electronics or computer stores, etc.). Describe your solution, along with the resource(s) used, in the format requested by your instructor (brief report, presentation, discussion, blog post, video, or other means).

Personal

1. **File Sharing Problems** You have configured your operating system to share some files with your parents using your home network, but your parents have informed you that they are unable to access the files on your computer. What are your next steps?

2. **Cannot Connect to Hot Spot** You are sitting in a fast food restaurant that offers free Wi-Fi. When you search for available hot spots using your computer, the restaurant's hot spot does not appear in the computer's list of wireless networks. What are your next steps?

3. **Wireless Connection Troubles** Your laptop normally connects to your home wireless network automatically, but recently you have to connect to the network manually by selecting the SSID and entering the network's password. Why might this be happening?

4. **Slow Internet Connection** Your Internet speed has suffered a sharp decline in performance recently. You have not added any computers or mobile devices to your house that might be accessing the network, and you are puzzled by the sudden performance problems. What might be the problem?

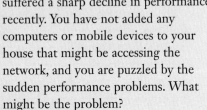
© artjazz / Shutterstock.com;
© Cengage Learning

5. **Wireless Network Coverage** You installed a new wireless network in your house. You notice that you sometimes have trouble connecting to the network from certain locations in the house, but other times you can connect from the same location without issue. What might be causing the problem?

Professional

6. **Broken Network Cable** The cable connecting your laptop to your work's network keeps falling out when you move the laptop or accidentally bump it with your hand. What steps can you take to correct this issue?

7. **Cannot Sign In** Your corporate network requires you to sign in with a user name and password as soon as your computer or mobile device connects. After entering your user name and password, the computer still does not connect to the network. What might be the problem?

8. **Too Many Networks** While attempting to connect to the wireless network at your job, you notice that five different wireless networks are available. How can you determine to which network you should connect?

9. **No Network Connection** You have unpacked, installed, and turned on a new computer at your desk. When the operating system starts and you run the browser to display a webpage, you receive an error message stating that you are not connected to the Internet. You check the network interface card on the back of the computer and although the cable is plugged in, the lights next to the port are not flashing. What are your next steps?

10. **Connecting Corporate Email** You are visiting your company's satellite office for the day and realize that you do not have the necessary information to connect to their wireless network. Your boss has asked you to check your email throughout the day, so it is important that you connect to the Internet. What are your next steps?

Collaboration

11. **Technology in Agriculture** Your employer owns hundreds of acres of orange groves and realizes labor and utility costs can be decreased by installing automated systems to manage the property. As a digitally literate employee of the organization, your supervisor asks you to research automated systems that can help decrease expenses. Form a team of three people to research automated agricultural solutions. One team member should research automated irrigation systems that water the trees only as needed. Another team member should research solutions that can keep the trees healthy and free from pests, and the third team member should create a list of reasons why these automated systems can decrease costs, bolster efficiency, and increase profit. Compile your findings and submit them to your instructor.

The Critical Thinking exercises challenge your assessment and decision-making skills by presenting real-world situations associated with chapter concepts. The Collaboration exercise should be completed with a team.

Critical Thinking

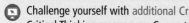 Challenge yourself with additional Critical Thinking exercises by navigating to this book's Critical Thinking resource on Computer Concepts CourseMate.

Instructions: Evaluate the situations below, using personal experiences and one or more resources available to you (such as articles on the web or in print, blogs, podcasts, videos, television, user guides, other individuals, electronics or computer stores, etc.). Perform the tasks requested in each exercise and share your deliverables in the format requested by your instructor (brief report, presentation, discussion, blog post, video, or other means).

1. Class Discussion

Transmission Media   You work as an intern in the IT department for a local newspaper. The newspaper's management team recently approved a budget for redesigning the interior of its century-old building as part of an urban rehabilitation project. Because the employees at the newspaper more often use mobile devices and laptops than desktops, the newspaper plans to set up a wireless LAN. Your boss has asked you to prepare information that summarizes the issues surrounding wireless network setup. He requested that you include the following information: What hardware is required for a wireless network? Could the thick walls in the building present a problem? If so, how can the issue be resolved? Does a wireless network present any health hazards? What security concerns exist for a wireless network? What advantages does a wireless network have over a wired network for the newspaper's needs?

2. Research and Share

Wireless Networking Standards   Several networking standards exist for wireless networks, including 802.11a, 802.11b, 802.11g, 802.11n, 802.11ac, and 802.11ad. You want to install a wireless network in your house and want to ensure that you choose the standard that best meets your needs. Use the web to research the various wireless networking standards and answer the following questions: Which was the first developed standard? Are any of the standards more susceptible to interference from other wireless devices in your home, such as alarm systems and mobile phones? Which standard is the fastest? Is the fastest standard always the best, or do other factors on your wireless network or on the Internet affect performance? Is equipment to support one standard more expensive than the equipment that supports the other standards? Which would you recommend? Why? Address the answers to those questions, as well as any other information you find pertinent. Compile your findings.

3. Case Study

Farmers' Market   You are the new manager for a group of organic farmers who have a weekly market in season. The market's office equipment consists of a few laptops and tablets, a printer, and several smartphones. The board of directors has asked you to investigate how the market might use Bluetooth technology in its offices. Review the uses of Bluetooth technology listed in Mini Feature 10-1 on page 428. Which uses might apply to the market? Can you think of other ways the market might use Bluetooth technology? What are the advantages to using Bluetooth technology? Use the web to find industry experts' recommendations for Bluetooth use in a small office. What other wireless technologies might the market's office use? Examine issues relating to bandwidth, speed, and reliability. What security concerns exist? Would you recommend the market use Bluetooth in its offices? Why or why not? Should the market replace its LAN with Bluetooth? Why or why not? Compile your findings.

© Fotolia

Collaboration

4. **Network Topologies**   You are a network administrator for a small security firm. The company's main office includes 20 workers, most of whom use laptops. This year, the company plans to upgrade the network. The company asks your team to compare different network topologies. Form a three-member team and assign each member a network topology (star, bus, or ring). Each member should use the web to develop a feature/benefit analysis of the network topology and answer the following questions: What hardware do you need? What is the initial cost of setting up that type of network? Is the network easy to install and maintain? Why or why not? What is the failure rate of the network? Can you easily add or remove devices to or from the network? What security concerns exist? What are advantages and disadvantages? Would you recommend the topology for a LAN? Why or why not? As a team, compile your findings and share your recommendation with the class.

✳ Beyond the Book

The Beyond the Book exercises expand your understanding of chapter concepts by requiring research.

Access premium content by visiting Computer Concepts CourseMate. If you have a Computer Concepts CourseMate access code, you can reinforce and extend your learning with MindTap Reader, practice tests, video, and other premium content for Discovering Computers. To sign in to Computer Concepts CourseMate at www.cengagebrain.com, you first must create a student account and then register this book, as described at www.cengage.com/ct/studentdownload.

Part 1 Instructions: Use the web or e-book to perform the task identified for each book element below. Describe your findings, along with the search term(s) you used and your web source(s), if appropriate, in the format requested by your instructor (brief report, presentation, discussion, blog post, video, or other means).

1. **Animation** 📄 Review the animation associated with this chapter and then answer the question(s) it poses (441). What search term would you use to learn more about a specific segment of the animation?

2. **Consider This** Select a Consider This in this chapter (419, 422, 423, 425, 427, 431, 433, 435, 438, 450) and find a recent article that elaborates on the topic. What information did you find that was not presented in this book or e-book?

3. **Drag-and-Drop Figures** 📄 Complete the Drag-and-Drop Figure activities associated with this chapter (430, 433, 442, 444, 445). What did you learn from these activities?

4. **Ethics & Issues** Select an Ethics & Issues in this chapter (421, 435, 443, 450) and find a recent article that supports one view presented. Does the article change your opinion about the topic? Why or why not?

5. **Facebook & Twitter** Review a recent Discovering Computers Facebook post or Twitter Tweet and read the referenced article(s). What did you learn from the article?

6. **High-Tech Talk** 📄 Locate an article that discusses topics related to The OSI Reference Model. Would you recommend the article you found? Why or why not?

7. **How To** Select a How To in this chapter (436, 437, 440, 445) and find a recent article that elaborates on the topic. Who would benefit from the content of this article? Why?

8. **Innovative Computing** 📄 Locate two additional facts about future Bluetooth uses or geocaching. Do your findings change your opinion about the future of this innovation? Why or why not?

9. **Internet Research** Use the search term in an Internet Research (418, 422, 427, 431, 437, 440) to answer the question posed in the element. What other search term could you use to answer the question?

10. **Mini Features** Locate an article that discusses topics related to one of the mini features in this chapter (428, 431, 440). Do you feel that the article is appropriate for this course? Why or why not?

11. **Secure IT** Select a Secure IT in this chapter (427, 429, 440, 446) and find a recent article about the topic that you find interesting. How can you relate the content of the article to your everyday life?

12. **Technology @ Work** Locate three additional, unique usages of technology in the agriculture industry (451). What makes the use of these technologies unique to the agriculture industry?

13. **Technology Innovators** 📄 Locate two additional facts about Robert Metcalfe, Bluetooth inventors Sven Mattisson and Jaap Haartsen, Cisco, and Verizon. Which Technology Innovator impresses you most? Why?

14. **Third-Party Links** 📄 Visit one of the third-party links identified in this chapter (426, 429, 435, 440, 442, 446, 450, 451) and read the article or watch the video associated with the link. Would you share this link on your online social network account? Why or why not?

Part 2 Instructions: Find specific instructions for the exercises below in the e-book or on Computer Concepts CourseMate. Beside each exercise is a brief description of its online content.

1. 📄 **You Review It** Search for and review a video, podcast, or blog post about news about computer networking.

2. 📄 **Windows and Mac** Enhance your understanding and knowledge about using Windows and Mac computers by completing the Connect Your Computer and Mobile Devices via Bluetooth activities.

3. 📄 **Android, iOS, and Windows Phone** Enhance your understanding of mobile devices by completing the Exchange Files over Bluetooth and Exchange Information between Mobile Devices in Close Proximity activities.

4. 📄 **Exploring Computer Careers** Read about a career as a network administrator, search for related employment ads, and then answer related questions.

5. 📄 **App Adventure** Find your way and see what is nearby using mapping apps on your smartphone or tablet.

Information and Data Management

Organizing, Verifying, Maintaining, and Accessing

11

Users interact with a variety of data and information daily.

"I check my grades on the school's portal. At home, I track my expenses and manage a personal budget. On weekends, I assist my neighbor, who owns a small manufacturing business, with billing her customers. What more could I learn about managing data and information?"

True, you may be familiar with some of the material in this chapter, but do you know . . .

Whether you should use a credit monitoring service?

What steps to take if your identity is stolen?

How to use a research database?

Which web databases you have used?

How to import data from a spreadsheet into a database?

Why data validation is important?

How technology is used in sports?

Which database management system would be best suited to your needs?

What the difference is between an attribute and a column?

Where you would find a knowledge base and inference rules?

When you would use SQL?

What is meant by the term, normalization?

Why enterprises use ERP?

When you might interact with a CRM information system?

For these answers and to discover much more information essential to this course, read this chapter and visit the associated Computer Concepts CourseMate at www.cengagebrain.com.

✓ Objectives

After completing this chapter, you will be able to:

1 Define the term, database, and explain how a database interacts with data and information

2 Define the term, data integrity, and describe the qualities of valuable information

3 Differentiate among a character, field, record, and data file

4 Describe file maintenance techniques (adding records, modifying records, and deleting records) and validation techniques

5 Differentiate between the file processing approach and the database approach

6 Discuss functions common to most database management systems: data dictionary, file retrieval and maintenance, data security, and backup and recovery

7 Describe characteristics of relational, object-oriented, and multidimensional databases

8 Discuss web databases

9 Identify database design guidelines and understand the responsibilities of database analysts and administrators

10 Describe various information systems used in an enterprise

Databases, Data, and Information

As presented in Chapter 4, a **database** is a collection of data organized in a manner that allows access, retrieval, and use of that data. As discussed in previous chapters, data is a collection of unprocessed items, which can include text, numbers, images, audio, and video. Information is processed data; that is, it is organized, meaningful, and useful.

Computers process data in a database to generate information for users. A database at a school, for example, contains data about its students and classes. When a student is admitted to a school, an admissions department specialist enters several data items about the student into a form or an application, which adds the data to a database. The specialist also uses a digital camera to take a photo of the new student. This photo, along with the other entered data, is stored in a database on a server's hard drive. A computer at the school then processes the new student data, assigns an ID number to the student, sends advising appointment information to a printer, and sends student ID card information to an ID card printer (Figure 11-1). The student ID is encoded on a magnetic stripe on the back of the ID card.

With **database software**, often called a **database management system (DBMS)**, users create a computerized database; add, modify, and delete data in the database; sort and retrieve data from the database; and create forms and reports from the data in the database.

How a School's Admissions Department Might Process New Student Data into Information

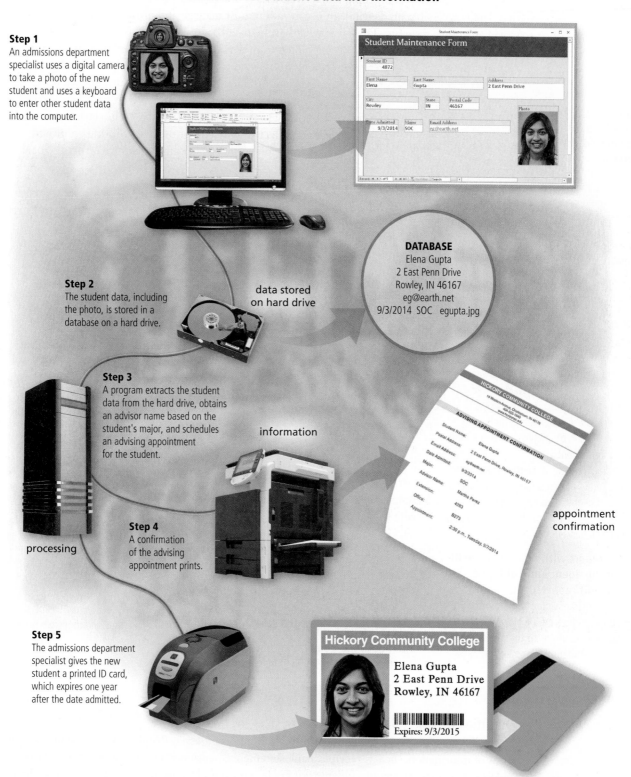

Step 1
An admissions department specialist uses a digital camera to take a photo of the new student and uses a keyboard to enter other student data into the computer.

Step 2
The student data, including the photo, is stored in a database on a hard drive.

data stored on hard drive

DATABASE
Elena Gupta
2 East Penn Drive
Rowley, IN 46167
eg@earth.net
9/3/2014 SOC egupta.jpg

Step 3
A program extracts the student data from the hard drive, obtains an advisor name based on the student's major, and schedules an advising appointment for the student.

information

processing

Step 4
A confirmation of the advising appointment prints.

appointment confirmation

Step 5
The admissions department specialist gives the new student a printed ID card, which expires one year after the date admitted.

student ID encoded on magnetic stripe

Figure 11-1 This figure shows how a school's admissions department might process new student data into information.

Data Integrity

Most organizations and people realize that data is one of their more valuable assets. To ensure that data is accessible on demand, an organization must manage and protect its data just as it would any other resource. Thus, it is vital that the data has integrity and is kept secure. For example, data in a database often is encrypted to prevent unauthorized users from reading its contents, and its access is restricted to only those who need to process the data. Read Secure IT 11-1 for steps to take if you become a victim of identity theft due to your personal data becoming unsecure.

For a computer to produce correct information from data in a database, the data that is entered must have integrity. *Data integrity* reflects the quality of the data. Storing an invalid number of credit hours for a course is an example of incorrect data. The more errors the data contains, the lower its integrity.

Data integrity is important because computers and people use information to make decisions and take actions. When you register for classes and pay with a credit card, a process begins that charges an amount to your credit card. If the value of the per-credit fee is not correct in the school's database, an incorrect amount will be billed to your credit card. This type of error costs both you and the registration specialist extra time and effort to remedy.

 BTW

GIGO

Garbage in, garbage out (GIGO) is a technology phrase that points out the accuracy of output depends on the accuracy of the input. If incorrect data is entered into a computer (garbage in), the computer will produce incorrect information (garbage out).

SECURE IT 11-1

Recovering from Identity Theft

Identity theft is the complaint most often reported to the Federal Trade Commission (FTC), with nearly 4 percent of Americans falling victim to this crime. Fraud related to government documents and benefits is the highest category of identity theft, with credit card, phone or utilities, and bank fraud declining in frequency.

On average, victims of identity theft spend 25 hours settling the resulting issues. Experts recommend people who have experienced identity theft should follow this advice as part of their resolution efforts:

• **File a report with a national credit reporting agency and obtain a free credit report.** Contact Experian, Equifax, or TransUnion to help prevent credit accounts from being opened in your name. (Refer to the How To: Your Turn student assignment on page 503 for details on contacting these

agencies.) One agency should report the theft to the other two companies, but you might want to contact all three to be certain the fraud has been noted. Once you file a fraud alert, you are entitled to receive a free credit report. Wait at least 30 days from the theft to obtain the report, however, because creditors may report activity on a monthly basis and your most current report may not have current information.

• **Obtain an FTC affidavit and file it with law enforcement agencies.** The FTC's Identity Theft Victim's Complaint and Affidavit is accepted as a proof of your identity. Download the form from the FTC's website and then file it with the police. The form also can be used to dispute claims with creditors.

• **Report Internet crime to the Internet Crime Complaint Center.** Report stolen finances or identities and

other cybercrime to the Internet Crime Complaint Center. This organization is a partnership between the Federal Bureau of Investigation and the National White Collar Crime Center.

• **Keep records of your actions.** Make a journal recording the names of people you called, phone numbers, dates, and correspondence sent.

• **Review financial accounts.** Look for unusual activity and check to see if any accounts were opened recently. Continue reviewing the accounts even if you do not see any questionable transactions.

✳ Do you know someone who has been a victim of identity theft? If so, which type of fraud occurred? What activity did this person take to report this crime and to restore personal records and accounts?

Qualities of Valuable Information

The information that data generates also is an important asset. People make decisions using all types of information, such as receipts, bank statements, pension plan summaries, stock analyses, and credit reports. At school, students use grade reports and transcripts to make decisions. In a business, managers make decisions based on sales trends, competitors' products and services, and production processes.

To assist with sound decision making, information must have value. For it to be valuable, information should be accurate, verifiable, timely, organized, accessible, useful, and cost effective.

- *Accurate information* is error free. Inaccurate information can lead to incorrect decisions. For example, consumers assume their credit reports are accurate. If your credit report incorrectly shows past-due payments, a bank may not lend you money for a vehicle or a house. Read Secure IT 11-2 to learn how you can monitor information in your credit report.
- *Verifiable information* can be proven as correct or incorrect. For example, security personnel at an airport usually request some type of photo identification to verify that you are the person named on the ticket.
- *Timely information* has an age suited to its use. A decision to build additional schools in a particular district should be based on the most recent census report — not on one that is 10 years old. Most information loses value with time. Some information, however, such as information about trends, gains value as time passes and more information is obtained. For example, your transcript gains value as you take more classes.
- *Organized information* is arranged to suit the needs and requirements of the decision maker. Two different people may need the same information presented in a different manner. For example, an inventory manager may want an inventory report to list out-of-stock items first. The purchasing agent, instead, wants the report alphabetized by vendor.
- *Accessible information* is available when the decision maker needs it. Having to wait for information may delay an important decision. For example, a sales manager cannot decide which sales representative deserves the award for highest annual sales if the December sales have not been entered in the database yet.
- *Useful information* has meaning to the person who receives it. Most information is important only to certain people or groups of people. Always consider the audience when collecting and reporting information. Avoid distributing useless information. For example, an announcement of an alumni association meeting is not useful to students who have not graduated yet.
- *Cost-effective information* should provide more value than it costs to produce. An organization occasionally should review the information it produces to determine if it still is cost effective to produce. Sometimes, it is not easy to place a value on information. For this reason, some organizations create information only on demand, that is, as people request it, instead of on a regular basis. Many make information available online so that users can access it as they need it. For example, printing a company directory could be quite costly. Instead, employees can access the directory when they need to review it. This also ensures they are accessing the latest information.

 SECURE IT 11-2

 Monitoring Credit Reports

Millions of consumers pay credit monitoring services to help protect against identity theft and unauthorized charges. Each of the three national credit reporting agencies and many credit card companies provide this service, which can cost more than $240 per year. The companies send messages to the subscribers when unusual activity is detected on a credit report to alert consumers to possible identity theft. While the services may offer convenience and peace of mind to consumers, some security experts criticize the practices as

being expensive and incomplete because the reports are made after the theft has occurred.

The monitoring services may be helpful for people who have been identity theft victims, have large balances in savings and checking accounts, travel frequently, or fail to check their bank statements and credit reports regularly. Consumer watchdog organizations, in contrast, state that people can monitor their own credit at no charge and may have this service already through their homeowner's insurance or credit card accounts. Consumers also can

contact the three national credit bureaus' fraud departments and request a fraud alert be placed on their accounts. This free service requires lenders to contact the account owners if a new request for credit is submitted. This fraud alert must be renewed every 90 days. For more information about monitoring your credit, read the How To: Your Turn student assignment on page 503.

Do you subscribe to a credit monitoring service? If so, do you think you could perform the monitoring yourself at no charge?

The Hierarchy of Data

Data is organized in layers. Information technology (IT) professionals classify data in a hierarchy. Each higher level of data consists of one or more items from the lower level. For example, a student has an address, and an address consists of letters and numeric characters. Depending on the application and the user, different terms describe the various levels of the hierarchy.

As shown in Figure 11-2, a database contains data files (sometimes called tables), a data file contains records, a record contains fields, and a field is composed of one or more characters. This sample School database contains four data files: Student, Instructor, Schedule of Classes, and Student Schedule. The Student file contains records about enrolled students. The Instructor file contains records about current instructors. The Schedule of Classes file contains records about class offerings in a particular semester, and the Student Schedule file contains records about the classes in which a student is enrolled for a given semester. Each field in a record contains many characteristics, one of which is the field size.

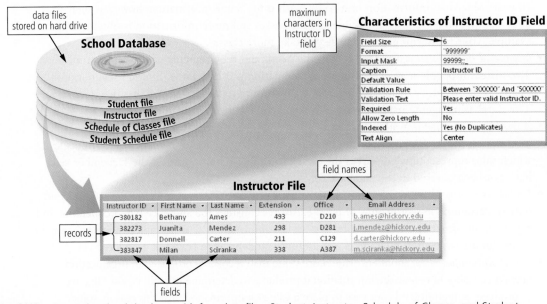

Figure 11-2 A sample school database with four data files: Student, Instructor, Schedule of Classes, and Student Schedule. The sample Instructor file contains four records. Each record contains six fields. The Instructor ID field can contain a maximum of six characters (bytes).
© Cengage Learning; Source: Microsoft

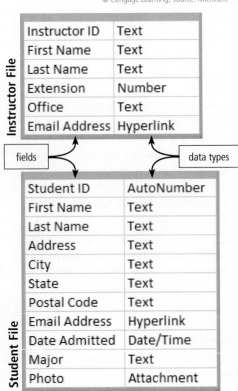

Figure 11-3 Data types of fields in the Instructor and Student files.
© Cengage Learning

Characters As discussed in Chapter 6, a bit is the smallest unit of data the computer can process. Eight bits grouped together in a unit constitute a byte. In the ASCII coding scheme, each byte represents a single **character**, which can be a number (4), letter (R), space, punctuation mark (?), or other symbol (&).

Fields A **field** is a combination of one or more related characters or bytes and is the smallest unit of data a user accesses. A **field name** uniquely identifies each field. When searching for data in a database, you often specify the field name. For example, field names for the data in the Instructor file are Instructor ID, First Name, Last Name, Extension, Office, and Email Address.

A database uses a variety of characteristics, such as field size and data type, to define each field. The field size defines the maximum number of characters a field can contain. For example, the Instructor ID field contains 6 characters and thus has a field size of 6 (shown in Figure 11-2).

The **data type** specifies the kind of data a field can contain and how the field is used. Figure 11-3 identifies the data types for fields in the Instructor and Student files.

 **CONSIDER THIS**

What are common data types?

Common data types include the following:

- Text: Letters, numeric characters, or special characters
- Number (also called numeric values): Positive or negative numbers, with or without decimal points
- AutoNumber: Unique number automatically assigned by the DBMS to each added record, which provides a value that identifies the record (such as a student ID)
- Currency: Dollar and cent amounts or numbers containing decimal values
- Date (also called date/time): Month, day, year, and sometimes time
- Memo (also called long text): Lengthy text entries
- Yes/No (also called *Boolean*): Only the values Yes or No (or True or False)
- Hyperlink: Email address or web address that links to a webpage on the Internet or document on a network
- Object (also called *BLOB,* for binary large object): Photo, audio, video, or a document created in other programs or apps, such as word processing or spreadsheet, stored as a sequence of bytes in the database
- Attachment: Document or image that is or apps attached to the field, which can be opened in the program that created the document or image (functions similarly to email attachments)

 **CONSIDER THIS**

Why do some fields that store only numbers have a text data type?

Fields that contain numeric characters whose values will not be used in calculations, such as postal codes or phone numbers, usually are assigned a text data type.

Records A **record** is a group of related fields. For example, a student record includes a set of fields about one student. A **primary key** is a field that uniquely identifies each record in a file. The data in a primary key is unique to a specific record. For example, the Student ID field uniquely identifies each student because no two students can have the same student ID. In some tables, the primary key consists of multiple fields, called a *composite key*. For example, the primary key for the Schedule of Classes file could consist of the fields Semester Code, Class Code, and Class Section, which together would uniquely identify each class listed in a schedule.

Data Files A **data file,** often simply called a file, is a collection of related records stored on a storage medium such as a hard drive or optical disc. A Student file at a school might consist of thousands of individual student records. Each student record in the file contains the same fields. Each field, however, contains different data. Figure 11-4 shows a small sample Student file that contains four student records, each with eleven fields. A database includes a group of related data files.

Sample Student File

Student ID	First Name	Last Name	Address	City	State	Postal Code	Email Address	Date Admitted	Major	Photo
2295	Milton	Brewer	54 Lucy Court	Charlestown	IN	46176		6/10/2013	EE	mbrewer.jpg
3876	Louella	Drake	33 Timmons Place	Bonner	IN	45208	lou@world.com	8/9/2013	BIO	ldrake.jpg
3928	Adelbert	Ruiz	99 Tenth Street	Sheldon	IN	46033		10/8/2013	CT	aruiz.jpg
2872	Benjamin	Tu	2204 Elm Court	Rowley	IN	46167	tu@indi.net	9/14/2014	GEN	btu.jpg

records   key field   fields

CONSIDER THIS

Would a Student file store multiple email addresses?

In addition to personal email addresses as shown in Figure 11-4 on the previous page, a Student file also would store a school-generated email address and a business address. It also probably would store multiple phone numbers, such as home, mobile, and work.

Maintaining Data

File maintenance refers to the procedures that keep data current. File maintenance includes adding records to, modifying records in, and deleting records from a file. Read Ethics & Issues 11-1 to consider how organizations use data they collect.

 ETHICS & ISSUES 11-1

Should Consumers Know How Data Collected about Them Will Be Used?

Function creep occurs when a company uses the technology intended for one purpose for another. One example of function creep is when companies sell customer data collected through sales transactions to businesses that perform marketing surveys or generate credit reports. Privacy advocates are concerned about any use of personal data, including library checkouts, medical records, and more, for purposes other than what the customer intended.

Social networking sites and search engines often use activity such as posts, pages viewed, and search terms to suggest

sponsored ads. Online vendors argue that the data enables them to provide custom product suggestions. Companies use stored data to streamline ordering processes and to send targeted marketing messages.

Some customers acknowledge that a company has the right to use data to enhance the customers' experience or to make business decisions. Others would like more control over their data. The FTC Fair Information Practice Principles attempt to address data privacy concerns. These principles state that companies must inform customers of their data use and must allow customers to provide or deny consent.

You can attempt to protect your data using a variety of techniques. Browsers often include settings that enable you to limit data tracking. Read privacy policies before you purchase an item from an online vendor, or use a social networking site that informs you of potential ways your data may be used.

Have you experienced examples of a website using your personal data? For what purpose? Do you read a company's data privacy policy before using their website or service? Why or why not? Should the government enforce data privacy laws? Why or why not?

Adding Records   Users add new records to a file when they obtain new data. If a new student is admitted to the school, an admissions department specialist adds a new record to the Student file. The process required to add this record to the file might include the following steps:

1. An admissions department specialist uses the database management system (DBMS) to display a Student Maintenance Form that provides access to the Student file. The specialist taps or clicks the New button to begin the process of adding a record to the Student file.
2. The specialist fills in the fields of the student record with data (except for the student ID, which automatically is assigned by the DBMS). In this example, the data entered is kept to a minimum.
3. The specialist takes a photo of the student using a digital camera. The DBMS stores this picture as an attachment to the Student file and prints it on a student ID card.
4. The admissions department specialist verifies the data on the screen and then instructs the DBMS to add the new student record to the Student file. The operating system determines where to write the record on the storage media. In some cases, it writes the new record at the end of the file. In other cases, such as illustrated in Figure 11-5 on the next page, it writes the new record for Elena Gupta between existing records in the file.

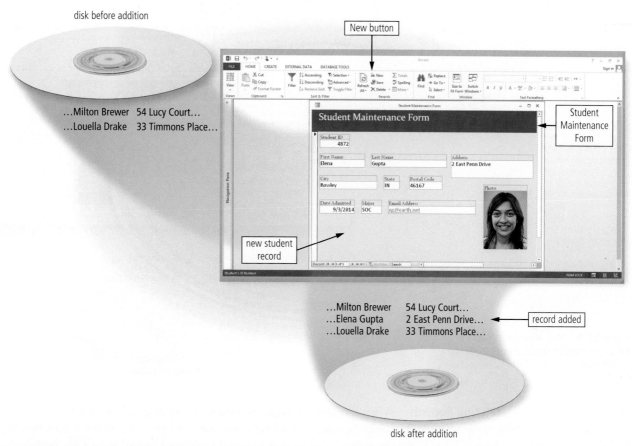

Figure 11-5   Using the Student Maintenance Form, an admissions department specialist adds a new student record for Elena Gupta.
© Warren Goldswain / Shutterstock.com; © Cengage Learning; Source: Microsoft

Modifying Records   Generally, users modify a record in a file for two reasons: (1) to correct inaccurate data or (2) to update old data with new data.

Suppose, for example, that Elena Gupta moves from 2 East Penn Drive to 76 Ash Street. The process to change the address and update Elena Gupta's record might include the following steps:

1. The admissions department specialist displays the Student Maintenance Form.
2. If Elena Gupta requests the change in person, she might provide her student ID card to the specialist. The specialist would swipe the ID card through a magnetic card reader to obtain Elena's student ID. The DBMS looks for the record matching her student ID and displays her student record on the screen. If Elena did not have her ID card or was not there in person to present it, the specialist could enter Elena's student ID number — if Elena knew it. Otherwise, the specialist could enter Gupta in the Last Name field, which would cause the DBMS to retrieve all students with that same last name. The specialist then would select Elena's first name to instruct the DBMS retrieve her student information. If multiple students have the name, Elena Gupta, the DBMS will display all matching records. The specialist then would locate the record in the list that contains this Elena's information.
3. The DBMS displays data about Elena Gupta so that the specialist can confirm the correct student record is displayed.
4. The specialist enters the new street address, 76 Ash Street.
5. The admissions department specialist verifies the data on the screen and then, if required, instructs the DBMS to modify the record in the Student file on the drive (Figure 11-6 on the next page).

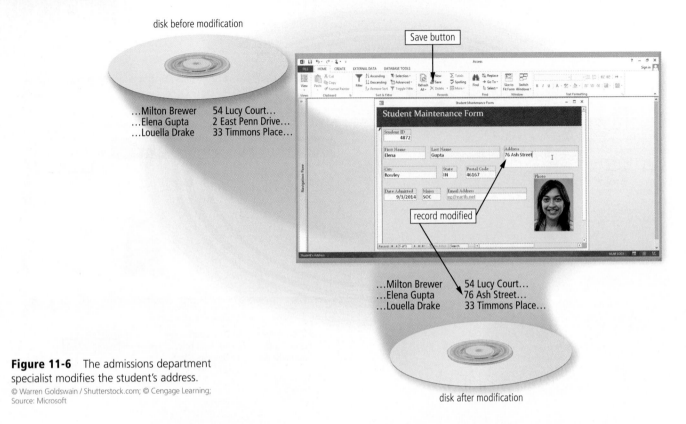

Figure 11-6 The admissions department specialist modifies the student's address.
© Warren Goldswain / Shutterstock.com; © Cengage Learning;
Source: Microsoft

Deleting Records   When a record no longer is needed, a user deletes it from a file. Assume a student named Benjamin Tu was accepted for admission but later notified the school that he chose to attend another college. The process required to delete a record from a file includes the following steps:

1. The admissions department specialist displays the Student Maintenance Form.
2. The specialist displays Benjamin Tu's student record on the screen.
3. The specialist confirms the correct student record is displayed. Then, the specialist instructs the DBMS to delete the record from the Student file and then, if required, saves the modified file.

DBMSs use a variety of techniques to manage deleted records. Sometimes, the DBMS removes the record from the file immediately, which means the deleted record cannot be restored. Other times, the record is flagged, or marked, so that the DBMS will not process it again. In this case, the DBMS places an asterisk (*) or some other character at the beginning of the record to indicate that it was deleted (Figure 11-7).

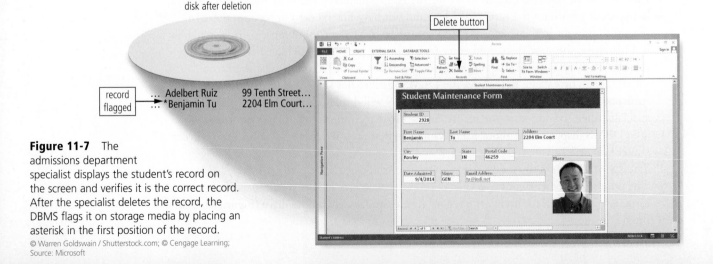

Figure 11-7 The admissions department specialist displays the student's record on the screen and verifies it is the correct record. After the specialist deletes the record, the DBMS flags it on storage media by placing an asterisk in the first position of the record.
© Warren Goldswain / Shutterstock.com; © Cengage Learning;
Source: Microsoft

DBMSs that maintain inactive data for an extended period commonly flag records. For example, a school might flag inactive students. When a DBMS flags a deleted record, the record remains physically on the drive. The record, however, is deleted logically because the DBMS will not process it. DBMSs will ignore flagged records unless an instruction is issued to process them.

 CONSIDER THIS

Can you permanently delete flagged records?
From time to time, users should run a program that removes flagged records and reorganizes current records. For example, the school may remove from the drive the names of applicants who chose to attend other schools instead. Deleting unneeded records reduces the size of files, thereby freeing up storage space.

Validating Data

Validation is the process of comparing data with a set of rules or values to determine if the data is correct. Many programs perform a validity check that analyzes data, either as you enter the data or after you enter it, to help ensure that it is correct. For instance, when an admissions department specialist adds or modifies data in a student record, the DBMS tests the entered data.

With an email address, you would expect to see a user name, followed by an at symbol (@), followed by a domain name (i.e., earth.net). For example, a valid email address is eg@earth.net. An entry of egearth.net is not a valid email address because it is missing the at symbol. If the data fails a validity check, the computer either should not allow the invalid data to be entered, or it should display an error message that instructs the user to enter the data again. Validity checks, sometimes called validation rules, reduce data entry errors and thus enhance the data's integrity.

Alphabetic/Numeric Check An *alphabetic check* ensures that users enter only alphabetic data into a field. A *numeric check* ensures that users enter only numeric data into a field. For example, data in a First Name field should contain only characters from the alphabet. Data in a Current Enrollment field should contain numbers.

Range Check A *range check* determines whether a number is within a specified range. Assume the lowest per credit hour fee at the school is $75.00 and the highest is $370.75. A range check for the Credit Hour Fee field ensures it is a value between $75.00 and $370.75.

Consistency Check A *consistency check* tests the data in two or more associated fields to ensure that the relationship is logical and their data is in the correct format. For example, the value in a Date Admitted field cannot occur earlier in time than a value in a Birth Date field.

Completeness Check A *completeness check* verifies that a required field contains data. For example, some fields cannot be left blank; others require a minimum number of characters. One completeness check can ensure that data exists in a Last Name field. Another can ensure that a day, month, and year are included in a Birth Date field.

Check Digit A *check digit* is a number(s) or character(s) that is appended to or inserted in a primary key value. A check digit often confirms the accuracy of a primary key value. Bank account, credit card, and other identification numbers often include one or more check digits.

 Internet Research
How do you know if a credit card number is valid?
Search for: luhn algorithm

 CONSIDER THIS

How are check digits calculated?
A program determines the check digit by applying a formula to the numbers in the primary key value. An oversimplified illustration of a check digit formula is to add the numbers in the primary key. For example, if the primary key is 1367, this formula would add these numbers (1 + 3 + 6 + 7) for a sum of 17. Next, the formula would add the numbers in the result (1 + 7) to generate a check digit of 8. The primary key then is 13678.

When a data entry specialist enters the primary key of 13678, for example, to look up an existing record, the program performs the calculation described above to determine whether the check digit is valid. If the specialist enters an incorrect primary key, such as 13778, the check digit entered (8) will not match the computed check digit (9). In this case, the program displays an error message that instructs the user to enter the primary key value again.

Other Checks DBMSs that include the hyperlink and attachment data types can perform validity checks on data entered in those fields. Hyperlink entries (web addresses and email addresses) can be tested to ensure that the address follows the correct format. Similarly, an attachment entry can be validated by confirming that the file exists.

 CONSIDER THIS

If a web address or email address is in the correct format, does that guarantee that the link works or that the address exists?
No. The validation check simply verifies that the address follows the correct format. It is possible that the link may not work or that the address is not an actual address.

Table 11-1 illustrates some of the validity checks just discussed and shows valid data that passes the check and invalid data that fails the check.

 Table 11-1   Sample Valid and Invalid Data

Validity Check	Field(s) Being Checked	Valid Data	Invalid Data
Alphabetic Check	First Name	Karen	Ka24n
Numeric Check	Current Enrollment	24	s8q
Range Check	Per Credit Hour Fee	$220.25	$2,120.00
Consistency Check	Date Admitted and Birth Date	9/19/2014 8/27/1992	9/19/2014 8/27/2015
Completeness Check	Last Name	Gupta	
Other Check	Email Address	eg@earth.net	egearth.net

 NOW YOU KNOW

Be sure you understand the material presented in the section titled Databases, Data, and Information, as it relates to the chapter objectives.
You now should know . . .

- How you might interact with a database (Objective 1)
- How you can determine if information has integrity (Objective 2)
- How you organize and maintain data (Objectives 3 and 4)

Quiz Yourself Online: Check your knowledge of related content by navigating to this book's Quiz Yourself resource on Computer Concepts CourseMate and then tapping or clicking Objectives 1–4.

File Processing versus Databases

Almost all applications use the file processing approach, the database approach, or a combination of both approaches to store and manage data. The next sections discuss these two approaches.

File Processing Systems

In the past, many organizations exclusively used file processing systems to store and manage data. In a typical **file processing system**, each department or area within an organization has its own set of files. The records in one file may not relate to the records in any other file. Many of these systems have two major weaknesses: redundant data and isolated data.

- **Redundant data:** Because each department or area in an organization has its own files in a file processing system, the same fields are stored in multiple files. If a file processing system is used at a school, for example, the Student file and the Student Schedule file both might store the same students' names and addresses.

  Duplicating data in this manner wastes resources such as storage space and time. When new students are added or student data is modified, file maintenance tasks consume additional time because employees must update multiple files that contain the same data. This duplication also can increase the chance of errors. If a student changes his or her address, for example, the school must update the address in each file that it appears. If the Address field is not changed in all the files where it is stored or is changed incorrectly in one location, then discrepancies among the files exist.

- **Isolated data:** It often is difficult to access data that is stored in separate files in different departments. Assume, for example, that the student email addresses exist in the Student files and class room numbers (locations) are in the Schedule of Classes file. To send an email message informing students about a room change, data is needed from both the Student file and the Schedule of Classes file. Sharing data from multiple, separate files to generate such a list in a file processing system often is a complicated procedure and usually requires an experienced programmer.

The Database Approach

When an organization uses a database approach, many programs and users share the data in the database. A school's database most likely at a minimum contains data about students, instructors, schedule of classes, and student schedules. As shown in Figure 11-8, various areas within the school share and interact with the data in this database. The database does secure its data, however, so that only authorized users can access certain data items. Read Secure IT 11-3 on the next page to consider the implications of unsecure data.

BTW

Forensic Databases
Innovative Computing:
You should be familiar with innovations of forensic databases.

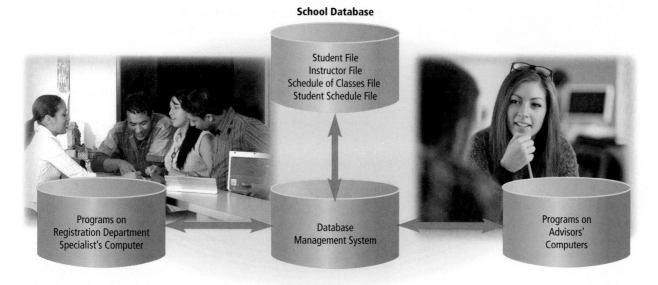

School Database

Student File
Instructor File
Schedule of Classes File
Student Schedule File

Programs on Registration Department Specialist's Computer

Database Management System

Programs on Advisors' Computers

Figure 11-8 In a school that uses a database, the computer used by the registration department clerk and the computers used by advisors access data in a single database through the DBMS.

⬡ **SECURE IT 11-3**

Genomes Project Database Donors Identified

International researchers are participating in the 1000 Genomes Project to study human genetics. They collected DNA from more than 1,000 people in various ethnic groups and countries and developed databases that the scientific community can access for free in the interest of studying human genetic variation. The project's goal is to locate genes associated with particular diseases in an effort to prevent and protect people from illnesses, such as cancer and Parkinson's disease.

The donors' identities were to remain anonymous. University geneticists not involved with the project, however,

matched the DNA with 50 people. They then compared the three-billion-digit genomes to data available in two popular genealogy websites and narrowed the results to eight surnames of people living in Utah. This connection between anonymous donors' identities eventually being revealed through DNA sequencing raises security and privacy issues, especially as more data becomes available and research techniques become more refined. Scientists now can sequence an individual's DNA within several weeks; the first human's DNA sequencing procedure took 13 years to complete.

The 200 TB of genetic data is stored in Amazon Web Services' cloud. According

to the White House Office of Science and Technology, this amount of data is equivalent to 16 million file cabinets or 30,000 DVDs. Researchers can access this data free of charge for use in disease research. The goal is to expand the number of donors from 1,000 to 2,600 from 26 specific worldwide populations.

✳ Would you be willing to donate your DNA to the 1000 Genomes Project knowing that your identity could be discovered? Should the university researchers disclose the names of the specific people they identified by matching the DNA in several databases? Why or why not? Should scientists secure permission from test subjects before using their samples for research?

While a user is working with the database, the DBMS resides in the computer's memory. Instead of working directly with the DBMS, some users interact with a front end. A *front end* is a program that generally has a more user-friendly interface than the DBMS. For example, a registration department specialist interacts with the Class Registration program by filling out a form. This front-end program interacts with the DBMS, which, in turn, interacts with the database. Many programs today use forms on a webpage as their front end. An application that supports a front-end program sometimes is called the *back end*. In this case, the DBMS is the back end.

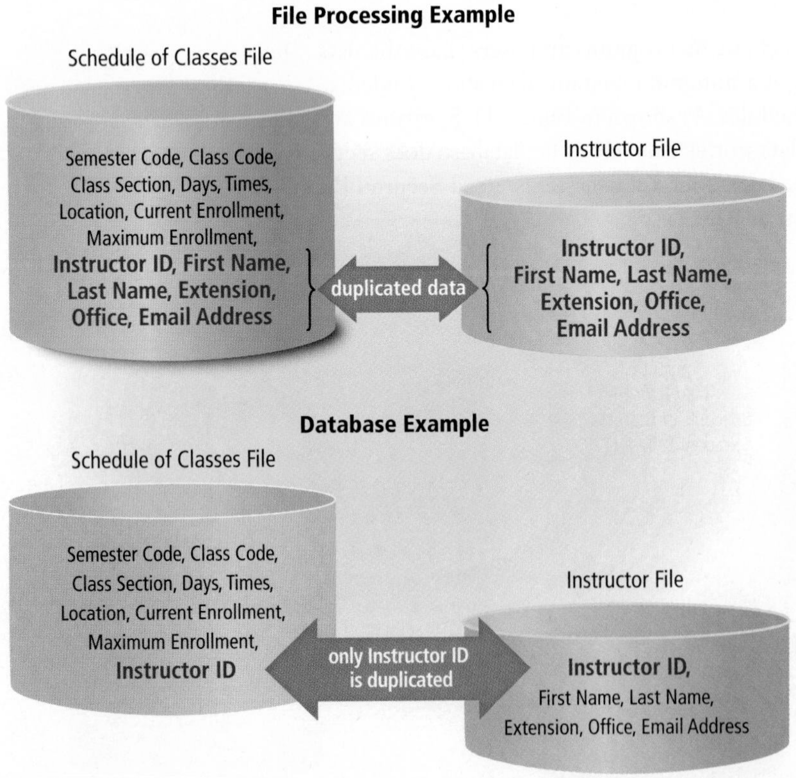

Advantages of a Database Approach
The database approach addresses many of the weaknesses associated with file processing systems. Advantages of the database approach include the following:

- **Reduced data redundancy:** Most data items are stored in only one file, which greatly reduces duplicate data. For example, a school's database would record a student's name and address only once. When student data is entered or changed, one employee makes the change once. Figure 11-9 demonstrates the differences between how a file processing application and a database application might store data.

File Processing Example

Schedule of Classes File
> Semester Code, Class Code, Class Section, Days, Times, Location, Current Enrollment, Maximum Enrollment, **Instructor ID, First Name, Last Name, Extension, Office, Email Address**

← duplicated data →

Instructor File
> **Instructor ID, First Name, Last Name, Extension, Office, Email Address**

Database Example

Schedule of Classes File
> Semester Code, Class Code, Class Section, Days, Times, Location, Current Enrollment, Maximum Enrollment, **Instructor ID**

→ only Instructor ID is duplicated →

Instructor File
> **Instructor ID,** First Name, Last Name, Extension, Office, Email Address

Figure 11-9 With file processing, both files contain all six instructor data fields. With a database, only the Instructor file contains the First Name, Last Name, Extension, Office, and Email Address fields. Other files, such as the Schedule of Classes file, contain only the Instructor ID — which links to the Instructor file when instructor data is needed.
© Cengage Learning

- **Improved data integrity:** When users modify data in the database, they make changes to one file instead of multiple files. Thus, the database approach increases the data's integrity by reducing the possibility of introducing inconsistencies.
- **Shared data:** The data in a database environment belongs to and is shared, usually over a network, by the entire organization. This data is independent of, or separate from, the programs that access the data. Organizations that use databases typically have security settings to define who can access, add, modify, and delete the data in a database. Read Ethics & Issues 11-2 to consider a database shared nationally.
- **Easier access:** The database approach allows nontechnical users to access and maintain data, providing they have the necessary privileges. Many computer users also can develop smaller databases themselves, without professional assistance.
- **Reduced development time:** It often is easier and faster to develop programs that use the database approach. Many DBMSs include several tools to assist in developing programs, which further reduces the development time.

 CONSIDER THIS

Can a database eliminate redundant data completely?

No. A database reduces redundant data; it does not eliminate it. Key fields link data together in a database. For example, a Student ID field will exist in any database table that requires access to student data. Thus, a student ID is duplicated (exists in more than one table) in the database.

Disadvantages of a Database Approach A database can be more complex than a file processing system. People with special training usually develop larger databases and their associated applications. Databases also require more memory and processing power than file processing systems.

Data in a database can be more vulnerable than data in file processing systems because it can store a lot of data in a single file. Many users and programs share and depend on this data. If the database is not operating properly or is damaged or destroyed, users may not be able to perform their jobs. Further, unauthorized users potentially could gain access to a single database file that contains personal and confidential data. To protect their database resource, individuals and companies should establish and follow security procedures.

Despite these limitations, business and home users often work with databases because of their numerous advantages.

 ETHICS & ISSUES 11-2

Should States Share Criminal Databases?

California was the first state to employ a controversial database listing names and addresses of people convicted of crimes against children. Megan's Law refers to a group of U.S. laws that require law enforcement agencies to share information publicly about criminals who prey on or commit unlawful acts on children. Most states' laws include requiring criminals convicted of these offenses to register changes of address. Updates over the years include outlining tiers of these offenders and banning them from participating in Halloween-related activities.

Today, all states employ similar databases and are required to share the data with a national database. States decide which information to make public and how to distribute the information. Often, states release criminals' names, photos, addresses, and information about the crime and time served on a searchable, public website. In some communities, when an offender moves in the area, police inform the local school system, which in turn sends parents a notification. Some states share information with each other regarding almost all criminals, and some allow citizens to search for these offenders by name.

Some feel that publishing this information makes it impossible for an offender to lead a normal life and can result in vigilantism. Proponents of these laws state that the public's right to know outweighs the rights of privacy of those convicted. These laws are considered by many to be a valuable tool in crime prevention.

What information should states provide to the public regarding people convicted of crimes? Why? What about for those who have committed other types of crimes? Who should have access to the database? Why?

Database Management Systems

 Internet Research

Which is the most widely used database?

Search for: database market share

As previously discussed, a database management system (DBMS), or database program, is software that allows you to create, access, and manage a database. DBMSs are available for many sizes and types of computers. Whether designed for a small or large computer, most DBMSs perform common functions. The following pages discuss these functions.

Data Dictionary

A **data dictionary**, sometimes called a *repository*, contains data about each file in the database and each field in those files. For each file, it stores details such as the file name, a description, the file's relationship to other files, and the number of records in the file. For each field, it stores details such as the field name, description, field type, field size, default value, validation rules, and the field's relationship to other fields. Figure 11-10 shows how a data dictionary might list data for a Student file.

A DBMS uses the data dictionary to perform validation checks to maintain the integrity of the data. When users enter data, the data dictionary verifies that the entered data matches the field's data type. For example, the data dictionary allows only dates to be entered in a Date Admitted field. The data dictionary also can limit the type of data that can be entered, often allowing a user to select from a list. For example, the data dictionary ensures that the State field contains a valid two-letter state code, such as IN, by presenting a list of valid state codes to the user.

 **BTW**

Metadata
Because the data dictionary contains details about data, some call it *metadata* (meta means more comprehensive).

A data dictionary allows users to specify a default value for a field to reduce the possibility of errors. A *default value* is a value that the DBMS initially displays in a field. If most students who attend the school live in Indiana, for example, then the DBMS initially could display IN in the State field. The user does not have to type in a default value. A user typically can override a default value if it does not apply for a certain record. For example, you can change the value from IN to OH if the student lives in Ohio.

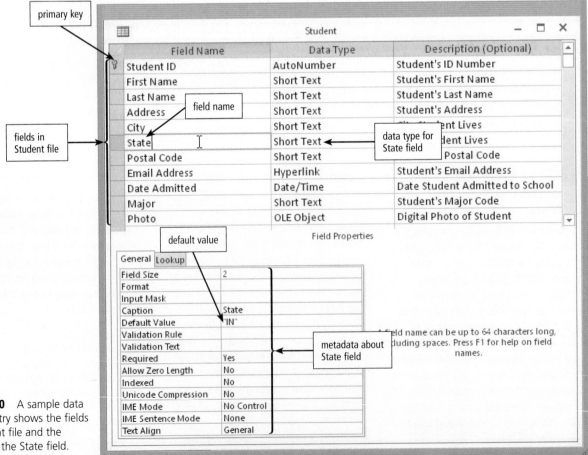

Figure 11-10 A sample data dictionary entry shows the fields in the Student file and the properties of the State field.
Source: Microsoft

File Retrieval and Maintenance

A DBMS provides several tools that allow users and programs to retrieve and maintain data in the database. To retrieve or select data in a database, you query it. A **query** is a request for specific data from the database. Users can instruct the DBMS to display, print, or store the results of a query. The capability of querying a database is one of the more powerful database features.

A DBMS offers several methods to retrieve and maintain its data. The four more commonly used are query languages, query by example, forms, and report writers. Another method is by importing data. Read How To 11-1 for instructions about importing spreadsheet data into a database and vice versa.

HOW TO 11-1

Import Spreadsheet Data into a Database and Export Database Data to a Spreadsheet

If you periodically use spreadsheets and databases, you may find it beneficial to import data from a spreadsheet into a database or export data from a database to a spreadsheet. As mentioned in this book, spreadsheet applications and database applications each have unique advantages; therefore, you may need to convert the data from one application's format to use in the other. For example, if you have a spreadsheet with many rows of customer data, you might want to import the data from the spreadsheet into a database so that you can perform simple or complex queries on the data. If you have a database with many records and you want to perform calculations or a statistical analysis of the data, you might export data from the database to a spreadsheet. The following steps describe how to accomplish these tasks.

Import Data from a Spreadsheet into a Database

1. Run the spreadsheet application. Open the spreadsheet you want to import to the database and make sure your data is organized properly. For example, each column should represent a field and each row should represent a record. The first row in the spreadsheet should contain the field names for each respective column. Make the necessary changes to the spreadsheet.

2. Save and close the spreadsheet.

3. Run the database application.

4. Create a new database or open the database to which you want to import the spreadsheet.

5. Navigate to and then tap or click the command to import data from an external file.

6. Select the type of file you want to import (spreadsheet, in this case). Some database applications may identify types of files by the name of the program that created them. For example, if you are importing an Excel spreadsheet into an Access database, you would select the option in Access to import an Excel file.

7. Navigate through the remaining steps to verify that the data in the spreadsheet will import properly. This includes:

    - Choosing the table to which you want to import the data in the spreadsheet

    - Verifying field names

    - Setting a field to act as a primary key

    - Choosing data types for each field

8. Tap or click the button or command to finish the import.

9. Open the table in the database with the data you just imported and verify it all was imported properly.

Export Data from a Database to a Spreadsheet

1. Run the database application. Open the database containing the data you want to export.

2. Open the table containing the data you want to export.

3. Navigate to and then tap or click the option to export the data.

4. Select the option to export the database to a spreadsheet. Some database applications might require you to select the name of the spreadsheet application to which you want to export the database. For example, in Microsoft Access, you should specify that you want to export to a Microsoft Excel file.

5. Specify a file name for the spreadsheet.

6. Tap or click the button or command to complete the export.

7. Run the spreadsheet application and open the file you have just created. Verify the data has been exported properly from the database.

What are some other reasons why you might want to import data from a spreadsheet into a database or export data from a database to a spreadsheet?

	A	B	C	D	E	F	G	H	I	J	K
1	Student ID	First Name	Last Name	Address	City	State	Postal Code	Email Address	Date Admitted	Major	Photo
2	2295	Milton	Brewer	54 Lucy Court	Charlestown	IN	46176		6/10/2013	EE	mbrewer.jpg
3	3876	Louella	Drake	33 Timmons Place	Bonner	IN	45208	lou@world.com	8/9/2013	BIO	ldrake.jpg
4	3928	Adelbert	Ruiz	99 Tenth Street	Sheldon	IN	46033		10/8/2013	CT	aruiz.jpg
5	2872	Benjamin	Tu	2204 Elm Court	Rowley	IN	46167	tu@indi.net	9/14/2014	GEN	btu.jpg
6											
7											

Source: Microsoft

Figure 11-11a (SQL statement)

```
SELECT CLASS_TITLE, CLASS_SECTION,
 MAXIMUM_ENROLLMENT - CURRENT_ENROLLMENT AS SEATS_REMAINING
FROM SCHEDULE_OF_CLASSES, CLASS_CATALOG
WHERE SCHEDULE_OF_CLASSES.CLASS_CODE = CLASS_CATALOG.CLASS_CODE
ORDER BY CLASS_TITLE
```

Figure 11-11b (SQL statement results)

Class Title	Class Section	Seats Remaining
Algebra 1	51	14
Art Appreciation	52	19
English Composition 1	02	5
Introduction to Sociology	01	14

Figure 11-11 A sample SQL statement and its results. Notice that the query results show meaningful column headings instead of the actual SQL field names.
Source: Microsoft; © Cengage Learning

Query Language A **query language** consists of simple, English-like statements that allow users to specify the data they want to display, print, store, update, or delete. Each query language has its own formats and vocabulary.

Structured Query Language (SQL pronounced S-Q-L or sequel) is a popular query language that allows users to manage, update, and retrieve data. SQL has special keywords and rules that users include in SQL statements. Figure 11-11a shows an SQL statement that creates the results shown in Figure 11-11b.

To simplify the query process, many DBMSs provide tools to guide nontechnical users through the steps of creating a query. Figure 11-12 shows how to use the Simple Query Wizard in Microsoft Access to display the First Name, Last Name, and Email Address fields from the Student file. Instead of using the Simple Query Wizard, you could enter the query language statement generated by the wizard (shown in Figure 11-12) directly in the DBMS to display the results shown in Step 3.

How to Use the Simple Query Wizard

Step 1
Select the fields from the Available Fields list you want to be displayed in the resulting query.

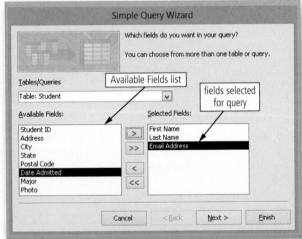

Step 2
Assign a name to the query, so that you can open it later.

```
SELECT FIRST NAME, LAST NAME, EMAIL ADDRESS
FROM STUDENT
```

query language statement generated by wizard

Step 3
View the query results on the screen.

Figure 11-12 This figure shows how to use the Microsoft Access Simple Query Wizard.
© Cengage Learning; Source: Microsoft

Query by Example Most DBMSs include **query by example (QBE)**, a feature that has a graphical user interface to assist users with retrieving data. Figure 11-13 shows a sample QBE screen for a query that searches for and lists students majoring in sociology; that is, their Major field value is equal to SOC. For more information about filtering data, read Mini Feature 11-1 (available in the e-book).

Figure 11-13a (all records in Student table)

Student ID	First Name	Last Name	Address	City	State	Postal Code	Email Address	Date Admitted	Major
2295	Milton	Brewer	54 Lucy Court	Charlestown	IN	46176		6/10/2013	SOC
2928	Benjamin	Tu	2204 Elm Court	Rowley	IN	46259	tu@indi.net	9/4/2014	GEN
3876	Louella	Drake	33 Timmons Place	Bonner	IN	45208	lou@world.com	8/9/2013	BIO
3928	Adelbert	Ruiz	99 Tenth Street	Sheldon	IN	46033		10/8/2013	CT
4872	Elena	Gupta	76 Ash Street	Rowley	IN	46167	eg@earth.net	9/3/2014	SOC

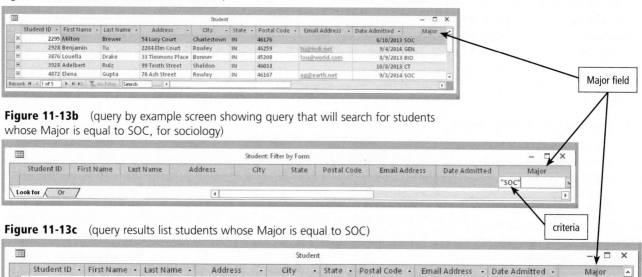

Figure 11-13b (query by example screen showing query that will search for students whose Major is equal to SOC, for sociology)

Figure 11-13c (query results list students whose Major is equal to SOC)

Student ID	First Name	Last Name	Address	City	State	Postal Code	Email Address	Date Admitted	Major
2295	Milton	Brewer	54 Lucy Court	Charlestown	IN	46176		6/10/2013	SOC
4872	Elena	Gupta	76 Ash Street	Rowley	IN	46167	eg@earth.net	9/3/2014	SOC

Figure 11-13 Shown here is a Microsoft Access QBE, which searches for students whose major is sociology.
Source: Microsoft

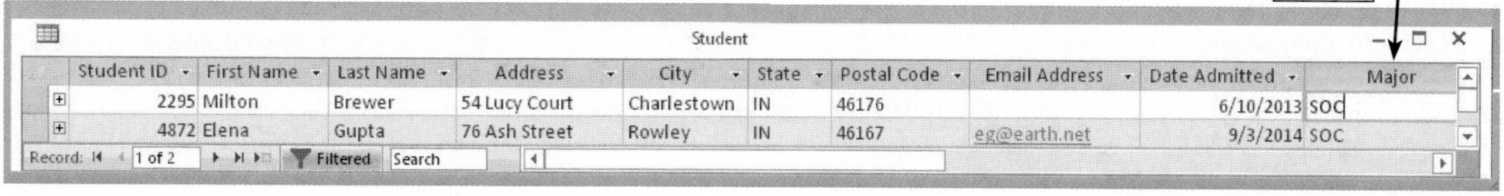

Form A **form**, sometimes called a *data entry form*, is a window on the screen that provides areas for entering or modifying data in a database. You use forms (such as the Student Maintenance Form in Figure 11-5 on page 471) to retrieve and maintain the data in a database.

To reduce data entry errors, well-designed forms should validate data as it is entered. When designing a form using a DBMS, you can make the form attractive and easy to use by incorporating color, shading, lines, boxes, and graphics; varying the fonts and font styles; and using other formatting features.

BTW
E-Form
A form that sends entered data across a network or the Internet is called an *e-form*, short for electronic form.

Report Writer A **report writer**, also called a *report generator*, allows users to design a report on the screen, retrieve data into the report design, and then display or print the report (Figure 11-14). Unlike a form, you use a report writer only to retrieve data. Report writers usually allow you to format page numbers and dates; titles and column headings; subtotals and totals; and fonts, font sizes, color, and shading. Many allow you to include images; for example, a product catalog could contain photos and descriptions of products. Some report writers allow you to create a report as a webpage, which can be interactive.

Student List by Major

Major	Last Name	Student ID	First Name	Address	City	Date Admitted
BIO						
	Drake	3876	Louella	33 Timmons Place	Bonner	8/9/2013
CT						
	Ruiz	3928	Adelbert	99 Tenth Street	Sheldon	10/8/2013
GEN						
	Tu	2928	Benjamin	2204 Elm Court	Rowley	9/4/2014
SOC						
	Brewer	2295	Milton	54 Lucy Court	Charlestown	6/10/2013
	Gupta	4872	Elena	76 Ash Street	Rowley	9/3/2014

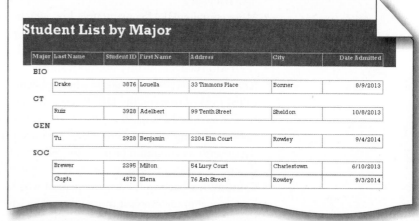

Figure 11-14 This report, created in Microsoft Access, displays student information by major.
Source: Microsoft

Data Security

A DBMS provides means to ensure that only authorized users can access data. In addition, most DBMSs allow different levels of access privileges to be identified for each field in the database. Access privileges define the actions that a specific user or group of users can perform on the data. For example, in the Schedule of Classes file, the student would have read-only privileges. That is, the student could view the list of classes offered in a semester but could not change them. A department head, by contrast, would have full-update privileges to classes offered during a particular semester, meaning he or she can view and modify the data. Finally, some users have no access privileges to the data; that is, they cannot view or modify any data in the database. Read Secure IT 11-4 for information about database security policies.

Many organizations adopt the *principle of least privilege policy*, where users' access privileges are limited to the lowest level necessary to perform required tasks.

Internet Research

What are recent data security breaches?

Search for: security breaches news

SECURE IT 11-4

Establishing Database Security Policies

Cyberthieves have targeted databases to obtain financial records, Social Security numbers, national security data, and other sensitive contents. Security administrators are responsible for preventing these unauthorized individuals from accessing databases, and their efforts should begin with developing a security policy for every database. This policy addresses who can access the database and their level of activity privileges.

At a minimum, each person accessing the database should have a profile that includes a user name, a strong password that must be changed frequently, and limits on database system-level access. For example, the database administrator should have access privileges to create and delete files. A typical user, in contrast, should not have the ability to create or delete files and should be allowed only to view records. Other users might be allowed to modify records but not to create or delete them.

Some database management systems allow the administrator to specify more than 100 distinct system privileges. In a highly secure environment, some users may be able to see limited data in each record or be restricted to accessing specific database files. They also can be limited to a specific number of sign-in attempts in one day. To help administrators monitor user access, a log file should identify the users, successful and failed sign-in efforts, and when the databases were accessed.

Have you accessed databases at school or work? If so, which access privileges do you have? What types of data might you be restricted from accessing in a school or work environment?

Backup and Recovery

Occasionally a database is damaged or destroyed because of hardware failure, a problem with the software, human error, or a catastrophe such as fire or flood. A DBMS provides a variety of techniques to restore the database to a usable form in case it is damaged or destroyed.

- A **backup**, or copy, of the entire database should be made on a regular basis. Some DBMSs have their own built-in backup tools. Others require users to purchase a separate backup program, or use one included with the operating system. Read How To 11-2 for ways to back up a database.
- More complex DBMSs maintain a **log**, which is a listing of activities that modify the contents of the database. If a registration department specialist modifies a student's address, for example, the change appears in the log.
- A DBMS **recovery utility** uses logs and/or backups, and either a rollforward or a rollback technique, to restore a database when it becomes damaged or destroyed. In a *rollforward*, also called *forward recovery*, the DBMS uses the log to reenter changes made to the database since the last save or backup. In a *rollback*, also called *backward recovery*, the DBMS uses the log to undo any changes made to the database during a certain period. The rollback restores the database to its condition prior to the failure. Depending on the type of failure, the DBMS determines which type of recovery technique to use.
- **Continuous backup** is a backup plan in which changes are backed up as they are made. This backup technique can cost more than other backup strategies but is growing in popularity for businesses whose data must be available at all times, because it provides recovery of damaged data in a matter of seconds. Organizations such as hospitals, communications companies, and financial institutions often use continuous backup.

HOW TO 11-2

Back Up a Database

Because backing up a database is an important step in protecting your data from loss, you should perform backups on a regular basis. Databases usually save changes as you make them, so undoing actions or closing a database without saving the changes you made often is not possible. For this reason, you also should back up a database: (1) before modifying or deleting data, (2) before performing any maintenance operations on the database (How To 11-4 on page 489 discusses maintaining a database), or (3) after adding data to the database. The following points discuss ways to back up a database:

- If your computer already has a backup program running, it might be backing up your database. Check your backups and determine whether your database is included in the backup. If not, configure the backup program to back up the database.

- Copy the database to another storage device. For example, if the database is stored on a server, you could copy the database to your computer. If the database already is stored on your computer, you can copy it to a server (if you have access to one) or to an external storage device, such as a USB flash drive.

- Copy the database to a different folder on the same storage medium as the original database. *Note*: Although this method is effective for keeping multiple copies of the database in an accessible location, you will lose both the original database and the backups if the storage device fails.

☀ How many backups should you keep of a database? Is one backup sufficient? If not, how can you determine an adequate number of backups to maintain?

Relational, Object-Oriented, and Multidimensional Databases

Every database and DBMS is based on a specific data model. A data model consists of rules and standards that define how the database organizes data. A **data model** defines how users view the organization of the data. It does not define how the operating system actually arranges the data on the storage media.

Three popular data models in use today are relational, object-oriented, and multidimensional. A database typically is based on one data model.

Relational Databases

A **relational database** is a database that stores data in tables that consist of rows and columns. Each row has a primary key and each column has a unique name.

As discussed earlier in this chapter, a file processing environment uses the terms file, record, and field to represent data. As shown in Table 11-2, a relational database uses different terms. A developer of a relational database refers to a file as a *relation*, a record as a *tuple*, and a field as an *attribute*. A user of a relational database, by contrast, refers to a file as a **table**, a record as a **row**, and a field as a **column**.

Table 11-2 Data Terminology Comparison

File Processing Environment	Relational Database Developer	Relational Database User
File	Relation	Table
Record	Tuple	Row
Field	Attribute	Column

In addition to storing data, a relational database also stores data relationships. A **relationship** is a link within the data. In a relational database, you can set up a relationship between tables at any time. The tables must have a common column (field). For example, you could relate the Schedule of Classes table and the Instructor table using the Instructor ID column. Figure 11-15 on the next page illustrates these relational database concepts. In a relational database, the only data redundancy (duplication) exists in the common columns (fields). The database uses these common columns for relationships.

Most relational database products for servers include support for SQL. Many personal computer databases also include support for SQL. The structure and wording in SQL statements may differ slightly among database management systems.

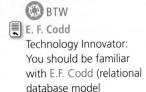

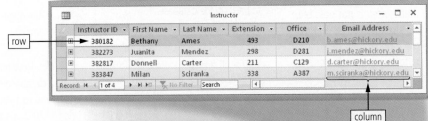

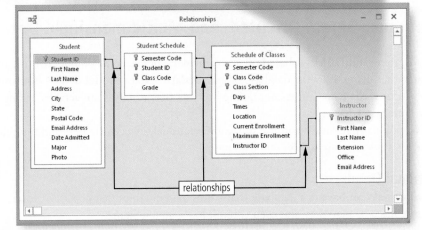

Figure 11-15 This figure shows
relationships among some tables in
the School database. For example, the
Schedule of Classes table is related to the
Instructor table through the Instructor ID
column.
Source: Microsoft

✳ **CONSIDER THIS** ────────────────

Who uses relational databases?
Applications best suited for relational databases are those whose data can be organized into a two-dimensional table, that is, tables with rows and columns. Many organizations use relational databases for payroll, accounts receivable, accounts payable, general ledger, inventory, order entry, invoicing, and other business-related functions.

Object-Oriented Databases

An **object-oriented database** (**OODB**) stores data in objects. An **object** is an item that contains data, as well as the actions that read or process the data. A Student object, for example, might contain data about a student, such as Student ID, First Name, Last Name, Address, and so on. It also could contain instructions about how to print a student transcript or the formula required to calculate a student's grade point average. A record in a relational database, by contrast, would contain only data about a student.

Object-oriented databases have several advantages compared with relational databases: they can store more types of data, access this data faster, and allow programmers to reuse objects. An object-oriented database stores unstructured data more efficiently than a relational database. Unstructured data can include photos, video clips, audio clips, and documents. When users query an object-oriented database, the results often are displayed more quickly than the same query of a relational database. If an object already exists, programmers can reuse it instead of re-creating a new object — saving on program development time.

Object-oriented and object-relational databases often use a query language called *object query language* (*OQL*) to manipulate and retrieve data. OQL uses many of the same rules, grammar, and keywords as SQL. Because OQL is a relatively new query language, not all object databases support it.

✳ **CONSIDER THIS** ────────────────────────

What applications use object-oriented databases?

Examples of applications appropriate for an object-oriented database include the following:

- A media database stores images, audio clips, and/or video clips. Examples include a *GIS* (geographic information system) database, which stores maps and other geographic data; a voice mail system database, which stores audio messages; and a television news station database, which stores audio and video clips.

- A groupware database stores documents such as schedules, calendars, manuals, memos, and reports (Figure 11-16). Users perform queries to search the document contents. For example, you can search people's schedules for available meeting times.

- A CAD (computer-aided design) database stores data about engineering, architectural, and

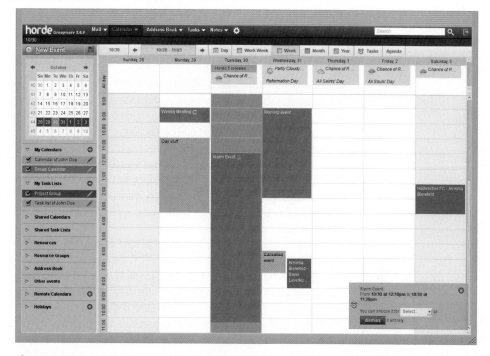

Figure 11-16 Using a groupware calendar, users can access a database of shared calendars.
Courtesy of Horde Groupware

scientific designs. Data in the database includes a list of components of the item being designed, the relationship among the components, and previous versions of the design drafts.

Multidimensional Databases

A **multidimensional database** stores data in dimensions. Whereas a relational database is a two-dimensional table, a multidimensional database can store more than two dimensions of data. These multiple dimensions allow users to access and analyze any view of the database data.

The number of dimensions in a multidimensional database varies (Figure 11-17). A retail business might have four dimensions: products, customers, regions, and time. A multidimensional database for a hospital procedure could have six dimensions: time, procedure type, patient, hospital, physician, and diagnosis. Nearly every multidimensional database has a dimension of time. The content of other dimensions varies depending on the subject.

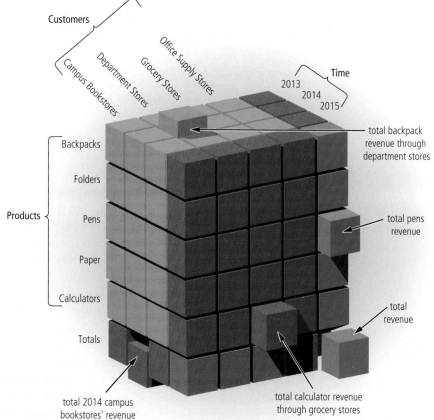

Figure 11-17 This figure shows a multidimensional database with three dimensions (products, customers, and time).
© Cengage Learning

The key advantage of the multidimensional database is that it can consolidate data much faster than a relational database. A relational database typically does not process and summarize large numbers of records efficiently. With a multidimensional database, users obtain summarized results very quickly.

 CONSIDER THIS

Where are multidimensional databases used?
One application that uses multidimensional databases is a data warehouse. A **data warehouse** is a huge database that stores and manages the data required to analyze historical and current transactions. Through a data warehouse, managers and other users access transactions and summaries of transactions quickly and efficiently. Some major credit card companies monitor and manage customers' credit card transactions using a data warehouse. Consumers also can access their own transactions in the data warehouse via the web. A data warehouse typically has a user-friendly interface, so that users easily can interact with its data.

The database in a data warehouse often is distributed. The data in a *distributed database* exists in many separate locations throughout a network or the Internet. Although the data is accessible through a single server, its location is transparent to the user.

Data warehouses often use a process called *data mining* to find patterns and relationships among data. A state government could mine through data to check if the number of births has a relationship to income level. Many e-commerce websites use data mining to determine customer preferences.

A smaller version of a data warehouse is the *data mart.* A data mart contains a database that helps a specific group or department make decisions. Marketing and sales departments may have their own separate data marts. Individual groups or departments often extract data from the data warehouse to create their data marts.

 NOW YOU KNOW

Be sure you understand the material presented in the sections titled File Processing versus Databases; Database Management Systems; and Relational, Object-Oriented, and Multidimensional Databases, as it relates to the chapter objectives.
You now should know . . .

- Why you would choose a database over a file processing environment (Objective 5)

- How you use a data dictionary, retrieve data in a database, keep data secure in a database, and back up a database (Objective 6)

- When you would use relational, object-oriented, and multidimensional databases (Objective 7)

 Quiz Yourself Online: Check your knowledge of related content by navigating to this book's Quiz Yourself resource on Computer Concepts CourseMate and then tapping or clicking Objectives 5–7.

Web Databases

The web offers information about jobs, travel destinations, television programming, photos, movies, videos, local and national weather, sporting events, and legislative information. You can shop for just about any product or service, buy or sell stocks, and make airline reservations. Much of this and other information exists in databases that are stored on or are accessible through the web. Some web databases are *collaborative databases*, where users store and share photos, videos, recordings, and other personal media with other registered users.

To access data in a web database, you fill in an e-form or enter search text on a webpage. The webpage is the front end to the database. Many search engines use databases to store website descriptions. Thus, the search engine's home page is the front end to the database. To access the database, you enter search text into the search engine.

A web database for an organization usually resides on a database server. A *database server* is a computer that stores and provides access to a database. For smaller databases, many desktop database programs provide a variety of web publishing tools that enable users without computer programming experience to create a home or small office database.

 BTW
IBM
Technology Innovator: You should be familiar with IBM.

 **MINI FEATURE 11-2**

Web Databases

A database service, or a website that acts as a portal for a database, enables government agencies, schools, and companies to share information with a wide audience. Some web databases are accessible to the public. Examples of public databases include shopping and travel databases. Other databases contain information accessible only to authorized users. Examples of protected databases include certain government databases or entertainment and research databases that are subscription-based.

Government

Government web database services can provide access to information about the government, as well as information created and used by government agencies. Some information that government agencies publish in databases is available to the public. Through these database services, for example, users can locate information about current laws. Other database services, such as those for criminal databases, allow access only to those individuals with necessary clearance. Government database services also enable officials around the world to share data.

Entertainment

You can search an entertainment web database service to find out who guest-starred on your favorite television program or locate video or audio clips. Using a subscription-based entertainment web database service allows you to access media content, such as music. These database services often enable you to create and share playlists. By drawing on your listening or viewing history, these database services also can recommend other media you might like.

Travel

Booking online travel through a travel web database service enables you to view multiple vendors and options. You can limit a search to desired locations and dates. These database services help you find deals on air travel, car rentals, hotel rooms, and vacation packages. Travel web database services can save your personal data and travel history and then inform you about upcoming travel deals in which you might be interested.

Shopping

Shopping web database services enable you to locate the right size and color, sort by price or featured products, and more. Vendors can use a web database service to show photos of items they sell and keep track of inventory. Some shopping database services search for bargains, presenting a variety of purchasing options so that you can find the lowest price. These database services also use your search and order history to suggest products in their databases that you may be interested in buying.

Research

You can interact with web databases to research product information when shopping for a new appliance or car. Information accessible through these web database services includes costs, safety concerns, and industry and user reviews. Some research web database services provide financial information for potential investors, including company histories and stock analysis. Research web database services are available to help you find a college or university and then provide information about admission requirements, financial information, and application advice. Read How To 11-3 on the next page for instructions about using a research database service at school.

Education

Teachers can search education web database services to locate and share curricula, worksheets, and lesson plans. Schools use web database service to store and distribute student contact information and grades. Students interact with web databases services when signing up for their courses online. Using these services during enrollment helps a school determine when a class has reached its maximum size.

Source: IXL Learning

✻ Which web database services have you used? How do web databases help you in your daily life? Would you use a web database for research? Why or why not?

HOW TO 11-3

Use a Research Database

Students often use one or more research databases to locate information about a particular topic. Research databases often can be accessed in a public or school library, through a library's website, or through the research database's website. The following steps describe how to use a research database:

1. Locate and then navigate to the research database that contains the information you are seeking. Consult a librarian if you need assistance in determining the exact database you should use.

2. Determine from where you can access the research database. For instance, you may need to access some research databases from a library computer. Other databases are accessible from anywhere if you can verify your identity as a library patron or a student. Some databases are available to the public at no charge or with no other restrictions.

3. Navigate to the research database you plan to use.

4. If the research database contains an option to perform an advanced search, tap or click the option to perform the advanced search.

5. Specify the search criteria. Note that not all research databases will request the same search criteria. The following list contains some common criteria:

   - Keywords
   - Author
   - Publication date
   - Publication type
   - Education level

6. Run the search.

7. Browse the search results and then tap or click the search result that interests you.

 What are some reasons why you might want or need to use a research database?

Source: EBSCO

 **Internet Research**

What are some examples of Big Data?

Search for: big data examples

 CONSIDER THIS

What is meant by the term, Big Data?

Big Data describes the widespread growth of data, the variety of formats in which this data is available, and the processing required to make this data accessible in a timely manner. Big Data originates from a variety of sources, such as databases, social media posts, text messages, email messages, web traffic, files, documents, audio, video, and sensors. Sensors that collect data are found in video cameras, medical devices and equipment, RFID tags, clothing, billboards, phones, and more. The goal of Big Data is to analyze its patterns and trends so that organizations can make effective decisions.

Database Administration

Managing a company's database requires a great deal of coordination. The role of coordinating the use of the database belongs to the database analysts and administrators. To carry out their responsibilities, these IT professionals follow database design guidelines and need cooperation from all database users.

The database analysts and administrators are responsible for managing and coordinating all database activities. The **database analyst** (**DA**), or *data modeler*, focuses on the meaning and usage of data. The DA decides on the proper placement of fields, defines the relationships among data, and identifies users' access privileges. The **database administrator** (**DBA**) requires a more technical inside view of the data. The DBA creates and maintains the data dictionary, manages security of the database, monitors the performance of the database, and checks backup and recovery procedures. The maintenance of a database is an ongoing task that organizations measure constantly against their overall goals. Read How To 11-4 to learn how to maintain a database. Read Ethics & Issues 11-3 to consider whether users should be reprimanded for accessing unsecure data.

In small companies, one person often is both the DA and DBA. In larger companies, the responsibilities of the DA and DBA are split among two or more people.

 BTW
Technology Certifications
For information about database and other technology certifications, see the Technology Certifications appendix (available in the e-book).

 HOW TO 11-4

Maintain a Database

As you add and delete tables and records from your database, you should maintain the database so that it can continue operating efficiently. If you neglect to maintain a database, chances increase that the data can become inaccessible. In addition to maintaining a database, you also should back up the database regularly. More information about backing up a database can be found in How To 11-2 on page 483. The following guidelines describe how to maintain a database:

- Back up the database.

- If the database contains a table that you do not need (and you do not foresee a future need for the data in that table), remove the table from the database.

- Evaluate the fields in all remaining tables and make sure they are assigned the proper data type. Make any necessary adjustments.

- Remove fields you no longer need from the tables in your database.

- If the database contains a large number of records, consider deleting records you no longer need.

- Navigate to and then tap or click the command to compact and repair the database (if available).

- If you want to protect the data in the database, consider selecting the option to encrypt the database.

✸ What are some advantages to maintaining a database?

 ETHICS & ISSUES 11-3

Should Users Be Punished for Accidentally Accessing Confidential Data?

A student discovered private student data on a publicly accessible area of a university computer. Instead of notifying authorities, he took the file to the student newspaper. After the newspaper published an article about the situation, the administration fired the newspaper's adviser for violating the university's computer policies and nearly expelled the student. Was the student obligated to report the vulnerability to the administration?

Should the student have been disciplined for not reporting the breach?

In another case, administrators charged a high school student with criminal trespassing after the student accessed information on the school's network. In this case, the student allegedly was attempting to profit from the data, which included personal data for school employees.

Institutions often attempt to resolve security breaches quietly, fearing that publicity may cause financial loss and may encourage hackers to target the institution. In some

cases, an institution may file lawsuits against those who make security breaches public, including reporters. Some feel that protecting data privacy is partially the responsibility of the person who uncovers the breach.

Who is responsible for personal data being made public — the institution for having an unsecured network or the person who accessed it? Even if a person is not trying to profit from detecting a data breach, should he or she still be held responsible for the discovery?

MINI FEATURE 11-3

Database Design

Database design is the process of determining the organization of a database. In designing a database, the database analyst or database administrator must identify the entities in the database, the entities' attributes, primary keys, and relationships.

The first step in designing a database is to determine its purpose. Next, the organization and structure of the database can be defined using the following guidelines:

1. **Examine the requirements and identify the entities (tables, files, or objects) involved.**
   - Each entity should contain data about one subject.
   - Assign names to the entities. If, for example, the design involves students and instructors, you could assign the names Student and Instructor.

2. **Identify the attributes (fields) for all the entities.**
   - The same attribute may be used in more than one entity. For example, students and instructors both have the attributes of first name, last name, street address, city, state, postal code, and so on.
   - Use separate attributes for logically distinct items. For example, a name could be stored in six fields: Title (Mr., Mrs. Dr., etc.), First Name, Middle Name, Last Name, Suffix (Jr., Sr., etc.), and Nickname.
   - Do not create attributes for information that you can derive from entries in other attributes. For example, do not include an attribute for age. Instead, store the birth date and compute the age.
   - Allow enough space for each attribute by determining the maximum character length.
   - Determine default values for frequently entered data to ease data entry and ensure consistency.

3. **Identify the functional dependencies that exist among the attributes.**
   - A functional dependency exists when one attribute can be derived only when another attribute is known.
   - When the value for one attribute enables you to determine a single value for a second attribute, the first attribute is said to determine the second attribute. Conversely, the second attribute is said to be functionally dependent on the first. For example, given a student ID, you can determine the student's email address. The Email Address attribute, therefore, is functionally dependent on the Student ID attribute. The location (room number) of a particular class, however, cannot be determined from a student ID. Thus, the Location attribute is not functionally dependent on the Student ID attribute.

4. **Use the functional dependencies to identify the entities.**
   - The attribute or attributes on which all other attributes in the entity are dependent will be the primary key, or unique identifier for each record in the entity. For a student entity, the Student ID attribute may be the primary key.
   - Some primary keys will consist of multiple attributes, called a composite key. For example, to determine a student's grade in a particular class, you need to know the semester, the student ID, and the class. This means that the grade is functionally dependent on the Semester Code, Student ID, and Class Code attributes. Thus, the primary key for this entity is a composite key that consists of the Semester Code+Student ID+Class Code attributes.
   - If no natural attribute exists as a primary key, you can use an AutoNumber data type.
   - Once you have determined all the attributes in an entity, you can name the entity.

5. **Identify any relationships between entities.**
   - Relationships are established through primary keys and foreign keys.
   - A *foreign key* is an attribute in one entity that exists in another entity as a primary key. For example, Instructor ID attribute is a primary key in the Instructor entity and a foreign key in the Schedule of Classes entity.

✳ What other attributes might you add to the Student entity in this example? What attributes might you add to the Instructor entity? What entities would be required for a retailer? Which attribute(s) would be the primary key in each entity you identified?

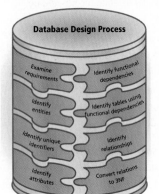

Database Design Process

Examine requirements · Identify functional dependencies · Identify entities · Identify tables using functional dependencies · Identify unique identifiers · Identify relationships · Identify attributes · Convert relations to 3NF

© Cengage Learning

Schedule of Classes
- 🔑 Semester Code
- 🔑 Class Code   } composite key
- 🔑 Class Section
- Days
- Times
- Location
- Current Enrollment
- Maximum Enrollment
- Instructor ID

foreign key

Instructor
- 🔑 Instructor ID ← primary key
- First Name
- Last Name
- Extension
- Office
- Email Address

Information Systems in the Enterprise

A system is a set of components that interact to achieve a common goal. Businesses use many types of systems. A billing system, for example, allows a company to send invoices and receive payments from customers. Through a payroll system, employees receive paychecks. A manufacturing system produces the goods that customers order. Very often, these systems also are information systems.

An **information system** is a set of hardware, software, data, people, and procedures that work together to produce information. Information systems support daily, short-term, and long-range activities of users in a company.

Some information systems are used exclusively by only one type of department, or functional unit, within the enterprise. Table 11-3 lists some of the more common information systems that typically are used within departments in an enterprise. Other information systems that support activities of several functional units include enterprise resource planning, content management systems, and document management systems.

Table 11-3	Information Systems Used Exclusively by Functional Units in an Enterprise
Functional Unit	**Information System**
Human Resources (HR)	• *A human resources information system* (*HRIS*) manages one or more administrative human resources functions, such as maintaining and managing employee benefits, schedules, and payroll.
Engineering or Product Development	• *Computer-aided engineering* (*CAE*) aids in the development and testing of product designs, and often includes CAD (computer-aided design).
Manufacturing	• *Computer-aided manufacturing* (*CAM*) controls production equipment, such as drills, lathes, and milling machines. • *Material Requirements Planning* (*MRP*) monitors and controls inventory, material purchases, and other processes related to manufacturing operations. • *Manufacturing Resource Planning II* (*MRP II*) is an extension of MRP that also includes product packaging and shipping, machine scheduling, financial planning, demand forecasting, tracking labor productivity, and monitoring product quality.
Marketing	• Market research systems analyze data gathered from demographics and surveys.
Sales	• *Salesforce automation* (*SFA*) helps salespeople manage customer contacts, schedule customer meetings, log customer interactions, manage product information, and place customer orders.
Customer Service	• *Customer relationship management* (*CRM*) manages information about customers, past purchases, interests, and the day-to-day interactions, such as phone calls, email messages, web communications, and instant messaging sessions.

Enterprise Resource Planning

Enterprise Resource Planning (**ERP**) integrates MRP II with the information flow across an organization to manage and coordinate the ongoing activities of the enterprise, including product planning, manufacturing and distribution, accounting and finance, sales, human resources, and customer support (Figure 11-18 on the next page).

Advantages of ERP include complete integration of information systems across departments, better project management, and improved customer service. Complete integration means information is shared rapidly and management receives a more complete and timely view of the organization through the information. Project management software often is standardized across an enterprise so that different parts of the enterprise easily can integrate and collaborate on their planning and logistics.

Figure 11-18 ERP encompasses all of the major activities throughout an enterprise.
© Morgan Lane Photography / Shutterstock.com; © Monkey Business Images / Shutterstock.com; © iStockphoto /Paul Mckeown; © BartlomiejMagierowski / Shutterstock.com; © Inti St Clair / Getty Images; © iStockphoto / choicegraphx; © John Penezic / Shutterstock.com; © lucadp / Shutterstock.com; © Andresr / Shutterstock.com; © baki / Shutterstock.com; © StockLite / Shutterstock.com; © wavebreakmedia / Shutterstock.com; © Tumar / Shutterstock.com; © Cengage Learning

Document Management Systems

Some organizations use document management systems to make collaboration possible among employees. A **document management system (DMS)** allows for storage and management of a company's documents, such as word processing documents, presentations, and spreadsheets. A central library stores all documents within a company or department. The system supports access control, security, version tracking of documents, search capabilities, and the ability of users to check in and check out documents. This information can be used for searches within the document repository. Web application document management systems allow individuals and any organization to enjoy the benefits of document management systems. Users are granted access to certain parts of the repository, depending on their needs.

Content Management Systems

A **content management system (CMS)** enables and manages the publishing, modification, organization, and access of various forms of documents and other files, including media and webpages, on a network or the web. CMSs include information about the files and data

BTW
DMS
A CMS (content management system) typically includes a DMS (document management system).

(metadata). For example, the metadata for a company's employee manual may include the author's name, revision number, a brief summary, and last revision date. A CMS also provides security controls for the content, such as who is allowed to add, view, and modify content and on which content the user is allowed to perform those operations. Read Ethics & Issues 11-4 to consider who is responsible when company data is compromised.

Users add content to a CMS through a graphical user interface or webpage. Based on the user's actions, the CMS processes content, categorizes the content, indexes the content so that it later can be searched, and stores the content. Users then access the content stored in the system through a website, company portal, or other application.

 CONSIDER THIS

What would be an application of a CMS?

Publishing entities, such as news services, use CMSs to keep websites and web feeds up to date. As news or information is published, it is categorized and updated on the appropriate sections of the website. For example, a sportswriter may submit a story to the CMS and add metadata that indicates the story is a headline story. The CMS categorizes the story so that it is displayed as the first item with a large headline on the sports section of the website and web feeds. The CMS indexes the information in the story so that users who search the website based on keywords in the story will find a link to the story.

 ETHICS & ISSUES 11-4

What Responsibility Does a Company Have to Protect Customer Data?

Hackers broke into a large entertainment company's server, disrupting service to its customers. The hackers also published personal data for millions of customers, including passwords and possibly credit card information. The breached company allegedly waited a week to inform customers about the attack.

The hackers who exposed this company's data were part of a well-known activist group. The group routinely targets large corporations and government agencies to expose data vulnerabilities and to protest

policies. The group claimed that the company had not encrypted the exposed data properly. The group's members are unknown, so officials are unable to hold them responsible for their actions.

Customers, however, are suing the company for the breach. One lawsuit stated that the company's lack of encryption and adequate firewalls makes it responsible for the hackers' actions. Officials agreed, with one stating, "If you are responsible for so many payment card details and log-in details, then keeping that personal data secure has to be your priority." Customers also are holding the company responsible for the delay in

notification. The attack ultimately cost the company an estimated $170 million. Since the breach, the company changed its user agreement policies. The new policy states that by agreeing to use its products, users give up the right to sue for security breaches.

Should hackers be punished for exposing customer data? Why or why not? What expectations of security should customers have when they enter personal data on a website or form? Should companies be able to prevent customers from suing them? Why or why not?

Other Enterprise-Wide Information Systems

Some enterprise-wide information systems focus on the collection, organization, and sharing of information so that users can make decisions based on an up-to-date and accurate view of the information. The following sections discuss these information systems.

 BTW

TPS

Transaction processing systems were among the first computerized systems that processed business data. Many people initially used the term, data processing, to refer to the functions of these systems.

Transaction Processing Systems   A **transaction processing system** (TPS) is an information system that captures and processes data from day-to-day business activities. Examples of transactions are deposits, payments, orders, and reservations. When you use a credit card to purchase an item, you are interacting with a transaction processing system. In an organization, clerical staff typically performs the following activities associated with a transaction processing system:

1. Record a transaction (i.e., airline reservation, customer order, employee time card, car owner's payment, etc.).

2. Confirm an action or cause a response (i.e., send an itinerary, send an order summary, print a paycheck, issue a receipt, etc.).

3. Maintain data (i.e., add new data, modify existing data, or delete unwanted data).

Information systems use batch or online transaction processing systems (Figure 11-19). With *batch processing*, the computer collects data over time and processes all transactions later, as a group. With *online transaction processing (OLTP)*, the computer processes each transaction as it is entered. For example, when you book a flight on the web, the airline probably uses OLTP to schedule the flight, book the flight, and send you a confirmation message.

Most transaction processing systems today use OLTP because users need information immediately. For some routine processing tasks, such as printing monthly invoices or weekly paychecks, they use batch processing.

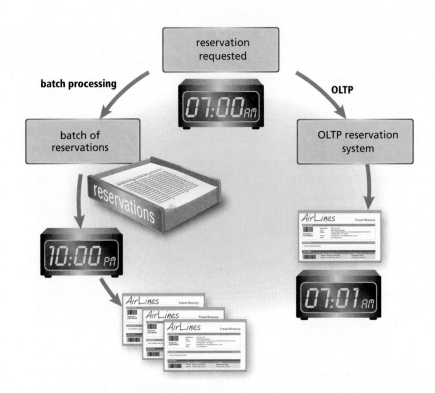

Figure 11-19 With batch processing, all airline reservations would be processed together at the end of the day. With OLTP, by contrast, reservations are processed immediately.
© Cengage Learning

Management Information Systems A **management information system (MIS)** is an information system that generates accurate, timely, and organized information, so that managers and other users can make decisions, solve problems, supervise activities, and track progress. Management information systems often are integrated with transaction processing systems and focus on creating information that managers and other users need to perform their jobs.

A management information system creates three basic types of reports: detailed, summary, and exception (Figure 11-20). A *detailed report* usually lists just transactions. For example, a Detailed Flight Report lists the number of passengers booked for a given flight. A *summary report* consolidates data usually with totals, tables, or graphs, so that managers can review it quickly and easily. An *exception report* identifies data outside of a normal condition. These out-of-the-ordinary conditions, called the *exception criteria*, define the normal activity or status range. For example, a Premier Club Booking Exception Report notifies the airline's marketing department that some flights have not met minimum goals for booking Premier Club members.

Detailed Flight Report for March 30

Flight #	Origin/ Destination	Class – Number of Passengers	Premier Club Members
1048	ORD – RSW	A – 5	A – 1
		B – 14	B – 12
		C – 89	C – 20
543	ORD – BMI	A – 2	A – 2
		B – 7	B – 5
		C – 15	C – 5
715	ORD – LAX	A – 12	A – 8
		B – 25	B – 15
		C – 123	C – 39
701	ORD – JFK	A – 9	A – 7
		B – 10	B – 0
		C – 7	C – 3

Summary Flight Report for March 30

Flight #	Origin/ Destination	Passengers	Premier Club Members
1048	ORD – RSW	108	33
543	ORD – BMI	24	12
715	ORD – LAX	160	62
701	ORD – JFK	26	10

Exception Flight Report for March 30

Flight #	Class	Origin/ Destination	Premier Club Members	Premier Club Member Goal
1048	A	ORD – RSW	1	4
701	C	ORD – JFK	3	5

Figure 11-20 Three basic types of reports generated in an MIS are detailed, summary, and exception.
© Cengage Learning

Decision Support Systems A **decision support system** (DSS) helps users analyze information and make decisions (Figure 11-21). Some decision support systems are company specific and designed solely for managers. Others are available to everyone on the web. Programs that analyze data, such as those in a decision support system, sometimes are called *online analytical processing* (*OLAP*) programs.

A decision support system uses data from internal and external sources. *Internal sources* of data might include databases, sales orders, MRP and MRP II results, inventory records, or financial data from accounting and financial analyses. Data from *external sources* could include interest rates, population trends, costs of new housing construction, or raw material pricing.

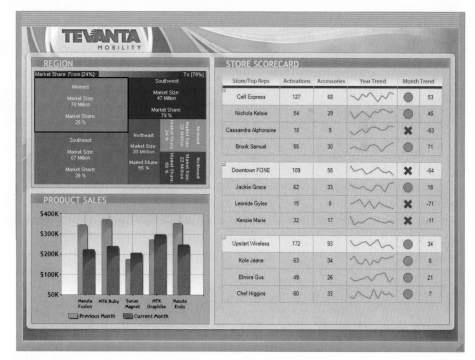

Figure 11-21 This decision support system helps managers analyze sales by product and by sales rep.
Courtesy of Dundas Data Visualation, Inc.

Some decision support systems include their own query languages, statistical analyses, spreadsheets, and graphics that help users retrieve data and analyze the results. Some also allow managers to create a model of the factors affecting a decision.

Expert Systems An **expert system** is an information system that captures and stores the knowledge of human experts and then imitates human reasoning and decision making (Figure 11-22). Expert systems consist of two main components: a knowledge base and inference rules. A *knowledge base* is the combined subject knowledge and experiences of the human experts. The *inference rules* are a set of logical judgments that are applied to the knowledge base each time a user describes a situation to the expert system.

Expert systems help all levels of users make decisions. Enterprises employ expert systems in a variety of roles, such as answering customer questions, training new employees, and analyzing data. Expert systems also successfully have resolved such diverse problems as diagnosing illnesses, searching for oil, and making soup.

Figure 11-22 This company's restaurant advisor expert system recommends a restaurant based on a user's answers to specific questions.
Courtesy of Exsys

Internet Research

What are recent developments in artificial intelligence?

Search for: artificial intelligence applications

☀ **CONSIDER THIS**

How do expert systems relate to artificial intelligence?
Expert systems are a component of artificial intelligence. **Artificial intelligence** (**AI**) is the application of human intelligence to computers. Artificial intelligence technology senses a person's actions and, based on logical assumptions and prior experience, takes the appropriate action to complete the task. Artificial intelligence has a variety of capabilities, including speech recognition, logical reasoning, and creative responses.

NOW YOU KNOW

Be sure you understand the material presented in the sections titled Web Databases, Database Administration, and Information Systems in the Enterprise, as it relates to the chapter objectives.
You now should know . . .

- Which web databases you might use (Objective 8)
- What you would consider if you were designing a database (Objective 9)
- Which enterprise information systems you have used (Objective 10)

> Quiz Yourself Online: Check your knowledge of related content by navigating to this book's Quiz Yourself resource on Computer Concepts CourseMate and then tapping or clicking Objectives 8–10.

Chapter Summary

This chapter discussed how data and information are valuable assets to an organization. The chapter also presented methods for maintaining high-quality data and assessing the quality of valuable information. It then discussed the advantages of organizing data in a database and described various types of databases. It presented the roles of the database analysts and administrators and database design guidelines. It also discussed information systems used in an enterprise.

 Test your knowledge of chapter material by accessing the Study Guide, Flash Cards, and Practice Test apps that run on your smartphone, tablet, laptop, or desktop.

TECHNOLOGY @ WORK

Sports

While watching your local football team play an out-of-state game on television, you watch various player and game statistics appear on the screen, alerting you to how many yards the offense must travel before making a first down. The camera then focuses on the large, colorful, high-resolution scoreboard at the stadium. While sports, such as football, have been around for many decades, the integration of technology has added significantly to the viewing experience.

While watching a baseball game, you notice that the scoreboard shows the number of balls and strikes for the player at bat, as well as other statistics. Behind home plate, an electronic radar gun calculates and records the speed of each pitch. This recorded data, along with the umpire's call (ball or strike) and the player's performance at bat (hit, home run, strike out, etc.) are entered in a computer, which updates the player's batting average automatically. A database stores information about the individual players and other aspects of the baseball game. During this entire time, the video display on the stadium's scoreboard plays audio and video

to entertain the fans. The computer storing the player and game statistics, audio, and video communicates with the scoreboard and video display using either a wired or wireless connection. At the same time, these computers send updated scores and statistics to webpages and mobile devices.

Technology not only is used to keep track of athlete statistics and communicate with scoreboards, but also in NASCAR to help measure a vehicle's performance before a race. Sensors installed on a vehicle can measure throttle inputs, airflow over the body, the distance between the vehicle's frame and the track, and more. The NASCAR teams then can modify the vehicle so that it achieves maximum

performance during a race.

Overall, technology adds enjoyment to various sporting events for many individuals. While waiting for a pitcher to throw the next ball or for a football team to start its next play, keep in mind that the integration of technology entertains you with interesting statistics and replays between the action.

How else might computers and technology be used in sports?

Study Guide

The Study Guide exercise reinforces material you should know for the chapter exam. You will find answers to items with the 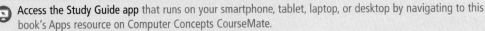 icon only in the e-book.

Access the Study Guide app that runs on your smartphone, tablet, laptop, or desktop by navigating to this book's Apps resource on Computer Concepts CourseMate.

Instructions: Answer the questions below using the format that helps you remember best or that is required by your instructor. Possible formats may include one or more of these options: write the answers; create a document that contains the answers; record answers as audio or video using a webcam, smartphone, or portable media player; post answers on a blog, wiki, or website; or highlight answers in the book/e-book.

1. Define these terms: database, data, and database software.

2. Explain the importance of data integrity. GIGO stands for _____.

3. List steps that you should take if you experience identity theft.

4. Identify characteristics of data that contribute to its value.

5. Identify the role of a file, record, and field in the hierarchy of data in a database.

6. In the ASCII coding scheme, each byte represents a single _____.

7. Define these terms: field, field name, and data type. List common data types.

8. Identify what is stored in a record. Explain the importance of a primary key.

9. Define the term, data file. Identify what is involved in file maintenance.

10. Explain the issues surrounding function creep.

11. Explain how a user might add a record to a database or modify a record.

12. Explain how a DBMS might manage deleted records.

13. Define the term, validation. Explain the role of a validity check.

14. List types of validity checks and explain what occurs in each.

15. Explain the disadvantages of typical file processing systems.

16. Describe the database approach to storing data. Differentiate between a front-end and back-end program.

17. 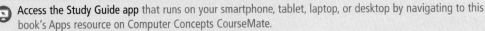 Explain the innovations of forensic databases.

18. Identify the uses of data and databases in the 1000 Genomes Project.

19. Explain how the database approach affects data integrity.

20. Explain the issues surrounding sharing of criminal databases.

21. List common functions performed by most DBMSs.

22. Define the term, data dictionary. Explain how a data dictionary uses default values.

23. Define the terms, query and query language. Explain what SQL allows users to do with data.

24. List steps to import data from a spreadsheet into a database.

25. Explain the QBE feature of a DBMS. 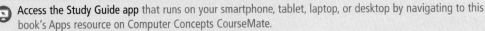 Explain how a database filters data.

26. Define the terms, forms and report writer.

27. Explain how access privileges contribute to data security. Identify differences between the security policies for a database administrator and a typical user.

28. List methods to restore a database. Differentiate between rollforward and rollback recovery.

29. List methods to back up a database. Explain why a business might choose continuous backup.

30. A(n) _____ defines how users view the organization of the data. List three popular data models.

31. Define the term, relational database.

32. 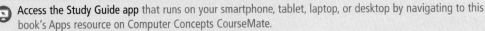 Identify the contributions of Larry Ellison and E.F. Codd with respect to databases.

33. Define the term, object-oriented database.

34. Describe how multidimensional databases store data.

35. Define the following terms: data warehouse, distributed database, data mining, and data mart.

36. Explain how you access data in a web database.

37. Identify steps to use a research database.

38. Explain what is meant by the term, Big Data.

39. Describe the roles of the database analyst and the database administrator.

40. List guidelines for maintaining a database.

41. Explain issues surrounding accidental access of confidential data.

42. Identify how to determine the organization and structure of a database.

43. Define the term, information system. List examples of information systems that support activities of several functional units.

44. Explain whether a company is responsible for protecting customer data.

45. Explain the role of a content management system.

46. List activities associated with a transaction processing system.

47. Define the terms: management information system, decision support system, expert system, and artificial intelligence.

48. Explain how the sports industry uses technology.

You should be able to define the Primary Terms and be familiar with the Secondary Terms listed below.

Key Terms

Access the **Flash Cards** app that runs on your smartphone, tablet, laptop, or desktop by navigating to this book's Apps resource on Computer Concepts CourseMate. **View definitions** for each term by navigating to this book's Key Terms resource on Computer Concepts CourseMate. **Listen to definitions** for each term on your portable media player by navigating to this book's Audio Study Tools resource on Computer Concepts CourseMate.

Primary Terms (shown in **bold-black** characters in the chapter)

artificial intelligence (AI) (496
backup (482)
character (468)
column (483)
content management
  system (CMS) (492)
continuous backup (482)
data dictionary (478)
data file (469)
data model (483)
data type (468)
data warehouse (486)
database (464)
database administrator
  (DBA) (489)

database analyst (DA) (489)
database design (490)
database management
  system (DBMS) (464)
database software (464)
decision support system (495)
document management
  system (DMS) (492)
Enterprise Resource
  Planning (ERP) (491)
expert system (496)
field (468)
field name (468)
file maintenance (470)
file processing system (475)

form (481)
information system (491)
log (482)
management information
  system (MIS) (494)
multidimensional
  database (485)
object (483)
object-oriented database
  (OODB) (483)
primary key (469)
query (479)
query by example (QBE) (481)
query language (480)
record (469)

recovery utility (482)
relational database (483)
relationship (483)
report writer (481)
row (483)
Structured Query Language
  (SQL) (480)
table (483)
transaction processing
  system (493)
validation (473)

Secondary Terms (shown in *italic* characters in the chapter)

accessible information (467)
accurate information (467)
alphabetic check (473)
attribute (483)
back end (476)
backward recovery (482)
batch processing (494)
Big Data (488)
BLOB (469)
Boolean (469)
check digit (473)
collaborative database (486)
completeness check (473)
composite key (469)
computer-aided engineering (CAE)
  (491)
computer-aided manufacturing
  (CAM) (491)
consistency check (473)

cost-effective information (467)
customer relationship management
  (CRM) (491)
data entry form (481)
data integrity (466)
data mart (486)
data mining (486)
data modeler (489)
database server (486
default value (478)
detailed report (494)
distributed database (486)
e-form (481)
exception criteria (494)
exception report (494)
external sources (495)
foreign key (490)
forward recovery (482)
front end (476)

function creep (470)
garbage in, garbage out
  (GIGO) (466)
GIS (485)
human resources information system
  (HRIS) (491)
inference rules (496)
internal sources (495)
knowledge base (496)
Manufacturing Resource Planning II
  (MRP II) (491)
Materials Requirements Planning
  (MRP) (491)
metadata (478)
numeric check (473)
object query language (OQL) (483)
object-relational database (483)
online analytical processing (OLAP)
  (495)

online transaction processing (OLT)
  (494)
organized information (467)
principle of least privilege policy (482)
range check (473)
relation (483)
report generator (481)
repository (478)
rollback (482)
rollforward (482)
salesforce automation (SFA) (491)
summary report (494)
timely information (467)
tuple (483)
useful information (467)
verifiable information (467)

data dictionary (478)

Checkpoint

The Checkpoint exercises test your knowledge of the chapter concepts. The page number containing the answer appears in parentheses after each exercise. The Consider This exercises challenge your understanding of chapter concepts.

Complete the Checkpoint exercises interactively by navigating to this book's Checkpoint resource on Computer Concepts CourseMate. **Access the Test Prep app** that runs on your smartphone, tablet, laptop, or desktop by navigating to this book's Apps resource on Computer Concepts CourseMate. After successfully completing the self-assessment through the Test Prep app, **take the Practice Test** by navigating to this book's Practice Test resource on Computer Concepts CourseMate.

True/False   Mark T for True and F for False.

_____ 1. The more errors data contains, the higher its integrity. (466)

_____ 2. In a data hierarchy, each higher level of data contains one or more items from the lower level. (467)

_____ 3. A field size determines the maximum number of characters a field can contain. (468)

_____ 4. Validity checks reduce data entry errors and thus enhance the data's integrity. (473)

_____ 5. A check digit often confirms the accuracy of a primary key value. (473)

_____ 6. File processing systems require more memory, storage, and processing power than a database. (477)

_____ 7. In a rollforward, the DBMS uses the log to undo any changes made to the database during a certain period. (482)

_____ 8. In a file processing system, you can set up a relationship between tables at any time. (483)

_____ 9. A relational database processes and summarizes large number of records efficiently and can do so much faster than a multidimensional database. (486)

_____ 10. A database administrator (DBA) focuses on the meaning and usage of data. (489)

_____ 11. An ERP allows for storage and management of a company's documents. (492)

_____ 12. With batch processing, the computer collects data over time and processes all transactions later, as a group. (494)

Multiple Choice   Select the best answer.

1. A(n) _____ check tests data in two or more associated fields to ensure that the relationship is logical and their data is in the correct format. (473)
   a. completeness
   b. consistency
   c. range
   d. alphabetic

2. Which of the following is *not* an advantage of a database approach? (476)
   a. improved data integrity
   b. reduced data redundancy
   c. shared data
   d. requires less memory, storage, and processing power than file processing systems

3. A _____ contains data about each file in the database and each field in those files. (478)
   a. query
   b. form
   c. data dictionary
   d. data mart

4. A developer of a relational database refers to a file as a _____. (483)
   a. dictionary
   b. relation
   c. tuple
   d. record

5. A(n) _____ database stores data in objects. (484)
   a. object-oriented
   b. multidimensional
   c. relational
   d. distributed

6. With _____, the computer processes each transaction as it is entered. (494)
   a. batch processing
   b. online transaction processing
   c. data mining
   d. query by example

7. A(n) _____ report usually lists just transactions. (494)
   a. detailed
   b. summary
   c. exception
   d. criteria

8. In an expert system, the _____ is the combined subject knowledge and experiences of the human experts. (496)
   a. inference rule(s)
   b. external source
   c. internal source
   d. knowledge base

Checkpoint

Matching   Match the terms with their definitions.

_____ 1. field (468)

_____ 2. data type (468)

_____ 3. primary key (469)

_____ 4. file maintenance (470)

_____ 5. validation (473)

_____ 6. query (479)

_____ 7. data model (483)

_____ 8. object (483)

_____ 9. data warehouse (486)

_____ 10. Big Data (488)

a. procedures that keep data current

b. defines how users view the organization of the data

c. field that uniquely identifies each record in a file

d. process of comparing data with a set of rules or values to determine if the data is correct

e. combination of one or more related characters or bytes and is the smallest unit of data a user accesses

f. term used to describe the widespread growth of data, the variety of formats in which the data is available, and the processing required to make the data accessible in a timely manner

g. huge database that stores and manages the data required to analyze historical and current transactions

h. specifies the kind of data a field can contain and how the field is used

i. item that contains data, as well as the actions that read or process the data

j. request for specific data from a database

Short Answer   Write a brief answer to each of the following questions.

1. What is function creep? (470) If you use a browser, what are some techniques you can use to protect your data? (470)

2. List reasons for backing up a database. (483) List some ways to back up a database. (483)

3. What are the responsibilities of database analysts and administrators? (489) How do their jobs differ? (489)

4. What is database design? (490) In designing a database, what must the database analyst or administrator identify? (490)

5. What is a decision support system? (495) What is an expert system? (496)

✳ Consider This   Answer the following questions in the format specified by your instructor.

1. Answer the critical thinking questions posed at the end of these elements in this chapter: Ethics & Issues (470, 477, 489, 493), How To (479, 483, 488, 489), Mini Features (487, 490), Secure IT (466, 467, 476, 482), and Technology @ Work (497).

2. What are the qualities of valuable information? (466)

3. Should you use a numeric field type for a phone number? Why or why not? (469)

4. Should companies sell customer data to other companies? Why or why not? (470)

5. Why might a DBMS flag records that contain inactive data? (473)

6. What are the advantages of a database approach to data storage? (476)

7. What is the purpose of a default value? (478)

8. What should security administrators consider when establishing database security policies? (482)

9. 📄 How does a database determine which type of recovery technique to use? (482)

10. How do developers and users of relational databases refer to files, records, and fields? (483)

11. What are the advantages of object-oriented databases over relational databases? (484)

12. For what purpose might an e-commerce website use data mining? (486)

13. How does the education field use web databases? (487)

14. What guidelines should you follow to maintain a database? (489)

15. How might an organization use a document management system? (492)

✳ How To: Your Turn

The How To: Your Turn exercises present general guidelines for fundamental skills when using a computer or mobile device and then require that you determine how to apply these general guidelines to a specific program or situation.

Instructions: You often can complete tasks using technology in multiple ways. Figure out how to perform the tasks described in these exercises by using one or more resources available to you (such as a computer or mobile device, articles on the web or in print, online or program help, user guides, blogs, podcasts, videos, other individuals, trial and error, etc.). Summarize your 'how to' steps, along with the resource(s) used, in the format requested by your instructor (brief report, presentation, discussion, blog post, video, or other means).

1 Plan a Database Structure

Designing a database is no easy task; proper planning not only can help a database store data efficiently, but also can reduce the possibility of returning incorrect results in a query or report. Before creating a database, you should plan its structure. The following steps guide you through the process of planning a database structure. Apply the guidelines in this exercise by planning the structure of a new database for a scenario of your choosing. Possible scenarios might include a database that a school might use to keep track of students and their grades or a database used by sales representatives in a small business to keep track of their customers.

a. Identify the tables and objects to be stored in the database. For example, if you are creating a simple database that keeps track of students and the grades they earn in each class, you might want to store information about each student (identification number, name, address, phone number, date of birth, etc.), information about each course (course identifier, title, instructor, day and time offered, etc.), and the grades that students receive in each course. Tables should store groups of related information; that is, every item the table stores should have the same characteristics. Information about students and courses should be stored in separate files or tables because students and classes have different characteristics. For example, students have a date of birth and courses do not.

b. Identify a unique identifier (primary key) in each file or table that will uniquely identify each record. In a table containing student information, the student identification number should uniquely identify each student. First or last names do not make good primary keys because multiple students might share the same name.

c. Determine the fields for each file or table. You should create a separate field for each item on which you want to sort, search, or filter. For example, you should store first names and last names as separate fields so that you can sort students by first name and/or last name.

d. Determine the type of data each field will store. If a field will store data that might be used in a calculation, that field should be stored using a numeric data type. If the field will not be used in a calculation, it is not necessary to store the field using a numeric data type.

e. Determine how the files or tables are related. This database contains information about students and courses. The relationship between these two categories of data is that students enroll in courses and courses contain students. In this example, students can take multiple courses, and courses can contain multiple students. This often is referred to as a many-to-many relationship. It is good practice to remove many-to-many relationships from the database, and this often is done by creating an additional file or table. The new file or table should contain the primary keys of each of the two tables in the many-to-many relationship. In this example, the new table would contain the student identifier and the course identifier. This new table now accurately depicts which students are enrolled in each course.

f. After creating a new table, determine what additional information might be stored in the table. In this example, students receive a grade in each class they take, so it would make sense to also store the grades in this table.

g. Review the database structure and make sure you are not storing the same data multiple times. For example, because you store the student's full name in the Student file or table, it is not necessary to store the name in the table containing the courses in which students are enrolled. Having redundant data can increase the potential for data to be updated in one location but not the other.

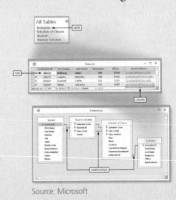

Source: Microsoft

How To: Your Turn ✳

Exercises

1. Why is it not ideal to store redundant data in a database?
2. What problems can occur from having a database that is not designed properly?

❷ Search a Web Database

Many people use web databases on a frequent basis. For example, you might use a web database to search for a flight for an upcoming vacation. The following steps guide you through the process of performing a basic and advanced search for a flight.

Basic Search

a. Navigate to a travel website that can search flights on multiple airlines.
b. Specify whether this is a round trip or one-way trip.
c. Select the originating city, departure date, destination city, and return date (if this is will be a round-trip ticket).
d. Run the search. Record the number of search results, and then locate the flight that best meets your needs and budget.

Advanced Search

a. Navigate back to the page where you can enter the search criteria.
b. If necessary, enter the same criteria from the previous set of steps (round trip or one-way, departure date, destination city, and return date).
c. For each flight, specify the time frame you prefer to leave and when you would like to arrive.
d. Specify up to three preferred airlines you want to fly.
e. Specify an acceptable airfare for the flight.
f. Specify whether you prefer a nonstop flight or a flight with one or more connections.
g. Run the search. Record the number of search results and then locate the flight that best meets your needs and budget.

Exercises

1. Do you typically perform basic searches where you enter the minimum amount of criteria required, or do you typically perform searches and specify additional criteria? In your opinion, which type of search is better? Why?
2. How long did it take you to locate an acceptable flight using the basic search? How long did it take you to

find an acceptable flight when you performed an advanced search?

❸ Obtain and Verify the Accuracy of a Credit Report

As discussed in this chapter, you might need to obtain or verify the accuracy of your credit report for a variety of reasons. It is important to obtain your credit report at least one time per year to verify its accuracy, as imperfections on a credit report can lead to problems such as financing being declined or higher interest rates on loans. The following steps guide you through the process of obtaining and verifying the accuracy of a credit report.

a. Run the browser and navigate to annualcreditreport.com.
b. When you arrive at the website, verify that the browser is using the "https" protocol, indicating a secure connection.
c. Select your state and then tap or click the button to request the report.
d. Provide the necessary personal information.
e. Select the agency or agencies from which you want a copy of your credit report.
f. Tap or click the button to continue to the credit reporting agency's website.
g. If necessary, enter the additional requested information to validate your request.
h. Follow the remaining instructions on the website to finish obtaining a copy of your credit report.
i. Save and/or print a copy of the credit report.

After you have obtained a copy of your credit report, you should verify it for accuracy. The following points describe what to look for when reviewing the report:

- Verify the list of accounts is accurate.
- Verify your payment history.
- Verify current balances are accurate.
- Review your personal information, and report any inconsistencies to the credit reporting agency.
- Review your rights under the Fair Credit Reporting Act.

Exercises

1. In addition to the reasons mentioned in this exercise, why else might you want to obtain a copy of your credit report?
2. What is a credit score? How can you obtain your credit score? What are the highest and lowest possible credit scores?

✳ Internet Research

The Internet Research exercises broaden your understanding of chapter concepts by requiring that you search for information on the web.

Instructions: Use a search engine or another search tool to locate the information requested or answers to questions presented in the exercises. Describe your findings, along with the search term(s) you used and your web source(s), in the format requested by your instructor (brief report, presentation, discussion, blog post, video, or other means).

1 Making Use of the Web

Entertainment and Media Americans, on average, spend nearly six percent of their income on entertainment, which includes tickets for concerts and movies, electronic equipment, hobbies, and services. They have scaled back their out-of-home activities in favor of in-home entertainment as they have invested in home theaters, high-speed Internet, and game consoles.

Many websites supplement cravings for amusement. For example, the Rock and Roll Hall of Fame and Museum has videos, stories, and a comprehensive "The Story of Rock" to enjoy. The Internet Movie Database has facts on more than two million movies and television programs, video highlights, quizzes, and movie showtimes. Other entertainment websites have a variety of content aimed at amusing visitors and relieving boredom.

(a) Use a search engine to locate the Rock and Roll Hall of Fame and Museum website and view the information about the latest inductees. What is the total number of inductees? Which artists have been inducted more than once? Describe two upcoming events. Which classes are being offered in the Rock and Roll Night School?

(b) Use a search engine to locate the Internet Movie Database website. Take the IMDb Top 100 Quiz. What score did you earn? What are three movies opening this week? What is the top news story of the day?

(c) Visit an entertainment website. What content is featured, such as humorous and sports video clips, pictures, animations, and audio clips? What categories are available? Are advertisements included in the content? Which content is available at no cost, and which requires a fee to access?

2 Social Media 📝

More than 100 companies collect data as people browse websites. Just seconds after individuals visit a specific webpage, advertisements are displayed matching their shopping patterns and favorite products. This tracking is prevalent in social media, too, as marketers match users' profiles and other posted information, such as status updates, with specific businesses. Facebook, for example, allows retailers to upload their databases containing email addresses, phone numbers, and other personal facts. This data then is compared with the Facebook users' data. When a match is found, specific advertisements are displayed. Social media may charge the advertisers each time a user clicks an ad, called CPC (cost per click) or PPC (pay per click), which could range from a few cents to several dollars. Another option is to charge for a specific number of times an ad is displayed, called CPI (cost per impression).

Locate at least two articles discussing targeting ads on social media websites. How do the businesses place their ads based on the users' online identities and profiles? What steps are taken to ensure the users' privacy? Should users expect companies to collect data about some of their online behaviors in return for using the websites at no charge?

3 Search Sleuth

(1) Three popular data models discussed in this chapter are relational, object-oriented, and multidimensional. Name one other type. (2) Which United States governmental agency was first associated with the expression garbage in, garbage out (GIGO) in April 1963? (3) What are three common SQL wildcard characters? (4) When did Microsoft release the first version of Access? (5) Records and sets are the fundamental constructs of which data model? (6) According to Amazon Web Services, which data model does the company offer for its database in the cloud? (7) Which company trademarked the phrase,

Source: The Rock and Roll Hall of Fame and Museum, Inc.

Courtesy of Exsys

database mining, for marketing its workstation? (8) Which organization markets the PeopleSoft human resource management system? (9) What are the 3V that describe aspects of Big Data? (10) At which conference was the term, artificial intelligence (AI), coined? In which year did this conference occur?

④ Green Computing

Companies are using databases to make an effort to conserve natural resources. Some sell reusable products, such as lead-free lunch bags, water bottles, and household items, and also educate consumers on how they can help reduce consumption of disposable items. The Electronic Product Environmental Assessment Tool (EPEAT) website has a searchable database showcasing greener electronics. Its rating system identifies computers, imaging equipment, and televisions manufactured by at least 60 companies worldwide.

Locate websites with databases providing information about earth-friendly products. How easy are the databases to use? What products are popular? Then, visit the EPEAT website. How are the environmentally preferable products identified? How was the Electronics Environmental Benefits Calculator (EEBC) developed? What measurable benefits for the environment are attained by using EPEAT-registered products? Which manufacturers are included in EPEAT database?

⑤ Security

When you use supermarket loyalty cards, enter contests, complete warranty registrations, apply for a credit card, and subscribe to newsletters, businesses automatically store personal data about you, your transactions, and your preferences in their marketing databases. They often use this data to analyze sales, develop advertising campaigns, and solicit more business from you. Unbeknownst to many consumers, some companies also sell or rent this data to other businesses for financial gain. Consumers can refuse to receive targeted email messages and marketing materials, but they often must search the websites or paper forms for check boxes to indicate these opt-out preferences. Some consumer advocates view this practice as an invasion of privacy and urge businesses to default to not adding consumers' information to databases unless the consumer opts in to receive additional materials.

Visit at least two websites that include opt-in or opt-out provisions and read the disclosure notices. What steps can you take to remove yourself from databases? Which organizations help protect consumers and offer information on maintaining online privacy? Then, search for at least two marketing companies that provide online direct advertising campaigns. How do these companies use databases to match consumers' buying preferences with targeted offers?

⑥ Ethics in Action

The term, Big Data, is described in the Consider This box on page 488. The massive amount of data collected about consumers is being used to predict events and to guide marketing campaigns. Whenever you post a message on social media, perform a search, make a purchase at a large retailer, or use a smartphone or tablet, you may be adding to a database that is storing details of your everyday behavior.

Marketers use the data to determine an individual's political views, marital status, and other demographics. Facebook's Data Science Team collects and analyzes the personal data posted and can develop a detailed record of each user's life and relationships. If, for example, a user is posting messages about a recent breakup with a significant other and listening to melancholy songs, marketers can use the information to send advertisements about similar albums or online social networks. On a larger scale, security agencies can use the data and predictive analytics to identify individuals who might commit a crime and then monitor their behaviors. Some individuals believe Big Data enriches lives by informing consumers of new products and services and also by adjusting prices to a price point that meets a budget. In contrast, privacy experts criticize the practice of collecting data in the interest of initiating direct marketing and changing behaviors.

Locate at least two articles discussing Big Data. Which states have proposed or passed legislation that would require companies to inform consumers about how personal data is collected and analyzed? Is it ethical for one company to share its database with another business in an entirely different context? For example, should a supermarket be permitted to share its customer purchases database with health insurance companies, which then can use the data to predict medical risks and possibly increase premiums for those customers purchasing unhealthy food? What steps can you take to minimize invasive Internet tracking?

✳ Problem Solving

The Problem Solving exercises extend your knowledge of chapter concepts by seeking solutions to practical problems with technology that you may encounter at home, school, work, or with nonprofit organizations. The Collaboration exercise should be completed with a team.

🖥 **Challenge yourself** with additional Problem Solving exercises by navigating to this book's Problem Solving resource on Computer Concepts CourseMate.

Instructions: You often can solve problems with technology in multiple ways. Determine a solution to the problems in these exercises by using one or more resources available to you (such as a computer or mobile device, articles on the web or in print, blogs, podcasts, videos, television, user guides, other individuals, electronics or computer stores, etc.). Describe your solution, along with the resource(s) used, in the format requested by your instructor (brief report, presentation, discussion, blog post, video, or other means).

Personal

1. **No Search Results** While searching a web database for a hotel room for an upcoming trip, a message is displayed stating that no search results match your criteria. What can you do to correct this problem?

2. **Incorrect Price** You are shopping for groceries and, after loading all items in your cart, it is time to check out. The cashier scans your items, but you realize that the register is not reflecting an advertised discount on one of the items. Why might this be happening?

3. **Invalid Email Address Format** You are creating an account to use some premium features on a website you currently are vising. Creating an account requires that you enter your name, email address, and billing information. When you enter your email address, an error message is displayed stating that your email address is formatted incorrectly. What might be wrong?

4. **Inaccurate Credit Report** You have obtained a free copy of your credit report and notice that multiple companies are accessing your credit report without your knowledge or permission. Your financial records are very important, and it is troubling that other companies are accessing this information. Why might this be occurring?

5. **Product Not Shipping** One month after placing an order with a well-known online retailer, the order still has not shipped, but your credit card has been charged. At first, you assume that the product you ordered is not in stock, but the retailer's website shows that the item is in stock. What might be wrong?

Professional

Source: Microsoft; © Warren Goldswain / Shutterstock.com

6. **Data Entry Issues** You are in charge of adding student information to your school's database using a front end. When you attempt to enter the street address for one of the students, the entire street name does not fit in the text box. What are your next steps?

7. **Incorrect Postal Codes** Your company's database stores information about its customers, including their names, addresses, phone numbers, email addresses, and order history. While reviewing the database to ensure data integrity, you notice that some of the postal codes, which should be five digits, are only four digits. What might be wrong?

8. **Database Restrictions** While updating information in your company's database, an error message suddenly appears, stating that you are not permitted to modify the data in one of the database tables. Why might this be happening, and what are your next steps?

9. **Database Recovery** Your boss has informed you that the main customer database for your company has become corrupt. Fortunately, you can attempt to use the recovery utility to salvage the data in the database. When you attempt to recover the database, you receive an error message that the recovery has failed. What are your next steps?

10. **Content Management System Updates** You are attempting to update your company's website using a content management system. When you make the requested changes in the content management system, they are not reflected on the company website. What might be the problem?

Collaboration

11. **Technology in Sports** You serve as an assistant coach for your former high school's baseball team. The head coach, who has a computer that is more than five years old, informs you that he would like to create an application that will allow him to keep track of his players' statistics. For instance, he would like to track each player's number of strikeouts, walks, hits, and home runs. Form a team of three people to determine the requirements for implementing his request. One team member will research the types of apps that can track this data, another team member will determine the specifications for a computer or mobile device capable of running the software and storing the data, and the other team member will determine the best way to collect the data during the game.

The Critical Thinking exercises challenge your assessment and decision-making skills by presenting real-world situations associated with chapter concepts. The Collaboration exercise should be completed with a team.

Critical Thinking ✸

 Challenge yourself with additional Critical Thinking exercises by navigating to this book's Critical Thinking resource on Computer Concepts CourseMate.

Instructions: Evaluate the situations below, using personal experiences and one or more resources available to you (such as articles on the web or in print, blogs, podcasts, videos, television, user guides, other individuals, electronics or computer stores, etc.). Perform the tasks requested in each exercise and share your deliverables in the format requested by your instructor (brief report, presentation, discussion, blog post, video, or other means).

1. Class Discussion

Online Movie Reviews   Information about movie titles and television shows is available from the web database IMDb (Internet Movie Database). Visitors can search IMDb using a movie's title, cast members, year produced, characters, genre, awards, or other criteria. Each movie's page offers a brief description and rating and includes links to such items as summary, trivia, reviews, quotes, and even streaming video options. Visit imdb.com and search for both recently released and classic movies. Discuss how visitors can query the movie database, how complete the information provided was, and who would benefit most from using the movie database and why. If possible, view the same movie title's webpage on both a computer and a mobile device. Did the information differ? Answer the following questions about your experiences. Did the information provided differ when viewing recently released titles versus classic movies? What did you learn from your queries? Can you identify a few fields that are included in the records for each movie?

2. Research and Share

Source: Microsoft

Spreadsheets versus Databases   Some individuals and small organizations prefer using spreadsheets instead of databases. People who use spreadsheets might argue that similar to databases, spreadsheets have rows and columns, and you can keep track of different sets of data in individual worksheets. This is similar to how you would use tables in a database to store different data sets. In addition, some find it easier to install, use, and maintain spreadsheet software than database software. After reading this chapter, you are convinced that databases have additional advantages. Advantages include the ability to store more data and more quickly search for data, as well as generate reports. Prepare information aimed toward individuals who prefer spreadsheets to databases. Include reasons why it is not advisable to store large amounts of data in spreadsheets, as well as the reporting and querying capabilities of databases. Compile your findings.

3. Case Study

Farmers' Market   You are the new manager for a group of organic farmers who have a weekly market in season. The market uses a database to store information about its vendors, customers, and products. The market's website uses information stored in the database about products available for sale online. The board of directors has asked you to investigate how the market should secure its database. Using information learned in the chapter as well as performing research on the web, prepare information about securing a database. What risks exist for databases? Who should determine the security measures to take? What should you include in the database security policy? Include recommendations for backing up data, data integrity, maintenance, and assigning different access levels to employees and vendors. Is the market responsible for security breaches that put customers' personal data at risk? Why or why not? Compile your findings.

Collaboration

4. **Data Models**   A major retail company has hired your team as database specialists to determine the data model — relational, object-oriented, or multidimensional — best suited for its applications. The retail company wants to allow different access to information for customers and employees. Form a three-member team and have each team member choose a different data model to research using the web. What are typical uses for the data model? What are the advantages and disadvantages of the data model? How does the database store data? What type of software is used to create the data model? Does the data model allow for query by example? How does the data model allow users to manage, update, and retrieve data? Can you use the data model to create a data warehouse? Would you recommend the data model to the retail company? Why or why not? As a team, compile your findings and share your recommendation with the class.

⊛ Beyond the Book

The Beyond the Book exercises expand your understanding of chapter concepts by requiring research.

Access premium content by visiting Computer Concepts CourseMate. If you have a Computer Concepts CourseMate access code, you can reinforce and extend your learning with MindTap Reader, practice tests, video, and other premium content for Discovering Computers. To sign in to Computer Concepts CourseMate at www.cengagebrain.com, you first must create a student account and then register this book, as described at www.cengage.com/ct/studentdownload.

Part 1 Instructions: Use the web or e-book to perform the task identified for each book element below. Describe your findings, along with the search term(s) you used and your web source(s), if appropriate, in the format requested by your instructor (brief report, presentation, discussion, blog post, video, or other means).

1. **Animation** 🖥 Review the animation associated with this chapter and then answer the question(s) it poses (465). What search term would you use to learn more about a specific segment of the animation?

2. **Consider This** Select a Consider This in this chapter (469, 470, 473, 474, 477, 484, 485, 486, 488, 493, 496) and find a recent article that elaborates on the topic. What information did you find that was not presented in this book or e-book?

3. **Drag-and-Drop Figures** 🖥 Complete the Drag-and-Drop Figure activities associated with this chapter (468, 478, 480, 483, 491). What did you learn from this activity?

4. **Ethics & Issues** Select an Ethics & Issues in this chapter (470, 477, 489, 493) and find a recent article that supports one view presented. Does the article change your opinion about the topic? Why or why not?

5. **Facebook & Twitter** Review a recent Discovering Computers Facebook post or Twitter Tweet and read the referenced article(s). What did you learn from the article?

6. **High-Tech Talk** 🖥 Locate an article that discusses topics related to Normalization. Would you recommend the article you found? Why or why not?

7. **How To** Select a How To in this chapter (479, 483, 488, 489) and find a recent article that elaborates on the topic. Who would benefit from the content of this article? Why?

8. **Innovative Computing** 🖥 Locate two additional facts about forensic databases. Do your findings change your opinion about the future of this innovation? Why or why not?

9. **Internet Research** Use the search term in an Internet Research (474, 478, 482, 488, 496) to answer the question posed in the element. What other search term could you use to answer the question?

10. **Mini Features** Locate an article that discusses topics related to one of the mini features in this chapter

(481, 487, 490). Do you feel that the article is appropriate for this course? Why or why not?

11. **Secure IT** Select a Secure IT in this chapter (466, 467, 476, 482) and find a recent article about the topic that you find interesting. How can you relate the content of the article to your everyday life?

12. **Technology @ Work** Locate three additional, unique usages of technology in the sports industry (497). What makes the use of these technologies unique to the sports industry?

13. **Technology Innovators** 🖥 Locate two additional facts about Larry Ellison, E.F. Codd, eBay, and IBM. Which Technology Innovator impresses you most? Why?

14. **Third-Party Links** 🖥 Visit one of the third-party links identified in this chapter (466, 467, 470, 476, 482, 484, 487, 489, 493, 497) and read the article or watch the video associated with the link. Would you share this link on your online social network account? Why or why not?

Part 2 Instructions: Find specific instructions for the exercises below in the e-book or on Computer Concepts CourseMate. Beside each exercise is a brief description of its online content.

1. 🖥 **You Review It** Search for and review a video, podcast, or blog post about Big Data.

2. 🖥 **Windows and Mac** Enhance your understanding and knowledge about using Windows and Mac computers by completing the Explore Data in a Web Database and Visualize Data in a Web Database activities.

3. 🖥 **Android, iOS, and Windows Phone** Enhance your understanding of mobile devices by completing the Find Your IMEI Number and Protect Your Data if Your Device Is Lost or Stolen activities.

4. 🖥 **Exploring Computer Careers** Read about a career as a database administrator, search for related employment ads, and then answer related questions.

5. 🖥 **App Adventure** Be an informed consumer using bar-code scanning apps on your smartphone or tablet.

Information Systems and Program Development

Designing and Building Solutions

12

Analysts and developers use a variety of tools and languages to build a system.

"My school is upgrading its computer system. The conversion process has been lengthy, but its new features are useful. When my boss needed to update his payroll program, he hired a software developer to make changes. Although these modifications are interesting, why do I need to learn about system development and programming languages?"

True, you may be familiar with some of the material in this chapter, but do you know . . .

Why you would use a Gantt chart?

When you might participate in a JAD?

Which finance apps are best suited to your needs?

Why information literacy is important to you?

How technology is used in the construction industry?

Why you would use a sandbox?

Which entertainment software developer refers to its programmers as software artists who can evoke emotions from game enthusiasts?

How you can record a macro?

How to protect your computer from macro viruses?

How to read a flowchart?

Where you would find HTML?

Why software developers use back doors?

How to determine which object-oriented programming language or application development tool to use?

When you might use CSS?

For these answers and to discover much more information essential to this course, read this chapter and visit the associated Computer Concepts CourseMate at www.cengagebrain.com.

✔ Objectives

After completing this chapter, you will be able to:

1 Define system development and list the system development phases

2 Identify the guidelines for system development

3 Discuss the importance of project management, feasibility assessment, documentation, and data and information gathering techniques

4 Discuss the purpose of and tasks conducted in each system development phase

5 Differentiate between low-level languages and procedural languages

6 Identify the benefits of object-oriented programming languages and application development tools

7 List other programming languages and application development tools

8 Describe various ways to develop webpages

System Development

Recall from the previous chapter that an information system is a collection of hardware, software, data, people, and procedures that work together to produce quality information. An information system supports daily, short-term, and long-range activities of users. The type of information that users need often changes. When this occurs, the information system must meet the new requirements. In some cases, members of the system development team modify the current information system. In other cases, they develop an entirely new information system.

As a user of technology in a business, you someday may participate in the modification of an existing information system or the development of a new one. Thus, it is important that you understand system development. **System development** is a set of activities used to build an information system. System development activities often are grouped into larger categories called *phases*. This collection of phases sometimes is called the **system development life cycle** (**SDLC**). Many traditional SDLCs contain five phases (Figure 12-1):

1. Planning
2. Analysis
3. Design
4. Implementation
5. Support and Security

Each system development phase consists of a series of activities, and the phases form a loop. In theory, the five system development phases often appear sequentially, as shown in Figure 12-1. In reality, activities within adjacent phases often interact with one another, making system development a dynamic iterative process.

System Development Guidelines

System development should follow three general guidelines: group activities into phases, involve users, and define standards.

1. **Group activities into phases**. Many SDLCs contain the same phases shown in Figure 12-1. Others have more or fewer phases. Regardless, all system development cycles have similar activities and tasks.

System Development

1. Planning
- Review project requests
- Prioritize project requests
- Allocate resources
- Form project development team

Ongoing Activities
- Project management
- Feasibility assessment
- Documentation
- Data/information gathering

5. Support and Security
- Perform maintenance activities
- Monitor system performance
- Assess system security

2. Analysis
- Conduct preliminary investigation
- Perform detailed analysis activities:
  - Study current system
  - Determine user requirements
  - Recommend solution

4. Implementation
- Develop programs and apps, if necessary
- Install and test new system
- Train users
- Convert to new system

3. Design
- Acquire hardware and software, if necessary
- Develop details of system

Figure 12-1   System development often consists of five phases that form a loop. Several ongoing activities also take place throughout system development.

2. **Involve users**. Users include anyone for whom the system is being built. Customers, employees, students, data entry specialists, accountants, sales managers, and owners all are examples of users. Users are more apt to accept a new system if they contribute to its design.

3. **Define standards**. *Standards* are sets of rules and procedures an organization expects employees to accept and follow. Standards help people working on the same project produce consistent results.

Who Participates in System Development?

System development should involve representatives from each department in which the proposed system will be used. This includes both nontechnical users and IT professionals. Although the roles and responsibilities of members of the system development team may change from organization to organization, this chapter presents general descriptions of tasks for various team members.

During system development, the systems analyst meets and works with a variety of people (Figure 12-2). A **systems analyst** is responsible for designing and developing an information system. The systems analyst is the users' primary contact person. Depending on the size of the organization, the tasks performed by the systems analyst may vary. Smaller organizations may have one systems analyst or even one person who assumes the roles of both systems analyst and software developer. Larger organizations often have multiple systems analysts. Some refer to a systems analyst as a system developer.

For each system development project, an organization usually forms a *project team* to work on the project from beginning to end. The project team consists of users, the systems analyst, and other IT professionals.

 CONSIDER THIS

What skill set should a systems analyst possess?

A systems analyst acts as the liaison between the users and the IT professionals. They convert user requests into technical specifications. Thus, systems analysts must have superior technical skills. They also must be familiar with business operations, be able to solve problems, have the ability to introduce and support change, and possess excellent communications skills, especially in interpersonal and group settings. Systems analysts prepare many reports, drawings, and diagrams. They discuss various aspects of the development project with users, management, other analysts, database analysts, database administrators, network administrators, web developers, software developers, vendors, and the steering committee. Read Ethics & Issues 12-1 to consider the impact of telecommuting employees.

 ETHICS & ISSUES 12-1

Is Telecommuting Good or Bad for Business?

Nearly 10 percent of workers realize the dream of leaving the confines of an office to work from the comfort of home. Although they may have an ideal work situation, some bosses do not agree. An Internet CEO, for example, made news when she reviewed data such as employees' sign-ins to the company's VPN and discovered that many employees were not working during company hours. As a result, the CEO made the decision to end telecommuting at her company.

Supporters of telecommuting provide evidence of reduced pollution and commuting time. Other benefits include increased

productivity due to lack of office gossip and politics. Many feel that they could not be as dedicated to their jobs without telecommuting because of the flexible hours and closeness to home. Others feel that trusted employees should have the privilege if they earn it.

Opponents of telecommuting claim that some lack the self-discipline to work remotely. Employees may be distracted more easily without direct management supervision. Productivity actually may decrease if employees stagger work hours to fit their schedule, limiting times when employees can schedule meetings. Some liken being idle on company time to stealing.

Many experienced workers agree that telecommuting cannot replace valuable face-to-face time with coworkers, vendors, and customers. Some workers fear telecommuting because they feel that the lack of a personal relationship with managers puts them at the top of the list for downsizing.

Is telecommuting good or bad for business? Why or why not? Are some businesses or positions better suited for telecommuting? If so, which ones? Do some people lack the self-discipline to be productive while telecommuting? If so, how should managers determine whether to allow this practice and who may participate?

BTW

Technology Careers
For additional information about careers in the technology field, see the Beyond the Book Computer Careers assignment in each chapter and the Technology Careers appendix (available in the e-book).

BTW

Steering Committee
A *steering committee* is a decision-making body in an organization.

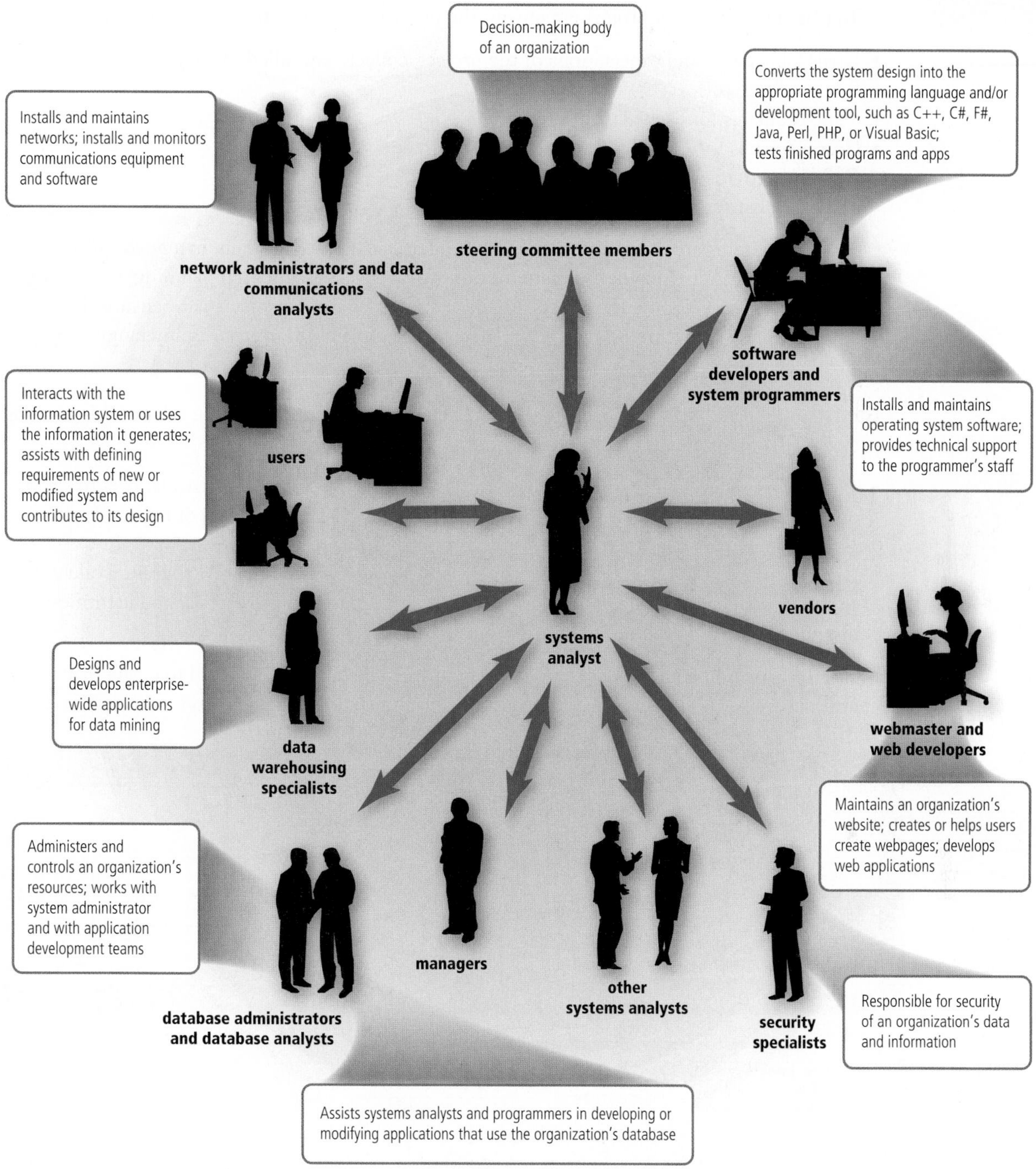

Installs and maintains networks; installs and monitors communications equipment and software

Decision-making body of an organization

Converts the system design into the appropriate programming language and/or development tool, such as C++, C#, F#, Java, Perl, PHP, or Visual Basic; tests finished programs and apps

network administrators and data communications analysts

steering committee members

software developers and system programmers

Interacts with the information system or uses the information it generates; assists with defining requirements of new or modified system and contributes to its design

users

Installs and maintains operating system software; provides technical support to the programmer's staff

systems analyst

vendors

Designs and develops enterprise-wide applications for data mining

data warehousing specialists

webmaster and web developers

Administers and controls an organization's resources; works with system administrator and with application development teams

Maintains an organization's website; creates or helps users create webpages; develops web applications

managers

other systems analysts

security specialists

Responsible for security of an organization's data and information

database administrators and database analysts

Assists systems analysts and programmers in developing or modifying applications that use the organization's database

Figure 12-2 A systems analyst meets with a variety of people during a system development project.
© Cengage Learning

Project Management

Project management is the process of planning, scheduling, and then controlling the activities during system development. The goal of project management is to deliver an acceptable system to the user in an agreed-upon time frame, while maintaining costs.

In smaller organizations or projects, one person manages the entire project. For larger projects, the project management activities often are separated between a project manager and a project leader. In this situation, the *project leader* manages and controls the budget and schedule of the project, and the *project manager* controls the activities during system development. Project leaders and/or project managers are part of the project team. If the systems analyst is not the project manager, he or she works closely with the project manager.

To plan and schedule a project effectively, the project leader identifies the following elements:

- Goals, objectives, and expectations of the project, collectively called the *scope*
- Required activities
- Time estimates for each activity
- Cost estimates for each activity
- Order of activities
- Activities that can take place at the same time

After these items are identified, the project leader usually records them in a *project plan*. Project leaders can use **project management software** to assist them in planning, scheduling, and controlling development projects. One aspect of managing projects is to ensure that everyone submits deliverables on time and according to plan. A *deliverable* is any tangible item such as a chart, diagram, report, or program file.

Gantt and PERT Charts   Popular tools used to plan and schedule the time relationships among project activities are Gantt and PERT charts (Figure 12-3).

- A *Gantt chart*, developed by Henry L. Gantt, is a bar chart that uses horizontal bars to show project phases or activities. The left side, or vertical axis, displays the list of required activities. A horizontal axis across the top or bottom of the chart represents time.
- Developed by the U.S. Department of Defense, a *PERT chart*, short for Program Evaluation and Review Technique chart, analyzes the time required to complete a task and identifies the minimum time required for an entire project.

PERT charts, sometimes called network diagrams, can be more complicated to create than Gantt charts, but are better suited than Gantt charts for planning and scheduling large, complex projects.

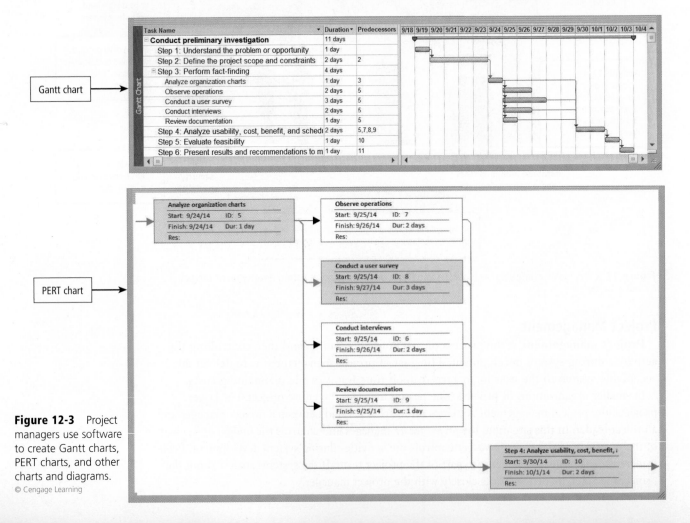

Figure 12-3   Project managers use software to create Gantt charts, PERT charts, and other charts and diagrams.
© Cengage Learning

✳ CONSIDER THIS ───

How do project leaders adjust when a project changes?

After the project features and deadlines have been set, the project leader monitors and controls the project. Some activities take less time than originally planned. Others take longer. The project leader may realize that an activity is taking excessive time or that scope creep has begun. *Scope creep*, also called *feature creep*, occurs when one activity has led to another that was not planned originally; thus, the scope of the project now has grown.

Project leaders should use *change management*, which is the process of recognizing when a change in the project has occurred, taking actions to react to the change, and planning for opportunities because of the change. For example, the project leader may recognize the team will not be able to meet the original deadline of the project due to scope creep. Thus, the project leader may extend the deadline or may reduce the scope of the system development. If the latter occurs, the users will receive a less comprehensive system at the original deadline. In either case, the project leader revises the first project plan and presents the new plan to users for approval. It is crucial that everyone is aware of and agrees on any changes made to the project plan.

Feasibility Assessment

Feasibility is a measure of how suitable the development of a system will be to the organization. A project that is feasible at one point during system development might become infeasible at a later point. Thus, systems analysts frequently reevaluate feasibility during the system development project.

A systems analyst typically uses at least four tests to evaluate feasibility of a project: operational feasibility, schedule feasibility, technical feasibility, and economic feasibility.

- *Operational feasibility* measures how well the proposed information system will work. Will the users like the new system? Will they use it? Will it meet their requirements? Will it cause any changes in their work environment? Is it secure?
- *Schedule feasibility* measures whether the established deadlines for the project are reasonable. If a deadline is not reasonable, the project leader might make a new schedule. If a deadline cannot be extended, then the scope of the project might be reduced to meet a mandatory deadline.
- *Technical feasibility* measures whether the organization has or can obtain the computing resources, software services, and qualified people needed to develop, deliver, and then support the proposed information system. For most information system projects, hardware, software, and people typically are available to support an information system. An organization's choice for using computing resources and software services in-house or on the cloud may impact a system's technical feasibility.
- *Economic feasibility*, also called *cost/benefit feasibility*, measures whether the lifetime benefits of the proposed information system will be greater than its lifetime costs. A systems analyst often consults the advice of a business analyst, who uses many financial techniques, such as return on investment (ROI) and payback analysis, to perform a cost/benefit analysis.

Documentation

During system development, project members produce much documentation. **Documentation** is the collection and summarization of data, information, and deliverables. It is important that all documentation be well written, thorough, consistent, and understandable. The final information system should be reflected accurately and completely in documentation developed throughout the development project. Maintaining up-to-date documentation should be an ongoing part of system development. Too often, project team members put off documentation until the end of the project because it is time consuming, but these practices typically result in lower-quality documentation.

CONSIDER THIS

How do team members collaborate?

Conferencing software includes tools that enable users to share documents via online meetings and communicate with other connected users. When a meeting takes place on the web, it is called a *web conference*. In an online meeting, the facilitator may share a document for all participants to see at the same time. This allows the participants to edit a document and see the changes being made. Many conferencing software apps allow the facilitator to share his or her computer's desktop screen to demonstrate software apps or show webpages in real time to meeting participants. During the online meeting, participants have the ability to open a chat window and type messages to one another. Conferencing software also usually includes audio and video capabilities.

 BTW

Wikimedia Foundation Technology Innovator: You should be familiar with the Wikimedia Foundation and Jimmy Wales (Wikipedia cofounder).

Internet Research

Does the Hawthorne Effect apply to development projects?

Search for: hawthorne effect

Data and Information Gathering Techniques

During system development, members of the project team gather data and information. They need accurate and timely data and information for many reasons. They must keep a project on schedule, evaluate feasibility, and be sure the system meets requirements. Systems analysts and other IT professionals use several techniques to gather data and information. They review documentation, observe, survey, interview, conduct joint-application design sessions, and research.

- **Review documentation:** By reviewing documentation such as organization charts, memos, and meeting minutes, systems analysts learn about the history of a project. Documentation also provides information about the organization, such as its operations, weaknesses, and strengths.
- **Observe:** Observing people helps systems analysts understand exactly how they perform a task. Likewise, observing a machine allows you to see how it works.
- **Survey:** To obtain data and information from a large number of people, systems analysts distribute surveys.
- **Interview:** The interview is the most important data and information gathering technique for the systems analyst. It allows the systems analyst to clarify responses and probe during face-to-face feedback.

- **JAD sessions:** Instead of a single one-on-one interview, analysts often use joint-application design sessions to gather data and information. A **joint-application design (JAD) session**, or *focus group*, consists of a series of lengthy, structured group meetings in which users and IT professionals work together to design or develop an application (Figure 12-4).
- **Research:** Newspapers, technology magazines and journals, reference books, trade shows, the web, vendors, and consultants are excellent sources of information. These sources can provide the systems analyst with information such as the latest hardware and software products and explanations of new processes and procedures. In addition, systems analysts often collect website statistics, such as the number of visitors and most-visited webpages, etc., and then evaluate these statistics as part of their research.

Figure 12-4 During a JAD session, the systems analyst is the moderator, or leader of the discussion. Another member, called the scribe, records facts and action items assigned during the session.
© Nyul / Dreamstime.com

⬡ MINI FEATURE 12-1

Information Literacy

Managing the vast amount of information inundating us daily can be an overwhelming task, not only for those involved in a system development project, but also for any digital citizen. This twenty-first century skill set, called *information literacy*, prepares students, employees, and citizens to manage information so that they can be knowledgeable decision makers.

Defining Information Literacy

More than 25 years ago, the American Library Association was the first organization to recognize the importance of information literate citizens. As the web and the Internet became a mainstay in education, business, and home environments, experts realized that the traditional basic literacy skills of reading, writing, and arithmetic were insufficient for living a productive life. According to the Association of College & Research Libraries, also needed are lifelong skills "to locate, evaluate, and use effectively the needed information."

Information Literacy Components

An individual's quality of existence depends upon obtaining quality information. Information literate people know how to locate meaningful sources that can be used to solve problems, make decisions, and set goals. The following five categories are recognized as integral literacy components:

- **Digital literacy:** Using computers, mobile devices, the Internet, and related technologies effectively is a necessity in business and society. Also important is an understanding of the general concerns of having computers in the world, including their integration in employment and education and their effects on national and personal security.

- **Library instruction:** Undergraduates rarely seek the help of librarians when performing academic research. This lack of help may be due, in part, to the fact that the students misunderstand the role of the reference librarian. Information literate individuals use the librarians' expertise in locating relevant sources. They also understand the necessity of using citations, how information is cataloged and organized, search strategies, and the process of locating and evaluating resources.

- **Media literacy:** Skills needed to understand how mass communication and popular culture affect learning and entertainment include the ability to evaluate and analyze how music, film, video, television, and other nonprint media are used effectively to persuade and inform.

- **Numerical literacy:** The ability to use basic math skills and interpret data is essential to solving

problems and communicating information. Also important are understanding how data is gathered and presented in graphs, charts, and other visuals and how to interpret and verify information presented in media.

- **Traditional literacy:** Individuals who can read and understand a variety of documents are likely to complete their educations, obtain employment, and participate in community groups. They also need to think critically about the material they have read and to express their thoughts by writing and speaking coherently.

© Nomad_Soul / Shutterstock.com

Steps in Effective Research and Composition

Locating appropriate material, organizing these sources, and producing the final document require effort and careful thought. The following paragraphs discuss steps you should take when crafting research, thinking critically, and drafting strategies:

- **Establish an appropriate topic.** Identify the purpose and audience. Determine an effective method of communicating the information, such as a written paper, oral presentation, or blog. Explore and narrow the topic so that it is manageable within time and logistical constraints. Determine the audience's familiarity with the topic and the need to find reference materials.

- **Identify sources.** Determine where to locate electronic and print resources, including websites, media, databases, and printed materials. Differentiate between primary and secondary sources, popular and scholarly articles, and current and historical materials.

© Pertusinas / Shutterstock.com

- **Evaluate materials.** Analyze the sources to determine reliability, accuracy, timeliness, and bias. Compare the materials to determine if the authors agree or disagree with topics.

- **Create the final work.** Organize and integrate the source material using direct quotations, paraphrases, and summaries. Document the work to credit sources and avoid plagiarism. Integrate photos, charts, and graphs when necessary to clarify the message. Use the writing process to create, review, revise, and proofread.

© Gary Arbach / Photos.com

Personal Portfolio Summary
- Securities
- Money Market Funds and Cash
- Certificates
- Annuities
- Mutual Funds

✱ Test your skills at effective research by examining a website for a household or personal care product you use regularly, such as laundry detergent or toothpaste. Describe the photos, colors, placement of objects, and description. Who is the intended audience? Is any information missing from the website? What message is the company attempting to send? Do you think the message achieves its purpose?

 **NOW YOU KNOW**

Be sure you understand the material presented in the sections titled System Development Guidelines, Who Participates in System Development, Project Management, Feasibility Assessment, Documentation, and Data and Information Gathering Techniques, as it relates to the chapter objectives.

You now should know . . .

- Why you should be familiar with system development and its phases (Objective 1)

- Why system development guidelines are important (Objective 2)

- How users are involved with project management, feasibility assessment, documentation, and data and information gathering tasks in a system development project (Objective 3)

 Quiz Yourself Online: Check your knowledge of related content by navigating to this book's Quiz Yourself resource on Computer Concepts CourseMate and then tapping or clicking Objectives 1–3.

 CONSIDER THIS

What circumstances initiate system development?

A user may request a new or modified information system for a variety of reasons. The most obvious reason is to correct a problem, such as an incorrect calculation or a security breach. Another reason is to improve the information system. Organizations may want to improve hardware, software, or other technology to enhance an information system.

Sometimes, situations outside the control of an organization require a modification to an information system. Corporate management or some other governing body may mandate a change. Mergers, reorganizations, and competition also can lead to change.

A user may request a new or modified information system verbally in a phone conversation or written as an email message (read Ethics & Issues 12-2 for a related discussion). In larger organizations, users write a formal request for a new or modified information system, which is called a *project request* or *request for system services*. The project request becomes the first item of documentation for the project. It also triggers the first phase of system development: planning.

 ETHICS & ISSUES 12-2

Do Digital Communications Have a Positive Effect on Relationships?

Carefully crafted handwritten letters, as well as long phone calls with friends and family, are rare in today's digital world. Nonverbal digital communications, such as email messages, text messages, and online social network posts, have replaced many social interactions. Although people often use these technologies to share thoughts, opinions, photos, and more, some question whether these types of communications are meaningful.

Many of today's digital communications enable you to keep hundreds of contacts informed about your life events. Without technology, you might not interact with most of these individuals on a regular basis. For example, you may receive numerous birthday wishes on a social networking site from people with whom you do not have a strong relationship. Are these good wishes genuine, or do they create a false social connection? Experts debate whether replacing face-to-face interactions with digital communications leads to social isolation. Mental health professionals characterize social isolation as a withdrawal from interactions with others. Some feel that social networking and the ease and immediacy of text messaging and email messages enable users to strengthen their existing relationships. Although technology can help introverted individuals connect with others, some experts believe that these communications can lead to isolation because they limit the need for face-to-face interactions. Further, users may feel pressure to share only positive events, leaving them to deal with negative experiences alone.

Do digital communications have a positive effect on your relationships? Why or why not? Have you ever shared events with others online that you would not share face-to-face? Why or why not?

Case Study: Hickory Community College

This chapter includes a case study to help you understand real-world system development applications. The case study appears shaded in light green immediately after the discussion of each phase in the chapter. The case is about Hickory Community College (HCC), a fictitious school.

Approximately 15,000 students are enrolled at HCC each year in its various programs. Students can earn A.S. (Associate of Science) or A.A. (Associate of Arts) degrees in many areas: accounting, anthropology, childcare, computer technology, electronics, construction technology, forensic science, graphic design, history, management, marketing, nursing, and sociology. The school also offers certificates and adult education classes in each of these areas. Some classes meet on campus, while others are offered online.

Although most areas of the school are automated, the bookstore still requires that instructors manually fill in book order forms. On these forms, the instructors fill in the course ID, course section, expected enrollment, and ISBN of the book, also indicating whether the book is required or supplemental. As instructors send in their completed book order forms,

bookstore staff enters each instructor's book order into bookstore database program. After book orders are entered, a separate group of bookstore staff compares the original forms with the entered orders to check for any errors that may have occurred during the data entry process. After all orders are verified, they are processed and sent to the book publishers.

Chad Goldstein, bookstore manager, has noticed that it takes a considerable amount of time for the bookstore staff to enter book orders and then to verify entered orders for accuracy. Chad would like to investigate the possibility of instructors using an online book order form, where instructors enter their book orders directly into the bookstore database. This change in procedure would save the bookstore a great deal of time and money and eliminate data entry errors.

Chad realizes this task will require substantial investigation and school resources. He sends an email message to the IT director. She agrees and asks him to fill out a Project Request form (Figure 12-5) and submit it to Juanita Mendez, chair of the steering committee at HCC.

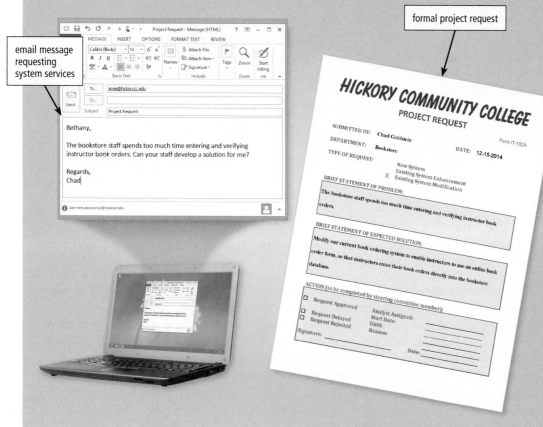

Figure 12-5 Users sometimes informally communicate a project request verbally or in an email message. In larger organizations, requests often are documented on a form such as this Project Request.

Planning Phase

The planning phase for a project begins when the steering committee receives a project request. This committee usually consists of five to nine people and typically includes a mix of vice presidents, managers, nonmanagement users, and IT personnel.

During the **planning phase**, four major activities are performed: (1) review and approve the project requests, (2) prioritize the project requests, (3) allocate resources such as money, people, and equipment to approved projects, and (4) form a project development team for each approved project.

 CONSIDER THIS

How are projects prioritized?

The projects that receive the highest priority are those mandated by management or some other governing body. These requests are given immediate attention. The steering committee evaluates the remaining project requests based on their value to the organization. The steering committee approves some projects and rejects others. Of the approved projects, it is likely that only a few will begin system development immediately. Others will have to wait for additional funds or resources to become available.

Case Study: Planning at Hickory Community College

After receiving the project request (Figure 12-5 on the previous page) from Chad, Juanita Mendez distributes it to all members of the steering committee. They will discuss the request at their next meeting. The steering committee members of HCC are Juanita Mendez, controller and chair of the steering committee; Milan Sciranka, professor; Suzy Zhao, web developer; Donnell Carter, training specialist; Karl Schmidt, systems analyst; and Bethany Ames, IT director. Juanita also invites Chad Goldstein to the next steering committee meeting. Because he originated the project request, Chad will have the knowledge to answer questions.

During the meeting, the committee decides the project request identifies modification to the system, instead of a problem. They feel the nature of the modification (where instructors enter book orders directly into the bookstore database) could lead to considerable savings for the school. It also will reduce data entry errors made by bookstore staff.

The steering committee approves the request. Juanita points out that the school has enough funds in its budget to begin the project immediately. Thus, Bethany assembles a system development project team and assigns Karl Schmidt, systems analyst, as the project leader. Karl and his team immediately begin the next phase: analysis.

Analysis Phase

The **analysis phase** consists of two major activities: (1) conduct a preliminary investigation and (2) perform detailed analysis.

The Preliminary Investigation The main purpose of the **preliminary investigation**, sometimes called the *feasibility study*, is to determine the exact nature of the problem or improvement and decide whether it is worth pursuing. Should the organization continue to assign resources to this project? To answer this question, the systems analyst conducts a general study of the project.

The first task in the preliminary investigation is to interview the user who submitted the project request. Depending on the nature of the request, project team members may interview other users, too. In addition to interviewing, members of the project team may use other data gathering techniques, such as reviewing existing documentation. Often, the preliminary investigation is completed in just a few days.

 CONSIDER THIS

What types of questions are asked during an interview?

Interviewers, including systems analysts, ask two types of questions: closed-ended and open-ended. Closed-ended questions generally are easy to answer, such as the number of years a system has been in place. Open-ended questions, by contrast, require more explanation. For example, an open-ended question may ask the interviewee to describe three problems with the current system.

Upon completion of the preliminary investigation, the systems analyst writes the feasibility report. This report presents the team's findings to the steering committee. The feasibility report contains these major sections: introduction, existing system, benefits of a new or modified system, feasibility of a new or modified system, and the recommendation (Figure 12-6).

HICKORY COMMUNITY COLLEGE
MEMORANDUM

To: Steering Committee
From: Karl Schmidt, Project Leader
Date: December 29, 2014
Subject: Feasibility Study of Book Ordering System

Following is the feasibility study in response to the request for a modification to our book ordering system. Your approval is necessary before the next phase of the project will begin.

Introduction

The purpose of this feasibility report is to determine whether it is beneficial for Hickory Community College to continue studying the book ordering system. The bookstore manager has indicated bookstore staff spends too much time entering and verifying book orders. This project would affect the bookstore and instructors.

Existing System

Background

Currently, the bookstore requires that instructors manually fill in book order forms. On these forms, the instructors fill in the course ID, course section, expected enrollment, and ISBN of the book, indicating whether the book is required or supplemental. As instructors send in their completed book order forms, bookstore staff enters each instructor's book order into bookstore's database program. After book orders are entered, a separate set of bookstore staff compares the original forms with the entered orders to check for any errors that may have occurred during the data entry process. After all orders are verified, they are processed and sent to the book publishers.

Problems

The following problems have been identified with the current book ordering system at Hickory Community College:

- Bookstore staff spends too much time entering and verifying book orders.

- During the check for errors of entered book orders, staff has been finding an excessive number of data entry errors.

FEASIBILITY STUDY
Page 2

Benefits of a New or Modified System

Following is a list of benefits that could be realized if the book ordering system at Hickory Community College were modified to enable instructors to use an online book order form, where instructors enter their book orders directly into the bookstore database:

- Data entry errors of book orders by bookstore staff would be eliminated.

- Cost of supplies, such as paper and ink, would be reduced by 10 percent.

- Through a more efficient use of bookstore staff time, the college could achieve a 25 percent reduction in temporary assistants in the bookstore.

Feasibility of a New or Modified System

Operational

A modified book ordering system will require instructors enter all book orders online.

Schedule

The established deadline for the book ordering system is reasonable.

Technical

Hickory Community College already has a functional database and server. To handle the increased volume and usage of data, however, it may be required to purchase a larger database server.

Economic

A detailed summary of the costs and benefits, including all assumptions, is available on our FTP server. The potential costs of the proposed solution could range from $15,000 to $20,000. The estimated savings in temporary clerks and supplies will exceed $30,000.

If you have any questions about the detailed cost/benefit summary or require further information, please contact me.

Recommendation

Based on the findings presented in this report, we recommend a continued study of the book ordering system.

Figure 12-6   A feasibility report presents the results of the preliminary investigation. The report must be prepared professionally and be well organized to be effective.
© Cengage Learning

CONSIDER THIS ————————————————————————————

Does the feasibility report always recommend that the project be continued?
In some cases, the project team may recommend not to continue the project. If the steering committee agrees, the project ends at this point. If the project team recommends continuing and the steering committee approves this recommendation, then detailed analysis begins.

Case Study: Preliminary Investigation at Hickory Community College

Karl Schmidt, systems analyst and project leader, meets with Chad Goldstein to discuss the project request. During the interview, Karl looks at the manual book order forms. He asks Chad how many data entry errors typically occur when his staff enters the book orders. Then Karl interviews the controller, Juanita Mendez, to obtain some general cost and benefit figures for the feasibility report. He also talks to several bookstore staff and instructors. He wants their opinion of the current book order process.

Next, Karl prepares the feasibility report (Figure 12-6 on the previous page). After the project team members review it, Karl submits it to the steering committee. The report recommends proceeding to the detailed analysis phase of this project. The steering committee agrees. Karl and his team begin detailed analysis.

Detailed Analysis   *Detailed analysis* involves three major activities: (1) study how the current system works, (2) determine the users' wants, needs, and requirements, and (3) recommend a solution. Detailed analysis sometimes is called *logical design* because the systems analysts develop the proposed solution without regard to any specific hardware or software. That is, they make no attempt to identify the procedures that should be automated and those that should be manual.

During these activities, systems analysts use all of the data and information gathering techniques. They review documentation, observe employees and machines, distribute surveys, interview employees, conduct JAD sessions, and conduct research.

While studying the current system and identifying user requirements, the systems analyst collects a great deal of data and information. A major task for the systems analyst is to document these findings in a way that can be understood by everyone. Systems analysts use diagrams to describe the processes that transform inputs into outputs and diagrams that graphically show the flow of data in the system. Both users and IT professionals refer to this documentation.

The System Proposal   After the systems analyst has studied the current system and determined all user requirements, the next step is to communicate possible solutions for the project in a system proposal. The purpose of the system proposal is to assess the feasibility of each alternative solution and then recommend the most feasible solution for the project, which often involves modifying or expanding the current system. The systems analyst presents the system proposal to the steering committee. If the steering committee approves a solution, the project enters the design phase.

When the steering committee discusses the system proposal and decides which alternative to pursue, it considers whether to modify the existing system, buy retail software from an outside source, use web apps, build its own custom software, and/or outsource some or all of its IT needs to an outside firm. The final decision often is a mix of these options.

- Retail software is mass-produced, copyrighted, prewritten software that meets the needs of a variety of users. Chapter 4 presented many types of software available for personal computers.
- As discussed in previous chapters, web apps are applications that are stored and run on a web server you access through a browser. Some are free; others charge a one-time or a recurring fee for access to their apps.
- Custom software is software developed by the user or at the user's request, typically to perform functions specific to a business or industry. The main advantage of custom software is that it matches the organization's requirements exactly. The disadvantages

 **Internet Research**
What is the difference between horizontal and vertical market software?
Search for: horizontal and vertical market software

 BTW
Crime Fighting Software
Innovative Computing: You should be familiar with custom crime fighting software.

usually are that it is more expensive and takes longer to design and implement than retail software or web apps.

- Organizations can develop custom software in-house using their own IT personnel or outsource its development, which means having an outside source develop it for them. Some organizations outsource just the software development aspect of their IT operation. Others outsource most or all of their IT operation. Depending on an organization's needs, outside firms can handle as much or as little of the IT requirements as desired. Read Secure IT 12-1 for issues related to outsourcing.

 SECURE IT 12-1

Security Issues Arising from Outsourcing

Outsourcing of noncore functions to outside vendors has been a trend among organizations in recent years. Noncore functions often include general business tasks such as maintaining and supporting an organization's information systems and processing customer payments on websites. Businesses outsource noncore functions because the third-party vendors may be more efficient and more cost effective than the businesses trying to perform the functions on their own.

Sometimes, however, when a business outsources, the external vendors are not as careful with security and customer

information as the business itself might be. The business that outsources this task has spent time and effort to cultivate and then forge a relationship with its customers, and it is in the company's best interest to treat its customers well. The outside vendor, however, has no such bond with the customers.

Security breaches might occur when work is contracted to third parties. For example, personal information about customers and employees, credit card numbers, and health records can be transferred to external hard drives or other storage media and taken outside the building. Companies should develop a computer security plan

that requires safeguards on the part of the outside vendors. These procedures might include running background checks on personnel, closely monitoring the level of database access and email messages, replacing Social Security numbers with another unique identifier, and conducting security audits.

✳ Does outsourcing lead to a lower level of security and privacy for customers? Why or why not? What can an organization do to ensure that vendors practice the same level of care of customer information as the organization practices? Should customers hold organizations or their vendors responsible for leaks of private customer information? Why?

Case Study: Detailed Analysis at Hickory Community College

Karl and his team begin performing the activities in the detailed analysis phase of the book ordering system. As part of the study and requirements activities, they use several of the data and information gathering techniques available to them. They interview employees throughout the bookstore and meet with some instructors. They observe instructors completing book orders. They prepare documents that become part of the project documentation. Members of the project team refer to these documents during the remainder of system development.

After two months of studying the existing system and obtaining user requirements, Karl discusses his findings with his supervisor, Bethany Ames. In

addition to instructors entering book orders online, Karl recommends that instructors also be able to enter course supply requests online, such as for calculators and safety goggles.

Based on Karl's findings, Bethany writes a system proposal for the steering committee to review. Suzy Zhao, web developer at Hickory Community College, developed the current website. Thus, Bethany recommends that Suzy's staff modify the website in-house. Bethany also recommends that the school invest in a larger database server to handle the additional requirements.

The steering committee agrees with Bethany's proposal. Karl and his team begin the design phase of the project.

Design Phase

The **design phase** consists of two major activities: (1) if necessary, acquire hardware and software and (2) develop all of the details of the new or modified information system. The systems analyst often performs these two activities at the same time instead of sequentially.

When the steering committee approves a solution, the systems analyst begins the activity of obtaining additional hardware or software or evaluating cloud providers that offer the

 BTW

Meg Whitman
Technology Innovator:
You should be familiar
with Meg Whitman
(technology leader).

computing services to meet the organization's needs. The systems analyst may skip this activity if the approved solution does not require new hardware or software. If this activity is required, it consists of four major tasks: (1) identify technical specifications, (2) solicit vendor proposals, (3) test and evaluate vendor proposals, and (4) make a decision.

Internet Research

What are popular online technology magazines?

Search for: online technology magazines

Identify Technical Specifications The first step in acquiring necessary hardware and software is to identify all the hardware and software requirements of the new or modified system. To do this, systems analysts use a variety of research techniques. They talk with other systems analysts, visit vendors' stores, and search the web. Many trade journals, newspapers, and magazines provide some or all of their printed content online.

After the systems analyst defines the technical requirements, the next step is to summarize these requirements for potential vendors. The systems analyst can use three basic types of documents for this purpose: an RFQ, an RFP, or an RFI.

- A *request for quotation* (*RFQ*) identifies the required product(s). With an RFQ, the vendor quotes a price for the listed product(s).
- With a *request for proposal* (*RFP*), the vendor selects the product(s) that meets specified requirements and then quotes the price(s).
- A *request for information* (*RFI*) is a less formal method that uses a standard form to request information about a product or service.

Solicit Vendor Proposals Systems analysts send the RFQ, RFP, or RFI to potential hardware and software vendors. Another source for hardware and software products is a value-added reseller. A *value-added reseller* (*VAR*) is an organization that purchases products from manufacturers and then resells these products to the public — offering additional services with the product (Figure 12-7).

Instead of using vendors, some organizations hire an IT consultant or a group of IT consultants. An *IT consultant* is a professional who is hired based on technical expertise, including service and advice. IT consultants often specialize in configuring hardware and software for businesses of all sizes.

Test and Evaluate Vendor Proposals After sending RFQs, RFPs, and RFIs to potential vendors, the systems analyst will receive completed quotations and proposals. Evaluating the proposals and then selecting the best one often is a difficult task. It is important to be as objective as possible while evaluating each proposal.

Systems analysts use many techniques to test the various software products from vendors. They obtain a list of user references from the software vendors. They also talk to current users of the software to solicit their opinions. Some vendors will provide a demonstration of the product(s) specified. Others supply demonstration copies or trial versions, allowing the organizations to test the software themselves.

Sometimes it is important to know whether the software can process a certain volume of transactions efficiently. In this case, the systems

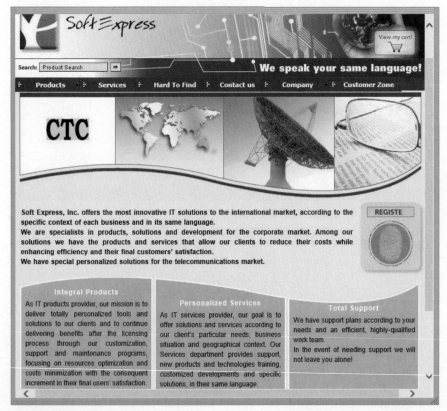

Figure 12-7 Many VARs provide complete systems, often called turnkey solutions.
Source: Soft Express, Inc.

analyst conducts a benchmark test. A *benchmark test* measures the performance of hardware or software. For example, a benchmark test could measure the time it takes a payroll program to print 50 paychecks. Comparing the time it takes various accounting programs to print the same 50 paychecks is one way of measuring each program's performance.

Make a Decision Having rated the proposals, the systems analyst presents a recommendation to the steering committee. The recommendation could be to award a contract to a vendor or to not make any purchases at this time.

Internet Research

What are the best benchmark tests for evaluating personal computers?

Search for: best pc benchmark tests

Case Study: Hardware Acquisition at Hickory Community College

Karl and his team compile a requirements list for the database server. They prepare an RFP and submit it to twelve vendors: eight through the web and four at local electronics stores. Ten vendors reply within the three-week deadline.

Of the ten replies, the development team selects two to evaluate. They eliminate the other eight because these vendors did not offer adequate warranties for the database server. The project team members ask for benchmark test results for each

server. In addition, they contact two current users of this database server for their opinions about its performance. After evaluating these two servers, the team selects the best one.

Karl summarizes his team's findings in a report to the steering committee. The committee gives Karl authorization to award a contract to the proposed vendor. As a courtesy and to maintain good working relationships, Karl sends a letter to all 12 vendors informing them of the committee's decision.

Detailed Design The next step is to develop detailed design specifications for the components in the proposed solution. The activities to be performed include developing designs for the databases, inputs, outputs, and programs.

- During database design, the systems analyst works closely with the database analysts and database administrators to identify those data elements that currently exist within the organization and those that are new. The systems analyst also addresses user access privileges. That is, the systems analyst defines which data elements each user can access, when they can access the data elements, what actions they can perform on the data elements, and under what circumstances they can access the elements.
- During detailed design of inputs and outputs, the systems analyst carefully designs every menu, screen, and report specified in the requirements. The outputs often are designed first because they help define the requirements for the inputs. Thus, it is very important that outputs are identified correctly and that users agree to them.

   The systems analyst typically develops two types of designs for each input and output: a mock-up and a layout chart. A *mock-up* is a sample of the input or output that contains actual data (Figure 12-8). The systems analyst shows mock-ups to users for their approval. Because users will work with the inputs and outputs of the system, it is crucial to involve users during input and output design.

Figure 12-8 Users provide their approval on inputs and outputs. This input screen is a mock-up (containing actual sample data) for users to review.
Source: Microsoft

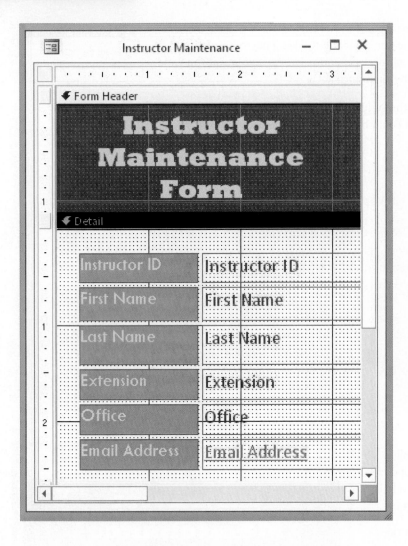

After users approve the mock-up, the systems analyst develops a layout chart for the software developer. A layout chart is more technical and contains programming-like notations. Many database programs provide tools for technical design (Figure 12-9).

Other issues that must be addressed during input and output design include the types of media to use (paper, video, or audio); formats (graphical or narrative); and data entry validation techniques, which include making sure the entered data is correct (for example, a state code has to be one of the fifty valid two-letter state abbreviations).

- During program design, the systems analyst prepares the *program specification package*, which identifies required programs and the relationship among each program, as well as the input, output, and database specifications.

Figure 12-9 Shown here is a technical view in Access of the mock-up in Figure 12-8 on the previous page.
Source: Microsoft

BTW
Ray Kurzweil
Technology Innovator: You should be familiar with Ray Kurzweil (technology futurist).

✺ CONSIDER THIS

How can systems analysts build relationships with users?
Systems analysts have much more credibility with users if the analysts understand user concerns and have empathy for how the workers are feeling. If users are involved, they are more likely to accept and use the new system — called *user buy-in*. One reason systems fail is because some systems analysts create or modify systems with little or no user participation.

Prototyping Many systems analysts today use prototypes during detailed design. A **prototype**, sometimes called a *proof of concept*, is a working model of the proposed system's essential functionality. The systems analyst actually builds a functional form of the solution during design. The main advantage of a prototype is users can work with the system before it is completed to make sure it meets their needs. As soon as users approve a prototype, systems analysts can implement a solution more quickly than without a prototype.

Case Tools Many systems analysts use computer software to assist during system development. *Computer-aided software engineering (CASE) software tools* are designed to support one or more activities of system development (Figure 12-10).

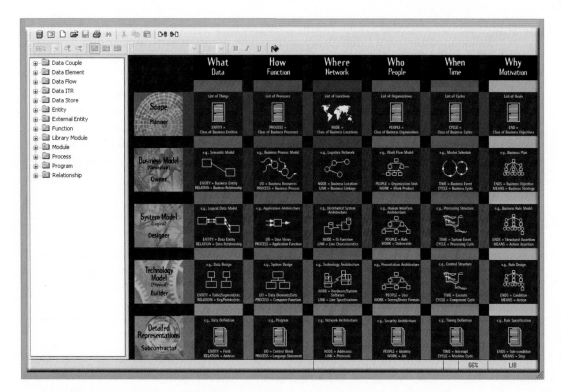

Figure 12-10 CASE programs assist analysts in the development of an information system.
Courtesy of Visible Systems Corporation

 CONSIDER THIS

Who reviews the detailed design?

Many people should review the detailed design specifications before they are given to the programming team. The purpose of their review is to ensure the design represents a finished product that will work for the user and the development is feasible. Reviewers should include users, systems analysts, managers, IT staff, and members of the system development team. If the steering committee decides the project still is feasible, which usually is the case, the project enters the implementation phase.

Case Study: Detailed Design at Hickory Community College

As approved by the steering committee, Karl and his team begin designing the book ordering system. After studying current vendor information and interviewing more users and vendors, the team designs changes to the school's database, website, and the associated programs. After completing the detailed design, Karl meets with several users and IT personnel to walk through the design. They locate two errors. He corrects the errors and then presents the design to the steering committee. The committee agrees with the design solution and consents to implement it.

Implementation Phase

The purpose of the **implementation phase** is to construct, or build, the new or modified system and then deliver it to the users. Members of the system development team perform four major activities in this phase: (1) develop programs and apps, (2) install and test the new system, (3) train users, and (4) convert to the new system.

Develop Programs and Apps If the organization purchases retail software or no modifications to existing custom software are required, the development team may skip this activity. For custom software that is new or requires modification, however, programs and apps are developed or modified either by an outside firm or in-house.

Software developers write or modify programs and apps from the program specification package created during the analysis phase. Just as system development follows an organized set of activities, so does program development. These program development activities are known as the *program development life cycle*. For information about program logic, read Mini Feature 12-2 (available in the e-book). Read Ethics & Issues 12-3 to consider why software developers use back doors when writing programs.

✳ CONSIDER THIS

What is a sandbox?

A *sandbox* is an environment that allows software developers to test their programs with fictitious data without adversely affecting other programs, information systems, or data. Sandboxes are used for testing purposes both by developers and users. Users often work with a sandbox to familiarize themselves with a new program or information system before they use it.

✳ ETHICS & ISSUES 12-3

 Should It Be Legal for Software Developers to Build in Back Doors?

As discussed in Chapter 5, a back door is a program or set of instructions that allows users to bypass security controls when accessing a program, computer, or network. Software developers often include a back door during product development to modify program code when troubleshooting. In these instances, a back door is necessary. What happens, though, when a hacker finds or creates a back door?

Hackers look for known security issues in software to access a computer through a back door. If a hacker is unable to find

and use a back door, they use trojan horses (previously discussed in Chapter 5) to deliver a payload that creates a back door. Hackers use back doors to gain control over a computer so that they can use its resources to mount further malware attacks or to send spam. Using an unsuspecting user's computer to distribute spam or malware enables the hacker to avoid detection from and identification by authorities.

Back doors pose a serious security risk because they allow unauthorized access to your computer's resources, files, and network whenever you are on the Internet. Not only can hackers control your computer, but they

can look through your files to find and steal your personal information. Users often are unaware of a back door's existence and when it is breached. If your computer acts strangely or performance decreases, you may have been the victim of a hacker. Do not connect to the Internet until you run an antivirus program.

Should software developers use back doors during product development? Why or why not? Have you ever been a victim of a back door infiltration? If so, how did you detect and resolve the issue?

Install and Test the New System If the organization acquires new hardware or software, someone must install and test it. The systems analysts should test individual programs. They also should be sure that all the programs work together in the system.

Systems analysts and users develop test data so that they can perform various tests.

- A *unit test* verifies that each individual program or object works by itself.
- A *systems test* verifies that all programs in an application work together properly.
- An *integration test* verifies that an application works with other applications.
- An *acceptance test* is performed by end users and checks the new system to ensure that it works with actual data.

Train Users **Training** involves showing users exactly how they will use the new hardware and software in the system. Some training takes place as one-on-one sessions or classroom-style lectures (Figure 12-11). Other organizations use web-based training, which is a self-directed, self-paced online instruction method. Whichever technique is used, it should include hands-on sessions with realistic sample data. Users should practice on the actual system during training. Users also should be provided access to printed or online user manuals for reference. It is the systems analyst's responsibility to create user manuals.

Convert to the New System

The final implementation activity is to change from the old system to the new system. This change can take place using one or more of the following conversion strategies: direct, parallel, phased, or pilot.

Figure 12-11 Organizations must ensure that users are trained properly on the new system. One training method uses hands-on classes to learn the new system.
© Goodluz / Shutterstock.com

- With *direct conversion*, the user stops using the old system and begins using the new system on a certain date. The advantage of this strategy is that it requires no transition costs and is a quick implementation technique. The disadvantage is that it is extremely risky and can disrupt operations seriously if the new system does not work correctly the first time.

- *Parallel conversion* consists of running the old system alongside the new system for a specified time. Results from both systems are compared. The advantage of this strategy is that you can fix any problems in the new system before you terminate the old system. The disadvantage is that it is costly to operate two systems at the same time.

- In a *phased conversion*, each location converts at a separate time. For example, an accounting system might convert its accounts receivable, accounts payable, general ledger, and payroll sites in separate phases. Each site can use a direct or parallel conversion. Larger systems with multiple sites may use a phased conversion.

- With a *pilot conversion*, only one location in the organization uses the new system — so that it can be tested. After the pilot site approves the new system, other sites convert using one of the other conversion strategies.

Case Study: Implementation at Hickory Community College

Upon receiving the program specification package, Karl forms an implementation team of Suzy Zhao, web developer; Adam Rosen, software developer; and Stephan Davis, data modeler. The team works together to implement the book ordering system.

Karl works closely with the team to answer questions about the design and to check the progress of their work. When the team completes its work, they ask Karl to test it. He does and it works great!

Karl arranges a training class for all instructors and also the employees of the bookstore. During the training session, he shows them how to use the new online book order form on the school's website. Karl indicates that he will send them the user manual via email; the user manual also will be available on the website.

Support and Security Phase

The purpose of the **support and security phase** is to provide ongoing assistance for an information system and its users after the system is implemented. The support phase consists of three major activities: (1) perform maintenance activities, (2) monitor system performance, and (3) assess system security.

Information system maintenance activities include fixing errors in, as well as improving, a system's operations. To determine initial maintenance needs, the systems analyst should meet with users. The purpose of this meeting, called the *post-implementation system review*, is to discover whether the information system is performing according to the users' expectations. In some cases, users would like the system to do more. Maybe they have enhancements or additional requirements that involve modifying or expanding an existing information system.

During this phase, the systems analyst monitors performance of the new or modified information system. The purpose of performance monitoring is to determine whether the system is inefficient or unstable at any point. If it is, the systems analyst must investigate solutions to make the information system more efficient and reliable — back to the planning phase.

Most organizations must deal with complex technology security issues. All elements of an information system — hardware, software, data, people, and procedures — must be secure from threats both inside and outside the enterprise. Read Secure IT 12-2 to learn about the role of an organization's chief security officer. Read Secure IT 12-3 for information about an organization's technology security plan.

 SECURE IT 12-2

Role of a Chief Security Officer

Organizations today often have a *chief security officer* (*CSO*), also called a chief information security officer (CISO) or director of corporate security, who is responsible for the physical security of an organization's property and people and for the digital security of computing resources. Additional responsibilities could include addressing privacy concerns and preventing loss and fraud.

It is critical that the CSO be included in all system development projects to address information security adequately. The CSO should use many techniques to maintain confidential or limited access to information, ensure integrity and reliability of systems, provide uninterrupted availability of systems, guarantee compliance with laws, and cooperate with law enforcement agencies.

Job qualifications include strong communication skills, experience with risk management, an understanding of security laws, knowledge of information technology, and experience with business planning. This person generally has earned a bachelor's degree in information or Internet security, computer science, or business administration. A CSO must continue his or her education by staying current in the latest international security breach developments, antivirus and malware software updates, and operating system upgrades. Some vendors offer product certifications for security systems administrators, which would benefit the skills and capabilities of a CSO.

✹ Would you consider becoming a CSO? If so, which skills do you have for the job, and which would you learn in classes or in on-the-job training?

 SECURE IT 12-3

Technology Security Plan Components

Most organizations never will experience a major information system disaster, but if they do, a computer security plan will guide the recovery process. Creating this document is part of a CSO's responsibility of protecting the organization's information assets. The plan should include all possible safeguards to detect, prevent, and recover from losses. It should identify all of the organization's information assets, which include hardware, software, documentation, procedures, people, data, facilities, and supplies. The document should identify all the security risks that may cause an information asset loss. Key components should include securing equipment, especially laptops and mobile devices, creating a strong disaster recovery strategy, developing a security breach detection and response plan, and providing for ongoing training.

The goal of the computer security plan is to match an appropriate level of safeguards against the identified risks. The CSO must realize that some degree of risk is unavoidable and that the more secure a system is, the more difficult it is for everyone to use. The security plan should be evaluated annually or more frequently if information assets have changed dramatically. Microsoft has developed a Security Development Lifecycle to guide the development, implementation, and review process. Its seven security practices phases — training, requirements, design, implementation, verification, release, and response – help increase security while reducing costs.

✹ What method should be used to communicate the plan to all employees and provide adequate training to ensure continued compliance? How can a CSO be assured that employees will comply with the computer security plan?

Case Study: Support and Security at Hickory Community College

During the post-implementation system review, Karl learns that the new book ordering system is working well. Instructors find it easy to use. The bookstore is saving time and money because employees no longer have to enter or verify book orders. Chad says his staff is working efficiently on other tasks, now that the book ordering system has been automated. Data in the system has been accessed only by authorized users, leading him to conclude security measures work as planned.

Six months after the book ordering system has been in operation, Chad would like to add the capability for email messages to be sent to instructors automatically when the books arrive in the bookstore. He sends a message to Karl requesting the change. Karl asks him to fill out a Project Request and adds this request to the agenda of the next steering committee meeting. Back to the planning phase again!

 **NOW YOU KNOW**

Be sure you understand the material presented in the sections titled Planning Phase, Analysis Phase, Design Phase, Implementation Phase, and Support and Security Phase, as it relates to the chapter objectives.
You now should know . . .

- What tasks are performed during the planning, analysis, design, implementation, and support and security phases (Objective 4)

 Quiz Yourself Online: Check your knowledge of related content by navigating to this book's Quiz Yourself resource on Computer Concepts CourseMate and then tapping or clicking Objective 4.

Application Development Languages and Tools

The previous sections discussed the system development phases. One activity during the implementation phase is to develop programs and apps. Although you may never write a program or app, information you request may require a software developer to create or modify a program or app. Thus, you should understand how software developers, sometimes called programmers, create programs and apps to meet information requirements.

To create a program, software developers sometimes write a program's instructions using a programming language. A **programming language** is a set of words, abbreviations, and symbols that enables a software developer to communicate instructions to a computer or mobile device. Other times, software developers use a program development tool to create a program or app. Software that provides a user-friendly environment for building programs and apps often is called an *application development tool*. An application development tool provides a means for creating, designing, editing, testing, and distributing programs and apps. Software developers use a variety of programming languages and application development tools to create programs and apps.

Several hundred programming languages exist today. Each language has its own rules, or *syntax*, for writing the instructions. Languages often are designed for specific purposes, such as scientific applications, business solutions, or webpage development. When solving a problem or building a solution, system developers often use more than one language; that is, they integrate the languages.

Two types of languages are low-level and high-level.

- A *low-level language* is a programming language that is machine dependent. A *machine-dependent language* runs on only one particular type of computer or device. Each instruction in a low-level language usually equates to a single machine instruction (discussed further in the next section).
- With a *high-level language*, by contrast, each instruction typically equates to multiple machine instructions. High-level languages often are machine independent. A *machine-independent language* can run on many different types of computers and operating systems. Examples of high-level languages include procedural languages, object-oriented languages, visual programming languages, and fourth-generation languages (discussed further later in this chapter). Read How To 12-1 for tips about determining whether programs are safe to use.

HOW TO 12-1

Determine Whether a Program or App Is Safe to Use

Anyone with programming knowledge can create a program or app using a programming language. Unethical software developers, however, can use their skills to develop malicious programs and apps that can harm a computer or mobile device or put confidential information at risk. Before installing and using a program or app, you should determine whether it is safe to use. The following guidelines describe how to determine whether a program or app is safe to use:

- If you are installing the program or app from installation media such as an optical disc, make sure you are installing it from the original, authentic installation media. Be leery of programs and apps on burned optical discs. Even if a program or app on a burned disc

is provided by a trusted source, your source may not be aware that it is malicious.

- If you are downloading a program or app from the web, make sure you are downloading it from a reputable website or app store. Reputable websites often include the software developer's website, as well as websites commonly used to distribute shareware and freeware.

- Do not automatically trust apps that are available in app stores and marketplaces. While the companies hosting these app stores and marketplaces try to keep malicious apps off their servers, some can slip through. Before downloading an app from an app store or marketplace, read the app's reviews and determine whether any risks are associated with downloading and installing the program. If the app does not

have many reviews, consider waiting for more reviews to appear before downloading and installing the app.

- Before installing a program or app from installation media such as an optical disc, perform a scan to search the installation media for any known malware. If you downloaded a program or app from the web, scan the installation files for malware before installing the program or app. If you decide to install the program or app, you also should perform a virus scan on your computer after the installation has completed.

☀ If you accidentally install a malicious program or app on your computer, what steps might you take to remove the program or app?

0000DE	5A50	35AA			015AC
0000E2	47F0	2100		00102	
000102	1B77				
000104	5870	304E			01050
000108	1C47				
00010A	4E50	30D6			010D8
00010E	F075	30D6	003E	010D8	0003E
000114	4F50	30D6			010D8
000118	5050	3052			01054
00011C	58E0	30B6			010B8
000120	07FE				
					00122
000122	50E0	30BA			010BC
000126	1B55				
000128	5A50	304E			01050
00012C	5B50	3052			01054
000130	5050	305A			0105C
000134	58E0	30BA			010BC
000138	07FE				

Figure 12-12 A sample section of a machine language program, coded using the hexadecimal number system. A hexadecimal number system can be used to represent binary numbers using letters of the alphabet and decimal numbers.
© Cengage Learning

Low-Level Languages

Two types of low-level languages are machine languages and assembly languages. **Machine language**, known as the first generation of programming languages, is the only language the computer directly recognizes (Figure 12-12). Machine language instructions use a series of binary digits (1s and 0s) or a combination of numbers and letters that represents binary digits. The binary digits correspond to the on and off electrical states. As you might imagine, coding in machine language is tedious and time consuming.

With an **assembly language**, the second generation of programming languages, a programmer writes instructions using symbolic instruction codes (Figure 12-13). Examples of these codes include A for add, C for compare, L for load, and M for multiply. Assembly languages also use symbolic addresses. A *symbolic address* is a meaningful name that identifies a storage location. For example, a programmer can use the name, RATE, to refer to the storage location that contains a pay rate.

Despite these advantages, assembly languages can be difficult to learn. In addition, programmers must convert an assembly language program into machine language before the computer can *execute*, or run, the program. That is, the computer cannot execute the assembly source program. A *source program* is the program that contains the language instructions, or *code*, to be converted to machine language. To convert the assembly language source program into machine language, programmers use a program called an *assembler*.

Procedural Languages

The disadvantages of machine and assembly (low-level) languages led to the development of procedural languages in the late 1950s and 1960s. In a **procedural language**, the programmer writes instructions that tell the computer what to accomplish and how to do it.

With a procedural language, often called a *third-generation language (3GL)* or *functional language*, a programmer uses a series of English-like words to write instructions. For example, ADD stands for addition, or PRINT means to print. Many 3GLs also use arithmetic operators such as * (asterisk) for multiplication and + (plus sign) for addition. These English-like words and arithmetic symbols simplify the program development process for the programmer. Hundreds of procedural languages exist. Only a few, however, are used widely enough for the industry to recognize them as standards. Read Ethics & Issues 12-4 to consider whether schools should teach students how hackers write code.

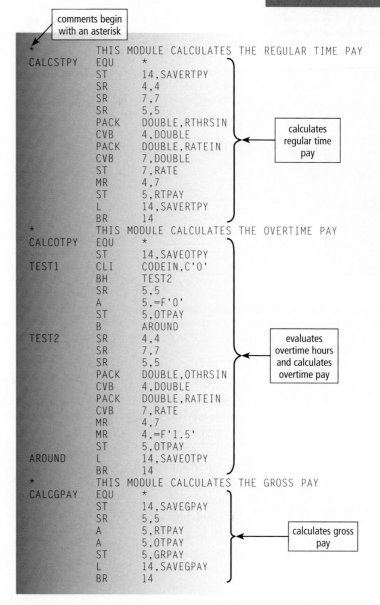

Figure 12-13 An excerpt from an assembly language payroll program. The code shows the computations for regular time pay, overtime pay, and gross pay and the decision to evaluate the overtime hours.
© Cengage Learning

✷ ETHICS & ISSUES 12-4

📄 Should Colleges Teach Hacking?

Investigators often try to understand criminal minds in an attempt to identify what motivates criminals to commit crimes. Similarly, to allow students to experience the mind-set of a hacker, some colleges offer courses that teach students how to write computer viruses and other malware. One instructor teaches students how to thwart antivirus software and how to generate anonymous email spam. He claims that if college students easily bypass antivirus software, then the products clearly are deficient. Is any benefit gained from teaching students to hack?

Proponents of such courses claim that these hacking skills enable the next generation of security experts to think like malicious hackers, thereby helping to stop the spread of malware. They liken the gained skills to physics students who learn about atomic weapons or biology students who learn how poisons work. One software company supports teaching hacking to help software developers evaluate code for security risks. Critics claim that this practice only encourages more virus authoring and hacking. Some developers of malware detection software have said they would not hire a student who had taken a hacking course. Others claim that knowing how to write malware does not make someone more capable of stopping malware. Questions remain about who is responsible legally, financially, and morally if a student uses the knowledge acquired in the course to release malicious code to the Internet or purposely infect other computers.

Should colleges teach hacking? Why or why not? Should companies hire people who are trained in creating malware and computer hacking? Why or why not? What precautions should schools take if they plan to offer such courses? Who is responsible if a student in such a course releases malware? Why?

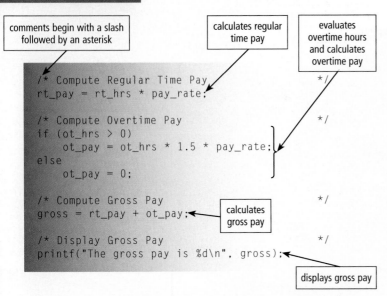

comments begin with a slash followed by an asterisk

calculates regular time pay

evaluates overtime hours and calculates overtime pay

```
/* Compute Regular Time Pay                */
rt_pay = rt_hrs * pay_rate;

/* Compute Overtime Pay                     */
if (ot_hrs > 0)
    ot_pay = ot_hrs * 1.5 * pay_rate;
else
    ot_pay = 0;

/* Compute Gross Pay                        */
gross = rt_pay + ot_pay;

/* Display Gross Pay                        */
printf("The gross pay is %d\n", gross);
```

calculates gross pay

displays gross pay

Figure 12-14 An excerpt from a C payroll program. The code shows the computations for regular time pay, overtime pay, and gross pay; the decision to evaluate the overtime hours; and the output of the gross pay.
© Cengage Learning

C A widely used procedural language is C. The C programming language, developed in the early 1970s by Dennis Ritchie at Bell Laboratories, originally was designed for writing system software. Today, many programs are written in C (Figure 12-14). C runs on almost any type of computer with any operating system, but it is used most often with the UNIX and Linux operating systems.

Compilers and Interpreters As with an assembly language program, the 3GL code (instructions) is called the source program. System developers must convert this source program into machine language before the computer can execute the program or app. This translation process often is very complex, because one 3GL source program instruction translates into many machine language instructions. For 3GLs, programmers typically use either a compiler or an interpreter to perform the translation.

- A *compiler* is a separate program that converts the entire source program into machine language before executing it. The machine language version that results from compiling the 3GL is called the *object program* or *object code*. The compiler stores the object program on storage media for execution later.

  While it is compiling the source program into the object program, the compiler checks the source program for errors. The compiler then produces a program listing that contains the source code and a list of any errors. This listing helps the programmer make necessary changes to the source code and correct errors in the program. Figure 12-15 shows the process of compiling a source program.

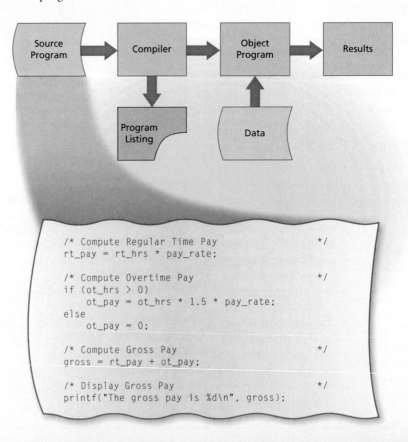

Figure 12-15 A compiler converts the source program (C, in this example) into a machine language object program.
© Cengage Learning

- An *interpreter*, by contrast, translates and executes one statement at a time. An interpreter reads a code statement, converts it to one or more machine language instructions, and then executes those machine language instructions. It does this all before moving to the next code statement in the program. Each time the source program runs, the interpreter translates and executes it, statement by statement. An interpreter does not produce an object program. Figure 12-16 shows the process of interpreting a program.

One advantage of an interpreter is that when it finds errors, it displays feedback immediately. The programmer can correct any errors before the interpreter translates the next line of code. The disadvantage is that interpreted programs do not run as fast as compiled programs.

Object-Oriented Programming Languages and Application Development Tools

System developers use an **object-oriented programming (OOP) language** or object-oriented application development tool to implement objects in a program. An *object* is an item that can contain both data and the procedures that read or manipulate that data. An object represents a real person, place, event, or transaction.

A major benefit of OOP is the ability to reuse and modify existing objects. For example, once a system developer creates an Employee object, it is available for use by any other existing or future program. Thus, system developers repeatedly reuse existing objects. For example, a payroll program and health benefits program both would use an Employee object. That is, the payroll program would use it to process employee paychecks, and the health benefits program would use it to process health insurance payments.

Programs developed using the object-oriented programming languages and application development tools have several advantages. The objects can be reused in many systems, are designed for repeated use, and become stable over time. In addition, developers create applications faster because they design programs using existing objects. Programming languages, such as Java and C++, and the latest versions of Visual Basic are complete OOP languages. Most object-oriented application development tools, such as Visual Studio, are referred to as an *integrated development environment* (IDE) because they include tools for building graphical interfaces, an editor for entering program code, a compiler and/or interpreter, and a debugger (to remove errors). Some work with a single programming language, and others support multiple languages. Read How To 12-2 for instructions about selecting the object-oriented programming language and application development tools best suited to your needs.

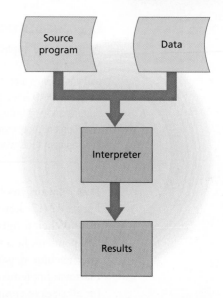

 Figure 12-16 With an interpreter, one line of the source program at a time is converted into machine language and then immediately executed by the computer or mobile device.
© Cengage Learning

BTW
Electronic Arts
Technology Innovator: You should be familiar with Electronic Arts (entertainment software developer).

 HOW TO 12-2 ───────────────────────────────────

Determine Which Object-Oriented Programming Language or Application Development Tool to Use

Software developers can choose from a variety of object-oriented programming languages and application development tools to write a program or app for a computer or mobile device. The following guidelines describe how to determine which language or tool to use:

- Determine the types of devices on which your program or app will run. For example, if you are writing an app for an iPhone or iPod Touch, limited languages and tools will be available for you to use. If you are

writing a program or app that will run on a computer, more options will be available. Perform research and determine which types of programming languages can be used for various operating systems.

- Determine the capabilities of the programming languages you are considering using. Some programming languages have greater capabilities than others.

- Consider the speed at which programs and apps run that are written in a particular programming language. For example, a program or app might run faster if it is written in one language as opposed to another.

- Consider whether you want to write a program using a text editor or an IDE. If you want to use an IDE, your choices of programming languages may be limited.

- Solicit recommendations from other developers. Explain the type of program or app you plan to write, and consider suggestions they might offer.

☀ If you are forced to write a program or app using a programming language with which you are not very familiar, what resources can you utilize to obtain assistance?

CONSIDER THIS

What is rapid application development?

RAD (*rapid application development*) is a method of developing software in which the software developer writes and implements a program in segments instead of waiting until the entire program is completed. An important concept in RAD is the use of prebuilt components. For example, software developers do not have to write code for buttons and text boxes on Windows forms because they already exist in the programming language or application development tools provided with the language. Object-oriented programming languages and application development tools work well in a RAD environment.

Java Java is an object-oriented programming language developed by Sun Microsystems. Figure 12-17 shows a portion of a Java program and the window that the program displays. When programmers compile a Java program, the resulting object program is machine independent. Java uses a *just-in-time* (*JIT*) *compiler* to convert the machine-independent code into machine-dependent code that is executed immediately. Software developers use various Java Platform implementations, which provide application development tools for creating programs for all sizes of computers and mobile devices.

```
public class BodyMassApplet extends Applet implements ActionListener
{
        //declare variables
        Image logo; //declare an Image object
        int inches, pounds;
        double meters, kilograms, index;

        //construct components
        Label companyLabel = new Label("THE SUN FITNESS CENTER BODY MASS INDEX CALCULATOR");
        Label heightLabel = new Label("Enter your height to the nearest inch  ");
            TextField heightField = new TextField(10);
        Label weightLabel = new Label ("Enter your weight to the nearest pound  ");
            TextField weightField = new TextField(10);
        Button calcButton = new Button("Calculate");
        Label outputLabel = new Label(
        "Click the Calculate button to see your Body Mass Index.");

            inches = Integer.parseInt(heightField.getText());
            pounds = Integer.parseInt(weightField.getText());
            meters = inches / 39.36;
            kilograms = pounds / 2.2;
            index = kilograms / Math.pow(meters,2);
            outputLabel.setText("YOUR BODY MASS INDEX IS " + Math.round(index) + ".");
        }

        public void paint(Graphics g)
        {
            g.drawImage(logo,125,160,this);
        }
}
```

```
Applet
THE SUN FITNESS CENTER BODY MASS INDEX CALCULATOR

   Enter your height to the nearest inch   67
   Enter your weight to the nearest pound   145
                    Calculate
   YOUR BODY MASS INDEX IS 23.


Applet started.
```

Figure 12-17 A portion of a Java program and the window the program displays.
© Cengage Learning

 Internet Research

What are examples of C++ applications?

Search for: C++ applications

C++ Developed in the 1980s by Bjarne Sroustrup at Bell Laboratories, **C++** (pronounced SEE-plus-plus) is an object-oriented programming language that is an extension of the C programming language. C++ includes all the elements of the C language, plus it has additional features for working with objects. Programmers commonly use C++ to develop database and web applications.

Visual Studio Developed by Microsoft, **Visual Studio** contains a suite of object-oriented application development tools that assists software developers in building programs and apps for Windows or any operating system that supports the Microsoft. NET Framework. Visual Studio also includes a set of tools for developing programs and apps that work with Microsoft's Office suite. OOPs included in the Visual Studio suite are Visual Basic (Figure 12-18), Visual C++, and Visual C#.

Creating a Visual Basic Desktop App

Step 1

The software developer designs the user interface, such as for the desktop app shown here. Enter Weight Loss is a button that, when tapped or clicked, displays a dialog box into which the user enters a weight loss value. The app then displays all weight loss values that the user enters in a list box, along with the team's average weight loss in a label. An image and label for the app's title (Fitness Challenge Team Weight Loss) adds visual appeal to the user interface.

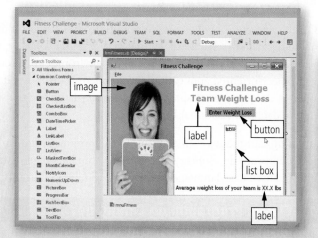

Step 2

The software developer assigns properties to each object. Objects include text boxes, list boxes, images, buttons, labels, and the form itself.

Step 4

The software developer tests the app. After the user enters a weight loss value, the app displays the value below any other values in the list box, calculates the average of the weight loss values shown in the list box, and displays the average in the Average Weight Loss label.

Step 3

The software developer writes code to define the action of each event that the user triggers, such as clicking a button or entering a value.

Figure 12-18 This figure shows how to create a Visual Basic desktop app.

Source: Microsoft; © Pando Hall / Getty images; © Cengage Learning

 CONSIDER THIS

What is .NET?

The Microsoft .NET Framework, or *.NET* (pronounced dot net), is a set of technologies that allows almost any type of program to run on the Internet or an internal business network, as well as stand-alone computers and mobile devices. Similarly, *ASP.NET* is a web application framework that provides the tools necessary for the creation of dynamic websites.

 CONSIDER THIS

What is a visual programming language?

A *visual programming language* is a language that uses a visual or graphical interface for creating all source code. The graphical interface, called a *visual programming environment* (VPE), allows system developers to drag and drop objects to build programs and apps.

BTW

Visual Basic
Visual Basic is based on the BASIC programming language, which was developed by Microsoft Corporation in the early 1960s. Because this language is easy to learn and use, beginning programmers often use it.

Internet Research

What is Visual Studio Express?

Search for: visual studio express

Other Languages and Application Development Tools

The following sections discuss a variety of other programming languages and application development tools.

4GLs A **4GL** (*fourth-generation language*) is a nonprocedural language that enables users and programmers to access data in a database. With a *nonprocedural language*, the programmer writes English-like instructions or interacts with a graphical environment to retrieve data from files or a database. Many object-oriented application development tools use 4GLs. One popular 4GL is SQL. As discussed in the previous chapter, *SQL* is a query language that allows users to manage, update, and retrieve data in a relational DBMS.

Classic Programming Languages In addition to the programming languages discussed on the previous pages, software developers sometimes use the languages listed in Table 12-1 to maintain legacy systems. These languages were more widely used in the past than they are today.

Table 12-1   Classic Programming Languages

Name	Description
Ada	Derived from Pascal, developed by the U.S. Department of Defense, named after Augusta Ada Lovelace Byron, who is thought to be the first female computer programmer
ALGOL	ALGOrithmic Language, the first structured procedural language
APL	A Programming Language, a scientific language designed to manipulate tables of numbers
BASIC	Beginners All-purpose Symbolic Instruction Code, developed by John Kemeny and Thomas Kurtz as a simple, interactive problem-solving language
COBOL	Common Business-Oriented Language, evolved out of a joint effort between the U.S. government, businesses, and major universities in the early 1960s; used primarily for business applications
Forth	Similar to C, used for small computerized devices
FORTRAN	FORmula TRANslator, one of the first high-level programming languages used for scientific applications
HyperTalk	An object-oriented programming language developed by Apple to manipulate cards that can contain text, graphics, and sound
LISP	LISt Processing, a language used for artificial intelligence applications
Logo	An educational tool used to teach programming and problem solving to children
Modula-2	A successor to Pascal used for developing system software
Pascal	Developed to teach students structured programming concepts, named in honor of Blaise Pascal, a French mathematician who developed one of the earliest calculating machines
PILOT	Programmed Inquiry Learning Or Teaching, used to write computer-aided instruction programs
PL/1	Programming Language One, a business and scientific language that combines many features of FORTRAN and COBOL
Prolog	PROgramming LOGic, used for development of artificial intelligence applications
RPG	Report Program Generator, used to assist businesses with generating reports and to access/update data in databases
Smalltalk	Object-oriented programming language

Application Generators An application generator is a program that creates source code or machine code from a specification of the required functionality. When using an application generator, a software developer or user works with menu-driven tools and graphical user interfaces to define the desired specifications. Application generators most often are bundled with or are included as part of a DBMS. An application generator typically consists of a report writer and forms, discussed in the previous chapter, and a menu generator. A menu generator enables you to create a menu for the application options.

Macros   A **macro** is a series of statements that instructs a program or app how to complete a task. Macros allow users to automate routine, repetitive, or difficult tasks in application software, such as word processing, spreadsheet (Figure 12-19), or database programs. That is, users can create simple programs within the software by writing macros. You usually create a macro in one of two ways: (1) record the macro or (2) write the macro.

※ **CONSIDER THIS** ───────────────────────────

Why and how would you record a macro?

If you want to automate a routine or repetitive task such as formatting or editing, you would record a macro. A *macro recorder* is similar to a movie camera because both record all actions until turned off. To record a macro, start the macro recorder in the software. Then, perform the steps to be part of the macro, such as taps, clicks, or keystrokes. Once the macro is recorded, you can run it any time you want to perform that same sequence of actions. For example, if you always print three copies of certain documents, you could record the actions required to print three copies. To print three copies, you would run the macro called PrintThreeCopies. When you become familiar with programming techniques, you can write your own macros instead of recording them. Read Secure IT 12-4 on the next page for a related discussion.

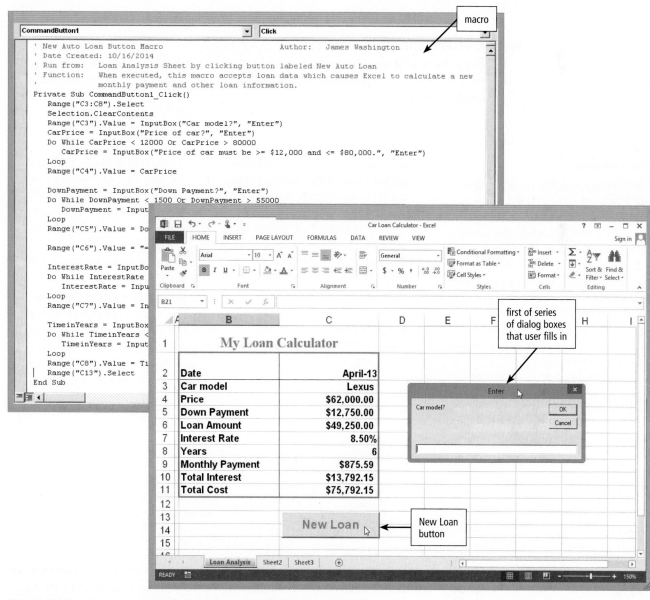

Figure 12-19   The top screen shows a macro used to automate an auto loan. After this macro is written, the user taps or clicks the New Loan button to run the macro. The bottom screen shows the macro guiding the user through part of the data entry process.
Source: Microsoft

SECURE IT 12-4

Protection from Macro Viruses

Microsoft accidentally shipped a CD-ROM labeled "Microsoft Compatibility Test" to hundreds of manufacturers in 1995. When these companies' computers read a Microsoft Word file on that disc, a message box with the number, 1, was the only item displayed on their monitors. This action occurred because the Word file was infected with the Word.Macro.Concept virus, one of the first macro viruses developed.

As the name implies, a macro virus hides in a program's macro language. Malware authors find that one of the easiest methods of spreading viruses and worms is by distributing files containing macro viruses.

This type of virus is easy to write, and the damage that results from infecting computers can exceed millions of dollars.

Because many companies' computers have acquired damaging macro viruses, antivirus and productivity software companies have strengthened their efforts to prevent this malware from infecting their products. One method, for example, disables the macros, which prohibits employees from running once-automated tasks on their computers. The employees, however, are frustrated when they now must perform routines manually. Other prevention measures include setting the software's macro security level to high,

not opening unexpected file attachments, and holding down the SHIFT key when opening a file that may be infected by a macro virus so that any automatic macros are prevented from running.

Many computer users claim the software companies should make it impossible for malware authors to take advantage of security problems in the software. The software companies, however, place the blame on users who open files from unknown sources.

✳ Should users or software companies be held accountable for macro security threats? Why? How can users best be educated about opening documents from unknown sources?

Web Development

The designers of webpages, known as *web developers*, use a variety of techniques to create webpages. The following sections discuss these techniques. Read How To 12-3 for instructions about posting webpages.

HOW TO 12-3

Post a Webpage

After creating a webpage, you will need to post it on a web server so that it is accessible online. The method you use to post a webpage can vary, depending upon a number of factors. For example, if you created a webpage using a web app, the webpage may automatically be available online or you may be able to use a feature in the web app to post the webpage. If you created the webpage using a program or app on your computer, the following sections describe various ways to post the webpage.

1. Identify the web hosting company you want to use.

2. Navigate to and review the documentation explaining how to post your webpage. Some web hosting companies require you to post the webpage using a specific set of steps, while others are more flexible.

3. Post the webpage using one of the web hosting company's recommended methods:

o Some web hosting companies will allow you to post your webpage using a web app or file transfer program that is part of their website. Select the files you want to transfer from your computer, select the destination (if necessary), and then tap or click the appropriate button or link that will initiate the transfer.

o Some web hosting companies, businesses, or universities allow you to post webpages using FTP or SFTP. Download and install a program or app that supports the required protocol (FTP or SFTP). Refer to How To 12-1 on page 532 for information about determining whether a program or app is safe to use. Run the program and enter the required information to connect to the web hosting company's server. (The required information, such as the server address, user name, and password, is available from the web hosting

company.) Next, connect to the server, select the file(s) you want to transfer from your computer, and the location on the web hosting company's server where you want to transfer the files, and then initiate the transfer.

4. Once the transfer has completed, run your browser.

5. Navigate to your webpage. Your web hosting company should have provided the web address for accessing the webpage.

6. If your webpage does not display properly, verify that you entered the correct web address and ensure the web server is functional. Lastly, consider contacting your web hosting company's technical support staff for additional assistance.

✳ Does one method of posting webpages have any advantages over another? Which method described in Step 3 above appears to be the easiest?

HTML   HTML (*Hypertext Markup Language*) is a special formatting language that programmers use to format documents for display on the web. You view a webpage written with HTML in a browser, such as Internet Explorer, Safari, Firefox, Opera, or Chrome. Figure 12-20a shows part of the HTML code used to create the webpage shown in Figure 12-20b.

Figure 12-20a (portion of HTML code)

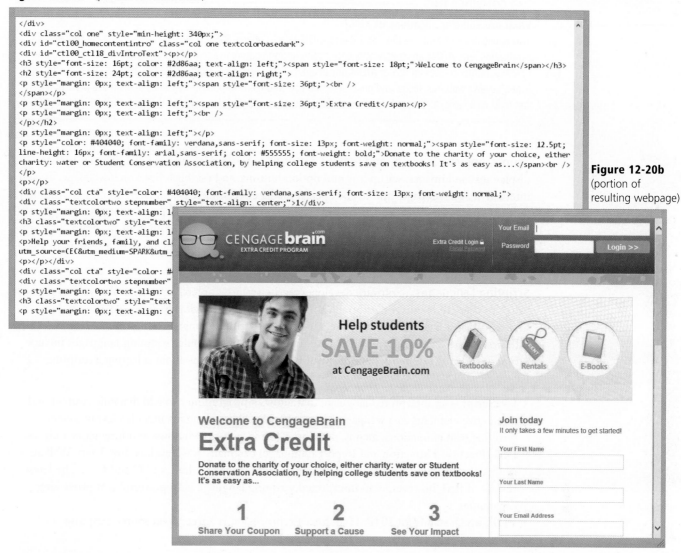

Figure 12-20b
(portion of
resulting webpage)

Figure 12-20 The portion of the HTML code in Figure 12-20a generates a portion of the Cengage Learning CengageBrain webpage shown in Figure 12-20b.
Source: Cengage Learning

 **CONSIDER THIS**

Is HTML a programming language?
HTML is not actually a programming language. It is, however, a language that has specific rules for defining the placement and format of text, graphics, video, and audio on a webpage. HTML uses tags or elements, which are words, abbreviations, and symbols that specify links to other documents and indicate how a webpage is displayed when viewed on the web.

BTW
Mobile Application Development
High-Tech Talk:
Application programmers use toolkits to develop mobile apps.

XML XML (*Extensible Markup Language*) is an increasingly popular format for sharing data that allows web developers to create tags that describe how information is displayed. XML separates the webpage content from its format, allowing the browser to display the contents of a webpage in a form appropriate for the display device. For example, a smartphone and a laptop both could display the same XML page or use different formats or sections of the XML page.

Wireless devices use a subset of XML called WML. *WML* (*wireless markup language*) allows web developers to design pages specifically for microbrowsers. Many smartphones and other mobile devices use WML as their markup language.

CONSIDER THIS

What are some applications of XML?
Two applications of XML are the RSS 2.0 and ATOM specifications. *RSS 2.0*, which stands for Really Simple Syndication, and *ATOM* are specifications that content aggregators use to distribute content to subscribers. The online publisher creates an RSS or ATOM document, called a web feed, that is made available to websites for publication. News websites, blogs, and podcasts often use web feeds to publish headlines and stories. Most browsers can read web feeds, meaning they automatically download updated content from webpages identified in the feed.

Scripts, Applets, Servlets, and ActiveX Controls Markup languages tell a browser how to display text and images, set up lists and option buttons, and establish links on a webpage. To add interactivity on webpages and to add special media effects, such as animated graphics, scrolling messages, calendars, and advertisements, web developers write small programs called scripts, applets, servlets, and ActiveX controls. These programs run inside of another program. This is different from programs discussed thus far, which are executed by the operating system. In this case, the browser executes these short programs.

Scripting Languages Software developers write scripts, applets, servlets, or ActiveX controls using a variety of languages. Although some use languages previously discussed, such as Java, C++, and Visual Basic, many developers instead use scripting languages. A *scripting language* is an interpreted language that typically is easy to learn and use. Popular scripting languages include JavaScript, Perl, PHP, and VBScript. Read How To 12-4 for tips about selecting a scripting language.

- **JavaScript** is an interpreted language that allows a programmer to add dynamic content and interactive elements to a webpage (Figure 12-21). These elements include alert messages, scrolling text, animations, menus, data input forms, pop-up windows, and interactive quizzes.
- **Perl** (Practical Extraction and Report Language) originally was developed by Larry Wall at NASA's Jet Propulsion Laboratory as a procedural language similar to C and C++. The latest release of Perl, however, is an interpreted scripting language with powerful text processing capabilities.
- **PHP**, which stands for PHP: Hypertext Preprocessor, is a free, open source scripting language. PHP is similar to C, Java, and Perl.

Ruby on Rails **Ruby on Rails** is an open source framework that provides technologies for developing object-oriented, database-driven websites. Ruby on Rails is designed to make web developers more productive by providing them an easy-to-use environment and eliminating time spent in development.

 HOW TO 12-4

Determine Which Scripting Language to Use

Before developing a webpage that requires the use of a scripting language, you first should determine which scripting language is best to use. The following guidelines describe how to determine which scripting language to use:

- If the scripts you are writing will be executed in a browser, select a scripting language that is compatible with the major browsers, such as Internet Explorer, Firefox, Chrome, and Safari.

- If the scripts you are writing will be executed on a web server, choose a scripting language that is compatible with the web server software running on the server.

- Research the various scripting languages and note whether any security vulnerabilities exist. Choose the scripting language that poses the least threat to your webpage and the server.

- To save development time, consider a scripting language with which you are most familiar.

- Research the various scripting languages to determine the capabilities of each one. Choose the language that contains all the features you require.

 In what situations might you need to use a scripting language?

Figure 12-21a (JavaScript code)

```
189
190
191  <script language="JavaScript" type="text/javascript">
192       jQuery(function() {
193           jQuery(".slidetabs").tabs(".images > div", {
194               effect: 'fade',
195               fadeOutSpeed: 1200,
196               fadeInSpeed: 1200,
197               rotate: true
198           // use the slideshow plugin. It accepts its own configuration
199           }).slideshow({autoplay: true, interval: 6000, clickable: false});
200
201           // Get access to the API - This has to be done after your Tabs instance is created
202           var api = jQuery(".slidetabs").data("tabs");
203
204           api.onBeforeClick(function() {
205               jQuery('.descriptor').hide();
206           });
207
208           //When the slidesh
209           api.onClick(functi
210               if (jQuery.
211                   jQuer
212               }
213               jQuery('.des
214           });
215
216       });
217  </script>
218
```

Figure 12-21b
(webpage)

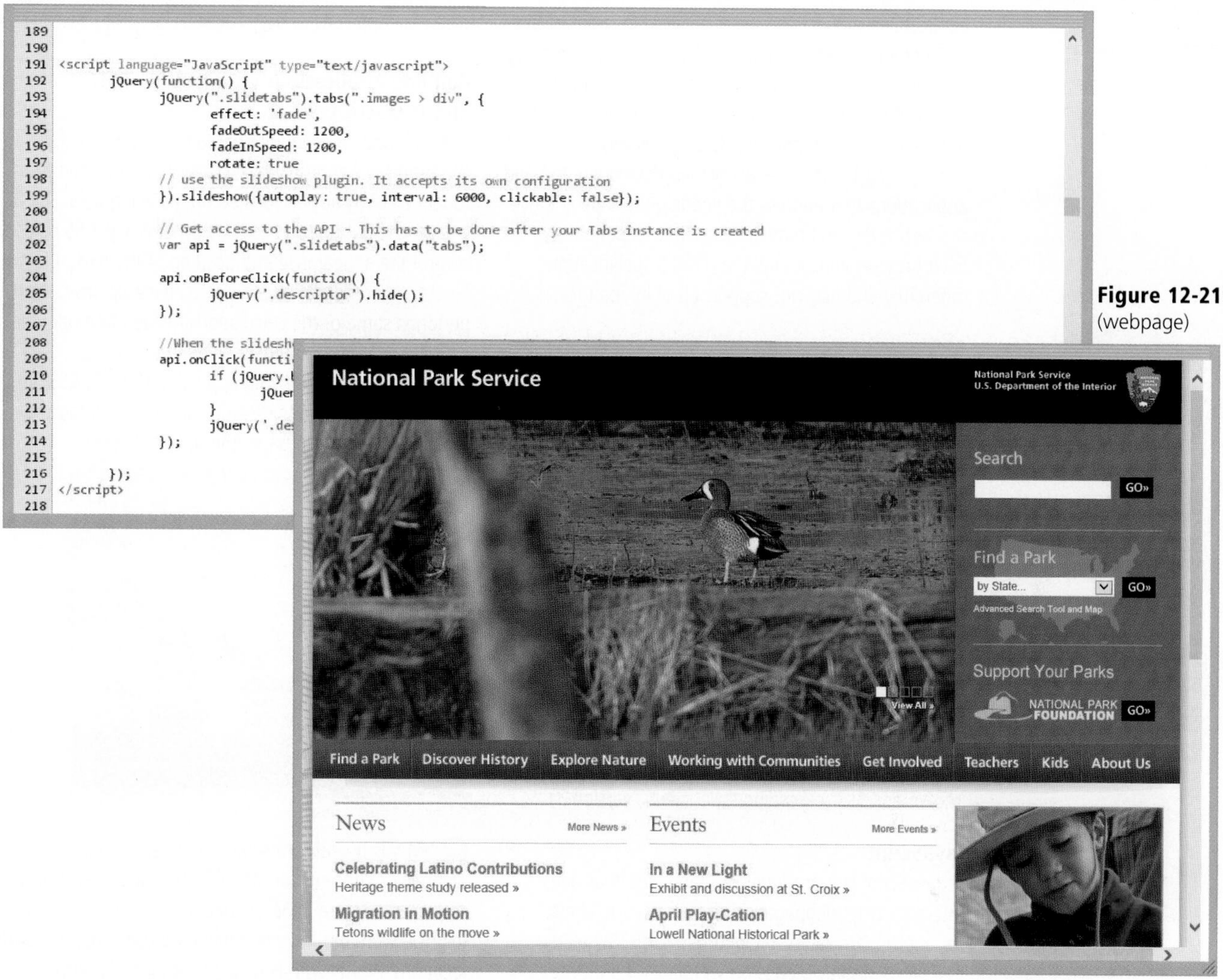

Figure 12-21   Shown here is a portion of the JavaScript code and its associated National Park Service webpage.
Source: National Park Service U.S. Department of the Interior

---

⊛ **MINI FEATURE 12-3**

Web Application Development

Three technologies form the foundation for many web applications: *HTML5* specifies the structure of content displayed on a web page; *CSS (cascading style sheets)* describes the design and appearance of information on a webpage; and JavaScript allows users to interact with a page's content. Many web applications also access applications running on a server, connect to a database, or access third-party content from online sources. Together, these technologies enable developers to create browser-independent web applications that run on a variety of devices.

The W3C (World Wide Web Consortium) is an international organization that sets the standards for the technologies and operation of the web. In addition, it defines the standards for HTML5 and CSS.

HTML5

HTML5 is the standard technology for creating websites and applications. Recall that HTML uses a set of codes called tags to instruct a browser how to structure a webpage's content. HTML tags specify how content is structured on a page, such as headings, hyperlinks, images, or paragraphs. This latest version of HTML has evolved to include new tags for playing audio and video files without relying on the use of third-party plug-ins, or modules, to perform these tasks. For example, Adobe Flash is a proprietary plug-in that many websites require to play audio, video, interactive games, or animations. Some mobile devices, such as Apple's iPhone and iPad, do not support displaying media content that requires Flash. Instead, they rely on HTML5-compliant browsers, which are capable of interpreting HTML5 tags, to handle these tasks. Additional HTML5 features include recognizing gestures popular on mobile

devices, such as swipe, or drag and drop; allowing applications to function in some limited fashion when no Internet connection is available; dynamically creating graphics, such as progress bars, charts, and animations; and *geolocation* (determining a user's location based on a device's GPS or connection to a cell tower).

These HTML5 features allow web developers to build applications that address the needs of how people use the web today and provide richer user experiences. Each browser implements the HTML5 specification differently and may not support all of its features.

CSS

While HTML describes the structure of a webpage's content as a collection of elements such as headings, paragraphs, images, and links, CSS allows web designers to separate the code that specifies a page's content from the code that specifies the page's appearance. For example, a webpage may contain two paragraphs of text that are presented using a variety of fonts and sizes, styles, colors, borders, thicknesses, columns, or backgrounds. CSS provides web designers with precise control over a webpage's layout and allows the designers to apply different layouts to the same information for printing or for viewing in browsers on smartphones, tablets, or computers with varying screen sizes. The current version of CSS is known as CSS3 (cascading style sheets, version 3).

JavaScript

JavaScript is a programming language that adds interactivity to webpages. It often is used to check for appropriate values on web forms, display alert messages, display menus on webpages, control the appearance of a browser window, read and write cookies, display alert boxes, and detect the browser version in order to display a page especially designed for that browser. JavaScript code is loaded with a webpage and runs in the browser.

Building Applications with HTML5, CSS, and JavaScript

Angry Birds is a popular game built using HTML5, CSS, and JavaScript in which players control a slingshot to launch birds at pigs located on a playing field. HTML5 creates the background screens dynamically; CSS helps control the appearance and position of the birds, pigs, blocks, and other on-screen game elements; JavaScript performs some of the calculations needed to model the physics for flight and other events in the game.

To create your own web app using HTML5, CSS, and JavaScript, complete the Beyond the Book Windows and Mac exercise on page 556 in this chapter.

Courtesy of Ricky Vermaat; Source: Rovio Entertainment Ltd.

✺ Why is it useful to separate the structure of a webpage's content from the CSS that specifies how it is displayed? Before HTML5's geolocation features, how might a web app have determined a user's approximate location? Words with Friends is another web app implemented using HTML5, CSS, and JavaScript. Name one feature of Words with Friends that might demonstrate a characteristic of these technologies.

✔ NOW YOU KNOW

Be sure you understand the material presented in the section titled Application Development Languages and Tools, as it relates to the chapter objectives.
You now should know . . .

- How your computer works with low-level and procedural languages (Objective 5)
- Why you would use an OOP language or application development tool (Objective 6)
- When you might use other programming languages and application development tools (Objective 7)
- How you can develop webpages (Objective 8)

Quiz Yourself Online: Check your knowledge of related content by navigating to this book's Quiz Yourself resource on Computer Concepts CourseMate and then tapping or clicking Objective 5–8.

Chapter Summary

This chapter discussed the system development phases. The guidelines for system development also were presented. Activities that occur during system development, including project management, feasibility assessment, documentation, and data and information gathering, also were addressed. This chapter also discussed various programming languages and application development tools used to create and modify computer programs. Finally, it described a variety of web development tools.

Test your knowledge of chapter material by accessing the Study Guide, Flash Cards, and Practice Test apps that run on your smartphone, tablet, laptop, or desktop.

TECHNOLOGY @ WORK

Construction

Walking the streets, you stop to admire a new skyscraper with the most striking architectural features you ever have seen. You think to yourself that those responsible for designing the building are nothing less than brilliant. While a great deal of physical labor as well as time is spent by people constructing and designing the building, computers and technology also play an important role in the process. In fact, the role of computers not only saves time and provides for more accurate results, it also allows us to preview how a building will look before construction even begins.

During the preliminary design process, architects and design firms use CAD software to design the appearance and layout of a new building and can provide clients with a 3-D walk-through of a building so that they can determine whether the proposed design will meet their needs. Later, the program can be used to include the placement of support beams, walls, roof shape, and so on, and also conform to building codes.

CAD software also allows engineers in various fields, such as mechanical and electrical, to design separate layers in a structure. The software then can superimpose the designs to check for interactions and conflicts, such as if a structural beam in one layer covers a drain in another layer. The CAD software makes it easy to modify and correct the structure before it is built, which can save time and money during the construction process. This software also eliminates most, if not all, of the manual drafting required.

Engineers use computers to determine the type of foundation required to support the building and its occupants; the heating, ventilating, and air conditioning (HVAC); the electrical requirements; and how the building may withstand external threats, such as hurricanes and tornadoes.

During construction, contractors and builders are able to use computer software to estimate accurately the amount of materials and time required to complete the job. Without computers, determining materials and time required is a cumbersome and time-consuming task.

The next time you notice a building under construction, stop to think about how computer technology has increased the efficiency of the design and construction process.

How else might computers and technology be used in the construction industry?

© iStockphoto / TommL

Study Guide

The Study Guide exercise reinforces material you should know for the chapter exam. You will find answers to items with the icon only in the e-book.

Access the Study Guide app that runs on your smartphone, tablet, laptop, or desktop by navigating to this book's Apps resource on Computer Concepts CourseMate.

Instructions: Answer the questions below using the format that helps you remember best or that is required by your instructor. Possible formats may include one or more of these options: write the answers; create a document that contains the answers; record answers as audio or video using a webcam, smartphone, or portable media player; post answers on a blog, wiki, or website; or highlight answers in the book/e-book.

1. Identify the five phases in the SDLC. Name three guidelines for system development.

2. Identify who participates in system development. Describe the skill set of a systems analyst.

3. Explain positive and negative issues surrounding telecommuting.

4. Define the term, project management. List elements the project leader must identify.

5. Define these terms: project management software, project plan, and deliverable.

6. Describe how Gantt and PERT charts are used.

7. Define the terms, scope creep and change management.

8. Identify tests used to evaluate feasibility of a project.

9. Explain the importance of documentation.

10. Describe ways that team members collaborate.

11. Identify data and information gathering techniques. A(n) _____ session also is called a focus group.

12. Identify the contributions of the Wikimedia Foundation and Jimmy Wales.

13. List components of information literacy.

14. Describe circumstances that can initiate system development.

15. Explain issues surrounding the effect of digital communications on relationships.

16. List the four activities of the planning phase. Explain how projects are prioritized.

17. Name the activities of the analysis phase. Identify questions to ask a user who submits a project request.

18. List the three activities of the detailed analysis phase. Detailed analysis sometimes is called _____ design.

19. Describe how a steering committee may decide on a system proposal.

20. Explain security issues surrounding outsourcing.

21. List the two activities of the design phase.

22. Describe how a systems analyst obtains hardware or software.

23. Differentiate among an RFQ, RFP, and RFI. Describe the roles of VARs and IT consultants when soliciting vendor proposals.

24. Explain what occurs when vendor proposals are tested and evaluated. A(n) _____ test measures the performance of hardware or software.

25. Identify circumstances that might influence the decision to accept a vendor proposal.

26. Explain the activities that occur during the detailed design phase and the people involved in the review.

27. Describe how systems analysts build relationships with users.

28. Define the terms, prototype and CASE software.

29. List the four activities of the implementation phase.

30. Define the term, program development life cycle. Identify considerations for program logic.

31. Explain issues surrounding the use of back doors in software development.

32. Define the term, sandbox.

33. List tests a systems analyst and users might perform.

34. Describe the activities that occur during the training phase.

35. Differentiate among the following conversion strategies: direct, parallel, phased, and pilot.

36. List the three activities of the support and security phase.

37. Explain the role of a CSO. Describe the components of a technology security plan.

38. Define the following terms: programming language, application development tool, and syntax.

39. Differentiate between low- and high-level programming languages.

40. Differentiate among machine, assembly, and procedural languages.

41. Explain issues surrounding colleges that teach students how to hack.

42. List guidelines to determine whether a program or app is safe to use.

43. Define the terms, compiler and interpreter.

44. List benefits of OOP languages. Name three types of OOP languages.

45. List guidelines to determine which programming language or development tool to use. Explain the RAD method.

46. Describe the following: 4GLs, classic programming languages, application generators, and macros. Explain how to protect yourself from macro viruses.

47. List steps to post a webpage. Explain how web developers use HTML, XML, CSS, and JavaScript.

48. Identify how web developers add interactivity. List guidelines to choose a scripting language.

49. Explain how the construction industry uses technology.

You should be able to define the Primary Terms and be familiar with the Secondary Terms listed below.

Key Terms

Access the Flash Cards app that runs on your smartphone, tablet, laptop, or desktop by navigating to this book's Apps resource on Computer Concepts CourseMate. View definitions for each term by navigating to this book's Key Terms resource on Computer Concepts CourseMate. Listen to definitions for each term on your portable media player by navigating to this book's Audio Study Tools resource on Computer Concepts CourseMate.

Primary Terms (shown in **bold-black** characters in the chapter)

4GL (538)
analysis phase (520)
assembly language (532)
C (534)
C++ (536)
design phase (523)
documentation (515)
feasibility (515)
HTML (540)
implementation phase (527)

JavaScript (542)
joint-application design (JAD) session (516)
machine language (532)
macro (539)
object-oriented programming (OOP) language (535)
Perl (542)
PHP (542)

planning phase (520)
preliminary investigation (520)
procedural language (533)
programming language (531)
project management (513)
project management software (514)
prototype (526)
Ruby on Rails (542)

support and security phase (530)
system development (510)
system development life cycle (SDLC) (510)
systems analyst (512)
training (528)
Visual Studio (536)
XML (541)

Secondary Terms (shown in *italic* characters in the chapter)

acceptance test (528)
application development tool (531)
ASP.NET (537)
assembler (533)
ATOM (542)
benchmark test (525)
change management (515)
chief security officer (CSO) (530)
code (533)
compiler (534)
computer-aided software engineering (CASE) software tools (526)
conferencing software (516)
cost/benefit feasibility (515)
CSS (cascading style sheets) (543)
deliverable (514)
detailed analysis (522)
direct conversion (529)
economic feasibility (515)
execute (533)
Extensible Markup Language (541)
feasibility study (520)
feature creep (515)
focus group (516)

fourth-generation language (538)
functional language (533)
Gantt chart (514)
geolocation (544)
high-level language (532)
HTML5 (543)
Hypertext Markup Language (540)
information literacy (517)
integrated development environment (IDE) (535)
integration test (528)
interpreter (535)
IT consultant (524)
just-in-time (JIT) compiler (536)
logical design (522)
low-level language (532)
machine-dependent language (532)
machine-independent language (532)
macro recorder (539)
mock-up (525)
.NET (537)
nonprocedural language (538)
object (535)
object code (534)
object program (534)

operational feasibility (515)
parallel conversion (529)
PERT chart (514)
phased conversion (529)
phases (510)
pilot conversion (529)
post-implementation system review (530)
program development life cycle (528)
program specification package (526)
project leader (513)
project manager (513)
project plan (514)
project request (518)
project team (512)
proof of concept (526)
RAD (rapid application development) (536)
request for information (RFI) (524)
request for proposal (RFP) (524)
request for quotation (RFQ) (524)
request for system services (518)
RSS 2.0 (542)
sandbox (528)
schedule feasibility (515)

scope (514)
scope creep (515)
scripting language (542)
source program (533)
SQL (538)
standards (512)
steering committee (512)
symbolic address (532)
syntax (531)
systems test (528)
technical feasibility (515)
third-generation language (3GL) (533)
unit test (528)
user buy-in (526)
value-added reseller (VAR) (524)
visual programming environment (VPE) (537)
visual programming language (537)
web conference (516)
web developers (540)
WML (wireless markup language) (541)

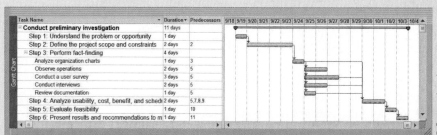

Gantt chart (514)

Checkpoint

The Checkpoint exercises test your knowledge of the chapter concepts. The page number containing the answer appears in parentheses after each exercise. The Consider This exercises challenge your understanding of chapter concepts.

Complete the Checkpoint exercises interactively by navigating to this book's Checkpoint resource on Computer Concepts CourseMate. **Access the Test Prep app** that runs on your smartphone, tablet, laptop, or desktop by navigating to this book's Apps resource on Computer Concepts CourseMate. After successfully completing the self-assessment through the Test Prep app, **take the Practice Test** by navigating to this book's Practice Test resource on Computer Concepts CourseMate.

True/False   Mark T for True and F for False.

_____ 1. Activities within phases of the SDLC often interact with one another, making system development a dynamic iterative process. (510)

_____ 2. Detailed analysis sometimes is called logical design. (522)

_____ 3. A mock-up is more technical than a layout chart and contains programming-like notations. (526)

_____ 4. One reason systems fail is because the systems analyst creates or modifies systems with little or no user participation. (526)

_____ 5. Only the systems analyst and developers should review detailed design specifications before they are given to the programming team. (527)

_____ 6. The purpose of the implementation phase is to construct the new or modified system and then deliver it to the users. (527)

_____ 7. With a high-level language, each instruction usually equates to a single machine instruction. (532)

_____ 8. A procedural language is the only language the computer directly recognizes. (532)

_____ 9. To convert machine language into an assembly language source code, programmers use a program called an assembler. (533)

_____ 10. The machine language version that results from compiling a 3GL is called the object program. (534)

_____ 11. One advantage of a compiler is that when it finds errors, it displays feedback immediately. (535)

_____ 12. HTML is not a programming language. (541)

Multiple Choice   Select the best answer.

1. System development activities often are grouped into larger categories called _____. (510)
   a. deliverables   c. phases
   b. standards   d. objects

2. During system development, the _____ is the users' primary contact. (512)
   a. web developer   c. steering committee
   b. systems analyst   d. programmer

3. _____ feasibility measures how well the proposed system will work. (515)
   a. Operational   c. Technical
   b. Schedule   d. Economic

4. Which of the following activities is not performed during the planning phase? (520)
   a. prototyping
   b. prioritizing the project requests
   c. allocating resources
   d. forming a project development team

5. With a(n) _____, a vendor selects a product(s) that meets specified requirements and then quotes the price(s). (524)
   a. RFP   c. RFQ
   b. RFI   d. VAR

6. A(n) _____ test verifies that all programs in an application work together properly. (528)
   a. acceptance   c. unit
   b. integration   d. systems

7. Which of the following activities is not performed during the support and security phase? (530)
   a. converting to the new system
   b. performing maintenance
   c. monitoring system performance
   d. assessing system security

8. Used as the markup language on many smartphones and mobile devices, _____ allows web developers to design pages specifically for microbrowsers. (541)
   a. WML   c. HTML
   b. XML   d. ATOM

Checkpoint

Matching   Match the terms with their definitions.

_____ 1. standards (512)

_____ 2. scope (514)

_____ 3. deliverable (514)

_____ 4. JAD session (516)

_____ 5. project request (518)

_____ 6. feasibility study (520)

_____ 7. benchmark test (525)

_____ 8. prototype (526)

_____ 9. sandbox (528)

_____ 10. machine language (532)

a. sets of rules and procedures an organization expects employees to accept and follow

b. tool used to measure the performance of hardware or software

c. any tangible item such as a chart, diagram, report, or program file

d. environment that allows software developers to test their programs with fictitious data without adversely affecting other programs, information systems, or data

e. formal, written request for a new or modified information system

f. working model of a proposed system's essential functionality

g. the first generation of programming languages and the only language the computer directly recognizes

h. goals, objectives, and expectations of a project

i. investigation to determine the exact nature of a problem or improvement and decide whether it is worth pursuing

j. series of lengthy, structured group meetings in which users and IT professionals work together to design or develop an application

Short Answer   Write a brief answer to each of the following questions.

1. Who belongs to a project team? (512) What skills should a systems analyst have? (512)

2. Differentiate between Gantt charts and PERT charts. (514) What is scope creep? (515)

3. What are a CSO's responsibilities? (530) What qualifications should a CSO have? (530)

4. Differentiate between low-level and high-level languages. (532) Differentiate between a compiler and an interpreter. (534)

5. What are HTML5 and CSS? (543) List some uses of JavaScript. (544)

✴ Consider This   Answer the following questions in the format specified by your instructor.

1. Answer the critical thinking questions posed at the end of these elements in this chapter: Ethics & Issues (512, 518, 528, 533), How To (532, 535, 540, 542), Mini Features (517, 528, 543), Secure IT (523, 530, 540), and Technology @ Work (545).

2. Should you involve users in system development? Why or why not? (512)

3. How does a project leader use a project plan? (514)

4. How does a systems analyst determine if a project is feasible? (515)

5. What steps ensure effective research and composition of strategies? (517)

6. Why is detailed analysis also called logical design? (522)

7. Should a business outsource noncore functions? Why or why not? (523)

8. How does a benchmark test evaluate software or hardware? (525)

9. What is the advantage of using a prototype? (526)

10. 📄 How does program logic influence a project's development? (528)

11. What is the disadvantage of a direct conversion? Why might a phased conversion be more effective? (529)

12. What is the goal of a computer security plan? (530)

13. Why might a system developer choose a compiler or an interpreter? (534)

14. How can you determine which object-oriented language or development tool to use? (535)

15. What features of HTML5 provide richer user experiences? (543)

✸ How To: Your Turn

The How To: Your Turn exercises present general guidelines for fundamental skills when using a computer or mobile device and then require that you determine how to apply these general guidelines to a specific program or situation.

Instructions: You often can complete tasks using technology in multiple ways. Figure out how to perform the tasks described in these exercises by using one or more resources available to you (such as a computer or mobile device, articles on the web or in print, online or program help, user guides, blogs, podcasts, videos, other individuals, trial and error, etc.). Summarize your 'how to' steps, along with the resource(s) used, in the format requested by your instructor (brief report, presentation, discussion, blog post, video, or other means).

1 **Conduct an Effective Interview**

As you learned in this chapter, gathering information is a critical element in system development, because without accurate facts, it is unlikely that the finished system will perform in the desired manner. An important means of gathering information is the personal interview. Interviews are used in several stages throughout system development, and they must be thorough and comprehensive. Prior to conducting an interview, you must determine that an interview is the best means for obtaining the information you seek. You have learned a variety of ways to obtain information, and you should use each of them appropriately. Because an interview interrupts a person's work and takes time, you must be sure the information gained in the interview justifies this interruption. Once you have determined you should conduct an interview to gather information required for system development, plan to ask questions that will generate useful answers. The following steps guide you through the process of conducting an interview that ultimately will generate useful answers.

a. Your questions should directly address the goals of the interview. Do not expect the person being interviewed to provide a tutorial. Your questions must generate answers that supply you with the information you need to make a decision.

b. Your questions should be thought-provoking. In general, do not ask questions requiring a yes or no answer. Your questions should not lead the interviewee to an answer — rather, the questions should be open-ended and allow the person to develop the answer. As an interviewer, you never should argue with the person being interviewed, you should not suggest answers or give opinions, you should ask straightforward questions rather than compound questions, you never should assign blame for any circumstance that might come up in the interview, and you must never interrupt while the person is talking. Finally, you, as the interviewer, should not talk much. Remember, you are conducting the interview to gain information, and it is the person you are interviewing who has that information. Let him or her talk.

c. Pay attention carefully, with both your ears and your eyes. What you hear normally is most important, but body language and other movements often convey information as well. Concentrate on the interviewee — expect that you will make much more eye contact with the person than he or she will with you. Allow silences to linger — the normal impulse in a conversation is to fill the silence quickly; in an interview, however, if you are quiet, the person being interviewed might think of additional information.

d. As you listen, concentrate on the interviewee. When points are being made, do not take notes because that will distract from what the person is saying; stay focused. When the information has been conveyed, then jot down a note so that you will remember.

e. Throughout the interview, offer reinforcing comments, such as, "The way I understand what you just said is …" Make sure when you leave the interview that no misunderstandings exist between you and the person you interviewed.

f. Before you conclude the interview, be sure all your goals have been met. You likely will not have another opportunity to interview the person, so ensure you have asked sufficient questions to gain the information you need to make a decision.

g. After the interview, it is recommended you send a follow-up letter or email message to the person you interviewed to review the information you learned. This document should invite the interviewee to correct any errors you made in summing up your findings. In addition, for all the people you interview, keep a record of the time and place of the interview. In this way, if any questions arise regarding the interview, you will have a record.

Exercises

1. Think about the last time you were involved in an interview (either as an interviewer or an interviewee). What types of questions were you asked? Do you feel the questions solicited useful answers?

2. If you were to interview a candidate for a technology-related position, what types of questions would you ask?

3. What advantages do open-ended questions have? When might a question requiring a brief answer be appropriate?

How To: Your Turn ☀

2 Create a Website Using a Website Authoring App

Website authoring apps simplify the process of creating a web presence for individuals with limited or no web development knowledge. Some website authoring apps are designed to create simple websites, while others can create large, complex websites. Some website authoring apps that create websites are available for free, and others charge a fee. In addition, some website authoring apps that initially are free may begin charging a fee either after a predefined period of time, or if you try to use premium or advanced features. If you want merely to create a simple, personal website, a free tool might be suitable. The following steps guide you through the process of creating a website using a website authoring app.

a. Run a browser.

b. Navigate to a search engine of your choice and search for website authoring apps that can create websites.

c. Tap or click the search results for website authoring apps that interest you and review the features of each app.

d. Before deciding on a website authoring app to use, perform research on the web and determine whether other users are satisfied with the app and its features. If the reviews are not favorable, consider using another app.

e. Navigate to the website authoring app you want to use to create a website.

f. Tap or click the button or link to sign up for a new account and then enter the requested information to create the account.

g. If necessary, tap or click the button or link to create a new website.

h. Select a design for the new website.

i. Add the desired elements to the page, including:
   1. Headings (titles and subtitles)
   2. Text boxes (lines or paragraphs of text)
   3. Media (photos, audio, and videos)
   4. Links to other webpages, websites, or email addresses

j. When you have finished adding all desired elements to the webpage, save it.

k. Tap or click the command to add another page to the website. Add the headings, text boxes, media, and links to create the additional webpage. Repeat these steps for each additional webpage you want to add to the website.

l. When you have created all webpages, revisit each webpage to make sure you have added appropriate links so that visitors properly can navigate the webpages in the website.

m. Save all pages in the website.

n. Record the web address of the website. The web address typically is assigned by the website authoring app and may include your user name and the website authoring app's domain name. Some website authoring apps will allow you to use a custom domain name either by registering one with them or using one you have previously registered. If you are using a free website authoring app, the option to use a custom domain name for your website may require a fee.

o. When you have finished, sign out of the app but do not close the browser window.

p. Navigate to the website using its assigned web address. Test the website to verify that:
   1. All text displays properly and is aligned as you intended.
   2. Photos and videos are displayed.
   3. All links work as intended and you are able to navigate through the webpages in the website.

q. To make changes to the website, you would follow these steps:
   1. Navigate to and sign in to the website authoring app.
   2. Navigate to the webpage you want to modify.
   3. Modify the webpage.
   4. Save all changes.
   5. Sign out of the account.
   6. Navigate to the website and verify all changes were made properly.

r. Exit the browser.

Source: Weebly, Inc.

Exercises

1. Which website authoring apps did you evaluate, and what do you like most about the website authoring app you used in this exercise?

2. Evaluate at least two website authoring apps that enable you to create webpages that charge a fee for their use. How much is the fee? What features are included? Do you feel the fee is worth the additional features? Why or why not?

3. Do you feel it is more efficient to create a website using a website authoring app or by writing HTML? Why or why not?

✳ Internet Research

The Internet Research exercises broaden your understanding of chapter concepts by requiring that you search for information on the web.

Instructions: Use a search engine or another search tool to locate the information requested or answers to questions presented in the exercises. Describe your findings, along with the search term(s) you used and your web source(s), in the format requested by your instructor (brief report, presentation, discussion, blog post, video, or other means).

1 Making Use of the Web

Careers and Employment   It is a good idea to acquire information before graduation about the industry in which you would like to work. While your teachers provide valuable training and knowledge to prepare you for a career, they rarely teach you how to begin a job search. You can broaden your horizon by searching online for career information and job openings.

Career websites provide details about training and education requirements, employment outlook, industry trends, and salary data. They also offer advice on writing a cover letter and resume, applying for jobs online, networking, and preparing for an interview. When you are offered a job, turn to these websites to obtain industry salary comparisons and negotiation techniques.

Job seekers can search employment websites for specific position openings worldwide. The jobs can be sorted by category, industry, location, date posted, job title, and keywords. Some websites list job fairs and separate the listings by categories such as entry level, part time, summer, and temporary.

(a) Visit at least two career websites and review the resources. What type of career advice is given? Are aptitude tests available? What tools are provided to manage a job search, such as tips for writing a cover letter and resume, job search mistakes to avoid, search strategies, and social networking tips?

(b) Use at least two employment websites to search for three job openings in your field. Which positions are available? What are their salaries, locations, required education and experience, and job descriptions? Can job seekers post a resume? Are company profiles and salary comparison available? Do these websites have mobile apps?

2 Social Media 📱

Companies have created policies that employees must follow when participating in social media and social networking sites. Intel, for example, considers participation in social media to be an opportunity, not a right, and requires its employees to disclose their identity, protect the company's confidential and classified information, and use common sense when writing and airing opinions. Apple employees are urged to use good judgment when using social networks and are barred from discussing the company on their own websites and from commenting on or posting messages regarding the company and its products on any related websites.

Locate at least two corporate policies for social media participation and summarize the requirements. Do you agree with the companies' guidelines? Are the policies too lenient or too strict? What actions are taken if an employee fails to abide by the policies?

3 Search Sleuth

(1) What large Internet search company eliminated the work-at-home option for their employees in 2013? (2) What is the correct MLA style to cite a Tweet? (3) Microsoft employees celebrate their employment anniversaries by sharing which chocolate candy with coworkers? (4) What is the name of Google's search algorithm that determines which links are the most relevant for a given query? (5) What was the original name of the programming language, Java? (6) What was the name of the computer in the 1983 film *WarGames* where a hacker uses a back door to access a military supercomputer that nearly starts World War III? (7) Who is the

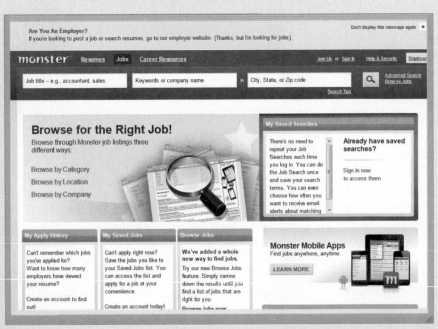

Source: Monster

Internet Research ✳

author of the study, *An Experiment in the Development of Critical Thinking*, published in 1941? (8) What is the name of the first computer virus that infected DEC PDP-10 computers in 1971? What message did it display? (9) What is the name of the annual hacking conference typically held in Las Vegas? (10) The hexadecimal number system uses 16 symbols to code machine language programs. What is the name of the Papuan language spoken in New Guinea that uses the quindecimal (base 15) number system?

4 **Green Computing**

The first Earth Day was celebrated in 1970 when 20 million Americans united to promote environmental awareness. This annual event now is recognized throughout the world, when more than a billion people in nearly 200 countries participate in activities that confront environmental challenges. Companies, too, have increased their commitment to protect natural lands, improve the manufacturing process, and provide eco-friendly work environments.

Locate articles discussing technology companies who promote their green computing practices. For example, look for usage of solar panels, net-zero energy, on-site wastewater treatment, and rainwater harvesting. Then, read the latest Greenpeace Guide to Greener Electronics. Which five companies scored highest? What three environmental criteria were used to evaluate the companies?

5 **Security**

Microsoft, Apple, Facebook, and Twitter are among the technology companies that have experienced a series of attacks exploiting security flaws in the Java plug-in for browsers. These security intrusions appear to have originated from hackers in China, Russia, or Eastern Europe who were attempting to obtain the companies' intellectual property, sensitive data, and users' personal information. The cyberthieves bypassed Java's built-in protections and installed malware on the compromised computers. Kaspersky Security estimates that more than one-half of the security threats in 2012 originated from Java flaws. Oracle, the company that develops Java, issues patches to address known security vulnerabilities, but the Department of Homeland Security and other experts recommend not using Java until it is needed in

browsers because new attacks may occur in the popular programming language.

Locate at least two articles discussing Java security flaws. How do Oracle and other companies inform users about the need to obtain updates to fix security holes? How many devices worldwide have Java installed? How can users discover if Java is installed on their computer or mobile device and, if it is, learn how to uninstall it?

© iStockphoto / Alexandru Nika

6 **Ethics in Action**

While gathering data and information during system development, employees are involved actively in the process. They complete surveys, participate in interviews, and are observed while performing their jobs. Many researchers suggest that during observation, employees may not exhibit everyday behavior and may perform above and beyond their normal workday activities. They feel important because they are being singled out to participate in a study and, in return, increase their productivity.

The researchers base this premise on the Hawthorne Effect, which is the result of a study performed in the 1920s at the Western Electric Company plant in Hawthorne, Illinois. The study discovered that productivity improved during observation, regardless of whether the workplace conditions, such as lighting, humidity, working hours, were made better or worse. Researchers concluded that productivity seemed to improve whenever the workers knew they were being observed.

Locate at least two articles discussing the Hawthorne Effect. Is such observation ethical, and can it have other psychological effects on employees? If productivity increases during observation, is observation a good data gathering technique in a system study? How have the conclusions from the Hawthorne study been interpreted in light of new research based on time-series analyses? Which workplace variables affect productivity?

✸ Problem Solving

The Problem Solving exercises extend your knowledge of chapter concepts by seeking solutions to practical problems with technology that you may encounter at home, school, work, or with nonprofit organizations. The Collaboration exercise should be completed with a team.

🖥 Challenge yourself with additional Problem Solving exercises by navigating to this book's Problem Solving resource on Computer Concepts CourseMate.

Instructions: You often can solve problems with technology in multiple ways. Determine a solution to the problems in these exercises by using one or more resources available to you (such as a computer or mobile device, articles on the web or in print, blogs, podcasts, videos, television, user guides, other individuals, electronics or computer stores, etc.). Describe your solution, along with the resource(s) used, in the format requested by your instructor (brief report, presentation, discussion, blog post, video, or other means).

Personal

1. **Missing Documentation**   After using a program on your computer for several months, you need to refer back to the printed documentation that was included with the program so that you can learn how to use some of the advanced features. You spend several hours looking for the printed documentation but are unsuccessful locating it. What are your next steps?

© Cengage Learning

2. **Macro Security**   Your friend sent you an Excel spreadsheet to modify, but you receive a warning about macros each time you open the file. You have heard in your Introduction to Computers class that macros can be malicious and that it is best to exercise caution before enabling macros. What are your next steps?

3. **Questionable Computer Program**   You just downloaded and installed a new app on your computer. When you try to run the app, the operating system displays a warning stating that it might not be safe to run the app. What steps can you take to determine whether the app is safe to use?

4. **Webpage Will Not Display**   You have created a personal website using a popular web app. When you attempt to view the website in a browser, an error message displays stating that the website cannot be found. What are your next steps?

5. **Malfunctioning Website**   While viewing a new website for a local business, an error message is displayed each time you click a link. As a result, you are unable to navigate to other pages in the website. What are your next steps?

Professional

6. **Project Behind Schedule**   A project you are managing has fallen behind schedule by more than three weeks. Your boss has stressed the importance of keeping the project on schedule, but factors beyond your control have contributed to this significant delay. What steps can you take to address this issue?

7. **Limited Hardware Budget**   A new program your company is developing requires more powerful servers to run properly. The chief financial officer, however, informs you that the budget lacks the funds to purchase new hardware. What are your next steps?

8. **Problems During Testing**   While testing a new system that is about to be implemented in your company, you discover multiple problems. What is the best way to document these problems, and to whom should you report them?

9. **Java Update**   When you run a newly installed program on your computer, a dialog box appears informing you that a Java update is available, and the program will not run without the update. When you attempt to proceed with the update, the operating system displays an error message stating that you need administrative privileges to proceed. What are your next steps?

10. **Problematic Portal**   While using the portal at your company to review recent sales information, you follow a link and a page is displayed that appears to have code from a scripting language. Knowing that this is not the proper behavior for this page, you navigate back to the previous page and then sign out of the portal. What might have happened?

Collaboration

11. **Technology in Construction**   As a student in a drafting class, your instructor has challenged you to design your dream home by using programs and apps wherever possible. Form a team of three people that will determine how to accomplish this objective. One team member should compare and contrast two programs or apps that can be used to create a two-dimensional floor plan, another team member should compare and contrast two computer-aided design programs or apps that can create a more detailed design of the house, and the third team member should compare and contrast two programs or apps that can assist with other aspects of the design process such as landscaping and interior design.

STUDENT ASSIGNMENTS

The Critical Thinking exercises challenge your assessment and decision-making skills by presenting real-world situations associated with chapter concepts. The Collaboration exercise should be completed with a team.

Critical Thinking ✳

 Challenge yourself with additional Critical Thinking exercises by navigating to this book's Critical Thinking resource on Computer Concepts CourseMate.

Instructions: Evaluate the situations below, using personal experiences and one or more resources available to you (such as articles on the web or in print, blogs, podcasts, videos, television, user guides, other individuals, electronics or computer stores, etc.). Perform the tasks requested in each exercise and share your deliverables in the format requested by your instructor (brief report, presentation, discussion, blog post, video, or other means).

1. Class Discussion

Offshore Outsourcing The consulting company where you work as a systems analyst has refused to use offshore outsourcing, claiming management prefers to employ homeland citizens. The company's competitors have been using offshore outsourcing for some time. Your company's management team wants to discuss outsourcing the company's accounting system to an overseas firm. Use the web and the material in Chapter 12 to research outsourcing. Address the following questions: Do you think systems should be developed entirely overseas? Why or why not? What are the major advantages and disadvantages of developing systems offshore? What security issues exist when using offshore developments? Does the United States have an obligation to help with employment overseas or in developing nations? Why or why not? What factors should a company take into consideration when determining whether to use offshore developers?

2. Research and Share

Programming Languages After becoming familiar with the SDLC, you are considering becoming a programmer. Use the web and what you have learned in this chapter to provide information and answer the following questions about programming languages. Would you prefer to use a compiler or an interpreter? Why? What are the advantages of each? What are the advantages of programs developed using object-oriented programming languages and application development tools? For what purpose would you use the Microsoft .NET Framework? Search for popular programming languages. Choose

three about which to find additional information. Find one interesting fact about each language's development, such as who developed it or what languages it was based on or compatible with. Find industry experts' reviews of each language. What is each language used for? Can you find an example of a program that uses each language? Compile your findings.

© Cengage Learning

3. Case Study

Farmers' Market You are the new manager for a group of organic farmers who have a weekly market in season. The market needs to build, customize, or purchase an information system to meet its needs. The information system should allow the market's vendors to enter information about current products, including quantities, dates of availability, and other characteristics, such as information regarding the use of pesticides or other products during the growing process. The board of directors asks you to determine what occurs during the planning phase. Using information learned in the chapter as well as performing research on the web, prepare information about the planning phase of the SDLC. Who needs to be involved from the market? What outside vendors or resources will you need? What types of requests or proposals will you need to prepare? How will you determine the priority of the requests? Compile your findings.

Collaboration

4. **Conversion Strategy** You are one of a team of systems analysts. Your company recently purchased a new custom-built information system that will replace an old system. You and your team are responsible for determining which conversion strategy to use. It is important that your users are able to remain productive during the conversion process; furthermore, you want minimal interruption of corporate activities. Form a four-member team and have each team member choose a different conversion strategy (direct, parallel, phased, and pilot) to research using the web. Each team member should compile a list of at least two arguments for and against each conversion strategy. Then, as a team, meet to discuss and compile your findings. Was it easy to reach a consensus as a team? Which conversion strategy does your team recommend? Why? How do the advantages of the chosen conversion strategy outweigh the disadvantages? As a team, share your recommendation with the class.

✳ Beyond the Book

The Beyond the Book exercises expand your understanding of chapter concepts by requiring research.

Access premium content by visiting Computer Concepts CourseMate. If you have a Computer Concepts CourseMate access code, you can reinforce and extend your learning with MindTap Reader, practice tests, video, and other premium content for Discovering Computers. To sign in to Computer Concepts CourseMate at www.cengagebrain.com, you first must create a student account and then register this book, as described at www.cengage.com/ct/studentdownload.

Part 1 Instructions: Use the web or e-book to perform the task identified for each book element below. Describe your findings, along with the search term(s) you used and your web source(s), if appropriate, in the format requested by your instructor (brief report, presentation, discussion, blog post, video, or other means).

1. **Animations** 📄 Review the animations associated with this chapter and then answer the question(s) they pose (528, 529). What search term would you use to learn more about a specific segment of the animation?

2. **Consider This** Select a Consider This in this chapter (512, 515, 516, 518, 520, 521, 522, 526, 527, 528, 536, 537, 539, 541, 542) and find a recent article that elaborates on the topic. What information did you find that was not presented in this book or e-book?

3. **Drag-and-Drop Figures** 📄 Complete the Drag-and-Drop Figure activities associated with this chapter (511, 513, 534, 535). What did you learn from this activity?

4. **Ethics & Issues** Select an Ethics & Issues in this chapter (512, 518, 528, 533) and find a recent article that supports one view presented. Does the article change your opinion about the topic? Why or why not?

5. **Facebook & Twitter** Review a recent Discovering Computers Facebook post or Twitter Tweet and read the referenced article(s). What did you learn from the article?

6. **High-Tech Talk** 📄 Locate an article that discusses topics related to toolkits used to develop mobile apps. Would you recommend the article you found? Why or why not?

7. **How To** Select a How To in this chapter (532, 535, 540, 542) and find a recent article that elaborates on the topic. Who would benefit from the content of this article? Why?

8. **Innovative Computing** 📄 Locate two additional facts about custom crime fighting software and the Mars Rover. Do your findings change your opinion about the future of this innovation? Why or why not?

9. **Internet Research** Use the search term in an Internet Research (516, 522, 525, 536, 537) to answer the question posed in the element. What other search term could you use to answer the question?

10. **Mini Features** Locate an article that discusses topics related to one of the mini features in this chapter (517, 528, 543). Do you feel that the article is appropriate for this course? Why or why not?

11. **Secure IT** Select a Secure IT in this chapter (523, 530, 540) and find a recent article about the topic that you find interesting. How can you relate the content of the article to your everyday life?

12. **Technology @ Work** Locate three additional, unique usages of technology in the construction industry (545). What makes the use of these technologies unique to the construction industry?

13. **Technology Innovators** 📄 Locate two additional facts about Wikimedia Foundation and Jimmy Wales, Meg Whitman, Ray Kurzweil, and Electronic Arts. Which Technology Innovator impresses you most? Why?

14. **Third-Party Links** 📄 Visit one of the third-party links identified in this chapter (512, 516, 518, 523, 526, 528, 530, 533, 535, 540) and read the article or watch the video associated with the link. Would you share this link on your online social network account? Why or why not?

Part 2 Instructions: Find specific instructions for the exercises below in the e-book or on Computer Concepts CourseMate. Beside each exercise is a brief description of its online content.

1. 📄 **You Review It** Search for and review a video, podcast, or blog post about creating web or mobile apps.

2. 📄 **Windows and Mac** Enhance your understanding and knowledge about using Windows and Mac computers by completing the Open a File in a Text Editor and in a Browser, and Create a Web App Using HTML5, CSS, and JavaScript activities.

3. 📄 **Android, iOS, and Windows Phone** Enhance your understanding of mobile devices by completing the View a Web App in a Mobile Browser, and Compare Web and Native Apps activities.

4. 📄 **Exploring Computer Careers** Read about a career as a systems analyst, search for related employment ads, and then answer related questions.

5. 📄 **App Adventure** Keep track of your funds using finance apps on your smartphone or tablet.

Acronym Reference

Acronym	Description	Page
3-D	three-dimensional	83
3GL	third-generation language	533
4GL	fourth-generation language	538
AC	alternating current	271
ACPA	Anticybersquatting Consumer Protection Act	60
ADA	Americans with Disabilities Act	321
ADSL	asymmetric digital subscriber line	433
AI	artificial intelligence	496
ALGOL	Algorithmic Language	538
ALU	arithmetic logic unit	253
AMOLED	active-matrix OLED	310
ANSI	American National Standards Institute	425
AOL	America Online	48
ARPA	Advanced Research Projects Agency	54
ASCII	American Standard Code for Information Interchange	259
ATC	advanced transfer cache	265
ATM	Asynchronous Transfer Mode	434
ATM	automated teller machine	114
AUP	acceptable use policy	101
B2B	business-to-business	77
B2C	business-to-consumer	77
BAN	body area network	421
BASIC	Beginners All-purpose Symbolic Instruction Code	538
BBS	Bulletin Board System	48
bcc	blind carbon copy	84
BD	Blu-ray Disc	356
BLOB	binary large object	469
BMP	bitmap	81
BSA	Business Software Alliance	215

Acronym	Description	Page
BSB	backside bus	271
BTW	by the way	90
C2C	consumer-to-consumer	77
CA	certificate authority	218
CAD	computer-aided design	170
CAE	computer-aided engineering	491
CAM	computer-aided manufacturing	38
CAPTCHA	Completely Automated Public Turing test to tell Computers and Humans Apart	212
CASE	computer-aided software engineering	526
CATV	cable television	433
CBT	computer-based training	174
cc	carbon copy	84
ccTLD	country code top-level domain	60
CD	compact disc	17
CD-R	CD-recordable	355
CD-ROM	CD-read-only memory	355
CD-RW	CD-rewritable	355
CDD	Center for Digital Democracy	459
CDMA	Code Division Multiple Access	447
CDP	continuous data protection	220
CERT/CC	Computer Emergency Response Team Coordination Center	208
CF	CompactFlash	348
CFO	chief financial officer	22
CIPA	Children's Internet Protection Act	232
CISO	chief information security officer	530
CMOS	complementary metal-oxide semiconductor	267
CMS	content management system	492
COBOL	COmmon Business-Oriented Language	538

Acronym	Description	Page
COPPA	Children's Online Privacy Protection Act	232
CPU	central processing unit	106
CRM	customer relationship management	258
CRT	cathode-ray tube	312
CSA	Cloud Security Alliance	259
CSC	common short code	118
CSI	Cellular Seizure Investigation	266
CSO	chief security officer	530
CSS	cascading style sheets	543
CTS	carpal tunnel syndrome	136
CUDA	Compute Unified Device Architecture	410
CVS	computer vision syndrome	137
DA	database analyst	489
DaaS	Data as a Service	258
DBA	database administrator	489
DBMS	database management system	464
DC	direct current	271
DDoS	distributed DoS	207
DDR SDRAM	Double Data Rate SDRAM	263
DHS	Department of Homeland Security	283
DIMM	dual inline memory module	262
DLP	digital light processing	320
DMCA	Digital Millennium Copyright Act	232
DMS	document management system	492
DNS	domain name system	61
DOE	Department of Energy	226
DoS	denial of service	206
dpi	dots per inch	314
DRAM	dynamic RAM	262
DRM	digital rights management	225
DSL	digital subscriber line	57
DSS	decision support system	495
DTP	desktop publishing	170
DTV	digital television	311
DV	digital video	300
DVD	digital versatile disc	17
DVD-R	DVD-recordable	355

Acronym	Description	Page
DVD-ROM	DVD-read-only memory	355
DVD-RW	DVD-rewritable	355
DVD+R	DVD-recordable	355
DVD+RW	DVD-rewritable	355
DVI	digital video interface	130
DVR	digital video recorder	440
EB	exabyte	338
ECPA	Electronic Communications Privacy Act	99
EDGE	Enhanced Data GSM Environment	447
EDI	electronic data interchange	419
EFT	electronic funds transfer	419
EIDE	Enhanced Integrated Drive Electronics	356
EPA	Environmental Protection Agency	49
EPEAT	Electronic Product Environmental Assessment Tool	505
ERP	Enterprise Resource Planning	491
eSATA	external SATA	356
ESRB	Entertainment Software Rating Board	10
EULA	end-user license agreement	215
EVDO	Evolution Data Optimized	447
FAQ	frequently asked questions	90
FC	Fibre Channel	358
FCC	Federal Communications Commission	443
FDDI	Fiber Distributed Data Interface	443
FOIA	Freedom of Information Act	232
FORTRAN	FORmula TRANslator	538
fps	frames per second	301
FSB	front side bus	271
FTC	Federal Trade Commission	74
FTP	File Transfer Protocol	88
FTTB	Fiber to the Building	434
FTTH	Fiber to the Home	434
FTTP	Fiber to the Premises	57
FWIW	for what it's worth	90
FYI	for your information	90
GB	gigabyte	58
GBps	gigabytes per second	339

Acronym	Description	Page
Gbps	gigabits per second	425
GHz	gigahertz	255
GIF	Graphics Interchange Format	81
GIGO	garbage in, garbage out	466
GIS	geographic information system	485
GPRS	General Packet Radio Service	447
GPS	global positioning system	66
GPU	graphics processing unit	311
gr8	great	8
GSM	Global System for Mobile Communications	447
GUI	graphical user interface	381
HD	high-definition	40
HDD	hard disk drive	339
HDMI	High-Definition Media Interface	311
HDTV	high-definition television	311
HIPAA	Health Insurance Portability and Accountability Act	232
HRIS	human resources information system	491
HTML	Hypertext Markup Language	540
http	Hypertext Transfer Protocol	64
HVAC	heating, ventilating, and air conditioning	545
IaaS	Infrastructure as a Service	258
IAD	Internet Addiction Disorder	331
ICANN	Internet Corporation for Assigned Names and Numbers	60
ID	identification	211
IDE	integrated development environment	535
IDEA	Individuals with Disabilities Education Act	322
IEC	International Electronics Commission	270
IEEE	Institute of Electrical and Electronics Engineers	133
IM	instant messaging	23
IMEI	International Mobile Equipment Identity	283
IMHO	in my humble opinion	90
IP	intellectual property	225

Acronym	Description	Page
IP	Internet Protocol	59
IPO	initial public offering	364
IR	infrared	429
IrDA	Infrared Data Association	429
IROC2	Institute for Responsible Online and Cell-Phone Communication	361
ISDN	Integrated Services Digital Network	433
ISP	Internet service provider	18
IT	information technology	211
JAD	joint-application design	516
JIT	just-in-time	536
JPEG	Joint Photographic Experts Group	81
KB	kilobyte	338
KBps	kilobytes per second	339
L1	Level 1	265
L2	Level 2	265
L3	Level 3	265
LAN	local area network	419
LCD	liquid crystal display	310
LED	light-emitting diode	310
LISP	LISt Processing	538
LOL	laugh out loud	8
LTE	Long Term Evolution	447
M2	Memory Stick Micro	348
M2M	machine-to-machine	128
MAC	Media Access Control	222
MAN	metropolitan area network	421
MB	megabyte	58
MBps	megabytes per second	339
Mbps	megabits per second	425
MFP	multifunction printer	317
MICR	magnetic-ink character recognition	307
MIS	management information system	494
MMA	MIDI Manufacturers Association	331
MMS	multimedia message service	119
MP	millions of pixels	122
MRP	Material Requirements Planning	491
MRP II	Manufacturing Resource Planning II	491

Acronym	Description	Page
ms	millisecond	267
NAS	network attached storage	359
NCIC	National Crime Information Center	34
NFC	near field communications	133
NIC	network interface card	439
ns	nanosecond	267
NUI	natural user interface	382
OCR	optical character recognition	304
OEM	original equipment manufacturer	388
OLAP	online analytical processing	495
OLED	organic LED	310
OLTP	online transaction processing	494
OMR	optical mark recognition	304
OODB	object-oriented database	484
OOP	object-oriented programming	535
OQL	object query language	484
OS	operating system	378
P2P	peer-to-peer	422
PaaS	Platform as a Service	258
PAN	personal area network	421
PATRIOT	Provide Appropriate Tools Required to Intercept and Obstruct Terrorism	232
PB	petabyte	338
PC	personal computer	4
PDF	Portable Document Format	81
Perl	Practical Extraction and Report Language	542
PERT	Program Evaluation and Review Technique	514
PHP	PHP: Hypertext Preprocessor	542
PILOT	Programmed Inquiry Learning Or Teaching	538
PIN	personal identification number	114
PL/1	Programming Language One	538
PNG	Portable Network Graphics	81
POS	point of sale	113
ppm	pages per minute	313
Prolog	PROgramming LOGic	538
ps	picosecond	267
PUE	power usage effectiveness	227

Acronym	Description	Page
QBE	query by example	481
QR	quick response	169
RAD	rapid application development	536
RAID	redundant array of independent disks	343
RAM	random access memory	262
RDRAM	Rambus DRAM	263
RF	radio frequency	446
RFI	request for information	524
RFID	radio frequency identification	303
RFP	request for proposal	524
RFQ	request for quotation	524
ROI	return on investment	515
ROM	read-only memory	265
RPG	Report Program Generator	538
rpm	revolutions per minute	342
RSI	repetitive strain injury	136
RSS	Really Simple Syndication	65
RTOS	real-time operating system	402
SaaS	Software as a Service	258
SAN	storage area network	359
SAS	serial-attached SCSI	356
SATA	Serial Advanced Technology Attachment	356
SCSI	Small Computer System Interface	356
SDHC	Secure Digital High Capacity	348
SDLC	system development life cycle	510
SDRAM	Synchronous DRAM	263
SDXC	Secure Digital Expanded Capacity	348
SFA	sales force automation	491
SIMM	single inline memory module	262
SLR	single-lens reflex	120
SMM	Sustainable Materials Management	256
SMS	short message service	118
SOPA	Stop Online Piracy Act	226
SQL	Structured Query Language	480
SRAM	static RAM	262
SSD	solid-state drive	16
SSID	service set identifier	222

Acronym	Description	Page
TB	terabyte	262
Tbps	terabits per second	444
TCP/IP	Transmission Control Protocol/Internet Protocol	426
TFT	thin-film transistor	310
TIFF	Tagged Image File Format	81
TLD	top-level domain	60
TPS	transaction processing system	493
TTFN	ta-ta for now	90
TYVM	thank you very much	90
UI	user interface	381
UMB	Ultra Mobile Broadband	447
UMTS	Universal Mobile Telecommunications System	447
UPC	Universal Product Code	305
UPS	uninterruptible power supply	135
URL	Uniform Resource Locator	64
USB	universal serial bus	131
USPS	United States Postal Service	305
UV	ultraviolet	312
UWB	ultra-wideband	429
VAN	value-added network	419

Acronym	Description	Page
VAR	value-added reseller	524
VoIP	Voice over Internet Protocol	88
VPE	visual programming environment	537
VPN	virtual private network	218
VR	virtual reality	83
W3C	World Wide Web Consortium	56
WAN	wide area network	421
WAP	wireless access point	222
WBT	web-based training	174
Wi-Fi	wireless fidelity	427
WiMAX	Worldwide Interoperability for Microwave Access	431
WLAN	wireless local area network	420
WML	wireless markup language	541
WORM	write once, read many	355
WPA2	Wi-Fi Protected Access 2	222
WWW	World Wide Web	61
XML	Extensible Markup Language	541
YB	yottabyte	338
ZB	zettabyte	338
µs	microsecond	267

Index

networks. 30, 418
architectures, 421–422
communications lines, 432–434
communications standards and protocols, 424–431
home, business, 31, 440–441
LANs, MANs, WANs, PANs, 419–421
monitoring network traffic, 427
operating system's controlling of, 391
overview, 418–419
securing wireless, 222
topologies, 423–424
unauthorized access and use, 210–214
neural network: A system that attempts to imitate the behavior of the human brain., 37
news feed: Terminology used on social networking sites to refer to activity updates from your friends that appear on a separate page associated with your account. 69
news mobile apps, 177
news websites, 71
newsgroups, 29
NFC: Type of wireless connection that uses close-range radio signals to transmit data between two
NFC (near field communication): Based on RFID, a protocol that defines how a network uses close-range radio signals to communicate between two devices or objects equipped with NFC technology. 430, 431. *See also* **near field communications**
NFC-enabled devices. 133
Nintendo, 125
nit: A unit of visible light intensity equal to one candela per square meter. 311
No Fly List, 235
node: Each computer or device on a network. 419, 423
noise, 443
nonimpact printer: A printer that forms characters and graphics on a piece of paper without actually contacting the paper. 313
nonprocedural language: A programming language in which the programmer writes English-like instructions or interacts with a graphical environment to retrieve data from files or a database 538
nonresident: Instructions that remain on a storage medium until they are needed, at which time they transfer into memory (RAM). 380
nonvolatile memory: Memory that does not lose its contents when power is removed from the computer. 261
normalization, 490
note taking software: An application that enables users to enter typed text, handwritten comments, drawings, sketches, photos, and links anywhere on a page and then save the page as part of a notebook. 162, 163
notebook computer: Thin, lightweight mobile computer with a screen in its lid

and a keyboard in its base, designed to fit on your lap. 4, 108. *See also* **laptop computer**
numeric check: Validity check that ensures that users enter only numeric data into a field. 473, 474
numerical literacy, 517
Nvidia, 256

O

object: A database item that contains data, as well as the actions that read or process the data. 484, 535
object code: The machine language version of a program that results from compiling a 3GL source program. *See also* **source code**
object program, 534
object query language (OQL): Query language used with object-oriented and object-relational databases to manipulate and retrieve data. 484
object-oriented database (OODB): A database that stores data in objects. 484, 485
object-oriented programming (OOP) language: Programming language used to implement objects in a program. 535
object-relational database, 484
OCR devices: Devices that usually include a small optical scanner for reading characters and sophisticated software to analyze what is read. 304
OCR software: Optical character recognition; software that can read and convert text documents into electronic files. 304
OEMs (original equipment manufacturers), and virus protection, 388
office productivity, increasing with web, mobile apps, 169
offline UPS: Uninterruptible power supply that switches to battery power when a problem occurs in the power line. 136. *See also* **standby UPS**
off-site: A location separate from the computer or mobile device site. 219
OLED: Organic LED; display technology that uses organic molecules that are self-illuminating and, thus, do not require a backlight. 310
OMR devices: Devices that read hand-drawn marks, such as small circles or rectangles. 305
onboard navigation systems, 36
online: Term used to refer to a the state of a computer or device being connected to a network. 6
online analytical processing (OLAP): Programs that analyze data, such as those in a decision support system. 495
online auction: Auction in which users bid on an item being sold by someone else on the web. 76
online gaming, avoiding risks, 206
online help, 176
online photo storage, 170

online security service: A web app that evaluates our computer or mobile device to check for Internet and email vulnerabilities. 208
online services, downloading digital media from, 82
online social network: A website that encourages its members in its online community to share their interests, ideas, stories, photos, music, and videos with other registered users. 21, 68. *See also* **social networking site**
online transaction processing (OLTP): Processing technique in which the computer processes each transaction as it is entered. 494
online UPS: Uninterruptible power supply that always runs off the battery, providing continuous protection. 136
on-screen keyboard: A keyboard that appears on a tablet or other mobile device. 5, 12, 118
Open Group, The, 397
open source software: Software provided for use, modification, and redistribution and has no restrictions from the copyright holder regarding modification of the software's internal instructions and its redistribution. 155, 398
Opera: Browser used on both computers and mobile devices. 64
operating system (OS), 378
open source software, 398
operating system: A set of programs that coordinates all the activities among computer or mobile device hardware. 25, 152
adding users to, 393
built-in security tools, 391
desktop, 394–399
examples by category (table), 393
functions, 380–393
mobile, 400–402
overview, 378–379
role of, 154–155
virus protection, 388
operational feasibility: Test that measures how well the proposed information system will work. 515
operators, search engine (table), 68
optical character recognition (OCR), 304
optical disc: Type of storage medium that consists of a flat, round, portable disc made of metal, plastic, and lacquer that is written and read by a laser. 17, 352
CDs, DVDs, 355–356
cleaning, fixing, 354
life span of, 354
overview, 352–353
optical fiber: Each strand of a fiber-optic cable. 444
optical mark recognition, 289
optical mark recognition (OMR), 304
optical mouse: Mouse that uses optical sensors that emit and sense light to detect the mouse's movement. 292
optical readers, 304–305

R

rack server: A server that is house in a slot (bay) on a metal frame (rack). Also called a rack-mounted server. 112

RAD (rapid application development): A method of developing software in which the software developer writes and implements a program in segments instead of waiting until the entire program is completed. 536

radiation from mobile phones, cellular antennas, Wi-Fi devices, 446

radio
  broadcast, 445
  cellular, 446
  frequency identification, 429

radiology, technology in, 41

RAID: Redundant array of independent disks; a group of two or more integrated hard disks. 343, 358

RAM (random access memory): Memory chips that can be read from and written to by the processor and other devices. 262. *See also* **main memory**
  applications using (fig.), 385
  types of, 263

random access: Access method where a device can locate a particular data item or file immediately, without having to move consecutively through items stored in front of the desired data item or file. 361. *See also* **direct access**

range check: Validity check that determines whether a number is within a specified range. 473, 474

RDRAM: Rambus DRAM; type of RAM that is much faster than SDRAM. 263

reading: The process of transferring these items from a storage medium into memory. 336

reading devices, and scanners, 303–307

read-only memory (ROM): Memory chips that store permanent data and instructions. 265

read/write head: The mechanism that reads items and writes items in the drive as it barely touches the disk's recording surface. 342

real time: Term used with online communications that means you and the people with whom you are conversing are online at the same time. 86

real-time clock: A separate battery-backed chip that keeps track of the date and time in a computer. 255

real-time operating system (RTOS): Operating system used by an embedded computer. *See also* **embedded operating system** 402

RECAPTCHAs, 361

receiving device: Device that accepts the transmission of data, instructions, or information. 416

record: A group of related fields. 469

recording
  macros, 539
  videos, 301

records
  adding, 470–471
  deleting, 472–473
  modifying, 471–472

recovery media, 381

recovery plan, 221

recovery utility: Tool that uses logs and/or backups, and either a rollforward or a rollback technique, to restore a database when it becomes damaged or destroyed. 482

Recycle Bin: Windows location for files that have been deleted. 345, 395

recycling
  computers, mobile devices, 256
  of electronics, 117
  of old computers, devices, 227

red-eye: The appearance of red eyes caused by a camera's flash. 172

redundancy: Built-in levels of duplicate components used in enterprise hardware that ensures that if one component fails or malfunctions, another can assume its tasks. 358
  reducing in databases, 476–477

redundant data in file processing systems, 475

reference apps, 169

registers: Small, high-speed storage locations that temporarily hold data and instructions. 254–255

relation: Term used by developers of relational databases for file. 483

relational database: A database that stores data in tables that consist of rows and columns. 483

relationship: A blink within the data in a relational database. 483

remote controls for home systems, 40

removing
  See also **deleting**
  apps, 185
  internal hard drives, 340
  media safely, 350

repair technicians holding private investigator licenses, 267

repetitive strain injury (RSI): An injury or disorder of the muscles, nerves, tendons, ligaments, and joints. 136, 292

report generator: DBMS feature that allows users to design a report on the screen, retrieve data into the report design, and then display or print the report. 481. *See also* **report writer**

report writer: DBMS feature that allows users to design a report on the screen, retrieve data into the report design, and then display or print the report. 481. *See also* **report generator**

reports, feasibility, 521–522

repository: A DBMS element that contains data about each file in a database and each field in those files. 478. *See also* **data Dictionary**

request for information (RFI): A less formal document that uses a standard form to request information about a product or service. 524

request for proposal (RFP): Document sent to a vendor during the system development cycle where the vendor selects the product(s) that meets specified requirements and then quotes the price(s). 524

request for quotation (RFQ): Document sent to a vendor during the system development cycle that identifies required products. 524

request for system services: A formal, written request for a new or modified information system. 518. *See also* **project request**

research and composition, information literacy, 517

research databases, 488

research web databases, 487

resize: To change the physical dimensions of a photo. 172

resolution: The number of horizontal and vertical pixels in a display device. 122, 310
  and print quality, 314

resources: Hardware, software, data, and information. 30
  in the cloud, 116

response time: The time in milliseconds (ms) that it takes to turn a pixel on or off. 311

restore: Copy backed up files to their original location on a computer or mobile device. 219

restore tool: Program that reverses the backup process and returns backed up files to their original form. 188

restoring deleted files, erased media, 345

retail apps, 169

retail software: Mass-produced, copyrighted software that meets the needs of a wide variety of users, not just a single user or company. 155

retail websites, 35

Retina Display: LCD technology developed by Apple that produces vibrant colors and supports viewing from all angles because the LCD technology is built into the screen instead of behind it and contains more pixels per inch of display. 310

revolutions per minute (rpm): The number of times per minute that a hard disk platter rotates. 342

RFID: Radio frequency identification; technology that uses radio signals to communicate with a tag placed in or attached to an object, an animal, or a person. 306, 429
  electronic tolls, 430
  tracking people's movements, 429

RFID (radio frequency identification): A protocol that defines how a network uses radio signals to communicate with a tag placed in or attached to an object, an animal, or a person. 429

RFID reader: Reading device that reads information on an RFID tag via radio waves. 289, 303, 306, 430